SAMUEL BECKETT IN

When Samuel Beckett first came to international prominence with the success of *Waiting for Godot*, many critics believed the play was divorced from any recognisable context. The two tramps, and the master and servant they encounter, seemed to represent no one and everyone. Today, critics challenge the assumption that Beckett aimed to break definitively with context, highlighting images, allusions and motifs that tether Beckett's writings to real people, places and issues in his life. This wide-ranging collection of essays from thirty-seven renowned Beckett scholars reveals how extensively Beckett entered into dialogue with important literary traditions and the realities of his time. Drawing on his major works, as well as on a range of letters and theoretical notebooks, the essays are designed to complement each other, building a broad overview that will allow students and scholars to come away with a better sense of Beckett's life, writings and legacy.

ANTHONY UHLMANN is a Professor of Literature and the Director of the Writing and Society Research Centre at the University of Western Sydney. He is the author of a number of works on Samuel Beckett, including *Beckett and Poststructuralism* (1999) and *Samuel Beckett and the Philosophical Image* (2006).

SAMUEL BECKETT IN CONTEXT

EDITED BY
ANTHONY UHLMANN
University of Western Sydney

CAMBRIDGE
UNIVERSITY PRESS

CAMBRIDGE
UNIVERSITY PRESS

32 Avenue of the Americas, New York NY 10013-2473, USA

Cambridge University Press is part of the University of Cambridge.

It furthers the University's mission by disseminating knowledge in the pursuit of education, learning and research at the highest international levels of excellence.

www.cambridge.org
Information on this title: www.cambridge.org/9781107454002

© Cambridge University Press 2013

This publication is in copyright. Subject to statutory exception and to the provisions of relevant collective licensing agreements, no reproduction of any part may take place without the written permission of Cambridge University Press.

First published 2013
First paperback edition 2015

A catalogue record for this publication is available from the British Library

Library of Congress Cataloguing in Publication data
Samuel Beckett in context / [edited by] Anthony Uhlmann, University of Western Sydney.
pages cm. – (Literature in context)
Includes an index.
ISBN 978-1-107-01703-0 (hardback)
1. Beckett, Samuel, 1906–1989 – Criticism and interpretation.
I. Uhlmann, Anthony, editor of compilation.
PR6003.E282Z819 2013
848'.91409–dc23   2012033220

ISBN 978-1-107-01703-0 Hardback
ISBN 978-1-107-45400-2 Paperback

Cambridge University Press has no responsibility for the persistence or accuracy of URLs for external or third-party internet websites referred to in this publication, and does not guarantee that any content on such websites is, or will remain, accurate or appropriate.

Contents

Notes on Contributors	*page* ix
Permissions and Acknowledgements	xix
List of Abbreviations	xxi
Chronology	xxiii

	Introduction Anthony Uhlmann	1

PART I. LANDSCAPES AND FORMATION

1.	Childhood and Portora Russell Smith	7
2.	Dublin and Environs John Pilling	19
3.	Trinity College, Dublin S. E. Gontarski	29
4.	École Normale Supérieure Anthony Cordingley	42
5.	Paris, Roussillon, Ussy Jean-Michel Rabaté	53

PART II. SOCIAL AND POLITICAL CONTEXTS

6.	Ireland: 1906–1945 Patrick Bixby	65
7.	France: 1928–1939 Garin Dowd	76

8.	England: 1933–1936 *Peter Marks*	87
9.	Germany: Circa 1936–1937 *Mark Nixon*	99
10.	France: World War Two *Lois Gordon*	109
11.	France, Europe, the World: 1945–1989 *Julian Murphet*	126

PART III. MILIEUS AND MOVEMENTS

12.	Modernism: Dublin / Paris / London *Paul Sheehan*	139
13.	The Joyce Circle *Sam Slote*	150
14.	Post–World War Two Paris *Shane Weller*	160
15.	Staging Plays *Anthony Uhlmann*	173
16.	Working on Radio *Ulrika Maude*	183
17.	Working on Film and Television *Graley Herren*	192

PART IV. 'THE HUMANITIES I HAD': LITERATURE

18.	Irish Literature *Seán Kennedy*	205
19.	English Literature *Mark Byron*	218
20.	French Literature *Angela Moorjani*	229
21.	Italian Literature *Daniela Caselli*	241

PART V. 'THE HUMANITIES I HAD': ARTS

22. Contemporary Visual Art — 255
    Nico Israel

23. Music — 266
    Catherine Laws

24. Cinema — 279
    Matthijs Engelberts

25. Popular Culture — 289
    Jane Goodall

PART VI. 'THE HUMANITIES I HAD': SYSTEMS OF KNOWLEDGE AND BELIEF

26. Philosophy — 301
    Matthew Feldman

27. Psychology — 312
    Laura Salisbury

28. The Bible — 324
    Chris Ackerley

29. The Occult — 337
    Minako Okamuro

30. Science and Mathematics — 348
    Hugh Culik

PART VII. LANGUAGE AND FORM

31. Language and Representation — 361
    Daniel Katz

32. Self-Translation — 370
    Corinne Scheiner

33. Theatre Forms — 381
    Enoch Brater

PART VIII. RECEPTION AND REMAINS

34. Initial Reception 397
James Gourley

35. Influence 405
Michael D'Arcy

36. Notebooks and Other Manuscripts 417
Dirk Van Hulle

37. Letters 428
Lois More Overbeck

Index 441

Notes on Contributors

CHRIS ACKERLEY is Professor of English at the University of Otago. He has annotated Beckett's *Murphy* and *Watt* (recently republished by the University of Edinburgh Press); he is, with S. E. Gontarski, author of the Grove Press and Faber *Companion to Samuel Beckett*; and he is completing a study of Samuel Beckett and science. A specialist annotator, he is part of the EMiC (Editing Manuscripts in Canada) project, preparing three works by Malcolm Lowry, including the long-lost but recently rediscovered novel *In Ballast to the White Sea*.

PATRICK BIXBY is an Associate Professor of English at Arizona State University and author of *Samuel Beckett and the Postcolonial Novel* (Cambridge University Press, 2009). He has served as an assistant to the editors of *The Letters of Samuel Beckett* (Cambridge University Press, 2009), and has published essays on Beckett, Joyce, Rushdie and others. He is currently writing a book on Nietzsche and Irish modernism.

ENOCH BRATER is the Kenneth T. Rowe Collegiate Professor of Dramatic Literature at the University of Michigan. He has recently published *Ten Ways of Thinking About Samuel Beckett: The Falsetto of Reason* (Methuen), and is well known for his seminal studies in the field, including *Beyond Minimalism: Beckett's Late Style in the Theater* and *The Drama in the Text: Beckett's Late Fiction*, both from Oxford University Press.

MARK BYRON lectures in Modern and Contemporary Literature in the Department of English at the University of Sydney. His current work is in developing digital scholarly editions of complex Modernist texts and their manuscripts, as well as critical and theoretical reflection on scholarly editing techniques. His ARC Discovery Project (2011–13) aims to produce a longitudinal study of literary text structures from the mid-nineteenth to the mid-twentieth century and the range of editorial methods (analogue and digital) used to represent those texts.

Notes on Contributors

DANIELA CASELLI is a Senior Lecturer in English at the University of Manchester. She is the author of *Beckett's Dantes: Intertextuality in the Fiction and Criticism* (Manchester University Press, 2005) and *Improper Modernism: Djuna Barnes's Bewildering Corpus* (Arena, 2009). She has published articles on Samuel Beckett, literary theory, modernism and gender. She is the editor of *Beckett and Nothing: Trying to Understand Beckett* (Manchester University Press, 2011) and co-editor, with Steven Connor and Laura Salisbury, of *Other Becketts* (Journal of Beckett Studies Books, 2001). With Daniela La Penna she has co-edited *Twentieth-Century Poetic Translation: Literary Cultures in Italian and English* (Continuum, 2008). She is the treasurer of the British Association of Modernist Studies.

ANTHONY CORDINGLEY is a Lecturer in English and Translation at the Université Paris 8–Vincennes-Saint-Denis. He has published on Beckett in specialist and general journals. He is co-editor of the electronic genetic edition of Beckett's *Comment c'est/How It Is*, and his monograph on that text will be published by Antwerp University Press. He is completing a book on Beckett's education in languages and philosophy and its effects upon on his fiction. Cordingley has also edited a collection of articles for Continuum's Studies in Translation series entitled *Self-translation: Brokering Originality in Hybrid Culture* (2012).

HUGH CULIK has worked with mathematics and neurology to understand Beckett's participation in long-simmering anxieties about inconsistency, incompleteness and the real. He has been the Chair of English at the University of Detroit Mercy and is co-founder of *Post Identity*. He is now an independent scholar.

MICHAEL D'ARCY teaches English literature at St. Francis Xavier University. He has published on modernist literature, film and literary theory, including articles on Beckett in *The Journal of Beckett Studies* and *Samuel Beckett Today/Aujourd'hui*. He is currently completing a monograph provisionally titled *Stratagems of Unnaming: Transnational Modernism and the Adventure of Narrative Stupidity*.

GARIN DOWD is Reader in Film and Media at the University of West London. He is the author of *Abstract Machines: Samuel Beckett and Philosophy after Deleuze and Guattari* (Rodopi, 2007), co-author (with Fergus Daly) of *Leos Carax* (Manchester University Press, 2003) and editor (with Lesley Stevenson and Jeremy Strong) of *Genre Matters* (Intellect Books, 2006).

MATTHIJS ENGELBERTS is based at the University of Amsterdam, where his current research is centred primarily on aspects of mediality in modern literature and (other) narrative art media. His publications include books, edited volumes and articles in French and English on (genre and media-related questions in) Beckett, surrealist theatre, the contemporary drama text, Tardieu, Duras, theatre sports, Molière, Philippe Claudel and other French authors, mainly those working at the intersections of literature and cinema or theatre. He is a member of the editorial board of the bilingual journal *Samuel Beckett Today/ Aujourd'hui*.

MATTHEW FELDMAN is a Reader in Contemporary History at Teesside University; a Senior Researcher with the Cantermir Institute, University of Oxford; and a Senior Research Fellow with the 'Modernism and Christianity' project at the University of Bergen, Norway. He co-edits the 'Political Religions' section of Wiley-Blackwell's online journal *Religion Compass* and, with Dr Erik Tonning, co-edits Continuum Books' *Historicizing Modernism* monograph series. He has published widely on twentieth-century literary modernism, particularly studies of Samuel Beckett, including the volumes *Beckett's Books: A Cultural History of Samuel Beckett's 'Interwar Notes'* (Continuum, 2006). With Dr David Addyman, he is currently preparing a critical edition of Samuel Beckett's interwar 'Philosophy Notes'.

S. E. GONTARSKI is the Robert O. Lawton Distinguished Professor of English at Florida State University, where he edited the *Journal of Beckett Studies* (new series) from 1992 to 2008. He currently serves as Co-Editor for the journal's present iteration published by Edinburgh University Press. Among his recent books are: (with C. J. Ackerley) *The Faber Companion to Samuel Beckett: A Reader's Guide to His Works, Life, and Thought* (Faber and Faber, 2006); *Beckett after Beckett* (edited with Anthony Uhlmann) (University Press of Florida, 2006), a finalist for the Theatre Library Association's George Freedley Award, and *A Companion to Samuel Beckett* (Wiley-Blackwell, 2010). He is currently editing *The Edinburgh Companion to Samuel Beckett and the Arts*.

JANE GOODALL was a Research Professor in the Writing and Society group until she moved to Queensland in 2007 to engage in full-time writing. She is the author of numerous essays on theatre and performance and three books: *Artaud and the Gnostic Drama* (Oxford University Press, 1994), *Performance and Evolution in the Age of Darwin* (Routledge, 2002) and *Stage Presence* (Routledge, 2008), which was shortlisted for the Theatre Book prize in London.

LOIS GORDON, University Distinguished Professor of English at Fairleigh Dickinson University, is the author of books on Donald Barthelme (1981) and Robert Coover (1983) and the first book in the United States on Harold Pinter, *Stratagems to Uncover Nakedness* (University of Missouri Press, 1969). She subsequently edited *Harold Pinter* (Garland, 1990) and *Pinter at 70* (Routledge, 2001). Her recent work includes *American Chronicle: Year by Year through the Twentieth Century* (Yale, 1999); *The World of Samuel Beckett, 1906–1946* (Yale, 1996); *Reading Godot* (Yale, 2002) and *Nancy Cunard: Heiress, Muse, and Political Idealist* (Columbia, 2007), which was reviewed on the front page of the *New York Times Book Review*. She has recently completed a book on Picasso.

JAMES GOURLEY is a member of the Writing and Society Research Centre, School of Humanities and Communication Arts, University of Western Sydney. He is the author of *Terrorism and Temporality in the Works of Thomas Pynchon and Don DeLillo*, forthcoming from Continuum.

GRALEY HERREN is a Professor of English at Xavier University in Cincinnati. He is the author of *Samuel Beckett's Plays on Film and Television* (Palgrave, 2007). He served on the executive board of the Samuel Beckett Society and edited its newsletter, *The Beckett Circle*.

NICO ISRAEL is the author of *Outlandish: Writing between Exile and Diaspora* (Stanford University Press, 2000) and *On Spirals: Metamorphoses of a Twentieth-Century Image* (Columbia University Press, forthcoming) and numerous academic essays on twentieth-century literature and critical theory. He has also published widely on visual art in museum catalogues, in *Artforum* and elsewhere. His essay on Beckett and earth artist Robert Smithson, 'At the End of the Jetty', appeared in *JOBS* 20:1. He is an Associate Professor of English at Hunter College and the City University of New York Graduate Center.

DANIEL KATZ is the author of *Saying I No More: Subjectivity and Consciousness in the Prose of Samuel Beckett* (Northwestern University Press, 1999), *American Modernism's Expatriate Scene: The Labour of Translation* (Edinburgh University Press, 2007) and *The Poetry of Jack*

Spicer (Edinburgh University Press, 2013). He teaches in the Department of English and Comparative Literature at the University of Warwick.

SEÁN KENNEDY is an Associate Professor of English and the coordinator of Irish studies at Saint Mary's University, Halifax, Nova Scotia. He is the editor of two special issues, 'Historicising Beckett' (*Samuel Beckett Today/Aujourd'hui,* 2005) and 'Queering Ireland' (*The Canadian Journal of Irish Studies,* 2011), as well as two edited volumes, *Samuel Beckett: History, Memory, Archive* with Katherine Weiss (Palgrave, 2009) and *Beckett and Ireland* (Cambridge University Press, 2010).

CATHERINE LAWS is a musicologist and a pianist specialising in contemporary music. She lectures in Music at the University of York and is a Senior Research Fellow at the Orpheus Institute, Ghent. Her current practice-led research focuses on processes of composer–performer collaboration and the relationship between physical and sonic gesture. Her musicological research examines the relationship between music, language and meaning, especially with respect to the work of Samuel Beckett and composers' responses to his texts.

PETER MARKS is an Associate Professor of English at the University of Sydney. He has published on a variety of topics including surveillance, literary periodicals, film adaptation, D. H. Lawrence, utopias and dystopias and socialist realism. His most recent books are *British Filmmakers: Terry Gilliam* (Manchester University Press, 2009), *George Orwell the Essayist: Literature, Politics and Periodical Culture* (Continuum, 2011) and (as editor) *Literature and Politics: Pushing the World in Certain Directions* (Cambridge Scholars Publishing, 2012).

ULRIKA MAUDE is a Lecturer in English at the University of Bristol. She is the author of *Beckett, Technology and the Body* (Cambridge University Press, 2009) and co-editor of *Beckett and Phenomenology* (Continuum, 2009) and *The Body and the Arts* (Palgrave, 2009). She also co-edited 'Beckett on TV', a special issue of the *Journal of Beckett Studies* (18: 1–2). She is currently writing a book on modernism and medical culture.

ANGELA MOORJANI is Professor Emerita of French and Intercultural Studies at the University of Maryland, Baltimore County. Her publications on repetition and mourning in artistic making fuse psychoanalysis and pragmatics with feminist thought and include *Abysmal Games in the Novels of Samuel Beckett* (University of North Carolina Studies, 1983), *The Aesthetics of Loss and Lessness* (Palgrave, 1991) and *Beyond*

Fetishism and Other Excursions in Psychopragmatics (Palgrave, 2000). She co-edited (with Linda Ben-Zvi) *Beckett at 100: Revolving It All* (Oxford University Press, 2008), and her recent essays investigate gaze deixis, multitiered effects and French cultural ghosts in Beckett. She is co-editor-in-chief of *Samuel Beckett Today/Aujourd'hui*.

JULIAN MURPHET is a Professor in Modern Film and Literature and the Director of the Centre for Modernism Studies in Australia at the University of New South Wales. He is the author of *Multimedia Modernism* (Cambridge University Press, 2009) and *Literature and Race in Los Angeles* (Cambridge University Press, 2001), as well as various pieces on modernism, postmodernism, film and cultural theory. He is currently completing a book on William Faulkner.

MARK NIXON is Reader in Modern Literature at the University of Reading, where he is also the Director of the Beckett International Foundation. He is an editor of *Samuel Beckett Today/Aujourd'hui* and the *Journal of Beckett Studies*, and the co-director of the Beckett Digital Manuscript Project. He has published widely on Beckett's work; recent books include the monograph *Samuel Beckett's German Diaries 1936–37* (Continuum, 2011) and the edited collection *Publishing Samuel Beckett* (British Library, 2011).

MINAKO OKAMURO is a Professor of Studies in Media, Body and Image at Waseda University. She is co-editor of *Samuel Beckett Today/Aujourd'hui 19: Borderless Beckett/Beckett sans frontièrs* (2008) and *Ireland on Stage: Beckett and After* (Peter Lang, 2007). She is co-founder of the Samuel Beckett Research Circle of Japan and director of the Waseda University Beckett Seminar for young scholars and served as the general director of the 'Borderless Beckett': International Samuel Beckett Symposium, Tokyo, 2006.

LOIS MORE OVERBECK is a Research Associate of The Laney School of Graduate Studies, Emory University, and a visiting lecturer in the Department of Theatre Studies. She was authorised by Samuel Beckett to serve as an associate editor and is now the managing editor of *The Letters of Samuel Beckett*. The first two of four volumes have been published by Cambridge University Press. She edited *The Beckett Circle* of The Samuel Beckett Society (1984–9), and has published widely on Beckett and modern drama, including a collection of essays edited with Paul Jackson on the plays of Adrienne Kennedy, *Intersecting Boundaries*

(University of Minnesota Press, 1992). She was a consultant for the Beckett Festival of Radio Plays, project director of Beckett/Atlanta (1987), and a coordinator of the Year of Beckett–2006, Atlanta, celebrating Beckett's centennial year.

JOHN PILLING is Emeritus Professor of English and European Literature at the University of Reading, where he is an advisor to the Beckett International Foundation. A past editor of the *Journal of Beckett Studies*, he still serves on its advisory board and acts in a similar role for *Samuel Beckett Today/Aujourd'hui*. He edited (with the late Seán Lawlor) the annotated *Collected Poems of Samuel Beckett* for Faber and Faber (2012) and recently published a monograph on *More Pricks Than Kicks* with Continuum (2011). His other books include *A Samuel Beckett Chronology* (Palgrave, 2006) and *Beckett before Godot* (Cambridge University Press, 1997).

JEAN-MICHEL RABATÉ, Vartan Gregorian Professor in the Humanities at the University of Pennsylvania, is one of the founders and curators of the Slought Foundation. He is a member of the American Academy of Arts and Sciences. He has authored or edited thirty books on modernism, psychoanalysis, contemporary art, philosophy and writers like Beckett, Pound and Joyce. Recent books include *Lacan Literario* (Siglo XXI Editores, 2007), *1913: The Cradle of Modernism* (Wiley-Blackwell, 2007), *The Ethics of the Lie* (Other Press, 2008) and *Etant Donnés: 1) l'art, 2) le crime* (Les Presses du Reel, 2010).

LAURA SALISBURY is a lecturer and RCUK Fellow in Science, Technology and Culture at Birkbeck, University of London. She is the author of *Samuel Beckett: Laughing Matters, Comic Timing* (Edinburgh University Press, 2012), co-editor of *Neurology and Modernity: A Cultural History of Nervous Systems, 1800–1950* (Palgrave, 2010) and co-editor of *Other Becketts* (Journal of Beckett Studies Books, 2002). She has published widely on Beckett, including essays on Beckett and Bion and on Beckett and neurology. Her current research project is a study of the relationship between modernism, modernity and neurological conceptions of language.

CORINNE SCHEINER is Maytag Associate Professor of Comparative Literature at Colorado College. Her research and publications focus on translation studies, Samuel Beckett, Vladimir Nabokov and the practice and teaching of comparative literature. Recent publications include: 'Collaborations and Self-Translation' (*Oxford's History of Literary Translation in English* [Oxford University Press, forthcoming]);

'Teaching Lolita with Lepidoptera' (*Approaches to Teaching Lolita*, ed. Zoran Kuzmanovich and Galya Diment [MLA, 2008] 49–54) and '"In Search of the Real" Smurov: Doubling and Dialogic Construction of Identity in Nabokov's *Sogladatay* (The Eye)' (*Poetics, Self, Place* [Slavica, 2007] 601–13).

PAUL SHEEHAN is a Senior Lecturer in the Department of English at Macquarie University, Sydney. He has published essays on Werner Herzog, W. G. Sebald and Cormac McCarthy, as well as numerous pieces on Samuel Beckett. He is the co-editor of a special issue of *Textual Practice* on 'The Uses of Anachronism' (2012), and the author of *Modernism, Narrative and Humanism* (Cambridge University Press, 2002) and *Modernism and the Aesthetics of Violence* (Cambridge University Press, 2013).

SAM SLOTE is an Assistant Professor in the School of English, Trinity College Dublin. He is the author of *The Silence in Progress of Dante, Mallarmé, and Joyce* (Peter Lang, 1999) and *"Ulysses" in the Plural: The Variable Editions of Joyce's Novel* (National Library of Ireland, 2004), and the co-editor of *Derrida and Joyce: Texts and Contexts* (State University of New York Press, 2012), *How Joyce Wrote "Finnegans Wake": A Chapter-by-Chapter Genetic Guide* (University of Wisconsin Press, 2007), *Genitricksling Joyce* (Rodopi, 1999) and *Probes: Genetic Studies in Joyce* (Rodopi, 1995). A monograph on Joyce's Nietzschean ethics is forthcoming. He is the co-director of the Samuel Beckett Summer School at Trinity College Dublin.

RUSSELL SMITH is a Lecturer in Literary Studies at the Australian National University, Canberra. He has published widely on Beckett, with essays in the *Journal of Beckett Studies* and *Samuel Beckett Today/ Aujourd'hui*, as well as *Samuel Beckett's* Endgame (Rodopi, 2007), *The International Reception of Samuel Beckett* (Continuum, 2009), and *Beckett and Nothing* (Manchester University Press, 2010). He edited the collection *Beckett and Ethics* (Continuum, 2009). He also writes on Australian literature and visual art, and is co-editor of *Australian Humanities Review* (www.australianhumanitiesreview.org). He is currently completing a book on the treatment of emotion in Beckett's postwar writing, provisionally titled '*All I Am Is Feeling*': *Beckett's Sensibility*.

ANTHONY UHLMANN is a Professor of Literature and the Director of the Writing and Society Research Centre at the University of Western

Sydney. He is the author of a number of works on Beckett including two monographs: *Beckett and Poststructuralism* (Cambridge University Press, 1999) and *Samuel Beckett and the Philosophical Image* (Cambridge University Press, 2006). He edited Beckett's notes to Arnold Geulincx in the first English edition of Arnold Geulincx's *Ethics*, which he co-edited with Han van Ruler and translator Martin Wilson (*Arnold Geulincx's Ethics with Samuel Beckett's Notes*, Brill, 2006). He is the editor of the *Journal of Beckett Studies*.

DIRK VAN HULLE, Professor of English Literature and Director of the Centre for Manuscript Genetics (University of Antwerp), is the current president of the European Society for Textual Scholarship. He edited *Beckett's Company* (Faber, 2009) and is the author of *Textual Awareness* (University of Michigan Press, 2004), *Manuscript Genetics, Joyce's Know-How, Beckett's Nohow* (University Press of Florida, 2008), and the first volume (2011) of the Beckett Digital Manuscript Project (www.beckettarchive.org). He is currently working with Shane Weller on *The Making of Samuel Beckett's 'L'Innommable/The Unnamable'* and with Mark Nixon on *Beckett's Library* (Cambridge University Press, forthcoming).

SHANE WELLER is a Professor of Comparative Literature and Co-Director of the Centre for Modern European Literature at the University of Kent. His publications include the monographs *A Taste for the Negative: Beckett and Nihilism* (Legenda, 2005); *Beckett, Literature, and the Ethics of Alterity* (Palgrave, 2006); *Literature, Philosophy, Nihilism: The Uncanniest of Guests* (Palgrave, 2008) and *Modernism and Nihilism* (Palgrave, 2011). Edited volumes include *The Flesh in the Text* (Peter Lang, 2007), with Thomas Baldwin and James Fowler; Samuel Beckett's *Molloy* (Faber, 2009), a special issue of *Comparative Critical Studies*, with Ben Hutchinson, on the theme of literary archives (2011); and *Modernist Eroticisms: European Literature after Sexology*, with Anna Katharina Schaffner (Palgrave, 2012).

Permissions and Acknowledgements

Letters, manuscripts and other unpublished documents written by Samuel Beckett and cited in this volume are cited by permission of the Estate of Samuel Beckett. These materials are © The Estate of Samuel Beckett and relate to the following:

Excerpts from Samuel Beckett's letters to Barbara Bray 7 September 1967 and Herbert Martyn Oliver White 5 April 1957 and to Hutchinson 21 January 1958; Barney Rosset 5 May 1959, 5 October 1960, 6 August 1960, 12 February 1961, 26 July 1962, and 20 October 1964; to Patrick Magee 26 February 1960; Barbara Bray 29 July 1959, 11 March 1959, 15 April 1959, 26 May 1959, 26 July 1959, 11 March 1959, 1 July 1963, 4 and 16 October 1960, 12 February 1959 and 26 May 1959; Thomas MacGreevy 19 August 1959; Ethna MacCarthy 22 April 1959; George Devine 5 March 1958; Aidan Higgins 17 May 1956 and 5 October 1960; A J Leventhal 9 February 1961 and 18 May 1961; Mary Hutchinson 9 July 1971; Robert Pinget 15 May 1962; Henri Lefébvre 12 May 1959; Avigdor Arikha 12 March 1959; Christian Ludvigsen 8 December 1966 and 7 October 1960; Klaus Herm 18 December 1976; Stefani Hunzinger 7 June 1961; Siegfried Unseld 1 July 1963; and Jacoba Van Velde 20 May 1961, 2 June 1961, and 20 October 1962; and manuscripts: HRHRC Notebook and 'Whorescope Notebook'; are reproduced by the kind permission of the Estate of Samuel Beckett c/o Rosica Colin Limited, London. ©The Estate of Samuel Beckett.

Permission to cite these materials has also been granted by the following owners of letters, manuscripts and other documents: The Beckett International Foundation, University of Reading; The Bibliothèque Nationale de France: Département des Manuscrits; John J. Burns Library, Boston College; Robert Pinget – Samuel Beckett Letters; Deutsches Literaturarchiv, Handschriftenabteilung, Marbach, SuhrkampArchiv; S. Fischer-VerlagGmH, Frankurt am Main; Grove Press Publishing Company Records, Special Collections Research Center, Syracuse University Library; Lilly Library, Indiana University, Avigdor Arikha Collection; Harry

Ransom Center, University of Texas at Austin; Manuscript Department, Library, Trinity College Dublin.

The cover photo to this volume was taken by Frank Serjack as part of a series captured during the production of *Film* in New York in 1964. Every effort was made to contact the estate of the late Frank Serjack.

I wish to thank the University of Western Sydney for its support of this project and James Gourley, Melinda Jewell, Liesel Senn, Suzanne Gapps and Gavin Smith for their work assisting with the editorial process.

Abbreviations

BECKETT

CDW	*The Complete Dramatic Works.* London: Faber and Faber, 1986.
CP	*Collected Poems in English and French.* New York: Grove Press, 1977.
CSP	*The Complete Short Prose, 1929–1989.* Edited by S. E. Gontarski. New York: Grove Press, 1995.
D	*Disjecta: Miscellaneous Writings and a Dramatic Fragment.* Edited by Ruby Cohn. New York: Grove Press, 1983.
Dream	*Dream of Fair to Middling Women.* New York: Arcade, 1992.
E	*Eleuthéria.* Translated by Michael Brodsky. New York: Fox Rock, 1995.
H	*How It Is.* Edited by Edouard Magessa O'Reilly, London: Faber, 2009.
M	*Murphy.* Edited by J. C. C. Mays, London: Faber, 2009.
M&C	*Mercier and Camier.* Edited by Seán Kennedy. London: Faber, 2010.
MD	*Malone Dies.* Edited by Peter Boxall. London: Faber, 2010.
Mo	*Molloy.* Edited by Shane Weller, London: Faber, 2009.
MPTK	*More Pricks than Kicks.* Edited by Cassandra Nelson. London: Faber, 2010.
NO	*Nohow On: Company Ill Seen Ill Said, Worstward Ho.* Edited by S. E. Gontarski. New York: Grove Press, 1996.
P	*Proust and Three Dialogues with Georges Duthuit.* London: Calder, 1965.
Poèmes	*Poèmes, suivis de mirlitonnades.* Paris: Minuit, 1999.
U	*The Unnamable.* Edited by Steven Connor. London: Faber, 2010.
W	*Watt.* Edited by C. J. Ackerley, London: Faber, 2009.

ARCHIVAL SOURCES

HRHRC	Harry Ransom Humanities Research Center, University of Texas at Austin.
TCD	Manuscript Department, Library, Trinity College Dublin
UoR	Department of Special Collections, University of Reading (Beckett Archives).

OTHER

B	Dierdre Bair, *Samuel Beckett: A Biography*. London: Vintage, 1978.
C	Anthony Cronin, *Samuel Beckett: The Last Modernist*. London: HarperCollins, 1996.
K	James Knowlson, *Damned to Fame: The Life of Samuel Beckett*. London: Bloomsbury, 1996.
L1	Edited by Martha Dow Fehsenfeld and Lois More Overbeck, *The Letters of Samuel Beckett: Volume I: 1929–1940*. Cambridge: Cambridge University Press, 2009.
L2	Edited by George Craig, Martha Dow Fehsenfeld, Dan Gunn, and Lois More Overbeck, *The Letters of Samuel Beckett: Volume II: 1941–1956*. Cambridge: Cambridge University Press, 2011.

Chronology

1906	Samuel Barclay Beckett born to May and William Beckett in their house 'Cooldrinagh' in upper-middle-class Foxrock, south of Dublin, on Good Friday, 13 April. He has a brother (Frank) who is his elder by four years.
1911	Attends kindergarten at Elsner's private academy (run by sisters Ida and Pauline Elsner) at nearby Leopardstown.
1913	Takes first communion at Tullow Church.
1915	Student at the Earlsfort House School in Dublin.
1920	Moves to Enniskillen in the north of Ireland to attend boarding school at the Portora Royal School.
1921	Is elected to the school's Literary and Scientific Society.
1922	Is made a Junior Prefect.
1923	Returns to Dublin and enters Trinity College Dublin (TCD) as a fee-paying student. Begins attending plays at the Abbey Theatre and other theatres in Dublin. Attends silent movies.
1924	Studies English, French and Italian at TCD.
1925	Studies English, French and Italian at TCD. Wins prize for Composition at Lectures.
1926	Travels to France on a cycling tour of the Loire Valley. Moves to College rooms at 39 New Square Dublin. Here he meets Alfred Péron, an exchange *lecteur* from the Ecole Normale Supérieure (ENS).
1927	Selected as an exchange *lecteur* with the ENS. Travels to Italy. Awarded his BA, first in the First Class.
1928	Moves to Belfast to teach English and French at Campbell College in January, but leaves the position in July. Meets his cousin Peggy Sinclair in Dublin then travels to visit her in Kassel and then in Vienna in September. Takes up his post as *lecteur* at ENS in November. Meets his compatriot Thomas McGreevy[1]

and forms a strong and enduring friendship. McGreevy introduces him to James Joyce and his circle. Beckett also meets Jean Beaufret and Eugene Jolas at this time. Beckett helps Joyce with the proofs to 'Work in Progress' (later published as *Finnegans Wake*). In December, Joyce suggests to Beckett that he write an essay on Work in Progress and gives advice on the topic and reading matter for what will become 'Dante…Bruno.Vico..Joyce'.

1929   Publishes both 'Dante…Bruno.Vico..Joyce' and his first short story, 'Assumption', in the journal *transition* with which he will be closely associated (as an occasional contributor and a regular, mostly uncredited, translator) both before and after World War Two. Publishes *Che Sciagura* in *TCD* magazine.

1930   Begins work with Alfred Péron on a translation of the *Anna Livia Plurabelle* section of Joyce's 'Work in Progress' into French. Submits his poem *Whoroscope* to the Hours Press, which offered a prize for a poem on time, and wins the prize. The poem is subsequently published with notes added at the request of the publishers. Begins writing his long essay *Proust*. Successfully applies for a lectureship in modern languages at TCD and returns to Dublin to take up the position in October, but confides to McGreevy from early on that he is not happy there. Corresponds with publisher on *Proust*, asking to add a chapter comparing the use of time in Bergson with that in Proust but finds himself too busy to add this chapter.

1931   *Proust* published in London by Chatto and Windus. Poem 'Alba' published in the *Dublin Magazine*. *Anna Livia Plurabelle* translation published in the *Nouvelle Revue Française* but Beckett's role in the translation is downplayed. Begins writing *Dream of Fair to Middling Women*.

1932   Visits his cousins and Peggy in Kassel. While there he sends a telegram submitting his resignation from TCD. Publishes 'Sedendo et Quiescendo' in *transition* and 'Dante and the Lobster' in *This Quarter*. Sends *Dream* to Charles Prentice at Chatto and Windus but it is rejected. It is subsequently rejected by Cape, Hogarth, Grayson and Grayson, Dent, Methuen and others. Has operation to remove a cyst on his neck.

1933   Peggy Sinclair dies of tuberculosis in May. In June his father dies of a heart attack. Abandons attempt to publish *Dream* and instead takes sections from it to add to his collection of short stories *More Pricks than Kicks*. Sends *MPTK* to Chatto and Windus who accept it for publication.

1934	Moves to London in January. Soon after begins psychoanalytic treatment (after a near breakdown he attributes to his response to the deaths that occurred in 1933) with Wilfred Bion. *MPTK* published by Chatto and Windus in May (the book sells poorly). In October it is banned in Ireland.
1935	Holidays with his mother, May, in England in July. Begins to write *Murphy*. George Reavey accepts a collection of poems and *Echo's Bones and Other Precipitates* is published by Europa Press in November. Returns to Foxrock in mid December and falls ill with pleurisy.
1936	Reads Geulincx in TCD library while finishing *Murphy*. Writes to the Russian film director Sergei Eisenstein and offers to work for him. Finishes *Murphy* and begins to send it to publishers (it is rejected by a number of publishers, including Chatto and Windus, Heinemann, Constable and Lovat Dickson). Leaves for an extended tour of Germany in September.
1937	Returns to Foxrock in April. Begins work on an ultimately unfinished play about Samuel Johnson called 'Human Wishes'. Moves back to Paris in October. *Murphy* is accepted for publication in December.
1938	Takes receipt of the eleven-volume *Complete Works of Kant*. Meets Hemingway. Around midnight on 6 January he is stabbed by a pimp on the Avenue d'Orléans and taken to hospital in the early hours of 7 January. Joyce visits him in hospital as does his future wife, Suzanne Deschevaux-Dumesnil. Beckett works on proofs of *Murphy* making late changes. Decides against translating the Marquis de Sade. Has affair with Peggy Guggenheim. *Murphy* published by Routledge in March. Begins writing poetry in French. Writes critical piece *Les deux besoins*.
1939	Last copies of *MPTK* pulped. Travels to Ireland briefly but returns to Paris the day after France declares war on Germany on 4 September.
1940	Finishes translating *Murphy* into French (which he worked on to begin with Alfred Péron). Germans break French lines in June and the French government and two million refugees leave Paris (among them Beckett and Suzanne). Beckett and Suzanne return to occupied Paris in September. Nazis require all Jews to register and carry identification papers.
1941	James Joyce dies in Zurich in January. Beckett begins *Watt*. In September he joins the Resistance group code named 'Gloria SMH'.

1942   In March Beckett's friend Paul Léon is transported to Auschwitz where he dies in April. Jews in Paris required to wear yellow Star of David on their outer clothing. From July the registered Jews in Paris begin to be deported en masse to Nazi extermination camps. On 16 August, Alfred Péron is arrested after 'Gloria SMH' is betrayed. Informed by Péron's wife, Beckett and Suzanne immediately flee their flat. Over two months they slowly make their way to Roussillon in the Vaucluse, which is outside the German occupied zone in 'Vichy' France. In November, Vichy France too is occupied by German troops.

1943   Beckett works on a farm for the Aude family. *Murphy* goes out of print having sold 600 copies. Beckett continues work on *Watt*.

1944   D-Day 6 June. Paris liberated on 24 August. Continues work on *Watt*.

1945   Beckett is awarded the Croix de Guerre by the French government in March. Makes his way to Dublin via London. War in Europe ends on 8 May. Finishes *Watt* and begins to send it to publishers. Experiences the 'vision' described in *Krapp's Last Tape*, which he tells Knowlson took place in his mother's room in Foxrock, through which he comes to understand how he should write from now on. Works at Saint-Lô in France as a volunteer with the Irish Red Cross. Beckett signs a contract with Bordas for the French *Murphy* and all subsequent work.

1946   Ends work at Saint-Lô and returns to Paris. Begins writing short story *Suite et Fin* first in English but then continues it in French. *Suite* is in part published by the Jean-Paul Sartre Simone De Beauvoir journal *Les Temps modernes* in July. Writes *The Capital of the Ruins*. Starts work on *Mercier et Camier* in July and completes it in October. Writes the short stories 'L'expulsé' and 'Premier amour' and begins 'Le Calmant'.

1947   Begins writing (in French) his first full-length play, *Eleutheria*, in January and completes it in February. The French *Murphy* is published in April. Begins *Molloy* in May and finishes it on 1 November. George Reavey unable to find a publisher for *Watt*. Reluctantly Beckett takes up an offer to work as a translator for the journal *Transition*, which has been revived under the stewardship of Georges Duthuit with whom Beckett discusses his aesthetic ideas in an important series of letters (see *L2*).

1948   Bordas rejects *Molloy*. Begins work on *Malone meurt* on 25 February and finishes it on 30 May. Publishes *Peintres de l'empêchement*. Begins *En attendant Godot* on 9 October.

1949	Completes *En attendant Godot* on 29 January. Begins *L'innommable* on 29 March. Publishes *Three Dialogues with George Duthuit* in *Transition* in December. Works on commissioned translations for UNESCO.
1950	Finishes first version of *L'innommable* on 21 January but revises it later in the year. Returns to Ireland in June due to his mother's ill health. May Beckett dies on 25 August. Suzanne, who has taken over as Beckett's French agent, has *Molloy*, *Malone meurt* and *L'innommable* accepted by Les Editions de Minuit (who will subsequently publish all Beckett's work in French). Publishes English extracts of *Molloy* and *Malone Dies* in *Transition* in October.
1951	Begins *Textes pour rien* in February and completes them all on 20 December. *Molloy* is published by Minuit in March. Roger Blin begins to try and stage *En attendant Godot* from April. Minuit publishes *Malone meurt* in November. From December he begins but abandons a number of works, with the extraordinarily productive period, which he called the 'siege in a room' (from 1946–51) coming to an end.
1952	Purchases land in Ussy sur Marne, where he will from now on spend a good deal of time, and which becomes a writing retreat from Paris. *En attendant Godot* is published by Minuit in September. Rehearsals for Blin's production of *Godot* begin in November.
1953	Rehearsals of *Godot* attended by critics, including Ruby Cohn, on 3 and 4 January, with official opening on 5 January. Finishes building a house at Ussy. *L'innommable* is published by Minuit in June. Publishers of erotic fiction *Merlin* agree to publish *Watt* and it appears under the 'Olympia Press' imprint in August. Beckett works on an English version of *Molloy* with Patrick Bowles and a German translation with Erich Franzen. Works on a French translation of *Watt* with Daniel Mauroc. Barney Rosset of Grove Press, New York, asks to see translations of *Molloy* and *Godot*, which are subsequently accepted. Minuit buy the rights to the French *Murphy* from Bordas.
1954	Tentatively begins work on *Fin de Partie*. Returns to writing in English 'From an Abandoned Work' in an effort to overcome writer's block. Grove Press publishes *Waiting for Godot* in September. Beckett's brother Frank dies the same month. Revises Bowles' translation of *Molloy*.
1955	Olympia Press publishes *Molloy* in English in Paris March and Grove publishes it in New York in August. Works, with difficulty

on *Fin de partie*. The first English production of *Godot*, directed by Peter Hall, is staged at the Arts Theatre in London beginning in August. It premieres in Dublin in October. *Nouvelles et Textes pour rien* is published by Minuit in November.

1956 *Godot* premieres in Miami in the United States in January and moves to New York in April. Faber publishes *Waiting for Godot* in London in February. Beckett sends *Mime du rêveur* to Minuit. Beckett works on *Fin de partie* and, having been asked by Martin Esslin at the BBC, for a radio play, begins work on *All That Fall*, which he finishes in September and sends to the BBC. Finishes *Fin de partie* about the same time. Grove publishes *Malone Dies* in October.

1957 *All That Fall* is broadcast by the BBC. Minuit publish *Fin de partie, suivi de Acte sans paroles*. The world premieres of these plays (in French) take place in London in April before moving to Paris. Finishes translation of *Endgame* in June. In August, Faber publishes *All That Fall* and a French translation prepared with Robert Pinget appears with Minuit in October. In November in San Francisco the San Francisco Actor's Workshop, directed by Herbert Blau, stages a famous production of *Waiting for Godot* in San Quentin Prison.

1958 World premiere of English *Endgame* in New York in January. Begins writing *Krapp's Last Tape*, which is published in the *Evergreen Review* in New York in July. Faber publishes *Endgame and Act Without Words* in April. *The Unnamable* is published by Grove in September. *Krapp's Last Tape* premieres in London with *Endgame* in October. Begins *Comment c'est* in December.

1959 French translation of *Krapp, La dernière bande* by Pierre Leyris published in *Les Lettres Nouvelles*. Beckett given honorary degree by TCD. Starts writing *Embers*, which is published in the *Evergreen Review* in November, with the French translation, *Cendres* published in *Les Lettres Nouvelles* in December. Grove and Olympia Press publish *Molloy, Malone Dies* and *The Unnamable* in a single edition. Faber publishes *Krapp* and *Embers*.

1960 Minuit publishes *La dernière bande, suivi de Cendres*. *Krapp* premieres in America in January and *La dernière bande* premieres in France in March. Calder publishes *Molloy, Malone Dies* and *The Unnamable* in a single edition. *The Old Tune*, an adaptation by Beckett of Robert Pinget's radio play *La manivelle*, is broadcast on the BBC. Both texts are published by Minuit in

September. Begins work on *Happy Days* in October. Finally finishes *Comment c'est*.

1961   *Comment c'est* published by Minuit in January. Marries Suzanne Deschevaux-Dumesnil in March. Begins translating *Comment c'est* into English. Finishes *Happy Days* in May, which premieres in New York in September and is published by Grove the same month. *Poems in English* is published by Calder in London. Begins writing *Cascando* in December.

1962   Finishes *Cascando* in January. 'The Expelled' published in the *Evergreen Review* in February. Starts work on *Play* in May. Faber publishes *Happy Days* in June. *Words and Music* is completed and broadcast on the BBC in November.

1963   Minuit publishes Beckett's translation of *Happy Days*, *Oh les beaux jours* in February. *Play* finished in March. Writes outline of *Film*, which he sends to Grove. Attends rehearsals of *Spiel* in Ulm, the German version of *Play*, which is also the world premiere of the play. Calder publishes *Murphy* and *Watt* in October.

1964   *Play* opens in New York in January. Attends rehearsals of *Endgame*. Meets Harold Pinter. Meets Billie Whitelaw. Faber publishes *Play, and two short pieces for radio* in March. *How It Is* published by Grove and Calder in April. Travels to New York to work on the production of *Film* between July and August. Begins *All Strange Away* in August. Attends *Godot* rehearsals in London in December.

1965   Begins writing *Eh Joe* in April and finishes it in May. *Film* shown at the New York Film Festival. Begins work on *Assez*. *Imagination morte imaginez* is published by Minuit in October and *Imagination Dead Imagine* is published in the *Sunday Times*. Begins work on *Le Dépeupleur*. Works with director Jean-Marie Serreau on film version of *Comédie*.

1966   Minuit publishes *Comédie et actes diverses* in January; *Come and Go* premieres in its German version in Berlin the same month. Begins *Bing* in June, which he finishes in September. It is published by Minuit in October. *Eh Joe* is broadcast by the BBC in July.

1967   Minuit publishes *D'un ouvrage abandonné*, and *Têtes-mortes* in February. Thomas McGreevy dies in March. *Eh Joe and Other Writings* published by Faber in March. Beckett directs his own production of *Endspiel* (*Endgame*) from August to September in Berlin. *No's Knife: Collected Shorter Prose* is published by Calder

	in November and as *Stories and Texts for Nothing* by Grove in December.
1968	*Poèmes* published by Minuit in March. Writes *Breath* for Kenneth Tynan's revue *Oh! Calcutta*. Minuit publishes French version of *Watt*.
1969	Beckett wins the Nobel Prize for Literature in October, while he is in Tunisia.
1970	Under pressure from Richard Seaver at Grove, Beckett removes publishing restrictions on *More Pricks than Kicks* and *Mercier and Camier*. Grove publishes *The Collected Works of Samuel Beckett*. Minuit publishes *Mercier et Camier* and *Premier Amour* in April. Calder publishes *Lessness* in July and Minuit publishes *Le Dépeupleur* in September.
1971	Undergoes operation to remove a cataract. Assists with a German production of *Happy Days*. Begins English translation of *Le Dépeupleur*.
1972	Calder and Grove publish the English translation of *Le Dépeupleur, The Lost Ones,* in January. Continues work on *Pour finir encore*, which he began in 1970. Writes *Still*. Writes *Not I*, which premieres in New York. Attends rehearsals for *Not I* in London.
1973	*Not I* premieres in London and is published by Faber in January. Works on translations of short prose works: *He is bareheaded, Horn came always, I gave up before birth*. *First Love* is published by Calder in July.
1974	Begins writing *That Time*. Attends rehearsals for London production of *Happy Days* in October and in December works on the Schiller Theater production of *Godot*.
1975	Directs *Godot* in Berlin and works on *Pas moi* in Paris. Finishes *That Time* and works on *Rough for Radio II*. Begins writing *Footfalls* and *Long Observation of the Ray*.
1976	Begins work on the TV play *Ghost Trio*. *Pour finir encore* published by Minuit in February. Works with Billie Whitelaw on a production of *Footfalls* and a production of *That Time*, which premiere in May. Meets composer Morton Feldman and sends him the short work *neither*. Begins the TV play *…but the clouds…* which he sends to the BBC in November and works on at the BBC in December. Begins writing the short poems in French he calls the *mirlitonnades*. James Knowlson and John Pilling found the *Journal of Beckett Studies* at Reading University.

1977	*Collected Poems in English and French* is published by Grove and Calder. Works on the *mirlitonnades*. The BBC broadcasts a programme called 'Shades,' which includes *Ghost Trio*, *...but the clouds...*, and *Not I* in April. He begins to write *Company* in May.
1978	Minuit publishes the French translation of *Footfalls, Pas* in May, and *Poèmes, suivi de mirlitonnades* in August. Jonathan Cape publishes Dierdre Bair's biography of Beckett in September. Works on German production of *Play* in Berlin.
1979	Sends *A Piece of Monologue* to critic and radio producer Martin Esslin and performer David Warrilow (it had been written some years before). Works on BBC TV production of *Happy Days* featuring Billie Whitelaw. Begins translating *Company* into French. Begins writing *Mal vu mal dit* in October. Premiere of *A Piece of Monologue* in New York.
1980	Minuit publishes *Compagnie* in Paris and Calder publishes *Company* in London in January. Stan Gontarski asks Beckett for a play to be performed at the forthcoming Beckett conference at Ohio State University. Begins writing *Rockaby*. Travels to London to direct the San Quentin Drama Workshop in *Endgame*. Begins writing *Ohio Impromptu*, which he completes in a few days on 1 December. Completes *Mal vu mal dit* and begins to translate it as *Ill Seen Ill Said*.
1981	*Mal vu mal dit* is published by Minuit in March. *Rockaby and Other Short Pieces* is published by Grove in April. *Ill Seen Ill Said* is published in the *New Yorker* magazine and by Grove in October. Writes *Quad*, which premieres on German TV in October.
1982	Finishes *Worstward Ho* in March. Invited by the Association internationale de défense des artistes (AIDA) to contribute a play in a benefit for imprisoned Czech playwright (later president of his country) Vaclav Havel, Beckett begins work on *Catastrophe*, which is presented at the Avignon festival of 1982 on 21 July 1982. Minuit publishes *Catastrophe et autres dramaticules* the same month. *Rockaby* opens in London in December.
1983	English version of *Catastrophe* published by the *New Yorker* in January. Writes *What Where*. *Worstward Ho* is published in April. *What Where* and *Catastrophe* premiere in New York in June. Tells friends he cannot translate *Worstward Ho* into French. *Disjecta: Miscellaneous Writings and a Dramatic Fragment*, edited by Ruby Cohn, is published by Calder in September.

1984	Works with the San Quentin Drama Workshop on a production of *Godot* that will tour the world. Faber and Grove publish *Collected Shorter Plays*. Calder publishes *Collected Poems 1930–1978* in May and *Collected Shorter Prose 1945–1980* in July. Begins work on *Stirrings Still* in November.
1985	Works on *Stirrings Still*. Recasts *What Where* as a TV play for German TV (*Was Wo*), which is produced by SDR in Stuttgart.
1986	Continues work on *Stirrings Still*. Has operation to relieve his emphysema.
1987	Begins the final section of *Stirrings Still*, which he is trying to finish for longtime publisher Barney Rosset. He completes the text in September and sends it to Rosset.
1988	Confined to a nursing home, he works on *comment dire*.
1989	Sections from *Stirrings Still* published in the *Guardian*. The full text comes out in a deluxe limited edition with illustrations by Louis le Brocquy with New Moon Books (an imprint founded by Rosset). Beckett translates *comment dire* as *what is the word*. Suzanne dies on 17 July, and Beckett attends her funeral. Beckett dies in Paris at 1 p.m. on 22 December and is buried in the Montparnasse cemetery on 26 December.

NOTES

This chronology is indebted to a number of sources, but the most important is *A Samuel Beckett Chronology* by John Pilling. Pilling's book is highly recommended to serious Beckett scholars and provides important information not easily found elsewhere. The other most important source is *K*. I also consulted the Table of Dates compiled by Cassandra Nelson and published as part of the new Faber editions of Beckett's works (see, for example, *Mo*, xxi–xxxi).

1 McGreevy changed his name to MacGreevy in 1943. To avoid confusion in this volume I have chosen to use McGreevy throughout (as the most important correspondence with Beckett occurs in the pre-war years).

Introduction
Anthony Uhlmann

When Samuel Beckett first came to international prominence with the success of *En Attendant Godot/Waiting for Godot*, what struck many critics was the sense that his works were virtually divorced from any recognisable context. The two tramps and the master and servant they meet seemed to represent nobody and everybody; the place where they waited might have been anywhere. Celebrated critic Richard Ellmann dedicated a long introductory essay to Beckett called 'Nayman of Noland'.[1] Yet while Ellmann and others struck by the apparent liberation from context in Beckett's works were correct in pointing to a strategy of negation in those works, they contributed to a critical tendency to overstate this freedom from context. This critical overstatement in turn led to misrepresentations and misunderstandings of the works. For example, Beckett was considered for many years to be an 'apolitical' writer. Emile Cioran famously wrote that Beckett remained above such concerns, in believing 'history is a dimension through which man must pass', and Alfred Simon cited this contention with approval in his obituary to Beckett published in *Le Monde*.[2] Clearly the belief that Beckett was apolitical and the first defence offered to this charge (that he was above such matters) share the common assumption that Beckett's works are divorced from the historical contexts from which they emerge.

Yet the assumption that Beckett definitively broke with contexts has come to be challenged by many critics who have brought to light images, allusions and motifs that cause Beckett's works to resonate with the real people, places and problems that marked his life and the world in which he moved. Beckett's notebooks, letters and manuscripts reveal how extensively he entered into dialogue with important intellectual, historical, social and scientific traditions. Theoretical readings have attempted to draw to the surface how far Beckett's use of language and form also confront the realities of the world in which he lived.

Scholars have come to recognise that, rather than being divorced from context, Beckett developed an aesthetic strategy that worked through deliberate negation. Yet just as negative theology seeks to reveal the reality of an omnipotent creator by tracing the outlines that reveal His absence from the world, Beckett's works evoke the power of the contexts from which they emerge by outlining their absence. This is a complex strategy, which Beckett himself described as 'non-relation', yet its methods can be traced within the works themselves.

In discussing Samuel Beckett's work for cinema, *Film*, Gilles Deleuze, who further develops the notion of exhaustion in Beckett in a later essay, contends that Beckett allows us to recognise key potentials of the filmic medium because he exhausts or negates those elements.[3] The same principle of exhaustion or negation might be seen in Beckett's aesthetic writings where he develops the concept of 'non-relation' in art, which he opposes to an artistic tradition that, he states, has always emphasised relation and the power of relation (see Beckett, 'Three Dialogues with Georges Duthuit' in *D* and *P* and the extensive correspondence with Duthuit in *L2*).

In his first novel, *Dream of Fair to Middling Women* (*Dream*), Beckett describes an aesthetic theory that emphasises the connections or relations between things rather than the nature of things themselves. In a later letter to Georges Duthuit (9 March 1949, *L2*, 134–43) Beckett outlines a somewhat different aesthetic understanding; one that emphasises *non*-relation or the refusal to fully draw connections or relationships. Beckett states:

As far as I'm concerned, Bram's painting ... is new because it is the first to repudiate relation in all its forms. It is not the relation with this or that order of encounter that he refuses, but the state of being quite simply in relation full stop, the state of being in front of ... the break with the outside world implies the break with the inside.... I'm not saying that he doesn't search to re-establish correspondence. What is important is that he does not manage to.[4]

In 'Peintres de l'Empêchement' (first published in 1948), Beckett states that all works of art have involved the readjustment of the relation between subject and object (*D*, 137), a relation that he claims has now broken down. He announced this crisis over a decade before and prior to World War Two in 1934 in another review, 'Recent Irish Poetry' (*D*). The breakdown might be understood to have taken place because, on one hand, the subject can no longer understand itself as a simple point of relation, and, on the other, the object is no longer something that can be simply represented, simply understood. A key problem with any attempt to represent (and therefore interpret) the object is that the interpretation,

Introduction 3

the representation (which for Beckett is always made by drawing a thing into relation with an idea), rather than revealing the object, simply adds another layer to it, one that serves to conceal it still more fully, 'Car que rest-t-il de représentable si l'essence de l'object est de se dérober à la représentation?' (*D*, 136).[5] This problem, which involves the thing itself constantly eluding any attempt to be portrayed, is something Beckett attempts to approach, strategically, from different sides at different times. Yet in 'Peintres de l'Empêchement' Beckett answers his own question as follows: 'Il reste à réprésenter les conditions de cette dérobade'(*D*, 136).[6] That is, another approach is the attempt to reveal the process of hiding, to create the effect of the power of an object by occluding rather than attempting to represent the essential components of that object.

What this amounts to in practice is a strategy through which Beckett would deliberately obscure or remove links that might serve to clearly situate his works or ideas in relation to a context. What needs to be very strongly emphasised with regard to Beckett's 'non-relation', however, is that it does not simply remove contexts altogether; rather, it still makes use of such associations, but it now obscures them.

This process of occlusion gives the works much of their power and allows them to generate a sense of abstraction that reconnects them with any place, any people, any time, rather than tying them once and forever to particular times and places. Yet, paradoxically, this is possible for Beckett because of the coherence and depth of analysis that have gone into the use of contexts and sources that he has then hidden. This very strategy, then, lends added weight to critical attempts to find points of connection that have been sundered, disconnected or suspended. These critical projects serve to help us to better understand the power of the works and their capacity for generating understandings of the sense, or senselessness, of our time and place.

This collection considers the question of context in relation to Beckett in two ways. The first three sections of the book, 'Landscapes and Formation', 'Social and Political Contexts' and 'Milieus and Movements', consider how the educational, sociopolitical and artistic milieus through which Beckett passed helped to form both the writer and his manner of writing. The next three sections look at how Beckett's extensive intellectual interests and knowledge (of literature, the arts and the human sciences and hard sciences) made their way into his works. If the first three sections might loosely be thought to involve 'external' influences, the second three might be thought to involve contexts that Beckett made his own. The next section, 'Language and Form', seeks to account for some of the textual strategies

Beckett developed to create his works. The final section, 'Reception and Remains', considers how Beckett and his works themselves have come to be an important context for contemporary artistic practice.

The essays published here offer clearly argued, lucid assessments of the importance of particular contexts to Beckett's works. This book, then, is a highly accessible resource for students first coming to Beckett's work. At the same time it offers a sustained attempt to understand Beckett's particular approach to working with contexts, and as such it will offer new insights that will be an important resource for Beckett scholars as well as general readers.

Finally, I wanted to offer a brief comment on two technical issues. First, I have chosen to use the spelling 'McGreevy' rather than 'MacGreevy' for Beckett's friend and correspondent (who changed his name to MacGreevy in 1941). Both versions of this name are given in the first two editions of Beckett's correspondence. I chose 'McGreevy' as the most important correspondence between Beckett and his friend came before World War Two. Clearly, however, there are arguments on both sides (Knowlson, for example, uses 'MacGreevy'). Second, I chose editions of the works that I felt were as definitive as possible and readily available, yet there are different American and English editions in most cases and choices had to be made. I leaned towards the new Faber editions for the novels as they are the most scholarly editions available. However, I prefer Gontarski's Grove editions of the *Complete Short Prose* and *Nohow On*.

NOTES

1 Richard Ellmann, 'Nayman of Noland', *The New York Review of Books*, 24 April 1986.
2 Simon, Alfred. 'Le mort de Samuel Beckett: L'auteur d' "En attendant Godot" est décédé vendredi 22 décembre à Paris'. *Le Monde*, 27 December 1989, Paris. Pages 1, 10.
3 Gilles Deleuze, 'The Greatest Irish Film', in *Essays Critical and Clinical*. Translated by Daniel W. Smith and Michael A. Greco. Minneapolis: University of Minnesota Press, 1997, 23–6.
4 This letter was first published in 2006 and is now included in *L2*. The original translation by Walter Redfern, which is cited here, can be found in Samuel Beckett, 'Letter to Georges Duthuit, 9–10 March 1949', translated by Walter Redfern, in *Beckett after Beckett*, S. E. Gontarski and Anthony Uhlmann (eds.), Gainesville: University Press of Florida, 2006. For George Craig's translation of this passage see *L2*, 140.
5 'Because what remains representable if the essence of the object is to evade representation?'
6 'What remains is to represent the conditions of this evasion'.

PART I

Landscapes and Formation

CHAPTER 1

Childhood and Portora

Russell Smith

INTRODUCTION

This chapter can do no more than give a very brief sketch of Beckett's childhood and schooldays, indicating in broad terms some of the strategies by which Beckett reworked autobiographical material in his writing. Readers interested in more detail should consult the biographical studies discussed throughout this chapter. By way of an introduction, however, I would like to outline a four-part schema with which these questions might be considered. It involves issues of presence and absence, of specific references and more generalised themes.

First, then, is the question of specific presences. Scholars have often noted how Beckett's mature writing, from the period of *Watt* onwards, say, constructs an abstracted world radically divorced from specific historical and geographical contexts, but in which, nevertheless, tiny concrete details and allusions remain – names or unique characteristics of people and places – which become all the more resonant for their comparative rarity. Beckett develops this tension most explicitly in *Company*, where 'one on his back in the dark' (*NO*, 3) listens to a voice speaking of a scene from childhood '[s]omewhere on the Ballyogan Road in lieu of nowhere in particular' (*NO*, 16). The Ballyogan Road (near Beckett's childhood home) functions as an indicator of specificity per se; the place name is *in lieu of* (in the place of) no place. Beckett's contextual details often have this ghostly quality, both necessary and arbitrary.

Second is the question of specific absences. This is a complex strategy, whereby Beckett's texts draw attention to specific lacunae, suggesting that what is *not* there is sometimes more important than what *is*. To give one example, Phil Baker has shown that all three postage stamps mentioned in *Molloy* are real stamps, but while two are accurately described, the one that is not described, 'your new Timor, the five reis orange' (*Mo*, 113), which Moran demands to see and which his son has hidden, shows 'an image of an upright-looking man with a moustache'[1]; it is an occluded portrait, in other words, of Moran himself, and indeed of Beckett's own father.

Third is the question of thematic presences, that is, more meaningful events or situations (not just 'details') that are reworked, sometimes repeatedly, through Beckett's oeuvre. James Knowlson relates in the preface to his biography how he confronted Beckett, who had insisted on a separation between his life and his work, with numerous examples of repeated childhood scenes. 'Beckett nodded in agreement: "They're obsessional," he said' (*K*, xx–xxi). Scholars often comment on two specific examples.[2] One is a scene where Beckett's father took him to the Forty Foot, a swimming hole near Dublin, and taught him to swim by ordering him to dive into the water. The scene is repeated in various forms throughout Beckett's writing life, from the uncollected poem 'For Future Reference' (1930), through *Watt* and *Eleutheria* to *Company*, written when Beckett was in his seventies. The thematic 'core' of the scene involves the child's fear and the father's stern command to 'Be a brave boy' (*NO*, 12). A second example involves a small boy out walking with his mother, asking a curious question and receiving a cutting retort, which is treated with significant variations in 'The End', *Malone Dies* and once again in *Company*. The thematic core here, amidst the shifting lacunae and variations of detail, is a feeling of apparent togetherness suddenly ruptured by the mother's angry response. As we shall see, Beckett's memories of his schooldays at Portora are of this type, for while there are few concrete details, scenes of mindless rote learning enforced by punishment are a recurrent theme, especially in *The Unnamable*.

The fourth category is the most difficult: the question of generalised themes notably absent from Beckett's writing. Beckett always insisted that he had a happy childhood; what can it mean, then, that children are almost entirely absent as characters in Beckett's oeuvre? That is, there are no imaginative reconstructions of the experience of childhood and schooldays as we see, for instance, in the opening chapters of Joyce's *Portrait*. The stories of Saposcat in *Malone Dies*, for instance, are self-consciously presented as fictional, with Malone even warning the reader 'Nothing is less like me than this patient, reasonable child' (*MD*, 18). Another way of putting this might be to say that there is no implicit *Bildungsroman* or childhood backstory in Beckett's mature writing; childhood exists in a separate universe radically divorced from the present. Seen from the estranged vantage point of adulthood, it appears complicated and compromised by the gaps, distortions, interpolations and embellishments of memory and its vicissitudes.

A brief word is in order on Beckett's biographers. Deirdre Bair, Beckett's first biographer, makes it clear in her preface that she found it difficult working with Beckett, and throughout the book one can discern an underlying hostility to her subject, by no means a prima facie fault in a biographer. Her 1978 biography was relentlessly criticised in Beckett studies for its factual errors and, more pointedly, for its negative portrayal of Beckett as a deeply disturbed man haunted by a tormented childhood and a lifelong guilt-ridden relationship with his domineering and neurotic mother. James Knowlson's authorised biography (1996) can be seen as a corrective to Bair's account, emphasising Beckett's emotional resilience, generosity and compassion, and consistently interpreting the negative aspects of his early years in the redeeming light of futurity. But Bair's biography was begun in 1971, and its depiction of Beckett's early years drew on many sources who had died before Knowlson began his account; Beckett and his contemporaries' views of their early years would have mellowed in the meantime. Knowlson's biography is faithful to the mature Beckett, while Bair's more tendentious account gives a glimpse of the intense sensibility that produced works like *The Unnamable*. The truth probably lies, as truth is wont to lie, somewhere in between (or nowhere in particular).

Lois Gordon's unjustly overlooked *The World of Samuel Beckett* (1996) concentrates on Beckett's first forty years and is particularly good on historical context, while Anthony Cronin's *Samuel Beckett: The Last Modernist* (1997) is astute and engagingly written, especially in its evocation of the Dublin of Beckett's childhood. Finally, Eoin O'Brien's *The Beckett Country* (1986) meticulously documents in photographs the actual people and places mentioned or alluded to in Beckett's work, but is guilty of occasional solecisms such as writing of the ancient graveyard at Tully near Beckett's childhood home: 'It was this graveyard that Moran chose for his final resting place'.[3] To suggest that the places in Beckett's fiction can be visited by a tourist with a map seems a radical misreading of Beckett's project as a whole.

FOXROCK

To begin at the beginning is never simple, and Beckett's case presents two difficulties. The first, thankfully, has been set to rest: Samuel Beckett was born in the front room of his family home on Good Friday, 13 April 1906. However, his birth was not registered until two months later, on 14 June, with the birth certificate giving his birthdate as 13 May, leading Bair to speculate whether this uncanny conjunction of Good Friday and Friday the thirteenth was myth making on Beckett's part (*B*, 1–2). The birth notice in the *Irish Times* of 16 April 1906 proves that Beckett's version is correct.[4]

The second problem is more difficult, for Beckett repeatedly claimed to have memories of his prenatal existence. 'My memoirs begin under the table, on the eve of my birth, when my father gave a dinner party & my mother presided', he wrote to Arland Ussher in 1937 (*L1*, 474). He told John Gruen in 1970: 'I have a clear memory of my own foetal existence. It was an existence where no voice, no possible movement could free me from the agony and darkness I was subjected to'.[5]

It seems that Beckett took these claims seriously. Prenatal memories of this kind are, however, impossible. While the foetus has a memory and undergoes various kinds of learning in utero, 'autobiographical memories' – that is, explicit recollections of events or episodes – do not begin until the age of three or older. Such 'false memories' are well known in psychoanalysis, where analysands produce memories – in which they genuinely believe – in an effort to please the analyst and advance the analysis. Moreover, many early childhood memories are likely to involve 'confabulation', in which individuals confuse actual memories and knowledge of events gained from others. Indeed, *The Unnamable* recognises the creative and collaborative nature of childhood memory: 'Enough of acting the infant who has been told so often how he was found under a cabbage that in the end he remembers the exact spot in the garden and the kind of life he led there before joining the family circle' (*U*, 36). Though it's appealing to imagine Beckett in utero scowling behind his spectacles at the inanity of dinner party chitchat, it is a fantasy on Beckett's part and tells us more about the adult Beckett than the unborn child. In its rejection of the idea of the womb as a lost Eden, it shows Beckett's insistence on understanding suffering as an ontological given, not a psychological contingency.

Beckett's father, William Frank Beckett (1871–1933), was a successful quantity surveyor, a man's man of practical good sense and robust energy, with a 'ready wit', but also a 'fiery temper' (*K*, 10). He was an excellent swimmer and keen golfer, but his greatest love was of long walks through the hills around Dublin, especially on Sunday mornings when, while May attended Tullow Parish Church, Bill would 'go to church with the birds up in the mountains' (*K*, 24). His early death plunged his younger son into profound depression, and Beckett's writing is repeatedly haunted by the wordless companionship of their walks together; 'they were absolutely tuned in', remembered Beckett's cousin Sheila Roe (*K*, 12). Memories of these walks in the Dublin hills provide the only moments of quasi-spiritual experience in Beckett's writing.

But Bill Beckett was, in his son's words, 'absolutely non-intellectual' (*K*, 10). Though he would have impressed upon his son the traditional manly virtues of courage, resilience and emotional self-restraint, there was another side to Bill Beckett. In his late twenties, as the son of a prosperous Protestant family, Bill had fallen in love with Eva Murphy, the daughter of a prominent Catholic businessman. Both families were appalled at the prospect of a marriage, and the girl, forced to renounce her lover at her mother's deathbed, hastily married an elderly Catholic surgeon (see *C*, 6). Bill lapsed into what would now be called depression and was admitted to the Adelaide Hospital with pneumonia, where he was nursed by a tall, thin, serious and practical girl, Maria Roe, known as May; they married within a year. But according to Mary Manning, a close childhood friend of Beckett's, Bill 'never got over' his first love (*K*, 13). By contrast with the more familiar image of his manly bonhomie, this story would have left a profound impression of masculine vulnerability and lasting hurt, though it is never directly evoked in Beckett's writing.

May Beckett (1871–1950) came from a once wealthy County Kildare family that fell on hard times, and when her father, Samuel Robinson Roe, died when she was fifteen, the family was in such financial straits that she had 'gone nursing' to ease the burden. Though May and Bill seemed an ill-sorted couple, Bill was seen as a good match for May and they married on 31 August 1901. The house Bill Beckett built for his new bride, Cooldrinagh, in the fashionable suburb of Foxrock, was a three-storey Tudor home with tennis court, croquet lawn, summerhouse, stables and extensive lawns and gardens. May was of a puritanical but also rather 'mercurial' temperament, 'extremely strict and demanding', with a rigid sense of decorum and a fierce temper, but also capable of 'acerbic wit' and even moments of elation that contrasted forcibly with her periods of 'dark depression' and self-imposed isolation (*K*, 5). She was threatened with expulsion during her convent schooldays for talking to a boy over the back wall, an episode she sometimes referred to as a married woman and of which she seemed rather proud (*C*, 8). In her married life, however, she displayed the intolerant perfectionism of the religious temperament, and, as Cronin observes, despite Beckett's claim to have little sympathy with this outlook, he would 'inherit this extremism rather than his father's adaptability and moderation' (*C*, 13).

Beckett's relationship with his mother – 'I am what her savage loving has made me', he confided to his friend Tom McGreevy (*L1*, 552) – is a source of constant dispute in Beckett studies. 'You might say I had a happy childhood', Beckett once said, 'although I had little talent for happiness. My parents did everything that they could to make a child happy. But I was often lonely. We were brought up like Quakers. My father did not beat me, nor did my mother run away from home'.[6] Bair astutely detects a sly message here: as the marriage progressed, Beckett's father was increasingly away from home, spending his evenings in the club and his weekends walking in the hills, while his mother almost certainly beat him, though how fiercely and how often is a significant point of variance between Bair and Knowlson's accounts (*B*, 13; *K*, 19–20). Whatever form they took, May's frequent punishments seem only to have ingrained more deeply her son's rebellious and risk-taking temperament (*K*, 21–2). However, although she sternly disapproved of her son's artistic ambitions and bohemian lifestyle, and they had blazing rows during his adult life whenever he stayed at Cooldrinagh, she supported him financially and paid for his two-year course of intensive psychoanalysis, a generous act for someone of her religious convictions and social mores.

Nevertheless, going by the prima facie evidence of Beckett's work, mother figures are often treated with hostility and aggression, sometimes of an extraordinarily violent nature. Though it would be wrong to read this as straightforwardly autobiographical, it would be equally disingenuous simply to follow Molloy's advice: '[I]f you don't mind we'll leave my mother out of all this' (*Mo*, 56). This phrase is of course an allusion to Freud's famous formulation in his essay 'Negation': '"You ask who this person in the dream can be. It's *not* my mother". We emend this to: "So it *is* his mother"'.[7]

Phil Baker's wonderful study *Beckett and the Mythology of Psychoanalysis* (1997) convincingly showed, before Beckett's notes became available to scholars, how well informed Beckett was about psychoanalytic theory. In particular, Beckett's use of themes such as birth trauma and the Oedipus complex are so overt that they become 'not unconscious symbols which need to be deciphered, but quotations of "unconscious symbols" which operate on a conscious thematic level and need to be recognised'.[8] This knowingness presents enormous problems for autobiographical and especially psychoanalytic readings of Beckett's work. For Baker, Beckett's 'hostile dialogue with psychoanalysis'[9] focuses 'particular aggression on one specific tenet: the formative effect of childhood on the adult'.[10] So, in terms of maternal aggression, the repressed material is presented in plain view, with no attempt at denial, 'turning the text inside out in a way which, far from being helpful to the Freudian reader, pre-empts this kind of psychoanalytic reading'.[11] In interpreting the influence of Beckett's childhood context on his work, we should be conscious that Beckett's treatment of childhood often involves significant exaggeration, distortion, inversion and irony. In terms of the schema outlined earlier, what is presented most overtly is often carefully crafted to mislead and frustrate the psycho-biographical reader.

Bair's biography related a childhood incident (told by Beckett's cousin Mollie Roe) in which Beckett tormented his mother by climbing to the top of a fir tree and throwing himself off to be caught by the lower branches. The scene is reproduced in *Company* (*NO*, 14–15), written a few years after Bair's biography was published, leading Bair to wonder 'if the work had truly sprung from Beckett's creative vision or if he might have been playing a joke on his biographer and her vision of his life' (*B*, xiii). This dichotomy seems a false one, however; the structure of *Company* insists that memories are ultimately no more than stories, and whether one's own or others' is ultimately undecidable: 'Repeatedly with only minor variants the same bygone. As if willing him by this dint to make it his. To confess. Yes, I remember' (*NO*, 10).

From the age of five until nine, Beckett attended a kindergarten near Foxrock run by the Elsner sisters; memories of the sisters, their cook, Hannah, and their dog, Zulu, reappear in *Molloy* (*K*, 24–5). From age nine to thirteen Beckett caught the 'Dublin Slow and Easy' from Foxrock to Harcourt Street Station in Dublin, where he attended a larger school at Earlsfort House (*K*, 30–6); details of this train journey and the two stations recur many times in Beckett's works, most notably in *All That Fall* and *Watt* (see *K*, 30–1).

PORTORA

Beckett attended Portora Royal School, Enniskillen, from Easter term 1920, when he was fourteen, until the latter half of 1923, when he entered Trinity College, Dublin. A primary reason for sending first Frank and then Sam to boarding school was, in Beckett's own words, 'to get us away from the Troubles'.[12] Beckett remembered being taken by his father, one night during the Easter Rising in 1916, up the Glencullen road to a spot where they could see the flames, an event Beckett later recalled with horror. Over the ensuing weeks, lists of rebels executed in secret by the British appeared daily in the Dublin papers;[13] in James Stephens' memorable words, 'it was like watching blood seeping from under a locked door' (*C*, 36). Gerry Dukes notes that there were twenty-three separate holdups by Republican irregulars or criminals on the Dublin 'Slow and Easy' line in the course of the Troubles.[14]

Portora was a school on the English public school model, renowned as 'tough' and offering 'the predictable package of discipline, prayers, bullying, and appalling food, but also a sound education'.[15] Reflecting the fact that the school was often referred to as the 'Eton of Ireland', the school's song was *Floreat Portora*, sung to the same tune as *Floreat Etona*. At the time, the school consisted of 120 pupils, mostly boarders, who resided in the school's imposing, square-set Georgian buildings, high on a hill overlooking Enniskillen and Lough Erne.

Portora Royal School was founded under the terms of a decree issued by James I of England in 1608, according to which 'there shall be a free school at least in each county, appointed for the education of youth in learning and religion'.[16] Portora's website wryly notes that, although the decree intended Royal Schools to be built in the 'county towns', 'at the time of the proclamation County Fermanagh had no town to which the description "county" could be applied, in fact it could be said that the county had no settlements to which the description "town" could be applied'.[17] The original school was therefore established in 1618 at the village of Ballybalfour, fifteen miles from Enniskillen. Ballybalfour's awkward role in serving as a 'county town', without any claim to either of these titles, cannot but recall Moran's description of the 'Molloy country' centred on Bally (from the Gaelic *baile*, meaning 'town' or 'village'), comprising 'a settlement, dignified by some with the name of market-town, by others regarded as no more than a village, and the surrounding country' (*Mo*, 139). Moran goes on to explain the system whereby the terms *Bally*, *Ballyba* and *Ballybaba* designate, respectively, the town, the town including its environs and the environs exclusive of the town. In transforming Ballybalfour into Ballybaba, Beckett seems to have drawn on this fragment of Portoran folklore.

Beckett excelled at the school in sporting pursuits – cricket, rugby, swimming and boxing – but as Portora's archivist David Robertson points out, his 'academic attainment at Portora was below his true potential'; Robertson notes that when Beckett left for Trinity in 1923, four of his contemporaries had won awards, but not Beckett.[18] His name does not feature on the scroll of academic prizewinners with the now restored name of Oscar Wilde, boarder from 1864 to 1872, whose name was removed after his conviction for homosexual offences in 1895 (*C*, 40).

Beckett's concentration on sporting rather than academic achievement was not atypical. A 1910 report by the Intermediate Education Board noted

Childhood and Portora

that '[a]ttention to sporting activities appeared to have been to the detriment of academic interests'.[19] Beckett made the school's cricket First XI in his first year, distinguishing himself, according to the school magazine, as 'an attractive batsman', a 'good field' and a 'very good medium-paced bowler with a sharp break-back'. He played halfback in the rugby side from his first year and in 1923 was captain of the First XV, 'blind without his spectacles, but bold as a lion in the scrum' as recalled by Douglas Graham, a contemporary and later headmaster of the school.[20] He was also a member of the school's swimming team and the school's light heavyweight boxing champion. There are almost no references to cricket, rugby, boxing or swimming in Beckett's writing.

Beckett appears to have fit in reasonably well at the school. As a boarder (rather than one of the despised 'day dogs'), a successful sportsman, and with an older brother who was a prefect and captain of the cricket First XI, Beckett's social status in the school hierarchy would have been secure. Nevertheless, Beckett's schoolmates remember him as moody and withdrawn; photographs typically show him with his head slightly lowered in a disdainful scowl, glowering behind his spectacles. Knowlson reports that during his first term, Beckett was bullied in the library by a gang led by a boy called Clark. Beckett, who had a violent temper, lashed out at the ringleader; having learnt boxing at Earlsfort House and being slightly heavier than Clark, Beckett gave him a savage beating. After that he was left alone (*K*, 38).

Although the school was more inclined to reward 'physical distinction on the playing field and knightliness expressed through the concept of "fair play"' (*C*, 40), it also accorded a certain prestige to intellectual achievement. Headmaster E. G. Seale awarded a gold medal each year to the winner of an essay competition, an honour Beckett won three times. It is not known whether Beckett contributed to the school magazine *Portora*, although a sonnet about a school performance of Haydn's Toy Symphony, signed 'John Peel', shows some features of Beckett's style and even includes a reference to Dante.[21] Both Sam and his brother Frank were unusual among their schoolfellows in taking piano lessons, and Sam was remembered for being word perfect across the range of Gilbert and Sullivan operas. He was also a keen chess and bridge player, participated in the school debating society and was an assistant to the school librarian. In short, he seems to have participated across the range of activities on offer.

Although never in serious trouble, Beckett was rebellious by inclination and was a ringleader in several pranks. Glimpses of this appear in the characterisation of Sapo in *Malone Dies*: 'He boxed and wrestled well, was fleet of foot, sneered at his teachers and sometimes even gave them impertinent answers' (*MD*, 14). One of the teachers who left a lasting impression was science and mathematics master W. N. Tetley, whom Beckett particularly loathed. Geoffrey Thompson remembers Beckett drawing lewd caricatures of Tetley, his face peering right side up from between his buttocks, and casually allowing Tetley to discover them, a streak of malicious daring that shocked his classmates (see *B*, 32–4). Tetley is the primary subject of the 1930 poem 'For Future Reference' – 'that little bullet-headed bristle-cropped / red-faced rat of a pure mathematician'[22] – indicating that Beckett's antagonism well outlived Portora (see *C*, 45–7). Eoin O'Brien even speculates that Tetley may have contributed to the creation of Basil in *The Unnamable*[23]: 'One in particular, Basil I think he was called, filled me with hatred. Without opening his mouth, fastening on me his eyes like cinders with all their seeing, he changed me a little more each time into what he wanted me to be' (*U*, 8).

Another memorable episode concerned Thomas Tackaberry, a hopeless disciplinarian who, though in his fifties, was still a junior master. One evening, when it was Tackaberry's turn to supervise the evening 'prep' in the study hall, Beckett and a fellow student orchestrated a concert of 'The Singular Sing-Song Singers'. Having received a song list beforehand, on a signal from Beckett the assembly 'spontaneously' burst into a series of songs. Tackaberry, spotting Beckett as the ringleader, descended on him and began to rain blows on his head with his fists. Beckett put up his guard until the beating stopped and then retorted: 'Why don't you hit someone your own size!' The effect was devastating: Tackaberry walked back to his dais, put his head in his hands and started to weep. 'To think I've come to this', he moaned, 'a convenient piss-pot for the whole school!' (*K*, 44–5). Along with his aloofness and sense of superiority, there was a streak of aggression and even cruelty in the younger Beckett that occasionally finds expression in his writing, especially in early works such as *Dream* and *Murphy*.

Though he often said his time at Portora was the last period of happiness for years to come, Beckett retained no affection for the school. Though one schoolmate, Geoffrey Thompson, became a lifelong friend, Beckett dropped all ties with the school and ignored later overtures for recognition. Eoin O'Brien's meticulous documentation of Beckett's Irish background is forced to concede that 'there are few references in Samuel Beckett's writings to the institutes in which he received his education'.[24] Indeed the principal literary legacy of Portora seems to have been a handful of names; G. T. Bor became surgeon Bor in 'A Case in a Thousand';

E. P. Mahood lent his name to the unfortunate pupil in *The Unnamable*, while both Mercier and Camier drew their names from Old Portorans.

What Beckett seems to have retained from Portora (whether or not he had it before) is self-discipline, physical toughness, self-reliance and a manly code of 'truth-telling, trustworthiness and fair play' (*C*, 40). What he did not retain, as his brother Frank did and as his mother would have wished, was religious faith: 'My mother and brother got no value from their religion when they died', Beckett later commented. 'At the moment of crisis it had no more depth than an old school tie'.[25]

The legacy of Portora, though short on detail, coalesces in two important themes in Beckett's work: a hatred of mindless educational methods based on coercion and a rejection of the conventional values they uphold. According to D. B. McNeill, a contemporary of Beckett's, the boys learnt large slabs of Latin by Ovid, Cicero and Virgil by heart, mainly taken from *Kennedy's Latin Primer*, the book favoured by the headmaster, E. G. Seale.[26] 'And out it all pours unchanged,' says the Unnamable. 'I have only to belch to be sure of hearing them, the same old sour teachings I can't change a tittle of. A parrot, that's what they're up against' (*U*, 49). An especially important theme is that of the pensum, 'a piece of schoolwork imposed as a punishment' (*OED*): '[I]f I have a pensum to perform it is because I could not say my lesson, and ... when I have finished my pensum I shall still have my lesson to say, before I have the right to stay quiet in my corner' (*U*, 21–2).

The disreputable behaviour of the insubordinate son and pupil who insists on thinking and acting for himself becomes a central figure in some of Beckett's most memorable writing (see, for instance, *Mo*, 22). One should not expect, therefore, to find Molloy's name among the lists of Old Portorans; 'the danger', as Beckett wrote in his first piece of literary criticism, 'is in the neatness of identifications' (*D*, 19). It is rather in the diffuse resonances, the ghostly after images and pointed lacunae, not the details, that the contours of Beckett's childhood and schooldays are to be discerned.

NOTES

1 Phil Baker, *Beckett and the Mythology of Psychoanalysis* (Basingstoke: Macmillan, 1997), 37.
2 See S. E. Gontarski, 'Introduction', *Nohow On: Company, Ill Seen Ill Said, Worstward Ho* (New York: Grove Press, 1996), xvii–xx.
3 Eoin O'Brien, *The Beckett Country: Samuel Beckett's Ireland* (Dublin: Black Cat Press, 1986), 26.

4 Reproduced in Gerry Dukes, *Samuel Beckett* (London: Penguin, 2001), 5.
5 Quoted in *C*, 2, see also James Knowlson and Elizabeth Knowlson (eds.), *Beckett Remembering/Remembering Beckett* (London: Bloomsbury, 2006), 68.
6 Alec Reid, 'The Reluctant Prizeman', *Arts* (29: 1969), 64. qtd. in *B*, 13.
7 Sigmund Freud, 'Negation', *On Metapsychology: The Theory of Psychoanalysis* (London: Penguin, 1991), 437.
8 Baker, *Beckett and the Mythology of Psychoanalysis*, xvi.
9 Ibid., 4.
10 Ibid., 18.
11 Ibid., 16–17.
12 Knowlson and Knowlson, *Beckett Remembering/Remembering Beckett*, 21.
13 See Lois Gordon, *The World of Samuel Beckett, 1906–1946* (New Haven: Yale University Press, 1996), 12–22.
14 Dukes, *Samuel Beckett*, 18.
15 C. J. Ackerley and S. E. Gontarski, *The Grove Companion to Samuel Beckett* (New York: Grove, 2004), 450.
16 'Portora Royal School – History.' <http://www.portoraroyal.co.uk/?tabindex=7&tabid=4443> Accessed 13 September 2011.
17 Ibid.
18 David Robertson, 'Sam's Schooldays', *The Irish Times*, 22 April 2006 <http://www.irishtimes.com/newspaper/weekend/2006/0422/1144908542147.html> Accessed 13 September 2011.
19 'Portora Royal School – History'.
20 Tom Peterkin, 'Sam Beckett's Schooldays', *The Telegraph* (UK), 13 April 2006 <http://www.telegraph.co.uk/news/uknews/1515563/Sam-Becketts-schooldays.html> Accessed 13 September 2011.
21 Reproduced in O'Brien, *Beckett Country*, 119.
22 Quoted in Lawrence Harvey, *Samuel Beckett: Poet and Critic* (Princeton: Princeton University Press, 1970), 299–301.
23 O'Brien, *Beckett Country*, 116.
24 Ibid., 111.
25 Tom Driver, 'Beckett by the Madeleine', in *Samuel Beckett: The Critical Heritage*, Lawrence Graver and Raymond Federman (eds.) (London: Routledge & Kegan Paul, 1979), 244.
26 Frances Green, e-mail correspondence with Anthony Uhlmann concerning reminiscences of D. B. McNeill, April–May 2002.

CHAPTER 2

Dublin and Environs

John Pilling

As is well known – even if readers do not always take matters very much further – it is by way of a 'commodius vicus of recirculation' that Joyce makes, or tries to make, *Finnegans Wake* an endlessly circular experience, 'bring[ing] us back' to Dublin with its familiar landmarks ('Howth Castle and environs'). Joyce had of course already given his hero Leopold Bloom an 'out and back' trajectory in *Ulysses* under the self-imposed pressure of matching the *nostos* or return of Homer's *Odyssey*.[1] Like his own Stephen Dedalus in *A Portrait*, Joyce had chosen silence, exile and cunning, but in the event, found it impossible to keep silent on the subject of Dublin once he had gone into permanent exile abroad, a Dublin to which (with the help of a small army of acolytes) he could not help but return afterwards in almost everything he wrote. It was only natural for the phrase 'the Joyce country' to take on a larger meaning than its literal equivalent in the remote hinterlands of Galway and Connemara. The idea of 'the Beckett country', by contrast, only took on reality with the splendid book of that title published by Eoin O'Brien at his Black Cat Press in Dublin in 1986, a book rendered even more indispensable by the addition of photographs by David H. Davison. The book's subtitle – 'Samuel Beckett's Ireland' – tied Beckett more firmly to his country of origin than he had ever been, or wished to be, during his lifetime, and the idea has now taken sufficient hold to be developed more or less successfully in a number of subsequent monographs. In this chapter I suggest some ways in which – if 'The time is perhaps not altogether too green[!]' (*D*, 94) – the picture might be supplemented and/or revised, so that 'without fear or favour' (*CP*, 28) matters can, if only temporarily, be put on a different footing and placed in a slightly more conflicted context.

The Irish scene in Beckett is never what it was in Joyce, or indeed in any number of other writers, whether traditionalist or modernist, or a bunch of 'thermolaters' and 'twilighters' (*D*, 70, 71). During and after World War Two, Beckett put 'his' Ireland to imaginative use in works as various as

Watt, *Mercier et Camier*, the so-called trilogy, *All That Fall*, *The Old Tune* and, very late, in *Company*, but he did so only intermittently. Indeed, by 1939 Beckett had clearly enough settled in his own mind that all returns to Ireland – other than those enjoined upon him by circumstances, notably the illnesses and funerals of family and friends – would only ever be imaginative journeys, and not long prolonged. How, or at least when, Ireland became an old tune can perhaps best be seen in a remarkable letter (dated 31 January 1938, *L1*, 598–600) to his close friend Thomas McGreevy – a closer friend before the war than he was after – which in its sinuous and essentially genial way anticipates the reservations Beckett felt reluctantly obliged to register in his 1945 review of McGreevy's book-length essay on writer and painter Jack B. Yeats for the *Irish Times*[2]:

I am inclined personally to think that the turning away from the local, not merely in [Yeats's] painting but in his writing (he has just sent me *The Charmed Life*), even if only in intention, results not so much from breakdown of the local, of the local human anyway, as from a very characteristic and very general psychological mechanism, operative in young artists as a naïveté (or an instinct) and in old artists as a wisdom (or an instinct). (*L1*, 599)

Beckett's letter speaks of 'inclinations' governing his inability to invoke '[t]he national aspects' (*D*, 96) – he is in fact obviously enough inclining *away* from them, with 'instinct' as his only real guide – and his syntax is sufficiently convoluted to remind us that at this point in time Beckett had resided in Paris for only a few short weeks, staying at the Hôtel Libéria, and that he was, with increasing desperation, looking for an apartment to rent. But the nub of the letter – 'the turning away from the local' – is perfectly clear, and the turning away in question had been taking place for the best part of a decade.

In investigating this turning away, an obvious first port of call is the novel *Dream of Fair to Middling Women*, written in 1931–2, but it can only be a port of call because it contains little of significance over against the experiences of the protagonist Belacqua in such charismatic places as Vienna, Paris and Kassel. Dublin is at the end of 'the dull coast road home' which opens section 'THREE', and this third section is largely concentrated upon, or orientated towards, a Christmas Eve party at the Fricas. The real-life equivalents of the Fricas, Susan and Mary Manning, lived outside the city centre, down by the Grand Canal, close to Ballsbridge (at 35 Wellington Place), and Beckett's interest lies in bringing the party guests there, exposing them for the chaff they are and moving on, having already left Dublin proper behind. There is nothing of the

Dublin and Environs

warmth and sentiment that infuses 'The Dead', the famous last story in Joyce's *Dubliners*, and none of these figures could possibly be co-opted, with or without their consent, into the Joycean project of writing a page in the moral history of their country, or forging race consciousness in the smithy of their souls. That kind of thing, Beckett implies, was over and done with; as he puts it in the 1932 poem 'Serena II', a far from serene affair as it happens, 'the fairy tales of Meath [are; and for 'Meath' read 'myth'] ended'. It is presumably no accident, as it were, that the mysterious Nemo, a kind of *éminence grise* throughout *Dream*, should be 'withdrawn' from the novel 'more dead than alive from under the stair of the Salmon Leap at Leixlip', only to fetch up at 'the Stillorgan Sunshine Home or was it the Lucan Spa Hotel'.[3] (A photograph of the Hotel is in the O'Brien book, and it was one of the few details of *Dream* that Beckett referred to in his private correspondence after the book had been, like Nemo, jettisoned.[4] How far the choice of the Salmon Leap at Leixlip was determined by the fact that his mother's family origins were in the vicinity can only be guessed at.)

Beckett's poems at this time are, naturally enough, more direct, and Dublin and its surroundings (especially the latter) figure largely in them. Here is a representative conspectus of some highly charged locales:

at Parnell Bridge a dying barge ('Enueg I')
on the hill down from the Fox of Geese into Chapelizod (ditto; Chapelizod is the *mise en scène* of *Finnegans Wake*; but the real point here is that the 'I' is moving southwest, away from the centre of the city)
Blotches of doomed yellow in the pit of the Liffey (ditto; cf. 'Clew Bay vat of xanthic flowers' in 'Serena II')
[...] like an anthrax
shining on Guinness's barges ('Enueg II')
[...] on Butt Bridge blush for shame ('Serena III')
the Bull and Pool Beg [lighthouses] that will never meet (ditto)
slow down slink down the Ringsend Road (ditto).

Here a landscape which could have been conceived of as merely indifferent (an epiphenomenal manifestation of the 'fate' which is half-heartedly assumed to be operating in the short story 'Walking Out', for example) seems to have turned into something actively hostile, and the places themselves seem to have lost any real connection with one another. Beckett was, of course, under no duress to be 'realistic' in what are self-evidently poems, and none of his poems (whether in Dublin or out of it) can be usefully put under the microscope, or in front of the mirror, of 'Realism'. But when Beckett was working (between 1929 and 1933) in the more 'conventional' genre of the short story he inevitably had to comply with a (limited) number of realistic conventions.

Beckett's short stories on first reading make it seem as if the places in them are simply what they would be in real life, backgrounds against which figures figure. In the heightened reality of the fiction, however, locations that have no option but to stay themselves take on different colourations in becoming something other:

> the Hill of Feltrim (cf. the mill at Feltrim in 'Fingal') as 'the Hill of the Wolves' ('Love and Lethe');
> the wood of 'Walking Out', 'Tom Wood', as 'fate';
> the Hibernian Dairy across Pearse Street as in some way implicated in the demise of a little girl 'run down' in her attempt to rejoin the cinema queue she has just left ('Ding-Dong');
> the Church of Saint Tamar – there *is* no Saint Tamar – at Glasnevin, close to the greatest and largest of Dublin cemeteries ('What A Misfortune');
> the Nursing Home in 'Yellow' transformed into a 'charnel house';
> the double-edged sword of Mr Taylor's pub in 'Fingal' (situated, appropriately enough, in Swords);
> Greystones cemetery (left unnamed; the resting place of Beckett's father from 1933) in 'Draff'.

Beckett's short stories depend for their effect on details, structures and ironies which have nothing to do with the storytelling impulse as such, which is one reason why they have largely been found ineffective. But, as with the poems, a personal geography, well beyond any putative map references, is at work in them. And Ireland (or a very small part of it) is unwittingly taking part in a complicated game in which Beckett is settling either old or recent scores with his native terrain, largely to its discredit.

The extremely unruly 'rules' of this game can be seen operating in another extraordinary personal letter, to Nuala Costello, a close friend of Lucia Joyce, sent to Nuala in Ireland by Beckett in London (*L1*, 184–9). As Miss Costello herself must have discovered, this is a more difficult nut to crack. Beckett ends up by telling her – she was looking after the mentally ill Lucia, the model for her father's Anna Livia in *Finnegans Wake*, whom she was in due course to help to bring to a hospital near London – 'I am all set now to give Liffey's stinking tide a long long miss'.[5] Beckett was almost certainly thinking of Lucia and the 'long long' river Liffey, and trying to school himself to keep away from her (an objective he only partly managed a year or so later). But earlier in the letter he had thought back to a junction of streets in Dublin ('if I have not forgotten my Dublin', which he very clearly had not, since he could pinpoint the 'petrified asp at the junction of D'Olier, College, Pearse and Townsend Streets'), and had then moved on to the specifics of whether one changes or 'alights from' buses in London (*LI*, 186). Nuala Costello was an intelligent woman, but could hardly have been expected to realise that she had been cast in a psycho-drama of Beckett's making, with him desperate to 'change', but desperate at the same time to find somewhere to stay put ('my anabases and stases', from the very first sentence of the letter; 'I must just stay as I am'), and desperate above all to stay away from the Dublin he could never really forget and to maintain some distance between himself and the Joyces, especially Lucia.

Beckett's letters, like his poems and short stories, are worthy of study in their own right, and I have obviously only scratched the surface of them here. All of them tell a story different from the one they appear to tell, and many of them are so difficult to decipher that they may never be satisfactorily decoded. But the clues are easier to follow in the poems, even with so much going on in them at once that they, too, can swiftly bring on a headache. Here, for example, is a single line from 'Sanies II':

> sailing slouching up to Puvis[6] the gauntlet of tulips[7]

This nods in the direction of Jack B. Yeats – a quite different painter from Puvis de Chavannes – but also the author of *Sailing Sailing Swiftly* (Wishart, 1933). But no sooner has it done so than it turns away from Jack towards his brother W. B. Yeats, among other things the poet of 'The Second Coming', which famously ends:

> And what rough beast, its hour come round at last,
> Slouches towards Bethlehem to be born?

When Beckett wrote 'Sanies II' he was imagining his *first* coming to Paris (he marked the HRHRC copy of *Echo's Bones and Other Precipitates* '1929' above this poem, which was not when it was written), and perhaps, in mid 1932, wondering whether he would ever return. But he would never have thought of an 'hour' coming round again (by a 'commodius vicus of recirculation' perhaps?), because for him an endless going ('[...] keep on the move / keep on the move'; 'Serena III'; cf. 'to move constantly from place to place' in 'Ding-Dong') has had to take over from any possibility of a second coming, or any kind of homecoming. The position is anticipated in line 67 of the (1929?) poem 'For Future Reference': 'if he can't come twice [...]'. But it is effectively confirmed by Beckett in his Philosophy Notes (1933?; TCD) in jotting down the famous Heraclitus dictum to the effect that no one can 'step down twice into the same stream' (the same motif is also found in the late 1933 jettisoned and still unpublished short story 'Echo's Bones', and is once again used *en passant* in 'Le Monde et le Pantalon'). Even more typically Beckettian is the dry additional note: 'For Cratylus not possible even once'!

In the mid 1930s Beckett obviously gave serious thought to a number of distinctively Irish matters – for a time he even considered a 'Trueborn Jackeen' project,[8] towards which he took notes from the *Encyclopaedia Britannica* – and was offered opportunities to express them in essay form ('Recent Irish Poetry'; 'Censorship in the Saorstat'[9]), and in reviews of friends' books (Thomas McGreevy's poems; Jack B. Yeats's novel *The Amaranthers*). Spot judgements intended to shock ('Balnibarbism has triumphed'; 'the Irish are a characteristic agricultural community' [*D*, 68, 87]) show Beckett in a poorer light than more considered estimates: of Jack Yeats's novel, for example, in which 'The Island is not throttled into Ireland' (*D*, 90). But it is not difficult to read between the lines, and more often than not there is no need to do so. Beckett's subsequent disavowal of the 'local', whether 'human' or a matter of landscape, was being prepared for by a disavowal of things national – very much a matter of concern in the years of nation building after gaining independence from Britain – but it was underpinned by Beckett's own sense of a 'rupture of the lines of communication' (*D*, 70), a product of psychological difficulties rather than an objective or semi-objective statement of fact. One of Beckett's few open admissions that this was at the root of the matter can be found in the claim made in the 'Recent Irish Poetry' essay, an acronym of which would obviously read 'RIP' for something or somebody, that 'what he [Thomas McGreevy] sees' is proof that 'it is the act and not the object of perception that matters' (*D*, 74).

These indicators, slight and trivial as they may seem in isolation, acquire a much greater significance as they accumulate over the years. Beckett's vision, whether microscopic or macroscopic, could hardly be more different from that of Joyce, who in exile liked (more than half seriously, it would seem) to claim that, were Dublin to suffer some terrible cataclysm, it could be rebuilt by a close reader of *Ulysses*. No such focus, no comparable notion of restitution and nothing so orientated towards integration, can be discerned in Beckett, for whom (as in the first version of the poem 'Serena II') 'all the chords of the earth [are] broken like a bad pianist's' (*L1*, 141). It is in the same spirit of disintegration that – in one of the most Irish of the *More Pricks* stories, 'Fingal' – Belacqua, on spotting what will become his getaway vehicle (a bicycle), sees 'The owner [...] out in the field, scarifying the dry furrows with a fork' (*MPTK*, 20), which inspires in him a 'longing to be down there in the clay, lending a hand', an impulse only modified in the nick of time by a 'soft chord of yellow' (*MPTK*, 21).

For Beckett 'turning away' was an 'act' which meant that in practice he was 'Always elsewhere', as in the first line of an unfinished, and in the event unfinishable, poem begun in Germany.[10] The abiding charm of this notion was that it could never be realised in reality, except of course at the most practical of levels. There was no longer a 'home' to go to ('Sanies I'), and the consummation devoutly to be wished was 'a setting out without the coming home' (*LI*, 334). Whether or not Beckett believed that Germany might be the way to realise this programme, it did not take long once he was there for him to discover that it had turned into 'a journey *from* and not *to*, as I knew it was, before I began it' (*LI*, 397), and once again he had to confront how impermanent all his moves away had turned out to be. In the early months back in Paris in late 1937 it was touch and go as to how he could make a going concern out of one more setting out, in the hope that it might prove to be (in the words of the poem 'Cascando') 'a last even of last times'. But Paris lasted, at least until the German occupation of France; the 'journey' became only too real, one reason perhaps why the journeys of Watt in the novel of that name possess such an odd and spectral quality, as if Watt himself were hardly there. It was only once he could be back in post-war Paris that Beckett could really take or leave Dublin much as he chose to do, which had certainly not been the case in the early to mid 1930s.[11] Very revealing in this connection is the long passage describing Ballyba, its economy wholly determined by the exchange values established for the production and recycling of faeces, which can only be found in the third holograph notebook of part II of *Molloy*.[12] Beckett subsequently jettisoned this long (circa twenty-four hundred words), wild, satirical passage, much of which was written between 9 and 11 October 1947, only a few months after he had returned from the 'summer rain' of Dublin, the Irish name for which (BaileAthaCliath) was obviously one of the partial prompts for creating the fictional Ballyba. In the manuscript, the reason Moran gives for writing the passage is strikingly in accord with Beckett's commitment to 'turning away from the local', as the wry tone, ostensibly nostalgic but desperately ironic, clearly enough indicates:

'C'est peut-être la dernière fois que j'aurais l'occasion de m'abandonner à une passion pour la chose régionale, pour ce qui donne à chaque terrain son bouquet unique, pour ce que j'appellece folklore de sous-sol.'[13]

(It is perhaps the last time I shall have the opportunity to indulge my passion for regional matters, for what gives each terrain its own peculiar bouquet, for what I call this folklore of the subsoil. [My translation])

Beckett may even have still had the Ballyba excursus in mind in writing to his friend McGreevy (letter of 27 March 1949; *L2*, 145): 'I think it is impossible to have health in Dublin. Of any kind', since it is of course highly questionable whether a political and social economy based entirely on faeces could ever really be healthy, even with the Irish already praised with faint damn for being 'a characteristic agricultural community' (*D*, 87), one reason why in 'Fingal' we are introduced to a labourer with a fork.

By 1949 and perhaps even two years earlier, it would seem Ireland could live or could be let live – not least by jettisoning a potentially offensive passage – because in Beckett's mind it was 'being given [...] birth to into death' (*MD*, 114). But even well beyond the 1940s, it was easier for Beckett to remember Dublin as a place of danger and near disaster. It seems somehow symptomatic that, in mentioning the Phoenix Park in a letter to Barbara Bray,[14] Beckett should remember how he had fallen off a horse there and had a 'hair-breadth escape'. This detail, which none of his biographers seem to have had to hand, can certainly be read as one more black mark against his country of origin, even if it could hardly be seen as the place's fault.

At the end of *Dream of Fair to Middling Women* (240), Beckett confronted the possibility that any engagement with landscape might be 'nostalgia'. But even at that early point Belacqua's gaze is being drawn towards the Welsh Hills: better to look away than to look back. Beckett's anti-Hibernian stance – sometimes brutally severe, sometimes delivered with more subtlety (making London, rather than Dublin, the focal point for *Murphy*, for example) – could be best maintained for so long as he could keep 'turning away from the local' in thought as well as in fact, and as time passed his relief at being free from the local was only really seriously threatened when he had no option but to return to Ireland. Two classic examples of the Irish authorities seeking to retrieve their great authors from deaths abroad (W. B. Yeats in 1939–40, and James Joyce in 1977)[15] seem to have prompted amusement and indignation in Beckett in just about equal measure, and it is not difficult to imagine what he would have thought of any comparable attempt in his own case to make of him, in death, something he had never been in life. But if we look closely, without (as it were) ourselves 'turning away', there is a certain value, over and above the kind of homage so memorably paid by books like *The Beckett Country*, in re-siting him among at least some of the familiar landmarks of his youth and young manhood, if only for a better understanding of what was at stake in what he chose to leave behind.

The Emerald Isle – perhaps already a little belittled by way of the name given to the Smeraldina in *Dream* – could be easily enough transformed into 'the haemorrhoidal isle',[16] and in due course 'Haemorrhaldia',[17] and ultimately 'the green unpleasant'.[18] More art, but also more waste matter, may be found at the point in the story 'Love and Lethe' where Belacqua, or his narrator, is moved to observe that 'A human turd lay within the rath [i.e. a fairy ring]'.[19] And with the passage of time greater subtlety could achieve more complex effects and still put Ireland in its place: *Murphy*, for example, moves all of its Irish characters ultimately to London; *Watt* generates motifs of Irish origin either in madcap schemes (Louit and the Mathematical Intuitions of the Visicelts; the unachieved millennium of the Lynch family), or similarly failed quests (Mr Hackett requesting information on the subject of Watt in the scene at the beginning, usually thought of as 'taking place' in the vicinity of the then Harcourt Street Station). There is also the (negative) evidence in the six *ur-Watt* notebooks at the HRHRC which show that a very large amount of distinctively Irish material was jettisoned. But Beckett's deep need, in the early days, was to dish the dirt on Joyce's 'dear old dirty Dub' as openly as he dared, as he attempted to make clear (albeit in a most oblique way) in a letter to McGreevy: 'Better Basel where love is not than D.D.D. with sentimental salmagundis and other on the mat' (*L1*, 119). In the end, as in the beginning, it was not to be Basel (or a number of other, equally unlikely as they seem now, European capitals), but – as with W. B. Yeats imagining himself 'Sailing to Byzantium', 'out of nature', and for good, in what for Beckett was both the temporal and the moral sense. Not so much 'Anywhere out of the world' as in Baudelaire, though with Beckett there was always something like that emotion to struggle with; but, failing that, (almost) anywhere out of Ireland.

NOTES

1 In the short story 'Ding-Dong' the narrator describes how Belacqua favours an 'out and back' or 'boomerang' trajectory; but it is questionable whether the story itself endorses this, rather than demonstrating that it is actually not achievable.
2 Collected in *D*, 89–90, with the original newspaper heading: 'An Imaginative Work!'.
3 *Dream*, 182–3.
4 Letter to Thomas McGreevy of 15 May 1935 (TCD).

5 This is a quotation from one of Jonathan Swift's poems to the 'Stella' who so intrigues Winnie Coates in the short story 'Fingal'.
6 French painter Puvis de Chavannes, referring to his murals at the Parthénon in Paris.
7 Cf. 'the green tulips' of a letter to McGreevy of 12 September 1931 (*L1*, 88).
8 See the letters to Nuala Costello (27 February 1934; *L1*, 188) and to A. J. Leventhal (letter of 7 May 1934; HRHRC).
9 These were written within a few weeks of each other in the summer of 1934. Neither of them was published by the magazine for which they were intended; both are collected, with the literary reviews, in *Disjecta*.
10 Mark Nixon, *Samuel Beckett's German Diaries 1936–1937* (London: Continuum, 2011), 117–18.
11 Not that Paris, with so much post-war reconstruction still to occur was, an unmixed blessing. In a letter of 31 October 1945 Beckett told George Reavey: 'Life in Paris is pretty well impossible except for millionaires'(*L2*, 24). Writing to McGreevy from Dieppe (either 21 or 31 December 1945; TCD) Beckett told him: 'Conditions in France are critical: life in Paris is almost impossible, naturally everyone is disappointed'. Writing to the same correspondent about two years later (4 January 1948), Beckett commented: 'The news of France is very depressing, depresses me anyhow. All the wrong things, all the wrong way. It is hard sometimes to feel the France that one clung to, that I still cling to' (*L2*, 72). Beckett then contrived to particularize what was threatening to become a more general critique: 'I don't mean material conditions, which are appalling. It is quite impossible for me to live now with my pittance. I had hoped that my books would make up the difference. But there is little chance of their pleasing here more than elsewhere'.
12 HRHRC notebook, 132–56; BIF, 'Knowlson Collection', A/4/12, folder 1, 211–24.
13 HRHRC notebook, ibid, 132. Whether the decision to jettison the Ballyba passage was Beckett's own, or the result of a 'prudent' intervention on the part of an editor, publisher or some other well wisher, is not known.
14 Letter of 21 August 1963 to Barbara Bray (TCD).
15 For Beckett's comments on the latter see the letter to his cousin John Beckett of 15 May 1977 (UoR).
16 In the 1932 poem 'Home Olga'.
17 Letter to Barbara Bray of 17 February 1959 (TCD).
18 From a late letter of 17 July 1983 (HRHRC) to Mary Manning Howe: a particularly demeaning description, given Beckett's feelings about the 'green and pleasant land' of Blake's 'Jerusalem'.
19 *L1*, 100. cf. the 'étron' in College Green – 'still there no doubt' – of the letter to Nuala Costello, *L1*, 185.

CHAPTER 3

Trinity College, Dublin

S. E. Gontarski

In the autumn of 1923, seventeen-year-old Samuel Beckett took up his third level education and enrolled as a junior freshman in Trinity College, Dublin. He would thus become part of the first new class at Trinity under the Saorstát Éireann, established the previous winter on 6 December 1922. Trinity Fellow Arthur Aston, that is, A. A., Luce (1882–1977) served as the young Samuel's advisor and tutor.[1] It proved a fortuitous conjunction, this middle-class, athletic student from the south Dublin suburb of Foxrock and the Doctor of Divinity, former Captain of the Late 12th Royal Irish Rifles, recipient of the Military Cross in 1917 and adept fly fisherman, a relationship, in some respects at least, as formative to the young Beckett's future as that of his acknowledged university mentor, Ruddy, Thomas Rudmose-Brown, whom Beckett would finally travesty as the Polar Bear in his first attempt at a novel, *Dream of Fair to Middling Women*. Luce would go on to become an international authority on Idealist philosopher George Berkeley, Bishop of Cloyne, writing Berkeley's biography, several critical books on his work, including *Berkeley's Immaterialism* (1945), editing, with Thomas Edmund Jessop, the complete works in nine volumes (1948–57) and compiling, again with Jessop, a bibliography of Berkeley's work. Almost every time the connection between Luce and Beckett is cited in the critical discourse, the emphasis falls on Luce's introducing Beckett to the Idealist, immaterialist philosophy of George Berkeley. But in 1921, Luce was preoccupied with another metaphysician, French philosopher Henri Bergson, Luce having delivered the prestigious Donnellan lectures that year, published, with the support of the board of Trinity College, by the Society for Promoting Christian Knowledge in March of the following year as *Bergson's Doctrine of Intuition*.[2] The Donnellan lectures, originally conceived as sermons 'for the encouragement of religion, sound learning, and good manners', were endowed by Anne Donnellan in 1794 and have been a fixture at Trinity continuously, if irregularly, since, sponsored at first by the School of Hebrew, Biblical and Theological Studies. The topic of the lectures, at least until 1919, was invariably religious. Luce was the first layman invited to deliver the lectures.

From our contemporary perspective, Luce's assessment of Bergson is misconceived, his analysis overly selective, his book too often oversimplified and wrongheaded, Luce reading Bergson's intuition, for example, not only as a doctrine rather than as a scientific method, as Bergson himself insisted it was, but aligning the doctrine almost exclusively with mysticism, particularly, but not exclusively, Christian mysticism, and too often confusing intuition with impulse and other like extra-rational methods. It is this emphasis on the extra rational that the great pacifist and analytic philosopher Lord Bertrand Russell picked in his review of *Bergson's Doctrine of Intuition*, and in which Russell manages to misconstrue Bergson as completely as does Luce, thinking of it as 'mystic intuition, which sees deeper than the mere analytic intellect'; so far so good, but Russell further notes that 'Bergson's "intuition", in the opinion of the present reviewer, is nothing but an invitation to abandon self-control in certain cases in which it is painful'.[3] Bertie Russell, no friend of Bergsonism in general, goes on in his review to call Luce, whom he nicknames 'Reverend Rifleman', a 'gallant divine', putting the emphasis on Luce as 'The Christian Warrior', the title he gives his review published in *The Nation and the Anthanaeum* (9 September 1922).[4] Russell further saw that, amid the peaceful aftermath of the Great War, *Bergson's Doctrine of Intuition* was a continuation 'of promoting Christian Knowledge',[5] and, in his opening paragraph, Russell notes that Luce's work captures 'the spirit of Irish Protestantism', adding the caveat 'not mentioned by name but implicit throughout the book',[6] and, further, that Luce's version of Bergson supports the tenants of the Church of Ireland. In his attack on Luce and Bergson and on the eve of the establishment of the Irish Free State, Russell takes up the Irish issue as well, suggesting economic motives for the British defeat in the Anglo-Irish war: 'We had an "intuition" that Sinn Fein ought to be put down', notes Russell, 'until we found that doing so would add a shilling to the income tax',[7] and so the spirit of intuition, which Russell admits is in 'closest touch with the spirit of the Western world of to-day', finally 'has led to the appalling outrages by all parties in Ireland'.[8]

Russell himself had thoroughly engaged and assessed Bergson's work for a lecture called 'The Philosophy of Bergson' delivered before 'The Heretics' at another Trinity College, that in Cambridge, a decade earlier on 11 March 1912 (erroneously cited as 1913 in the published volume), just two years after the bulk of Bergson was published in English in 1910. Russell had met Bergson in Paris the year before, in March, and he would see him again at the meeting of the Aristotelian Society on the last Monday in October 1911, where Russell would present a lecture on 'universals and particulars' for which he prepared by reading 'a great deal of Bergson'.[9] He had dinner with Bergson on 28 October, on which he reported, 'all England has gone mad about him for some reason. It was an amusing dinner'.[10] But Russell's take on Bergsonism was severe: 'Bergson's philosophy, though it shows constructive imagination, seems to me wholly devoid of argument and quite gratuitous; he never thinks about fundamentals but just invents pretty fairy tales. Personally, he is urbane, gentle, rather feeble physically, with an extraordinarily clever mouth, suggesting the adjective "fin" [that is, delicate, perhaps]. He is too set to be able to understand or answer objections to his views'.[11] Lord Russell's talk to The Heretics was first published in *The Monist* on 22 July 1912 (321–47), then as a monograph, *The Philosophy of Bergson*, in 1914,[12] revised and collected in his *A History of Western Philosophy* in 1945[13] and, finally, shortened, as Bergson's philosophical reputation declined and so was less formidable an adversary, for the edition of 1961.

Russell's talk was designed, at least in part, to counter the enthusiastic championing of Bergson by T. E. Hulme, who himself delivered a talk before The Heretics on 'Anti-Romanticism and Original Sin' on 25 February 1912, which 'anti-Romanticism' formed much of the core of what would become imagism, if not modern poetry, and shortly thereafter delivered a lecture specifically on Bergson, 'Bergson's Theory of Art', which theory he finds 'is exactly the same as Schopenhauer's',[14] to the students at Girton College (the residential college for women at Cambridge), and four subsequent lectures in London in 1913 collected in *Speculations* as 'The Philosophy of Intensive Manifolds', these as Hulme was translating, along with F. S. Flint, Bergson's *An Introduction to Metaphysics* (1903 French, 1913 English), which translation Luce read for his lectures.[15] Russell's attack on Bergson's 'intuition' was countered in part by his niece, Karin Costelloe, whom he had tutored as she prepared for her Tripos (on which she received a First) and writing a paper on Bergson at Newnham in 1910.[16] She published a pointed response to her tutor, 'An Answer to Mr. Bertrand Russell's Article on the Philosophy of Bergson', in 1914 in *The Monist*,[17] where she notes straightforwardly, 'Mr. Russell is therefore wrong' and that he 'caricatures this theory'. For Costelloe, 'Thought about, knowledge by, concepts, involves the distinction between subject and object. It is only in pure intuition that Bergson ever claims that this distinction is transcended. It may fairly be questioned whether such a claim can be justified, but in any case criticisms leveled against Bergson's theory and perception as though it applied to conceptual thought will always be wide of the mark'.[18]

The Russell–Hulme conflict at Cambridge played out before the Heretics Club was one between amateur and professional philosopher at a University dominated by ordinary language philosophy, and the Vienna school in general, even as Hulme's strong opposition to and Russell's strong advocacy of pacifism fuelled the animosity.[19] For Russell and his band of New Philosophers, Bergson lacked method.[20] Luce's book, then, might have placed him amidst the very foundations of Modernist discourse, the strand at least leading from Bergson through Hulme to Pound, Eliot, Woolf and Joyce. Knowingly or not, then, Luce stepped into one of Modernism's great early conflicts, between metaphysicians and analytic philosophers, the early battle played out before The Heretics at Cambridge University, and one which Russell's sometime student Karin Costelloe Stephen and Luce's student Samuel Beckett would also take up.

With Luce's assessment in 1921 and 1922, rather his précis of Bergson, he joins the Modernist discourse in philosophy and literature, placing a strong emphasis on evolution, particularly the evolution of mind or consciousness as outlined by Bergson, while omitting all mention of Bergson's powerful critique of nothingness.

Luce does, however, make a strong argument for what we might call Bergson's Doctrine of Failure. Very little of Luce's argument would have struck a sympathetic chord with the callow Beckett of 1923, fresh from his mother's religiosity, but the denigration of the rational process and the description of a universe in perpetual flux, without fixity, matter and memory inseparable if not indistinguishable, a point to which Russell vehemently objected, may have struck a chord in Beckett's growing rebellious spirit. At least it did at some point; that is, something triggered a rebellious spirit in the University student, and Luce's book, in its own timid way, can be read as a call to overthrow the old order. But Luce, at least nominally Beckett's tutor for his first two years at Trinity, found the young Beckett an indifferent, unreceptive student at best, according to Deirdre Bair, showing none of the promise that would blossom in his third year under the tutelage of Professors of Romance Languages Thomas Rudmose-Brown and Walter Starkie. Much has been written about those latter relationships.[21] Some also has been written about A. A. Luce's direct influence on Samuel Beckett, particularly Luce's work on George Berkeley.[22] But the possibility of this shy, lacklustre student paying any attention to the work and publication very much on Luce's mind when Beckett entered University in the autumn of 1923, Luce's second book, which Luce had recently completed editing and revising for publication, is almost wholly ignored. Deidre Bair suggests that Beckett's relationship with Luce was distant since Beckett lived at home for his first two years at Trinity, and Luce himself admitted that Beckett had 'very little need for a college tutor'; in his first two years, Luce notes, 'he hadn't found his métier [...] his first two years were actually quite dismal' (*B*, 37–8). Anthony Cronin reminds us that Beckett's 'main interests, amounting almost to passions into which all other passions were sublimated, were golf, cricket and motor-bikes" (*C*, 53). What is clear, however, is that Luce would outline to this lacklustre student, through his assessment of Bergson, what became the central preoccupations of Beckett's life work.

The book Luce published as *Bergson's Doctrine of Intuition* is divided into four parts, the format following that of the lectures delivered in the Trinity College Exam Halls off Parliament Square (the venue alluded to on page 87): 'The Method of Intuition' essentially focuses on *Creative Evolution*; 'Free Will' takes as its starting point *Time and Free Will*; 'Mind and Body', perhaps the most important chapter in both the book and for Beckett's future, explores *Matter and Memory*, and finally 'Theory of Evolution' returns to Bergson's magnum opus, *Creative Evolution*, by way of summary. Despite its overriding Christian framework and the added aegis of the publishing house, its themes are flux, failure and inadequacy, 'The inability of the conceptual mode of thinking to express duration [...]',[23] that is, the process, the continual evolution of life itself, and hence the ineluctable process of movement and change, becoming. In terms of classical philosophy we find 'In Bergson', Luce tells us, 'Heraclites asserting his primary conviction and tracing to its source the error of Parmenides' (Luce, 4), a comparison Luce returns to regularly. Bergson, according to Luce, requires of us a new way of thinking: 'the stock in trade of intellect will serve our purposes only as long as we are dealing with a universe that is [static]; a universe that becomes, a universe in the making, demands more [...]. It requires the growth of new powers of apprehension' (Luce, 4), what Luce calls 'a binocularity of inner vision' (Luce, 6). The function of intelligence, then, 'is to enable the organism to act upon its environment' (Luce, 11). The objection is to 'structure', 'the abiding structure under which man [humanity] thinks', structure that 'we call categories' (Luce, 12), which fix and make manageable 'the flux of things' (Luce, 13),[24] which is the 'multiplicity of heterogeneous elements' (Luce, 16). The focus then is the collapse of cause and effect, which suggests linear thinking as opposed to the rhizomatic approach that Luce, after Bergson, advocates here, as he develops the analogy of attempting to eradicate the single dandelion only to 'find it a hydra containing the possibilities of an unlimited number of similar hydras' (Luce, 13). Luce in his 1921 lecture summarising Bergson anticipates Giles Deleuze. In his 1931 postgraduate essay on Marcel Proust, Beckett chastises Proust for remaining tied to cause and effect. Beckett's Proust cannot ignore *causality*; he must accept 'the sacred ruler and compass of literary geometry' (*P*, 12).

It is Arsene who lectures Watt on the slippage of causality, on the failures of the step-by-step approach of precepts to concepts, the slippage that is life off the ladder. The change Arsene tries to explain is the slippage from an incremental change of degree to a change of kind, or at least 'a change, other than a change of degree had taken place'. It is now life off the metaphorical sequence of the ladder: 'Do not come down the ladder, Ifor, I haf taken it away' (*W*, 36). Happiness, however, in Beckett's version of the myth of Sysiphus, resides in the continued longing for the impossible ladder: 'The glutton castaway, the drunkard in the desert, the lecher in prison, they are the happy ones. To hunger, thirst, lust, every day afresh and every day in vain, after the old prog, the old booze, the old whores, that's the nearest we'll ever get to felicity [...]' (*W*, 36).

Much of the oral quality of the original lectures remains in the printed record. Luce may be overly fond of clichés and of sports metaphors, particularly to golf and tennis, but he includes salient anecdotes as well. In one, Luce speaks of discussing Bergson with Trinity's provost and leading Kantian, John Mahaffy, whom, he says, 'was too good a Kantian to approve the substance of this new doctrine. But he was unstinting in praise of its literary form. He spoke in the highest terms of the charm of Bergson's pen' (Luce, 17). Summarising that eloquence, Luce, presumably, dubs Bergson 'Chrystostom' (Luce, 17), a compliment that evidently could not be returned. The term would appear in February that same year, the year before Beckett entered Trinity, in James Joyce's landmark novel *Ulysses* when Buck Mulligan's oratory and gold-tipped teeth earn him the title, which St. John Chrysostom's preaching earned him, 'golden-mouthed', 'Chrysostomos'. As Stephen, Joyce's independent, exiled genius notes of Mulligan: 'He peered sideways up and gave a long low whistle of call, then paused awhile in rapt attention, his even white teeth glistening here and there with gold points. Chrysostomos'. The reader need not labour too deeply into *Ulysses* to come across the allusion since it appears on the novel's first page so that even those reading it for the wrong reason might come across it. The web of allusions here to Mahaffee, whose book not on Kant but on Descartes Beckett studied closely enough to plunder for his own Bergsonian poem about time, *Whoroscope*,[25] and Beckett would certainly have come across Stephen Deadelus's praise of the oratory of Buck Mulligan in terms of St. John Chrysostom, Archbishop of Constantinople, images of whose legendary living like a beast for his sins of sexuality and, finally, murder, were painted or engraved by any number of artists including Albrecht Durer, a favourite of Beckett. It is difficult not to conclude that the young Beckett's introduction to Bergson and Bergsonism would come through his first tutor. The difficulty is to gauge the depth of that early influence.

In his second chapter, Luce turns to an earlier book, Bergson's *Time and Free Will*, where he takes up the issue of 'intensity', which 'gives us the picture of a multiplicity of interpenetrating psychic states', which is decidedly different from quantity, the multiplicity of number (Luce, 37). Much of the focus, however, is on time, but 'Time thought *in abstracto* is nothing; time lived is for Bergson the stuff of reality. Real time is the time whose lapse we feel. He calls it duration', that is, time undifferentiated, instant inseparable from instant (Luce, 39). Freedom, then, is the release from mechanism, necessity, the release from the linearity of cause and effect, which is spatial: 'There is no room for freedom in space or in spatial time. In space each part determines the position of each other part. In linear time each instant determines the next instant'; it is thus time on the ladder (Luce, 42). Freedom finally constitutes the deniability of prediction, at least in the psychic field; a free act is an uncaused act, not simply a matter of alternate choices, possibilities not pursued. Beckett will finally find such a breakdown across the modernist landscape, in the 'acte gratuit' from Gide to Camus, from Lofcadio to the *Pied-noir* Meursault, and among the emergent surrealists, but its nearest iterations were in Bergson, perhaps through, at first, Luce.

Luce begins his third lecture with an apology since despite its title, 'Mind and Body', his focus will be on perception, our primary connection to the world or to matter or to the real, and through which Luce explains away the mind–body conflict of Descartes, 'We see with the eye and hear with the ear, because in the sensory cerebral process mind and body meet. Perception then is a union of mind and body, a solution of the problem of perception is our quest' (Luce, 64). 'Both idealist and realist methods', Luce continues, 'set up a barrier between thought and thing. Both make a clean cut between percipient and percipienda, and thus they never touch the concrete perception. [...] Every sense action is an interaction' (Luce, 65). The resolution of the mind–body split and the separation of perceiver and perceived are resolved in the Bergsonian image, as Luce summarises almost verbatim the opening pages of *Matter and Memory*, '"Image" is an existence [that is, matter], more than a representation and less than a thing', that is, 'surrounding objects act on the brain and the brain [acts] on those objects' (Luce, 67). Beckett explored this philosophical and aesthetic position for the whole of his creative life, stated most discursively at the opening of his 1934 essay 'Recent Irish Poetry'. In fact, Beckett will go further to adopt the position as expressed by T. E. Hulme in his Bergson essays whereby the process of perception is an inherently distortive habit of mind: 'The habit of mind which [Bergson] thinks distorts instead of revealing is simply the ordinary use of the logical intellect'.[26] The entire process of perception is thus inevitably ill seen, ill heard and ill represented. Representation itself is, by definition, distortion.

The brain, rather the mind, or particularly 'The cerebrum is not an information bureau, nor a storehouse of memory, but a distribution centre of action. [...] The body is the centre of perceptions not its source" (Luce, 71). This is Bergson's alternative both to realist and idealist philosophers, and Luce uses an image that Beckett will later associate with Berkeley: 'This theory rules out the subjective origin of things; it shows that there is more in their *esse* than their *percipi*' (Luce, 73). The conclusion: 'perception [is] a purely material process. [...] the stimulus from without and the nervous process within the body form one homogeneous movement", "concrete perception", that effected by memory; that is, the body is "grafted" onto "pure perception"' (Luce, 75). It is difficult to resist reading such observations through Beckett's own study of immaterialism, *The Unnamable*, as Luce discusses the possibilities of 'disembodied mind. The first effort of intuition gave us a picture of mindless perception: the second will offer a picture of disembodied mind' (Luce, 76). All 'Vision is [thus] re-vision' or the interplay of 'concrete memory', that is, voluntary memory, a bodily mechanism, on one hand, and what Luce here calls 'spontaneous memory' (Luce, 77, 83). As he concludes the chapter, Luce returns to his and Bergson's central points: pure and concrete perceptions, spontaneous and voluntary memory and a central observation for Bergson and Beckett that our 'perception forms part of the things, the things participate in the nature of our perception' (Luce, 93). Again, the issues are those that dominate *The Unnamable*: 'Mind is not brain; nor is memory stored in protoplasm or in brain cells. [...] Mind then depends on the body for its power of acting into space, but not for its being. Thought thinks in its own right' (Luce, 96–7). Such revelation is the result of 'intuition' and, as Karin Costelloe puts it, 'The theory that in pure intuition the subject which knows becomes its object, is certainly of very fundamental importance for Bergson', and for Beckett, we might add (Luce, 145).

After such startling observations most of which run counter to received wisdom or common sense, especially for their time, Chapter IV (or lecture 4) could only be anticlimactic, but Luce rises to the occasion of a classical peroration. It is his most passionate, elegant and aphoristic chapter, where he even seems to predict the young Beckett's transformation at university: 'The student knows that his Senior Freshman self is not the same as his Junior Freshman self'; this is 'the truth of personal existence' (Luce, 101). The emphasis on such personal existence is the subject of Luce's final chapter, as Luce tells us, 'Bergson intuites the essence of personal existence as an incessant tendency to self creation' (Luce, 103). In his critique of 'nothing' in *Creative Evolution* Bergson put such radical regeneration thus:

> When I no longer know anything of external objects, it is because I have taken refuge in the consciousness that I have of myself. If I abolish this inner self, its very abolition becomes an object for an imaginary self which now perceives as an external object the self that is dying away. Be it external or internal, some object there always is that my imagination is always representing. My imagination, it is true, can go from one to the other, I can by turns imagine a nought of external perception or a nought of internal perception, but not both at once, for the absence of the one consists, at bottom, in the exclusive presence of the other.[27]

In 1931 Beckett put the matter more sharply: we are not simply more weary because we are further on the way, but we are other, 'no longer what we were before the calamity of yesterday' (*P*, 13). It is a position that Samuel Beckett will adopt for his life's work, yet a process that his characters, his creatures, from *Watt* onwards, resist. The rendering of that process, however, is inevitably doomed to failure. In Luce's understatement, 'It is hard to put into words what personal existence feels like', yet this will be that task that Samuel Beckett will set for himself, and it is feeling not philosophy that Beckett will emphasise (Luce, 101). The élan is neither aimless nor predictable, and so, as Luce notes, 'A biography cannot be written in advance' (Luce, 102). That is, for the biography to be written or completed, change must have ceased. In her retort to Russell, Karin Costelloe argued: 'if we try to describe change we have always to regard it as change completed and not in the process of changing'.[28] Beckett put the matter concisely in his novel *Molloy*: 'Perhaps there is no whole, before you're dead' (*Mo*, 24).

This feature of incompleteness, the inability to capture the whole of a life, in biography, autobiography or fiction, the inability of characters or narrators to tell their stories, will consume Beckett's art, but what dominates is the need, the persistent desire to do so. All we can capture, perhaps, is how it feels to try. In the outline for a book on 'Modern Theories of Art', Hulme suggests in an outline to an unwritten chapter 4, 'French – Bergson', where he says of Bergson: 'least apriori of all theories – springs from actual and intimate acquaintance with emotions involved'.[29] Russell will call such emphasis on emotions a lack of system. Luce deals with the great Bergsonian subjects, evolution and endurance, but evolution not of the species, not physical, biological evolution, but that of the individual organism, the individual psyche. The 'ego', Freudian or otherwise, however, is what Luce calls 'an arrest of a current of being', and, as Luce grows more eloquent, he calls it 'the hanging wave of a flowing tide' (Luce, 102); being, thus, cannot be described or represented without distortion or contradiction since it entails arresting the élan vital, stopping time, ending the process of dureé. All attempts at representation, of the élan, of dureé, of time and being, that is, all attempts to make a life-like copy, must end in failure. Being, what Luce calls 'the living body', 'is a closed system, not an artificially closed system like those postulated by science or made by human perception, but closed by nature' (Luce, 103). Beckett will take up the issue in the novel *Murphy* and thereafter. The feel of life, the organism that endures, impossible to capture on Krapp's tapes, or in the photographs of *Film* or 'A Piece of Monologue', impossible to capture completely in language, is the great subject of Samuel Beckett's work and the core of Henri Bergson's mystical metaphysics: 'Duration is [...] the ultimate reality'. Luce tells us, 'Duration is not spatialised time; it is not passive continuance while something else continues [...] it is the interpenetration of past and present events, a cumulative carrying forward of past into the future' (Luce, 104–5).

All this Beckett will study and embrace. When he does so is not yet possible to ascertain with any certainty. We do know that Beckett was curious enough to read the works of his tutors and dons. This fact has been thoroughly documented by critics and biographers. We do know as well when the young Beckett would have had the opportunity to engage Bergson, on his own or at the suggestion of his tutor. If we cannot determine when Beckett read Luce on Bergson, we can say that Luce's little book on Bergson would have been his first opportunity to study the evolution of the individual psyche.

NOTES

1 Discussions of other important teachers Beckett encountered at TCD can be found in Chapters 20 and 21.

2 It is difficult to ascertain the degree of interest Samuel Beckett may have had in the Donnellan lectures, but it is worth noting here that the series of three lectures for 1924, in June of that year so at the end of Samuel Beckett's first year at Trinity, were delivered by F. C. Burkitt. Their subject was 'The Religion of the Manichees', and Cambridge University Press published them under that title in 1925. Surely Dr Luce attended those lectures, but whether or not he persuaded his young student to attend as well we can only conjecture. If he did one might guess that something of at least Burkitt's conclusion may have been retained: 'this view of human life taught that Man went and still goes wrong because he had always lived in a Dualistic world, a world where the Light and Dark existed in opposition before Man was, and where though the Light is stronger than the Dark it will never quite illuminate it altogether', F. C. Burkitt, *The Religion of the Manichees: The Donnellan Lectures for 1924* (Cambridge: Cambridge University Press, 1924), 104. See particularly James Knowlson's analysis of Manicheanism in *Light and Darkness in the Theatre of Samuel Beckett*, delivered as a public lecture at Trinity College, Dublin on 17 February 1972 and published in an edition of 1,000 copies by Turret Books that same year. See also Knowlson's collaboration with John Pilling, *Frescoes of the Skull: The Later Prose and Drama of Samuel Beckett* (London: John Calder, 1979), particularly 86–7: 'Krapp is clearly following here in a Gnostic, even specifically Manichean tradition [...]'. Knowlson also references Beckett's theatrical notebook for his production of *Krapp's Last Tape* in 1977: 'Krapp decrees physical (ethical) incompatibility of light (spiritual) and dark (sensual) only when he intuits [!] possibility of their reconciliation as rational-irrational', what is finally a most Bergsonian statement. Further, Knowlson notes, 'Krapp created a prison for himself by choosing at the age of thirty-nine to plumb the darkness of his own being in an attempt to create an *opus magnum* in which light and darkness would be reconciled' (93). Knowlson also references Kenneth and Alice Hamilton, *Condemned to Life: The World of Samuel Beckett* (Grand Rapids: W. B. Eerdmans, 1976), 51–8. Of late the Donnellan lectures have been offered roughly triennially by the Department of Philosophy and have been delivered by the likes of Martha Nussbaum (1992), Richard Rorty (on pragmatism in 1998) and Stanley Cavell (2002).
3 Bertrand Russell, *Uncertain Paths to Freedom: Russia and China 1919–1922: The Collected Papers of Bertrand Russell*, Volume 15. Richard A. Rempel and Beryl Haslam (eds.) (London: Routledge, 2000), 378.
4 Ibid., 379.
5 Ibid., 378.
6 Ibid.
7 Ibid., 379.
8 Ibid.
9 Nicholas Griffin (ed.), *The Selected Letters of Bertrand Russell: Volume I, The Private Years, 1884–1914* (New York: Houghton Mifflin Company, 1992), 394.
10 Ibid., 399.

11 Ibid., 400.
12 Published for 'The Heretics' by Bowes and Bowes, Cambridge, 1914, [ii]–36, (2). Joint publishers include Macmillan and Co., Ltd, London and Jas. MacLehose and Sons, Glasgow.
13 Bertrand Russell, *A History of Western Philosophy* (London: George Allen and Unwin, 1946).
14 T. E. Hulme, *Speculations: Essays on Humanism and The Philosophy of Art*, Herbert Read (ed.) (London: Kegan Paul, Trench, Trubner & Co. Ltd., 1924), 149.
15 Both of these lectures, along with notes for four subsequent London lectures on Bergson, were published after Hulme's death in 1917 as *Speculations*, edited by Hulme's friend Herbert Read and published under the auspices of the International Library of Psychology, Philosophy, and Scientific Method, C. K. Ogden, general editor, by Keegan Paul, Trench, Trubner & Co., Ltd. in London and Harcourt, Brace & Co., Inc. in New York in 1924.
16 Griffin, *Selected Letters of Bertrand Russell*, 336.
17 Karin Costelloe, 'An Answer to Mr. Bertrand Russell's Article on the Philosophy of Bergson', *The Monist* (24.1: 1914), 145–55.
18 Ibid., 146. She also published 'What Bergson Means by "Interpenetration"', *Proceedings of the Aristotelian Society*, New Series, Volume 13, (1912–13), 131–55 (Published by Blackwell Publishing on behalf of The Aristotelian Society). This is doubtless the lecture that Virginia Woolf attended on 4 February 1913; see Ann Banfield, *The Phantom Table: Woolf, Fry, Russell and the Epistemology of Modernism* (Cambridge: Cambridge University Press, 2000), 34. Almost a decade later and under her married name, Karin Stephen, Costelloe published *The Misuse of Mind – a Study of Bergson's Attack on Intellectualism*, which includes a *Prefatory Letter by Henri Bergson* (London: Kegan Paul, Trench, Trubner & Co., Ltd., 1922), which Leonard Woolf claims his wife Virginia never read (Ann Banfield, *The Phantom Table: Woolf, Fry, Russell and the Epistemology of Modernism* [Cambridge: Cambridge University Press, 2000], n393).
19 They would also be at odds over the ideology of WWI: Russell the pacifist and Hulme the militarist who would finally lose his life in that war.
20 See Edward P. Comentale and Andrzej Gasiorek (eds.), *T. E. Hulme and the Question of Modernism* (London: Ashgate Publishing, 2006).
21 See for example Roger Little, 'Beckett's Mentor, Rudmore-Brown: Sketch for a Portrait', *Irish University Review* (XIV.1: spring 1984), 34–41.
22 See for example David Berman, 'Beckett and Berkeley', *Irish University Review* (XIV.1: spring 1984), 42–5.
23 A. A. Luce, *Bergson's Doctrine of Intuition: The Donnellan lectures for 1921* (London: Society for Promoting Christian Knowledge, 1922). Online from the University of California at http://ia351405.us.archive.org/2/items/bergsonsdoctrine00lucerich/bergsonsdoctrine00lucerich.pdf, 4. [Hereafter this source will be cited in the body of the text as 'Luce' followed by a page number.]
24 Henri Bergson, *Creative Evolution* (London: Dover, 1998), 174.

25 Francis Docherty, 'Mahaffy's *Whoroscope*', *Journal of Beckett Studies* (2.1: Autumn 1992), 27–46.
26 Hulme, *Speculations*, 123.
27 Bergson, *Creative Evolution*, 303.
28 Costelloe, 'An Answer to Mr. Bertrand Russell's Article on the Philosophy of Bergson', 148.
29 Hulme, *Speculations*, 263.

CHAPTER 4

École Normale Supérieure

Anthony Cordingley

No other institution in France, public or private, has the unique culture of the École Normale Supérieure, where unparalleled intellectual elitism is tempered with an ideological commitment to defend the values of the French republic. Known as 'Normale sup', 'the ENS' or simply 'Ulm', owing to its location at rue d'Ulm on Paris's left bank, the university is situated in the student precinct of the Latin Quarter only a few hundred metres from the Sorbonne, over the hill upon which the Pantheon presides. It is France's most prestigious institution of higher learning in the humanities, attracting the nation's best students and consistently producing leading French intellectuals – when Samuel Beckett arrived in November 1928, having been selected by Trinity College Dublin to take up the one-year post (renewable) of *lecteur d'anglais* (English tutor), Simone de Beauvoir, Maurice Merleau-Ponty, Jean-Paul Sartre and Simone Weil had recently made the passage into its famous quadrangle. The two years Beckett spent at the ENS marked his transition from student to apprentice writer and translator. Beckett published poetry, fiction, translations and literary criticism; he met James Joyce and integrated himself into Joyce's circle, progressively distancing himself from university culture. In *Damned to Fame*, James Knowlson offers a thorough and enchanting portrait of 'The Paris Years' (*K*, 87–110). Revisiting this period after the publication of the first volume of Beckett's *Letters* (1929–40), a complementary narrative becomes perceptible in which Beckett affirms his intellectual liberty against the institution of the École Normale and its elite of young intellectuals.

The École Normale Supérieure was established after the French Revolution and in opposition to the Sorbonne, the historic centre of learning closely affiliated with church and aristocracy. Its mission was to train future university professors and high school teachers in the secular, liberal values of the new republic. In November 1928, this division had become less marked as numerous reforms had resulted in the need for ENS students to take classes at the Sorbonne. Nevertheless, professors still gave certain courses at rue d'Ulm, and *Normaliens* otherwise returned to the residential campus for lectures, tutorials, study, meals or sleep. These students entered the ENS by passing extremely competitive and demanding examinations – one usually spends two years following the high school baccalaureate studying in one of the many preparatory colleges (*prépas*) dotted across France. Each year hundreds of students sit exams that, as in Beckett's day, last six hours each in most cases. Examinations for the humanities stream focused on either translation or essay composition: Latin translation, Latin composition, Greek translation (replaceable with a modern language for those aiming to teach a modern language in a secondary school) and three separate exams responding to a single essay question in French literature, philosophy and history.[1] Once admitted, the student becomes in effect a public servant: for the privilege of receiving a relatively generous stipend during one's studies, one agrees to offer at least ten years of service to the state, typically in teaching or research. Yet one is, in effect, *Normalien* for life: in a society which places so much emphasis on one's *culture* (the accumulation of learning) a *Normalien* is armed with the incomparable public recognition of his intellectual excellence – and few women were admitted in Beckett's day. George Pompidou points to the perennial cultural capital of the intellectual aristocracy to which Beckett became associated when he commented, '*On est normalien comme on est prince du sang*'.[2]

Yet Beckett, on the whole, kept his distance from these highly confident, motivated students and his contact with the student body was minimal, having one first year student only and two students studying for the postgraduate *agrégation* exams. However, Alfred Péron, one of the latter group, had been Beckett's *lecteur* in French at Trinity College Dublin. Two years Beckett's senior, Péron had helped Beckett immensely with his French and the two of them had become good friends. Their friendship continued in Paris, and when Beckett wrote *Dream of Fair to Middling Women*, he turned Péron into his hero Belacqua's 'dear friend, Jean du Chas' (*Dream*, 141). The two remained friends until Péron's tragic death after the Liberation in May 1945. He recruited Beckett into the Resistance cell 'Gloria SMH' in September 1941, but in February 1943 was captured by the Gestapo and finally expired on his way home after two years of forced labour at the Mauthausen Nazi concentration camp (*K*, 305–14, 341–2).

But in 1928, the ENS offered Beckett a secure base from which to explore Paris's rich cultural life, far from the ties of family, from the weight of conservative, censorious Ireland and from the stuffy pretentions of

Trinity College Dublin. It gave him, above all, precious time to think. If Beckett harboured literary ambitions upon his arrival at the ENS, and if he spent many a night enjoying his newfound liberty, he also used his time diligently, applying himself to his studies. His partner in many of these activities, serious and ludic, was his compatriot Thomas McGreevy, and the experiences they shared at the École forged the deep friendship attested by the rare confidence Beckett accords McGreevy in his (published) letters. Most important, the debonair and immensely likable McGreevy, who later became an accomplished poet and the director of the Irish National Gallery, was in the late 1920s intimately connected with the expatriate literary and artistic scene in Paris. James Knowlson's biography of Beckett, *Damned to Fame*, sketches a compelling portrait of the friendship which developed between these two very different characters: importantly McGreevy offered Beckett a passage into the 'Joyce circle', where he was to make important literary acquaintances such as Eugene Jolas, editor of *transition* (*K*, 87–119).

Beckett had read *Dubliners* and *Portrait of the Artist as a Young Man* and was keen to meet the author of *Ulysses*; by the end of 1928 Beckett had fallen swiftly under the influence of the literary giant. Joyce's impact upon Beckett and Beckett's subsequent need to 'get over J.J. ere I die', as he wrote to Samuel Putnam on 28 June 1932 (*L1*, 108), has furnished whole shelves of research libraries. Beckett's turn towards a literature of minimalism and sparsity, with its longing for silence and an escape from the haunting of memory and erudition, away from Joyce's expansive, heroic modernism was a defining moment in literary history, one whose consequences were only just beginning to be realised when John Barth wrote his seminal essay in 1967 on the new, postmodern literature, 'The Literature of Exhaustion'. Beckett was also a great admirer of McGreevy's poetry, lauding McGreevy as 'probably the most important contribution to post-War Irish poetry' in his article 'Recent Irish Poetry' (*D*, 74). Through the ENS Beckett therefore came into contact with two models for being a modern Irish author; worldly and cosmopolitan, Joyce and McGreevy surpassed the parochial concerns of a religiously divided Ireland. Indeed, at the ENS Beckett began seriously to write.

At Joyce's request, Beckett composed the essay 'Dante...Bruno.Vico.. Joyce', with punctuating points marking the centuries separating each author. First published in *transition* 16–17 (June 1929), revised and republished in Eugene Jolas's book celebrating Joyce's *Work in Progress* entitled *Our Exagmination Round His Factification* ..., Beckett's essay has often been judged as a hasty arrangement of ideas largely derivative of secondary sources (such as McIntyre, Croce, de Sanctis, Michelet and Symonds). In this essay one nonetheless witnesses Beckett rising to Joyce's challenge to think mythically. Notably, the essay closes on a comparison between the conical purgatory in Dante, which is essentially teleological, and Joyce's purgatory, which is spherical and interminable. Beckett emphasises that motion in Joyce's purgatory is not redemptive, existing in the absence of the Absolute. Without heaven or hell, Joyce's 'Purgatory is a flood of movement and vitality released by the conjunction of these two elements' (*D*, 33).

Beckett had studied foreign languages in Ireland, but now, immersed in French at the École Normale, he was traversing a cosmopolitan space where multilingualism was integrated into everyday life. Beckett's letters during his tenure at the ENS reveal the extent to which literary creation and translation grew intimately connected. An otherwise banal note he wrote to the director of the École Normale on 10 May 1929 justifying his application for a second year as *lecteur d'anglais* because of his need to spend a year preparing a doctoral thesis at the Université de Paris demonstrates how Beckett was acquiring an ear for the bureaucratic French he would later undermine with caustic irony in his French novels and plays: 'Je vous écris dans l'espoir que vous voudrez bien ratifier mon désir de passer l'année scolaire prochaine à l'Ecole comme lecteur d'Anglais' (*L1*, 9). Only in formal contexts would one use a phrase such as '*ratifier mon désir*' ('approve my wish'), which must have presented itself like a bilingual joke to the Anglophone ear, for Beckett would surely have heard himself asking the director of the École Normale to 'ratify my desire'. Using a verb normally reserved for matters of treaty and state to express one's private hopes is in fact a typically Beckettian strategy to generate irony through a sudden shift in register, and such an interplay between French and English became essential to Beckett's bilingual poetics, offering him the ability to exploit bilingual puns and literal (mis)translations to engender knowing intratextual humour between the French and English versions of his work.[3]

Yet at this point in his career Beckett is very much the apprentice in multilingual poetics, and never more so than when serving the master. Addressed to James Joyce on 26 April 1929, the second of Beckett's published letters shows the kind of work Beckett conducted for the author of 'Work in Progress'. Like a research assistant Beckett copies out a phrase in ancient Greek, which the notes to the *Letters* translate as 'proceeding from the Father', clarifying the allusion to 'John 15:26 ... central to the *Filioque* debate that divided the Roman Catholic and Eastern Orthodox churches' (*L1*, 8–9). Beckett offers a gloss on the grammar, pointing to infinitive and substantive forms (though he likely sought assistance to do this, having no command of ancient Greek). Translation was becoming more and more part of Beckett's everyday life: a letter dated 1 March 1930 shows that Beckett covered for McGreevy, who was away in Ireland, by doing a spot of translation work for *Formes*, rendering in English titles of articles and 'an archaeological chronicle by Delaporte and two lists of illustrations – Maillol & Picasso' (*L1*, 19). This letter also shows that at the same time Beckett had turned his hand to writing poetry, albeit referring to his poem's rejection from *The Irish Statesman*. Pilling suggests that this work is 'Sonnet', a poem subsequently integrated into the short story 'Sedendo et Quiesciendo', published in *transition* 21 (March 1932) and reworked into Beckett's first novel, *Dream of Fair to Middling Women*.[4] The poem's history in many ways prefigures the development of Beckett's aesthetics of transformation, recycling content through different genres and contexts. This technique is coupled with the appearance of intratextual migrants; characters from past works pop up in later works with capacities to remember their textual histories. The *Letters* show Beckett working with Greek, French and now Italian: on 14 May 1930 he translated poems by Raffaello Franchi (1899–1949), Eugenio Montale (1896–1981) and Giovanni Comisso (1895–1969) for Samuel Putnam, associate editor of the *This Quarter* literary review.

Translation took a much more difficult turn, however, when it came to rendering Joyce's polyphonic, polyglot English into Beckett's non-native French: with Alfred Péron, he translated an extract (one third) of the 'Anna Livia Plurabelle' section from Joyce's *Work in Progress* for the review *Bifur*. Not unsurprising, Beckett found the task exceedingly difficult, and when Péron went on holiday in August 1930, Beckett lamented: 'I cannot go on with the translation alone. I can't do it' (*L1*, 5). While Beckett missed the help of Péron's native French in August 1930, he relied on it in 1938 when working on the French translation of *Murphy*. However, the experience of working on the English *Molloy* with Patrick Bowles in 1954 led Beckett thereafter to shun collaborative translation when working in English and French, with the exception of the French *Watt* (a task Beckett could not stomach). Indeed translating himself 'alone' would become one of the most distinguishing features of Beckett's literary career, and perhaps its single greatest innovation: Rainier Grutman has demonstrated that while many authors flirt with self-translation only to abandon the task after finding the experience disagreeable, Beckett is atypical in his dogged persistence in self-translating systematically almost the entirety of his works between two major languages.[5] It is interesting to consider this feature of Beckett's œuvre in light of Belén Bistué's recent argument that theoretical descriptions of translation which assert its legendary 'difficulty', not to mention its infamous 'impossibility', are the inheritance of a rhetorical conflict dating from the early modern period, when the historical fact that translation was typically performed collaboratively by teams of individuals specialised in different languages was challenged by 'an ideological demand for unity ... in the context of political unification processes – and of the linguistic and stylistic ideologies that accompanied them'.[6] By devolving upon the individual the task previously done by many, the singular translator could be imagined as a text's surrogate author and given the daunting task of equalling the comprehension of the author in the author's tongue and matching that author's skill and style in another. No other figure embodies this ideological trajectory in thinking about translation as much as the self-translator, and Beckett is its most famous exemplar. His time at the École Normale Supérieure was pivotal because it offered Beckett the ideal conditions from which to launch himself towards a career of bilingual writing: through McGreevy Beckett was given the task of figuratively embodying Joyce in translation – for the discourse around translation over the last 500 years had come to demand nothing less. In having to *become* Joyce Beckett stepped into the shoes of multilingualism personified.

Beckett's enthusiasm for Joyce resulted in his desire to change tack in his research. Beckett had originally planned to use his time at the ENS to do research for a doctorate on Pierre-Jean Jouve and the 'Unanimisme' literary movement; Beckett admired Jouve's pre-war poems but was disappointed with the latter's mystical and psychoanalytic turn, and hoped to devote his energies to a comparative study of Proust and Joyce (*K*, 100–1). Beckett was probably aware that at this time in France it would have been unusual to study such contemporary authors. However his first term at the ENS coincided with the arrival of a new influence upon the institution's direction. The transition from Gustave Lanson's dour and authoritarian reign as director began when Célestin Bouglé became the ENS's vice director in 1928. Bouglé was an ex-*Normalien* and radical socialist associated with Emile Durkheim's circle; he eventually became director of the ENS from 1935 until his death in 1940, and was known to be sympathetic to students.[7] Nevertheless, Bouglé was not about to break with French academic tradition by accepting Beckett's doctoral proposal, for Proust had been dead a mere eight years and Joyce's œuvre was still in evolution (*K*, 100–1). Still, Beckett went on to publish on both authors, outside of an academic setting. In working on 'Dante...Bruno.Vico.. Joyce' Beckett had complemented his knowledge of Dante with readings of Bruno, Vico and appropriate secondary sources. In his first year at the École Normale he worked on Descartes for 'some months' in its library, amassing a body of notes (*K*, 111). Deirdre Bair reports of Beckett's 'total immersion in Descartes' (*B*, 90) in 1929, while Ackerley and Gontarski date the apprenticeship from November 1928 to September 1930, citing Beckett's reading Adrien Baillet's *La Vie de Monsieur Des-Cartes* (1691) and 'the twelve volume *Œuvres de Descartes* by Charles Adam and Paul Tannery (1897–1910)'.[8]

Beckett's labour bore immediate fruit in the form of his prize-winning poem, *Whoroscope*, which stars René Descartes as its narrator – the story of whose composition has become more legendary than the work itself. Nancy Cunard's Hours Press was offering ten pounds for a poem of no more than 100 lines on the subject of time, and McGreevy, aware that the press was not happy with the poems already submitted, wryly suggested to Beckett on the afternoon of 15 June 1930, the eve of the competition deadline, that Beckett could still write the poem and drop it into Nancy Cunard's office on the rue Guénégaud before midnight. The fact that the poem was so rushed, not to mention that it was a ludic, non-scholarly piece of work, perhaps explains why many of the phrases which refer to Descartes' personal habits were apparently drawn only from *Descartes*, a short biography by John Mahaffy.[9]

Beckett's study of Descartes was nonetheless more serious, and Lawrence Harvey's seminal study of *Whoroscope* in *Samuel Beckett: Poet and Critic* – a study which Beckett vetted and approved for publication only after the removal of objectionable material – refers to Beckett's extensive research on Descartes gathered in the 'thick notebook'.[10] Unfortunately, unlike Beckett's notes from Wilhelm Windelband's *A History of Philosophy*, this notebook has since been lost. The record of Beckett's reading while he was at the ENS remains deficient, though occasional jewels of information sparkle in his published letters. Beckett writes, for instance, to McGreevy in a letter dated 18–25 July 1930 that the 'Bowsprit' – their friend, the young philosopher Jean Beaufret – 'comes & talks abstractions every second day, and déniche [digs out] books for me in the library' (*L1*, 32). Beaufret was 'particularly interested in Greek thought' and Beckett sought out Beaufret's help in grounding himself in 'some of the major classical and more modern European philosophers' (*K*, 96–7). Indeed Beckett used Beaufret as the model for Lucien in *Dream of Fair to Middling Women*, who 'used to tell stories – mostly of his own invention – about the grouch of

Descartes against Galileo'. (*Dream*, 47) Beckett appears to have been filling gaps in his learning and his focus on reading philosophy was no doubt strongly influenced by living in France, where the discipline of philosophy has a much broader reception and higher cultural standing than in the Anglophone world. In France, philosophy is a compulsory subject studied intensively in the terminal year of high school, and any serious young man or woman of letters needs to have a grounding in the subject. Yet neither at high school nor at university had Beckett studied philosophy. At the École Normale he must have felt this deficiency most acutely, for the vast majority of humanities students had already performed outstandingly when examined after two years of gruelling study of philosophy in their *classes préparatoires* – the only exceptions were the few brilliant enough to bypass *prépa* altogether and enter the ENS directly.

However at the ENS Beckett acquired a taste for philosophy, and having become so intrigued by Descartes' affirmation of hyperbolic doubt, he was drawn to delve deeper and deeper into seventeenth-century rationalist philosophy after he left the École. He went on to read Malebranche, Spinoza and Leibniz, probing into even more arcane corners of this period until pursuing a philosopher who spoke to him as no other had. In the thought of the seventeenth-century occasionalist, Arnold Geulincx, Beckett discovered an exaltation of the virtue of the *despectio sui*, or 'disregard of oneself', which enabled him to part ways with Descartes and substitute the positivism of Descartes' *cogito ergo sum* with Geulincx's self that affirms its ignorance.[11] The 'I' which searches for but does not find any grounded first principles and which can express only the knowledge of its ignorance is certainly a self readers of Beckett's works recognise. Yet it is important to appreciate that Beckett's reception of such ideas was conditioned by his Protestant upbringing in Ireland, belonging to a minority, albeit well-off, Anglo-Irish class. Furthermore, at the École Normale, his reading of Schopenhauer attuned his intellect to a philosophy of the negative. Beckett wrote to McGreevy in July 1930 (*LI*, 32–3) that he was inspired by Schopenhauer's pessimistic 'intellectual justification of unhappiness' and its relevance to one (like himself) 'interested in Leopardi and Proust rather than in Carducci and Barrès'. Yet Beckett's declaration that Schopenhauer's defence of unhappiness was 'the greatest that has ever been attempted' might appear somewhat defensive: How could one with so little reading in philosophy make such a confident, categorical assertion? Even if he was perhaps parroting something he had picked up from Joyce, Beckett's championing of Schopenhauer might say more about his affirming his own difference from those around him, given that in the same breath he suggests that he has made himself ridiculous in the eyes of the very learned young intellectuals with whom he had come into contact at the ENS: 'Everyone laughs at that. Beaufret and Alfy [Péron] etc.'. One suspects that Beckett may even have been conscientiously suffering for his very identification with the philosopher of suffering, and where scholars are beginning to see in Beckett's 'poetics of ignorance' an alternative to Joyce's encyclopaedic modernism, one might also consider that the trajectory of this poetics began at the ENS: at this critical period, the debut of Beckett's writing career, despite his considerable learning, Beckett found himself outflanked on a number of important intellectual fronts.[12] As his letter to McGreevy continues, one can observe Beckett forging his own personal space in reaction to this situation, insisting that he does not read like 'Everyone' surrounding him: 'But I am not reading philosophy, nor caring whether he is right or wrong or a good or worthless metaphysician'. It is a credit to Beckett's intellect that he could perceive immediately the literary qualities and the rhetorically constructed nature of philosophical narrative, but he might just have been spurred into such precocious reading by his need to justify his own deficiencies at the École Normale, his very lack of philosophical *culture*. The importance of how Beckett reads philosophy manifests in his ability to generate narratives pregnant with philosophical significance without flaunting their learning or pronouncing on the 'right or wrong or a good or worthless' reasoning, that quality which has spoken directly to contemporary philosophers such as Adorno, Deleuze, Derrida, Cixous and Badiou.

The impact of Beckett's reading of Schopenhauer upon his *Proust* monograph especially, and upon his early prose works generally, has received a good deal of attention from scholars: a useful introduction is offered in the entries for 'Schopenhauer', 'Proust' and Beckett's '*Proust*' in the *Faber Companion to Samuel Beckett*. Published in March 1931 by Chatto and Windus, facilitated by Tom McGreevy, Thomas Prentice and Richard Aldington, and for which Beckett read and reread the entire *À la Recherche du temps perdu*, Beckett's *Proust* is a highly idiosyncratic piece of criticism. Not only does it anticipate many of the preoccupations within Beckett's own œuvre (memory, habit, time), it also breaks definitively with the French tradition of historical-biographical literary scholarship. This tradition, epitomised by Charles-Augustin Sainte-Beuve, who lectured at the École Normale from 1858 to 1861, was in Beckett's time embodied and publically championed by Gustave Lanson, who presided over the ENS while Beckett was writing *Proust*. Sainte-Beuve and Lanson's 'scientific' literary method consisted in thoroughly reconstituting the biography of an author so as to explain with the greatest 'objectivity' the meaning of his (and rarely her) text. The very first line in the 'Foreword' to Beckett's *Proust* proclaims its dissent from this tradition: 'There is no allusion in this book to the legendary life and death of Marcel Proust, nor to the garrulous old dowager of the Letters, nor to the poet, nor to the author of the Essays ... ' (*P*, i). Beckett discussed Sainte-Beuve on 5 December 1932, when he wrote to Thomas McGreevy, after discussing his rereading of the first volume of Proust's *Le Temps retrouvé*: 'I have a great admiration for Sainte-Beuve & I think his was the most interesting mind of the whole galère [crew] but I can't help regretting that it was applied to criticism' (*L1*, 145). Indeed in *Proust* Beckett found a kindred spirit hostile to the reduction of literature to biography, as became publically known with the eventual publication in 1954 of Proust's *Contre Sainte-Beuve*.

Beckett finished his *Proust* manuscript in a rush over the summer of 1930, before leaving the École Normale definitively in September to return home via England. Ultimately, it is perhaps not surprising that Beckett should open *Proust* with a riposte to the institution which had been the bastion of 'objective' literary criticism and which blocked his writing a dissertation on *La Recherche* for reasons of its author's biography rather than the quality of Proust's writing. This situation encapsulates the complexity of Beckett's relationship to the École Normale. He was wholly indebted to the ENS for the window it opened upon a privileged world of intellectuals and artists and for the freedom it gave him to explore that world and embark upon his practice of professional writing and translation. Beckett set the terms of much critical debate of his work by saying in 1956, almost three decades after meeting Joyce, that his personal exploration of 'impotence' and 'ignorance' diverged from the aesthetics deployed by Joyce, who was 'tending toward omniscience and omnipotence as an artist'.[13] However, an unobserved and perhaps even unconscious factor in this 'exploration' is that in resisting the conservatism of some of the intellectual traditions of the ENS and needing to differentiate himself from the young French intellectuals he encountered there who were armed with a potentially intimidating *culture*, Beckett was forced to embark upon an intellectual swerve that would have enduring consequences on his writing. He returned to Ireland profoundly changed and unable to commit himself to teaching at Trinity College Dublin; his time at the ENS had confirmed his need to strike his own path outside of institutions of learning and their discourses that aspire to universal and objective claims to truth.

NOTES

1. Célestin Charles Alfred Bouglé, *The French Conception of Culture Générale and its Influences Upon Instruction* (New York: Columbia University, 1938), 15–16.
2. Georges Pompidou, 'Forward', in Alain Peyrefitte *Rue d'Ulm, chroniques de la vie normalienne* (Paris: Flammarion, 1963), 14; One is a *Normalien* like a prince's blood runs blue.
3. See Daniel Katz, 'Beckett et les huit langues', *Samuel Beckett Today/Aujourd'hui* (10: 2000), 223–9, and Will Noonan, 'Self-translation, Self-reflection, Self-derision: Samuel Beckett's Bilingual Humour', in Anthony Cordingley (ed.) *Self-translation: Brokering Originality in Hybrid Culture* (London: Bloomsbury, 2013).
4. John Pilling, *A Samuel Beckett Chronology* (Basingstoke: Macmillan, 2006), 23.
5. Rainier Grutman, 'A Sociological Glance at Self-Translation and Self-Translators', in Anthony Cordingley (ed.) *Self-translation: Brokering Originality in Hybrid Culture* (London: Bloomsbury, 2013).
6. Belén Bistué, 'The Task(s) of the Translator(s): Multiplicity as Problem in Renaissance European Thought', *Comparative Literature Studies* (48.2), 140.
7. Paul W. Vogt, 'Un Durkheimien ambivalent: Célestin Bouglé, 1870–1940', *Revue française de sociologie* (20.1), 123–40.
8. C. J. Ackerley and S. E. Gontarski, *The Faber Companion to Samuel Beckett* (New York, Grove, 2004; New York, Faber, 2006), 644.
9. Frances Doherty, 'Mahaffy's Whoroscope', *Journal of Beckett Studies* (2.1), 27–46.
10. Lawrence Harvey, *Samuel Beckett: Poet and Critic* (Princeton: Princeton University Press, 1970), 34.
11. Anthony Uhlmann, *Samuel Beckett and the Philosophical Image* (Cambridge: Cambridge University Press, 2007), 86–113.
12. For a discussion of Beckett's 'poetics of ignorance' see Dirk Van Hulle, 'Samuel Beckett's Faust Notes', in Matthijs Engelberts, Everett Frost with Jane Maxwell (eds), *Notes diverse holo: Catalogues of Beckett's reading notes and other manuscripts at Trinity College Dublin, with supporting essays* (New York: Rodopi, 2006), 291.
13. Quoted in Lawrence Graver and Raymond Federman, *Samuel Beckett: The Critical Heritage* (London: Routledge, 1979), 148.

CHAPTER 5

Paris, Roussillon, Ussy

Jean-Michel Rabaté

Even though the epithet may sound incongruous, I want to speak of Beckett as a Parisian. Didn't he spend half a century in Paris? This is the city in which he lived most of his adult life, and it is also the city in which he died. However, if Paris can indeed be taken as Beckett's city more than Dublin, one cannot say that it figures massively in his work. Beckett's latent pastoralism, a cynical pastoralism to be sure, often comes in the way of any attempt to render the city in literature; not for him the lush or drab urban scenes that one associates with modernist cityscapes. He rarely uses the city as a backdrop for local colour and idiomatic characterisation as one sees in the works of Eliot, Joyce, Céline or Proust. This is perhaps because Paris meant, above all, people more than places for Beckett. Paris had been first a cultural milieu, defined by social networks and a specific use of language. It was the place where a certain French was spoken, and this slangy idiom durably impacted Beckett's works. Parisian French bathes the texts in all its changing moods, from racy slang to abstract concepts and the murmurs of marital bickering. Besides its layered idioms, for a while Paris offered a convenient site for productive work. Fears of sterility would be assuaged by late night drinks and conversations, until the network of friendships and obligations that this entailed would become too heavy a burden.

I will rapidly sketch the four moments of Beckett's progressive introduction to Paris, which correspond to different modalities of being a Parisian. The first period is that of the gifted graduate student, and it goes from November 1928 to September 1930. These are the years Beckett spent at the École Normale Supérieure as the exchange language instructor sent by Trinity College Dublin. Beckett's meeting with Thomas McGreevy opened the doors to the Joyce family, a nuclear family that expanded and soon included an 'Odeonia' dominated by Adrienne Monnier and Sylvia Beach and the dynamic group of experimental writers and artists gathered by Eugene Jolas around the international review *transition*. Next to Dublin, which then felt provincial and Puritan, Paris seemed to offer everything at once. It was the Paris of the *Quartier Latin* that Beckett knew intimately, with inroads near the Invalides and the quays of the Seine explored during regular walks with Joyce. During those two years, Beckett went out a lot, visited the Louvre and galleries, was a regular theatre goer and devoured the new magazines and little reviews. Often taken for Joyce's secretary, he was in the habit of ending up dead drunk at the end of the dinners launched by Joyce to mark birthdays, publications and other rituals. It was in Paris that Beckett discovered Surrealism, a movement that left a deep imprint on him. It was in Paris finally and above all that Beckett became a writer and started publishing poems and essays.

The second period is brief but important; it goes from the end of January 1932 to 12 July 1932 and corresponds to the first decision to be a writer – the Proustian moment, one might say, when the narrator refuses to waste his time any longer at the end of *La Recherche du Temps Perdu*. This moment follows the breakup with Joyce and with Peggy Sinclair and corresponds to the momentous refusal of an academic career in Dublin. This is when Joyce, realising that Lucia's plight had not been caused by Beckett, invited him back to his circle. Hence the collaboration with *transition* turned into a regular partnership, and Beckett completed the redaction of *Dream of Fair to Middling Women*.

The third period is more dramatic, after the stay in London and the trip to Germany, as it contains instances of near death, first when he was stabbed by a pimp in the street, then when he was almost caught by the Gestapo. It goes from October 1937, when Beckett settled in Paris, to August 1942, when he rushed out of his apartment fleeing the police, who were arresting the members of the 'Gloria' resistance network. This defines Beckett's true maturity: he leaves behind the immaturity of the 'artist as a young man', becomes a writer who shares his place with a woman and is ready to make life-changing decisions. In the autumn of 1937 Beckett left Dublin for Paris, where, after a few attempts and delays he found a lasting refuge, the small apartment of 6, rue des Favorites, in the fifteenth arrondissement, not very far from the metro station Vaugirard. Visitors would say that the place looked more like a studio than an apartment, and they found it situated too far from the fashionable sixteenth arrondissement or the more lively areas of Montparnasse or the Latin Quarter. But such distance was needed by Beckett, by then engaged in various liaisons with women. Finally, after the near-fatal stabbing in January 1938, Suzanne Deschevaux-Dumesnil came to live with him in the rue des Favorites apartment.

Some French poems evoke this period, with themes revolving around sterile love making, solipsist isolation, the *taedium vitae* and the recurrent fear of death. They are markedly different from the first poems in English; the style is less allusive, polyglot puns are rare. This paring down of the language corresponds to Beckett's immersion in spoken French. At times, we see an older, even medieval Paris called up, as in the poem '*être là sans mâchoires sans dents*', which names Roscelin, the nominalist teacher of the notorious Abélard:

> être là sans mâchoires sans dents
> où s'en va le plaisir de perdre
> avec celui à peine inférieur
> de gagner
> et Roscelin et on attend
> adverbe oh petit cadeau (*Poèmes*, 9)

(to be there without jaws without teeth / to where goes the pleasure of losing / with that pleasure barely inferior / of winning / and Roscelin and we are waiting / adverb oh my little gift)

The eleventh-century philosopher who founded nominalism insisted that all words have to refer to something real in some way. In the end, Abélard turned against him and denounced him as a heretic. The famous castration of the latter for his dalliance with Heloise is evoked in the first line, as being 'without jaws without teeth'. More astonishing is the use of *on attend*, here characterised as an adverb. Normally, one would say *en attendant* as in *Waiting for Godot*. Beckett implies slyly that *waiting* would be less a present participle than an adverb attached to any verb. This suggests an empty time that will nevertheless not be lost by the prostitute of Les Halles: paid by the hour, she is waiting for her '*petit cadeau*' (a euphemism for the payment of a prostitute's services). Yet time cannot be 'killed' by mindless coition – the subject is always waiting there and this defines his condition. The same poem has the slang expression '*qu'elle mouille*' ('that she becomes all wet') to highlight delayed or impossible sexual enjoyment. At the end, a lyrical finale conquers the hesitations marked in a diction full of submerged puns:

> et vienne
> à la bouche idiote
> à la main formicante
> au bloc cave à l'œil qui écoute
> de lointains coups de ciseaux argentins (*Poèmes*, 9)

(that she should come / to the idiot mouth to the formicating hand / to the vena cava of the heart to the eye listening / for distant and silvery scissors strokes)

The pun on '*fourmi*' (ant) and 'fornication' will not be lost. It will reappear in *Happy Days*, where it triggers a rare moment of hilarity. Here, in this wry Parisian vignette situated in a brothel of Les Halles, one cannot remain deaf to the tinkling of scissors wielded by the Parchae who announce an ethereal death.

The dialectics of this Parisian period, whether nominalist or idealist, absorb the negative and convert it into a positive, as we see in the short poem 'Rue de Vaugirard':

> à mi-hauteur
> je débraye et béant de candeur
> expose la plaque aux lumières et aux ombres
> puis repars fortifié
> d'un négatif irrécusable (*Poèmes*, 16)

(half-way, / I declutch and gaping with candor / expose the plate to lights and shadows / then start off again strengthened / by an irrefutable negative)

Images coming from two different technologies are spliced together here, those of the bicycle often used by Beckett to go from rue des Favorites (it merges with rue de Vaugirard, halfway in that long street) to Montparnasse, and those of photography: the subject sees himself as a camera recording a vision in black and white. The darkness of a negative is kept in reserve, as it were, after the poet stops to observe and starts again. Darkness will highlight his 'white' or naive candor thanks to a process of purification by progressive evacuation. As in many poems of this period, the process relies on a series of oppositions: shadows and light, love and indifference, isolated self and the vastness of the world.

Such oxymoronic couplings can lead to a de-doubling of the self, as one witnesses in 'Arènes de Lutèce', one of the most descriptive Paris poems. It depicts precisely the Gallo-Roman ruins of a huge amphitheatre situated between rue Monge and rue des Arènes, two street names quoted in the poem. A character is seen entering with a woman, but from higher up than the steps, and he thus sees himself walking. Is this a doppelganger? Has he seen himself entering the space? A green dog is running, little girls push a hoop, it is cold, rainy and misty; the narrator shudders and suddenly feels reunited with himself. Some details are extremely specific: we are told that the basis of the neoclassical statue to be seen there is that of Gabriel de Mortillet, but the ending suggests a general swooning. The urban space ('the empty steps, the high houses, the sky / giving us its light too late') is a backdrop for a metaphysical quest for identity. The last lines leave undecided who is accompanying the narrator, either the woman he was with at first or himself: 'I turn around, I am astonished / to find there her (or his) sad face'. Perhaps Beckett had been amused by the fact that the statue dedicated to the staid and bearded scientist Gabriel de Mortillet visible in the Arènes de Lutèce actually represents a young woman. It is not an exaggeration to say that this impressionist vignette contains the blueprint for *Film*. While Buster Keaton haphazardly flees the camera's gaze and his own along high walls coming straight out of the New York of the Great Depression, here we have a Parisian hymn to a no less depressed urban and antique 'arena', an arena in which the struggle continues, not only between self and other, but also between self and self.

In spite of the rather dispirited tone of those early Paris poems, this period corresponded to a moment of relative peace and hard-won equanimity. Beckett was fully integrated in the group of *transition*; he was at ease among the second wave of the English-speaking 'pilgrims' who spent their nights chatting and drinking in Montparnasse. Montparnasse was the hub for the American expatriates whereas French misfits like Jean Genet preferred the pimps and transvestites of Montmartre, Clichy and Pigalle to those of Montparnasse. In a similar manner, Beckett did not follow the Surrealists, then relayed by Walter Benjamin in exile, to the small cafés of the nineteenth-century *passages* around the *grands boulevards*. The Paris *rive droite* was largely ignored by Beckett, except in the poem mentioning Les Halles. Most of his friends lived between Odéon and Les Gobelins, like Geer van Velde who lived in Boulevard Arago. At the time, Joyce had come back to the seventh arrondissement, living at 7 rue Edmond Valentin from 1934 to 1939.

Very soon, Beckett perceived his neighbourhood as the '*commune de Vaugirard*', which implies a sense of community with the locals (*L1*, 643). If he could deplore his relative distance from Montparnasse, he felt obviously comfortable there, in spite of the noise made by the neighbours – or perhaps because of the noise (*L1*, 626). The French poems 'Ascension', 'The Fly' and 'Prayer' were written soon after his taking possession of the new premises, and all three rehearse the main features of this new life. An inner silence is opposed to the noise from outside, and from this confrontation the way out is a lyrical unleashing of dreams and fantasies. All three open up new possibilities for a contemplation of the soothing Nothing. If the voice of a young neighbour comments too loudly on the soccer championship, this does not distract the speaker enough. He will have to relive the ghastly vision of his loved one dying, blood spurting from her mouth and covering her bed sheets. In another poem, the fly on the windowpane reminds him that the divider between the world and his subjectivity, although transparent, is material. When the fly is squashed by the poet's thumb, it makes the sea and the sky tumble together in a cosmic shipwreck.[1] Finally, 'Prayer' (without title in the poems) offers a simple prayer to the 'music of indifference', asking that this music should prevent the poet from listening to his own silence.

The fourth period is by far the longest and the most stable, and it leads to a writer who has to fight against his notoriety. Beckett came back to Paris in 1946 and reoccupied his apartment on rue des Favorites. From 1953, he spent more and more time in his country cottage at Ussy, a point to which I return later. Finally, in January 1971, he moved to 38 Boulevard Saint Jacques, a nicer apartment where he stayed until his final illness forced him to go to a clinic. The Paris in which Beckett lived was thus mainly the *rive gauche* Paris from the Latin Quarter before it was trivialised in the 1970s to Saint-Germain and Montparnasse, going then further south into the fifteenth arrondissement and towards the river. The place names mentioned in the texts are most often to be found there, from rue de Vaugirard to the arênes de Lutèce. Beckett spent a lot of time in the cafés of Montparnasse like le Dôme, le Select and la Coupole. Quite regularly, he would meet his friends in the restaurant Les Iles Marquise rue de la Gaieté, famous for its fish dishes, and whose Beaujolais Beckett never stopped praising.

Beckett's Paris was to accrue new memories as years went by. In 1965, in an untypical outburst of enthusiasm, he told Lawrence Harvey that 'every building, every bench' in Paris held memories for him (qtd. in *K*, 533). And yet, even talking of his wish to go to Paris in April 1933, when he was obliged to stay in Dublin, he mentions his refusal to take root anywhere: 'I am sure you were right to go to Paris. (...) Of course your letter made me wish very much to be there. The sensation of taking root, like a polypus, in a place, is horrible, living on a kind of mucous [*sic*] of conformity' (*L1*, 153). Of course, more than thirty years elapsed between those two letters, but, as we will see, Beckett never wanted to 'take root' in Paris. This he reserved for Ussy.

It would be idle to look for precise references to Paris in Beckett's texts. Paris is both everywhere and a nowhere, a shifting referential tissue. The ending of the eighth 'Text for nothing' gives us a good warning whenever we are seized by the wish to look for local references. At the end of this short text opening with a meditation on how language alone can break the silence, the narrator finally zooms on a specific place. He daydreams of being a blind and deaf passerby, wandering aimlessly in Paris until the moment when he gropes his way to a metro station and there begs for money. But where is he? He is at first on Place de la République, and more precisely 'at pernod time', that is at the sacred hour of the *apéritif* (*CSP*, 134). A little later, he passes along the 'United Stores', but then wonders whether he is not on Place de la Bastille instead, and whether his infirmities will not soon lead him to the cemetery of Père-Lachaise. This shows how warped, twisted and unreliable Beckett's Parisian geographies are. They never rely on an exact topography, and more often exploit objective puns, like the fact that there was indeed an Impasse de l'Enfant-Jésus near the rue des Favorites. This will not be lost in the French version of *Murphy*. To imagine Christ in a dead end or blind alley is tantamount to having T. S. Eliot meditating on the mystical meaning of 'the Word without a word' via Lancelot Andrews's *verbum infans*.[2] But it adds a modernist twist to an ancient paradox by hinting at the aesthetics of 'found objects', since the street still exists today, leading from hospital Necker to rue Vaugirard.

This is why Parisian places are so rarely described. Beckett may have agreed with André Breton's anathema against descriptions. This prohibition led Breton to replace local allusions, especially to Paris streets, squares, hotels or monuments with black-and-white photographs in *Nadja*. The result paradoxically reinforces the sense of an urban background to the story. One would not imagine Beckett's texts decorated with photographs, except perhaps for the three Paris poems already mentioned. In a sense, we feel that Paris is above all a literary space in which one catches a glimpse of the ghosts of other writers, like those emblematic Parisians, Apollinaire, whose *Zone* he translated so well, and Céline, whose dark *Voyage au Bout de la Nuit* he admired. Finally, Paris may stand as a synecdoche for Europe, since, like Joyce, Beckett felt that he was a European, albeit a strangely nihilistic one : 'to my certain knowledge I'm dead and kicking above, somewhere in Europe probably, with every plunge and suck of the sky a little more overripe, as yesterday in the pump of the womb' (*CSP*, 133).

The two other French places I would like to pair, even though they look like polar opposites, are Roussillon and Ussy. Thanks to Knowlson's biography, we have a very accurate picture of Roussillon during the war when Beckett was in hiding. I have always been struck by the coincidence that from the top of the village, across the valley, one can see in front and to the south the castle of Lacoste, the site of Marquis de Sade's last orgies. Beckett may not have noticed this. He did not seem interested in learning the rich history of the Vaucluse with its ferocious wars of religion, wars that left scars visible in the villages today. He does not seem to have noticed, as Ezra Pound did in his fourth Canto, that Roussillon merited its inscription in the book of fame of troubadour legend. Pound knew that the castle of Roussillon had been destroyed after a murder that had mythical proportions: it was after the troubadour Cabestan had been killed by the jealous Lord of Roussillon, who then served his heart to his unfaithful wife. After learning what the dish was, she proudly said that she would never taste any other meat, and threw herself out of the window. This excessive deed brought the downfall of the lord, who was then murdered, and the destruction of the castle. A similar fate awaited Sade's own castle. But there was enough destruction at the time around Beckett for him to chase after mythical parallels. He was also oblivious to the more active struggle of his immediate neighbour René Char, who invented a poetic language of packed images and taut action to jot down his impressions as a *maquis* leader in the region. Thus Char finds the right words to vent his anger when one of his men is shot by the Germans and he watches hidden not far away, refusing to risk the lives of the others, or when the entire population of the village of Céreste banded together against the SS, refusing to divulge where he was hiding – all this in the wonderful *Feuillets d'Hypnos*. Beckett's equivalent to *Feuillets d'Hypnos* was *Watt*, but whereas Char's prose pieces still carry the smell, heat and stony feel of the Lubéron landscapes, *Watt* systematically explodes an Irish landscape. Nevertheless, his creative immersion, his excavation, while in line with the programme outlined in *Proust*, may have owed something to the peculiar geography of Roussillon, with its abandoned ochre quarries and steep caves offering so many welcome hiding places in times of war.[3]

What Beckett experienced in Roussillon, a village which in 1942 lived more or less as in the nineteenth century, without running water and hot baths, and in which someone called Samuel must be Jewish, was so different from the luxury of Foxrock or the sophistication of Paris that it is surprising to see that this became the model for Beckett's construction of his own space in Ussy. When Beckett had his country house built in Ussy-sur-Marne in 1953, he eschewed luxury and was pursuing the dream of a place where he could 'disappear' – become invisible, as he had in 1942. The idea of disappearing is sounded as early as 1948 (*L2*, 95, 97). 'All I want is to disappear in the country' is a leitmotiv that runs through the correspondence (*L2*, 555). Whereas Paris is more and more seen as a social hell peopled of old friends or new bores who impose their schedules and obligations, Ussy is always associated with stillness, silence, solitude, teeming wild animals and also, of course, creativity.

What is striking in all the letters documenting Beckett's everyday life in Ussy is that one catches him repeating gestures or chores learned when working for food in the Audes' farm near Roussillon: digging, weeding, cutting, planting, attacking roots, fighting against pests like moles or wild boars. Digging became an obsession in Ussy, it seems, since many of the trees that Beckett planted in his garden would die year after year. This mindless activity became soothing particularly after the death of his mother. Beckett did not need another Bion to point out to him the obvious link between digging and mourning, and several letters show that he was aware of the association; here is one from January 1951 to Georges Duthuit: 'I long to be digging, digging over (*labourer*) as they say here. Went for a long walk yesterday, met no one, – yes, I did, a gravedigger coming out of a cemetery pushing a wheelbarrow' (*L2*, 217). Then follows a hilarious account of having gone to a local café where an old man comes in a state after his wife has fallen and broken her hip, wishing he could finish her off with his shotgun. The stories overheard from the locals and the peasants who remain close to nature are all wickedly funny, as when Beckett in a sort of dead pan, just after mentioning proofs for *Waiting for Godot*, adds: 'It is snowing. The farm-workers are fucking the cows, perched on 3-legged milking stools. Bad for the cows, it seems. They are called "juniors" and are driven away pitilessly' (*L2*, 332). This digging, for Beckett, is not a metaphor for writing, as it is in a famous poem by Seamus Heaney. For him, digging means really digging the earth, that is making holes into a communal tomb that links us all with nature.[4]

I have mentioned Beckett's cynical pastoralism, and it is on display in the letters from the fifties in which the difference between animality and humanity tends to vanish. Men, women and animals appear all as puppets in a theatre of futility, caught up in the great swells of unconscious survival and also drifting towards final extinction. This surfaces in one of the most tender pastoral evocations: 'in the fields, on the roads, I give myself over to deductions on nature, based on observation! No wonder I am irritable. It produces grim results. (...) One evening as we were on our way back to Ussy, at sunset, we suddenly found ourselves being escorted by ephemerids of a strange kind, "may-flies", I think. They were all heading in the same direction, literally following the road. (...) In the end I worked out that they were all going towards the Marne to be eaten by the fish, after making love on the water' (*L2*, 162). At least, one might interject, they have known love! In other passages, Beckett's humour is even grimmer – as when he compares beetles with humans and himself. His garden has been invaded by Colorado beetles, in French *doryphores,* a common pest in those regions. He comments thus: 'I keep an eye on the love-life of the Colorado beetle and work against it, successfully but humanely, that is to say by throwing the parents into my neighbour's garden and burning the eggs. If only someone had done that for me!' (*L2*, 232). Here we see once more the old fantasy of 'not being born' acted out with a vengeance.

We can thus understand the relentless dynamism inscribed in Beckett's spaces – there must always be a double pole, first following a Dublin–Paris axis, then replaced by a Paris–Ussy axis. Life and death mark the extreme points for the course of the swinging pendulum, but they are not empty allegories; they are visible in the soil, in the earth, in the animals. Hence writing will become another way of 'burning' all those eggs, seeds, weeds, pests, and the remainders of all too painful memories, in a process that consists in leaving traces on neutral spaces. If Beckett's landscapes all look like *paysages moralisés*, they are never static; like the best metaphysical poets of the English tradition, he knew how to move through them. Even the place he had elected for his relative solitude, Ussy, would combine signifiers conjuring up a collective spirit (*Us*) and a calculation of practical utility combining frugality and disappearance ('use value'), all the while pointing to a shifting deictic. Here, here I am: *Ici!*

NOTES

1 The poems accompany Beckett's letter from 15 June 1938 to Thomas McGreevy in which he mentions his new apartment. See *LI*, 630–2.
2 See T. S. Eliot's poem 'Gerontion'.
3 'The only fertile research is excavatory, immersive, a contraction of the spirit, a descent' (*P*, 65).
4 See Daniel Gunn's excellent 'Introduction' to *L2*, lxxi–lxxv, for a wonderful discussion of 'digging' and 'digging in', with the added dimension of going deeper in the exploration of despair.

PART II
Social and Political Contexts

CHAPTER 6

Ireland: 1906–1945

Patrick Bixby

It would be an understatement to say that the years of Samuel Beckett's youth and young manhood were a tumultuous epoch in Irish history. Between 1906 and 1945, the small island nation experienced the continued frustration of the Home Rule movement, the radicalisation of republican interests, a heroic but failed rebellion, a bloody war of independence, a still bloodier civil war and the difficult efforts of state and nation building, not to mention the impact of two world wars. Given the almost unremitting turbulence of these years, the formative period of Beckett's life and career, it is all the more surprising that critics and scholars of his writing, until very recently, have given so little attention to the question of Ireland.[1] No doubt some of this negligence can be attributed to the predominance of a succession of formalist critical schools during the second half of the twentieth century and to the now lapsed critical consensus regarding the cosmopolitan nature of literary modernism. Beckett's writing seemed to exemplify a 'pure aesthetics' or a 'metaphysics of absence' untainted by political commitments or references to what the writer called 'the local accident, the local substance'.[2] Even as literary studies has turned increasingly towards historical and political concerns over the last two decades, generating new insights into the work of W. B. Yeats, J. M. Synge, James Joyce and other Irish writers, most modernist scholars have continued to assume a relative detachment from Irish matters in Beckett's writing, which largely resists the kind of archaeological investigation that has yielded so many new discoveries for Joyce studies, in particular. Now, as Beckett studies has begun to direct attention more insistently to the question of his status as an 'Irish writer', a postcolonial subject, a member of the Protestant minority, even an eccentric historian or political commentator of sorts, it necessarily takes on the challenges of Irish historiography and the ongoing debates regarding the significance of Irish nationalism, sectarianism and political independence during his lifetime. At the same time, it must account for the persistent movement towards elision and indeterminacy in his mature writings, which attenuate all referential gestures to the social and political world beyond the text. What begins to emerge from this effort is the recognition of a remarkable postcolonial aesthetic, structured by unrelenting tensions between a literary imagination and a set of vexed and vexing historical circumstances that can never be completely forgotten or abandoned.

In considering Beckett's positioning within these circumstances, the effort to account for his social affiliations and political surroundings should be made with great care, not just to avoid overly reductive or insensitive accounts of Irish history, but also to evade the hazard of reducing his aesthetic too easily to partisan or sectarian determinants. Here, with that very much in mind, I can only begin to sketch the outlines of Beckett's Ireland. Growing up in Foxrock, a wealthy suburb south of Dublin, the writer spent his childhood primarily amongst the Protestant middle classes, who remained implicitly loyal to the Union through the early decades of the twentieth century. Yet 'low church' Protestants like the Becketts had relatively little in common with their Presbyterian neighbours to the north, who enjoyed a majority status in Belfast and the surrounding counties. Anthony Cronin has warned against the mistake of confusing Beckett's background with that of the Protestant landowning aristocracy referred to most often as the Anglo-Irish. Southern Protestants of the business and professional classes were unlikely to have close familial or financial ties with England, and were even less likely to cultivate such ties by sending their children to English schools (*C*, 10). Nor were members of the Protestant middle classes closely associated with the Big House culture of the Anglo-Irish Ascendancy, whose often callous exploitation of Catholic tenant farmers had earned them increasing resentment through the course of the nineteenth century. To be sure, Beckett had relatively little contact with Catholics in his youth, though, as his biographers have pointed out, he would undoubtedly have met with members of the Catholic working classes who served as maids and gardeners in Foxrock, and likely with members of the poorer Catholic community living in cottages at the edge of the enclave (*C*, 24; *K*, 50).[3] Yet this relative insularity seems to have bred as much contempt for the limitations of Irish Protestant life as aversion to any apparent differences in Irish Catholic culture. Beckett's contact with that culture during his youth would have underscored, more than anything, the increasingly marginalised location occupied by southern Protestants who, despite their traditionally privileged position, faced ever more pressing questions about their place in Irish society and even their fundamental 'Irishness'.

The currents of history only swept the Protestant community in Foxrock farther to the margins of Irish society. The decade leading up to Beckett's birth in 1906 saw the rise of groups such as the United Irish League and the Ancient Order of Hibernians, which campaigned for the redistribution of land and the political representation of Catholic values. Meanwhile, the Gaelic League, established to combat the erosion of the Irish language and native culture, appealed to its growing membership with the call for de-Anglicisation, idealising the lifestyle of the rural western counties of Ireland over and against the perceived materialism of English urban life. A year before Beckett's birth, the great nationalist polemicist Arthur Griffith founded Sinn Féin (We Ourselves or, as it is often translated, 'Ourselves Alone'), a party combining the new emphasis on cultural autonomy with a desire to extend Irish self-reliance to the political sphere. The Irish Parliamentary Party, which had campaigned for Home Rule since its foundation by Charles Stewart Parnell in 1882, thus gradually found itself sharing the national scene with an increasing number of more extreme political forces. By the time the First World War broke out on the Continent, drawing British attention almost entirely away from the Irish question, it seemed that the nationalist movement had at last found a radicalised Catholic leadership positioned to advance the cause of Irish republicanism. Chief among its leaders was Patrick Pearse, a young lawyer and educator turned political activist and ideologue, who drew on a strain of mystic Catholicism and the mythic heroes of Gaelic antiquity, especially Cuchulain, in his advocacy of sacrificial violence: 'there are many things more horrible than bloodshed', he famously declared, 'and slavery is one of them'.[4] On Easter Monday 1916, Pearse guided about fifteen hundred troops from the Citizen Army and Irish Volunteers in seizing five groups of large buildings in central Dublin, including the General Post Office, where he read out the Proclamation of the Irish Republic. The Easter Rising was suppressed by British troops after seven days of fierce fighting. If the Dublin middle classes initially disapproved of what they saw as little more than an ill-planned fiasco resulting in widespread looting and the gratuitous loss of life, Foxrock Protestants were likely even less sympathetic with the events of Easter week. Public opinion was about to take a dramatic turn, however, when the British government commenced its draconian response, court marshalling, executing and effectively martyring Pearse and fourteen other leaders of the rebellion within two weeks after their surrender (though sparing future President and Prime Minister Eamon de Valera due to his American citizenship).

In many ways, the Easter Rising was only the beginning of the struggle that would lead to Irish independence and the establishment of a legitimate native government in Dublin. The shift in communal sentiment towards the leaders of the rebellion paved the way for the rise of Sinn Féin as a powerful political force, which quickly gained support from members of the public disenchanted with the inefficacy of the old Parliamentary Party. Soon after his release from penal servitude in 1917, de Valera was elected president of the ascendant party, his popularity as the senior survivor of the Rising garnering increasing support for Sinn Féin among the Irish people and facilitating the declaration of an independent parliament, the first Dáil Éireann, in January 1919. Under the leadership of Michael Collins, extreme elements in the volunteer movement, now known as the Irish Republican Army, presently commenced an extended guerrilla campaign against British interests in Ireland, which responded with brutal reprisals of their own against both soldiers and civilians. With political pressure from the War of Independence mounting on both sides, negotiations for a peace finally commenced in October 1921, as Sinn Féin sent a delegation to London headed by Collins and Griffith. The delegates returned to Dublin on 6 December having established the Irish Free State as a self-governing domain, but having relinquished the six northeastern counties of the island and, just as galling, having accepted a pledge of allegiance to the king on behalf of the new state, which was much less than the desired unified and sovereign republic. A split within Sinn Féin was all but inevitable. After the Anglo-Irish treaty was narrowly ratified by the Dáil, de Valera walked out of the chambers with his political allies and summarily resigned his presidency, actions that eventually led to civil war between pro-treaty and anti-treaty forces the following year. Once initiated, the conflict quickly spread across the country, sundering families and friendships in the process and resulting in terrible loss of life – about 800 Free State soldiers and many more of the opposition – before anti-treaty forces were compelled to dump their arms rather than continue a battle they could not win.

Though it has seldom been remarked, the events surrounding the foundation of the new state did not fail to have an impact on Beckett's literary imagination: I would suggest, moreover, that it is only in relation to the Irish story of rebellion, civil war and independence that we can begin to appreciate the political sensibility expressed in his mature writings. This sensibility can be glimpsed, for instance, in Molloy's pronouncement that 'for my part I have always preferred slavery to death, I mean being put to death', which ironically reverses Pearse's declaration of blood sacrifice leading up to the Easter Rising, even as it acknowledges his martyrdom at the hands of a British firing squad (*Mo*, 68). The allusion, in response to Molloy's unheroic personal plight, may seem to diminish the power of Pearse's unyielding assertion, but not without recalling the fervency of his political commitment – and its cost. In *Malone Dies*, we encounter something similar when Beckett's narrator, in reaction to his own prolonged hunger, wonders, 'how long can one fast with impunity? The Lord Mayor of Cork lasted for ages, but he was young, and then he had political convictions, human ones too probably, just plain human convictions' (*MD*, 103). This time the allusion is to the seventy-four-day hunger strike of Terence McSwinney, the Sinn Féin leader who undertook the protest in response to his imprisonment by a British military court during the War of Independence. His subsequent death assured him a place amongst the martyrs for the republican cause and served as a forceful gesture towards his belief, shared with Pearse, that 'it is not those who can inflict the most, but those who suffer most who will conquer'.[5] In his most admired fictions, often read as examples of the modernist obsession with privatised interiority, Beckett appears in fact to acknowledge the continuing hold that the trials of national history have on postcolonial subjects, who cannot, in spite of themselves, escape the haunting memory of these sacrificial figures. Crucially, the recollections also raise the question of Malone's very humanity, insofar as he is unable to share in McSwinney's political enthusiasm or, more generally, the liberal humanist notion of a coherent human subject that is vital to both nationalist and imperialist historical narratives. The oblique, sceptical and even parodic manner in which Beckett renders these memories betrays a desire to interrogate the national icons of Irish history and to question the heroic narrative of colonial resistance in order to open a space for the articulation of a postcolonial subjectivity that might be freed from residual resentments, conflicts and entanglements.

The trouble, of course, is that neither Beckett nor his characters have managed to free themselves entirely from Irish history, even if his writing continually problematises any direct reference to the historical realm. The effort to understand the political significance of his work requires accounting for the tensions between formalism and representation, detachment and engagement, private consciousness and public imperatives, rather than writing off the problem of reference as the sign of modernist interiority or postmodernist *écriture*. In doing so, one might even hazard to assert that, in his oblique way, Beckett offers not simply a subversion or negation of historical representation, but his own incisive reassessment of Irish history. Take for example Malone's claim earlier in the novel:

> Yes, that's what I like about me, at least one of the things, that I can say, Up the Republic!, for example, or, Sweetheart!, for example, without having to wonder if I should not rather have cut my tongue out, or said something else. Yes, no reflection is needed, before or after, I have only to open my mouth for it to testify to the old story, my old story ... (*MD*, 63)

For Leslie Hill, who reads the phrase in Derridean terms, the repetition of 'Up the Republic!' demonstrates 'an irreducible friction between discourse and writing, political statement and textual irony, since the effects of recontextualising the slogan are complex and difficult to control'.[6] To be sure, the allusion, which lifts a declaration of political commitment from its original context and places it in an entirely new one, produces a certain amount of ambiguity, but this hardly dampens the historical resonance of the phrase. Rather, I would argue, it confirms the hold that the discourse of a decolonising nationalism (in this case, a radicalised republicanism) continues to have on the postcolonial subject. Once the rallying call for anti-treaty forces during the Irish Civil War, and later the slogan for Eamon de Valera's 1932 presidential campaign, 'Up the Republic!' has become part of Malone's autobiographical narrative, unthinkingly reiterated as a vestige of his political education, much like the exclamation 'Sweetheart!' is repeated as a trace of his romantic socialisation, something that has been imposed, managed and normalised by the ritualised reiteration of verbal formulas. Beckett may even be recalling his own repetition of the phrase, capitalised and Iberian-ised as '¡UPTHEREPUBLIC!' when he was asked to comment on the Spanish Civil War for the *Left Review* in 1937. Malone's repetition of the phrase can be read as a recognition that the past, because it cannot be entirely forgotten or abandoned, must continually be revisited – albeit with politically charged irony, from the perspective of Beckett and his readers. Indeed, his oeuvre is scattered with such ironies, which, when viewed against the background of Ireland, suggest a complex relationship, an ambivalent push and pull, between his literary imagination and an (image of) history that threatened to limit the consciousness of the Irish well into the postcolonial period.

To more fully appreciate these ironies it is necessary to consider Beckett's sense that the independent state established after so much republican sacrifice was profoundly disappointing, largely because it stifled the very revolutionary energies that gave it birth with a seemingly innate social and political conservatism. In fact, many contemporary historians have gone so far as to claim that the Civil War was, in effect, a counterrevolution which initiated the emergence of an illiberal nationalist agenda backed by the Irish middle classes and the Catholic Church.[7] It may not be surprising, given the upheavals attending independence, that the new government in Dublin gave so much of its attention to establishing law and order. It is perhaps dismaying, however, that this was primarily accomplished by readopting many elements of the former British regime, including English-style court procedures and a centralised police force, the Garda Síochána na hÉireann, modelled on the old Royal Irish Constabulary. The new government also made great efforts to enforce Catholic social values amongst its citizens, so that, by the end of the twenties, the state had expanded its bureaucratic and judicial influence into the realms of divorce, contraception and the censorship of film and literature. The social and political developments of this period were profoundly unsettling for many Protestants, and perhaps even more so for a young man with cosmopolitan cultural aspirations such as Beckett, who found little to his liking in a public life defined almost exclusively by Catholic and Gaelic interests. While still a student at Trinity College, Dublin, Beckett published a satirical dialogue titled 'Che Sciagura' deriding the recent ban on the sale and advertising of contraceptives by reiterating the eunuch's cry from Voltaire's *Candide*, 'what a misfortune to be without balls'.[8] A few years later, after his first work of fiction had been banned by the Censorship Board, Beckett returned to these issues in a scathing article for the *Bookman* titled 'Censorship in the Saorstat', which joined the uproar from a host of other Irish writers, including G. B. Shaw, W. B. Yeats and George Russell. Even more vehemently than his older compatriots, the young writer voices a penetrating complaint about the governance of the postcolonial state, which had resorted to 'panic legislation' in the name of conservative nationalism (*D*, 86).

Beckett's early fiction offers a satirical portrait of public life in the new state. Yet this satire is not without a certain poignancy insofar as it registers the alienation of Beckett's first protagonist, Belacqua Shuah, whose formative subjectivity remains stunted, at least in part, by his inability to develop a sense of national belonging in these surroundings. In *Dream of Fair to Middling Women*, Belacqua travels to the Continent and back to Dublin, where he creeps through the crowded streets in the hopes of avoiding figures such as the 'homespun poet' in his 'Donegal tweeds' and the 'little macaco of anonymous politic-ploughboy', both mocking representatives of an ever narrower vision of cultural nationalism in post-independence Ireland (*Dream*, 203). Meanwhile, the 'the Polar Bear', a man of 'culture and distinction' modelled on Beckett's outspoken mentor at Trinity, Thomas Rudmose-Brown, engages in verbal warfare with a Jesuit priest and, later, a Gaelic-speaking tram conductor, revealing to Beckett's sardonic narrator the emergence of a 'dogocracy' in Ireland, where the 'scurvy dog has taught the snarl to his scurvy master' (*Dream*, 159). The new dispensation leaves Beckett and his narrator – 'we', as they are identified – in a difficult position:

> The point it seems almost worth our while trying to make is not that the passing of the Castle as it was in the days of the Garrison is to be deprecated. Not at all. We hope we know our place better than that. We uncover our ancient Irish wedgehead in deference to that happy ejection. Nor are we the least prone to suggest that the kennel is a less utopian community than the pen or coop or shoal or convent or any other form of natural or stylicised pullulation. (*Dream*, 159)

This is not to suggest that Beckett, or his narrator, or his protagonist, have sided with a displaced Anglo-Irish Ascendancy with its lingering Unionist sympathies and its resentment towards an ascendant Catholic community. Rather, the end of the British occupation, signalled by the departure of the English garrison from Dublin Castle, has touched their sympathies with Ireland and its national traditions, though it has also intensified questions about the place of a shrinking Protestant minority in an ostensibly Catholic and Gaelic nation. What follows in the novel is an extended effort to re-imagine the postcolonial community in a radically eclectic and utopian fashion, but this effort fails to produce a coherent alternative to the dominant modes of cultural nationalism. Belacqua's story ends with him stranded and alone in the street on a rainy Dublin evening, only to be confronted by the authority of the state in the form of a Garda who enjoins him to 'move on', since he is not welcome there (*Dream*, 241).

Protestants' anxieties about their position in the Free State were only exacerbated by the return to power of Eamon de Valera and his new Fianna Fáil party in the 1932 elections, which confirmed, for many observers, the destiny of Ireland as a both an independent nation and a Catholic democracy. Although Beckett toyed with the idea of voting for de Valera, the new regime, once in place, seems to have confirmed the young writer's perspective as an outsider, critical of the illiberal social and political ethos of post-independence Ireland. *Murphy* may be read as a chronicle of Irish disaffection, its eponymous protagonist abandoning the limiting social norms and economic policies of the Free State, which were increasingly legislated into place under De Valera's government, for the wider opportunities on offer in London – even if Beckett's hero is singularly unfit to capitalise on such opportunities. The new prime minister's advocacy of a conservative, confessional nation sustained by small agricultural units and protected by high tariff barriers largely failed to overcome the effects of the worldwide depression or to stem the rising tide of emigration. But he attempted to appease the Irish public with symbolic calls to the ongoing struggle against the neocolonial menace of Great Britain, and to the heroic battle for national independence waged almost two decades earlier. On 21 April 1935, for instance, de Valera commemorated the nineteenth anniversary of the Easter Rising by dedicating a statue of the mythic hero Cuchulain at the Dublin GPO, an event accompanied by large-scale parades and military demonstrations.[9] The prime minister's appeals to mythology can be read as an effort to exploit national tradition in order not only to cover over the presence of social and political difference in the new state, including more radical republicanisms, but also to assure the closure of Irish history. In the fourth chapter of Beckett's novel, written within a few months of de Valera's dedication, Murphy's mentor, Nr. Neary, expresses his resistance to this ideological manoeuvring by entering into the GPO, examining the statue of Cuchulain and unceremoniously attacking the figure's buttocks with his bared forehead before he is ushered away by a muscular Garda. The story of Murphy, with his most Irish of surnames, betrays a particular variety of postcolonial consciousness, caught between alienation and belonging, between self-imposed exile and communal accommodation, thus belying the familiar modern narratives of personal development and national integration while protesting the stifling insularity of De Valera's Ireland. Although he chooses to live his life abroad, like so many other Irishmen of his generation, Beckett's protagonist desires nonetheless that his last resting place should be Dublin's Abbey Theatre, an institution founded on the restoration of Irish folklore and mythology and on the resistance to British culture and influence. Though, at the time of his death, Murphy can only be identified as 'a native of the city of Dublin', his ashes never make their way back to the city of his birth, instead ending up scattered across a pub floor in London, an image which registers the comic pathos of his emigrant narrative (*M*, 171).

It is a telling coincidence that Beckett left Ireland, never to live there again, in 1937, the same year that the de Valera's vision for national independence was validated by the ratification of a new constitution. Beckett's alienation from this vision was only reinforced by de Valera's decision to follow a policy of scrupulous neutrality during the so-called 'Emergency' of the Second World War, as Beckett witnessed firsthand the costs of political and military catastrophe in occupied France. There is a further irony for Beckett studies in the coincidence that, as the writer was at work with the French Resistance, fully immersed in the historical and political world, Ireland was trying, in a sense, to lift itself out of modern history, as de Valera attempted to protect his dream of 'Irishness': in the middle of the war, on St. Patrick's Day 1943, the prime minister delivered an address containing his most famous images of the bucolic island nation, a land of industrious 'fields and villages' and 'cosy homesteads' occupied by 'sturdy children', 'athletic youths', and 'comely maidens' – 'a people who were satisfied with frugal comfort and devoted their leisure to things of the spirit'.[10] When Beckett notoriously declared that he preferred 'France at war to Ireland at peace', he was implicitly rejecting this image of a pious and pastoral nation, which failed to acknowledge the social, cultural and economic growing pains of postcolonial independence (*C*, 310). Yet, despite his disaffection with Ireland, Beckett continued his negotiations with Irish history: satirising Big House culture and nationalist anthropology in *Watt*, revisiting the militarist ethos of the Civil War in *Mercier and Camier*, examining a sense of Protestant dislocation in the *nouvelles* and *All That Fall*, parodying republican rhetoric in the trilogy, even registering the traumas of the Great Famine in *Waiting for Godot* and *Endgame*.[11] This does not mean, however, that Beckett sought to overcome a sense of displacement by reclaiming an image of Ireland for himself. Rather, his eccentric history of Ireland challenges the ability to provide a totalising vision of national unity or communal destiny, giving lie to those historicist pedagogies that that derive their authority from patriotic essences or humanist ideals. What we might call Beckett's 'counter-narratives' of the nation interrogate the constitution of identity and the constituent ingredients of language and tradition while probing the very ambivalences that structure postcolonial subjectivity and its cultural representation.

NOTES

1 Important exceptions include John Harrington, *The Irish Beckett* (New York: Syracuse University Press, 1991); David Lloyd, *Anomalous States: Irish Writing and the Post-colonial Moment* (Dublin: Lilliput, 1993), 41–58; Declan Kiberd, *Inventing Ireland* (Cambridge: Harvard University Press, 1995), 454–64.
2 Peter Boxall, 'Samuel Beckett: Towards a Political Reading', *Irish Studies Review*, (10.2: 2002), 159. Seamus Deane, 'Joyce and Beckett', in *Celtic Revivals: Essays in Modern Irish Literature 1880–1980* (Winston-Salem: Wake Forest University Press, 1988), 130. *D*, 97.
3 See also Seán Kennedy, '"A lingering dissolution": *All that Fall* and Protestant fears of engulfment in the Irish Free State', *Assaph: Studies in the Theatre* (17/18: 2003), 255.

4 Patrick Pearse, 'The Coming Revolution' in F. X. Martin (ed.) *The Irish Volunteers, 1913–1915: Recollections and Documents* (Dublin: J. Duffy, 1963), 65.
5 Quoted in Richard Kearney, *Postnationalist Ireland: Politics, Culture, Philosophy* (London: Routledge, 1996), 89.
6 Leslie Hill, *Beckett's Fiction: In Different Words* (Cambridge: Cambridge University Press, 1990), 912–13.
7 See, for instance, John M. Reagan, *The Irish Counter-Revolution, 1921–1936: Treatyite Politics and Settlement in Independent Ireland* (London: Gill, 1999); Mike Cronin and John M. Reagan, *Ireland: the Politics of Independence, 1922–49* (London: Macmillan, 2000); Kevin Whelan, 'The Revisionist Debate in Ireland', *boundary 2* (31.1: 2004), 179–205.
8 Samuel Beckett, 'Che Sciagura', *T.C.D.: A College Miscellany*, (XXXVI: 17 November 1929), 42.
9 'Mr De Valera Unveils 1916 Memorial', *Irish Times* (22 April 1935), 8.
10 Eamon De Valera, *Speeches and Statements by Eamon de Valera 1917–1973*, Maurice Moynihan (ed.) (New York: St Martin's, 1980), 466.
11 In recent years, the scholarly and editorial work of Seán Kennedy has been instrumental in turning critical attention to Beckett's relationship with Irish history. See Seán Kennedy (ed.), 'Historicising Beckett', *Samuel Beckett Today/Aujourd'hui* (2005), 21–131; Seán Kennedy and Katherine Weiss (eds.), *Samuel Beckett: History, Memory, Archive* (London: Palgrave, 2009); and Seán Kennedy (ed.), *Beckett and Ireland* (Cambridge: Cambridge University Press, 2010).

CHAPTER 7

France: 1928–1939

Garin Dowd

The decade in which Samuel Beckett undertook his chaotic version of the European tour, with Paris the closest thing to home, was, by any standards, and at the not inconsiderable risk of understatement, an extraordinary one.[1] At the beginning of his most peripatetic decade Beckett found himself back in Dublin following the two years he had spent at the École Normale Supérieure in Paris (from the end of October 1928 to September 1930). He was back in Paris when Eamon de Valera's Fianna Fáil won the election in the Irish Free State and stayed until August 1932 when he returned to Dublin. His experience of London from 1933 onwards was far from felicitous, as his letters of the period attest. While on a lengthy holiday sojourn in Germany between late September 1936 and March 1937, Beckett witnessed with some detachment a state building towards the *Anschluss* and perceived elements of the inexorable logic which would lead to the development of technologies (in soft and hard forms) of mass persecution, genocide and expansionism.[2] Following a spell in Dublin, his return to France in October 1937 meant that he was not there to witness the short tenure of the Popular Front government of Léon Blum, although he was in France during the brief revival of Blum's administration between March and April 1938. Following this period, the France in which Beckett resided would be propelled by the impetus of the hard turn to the right of the elite cadre trained in the Sciences Po towards the decade's end, and by the technocratic Daladier regime. That a writer of Beckett's intellectual stature, extensive cultural knowledge and linguistic prowess should encounter, and for significant periods reside in, nations in the throes of such unprecedented reconfiguration and flux merits consideration.

By 1930, the ENS had said farewell to its indolent *lecteur* (whose only student, Georges Pelorson, he saw at the Dôme) and Beckett had returned to Ireland to take up a teaching post at Trinity College, Dublin. No sooner had he embarked on this venture than he swiftly rejected the career for which his studies and his mentor, Rudmose-Brown, had so thoroughly prepared him. In 1939, at the onset of the Second World War, Beckett was back in Paris. The French capital therefore bookends the period discussed in this chapter. The momentous events of 1939, followed by the armistice of June 1940, would see the literary aspirations fed by Beckett's wanderings abruptly supplanted by the struggle to survive in a wartime France divided into the occupied zone and the territory administered by the Vichy regime under Pétain. That his experiences in the decade leading up to the war and the war itself combined to forge the specificity of post-war Beckett is undeniable.

The major difficulty in assessing the impact of social and political contexts in France on Beckett and his work arises from the extent to which he is absent from the country during the decade. In fact, he only resided in Paris between 1928 and 1930; he stayed there briefly again in 1932 and he returned to live there in December 1937. Despite being physically absent from the country for more than half of the decade, insofar as the political and social contexts of France impinge on Beckett's life and work, a number of salient delineations of influence and absorption may, nonetheless, be identified. The first concerns apprenticeship and participation in the great avant-garde movements centred in France in the 1920s and in which Beckett, arriving in 1928, was well placed to participate. The second is the social and economic deprivation of France in this period (the decade begins with the Great Depression), which recent research has shown to have directly influenced some of the post-war work.[3] The third is the various attempts at nation building under way in 1930s France.

CULTURE AND POLITICS

Each of the resting points in Beckett's nomadic decade offers interesting perspectives on diverse approaches to national construction and reconstruction in the aftermath of the Great War and the stock market crash of 1929. It is a key decade for Ireland in what was in effect the first successful decolonisation project, a project which, as many commentators have pointed out, placed Beckett in a highly ambiguous position. His disdain for the Irish Free State of the post-civil war decade (1922–32) and especially for de Valera's Ireland (Fianna Fáil won the 1932 election by a narrow majority) is directed at its pieties and in particular its enshrining (through the Constitution of 1937) of the role of the Catholic Church in state affairs, rather than at independence itself. The cult of the leader, in which de Valera participated, would find an altogether more extreme (at the risk of understatement) manifestation in the shape of Hitler in Germany, to whom Beckett refers negatively in the German diaries and in response to a radio broadcast by Hitler which he heard in Paris; Beckett refers derisively to the Führer as 'Adolf the peacemaker'.[4] While each case is specific, Ireland and Germany were, like France, engaged in nation building. If Ireland had embarked on a hugely compromised reconstruction of a democracy after centuries of occupation, Germany was the laboratory of a maximisation of the cult of the leader driven by an autocratic and anti-democratic ideology. They were each in their different ways, and in their incomparable scales, engaged in a mythologising which is central to all nation building. De Valera's rhetoric was steeped in the Catholic ideology of purity which achieved retrospective hegemony in 1916, and in so doing almost rendered to oblivion the class-centred syndicalism of James Connolly.[5] The rhetoric of exclusion is a necessary stage of nation building, even if, as Etienne Balibar points out, that exclusion need not be essentialist and can be democratic.[6] Beckett seems to react, from the distance of some of his reviews and letters, to the essentialist form this took in Ireland of the 1920s and 1930s, abetted in the era of de Valera by aggressive economic nationalism and protectionist tariffs and culminating in the Constitution of 1937 with its enshrining of the 'special position of the Holy Catholic and Apostolic Roman Church as the guardian of the faith professed by the great majority of its citizens'.[7] The case of Germany is of course extreme and sees the nation founded on an idea of the *Volk* and of purges, pogroms and genocide launched against Jews and others deemed alien, degenerate or irrecuperable. France remained in the position of possessing colonies, but in the decade often described as one of *immobilism*, the Third Republic embarked on a dangerous course away from democracy towards fascism, a trajectory which culminated in the collaborationist regime under Pétain. On the way, a new ideology of nation building which emphasised the demolition of the old France gained ground. Publications such as Robert Aron's *Décadence de la nation française* in 1931 and the widespread repudiation of centralising Jacobinism helped to generate ideas of regionalisation and strengthened the influence of reactionaries such as L'Action française.

The year 1939 would radically alter the course of world history and in particular would begin the dismantling of Europe and would initiate the radical redrawing of boundaries and the profound reconfiguration of political and ideological alliances across the continent. The whole of Europe – both its outposts, such as Ireland, and its centres (in several of which, Paris, London, Berlin, Beckett resided in the decade) – would feel the reverberations of the war. The story of Beckett under the occupation, which has been a major focus for biographers and scholars of his work, and which will be explored in a fresh light elsewhere in the present volume, however, can only, like that of the occupation, Vichy and collaboration, be told by taking due account of the contributing factors in the lead up to war. In recent decades, there have been some important correctives to a certain mythologised portrait of the decade (including micro-periods within the encompassing decade – summarised in the title of Pascal Ory's book on the Popular Front, *La Belle Illusion*), despite its economic torpor, as a golden era (perceived in the light of the horrors which were to come). These correctives serve to reconfigure our understanding of the complexities both of Vichy and what has come to be known as *Vichy avant Vichy*. If the accounts put forward by Marrus, Nord and Weber, among others, are to be given credence, this defines the social and political climate of France in the 1930s and is the context against which part of the formation of Beckett the man and Beckett the writer must be considered.[8]

'Never has humanity joined so much power and so much disarray, so much anxiety and so many playthings, so much knowledge and so much uncertainty'.[9] According to Weber, an account of the decade 'must be, directly or indirectly, a book about the wounds and mind-set of a host of survivors – veterans, widows, orphans, parents – grieving for the slaughtered'.[10] It is against this backdrop that an emerging discipline must be considered. One of the focal points of the French political elites in the 1930s is demography. As Weber's research shows, between 1900 and 1939 the French population grew by only three per cent, whereas in Britain growth was twenty-three per cent. In 1936, fifteen per cent of the French population was over sixty and ten per cent over sixty-five.[11] In 1934, Adolphe Landry published *La Revolution demographique* (1934); there he argued for the notion of demographic transition.[12] The concern with demography, and in extreme cases the advocacy of eugenicist policies, manifested itself in many different areas of policy. One of the consequences, however, was a yoking together of demographic science and morality. As Philip Nord states, 'The crisis of the thirties re-routed the pronatalist movement, taking it in a familialist direction that yoked demographic science to a much larger project of moral, not to say Christian, regeneration'.[13] The middle of the decade also saw Alexis Carrel become a bestseller in the United States and France with the eugenicist *L'Homme, cet inconnnu* (1935). The anti-Semitic and anti-communist Carrel is associated with a theory of the decline and inadaptation of the human to industrialisation and the need to do away with democracy and to install firm authoritarian leadership. The fascist Parti Populaire Français established by Jacques Doirot may be regarded as a formalisation of the hard-fisted policy advocated by Carrel. Within the same context, historians have noted the institutional anti-Semitism of the cradle of policymakers, Sciences Po. Blum was both Jewish and socialist. When the Daladier administration of 1938–40 succeeded that of Blum, the long-standing pronatalist policies (which included the financial incentivisation of having large families) were augmented and underpinned by a new moralistic and disciplinary rhetoric.[14] Beckett displays his awareness of these debates in both France and Ireland in his essay 'Censorship in the Saorstat'.

If Beckett was itinerant during the 1930s, the decade is often described by historians as that of France's own 'immobilism' as a nation. Daniel Linderberg in his study of French culture in the period 1937–47 has suggested that the 'ambiance eschatologique' of the time manifests itself in various 'soft' forms, and these include Beckett's post-war studies of a Europe in ruins.[15] We know of Beckett's admiration for the works of Céline, an author with right-wing beliefs expressed at their most extreme in his pamphlet, published in 1938, *L'École de cadavres*. Regardless of the latter, which Beckett would have had no hesitation in denouncing, he was no doubt drawn to something of the eschatological ambiance of Céline's earlier novels (for which Beckett professed an admiration). Another manifestation of this tendency in the writers of the period is evident in the pre-war non-fiction writings of Maurice Blanchot for *Combat*.[16] In declaring France the real enemy in his pre-war journalism, for Linderberg (in what is perhaps too straightforward an extrapolation), the Blanchot who retreats into pure literature 's'inscrit, de manière extrême, comme à sa habitude, dans un mouvement qui avait conduit la littérature française a prendre pour objet l'attente de l'Apocalypse'.[17] Arguably, there is a sense in which Beckett absorbs some of this ambiance.[18] Nonetheless fascism failed in France, and as Robert Paxton and others have argued, the collaborationist administration (in which Beckett's friend Georges Pelorson would play a part) was formed from the traditional rather than the extreme left.[19]

PARIS AND THE AVANT-GARDE

As Terence Brown has pointed out, for Irish artists with European cultural sensibilities, in the years between the wars Paris was of central importance. Beckett and those like him, McGreevy included, recognised that 'Irish cultural provincialism could be redeemed only if a proper concern with nationality was combined with an acceptance of the riches of European culture'.[20] Avant-garde Paris acts as the mediating space between Beckett and politics. This context after all is far from being exclusively cultural as even a glance at the manifestos of the decade will attest. Indeed, the avant-garde and the intelligentsia at the forefront of debate, not least in the little magazines of the 1930s, would become hosts to a burgeoning right-wing contingent as the decade wore on. Beckett has political affiliations only by means of association. As many have commented, his relative politicisation in the shadow of anti-Semitism may derive as much from his friendship with Alfred Péron (with whom Beckett first became acquainted in 1926) as from a sense of horror at developments in Germany. Never exercising his right to vote in his lifetime, the only directly political statements of the 1930s which come to us from the archives are contained in letters and entries in his diary from his stay in Germany and his '¡Uptherepublic!' contribution to Nancy Cunard's *Authors Take Sides on the Spanish Civil War*. One might argue that the 'Poetry is Vertical' manifesto, published in *transition* 21, often attributed at least in part to Beckett, displays a Beckett by association firmly on the left, albeit formally apolitical.[21]

The Parisian avant-garde, then, and the access to it provided by Beckett's acquaintance – almost immediately upon his arrival – with Joyce directly contributed to Beckett's development. He published in its journals ('Whoroscope and 'Assumption' being published in *transition* in 1929), interacted with its principal players and patrons (Eugene Jolas, Joyce, Peggy Guggenheim), played notable editorial roles (sitting in for McGreevy at the journal *Formes* and working for Joyce) and translated key experimental authors, among them Apollinaire, Eluard and Rimbaud.[22]

Pascal Ory's account of the mélange of the literary and the political as it was operative at the journal *Soutes*, which would also publish Beckett, is a useful index of the extent to which culture and politics overlapped in the small reviews. Ory quotes some of the *Soutes* mantras: 'L'action est la forme supérieure de la pensée'; 'la vie – la poésie – la révolution sont même chose'.[23]

SOCIAL AND ECONOMIC DEPRIVATION

(Vichy avant Vichy)

As studies by Emilie Morin and others have shown, the aesthetics of poverty discernible in Beckett's post-war work has double roots in the events of Irish history and the French context (even in its intermittency) in the 1930s and during the German occupation.[24] In 1931, following the Wall Street crash of 1929, which served to exacerbate economic problems created by the Great War from which Europe was struggling to recover, France was, according to Weber, 'not an underdeveloped country, but a developed one in an advanced state of decay'.[25] Beckett may have already left at this juncture – though he was in France with his brother in the summer of 1931 – but in a sense he never completely left the French capital in the decade between his appointment at the ENS and his definitive return in 1937. Throughout his absence from France between 1932 and 1937 he was in communication with French publishers and editors.

Andrew Gibson has convincingly argued that Vichy France is present in the Trilogy and *Waiting for Godot*. Beckett's experience of the resistance and the risks that he, like so many other foreign nationals residing in France, had to take, and the assistance he received from others are factors which lie outside our concerns.[26] However, the idea of *Vichy avant Vichy* is important for a consideration of the political and social contexts contributing to our understanding of Beckett's work. As Nord has argued, 'the Liberation movement does not stand alone facing toward the future but comes at the end of a longer history, representing a denouement as much as a fresh start'.[27] In his account of Vichy before Vichy, Nord has described the troubled 1930s as incubating 'a vision and cadre of personnel that would come into its own under Pétain'.[28] This cadre, delivered to its destiny under Pétain, spearheaded the authoritarian turn in the declining Third Republic.[29]

Beckett has his own miniature *Vichy avant Vichy* in the guise of his friendship with Georges Pelorson, with whom Beckett became acquainted at the ENS and at Trinity College, Dublin, where Pelorson had the post of *lecteur*. Pelorson who is also known – under his post-war nom de plume Georges Belmont – for his translations (among them of the poetry of Emily Brontë and novels by Henry Miller, Graham Greene and Henry James as well as Anthony Burgess) wrote provocative articles in the pre-war journal *Volontés* (which he founded) and would later be a staunch collaborator and member of the Vichy regime. Beckett's friendship had been forged largely during Pelorson's time at Trinity College, Dublin, where they infamously staged Pelorson's parody *Le Kid* (Beckett's first creative encounter with the stage and his only known acting part). The letters attest to a growing distance from Pelorson – who just fell short of becoming a minister, but whose extremism saw him unfavoured by Pétain – but make no reference to the essentially fascist turn his work as an author took in the years leading up to the war. In a letter dated 11 February 1938, Beckett merely mentions the angry and negative tenor of Pelorson's editorials for *Volontés*, whose editorial board included Eugene Jolas, Raymond Queneau and Henry Miller.[30] He is not alone in his failure to notice the incipient fascism, as the correspondence with Péron shows. Beckett's formally apolitical nature is nonetheless evidenced by the restoration of his friendship and correspondence in the 1950s.[31]

During Beckett's absence the short-lived utopian hopes of the Popular Front government were fired and extinguished. As Nord points out, the Third Republic had been laissez-faire in the matter of culture to the point of negligence.[32] Coming to power on 3 May 1936, Léon Blum's regime was, in Nord's account, 'a moment of cultural adventure when a socialist-leaning state encouraged an upwelling of youthful and antifascist expression in a dizzying variety of media'.[33] The Popular Front was an administration of socialists and radicals committed to a new democratic form of public life; it was antifascist and directly responded to the rise of fascism in Europe, and it sought a new deal for working people.[34] Despite its commitment, however, in its failure to revive the economy and with the looming threat of German expansionist intentions, the Popular Front came to provide yet another chapter in the narrative of stasis, even if this can be overstated.[35] When Beckett returned from Germany in 1937 it is possible that he associated the failure of the Popular Front with those inexorable forces he had observed at closer quarters on his German tour.

Beckett's experience of both presence in and absence from France in the decade leading up to 1939 could not condense and inform a body of work written directly out of this experience. While there is no denying the acuity of Beckett's awareness of his social surroundings and undoubtedly this feeds his writing (as contained in the German diaries for example), it remains true that the Beckett of 1939 did not have the opportunity to develop this raw material into literature as such. The presence of France in Beckett's published work in the 1930s is felt intermittently throughout the decade in commissions, such as *Proust*, his work as a translator (for *transitions* for example) and his own forays into writing poetry in his adopted tongue. If Beckett later came to draw on his experiences of France between 1928 and 1939, the resource would be subject to the palimpsest of the enforced peripateticism and deprivations of wartime and viewed, therefore, through a glass darkly.

NOTES

1 See the letter of 10 October 1930 in which Beckett refers to life in Paris as 'an approximation to something reasonable' (*L1*, 50).
2 Beckett observed in his diary: 'They must fight soon (or burst)', 6 October 1936, cited by Mark Nixon, *Samuel Beckett's German Diaries 1936–1937* (London: Continuum, 2011), 7.

3 See, for example, Emilie Morin, *Samuel Beckett and the Problem of Irishness* (Oxford: Oxford University Press, 2009) and Andrew Gibson, *Samuel Beckett* (London: Reaktion Books, 2010).
4 See the letter to George Reavey dated 27 September 1938, in which Beckett makes a matter of fact reference to mobilisation and evacuation (with explicit reference to the flight of Péron) in the capital (*LI*, 642).
5 As Terence Brown argues, 'A recurrent intellectual motif in the writings of Irish Ireland's thinkers is the provision of historical accounts of Ireland's European uniqueness. The authentic Gaelic life which must be the basis of an Irish resurgence in the twentieth century, the argument runs, is a way of life that has traditionally escaped the universalising forces that have disturbed local life throughout most of the rest of Europe'. See Terence Brown, *Ireland: A Social and Cultural History 1922–2002*, (London: Harper, 2004), 57.
6 See Etienne Balibar, *We, the people of Europe? Reflections on Transnational Citizenship*, trans. James Swenson (Princeton: Princeton University Press, 2004).
7 Ibid., 152.
8 Michael Marrus, 'Vichy avant Vichy', *Histoire* (3: 1979), 77–92; Eugen Weber, *The Hollow Years: France in the 1930s* (New York: Norton, 1994); Philip Nord, *France's New Deal: from the Thirties to the Postwar Era* (Princeton: Princeton University Press, 2010).
9 Weber, *The Hollow Years*, 9.
10 Ibid., 8.
11 Ibid., 21.
12 Ibid., 51.
13 Ibid., 54.
14 Ibid., 60.
15 Daniel Lindenberg, *Les Années souterraines: 1937–1947* (Paris: Editions de la découverte, 1990), 371.
16 As Leroy and Roche assert, *Combat*, published between January 1936 and July 1939, embodies the diversity, contradictions and ambiguities of the French intellectual right (Leroy and Roche, *Combat*, 72). Blanchot himself, in an article entitled 'La grande passion de modérés', would denigrate Blum and the Popular Front in crypto-fascist terms: 'une bande de dégénérés et de traitres déshonore le pays sans resistance' (9 November 1936), a somewhat milder version of the more extreme views expressed elsewhere in the journal. The recent publication of a letter written by Maurice Blanchot to Dionys Mascolo in the 1980s describing the context in which his pre-war journalism appeared, especially when considered in the light of Jean-Luc Nancy's introduction, serves as a corrective to certain overly sensationalist accounts of Blanchot's politics in this period. Blanchot's right-wing liberalism of the pre-war years is always vigilant against the extremism represented by Nazism. See Jean-Luc Nancy, *Maurice Blanchot, passion politique: lettre-récit de 1984 suivie d'une lettre de Dionys Mascolo* (Paris: Galilée, 2011).
17 Lindenberg, *Les Années souterraines*, 22.

18 Paul Ricoeur for example notes that in his confusion in part brought about by a massive propaganda campaign as late as 1941 he still considered that the defeat of France might have been the best way to rebuild. Ricoeur's testimony is cited by Paxton in Robert O. Paxton, Olivier Corpet and Claire Paulhan (eds.), *Archives de la vie littéraire sous l'Occupation: À travers le désastre* (Paris: Tallandier, 2009), 7.

19 Robert O. Paxton, *The Anatomy of Fascism* (London: Penguin Books, 2005), 68–73.

20 Ibid., 156.

21 A point which may be illustrated by the fact that Georges Pelorson is also a signatory. Indeed the immensely contradictory Pelorson is published in all but one of the numbers of the 'New *transition*' between 1932 and 1938 during a period in which his political views, as expressed in print, have yet to consolidate into the quasi-fascistic form they would soon take in his own journal *Volontés*. See Vincent Giroud's indispensable study of Pelorson, 'Transition to Vichy: The Case of Georges Pelorson', *Modernism/Modernity*, (7.2: 2000), 221–48. Le Corbusier, writing in *Volontés*, makes a chilling reference to the creation of a 'solid, beautiful, healthy race', while in an editorial of his own Pelorson advocates 'policies of racial maintenance'. Elsewhere Pelorson shows himself to be susceptible to the rhetoric of soil, blood and destiny, while he also records his clear, albeit qualified, support for the Munich accords. Giroud's article should dispel any doubt that might remain among Beckett scholars as to the virulence of Pelorson's fascism. Biographers (with the exception of Cronin) have tended to avoid the issue of Pelorson's wartime activities. In a letter of 12 April 1938 Beckett refers to 'the turn his writing has taken'. Liebert in *Dream* is in part based on Pelorson. See their entry on Pelorson in C. J. Ackerley and S. E. Gontarski (eds.), *The Grove Companion to Samuel Beckett: A Reader's Guide to his Works, Life and Thought* (New York: Grove Press, 2004). See Pelorson's own account (which studiously avoids his wartime activities) of his relationship with Beckett in Georges Belmont, *Souvenirs d'outre monde* (Paris: Calmant Levy, 2001).

22 McGreevy was the secretary of the English edition of *Formes: an International Review of Plastic Art* (December 1929–March 1933). Beckett stood in for McGreevy as translator for a period. Beckett's translations of Bréton and Eluard appeared in the surrealist number of *This Quarter* in 1931. His ambitious translation of *Le bateau ivre*, which is in *Disjecta*, was not published.

23 Pascal Ory, *Le Belle Illusion: Culture et politique sous le signe du Front Populaire 1935–1938* (Paris: Plon, 1994), 216. Péron's translation of 'Alba' appeared in *Soutes* in April 1938.

24 Beckett was not well off, even though he received an allowance from his parents. His letters attest to his relative penury – and how he was the frequent recipient of shoes and clothes from Joyce and others.

25 Weber, *The Hollow Years*, 7.

26 See Gibson, *Samuel Beckett*. Beckett applied to serve France, having returned to the country the day after the declaration of war. He doggedly pursued this

despite not receiving a reply. This led eventually to his volunteering to assist the Irish Red Cross in Normandy after the war.
27 Gibson, *Samuel Beckett*, 11.
28 Ibid.
29 Ibid., 12.
30 In a letter dated 11 February 1938 Beckett writes: 'Editorials negative and far too angry' (cited *L1*, 616, n. 9). He adds comments on Pelorson's journal in letters to McGreevy of 12 April 1938 (where he declares a lack of interest) and 26 May 1938 when he describes issue 5 of the journal as 'considerably more ignominious than any of the former ones' (*L1*, 614; 627 respectively).
31 Marie-Claude Hubert claims (erroneously) that contact was definitively severed following the war (Marie-Claude Hubert, 'Pelorson', in Marie-Claude Hubert (ed.), *Dictionnaire Beckett* (Paris: Honoré Champion, 2011), 790), whereas letters attest to a resumed and apparently friendly acquaintance. Beckett did have at least one direct dealing with a French politician. In the course of his (ultimately successful) attempt to help out his friend Thomas McGreevy, he corresponded with a member of the cabinet of foreign affairs – Henri Laungier – and became acquainted with him socially. See the letter by Beckett dated 22 December 1937.
32 Nord, *France's New Deal*, 14.
33 Ibid., 13. This welling up is the topic of Pascal Ory's *La Belle Illusion*, the title being a composite of the two most famous films of the Popular Front tenure, Julien Duvivier's *La Belle Équipe* (1936) and Jean Renoir's *La Grande Illusion* (1937). A scene in the latter film provides one of the visual sources for *En attendant Godot*.
34 The essential volume edited by Morin and Richard contains a rich collection of visual materials. See Gilles Morin and Gilles Richard, *Les Deux France du Front populaire*, (Paris: l'Harmattan, 2008). See also the invaluable reproductions of archival materials from France under the occupation edited by Robert Paxton, Olivier Corpet and Claire Paulhan.
35 Nord, *France's New Deal*, 25.

CHAPTER 8

England: 1933–1936

Peter Marks

Having no alternative, the sun that shines in *Murphy* – but not on Murphy himself – at the opening of Samuel Beckett's first published novel shines on the nothing new of London. Specifically, it shines on 'a mew in West Brompton' (*M*, 3). More specifically still, it shines on an area encompassing Edith Grove, Cremorne Road, Lot's Road and Stadium Street, where the streetwalking Celia Kelly first spies Murphy. As the narrative begins, he sits out of the sun, 'as though he were free', struggling to disengage himself physically from the world: 'These were sights and sounds that he did not like. They detained him in the world to which they belonged, but not he, as he fondly hoped' (*M*, 3). While Murphy ostensibly lives in London, he does so, as he might do anywhere else, under sufferance, actively detaching himself from the metropolitan context. From late January 1933 until the end of 1935 Beckett himself lived not a ten-minute walk away, first in Paulton's Square and then, after returning from a short visit to Dublin in May 1934, nearby in Gertrude Street. He had moved from Dublin to London to undergo psychotherapy at the suggestion of his friend from Trinity College, Dublin, Geoffrey Thompson, in the hope that it might cure symptoms including heart palpitations and panic attacks brought on by the sudden death of his father, Bill, in June 1933. That unexpected calamity followed shortly after another, the death of his cousin Peggy Sinclair in Germany.

Thompson suggested the Tavistock Clinic, a leading centre for psychotherapy in Britain. The treatment would cost £200, more than Beckett could afford on the annual allowance from his father's will. His mother, May, agreed to supply the required funds, although given her concerns about her son's prospects this investment in his well-being possibly added tension to their always complex relationship. Beckett had found his mother's extended mourning for her dead husband oppressive; in addition to therapy, then, London offered him some respite from the anxious domestic environment of Dublin.

Perhaps to offset costs, between Thompson's diagnosis and Beckett's departure for treatment Beckett applied, 'in a moment of gush', for a job at the National Gallery in London, using as referees Jack Yeats and Charles Prentice. The latter was a supporter of Beckett's writing as well as a senior partner at London publisher Chatto and Windus. Beckett wrote to Thomas McGreevy, then living in Paris: 'I think I'd be happy there for a time among the pigeons and not too far from the French charmers in the Garrick [Theatre]' (*L1*, 167). Despite these hopes, the application failed. In a December 1933 letter to McGreevy, by now in London, Beckett wrote of his interest in another possible form of employment: 'I thought of apprenticing myself to some advertising firm in London. At least it would get me out of here [Dublin] and it might be entertaining' (*L1*, 171). He explained that the idea:

has been in my mind for a long time and I had often been on the point of putting it to father. Now I can put it up to mother. There is always someone to whom one can put it up. If there was always someone *in* whom.... (*L1*, 171)

Again, nothing came of this plan. McGreevy, meanwhile, had found Beckett lodgings in Paulton's Square, close to his own accommodation in Chelsea and across the Thames from Battersea Park, home of the four caged owls Murphy thinks about when he comes to consciousness near the end of chapter five (*M*, 67).

Beckett's motivation for living in London, then, was not literary, that city providing as much an escape as a favoured destination. Indeed, a previous visit on his way back from Paris in 1932 had created few positive associations. He did get his reader's ticket for the Reading Room of the British Museum, stating that he wanted to look at 'minor pre-Revolutionary writing of the 18th century' (*L1*, 109). But by August 1932 he wrote to McGreevy that 'here I am, perfecting my methodol[og]y of sleep, and little else. No courage for galleries or palaces. I went into St Paul's and found it hideous.... I couldn't stand the British Museum any more' (*L1*, 111). His main reason for being in London in 1932 was neither sightseeing nor minor pre-Revolutionary writing, but to make literary connections, to perhaps pick up some work from literary papers and periodicals and to find a publisher for *Dream of Fair to Middling Women*, completed earlier that year. Encouraged by the well-connected McGreevy, Beckett began, as Anthony Cronin puts it, 'to do the rounds, or in, other words, perform the necessary penances that residence in London imposed on a troubled and guilt-ridden young literary man' (*C*, 175). He visited literary journalist, critic and Bloomsbury Group member Desmond MacCarthy (who had reviewed *Proust* for the *Sunday Times*),[1] as well as Leonard Woolf at the Hogarth Press (Woolf was out of town) and the literary editors of *The Spectator* and *New Statesman* (*C*, 175-7). But nothing substantial came of these efforts.

The manuscript of *Dream of Fair to Middling Women*, which he fruitlessly carried with him to the Hogarth Press, potentially was far more significant for Beckett's literary prospects. Realising that Irish censorship made it impossible for the book to be published in his homeland, and knowing that it could not be translated easily into French, Beckett also visited Chatto and Windus – which had published *Proust* – and Jonathan Cape. Even with Beckett's connection to Prentice, though, Chatto and Windus turned down *Dream of Fair to Middling Women*, as did the Hogarth Press and Cape. Beckett wrote bitterly to George Reavey soon after his return to Dublin: 'The novel doesn't go. Shatton and Windup thought it was wonderful but they couldn't they simply could not. The Hogarth Private Lunatic Asylum rejected it the way Punch would. Cape was écoeuré [disgusted] in pipe and cardigan and his Aberdeen terrier agreed with him' (*LI*, 125). As it had been for centuries, London in the 1930s was an international literary hub, but as Valentine Cunningham notes: 'It's been too little observed about the '30s how small an area was actually occupied by its characteristic centres. Then, as now, England's literary and political life was managed from Central London and from a tiny part of Central London at that'.[2] It says something about the compact – if in this case unsympathetic – London literary world that an energetic walker like Beckett could have strode from Chatto and Windus (St Martin's Lane) to Jonathan Cape's (Bedford Square) and then on to the Hogarth Press (Tavistock Square) in twenty minutes. The disappointed writer put aside *Dream of Fair to Middling Women* for another sixty years. But between Thompson's examination in Dublin and Beckett's departure for London in 1933 Beckett received better news, Prentice informing him in September that Chatto and Windus had accepted his collection of short stories. The publisher, however, wanted a new title to replace *Graff*; Beckett suggested *More Pricks than Kicks*, which it accepted. As he noted ruefully to Nualla Costello, though: 'Can't get it taken in U.S.A' (*LI*, 188). *More Pricks than Kicks* was offered unsuccessfully to American publishers Viking Press, Farrar and Rinehart, Harrison Smith and Hass, Doubleday Doran and Grundy (*K*, 183), and by October 1934 had been placed on the 'Index of Forbidden Books in Ireland'. Whatever London's drawbacks, it provided one of the few places where Beckett enjoyed even the chance of being published.

Ironically, as well as housing the 'Hogarth Private Lunatic Asylum', Tavistock Square also was the original site of the Tavistock Clinic, where, James Knowlson records, Beckett's intensive sessions began 'shortly after Christmas 1933' (*K*, 174). The clinic itself had been set up by the pioneering Hugh Crichton-Miller in 1920, and in the early 1930s was well established and expanding (requiring the move to larger Malet Street premises in 1932, where Beckett was treated). By then there were 'twenty-five "full physicians", as well as some psychologists and social workers'.[3] The number of new cases seen by the clinic in that year 'increased from some 500 to well over 700'.[4] Largely as the result of the 1930 Mental Treatment Act, which drew on Crichton-Miller's ideas, psychotherapy was on a firm footing in Britain, and the Tavistock Clinic took a largely non-doctrinaire approach to the various branches of treatment then current. Beckett was assigned a young and relatively inexperienced therapist, Wilfred Bion, with whom he quickly struck up an easy and mostly beneficial relationship. (Bion himself would develop into a highly regarded and influential international figure in psychotherapy.) He responded positively to the treatment at first, which comprised intensive sessions of dream analysis and free association. Interviewed in 1989, he revealed that he 'used to lie down on the couch and try to think back into my past', explaining that 'I certainly came up with some extraordinary memories of being in the womb. Intrauterine memories'. He added: 'I used to go back to my digs and write on what happened', judging that 'I think it all helped me to understand a bit better what I was doing and what I was feeling' (*K*, 177). Beckett's initial feelings at the time were also positive. Writing to Morris Sinclair on 27 January 1934, he explained:

Three times a week I give myself over to probing my depths with my psychiatrist which has already, I think, done me some good in the sense that I can keep a little calmer, and that the panic attacks in the night are less frequent and less acute. But the treatment will necessarily be long, and I may have months more of it yet. (*L1*, 182–3)

In fact the treatment would continue for nearly two years, analysis prompting advances, relapses and resistances at different stages. It also provoked searching personal insights. A March 1935 letter to McGreevy blended assessments of Beckett's long-term unhappiness with the realisation that his recent physical symptoms had deeper causes:

It was with a specific fear & a specific complaint that I went to Geoffrey, then to Bion, to learn that the 'specific fear and complaint' was the least important symptom of a diseased condition that began in a time which I could not remember, in my 'pre-history', a bubble on the puddle; and that the fatuous torments which I had treasured as denoting the superior man were all part of the same pathology. That was the picture and I was required to accept it, and that is still largely the picture.... (*L1*, 259)

This searing self-portrait shows the clear impact of the sessions, and while Beckett at times would become frustrated, sceptical or cynical about the efficacy of the therapy, the fact that he continued with it, 'read widely on the subject of psychology and psychoanalysis' (*K*, 177), and maintained a longer-term interest in psychoanalysis, register Bion's effect in this period.

Beyond this necessarily highly personal focus, the London Beckett lived in was, as Cunningham suggests, also the political centre of Britain, and the decade as a whole experienced high political turbulence. The massive impact of the Great Depression, which called into question the viability of capitalism, the rise of Hitler and the consolidation of fascism in Spain (in Italy, of course, it had been established for more than a decade), along with the competing arguments for socialism often based on the supposed success of the USSR, created a fevered international environment. But if the 1930s generally (though somewhat erroneously) is labelled the Red Decade, during the years Beckett lived in London Britain was governed by a Conservative-dominated coalition. Led by the former Labour Party leader Ramsay MacDonald but essentially controlled by Conservatives, the 'National Government' had taken control in the landslide victory of 1931, its success reinforced by the 1935 elections. By contrast to much of Europe, Britain politically was stable, though not politically inert: high unemployment, the rise of the British Union of Fascists (exemplified by the infamous gathering at Olympia Exhibition Hall in June 1934) and the consolidation of a sizeable left-wing community ensured that political contestation was pervasive. But for all the undoubted politicisation of the decade, in actuality political engagement in Britain absorbed a relatively small section of society, and it was possible to live in London without participating in any way in ideological debates or divisions. This might be especially true for a young, aloof, intellectual Irishman undergoing psychotherapy, especially one whose friends in London predominantly were Irish as well. Beckett's letters show no indication of any interest in local political matters. But his Jewish uncle Boss Sinclair had taken his family and fled anti-Semitism in Germany soon after the Nazis came to power, and Beckett's assessment of the Berlin Philharmonic Orchestra at Queen's Hall in London attacks its conductor, 'the ignoble [Wilhelm] Furtwängler, who, it appears, has the better part of his nudity covered with interwoven swastikas' (*L1*, 182). Even Beckett could not completely escape the political climate.

As a global cultural centre, London afforded many opportunities to hear large and small ensembles, and the Berlin Philharmonic concert was only one of many Beckett went to during his time in London. Early on he also mentions in a letter to Morris Sinclair hearing 'a superb concert by the Pro Arte Quartet' and another by the Busch Quartet. But money was tight, and although he was not desperately poor, he had to carefully husband his funds. In the same letter, consequently, while recording 'a positive storm of music in London just now' (*L1*, 197), he adds that 'even if one could afford them all it would be hard to choose between concerts happening on the same day. Now there is a dilemma that costs me no sleep! Alas!' (*L1*, 198). When money permitted, though, Beckett enjoyed the quality and variety of London's musical offerings. Equally enticing, and far less expensive, was London's profusion of major and minor art galleries, many of which he visited with an equally enthusiastic McGreevy. The National Gallery gave him the chance to see one of Cézanne's landscapes, his response giving a telling sense of his ideas about the potential overlap of painting and writing:

What a relief the Mont Ste. Victoire after all the anthropomorphised landscape.... How far Cézanne had moved from the snapshot puerilities of Manet & Cie when he could understand the dynamic intrusion to be himself & so landscape to be something by definition utterly alien, unintelligible arrangement of atoms.... Perhaps it is the one bright spot in a mechanistic age – the deanthromorphizations of the artist [*sic*]. (*L1*, 222–3)

Only a few months earlier, writing to Morris Sinclair in May 1934, Beckett had mused almost plaintively about the Irish landscape, admitting that '[s]taying in this town [London] gives me little pleasure', this dismissal preceding an almost romanticised evocation of Ireland, were it not for the final sting: 'Sometimes I long for those mountains and fields, which I know so well, and which create a completely different calm from the one associated with this coarse English landscape. If only Dublin were unfamiliar, then it would be pleasant to live somewhere nearby' (*L1*, 205).

Beckett did return to Dublin three times during his time in London, first in September 1934, then for the Christmas break at the end of the year, returning to London with his brother Frank, and again in Easter 1935. The follow-up to that trip was an invitation for his mother to visit, which she did for three weeks in July 1935. Despite their troubled relationship and those disparaging comments on the coarse English landscape,

England: 1933–1936

the two holidayed in Devon and journeyed up to Stratford-upon-Avon, which he found 'unspeakable' (*K*, 203), as well as to Winchester and Bath, towns associated with Jane Austen, whom he was reading for literary instruction. Once he had despatched May back to Ireland Beckett visited Samuel Johnson's birthplace in Lichfield, what Knowlson labels a 'pilgrimage' (*K*, 203). Given Beckett's own ambivalence about London, Johnson's declaration to Boswell, 'No, Sir, when a man is tired of London, he is tired of life; for there is in London all that life can afford' might suggest an unbridgeable gap between the eighteenth-century polymath and the twentieth-century apprentice writer.[5] But Johnson had already fascinated Beckett, and Linda Ben-Zvi contends that Johnson 'proved in many ways one of the most compelling and the most intractable' of inspirations.[6] The traces of this trip followed Beckett; for the following year, after leaving England, he committed substantial time and creative energy to a proposed play on Johnson's agonising relationship with Mrs Thrale, Ben-Zvi considering that his 'work on the project was one of the most protracted of his career'.[7]

Even with these cultural activities, Beckett did not feel prompted to write anything substantial in his first year in London.[8] Because of the lag time between completion and publication, his translations for Nancy Cunard's *Negro* anthology appeared a few months after his analysis began, while the finalising of his poetry collection *Echo's Bones* dragged frustratingly on. Short works did begin to appear in London and Dublin periodicals, including one review in *The Spectator*, and another, of a translation of *Poems* by Rainer Maria Rilke, in *The Criterion*. This piece – submitted by McGreevy, who knew T. S. Eliot – was Beckett's only contribution to that cultural juggernaut, although Anthony Cronin writes off the lack of other Beckett input to *The Criterion* as proving 'nothing either way' (*C*, 203). Beckett also had his poem 'Gnome' and a review of McGreevy's *Poems* published in *Dublin Magazine*. He contributed several reviews to *The Bookman*, and that periodical gave 'a favorable [sic] review' to *More Pricks Than Kicks* in July 1934, asking its author for an article on censorship in Ireland.[9] Beckett rather reluctantly began and eventually completed that piece, called 'Censorship in the Saorstat', but it was not published. *The Bookman*, although 'a long-running tradition in British letters since 1891', suffered the fate of many a literary journal, being 'amalgamated into *The London Mercury*, initially creating *The London Mercury with which is Incorporated The Bookman*'.[10] That ludicrously unwieldy title soon disappeared, as did the *Mercury* itself in 1939. But in August 1934 it published both Beckett's article on 'Recent Irish Poetry', under the pseudonym Andrew Belis, and his short story 'A Case in a Thousand' in a special number 'devoted to Irish writing'.[11] Knowlson argues that 'A Case in a Thousand' 'already shows the influence of Beckett's own psychotherapy and his reading around on the subject', something that 'is much more obvious and direct than it would later become' (*K*, 181). Rubin Rabinovitz offers a different interpretation, for while recognising the obvious psychological dimensions of the story, he links it to later works such as *Watt* and *Molloy*, which 'are about quests and failures' in which 'Beckett encourages his readers to become involved in the quests in order to experience the failures more sharply'.[12] The most substantial of the works published while Beckett was in England clearly was *More Pricks Than Kicks*, published in May 1934. Although it sold modestly, for a collection by a barely known author in his late twenties it attracted the critical attention of some of the better London literary journals and papers, including *The Observer*, *The Spectator*, *New Statesman*, *The Listener*, *The Bookman* and the *Times Literary Supplement*. As well as a powerful and established book publishing culture, London provided one of the most vibrant periodical cultures, and while reviews were mixed (*C*, 204; *K*, 184), short story collections are a hard sell at any time, especially ones that test the mettle of even highly intelligent reviewers. To be noticed in London was no small thing, Raymond Federman and John Fletcher indicating that the publication of 'A Case in a Thousand' in *The Bookman* exposed Beckett 'to a wider public than he ever again would be, at least until the staging of *Waiting for Godot*'.[13]

Although London was the undoubted centre of literary life in Britain, with a diverse and active range of individuals and groups including the Bloomsbury set, the so-called Auden Generation and the politically engaged writers associated with journals such as the *Left Review* (1934–8), Beckett's therapy, his relative anonymity and his natural reticence meant that his contact with local literary figures was very occasional and largely inconsequential. McGreevy's contacts helped him meet T. S. Eliot, and in a letter to Nualla Costello early in 1934 he mentions 'a brief interview' with Rebecca West, 'the Author of *Strange Necessity* (positively surprising my dear)', which provoked a limerick and attendant comment:

> There once was a woman called West
> Whose distinction it was to be blessed
> With so unremitting
> A sense of the fitting
> That she never if ever, undressed.

(Until [H.G.] Wells, and then I supposed she had to). This poemetto has been well-received in certain quarters. (*L1*, 187)

Deirdre Bair reports another meeting in 1935 with Cyril Connolly, who lived near Gertrude Street, and from whom Beckett hoped to get some work in literary journalism. Then a highly promising young writer (although he never fulfilled that promise), Connolly was well connected to powerful literary figures and to some of the better placed literary papers and periodicals in London. Rather than give Beckett work, though, Connolly 'thought it best', Bair suggests, 'that he "suffer a bit more, perhaps with the job as a dishwasher", to give him the needed experience to become a true writer' (*B*, 198–9). Bair does not specify the precise date of this meeting, and while it must remain speculative, Connolly's peculiar and peculiarly specific advice about useful occupations for aspiring writers perhaps drew on the example of Eric Blair, a friend of Connolly's from Eton with whom he had only recently re-established contact. Connolly was surprised to find that Blair had taken the pseudonym George Orwell, using his dishwashing experience and occasional forays into the suffering underclass in his first major publication, *Down and Out in Paris and London* (1933).

In any case, Beckett began work in August 1935 on the manuscript that became *Murphy*. Both Knowlson and Cronin state that Beckett drew particular inspiration from two London experiences: watching old men flying kites near the Round Pond in Kensington Park, and visits to the Bethlem Royal Hospital, where Geoffrey Thompson had become Senior House Physician in February 1935. The kite flying had caught Beckett's eye during his long regular walks around London (Kensington Park is ten minutes from Gertrude Street), and Celia's grandfather, Willoughby Kelly, indulges in it during the final chapter of *Murphy*. Thompson invited Beckett to visit Bethlem several times. He was fascinated by the patients, some of whom made a lasting impression. Knowlson notes that 'Three decades later, Beckett could still remember very clearly "standing five or six feet away from a schizophrenic who was 'like a hunk of meat. There was no one there. He was absent'"' (*K*, 209). These visits provided material for the Magdalen Mental Mercyseat where Murphy works briefly as a male nurse. Knowlson states that 'Beckett made extensive use of his knowledge of London in *Murphy*' (*K*, 204), and the novel certainly abounds with the names and spaces of London: the streets of West Brompton, Battersea Park and Hyde Park, 'the Piccadilly tube from Caledonian Road to Hyde Park Corner' (*M*, 95), the British Museum and Pentonville Prison. But for all these contextual markers *Murphy*'s 'London' has an alien and alienating quality, reflecting the narrator's comment that 'All the puppets in this book whinge sooner or later, except

Murphy, who is not a puppet' (*M*, 78). London is less an actual city than a series of theatrical flats in front of which the puppets perform. Murphy himself finds solace from the reality of London in curtained rooms and garrets, with the padded cells in the Magdelan Mental Mercyseat surpassing 'by far all he had ever been able to imagine in the way of indoor bowers of bliss' (*M*, 113). Readers are told that, from Murphy's perspective, the issue:

lay between nothing less fundamental than the big world and the little world, decided by the patients in favour of the latter, revived by the psychiatrists on behalf of the former, in his own case unresolved. In fact, it was unresolved, only in fact. His vote was cast. 'I am not of the big world, I am of the little world' was an old refrain of Murphy's.... (*M*, 112)

While much of *Murphy* apparently is set in the big world of London, Murphy retreats to his own little world. The first *London A-Z* was published in 1936, and if we take that street directory as our model, *Murphy* supplies parts of the index, but not the detailed and informative maps that bring London cartographically to life.

By the time he began *Murphy*, Beckett was determined to finish treatment with Bion by the end of the year, although in October 1935 he did dine with his therapist and then attend a lecture given at the Tavistock by Carl Jung. His account conveys the ongoing tension between his scepticism and curiosity, Beckett noting to McGreevy that Jung's mind was 'infinitely more ample, provocative and penetrating [than A. E. Russell's], but the same cuttle-fish's discharge & escapes from the issue in the end [*sic*]. He let fall some remarkable things nevertheless' (*L1*, 282). By this point *Murphy* was under way, letters to McGreevy charting its early progress: 'I have been forcing myself to keep at the book, & it crawls forward. I have done about 9000 words. It is poor stuff and I have no interest in it' (*L1*, 277), Beckett writes in September, although when he had completed twenty thousand words by October some of that negativity had passed: 'I have been working hard at the book & it goes very slowly, but I do not think there is any doubt now that it will be finished sooner or later. The feeling that I must jettison the whole thing has passed, only the labour of writing the remainder is left' (*L1*, 283). He would not complete *Murphy* until June 1936, six months after he left England for Dublin. The difficulties of finding a publisher meant that inevitably he sent the manuscript to Chatto and Windus. Charles Prentice had retired; however, his replacement, Ian

Parson, wrote a letter that proved a model for the prevailing response: 'the novel racket has reached such a pass today that a book, such as yours, which makes real demands on the reader's intelligence and general knowledge has less chance than ever of gaining a hearing' (*L1*, 357). In a June 1936 statement from the publisher, Beckett learnt that only two copies of *More Pricks Than Kicks* had been sold in the past year (*L1*, 347), so Parson's reluctance was sound commercially. *Murphy* would do the frustrating rounds of publishers on both sides of the Atlantic for more than a year before Routledge finally accepted it in December 1937. Jack Yeats had enthused about the novel to Routledge's T. M. Ragg, who replied astutely that 'it will bring great joy to the few' (*K*, 292). Beckett received the contract in Paris. Since beginning *Murphy* in London over two years earlier he had travelled to Germany and later to France. Tellingly, while *Murphy* would not be published in the United States until 1957, London's array of publishers in 1937 included just the type of highly intelligent, courageous company the novel required, and without which it might never have appeared. We can only imagine the effect on Beckett's still highly precarious literary career had *Murphy* not been published.

NOTES

1 Raymond Federman and John Fletcher, *Samuel Beckett: His Works and His Critics: An Essay in Bibliography* (Berkeley: University of California Press, 1970), 236.
2 Valentine Cunningham, *British Writers of the Thirties* (Oxford: Clarendon Press, 1989), 108.
3 H. V. Dicks, *Fifty Years of the Tavistock Clinic* (London: Routledge & Kegan Paul), 50.
4 Ibid., 47.
5 R. W. Chapman (ed.), James Boswell, *Life of Johnson* (Oxford: Oxford University Press, 1980), 859.
6 Linda Ben-Zvi, 'Biographical, Textual and Historical Origins', in Lois Oppenheim (ed.), *Palgrave Advances in Beckett Studies* (Basingstoke: Palgrave Macmillan, 2004), 133–53, 140.
7 Ibid., 145.
8 Deirdre Bair has him beginning to write a story that 'gradually evolved into the novel *Murphy*' in 'the fall of 1934' (*B*, 196), although Cronin and James Knowlson date its genesis to August 1935 (*C*, 217; *K*, 203).
9 Federman and Fletcher, *Samuel Beckett: His Works and His Critics*, 14–16.
10 J. Matthew Huculak, '*The London Mercury* (1919–39) and Other Moderns', in Peter Brooker and Andrew Thacker (eds.), *The Oxford Critical and Cultural*

History of Modernist Magazines, Volume 1: Britain and Ireland 1880–1955 (Oxford: Oxford University Press, 2009), 240–59, 256.
11 Federman and Fletcher, *Samuel Beckett: His Works and His Critics*, 15.
12 Rubin Rabinovitz, *The Development of Samuel Beckett's Fiction* (Chicago: University of Chicago Press, 1984), 69.
13 Federman and Fletcher, *Samuel Beckett: His Works and His Critics*, 15.

CHAPTER 9

Germany: Circa 1936–1937
Mark Nixon

Eight months after returning from his journey through Nazi Germany, which he undertook between October 1936 and April 1937, Samuel Beckett acquired a copy of the complete works of German poet Friedrich Hölderlin. His personal copy, preserved at the Beckett International Foundation's archive in Reading, contains various annotations and carries the inscription '24/12/37'. Beckett first encountered Hölderlin's writing in the early 1930s, and during his reading of Robertson's *History of German Literature* had noted that Hölderlin was not 'romantic like Richter, but combination of Sturm u.[und] Drang & Hellenism. Insane from 1802 till his death', and that his work was imbued with the 'melancholy of late 19th century'.[1] The marked passages in Beckett's copy of Hölderlin, dating from 1938 and 1939, relate to such moods of nostalgia and melancholy. Moreover, Beckett invoked the German poet in his review of Denis Devlin's poems ('Intercessions') in 1938, citing the poem 'Der Spaziergang', which impressed him to such a degree that it influenced the writing of his own poem 'Dieppe' that same year. As the Devlin review makes clear, Beckett was in particular attracted to Hölderlin's late, fragmentary poetry, written in madness and isolation in his tower at Tübingen. Beckett referred to these poems in a letter to Arland Ussher, written in June 1939, as the 'terrific fragments of the Spätzeit [late period]' (*LI*, 665).

Beckett's response to Hölderlin in these years stands in stark contrast to the appropriation of the poet by the National Socialist regime in Germany, which turned him into a symbol of cultural nationalism and German purity. Already in 1915, the influential editor of Hölderlin's work, Norbert von Hellingrath, had called him the 'most German poet', a designation which, with far-reaching consequences, was taken up by poet Stefan George.[2] In 1919, George called Hölderlin 'the great seer of his *Volk* [...] the cornerstone of the imminent German future and the herald of the New God'.[3] Similarly, in a series of lectures in the 1930s, Martin

Heidegger spoke of Hölderlin as the prophet of a new German dawn, reinforcing this with the idea that the poet's vocation is to have an affinity with the people, the *Volk*. By 1943, when the Hölderlin Society was established in Germany (with Goebbels as honorary patron), the manipulation of the poet's reputation was complete; that same year, to mark the centenary of the poet's death, one hundred thousand copies of a new edition were sent to soldiers on the front line to remind them of the honourable sacrifices demanded by the Fatherland.

It is unclear whether Beckett was aware of these attempts to turn Hölderlin into a model of patriotism, but his annotated copy reveals that he made a connection between the Nazis' rhetoric and the poet's work. He thus appended – beside a passage from *Hyperion* – the words 'fit for Das I.R.', a reference to the journal *Das Innere Reich* which Beckett had encountered during his trip through Nazi Germany. Thus Beckett noted the similar use of heroic terminology in the following passage: 'Von ihren Taten nähren die Söhne der Sonne sich; sie leben vom Sieg; mit eignem Geist ermuntern sie sich, und ihre Kraft ist ihre Freude [The sons of the sun nourish themselves from their deeds; they live on victory; their own spirit rouses them, and their strength is their joy]'.[4]

While the Nazis could easily appropriate such sentiments, they struggled to accommodate Hölderlin's madness within their visions of the new master race, ultimately turning the poet into a symbol of betrayal instead. Beckett, however, found aesthetic concerns in the German poet's work which mirrored his own in the late 1930s: notions of speechlessness, incompetence and fragmentation. Indeed, it will be my point in this chapter to show that Beckett turned to Hölderlin precisely *because* he offered an aesthetic that could be set against totalising narratives. As Beckett told Patrick Bowles in 1955, Hölderlin:

> ended in something of this kind of failure. His only successes are the points where his poems go on, falter, stammer, and then admit failure, and are abandoned. At such points he was most successful.[5]

Beckett saw this admittance of failure as diametrically opposed to Goethe's work, which he had read extensively in the two years leading up to his German trip. In his letter to Axel Kaun of July 1937, Beckett drew attention to the fact that Goethe was the kind of poet who carried on writing even when he had nothing to say. If Goethe was the poet of progressive 'onwardness', Hölderlin was the writer who renounced such a belief and embraced silence and failure. Beckett's trajectory from the former to the latter poet is brought into sharper focus by the journey through Nazi

Germany, as the German diaries, with their criticism of totalitarian discourse, reveal.

Beckett's reading of Goethe in the first half of the 1930s needs to be seen in the context of his wider engagement with German culture and thought, which was in part provoked by his relationship with Peggy Sinclair and his five trips to Kassel between 1928 and Christmas 1931. From an early stage, Beckett appears to have sought a melancholy strain in German thought and art, and found it in Schubert's *Lieder* and Schopenhauer's philosophy. In 1934, Beckett began to study the German language more intensely as two German vocabulary notebooks testify[6]; he familiarised himself with German literary history by taking copious notes from J. G. Robertson's *A History of German Literature*.[7] He subsequently read, amongst other German texts, Goethe's *Dichtung und Wahrheit*, and then, from August 1936 onwards, the epic poem *Faust*; as he told Thomas McGreevy, he had 'been working at German and reading Faust' (Beckett to McGreevy, undated [19 August 1936]; *L1*, 368). Beckett's correspondence, as well as his extensive transcriptions from Robert Petsch's introduction and the first two parts of *Faust* in two notebooks, reveal much about his creative thinking at this time.[8]

While finding much to admire, Beckett's main criticism of *Faust* was that 'the *on and up* is so tiresome [...] the determined optimism à la Beethoven' (Beckett to McGreevy, undated [19 August 1936]; *L1*, 368). As Dirk Van Hulle has shown, Beckett in this letter is commenting on Petsch's introduction to the book, which comments on the fact that 'Faust [...] stetig *aufwärts* streben muss [must always strive upward]'.[9] Beckett's dismissal of this Faustian *Vorwärtsstreben* is compounded by what he perceived as a 'surprising amount of irrelevance' in the text, partly because Goethe 'couldn't bear to *shorten* anything' (Beckett to McGreevy, 7 August 1936; *L1*, 366). This is undoubtedly the evaluation that lurks behind Beckett's statement made a year earlier in his letter to Kaun: that Goethe's opinion was '*better to write NOTHING than not to write*' (*L1*, 517).

The Faustian spirit, defined by the attempt to overcome internal and external limits, was harnessed by the Nazi regime in the 1930s. The *Völkischer Beobachter* for example noted in a review that *Faust* epitomised the 'germanische dynamische Wesen der Weltüberwindung und des Kampfes [Germanic, dynamic overcoming of the world and struggle' (23 May 1933). Beckett was aware of this narrative in its cultural and political guises, as a diary entry of January 1937 attests. Having read a German novel by Walter Bauer, *Die Notwendige Reise* (*The Necessary Journey*),

Beckett distanced himself from the 'heroic, the nosce te ipsum, that these Germans see as a journey':

> *Das notwendige Bleiben* [the necessary staying put] is more like it. That is also in the figure of Murphy in the chair, surrender to the thongs of self, a simple materialisation of self-bondage, acceptance of which is the fundamental unheroic. (German diaries, 18 January 1937, quoted in *K*, 230)[10]

Beckett's own journey to Germany was made in the awareness that it was 'a journey *from*, + not *to*', as he told Mary Manning Howe on 13 December 1936 (*L1*, 397). Beckett arrived in Hamburg in October 1936 at a rather pivotal historical moment. By this time, the Nazis had established complete control over political, social and cultural life within Germany's borders, and their expansionist intentions had, since the occupation of the demilitarised Rhineland (March 1936), become clear. Beckett acknowledged in his diary that he was travelling through a country that would most probably be at war in the near future: 'They *must* fight soon (or burst)' (German diaries, 6 October 1936 quoted in *K*, 261). Beckett's political awareness of what was happening in Germany prior to his journey is evident from his correspondence, punning for example on Hitler's *Mein Kampf* by writing 'Mein Krampf [My Cramp]' (letter to A. J. Leventhal, May 1934) or by mocking the conductor Furtwängler as a 'good Nazi' who has his 'nudity covered with interwoven swastikas' (letter to Morris Sinclair, 27 January 1934; *L1*, 182).

The daily diary entries that Beckett kept during his journey give an insight into the realities in Nazi Germany at this time, as well as Beckett's response to what he was experiencing. He was attentive to the main political events as reported in German newspapers and on the radio, listening for example:

> like a fool to 2 hours of Hitler & an hour of Goering (opening of Reichstag, Goering reelected President, laws controlling 4 years plan extended for another 4[)], the usual from A.H. with announcement of a 20 yr. plan for development of Berlin, 'reply' to Eden consisting mainly in repeated assertion that Germany's policy is not one of isolation. (German diaries, 30 January 1937)

He would also jot down passages from the papers he was reading, either in his diary or in one of the other notebooks he carried with him, copying out quotations by Goebbels, Hitler or Hess, or for example the following sentence from the *Frankfurter Zeitung*: 'War an accelerator of historical process, what in chemistry is called a catalysator' (German diaries, 14 March 1937). In recording such events, the diaries become historical documents, and this is even more the case when we consider Beckett's

Germany: Circa 1936–1937

shrewd and perceptive observations of daily life (the *Winterhilfswerk*, Hitler Youths on the street, *Eintopfsonntag*) and his notes preserving conversations with people from various walks of life, registering the range of opinion within German society regarding the political and cultural situation. One of his fellow guests at his lodgings propounds Germany's right to colonies, and in Leipzig a waiter explains that 'the Pelz [fur] trade has gone to hell because of Jews' (German diaries, 28 January 1937). He also noticed the '[p]hotographers outside Jewish shops' (German diaries, 21 January 1937).

Rather more instructive were Beckett's meetings with two young booksellers Axel Kaun and Günter Albrecht, who both possessed a more liberal outlook, as underlined by Beckett's description of Albrecht as 'not at all a Hitler Jüngling [youth]' (German diaries, 6 November 1936). Beckett endorsed Axel Kaun's analysis of 'the new Germany as one half sentimental demagogies and one half the brilliant obscurantics of Dr G. [Goebbels]', and further noted that Kaun 'deplores the failure of the Jews in exile to establish a *spiritual criticism* & the futility of their protest against the inessential' (German diaries, 11 January 1937). Beckett again agreed with Kaun's views a week later: 'The Kaun (young Germany?) view of Goebbels as the sinister controlling force, & Hitler & Goering the sentimental thunderers, strikes me also as more correct' (German diaries, 19 January 1937).

This 'sinister controlling force' is discernable throughout Beckett's diaries, and often elicits a sense of surveillance, menace and repression. This is evident from an entry dated 15 October 1936: 'Crawl home [...] past Jüdischer Friedhof [Jewish cemetery] (a desolation, cf. Ruysdael's *Judenkirchhof* in Zwinger [Dresden art museum], which I wonder if by now burnt)'. As this reference reveals, Beckett was in particular attentive to the way in which the Nazis were rewriting history, specifically through the censorship of books, journals and newspapers, as well as through the persecution of artists and writers and the removal of 'decadent' art from museums. Beckett's criticism of the Nazis' revision of history becomes clear when we examine his comments on literary histories. As he tried to buy a German literary history in Hamburg, he realised that '[e]verything in way of history of literature, art, m. [music], prior to Machtübernahme, disparaged'. Distrusting Nazi propaganda, Beckett proceeded to buy a German literary history by Karl Heinemann because it was 'written before the Machtübernahme' (German diaries, 21 October 1936), and similarly, when buying a book on architecture, noted that the author had been relieved of his position by the Nazis: 'when I hear that the author is in "retirement",

I know I am on the right thing' (German diaries, 24 February 1937). At the same time, Beckett struggled to acquaint himself with contemporary German literature; his reading during his journey largely consisted of writers judged acceptable by the Nazis, an indication of the success of their ideological and cultural repressions. Reading books recommended to him by people he met, Beckett was introduced to active proponents of Nazi literature. For example, his description of works inspected at a book exhibition in Hamburg's Kunsthalle includes most of the prominent authors of the National Socialist regime: Friedrich Griese, Gerhard Schumann, Hans Heyse and Hans Grimm, whose influential novel *Volk ohne Raum* was one of the earliest literary books to conform to Nazi ideology. Moreover, exhibitions and lectures, such as the one promoting 'Volkhafte Dichtung der Zeit' in Berlin, made Beckett aware of the way in which the Nazis turned art into propaganda. Although he did not attend any of the lectures, Beckett copied some phrases from a newspaper following a lecture by Gerhard Schumann into his diary:

Die heilige[n] Begriffe: Führer, Bewegung, Blut u. Boden, Freiheit u. Ehre dürfen nicht dem Geschwätz der Verwandlungskünst[l]er überlassen werden, die mit der Weltanschauung des NS ein Geschäft zu machen suchen. [The holy terms: Führer, Movement, Blood and Soil, Freedom and Honour must not be given over to the babble of the fraudsters who seek to make a business out of the world view of National Socialism]. (German diaries, 28 October 1936; my translation)

The only book of overtly Nazi persuasion that Beckett purchased during his trip was Hans Pferdmenges's *Deutschlands Leben* (1930), which explicitly propounds Germany's destiny of superiority. Beckett, who bought the book following several recommendations, quickly discerned that it 'seems NS Kimmwasser [bilge]' (German diaries, 4 November 1936).

The Nazis' cultural politics also inhibited Beckett's attempts to study the vast treasures of modern art in Germany. While he was in Germany, the regime stepped up its campaign against 'decadent' art, and on 30 October 1936, the first of the large museums, the Nationalgalerie in Berlin, closed its contemporary rooms in the Kronprinzenpalais, and across Germany non-conform paintings were removed from public view. As Beckett wrote to Mary Manning Howe, all 'the modern pictures are in the cellars' (13 December 1936; *L*I, 397). Beckett was particularly aware of the repressions carried out by the National Socialists when he met persecuted and marginalised painters, writers and academics such as Karl Ballmer, Gretchen Wohlwill and Rosa Schapire early on in his trip, in Hamburg. Through these people Beckett became aware of the atmosphere of surveillance in which utterances of political opposition to the regime were not taken lightly. The delicate nature of the situation was brought home to Beckett by art collector Margaritha Durrieu, who 'hint[ed] how unpleasant it could be for her & Frau Fera if I published disparagements of Germany' (German diaries, 2 December 1936).

Beckett naturally gravitated towards people who stood in opposition to the Nazis. He was thus for example drawn to the eminent (but under the Nazis disgraced) art historian Will Grohmann, with whom he spoke at length about the 'position of [the] German intellectual'. Grohmann told Beckett that:

it is more *interesting* to stay than to go, even if it were feasible to go. They can't control *thoughts*. [...] If [regime] breaks down it is fitting for him + his kind to be on the spot, to go under or become active again. (German diaries, 2 February 1937)

Such conversations led Beckett to think about the role of art in society, and the position of the artist within communities. In many ways, his experience of the difficulties faced by artists within Germany confirmed his opinion that 'the artist is never comfortable by definition' (German diaries, 4 February 1937). Nevertheless, this did not appease his opposition to all forms of censorship; when he learnt that art critic Max Sauerlandt's study *Kunst der letzten dreißig Jahre* had been banned, his response was quite simply: 'Pfui!!!!' (German diaries, 29 October 1936).

Beckett, however, could still view some contemporary art in Germany, either in private collections or in so-called Schreckenskammer des Entarteten, anti-modernist exhibitions such as the one at the Moritzburg in Halle in January 1937 where Beckett saw a wide selection of paintings by German expressionists. Three months after Beckett's departure from Germany, however, the infamous exhibition 'Entartete Kunst' ('Degenerate Art') opened in Munich on 19 July 1937, aimed at presenting the shameful decadence of modern artists to the indignation of the public. At the same time, an exhibition 'Grosse Deutsche Kunstaustellung' with Nazi-approved art opened, also in Munich, in the Haus der Deutschen Kunst. Beckett's response on reading an announcement of the approved exhibition, which stated that 'the period of Nolde, the Brücke, Marc etc has been überwunden [overcome]', is indicative of his attitude towards cultural repression: 'Soon I shall really begin to puke. Or go home' (German diaries, 15 January 1937).

Throughout the diaries, Beckett deflates the harsh realities of Nazi Germany through humour, often by mocking the overblown Nazi rhetoric or by the use of satirical word play. Such a humorous treatment of political discourse occurs when Beckett listens to an '[i]nterminable harangue by Goering on Vierjahresplan [Four Year Plan] relayed from Berlin. Sehr volkstümlich. Kolonien, Rohstoffe, Fettwaren [Very traditional. Colonies, raw materials, fats]' (German diaries, 28 October 1936). In response, Beckett entered the word 'Bierjahresplan [beer-year-plan]', rather than 'Vierjahresplan', in his *Whoroscope* notebook.[11] Early during his stay in Hamburg, he attended a charity event for German exiles in Spain which featured a 'SS Blasekapelle [brass band], bit of documentary film (Moskau droht [Moscow threatens]), speech from one Lorenz (I stretched out the wrong arm to Horst Wessel & Haydn), then more blasts from the Kapelle' (German diaries, 11 October 1936). Two months later he was pleased to observe the irony inherent in the fact that Horst Wessel was 'whelped, not least suckled' in the Judenstrasse [Jewish Street] in Berlin (German diaries, 19 December 1936).

At times, however, Beckett's distaste for the Nazis is expressed more clearly, as in his dealings with his German conversation partner Claudia Asher, assigned to him through the Akademische Auslandsstelle in Hamburg: having listened to her talk of 'national soul, of unity & might of her country' on several occasions (German diaries, 19 November 1936), he at one point remarked that '[h]er Kraft durch Freude conversation kills me' (German diaries, 1 November 1936). And his antipathy against Nazi Germany grew with the duration of his stay; in Braunschweig he noted: 'Sausages in Bierstube. HH [Heil Hitler] without ceasing. Reunion of WH [Winterhilfs] Werker. Damned again' (German diaries, 5 December 1936). Beckett clearly grew tired of hearing the same Nazi propaganda over and over again. After a train journey in January 1937 he remarked: 'Rest of conversation the usual politics, almost the same words that I have heard so often' (German diaries, 21 January 1937). As a result, he could discern that a 'Little waiter reels out the NS Evangile with only one or two errors & omissions' (German diaries, 28 January 1937). Beckett's ironic comparison of Nazi discourse with biblical 'truth' appears several times in the pages of his diaries; in Erfurt, Beckett received 'the NS Gospel from the waiter', and in Berlin an 'appallingly Nazi' man 'reels off the entire Gospel, as conceived for interior & exterior' (German diaries, 24 January and 20 December 1937).

Beckett's distrust of the political and historical assertions encountered in Nazi Germany, and the totalitarian discourse in which it was couched, is most evident when he attempted to buy a book on German history. Axel Kaun had recommended a work by Friedrich Stieve, but Beckett was not impressed: 'Just the kind of book that I do *not* want. Not a *Nachschlagewerk* [reference book], as proudly proclaimed from wrapper,

Germany: Circa 1936–1937

but the unity of the German Schicksal [destiny] made manifest'. As he went on to argue in conversation with Kaun:

> I say I am not interested in a 'unification' of the historical chaos any more than I am in the 'clarification' of the individual chaos, & still less in the anthropomorphisation of the inhuman necessities that provoke the chaos. What I want is the straws, the flotsam, etc., names, dates, births + deaths, because that is all I can know. [...] I say the expressions 'historical necessity' & 'Germanic destiny' start the vomit moving upwards. (German diaries, 15 January 1937)

There is no doubt that the trip through Nazi Germany, as evidenced by this statement, sharpened Beckett's understanding of historical narratives. Moreover, it also made a significant contribution to the development of his poetics. Having returned to Dublin in April 1937, Beckett emphasised in a letter to McGreevy that he had 'no sense of history' (4 September 1937), and by January 1938 the question of history had led to a difference of opinion between the two men, from which their friendship never fully recovered. Beckett was overtly critical of McGreevy's study of Jack B. Yeats, in which the painter was characterised as being a specifically Irish artist: 'You will always, as an historian, give more credit to circumstance than I, with my less than [suilline?] interest and belief in the *fable convenue*, ever shall be able to' (letter to McGreevy, 31 January 1938; *LI*, 599).

It is surely no coincidence that much of Beckett's reading after his return from Nazi Germany relates to texts that disrupt totalitarian narratives. Beside Hölderlin, Beckett in particular turned to reading Fritz Mauthner's *Beiträge zu einer Kritik der Sprache*, which contained, as Emilie Morin has shown, stark criticisms of Aryanism and the concepts of *Ursprache* and *Urvolk*.[12]

Moreover, it is during 1937 and 1938 that Beckett's idea of a 'literature of the unword' is most clearly formulated, which resonates across various concomitant aesthetic concerns, from irrationality to incompetence. In this context, Beckett's 1938 review of Devlin's poetry is a barometer of his thinking at this time, as he declares that 'art has nothing to do with clarity, does not dabble in the clear, and does not make clear' (*D*, 94). It is telling that Beckett also cites Hölderlin in this review when praising Devlin's piece 'The Statue', stating that 'the extraordinary evocation of the unsaid by the said has the distinction of a late poem by Hölderlin' (*D*, 94). Finally, as he told Mary Manning Howe in a letter of 13 December 1936, Beckett had understood that the 'unsaid' was more important than what was said, having achieved an instinctive respect, at least, for what is real, & therefore has not in its nature, to be clear. Then when somehow this goes over into words, one is called an obscurantist. The clarifiers are the obscurantists. (*L1*, 397)

NOTES

1 TCD MS10971/1, 31v.
2 Quoted in Robert Savage, *Hölderlin after the Catastrophe: Heidegger, Adorno, Brecht* (New York: Camden House, 2008), 9.
3 Quoted in Allan Megill, *Prophets of Extremity: Nietzsche, Heidegger, Foucault, Derrida* (Berkeley: University of California Press, 1985), 172.
4 Friedrich Hölderlin, *Sämtliche Werke* (Leizpig: Insel Verlag, 1926), 453; *Hyperion and Selected Poems*, Eric L. Santner (ed.) (London: Continuum, 1990), 21.
5 Patrick Bowles, 'How to Fail: Notes on Talks with Samuel Beckett', *PN Review* 96 (20.4: March–April 1994), 31.
6 The German Vocabulary notebooks, Beckett International Foundation, University of Reading, UoR MS5002 and MS5006.
7 TCD MS10970.
8 UoR MS5004 and MS5005.
9 UoR MS5004, 17r-18r. See Dirk Van Hulle, 'Beckett's *Faust* Notes', *Samuel Beckett Today/Aujourd'hui* 16, ed. by Matthijs Engelberts and Everett Frost, with Jane Maxwell (Amsterdam: Rodopi, 2006), 283–97.
10 'German Diaries' [six notebooks], Beckett International Foundation, University of Reading. Hereafter these will be noted as 'German diaries' followed by a date.
11 UoR MS3000, 34r.
12 See Emilie Morin, 'Samuel Beckett, the wordless song and the pitfalls of memorialisation', *Irish Studies Review* (19.2: May 2011), 185–205.

CHAPTER 10

France: World War Two
Lois Gordon

After the Germans occupied Paris, Beckett might have remained in Ireland as a neutral alien. Instead, in the fall of 1940, he returned to France and joined the fledgling Resistance to fight 'against the Germans', who 'were making life hell for my friends'. The war had become 'something personal', and Beckett refused to stand by 'with his arms folded'.[1] Like Joyce, he had many Jewish friends and was incensed by their constant humiliations and maltreatments. He was enraged by the Germans' murder of all the non-combatants they were taking as hostages.

Beckett had powerful convictions regarding his moral obligations. Friendship was a sacred responsibility, but as he had often discussed with Joyce, he was, as a human being, compelled to stand up for every 'innocent' – friend or not.[2] Intentional cruelty required action, regardless of personal risk. Common decency was based, as his friend Thomas McGreevy said, on the commandment that 'Every place in which there are human beings matters'. In a sense, Beckett looked upon all of suffering humanity as his 'friend'.

Like most thoughtful people, he had become aware of the potential for unkindness and cruelty in human society. In the 1930s, in London, he was deeply affected by the hunger marches and the indifference and exploitation with which the starving and the ill were treated. More recently he had witnessed leaders of the free world behaving like cowards, abdicating their moral responsibilities to their friends in Ethiopia, Czechoslovakia, Spain and China, as well as the forsaken Jews in Germany – all in desperate need of help against the fascist machines. Hitler had not only been virtually granted permission to dismember democratic Czechoslovakia, but he had publicly written of his intention to annihilate all the Jews in Europe. Where were the world's decent people when the fleeing refugees approached border after border? Indeed, after the stunning Russian–German pact and the French capitulation, could one be certain that any nation would stand up for moral justice?

Beckett may have dismissed his World War II activities as 'boy-scout stuff', a typically modest response, but he was one of the earliest to join the Resistance in Paris in 1940. In addition, when his circuit was discovered in 1942 and he became 'a wanted man', he took refuge in Roussillon and rather than cower in hiding, fought with the *maquis*. After the war, he joined a civilian rescue unit in Saint-Lô to rebuild a hospital. Only after that, in 1946, was he ready to begin his own 'siege in the room', one of prolific creativity. His *Waiting for Godot* was a product of the war and his response to the complexity of human goodness and evil. It was about the most basic elements of survival in an unpredictable universe and the obligation to reaffirm one's humanity by helping and protecting strangers and those one loves from gratuitous suffering.

Beckett's acute awareness of totalitarianism, on both a small and grand scale, like his unequivocal sense of right and responsibility, should not surprise us. Since childhood, he had demonstrated a mature sense of justice and an acute sensitivity to suffering. In his early youth he witnessed the ongoing civil war in Dublin (He would never forget seeing O'Connell Street in flames) and the beggars and war-torn residents of the hospital facilities near his home in Foxrock. During his early manhood, he had participated in debates at Trinity College, Dublin about national and international warfare; teaching in Belfast, he had seen the terrible discrimination against the Catholics. During his 'bad years' of living in Depression England, as well as his travels through Germany in 1937, he had seen humanity in desperate straits – under enormous economic, physical, mental and spiritual distress. Until his death, he was pained by the slightest manifestation of human suffering, and he was never free from the memory of those who perished during the strife he had witnessed – from civil war to international war.

Given the vast topic of 'France: World War Two', I attempt to present the major events in Paris and Roussillon that Beckett knew about and responded to. In a brief coda, I discuss his restorative work in St. Lô, as he helped build a hospital, his first response after the war, which prepared him for his great work to follow, especially *Waiting for Godot*.

Armoured cars, steel tanks and gray-clad soldiers paraded up the Champs-Elysées on the afternoon of 14 June 1940, as the Germans entered Paris. In triumph, they proclaimed 'the Reich will last a thousand years'. Swastikas were mounted on the Eiffel Tower and public buildings. Posters on the kiosks encouraged citizens to 'TRUST THE GERMAN SOLDIER'. Newspapers, including *L'OEuvre*, *La Victoire*, *Le Matin* and

Paris-Soir, printed Nazi propaganda, and new, German-inspired papers appeared virtually overnight: *Aujourd'hui, Dernières Nouvelles de Paris, La France au Travail, Temps Nouveaux*.[3]

The French army had been crushed. In just five weeks it had suffered its worst defeat in history. An estimated ninety-five thousand were dead and two hundred fifty thousand wounded; one and a half to two million became prisoners of war.[4] On 16 June, after presenting a plan for union with Britain and the withdrawal of French forces to North Africa, Prime Minister Paul Reynaud was defeated by his own cabinet. Marshal Pétain, chief of the new government in the southern spa town of Vichy, was mandated to request an 'honourable armistice' from Hitler. Pétain had the support of his vice president, Camille Chautemps, and cabinet, including the brilliant Pierre Laval, famous for declaring that parliamentary democracy had caused the war and must 'give way to an authoritarian, hierarchical, national and social regime'.[5]

Pétain, the nearly eighty-five-year-old Verdun hero and France's 'father' symbol, addressed the French 'state': 'We must try to put an end to the fighting. Tonight I have contacted the enemy to ask if they are prepared to join us, as honorable soldiers, in seeking ... the means whereby hostilities will be terminated'.[6] According to the armistice of 22 June, France would be divided into two zones. The occupied zone, including Paris, would incorporate both the Channel and Atlantic coast areas (two-thirds of France); the unoccupied area would include the central mountains and the Rhône Valley. Alsace and Lorraine would be incorporated into Germany.

On 10 July, the parliament overwhelmingly voted to give over its powers to the new authoritarian Vichy government. Parliamentary leaders were imprisoned or placed under house arrest. The French agreed to fully fund the German army of occupation, give up their weapons, disarm their large fleet and retain only a small number of soldiers to maintain local order.

The acquiescence to Vichy, degrees of submission or resistance ('collaboration' or 'neutrality'), remain subjects of historical discussion.[7] It is true that Roosevelt remained friendly with Vichy through November 1942 and that Churchill, while 'privately and publically short with Pétain', kept in touch with him unofficially. Nonetheless, after the D-Day landings in Normandy, Pétain called for the French to remain neutral, and Laval went further and called the Allied landings 'an act of aggression'. Even in August 1944, Vichy called upon the United States to act as a neutral arbiter rather than a liberator.[8]

Following the defeat of the French army, on 18 June 1940, Charles de Gaulle, a little-known career officer and undersecretary of state, pleaded with a defeated nation to reject Pétain's call for an armistice and to continue to fight the enemy invader. Driven by a romantic and mystical vision of France's greatness, he saw the military as necessary for France to achieve its glorious destiny.

In fact, de Gaulle's challenge served to exacerbate his criminal status. A military tribunal had sentenced him *in absentia* to death, and anyone who joined him would have been similarly condemned. Moreover, the nation was not psychologically or materially prepared to respond. What was presumed to be the most powerful fighting machine in Europe had been devastated. The supposedly impregnable border defence, the Maginot Line, had been rendered useless. Paris had been occupied by its historic German enemy, even as the French nation remained haunted by the shadow of the more than a million slaughtered in World War I.

By June 1941, the situation changed dramatically. Ordinary citizens had begun printing anti-Nazi propaganda, and action groups had begun burning German vehicles and cutting telecommunications wires. A sizable Resistance had taken shape. By sheer force of will, it seemed that de Gaulle, with his symbolic Cross of Lorraine, had become the leader of the 'Free French'. His words were unforgettable: 'Should all hope be abandoned? ... No! ... No matter what happens, the Flame of French Resistance must not and will not be extinguished'.[9]

In the first weeks of the occupation, German soldiers tried to befriend the French, but they soon became brutal in their response to the smallest acts of resistance. Rations were increasingly sparse; by September, Jews were required to officially identify themselves as such. Almost immediately thereafter Vichy passed its own anti-Semitic statutes and decreed that all dissidents be interned. Beckett was in Paris in October when the Paris police arrested 871 people and seized thirty-five printing presses. Massive student protests arose, members of the Sorbonne faculty were dismissed and classes in the New Order were instituted. Despite threats against protests, an estimated five thousand to ten thousand people gathered on Armistice Day at the Étoile and decorated Clemenceau's monument. German troops made over 140 arrests and killed at least five students.

The dreaded Milice – the French version of the German SS – was informally organised shortly after the occupation, along with youth camps for boys and girls modelled on Hitler Youth organisations. The 'purification' of the nation proceeded with prodigious speed. All Jews were issued identity cards stamped 'Juif'. Anti-Jewish demonstrations were whipped up in cities throughout the country. By the end of 1941, businesses displayed black and yellow cards warning 'Jüdisches Geschäft'; factories had fired Jews and foreigners, and most Jews were excluded from the civil and military services, the professions and businesses. Jewish property, including everything from land to art, was confiscated. All of this was common public knowledge.

Following the arrest of his Jewish friend Paul Léon, subsequently tortured to death, Beckett joined Alfred Péron in the Resistance. Eminent Resistance scholars like Henri Michel remind us that regardless of one's specific affiliation – in the Free French, SOE, a Polish, communist, or occupational group (and many joined more than one group) – each group retained its autonomy while sharing similar goals, activities, rules of survival and possible mortal retaliation.[10] Beckett's 'Gloria' was funded by Churchill's SOE organisation 'Prosper', but its manner of doing business was its own.[11] The same independence was true of 'Étoile', Beckett's second group.

There were common rules among most circuits, and the limited materials with which they worked were often the same. They sabotaged factories by pouring sand into machinery, set oil tanks on fire, derailed railway cars and cut telephone and telegraph cables. Those caught were killed instantly. Beckett's activities first included collecting information (sometimes in code) regarding German troop movements, which he deciphered, classified and typed before it was smuggled out to London; later on, he transferred the information via microfilm.

Foot, in his landmark study of the SOE, describes Beckett in his circuit loosely connected with 'Prosper'. The small circuits looked to Prosper for 'arms and money but not ... orders'. They knew enough 'of the fundamentals of clandestine work to keep to themselves'. Some of the cell's members, he also notes, like Samuel Beckett, knew when to hide and when they could meet their leaders, Guerne (a translator) and Suttill (a poet), and other resisters at a black market restaurant near the Arc de Triomphe or at a café near Sacre-Coeur. Here they attended to business – and even played cards – despite the presence of Nazi waiters.[12]

Some information about the Resistance was common knowledge. If a man was caught – and no one was invulnerable to torture – he was expected to say nothing for two days, even under duress of having his teeth pulled, one by one. The delay would give his companions time to escape. The optimal way to survive was to cultivate a life of privacy, since arrest was inevitably fatal.

Acts of sabotage could be as subtle as the imagination could contrive. The 'fat hammer' used thirty minutes in a factory could destroy optical glassworks that had taken six months to produce. Abrasive grease, which would actually wear out the parts it only appeared to lubricate, was unparalleled for railway sabotage. Mismarking seals on goods and rewriting directions might (as it once did) send a truckload of women's underwear to the German airfields.[13]

Plastic explosives were widely used for industrial sabotage. One looked like butter and could be smeared anywhere – on aircraft, a ship rudder, building or helmet. Pocket incendiaries and tire busters were efficient for brief acts of sabotage when one was walking towards a more ambitious assignment.

Coded messages, alternating vowels and consonants in four-letter phrases set in columns, contained prearranged meanings. AKAK FORU DODO LONA, for example, meant 'parachute at next opportunity for container-loads and gun ammunition'. While gibberish to the Germans, it was vital to the Resistance and to the Allies. So too the Free French and SOE worked out ingenious messages in phrases like 'Josephine wears a blue dress' or 'Uncle Jacques has lost his umbrella'.[14] Many hid their forbidden radios and later wrote down messages that were subsequently printed in clandestine papers.

Extraordinary 'props' were the inventions of a former scenic artist at the Drury Lane Theatre: 'invisible' ink, visible only under infra-red light; tiny microfilm documents sealed in tiny containers and hidden in body orifices, on a matchstick or within toothpaste tubes.[15] Microdots, smaller than a speck of dust, fit on the lens of an eyeglass. The explosives were highly imaginative – from fountain pens, cigarettes and nuts and bolts that squirted ammunition to coal lumps, logs, milk bottles and bread loaves. Another impressive explosive was the (plastic and hand-painted) horse, camel, mule and horse dung. One drop in front of a parked SS car worked miracles.

Gradually, as assassinations of German soldiers increased, retaliation became increasingly random and large scale. In the fall of 1941, with the siege of Leningrad well begun, General Wilhelm Keitel announced that 100 to 500 communists would be shot for every German killed. Shortly thereafter, the Soviet Union recognised the Free French as the official government of France, bringing many more communists into the Resistance. The British also recognised de Gaulle as the leader of the French government. In December, a week after the Japanese attack on Pearl Harbor, 100 Jews were executed in Paris; 100 'notable' Jews were arrested, and a billion-franc fine was imposed on the occupied zone.

The large-scale deportation of Jews in February 1942, which brought massive protests and reprisals, was not only shocking in its reality but in the diabolical strategies by which the Jews were captured. Organisations masqueraded as emergency aid programmes, and Jews seeking assistance were picked up by the police. The year 1942 was indeed a time of 'Nacht und Nebel' ('Night and Fog'), the phrase coined by the authorities for the dark and repulsive activities that marked the times.

That summer was a grave turning point in the treatment of Jews, as Laval gained more power and Pétain intensified Vichy's collaboration with the Nazis. The notorious racist Darquier de Pellepoix also became 'Commissar-General of Jewish Questions'. Two days after Rommel's offensive in Libya, the Germans decreed that Jews (all wearing the yellow star) could no longer enter public buildings like libraries, movie theatres and restaurants. Those who protested (or forgot) were executed.

In the middle of July, de Gaulle's Committee became 'France Combatante', after which activities against Jews escalated even further. Terrible raids occurred in Paris and the suburbs; all so-called foreign, stateless Jews were arrested by the French police. Families with children were sent to 'Vel d'Hiv', the sports arena south of the Eiffel Tower, where they were held eight days before being sent to their doom at Auschwitz. Treatment of the children, of infants and babies, was indescribably cruel. In all, twelve thousand eight hundred eighty-four were arrested, including four thousand fifty-one children; one hundred six adults, who committed suicide; hundreds were shot; many joined the Resistance. By the end of the year, a total of forty-two thousand five hundred Jews were similarly arrested.[16] By this time, the French and German police officially agreed to coordinate their activities with the Gestapo.

Concentration camps had been built throughout France, and those set up in the south during the Spanish Civil War for the Spanish Republicans were put to new purpose.[17] By the summer of 1942, an estimated twenty-six thousand Jews were incarcerated in French concentration camps in the unoccupied zone alone – again, for the crime of being Jews (for the sin of 'being born', as Beckett evokes the human tragedy in *Godot* and *Proust*).

All activities of the Resistance exposed its heroes to sudden torture and death, and Beckett witnessed the courageous deaths of some of its unheralded heroes. One Frenchman, known as 'Honoré', of no particular fame or oratorical talent, said to those at his public execution, 'Remember that you have had the honor of fighting for France.... God allow us to die honorably!'[18] There are many erudite explanations as to why Beckett erased the specifics of time, place and person in his work, but a simple explanation presents itself in the courage he witnessed in the seemingly most 'ordinary' of humankind.

Interestingly, Foot attributes the inspiration of the Resistance throughout Europe to a person still 'within living memory': Michael Collins, military chief of the IRA during the Troubles of 1916–1922, which Beckett witnessed in Dublin. 'The greatest resistance leader of the twentieth century', writes Foot, Collins understood the basic grammar of sabotage and Irish resistance, and he showed the rest of the world how to fight economically in guerrilla warfare. Foot even compares de Gaulle's great agent, Jean Moulin, and other disparate resisters against Hitler to Collins.[19] Although Foot admits that not many Europeans would have heard of Collins, Beckett certainly would have.

Beckett left Paris in August 1942. After one of Gloria's members had been tortured into a confession, Beckett's friend Alfred Péron was arrested, and the rest of the group faced imminent exposure. Only thirty out of eighty survived. At 11 A.M. on 15 August, Péron's wife sent Beckett and his wife a telegram: 'Alfred arrêté par Gestapo. Prière faire nécessaire pour corriger l'erreux'. By 3 P.M., they were gone. Beckett set out, mostly on foot and at night, for Roussillon, in the unoccupied zone. Jack MacGowran speaks of Beckett in flight as a 'key man' for whom Nazi bullets were marked.[20]

ROUSSILLON

An Outlaw Is Braver than a Soldier,
Because He Acts for Himself – Louis Aragon

Beckett arrived in the south after Germany's November failures in North Africa and on the Russian Front. The Germans had invaded this previously unoccupied zone, destroying any illusion that the south was safe. Any Jews not in hiding were routinely picked up. Military recruitment was intensified and all available *French* males were conscripted into the German factories. The new STO compulsory labour law gave new meaning to the *maquis* – so named after the wild Corsican brush country that had been a hideout for outlaws. Until now, only a few hundred guerrilla forces had organised in the mountains. After the STO and by February 1943, an estimated thirty thousand to fifty thousand had volunteered, including Alsatians, Lorrainers, Belgians, Danes, Poles, Yugoslavs, Jews and anti-Hitler Germans.[21] As the Gestapo sought out thousands of saboteurs, every circuit in the north and south was in danger. Meanwhile, the American war machine was moving to full capacity.

As a group, the *maquisards* lacked arms and military experience but young, homeless and angry, they wanted to fight a real war. They stole whatever weapons they could; as farmers and peasants, they made them out of pitchforks and other farm equipment. They were fearless and envisioned themselves as a secret army taking part in the Allied military operations to come. Such fervour and anarchical structure worried de Gaulle and Moulin, who feared that they would not wait until D-Day.

Christian Durandet writes of their activities in the very area and time period during which Beckett fought in the *maquis*. He insists that they 'were perfectly organized' once under the leadership of Jean Moulin and Jean Garcin. That is, Resistance organisations provided food, clothing, forged papers and ration cards. In addition, the Comités de Resistance Ouvriere connected the *maquis* with the FFI (Forces Françaises de l'Intérieur), which trained many of the soldiers, who came to be 'the most hardened, if not the most experienced, part of the FFI'.[22]

Beckett took part in one of the *maquis*' primary activities – the destruction of railroad sites. This involved setting up contacts between other workers and the pickup, hiding and delivery of supplies and ammunition for the destruction of key rails involved in transporting German supplies. The job required absorbing complex information: details about drops of clothes and boots, as distinguished from small arms (which went to over a million people), explosives (for thousands of demolitions) and even jeeps (loaded with machine guns). Finding a safe hiding place was always difficult. One of the *maquis*' most memorable activities would occur immediately after D-Day: 180 German trains were derailed, and within three weeks, three thousand railways became inoperative, necessitating German travel by land, at which point street signposts were changed and vehicles destroyed. The Germans were forced to travel by foot.

With the *maquis* working primarily after dark, Beckett's life was often a mixture of uneventful days and dangerous nights. We are fortunate in learning some of the particulars of Beckett's days during the last two and a half years of the war from the extensive research of Laurence Wylie.[23]

Roussillon was situated between *maquis* centres and Nazi strongholds, but the first thing Beckett would have noticed was its brilliant colouration, its dramatic reds ('There, everything is red', he writes in *Godot*). Together with its countless ramparts from the ancient past, the village has remained a place of such natural beauty that it continues to provide some of France's most widely circulated photo images. Beckett lived in a house, still called 'la maison Beckett', at one end of the village, next to the local leader of the *maquis* who, after the war, became mayor.

At the opposite end of the town, was 'la maison de Miss Beamish', a writer rumoured to be Winston Churchill's cousin who invited Beckett to live there.

The wealthy Vichy-appointed mayor was proud of his success in maintaining the peace. The village was untouched by German raids ('The only Germans likely to have stopped in Roussillon would have been vacationing officers'[24]); at the same time adjacent villages suffered the consequences of Nazi brutality. Many Roussillians, including Beckett, joined these neighbouring towns in their *maquis* activities, but they remained silent about it. They shared, in addition, a unique attitude towards life. They cultivated a sense of '*d'broussillement*' or '*systeme d-*' – a stoic accommodation to the requirements of endurance.[25] They fought the enemy at night but picked grapes during the day, indulging in the 'now', not worrying about the future. They assumed, first, that not everything was under the eye of the Germans, and second, that there was a way to 'wrangle' anything they wanted. Vichy may have made the rules, but one made one's way around them. The point was 'to learn to live with the life around you without suffering too much'. Pursuing their '*systeme d-*' provided Beckett with another model of human durability.

The Roussillians also lacked the negative qualities often associated with villages: gossip and provincialism. They contented themselves farming the crops and making ends meet. Routine was a great comfort, for it reinforced their sense of identity and gave them a clear concept of their limits. ('Habit is a great deadener', say *Godot*'s heroes.) They were also unusual in lacking any suspicion regarding strangers – the result of their equally unusual need for privacy. As a result, Beckett was not viewed as a curiosity but perhaps as one of the many refugees who had moved there. Many villagers who became his friend agreed that he felt comfortable here. Interestingly, he registered at the town hall as Samuel Beckett from Dublin, England.

Beckett spoke of his boredom and anxiety in Roussillon, that state of waiting and uncertainty he later evoked in *Waiting for Godot*. During the day, he often took long walks in the countryside. He welcomed structured activity, such as a job in the fields, which he took out of friendship with his neighbours. On rainy days, he joined in the farmers' favourite activities – travelling from one vineyard to the next to sample the wines. At night, he watched groups of armed *maquisards* roam the village in search of supplies and food. His own noctural Resistance activities gave purpose to his life. He also wrote *Watt* here 'to get away from war and Occupation' and, as he said, a means of 'staying sane'.[26]

By the spring of 1944, important radio news was announced twice a month, on the first and fifteenth, at 7:30 and 9:15 P.M., to alert agents about D-Day. On 5 June, when the call for action arrived, an epidemic of explosives followed at railway stations and telecommunication centres, as well as various sabotage activities throughout France, Belgium and Holland. The signal had been two lines from Verlaine's *Autumn Song*.[27] '*The long sobbing of the victims of autumn*' indicated that the invasion date had been set; '*Wound my heart with monotonous languoir*' (amidst jumbled phrases like 'The doctor buries all of his patients'), meant that the attack would begin within forty-eight hours and sabotage activities should begin simultaneously (which was carried out meticulously).

When the Allies landed in Normandy on 6 June 1944, Jean Luchaire, the foremost of the Parisian journalist-collaborators, issued an official directive. It was the 'duty' of all French citizens 'to hate' both the Anglo-Americans (the enemy) and their *maquis* or Resistance partners. Vichy mobilised the Milice and called on all French citizens to join in a counterattack against the enemy.[28]

In response, members of the *maquis*, dressed as Milice, entered the offices of the Ministry of Information and shot the minister, Philippe Henriot. A twenty-million-franc reward failed to uncover their whereabouts. By this time, the *maquis* and all the underground armies of the Resistance, now working with the FFI, were brought together with the Allied forces under Dwight Eisenhower and were instrumental in the final efforts towards victory. Because of the *maquis*' continued sabotage of communications, for example, the Germans were incapable of bringing adequate forces to the Normandy beachheads.

After the landings, in the late summer of 1944, the air was filled with reports of German massacres. Although many German troops and the entire Vichy regime had fled to Sigmaringen in southern Germany, others remained behind. Supported by the Milice, they went up and down the Rhône Valley in search of villages with Jews or members of the Resistance or *maquis*. Seven hundred, including 250 children, were killed at Oradour-sur-Glane. By D-Day, thirty thousand Resistance members and *maquis* had been executed; another thirty thousand died battling the enemy. Of the one hundred fifteen thousand deported to the Buckenwald, Ravensbruck, Dachau and Mauthausen camps, and countless others deported for forced labour, only thirty-five thousand returned alive.[29]

The Germans fled the Roussillon area, and the 'momentous' day the victorious *maquis* marched into Roussillon was 'more joyously celebrated than any other event in history'. The townspeople heard the sound of drums and great fanfare, and as the heroes approached, they entered the village with Beckett at the front of the procession, carrying the flag.[30]

Following the war, Beckett was decorated by de Gaulle with the Croix de Guerre – for his 'distinguished noncombatant activities'. His medal, with a silver star, indicated specific acts of bravery 'in divisional despatch', suggesting his alignment with a fighting unit, such as the FFI, which had amalgamated members of the SOE, Resistance, and *maquis*.[31] He also received the Medaille de la Resistance. To both these honours, he responded with typical humility. After the war and a brief visit to his family, he wanted to return to Paris, but his plans were suspended because of new restrictions on aliens. The resourceful Beckett secured work with the Red Cross in Saint-Lô.

SAINT-LÔ

The arrival of Allied aircraft in Normandy had prefaced the most momentous military feat in military history. Saint-Lô was targeted because its topography and location were unique. From the air it resembled a hub of a bicycle wheel with eight major roads radiating from its centre – an optimal jumping-off point to the entire area. In addition, its nearly impenetrable hedgerows had to be destroyed. They enclosed small fields that protected the Germans and allowed them the time and space to build important communications networks.

A force of over three thousand planes with seven thousand to eight thousand tons of bombs entered in three waves – each fifteen minutes long – with bombs falling at the rate of one per second, with five minutes in between. After their final successful assault, on 25 and 26 July, the 'milk and honey' landscape of Saint-Lô was transformed into a world of rubble and maimed and unburied bodies. The Allies' victory unhinged the entire west end of the German line, permitting a breakthrough to Marigny and St. Gilles, which destroyed the German Seventh Army. After this, they moved on to Brittany. The French nicknamed the village *The Capital of the Ruins*, the title of a radio address Beckett wrote.

The same altruistic impulse that had motivated Beckett at the start of the occupation prompted him to go to Saint-Lô, where the Irish and French

Red Cross were building a hospital. Now, doing menial and boring tasks, he was working in the cause of healing. His radio announcement would reveal his pride in joining his Irish kinsfolk in a collaborative activity with the French to save lives. Beckett seems to have been determined to battle suffering – whether combating an evil invading force or alleviating the destruction caused by friendly fire.

Now in the restoration of one of the post-war ruins of the world, he would wear the uniform of the medical orderly. Working with an Irish group in France, Beckett could connect his past with the nation that would become his permanent home. Finally, the Saint-Lois illustrated the combination of human misery and resilience – the absurd victory – that Beckett would write about shortly. They had achieved liberation through unspeakable suffering, enduring the bizarre paradox of a relatively peaceful, if humiliating, enemy occupation, followed by a horrific and destructive, if liberating, victory. Gratitude at salvation – freedom through despair – such would be the subject of Beckett's future *Waiting for Godot*.

Ultimately, the experience at Saint-Lô provided Beckett with a long-awaited equanimity, a sense of balance, of what in *Godot* he would call the 'tears' and 'laughter' of the world – the alternation of elation and despair that is the individual's lot, as well as the nature of history. It provided him with a living example of the human capacity for stoical forbearance, kindness and even humour in the face of brutal devastation. It could only have stirred resonances of what he had seen in Dublin and Belfast, in London and Germany, and, of course, during wartime France. *The Capital of the Ruins* would celebrate the dignity of survival in a contingent universe.

In August 1945, an advance party from Dublin, including Beckett, 'Quartermaster [and Storekeeper]-Interpreter', had arrived to survey the situation. About 174 tons of equipment would arrive for the 100 wooden huts in the new facility that would handle 200 outpatients and 115 inpatients – all survivors of the bombings and concentration camps, and all suffering from tuberculosis and the diseases of wartime.[32] Flowers and trees would also be planted.

Beckett's first tasks included picking up supplies and driving staff to and from various destinations – generally doing whatever was called for, all of which he performed with enthusiasm and generosity. When he picked up new arrivals from Ireland at Dieppe and drove them to Saint-Lô, he arrived in his large Ford V-8 utility wagon and always presented them with enormous bags of plums, grapes and pears (his favourite fruits). When 250 tonnes of supplies arrived, Beckett helped to organise, stack and record them on cards.

Beckett worked alongside the medical staff, with local labourers and 1,000 German POWs on loan from the French government. They socialised at picnics on the beach. One attending physician described Beckett's caring and good nature: 'terribly conscientious about his work and enthusiastic about the future of the hospital; [he] like[s] a game of bridge and in every way [is] a most likeable chap, aged abut [sic] 38–40, [of] no religious persuasion; I should say a free thinker – but he pounced on a little rosary beads which was on a stall in Notre Dame to bring back as a little present to Tommy D. It was very thoughtful of him'.[33]

After Beckett returned to Paris – the time of his great creative 'siege in the room', he wrote his radio speech. It was occasioned by Dublin press coverage of France's ostensible lack of appreciation of the Irish effort in Saint-Lô. Beckett's intention – clearly reconciliatory – was to praise both the French and Irish. However, his decision to make a *public* statement – exceptional for this man – and the nature of that statement are important, since it was unlike Beckett to explicitly state his personal and philosophical reflections. Although Beckett is often said to have attributed his writing to 'impotence' and 'ignorance', perhaps at this moment he had a sense of confidence in his observations of human nature and a realisation of his own personal courage. The war may have synthesised everything he had seen and studied thus far in his life and allowed him to retreat to 'the room' in order to engage the world of his imagination. Beckett was forty when he wrote the speech.

In it, he exalts the comfort to be gained in surmounting the gravest of events and the sustenance to be gained in moments of camaraderie. He also sets forth several articles of faith that will resonate in his great works to come.[34] The first is his awareness of the human capacity to observe and take comfort in one another's acceptance of the common condition – seeing in the patients, as they see in us, 'that smile at the human condition as little to be extinguished by bombs as to be broadened by the elixirs [medication]'. It is an awareness that derides material possessions and accepts the precarious nature of life, 'the having and not having, the giving and the taking, sickness and health'.[35] In *Godot*, he would say 'The tears of the world are a constant quantity' and its corollary, about the smile that brings consolation and joy: 'The same is true of the laugh'.

Beckett's second point is that while the material universe is 'provisional' and ephemeral, acts of mundane generosity are not: 'The hospital ... will continue to discharge its function and its cured ... long after the Irish are gone'. That is, as others come and serve the ill, they too will demonstrate the impulse to give of themselves to the suffering, because healing and caring are the steadfast threads in the human fabric. Implicit is his faith, as he will write in *Godot*, that regardless of circumstance, humanity will 'represent worthily the foul brood to which a cruel fate has consigned us'. In perhaps his most optimistic statement, Beckett declares that the act of giving uplifts the giver as well as the recipient: 'Those who were in Saint-Lô will come home realizing that they got at least as good as they gave'. This may be our salvation as we await Godot.

Finally, summarising St. Lô's lasting 'gifts' as a product of the eternal Irish and French spirit working together, he returns to his kinsmen, who helped the French to rebuild, and with evident Irish pride says: 'I think that to the end of its hospital days, it will be called the Irish Hospital, and after that the huts, when they have been turned into dwellings, the Irish huts'. Then, revealing what was perhaps for him the crucial wisdom that would direct his future work, he amplifies what he has just suggested: 'I may perhaps venture to mention another [possibility], more remote but perhaps of greater import', the possibility that those who walked the earth both bombed and restored '*got ... a vision and sense of a time-honored concept of humanity in ruins, and perhaps even an inkling of the terms in which our condition is to be thought again*. These will have been in France'. (*CSP*, 278, My italics)

The willingness to give of oneself to the suffering is not only an abiding part of human nature. It is the very means through which one sees recovery and can gain an 'inkling' of the mystery of the human condition. Beckett's remark about the generosity of the Irish, whose lessons will have been consummated in France, reconcile the land of his origin with the land of his destiny. In addressing 'our condition to be thought again', Beckett braces himself for the great creative task now facing him.

NOTES

1 Alan Simpson, *Beckett and Behan and a Theatre in Dublin* (London: Routledge & Kegan Paul, 1962), 50; Alec Reid, 'The Reluctant Prizeman', *Arts* (29: October 1969), 68.
2 See Lois Gordon, *The World of Samuel Beckett* (New Haven: Yale University Press, 1996), 71, 78, 106.
3 Frida Knight, *The French Resistance* (London: Lawrence and Wishart, 1975), 54.
4 See Marshall Cavendish, *Nazi Europe* (London: Cavendish House, 1984), 359. For more specific statistics, see Chris Cook and John Paxton, *European Political Facts*, 1918–84 (New York: Facts on File, 1986), 242, and Robert Goralski, *World War II Almanac, 1931–1945* (New York: G.P. Putnam's, 1981), 421.
5 Arthur Marwick, *War and Social Change in the Twentieth Century* (New York: St. Martin's Press, 1974), 188.

6 Quoted in Claude Chambard, *The Maquis*, trans. Elaine P. Halperin (Indianapolis: Bobbs-Merrill, 1970), 2.
7 See, for example, Frida Knight, *French Resistance*; Robert O. Paxton, *Vichy France: Old Guard and New Order* (New York: Knopf, 1972), and with Michael R. Marrus, *Vichy France and the Jews* (New York: Basic Books, 1981); Susan Zuccotti, *The Holocaust, the French, and the Jews* (New York: Basic Books, 1993); Stanley Hoffmann, *In Search of France* (Cambridge: Harvard University Press, 1963), Jacques Adler, *The Jews of Paris and the Final Solution: Communal Response and Internal Conflicts, 1940–1944* (New York, Oxford University Press, 1987).
8 Regarding FDR and Churchill, see M. R. D. Foot, *Resistance: European Resistance to Nazism, 1940–1945*, London: McGraw-Hill, 1977, 235–6; on Pétain, Paxton, *Vichy France*, 326. On Laval, see David Littlejohn, *The Patriotic Traitors* (London: Heinemann, 1972), 274. On Vichy, see Paxton, *Vichy France*, 301.
9 Quoted in Claude Chambard, *The Maquis: A History of the French Resistance Movement* (New York: MacMillan, 1976), 3.
10 Henri Michel, *Histoire de la Résistance en France* (Paris: Presses Universitaires de France, 1972). See also his *Bibliographie critique de la Résistance* (Paris, Sevpen, 1964) and P. J. Stead, *Second Bureau* (London: Evans, 1959); Edward Spears, *Assignment to Catastrophe*, 2 vols. (London: Heinemann, 1947); Rémy [Gilbert Renault-Roulier], *The Silent Company*, trans. L. C. Shepherd (London: Barker, 1948) and *Courage and Fear* (London: Barker, 1950); Patrick Howarth, *Special Operations* (London: Routledge, 1955); Vincent Brome, *The Way Back* (London: Cassell, 1957); and Philippe de Vomécourt, *Who Lived to See the Day* (London: Hutchenson, 1961).
11 M. R. D. Foot, *SOE in France* (London: Her Majesty's Stationery Office, 1966), 319.
12 M. R. D. Foot, *An Outline History of the Special Operations Executive 1940–1946* (London: BBC, 1984), 138, 89, 122.
13 See M. R. D. Foot, *Resistance: European Resistance to Nazism, 1940–1945* (New York: McGraw-Hill, 1977), 22–69, and *SOE in France*, 40–60. See also E. H. Cookridge, *Set Europe Ablaze* (London: Pan, 1969), 65ff.
14 Foot, *SOE in France*, 505–17, 110, 112; Cookridge, *Set Europe Ablaze*, 96–7.
15 Colonel Elder Will, at the Drury, was also an art director in film. E. H. Cookridge, *Set Europe Ablaze*, 37.
16 Philip Hallie, *Lest Innocent Blood Be Shed* (New York: Harper & Row, 1979), 105. See also Claude Lévy and Paul Tilliard, *Betrayal at the Vel d'Hiv*, trans. Inea Bushnaq (New York: Hill and Wang, 1969).
17 Lois Gordon, *Nancy Cunard: Heiress, Muse, Political Idealist* (New York: Columbia University Press, 2007), chap. 12.
18 Quoted in Claude Chambard, *The Maquis*, trans. Elaine P. Halperin (Indianapolis: Bobbs-Merrill, 1970), 11.
19 'The IRA and the Origins of SOE', *War in Society*, M. R. D. Foot (ed.) (London: Paul Elek, 1973), 68, 61.
20 Kathleen McGrory and John Unterecker (eds.), 'Interview with Jack MacGowran', *Yeats, Joyce, Beckett* (Lewisburg: Bucknell University Press, 1976), 173–4.

21 Studies of the *maquis* include Claude Chambard, *The Maquis*; George Millar, *Hoaned Pigeon* (London: Heinemann, 1945); Anne-Marie Walters, *Moondrop to Gascony* (London: Macmillan, 1946); Alexander Werth, *France, 1940–1955* (Boston: Beacon Press, 1966).
22 Christian Durandet, *Les Maquis de Provence* (Paris: Editions France-Empire, 1974), 35, 222.
23 Wylie pursued my questions with the older Roussillon villagers during subsequent trips there. See his *Village in the Vaucluse* (Cambridge: Harvard University Press, 1974) and 'Roussillon, '87', in *French Politics and Society* (7: Spring 1989), 1–26; Francis Berjot (ed.), *Roussillon* (Apt: Archipal, 1992) and *Roussillon: Le Temps Retrouvé* (Mas du Sacré-Coeur, Marguerittes: Equinoxe, 1992).
24 Telephone conversation with the Robert O. Paxton, 2 May 1992.
25 Wylie to author, 19 May, 1992. On 'system d-' see John F. Sweets, *Choices in Vichy France: The French under the Occupation* (New York: Oxford University Press, 1986).
26 On escaping from war, see John Fletcher, *The Novels of Samuel Beckett* (London: Chatto and Windus, 1964), 59; on escaping madness, John Harvey, *Samuel Beckett: Poet and Critic* (Princeton: Princeton University Press, 1970), 222.
27 Douglas Botting, *The Second Front* (New York: Time-Life, 1978), 93.
28 David Littlejohn, *The Patriotic Traitors* (London: Heinemann, 1972), 274.
29 Hallie, *Lest Innocent Blood Be Shed*, 238. Werth confirms these figures from SHAEF, in *France 1940–1955*, 168. They vary from scholar to scholar. Paxton cites lower figures from Gordon Wright's 'Reflections on the French Resistance', *Political Science Quarterly*, (77: September 1962), 49.
30 Francis Berjot, *Roussillon: Le Temps Retrouvé* (Mas du Sacré-Coeur, Marguerittes: Equinoxe, 1992), 71, and verified by dozens of Roussillians to Wylie in 1950–1.
31 The Croix de Guerre was associated with Churchill's SOE; the Ordre de la liberation, almost always with de Gaulle's Free French. See Robert Werlich, *Orders and Decorations of All Nations* (Washington, DC: Quaker Press, 1974), 134; 'Medals', *Encyclopedia Brittanica*, 1973 ed., 64; and Guido Rosignoli, *Ribbons of Orders, Decorations and Medals* (New York, Arco Publishing, 1977), 86.
32 Eoin O'Brien, *The Beckett Country* (Dublin: Black Cat Press, 1986), 342, 384.
33 Ibid., 384, 327.
34 Although most scholars believe that the broadcast did occur, Eoin O'Brien (*Beckett Country*), 385, remains uncertain. However, the speech has been widely published. My citations are from O'Brien's full typescript signed by Beckett, 333–7. Unless otherwise noted, they are from 337.
35 Eoin O'Brien, *Beckett Country*, 335.

CHAPTER 11

France, Europe, the World: 1945–1989

Julian Murphet

The first thing to say about the historical context of Samuel Beckett's post-1945 writings is that it is denied admission to the works themselves. Beckett's works are 'startlingly lacking in historical clutter, the traces of historical circumstance'.[1] Beckett's texts are the ciphers of history rather than its testimony; yet this negative relation is itself profoundly historical. As historicism swamps independent thought, revulsion from it bespeaks nobility of mind and is historical through and through. No interpretive strategy is more tempting, or more futile, than to suppose a direct correspondence between a Beckett work and its historical situation – equally, however, not to hazard the connections is to betray the formal promise of each work's rigorous self-enclosure: that it safeguards the unvoiced, nameless suffering written out of official histories. Such paradoxes bedevil any historical approach to a sequence of masterpieces, each more contextually forlorn and bereft of novelistic 'chatter' than the last, yet each testifying more eloquently to the material pressures on the imagination than a metric tonne of more voluble texts. If abstraction is the formal law of the later work,[2] empty universality is its interpretive curse, and finding history's place in such arid textual spaces is the responsibility of all who would resist Beckett's canonisation as the gaunt saint of secular Man.

Heir presumptive to Joyce's crusade against Irish provincialism and Anglo-European imperialism both, Beckett took up Stephen Dedalus' view that 'History is a nightmare from which [we are] trying to awake', and drained that effort of heroic faith. Exposed as he was (unlike Stephen) to the ruinous apotheosis of the Enlightenment in Germany's factories of mass extermination, the fifty-two million dead of the Second World War and the blasted wasteland of civilisation it left behind, such drainage was advised. A volunteer for the Irish Red Cross posted in 1945 to Saint-Lô in Normandy, Beckett the ex-Resistance worker confronted the wreckage of his beloved France as a literal levelling of possibility. In a letter he writes: 'St[-]Lô is just a heap of rubble, la Capitale des Ruines as they call it in

France. Of 2600 buildings 2000 completely wiped out, 400 damaged and 200 "only" slightly. It all happened in the night of the 5th to 6th June. It has been raining hard ... and the place is a sea of mud' (quoted in *K*, 345). As a synecdoche of Europe's pulverised state, the town also anticipates some of Beckett's fictional spaces, in which homeless men crawl in mud for all eternity. He was moved to create a poetic image of its 'havoc' around the river Vire:

> *Saint-Lô*
> Vire will wind in other shadows
> unborn through the bright ways tremble
> and the old mind ghost-forsaken
> sink into its havoc. (*CP*, 32)

Arguably, Beckett's 'ghost-forsaken' mind sank so deep into the mud of this collapsed town that it never fully emerged.

Auschwitz may have been an actuality of the war years, but its full impact as a collective trauma awaited realisation in the years after 1945. The Nuremburg Trials of 1945–6 brought forensically to public consciousness the full horror of National Socialist barbarism, an affront to all thoughts of 'progress' and the civilisational ideal. As the Shoah of European Jewry became the accepted centrepiece of Europe's most recent history, the consequences for historical thinking were grim. The immediate implications for aesthetic labour after Auschwitz were bleak beyond compare. Theodor Adorno's infamous injunction, 'To write poetry after Auschwitz is barbaric. And this corrodes even the knowledge of why it has become impossible to write poetry today', neatly expresses the dilemma faced by Beckett the secular artist.[3] What good is literature, if two centuries of masterpieces since Goethe's birth could not prevent Zyklon B? But believing as much was as futile as the rote production of 'spiritually uplifting' letters. Beckett's inestimable solution to the impasse was that enshrined at the culmination of his long prose masterwork, *The Unnamable*: 'I can't go on, I'll go on' – raising the paradox to an aesthetic principle (*U*, 134). 'Imagination Dead Imagine' is another paraphrase. 'First Love's' opening salutation to the human graveyard sets the scene for a long litany of 'corpsed' paralyses before the six million dead.

That Beckett felt the legacy of Nazism and its aftermath as an antifascist Irishman in France, first and foremost, inflects his specific awareness of the stakes involved in resuming the labours of civilisation. For France's situation was one of utterly compromised nationality, just as Ireland's had been in the lead-up to independence and its first years as a free state.

The fracturing of national soil into the occupied north and the Vichy south during the war, and thus of political and psychological identities throughout the land, persisted like a dark afterimage into the post-war years, as did the guilt of collaboration and the heroism of Resistance, as new myths of the 'true' France took hold under the charismatic leadership of Charles de Gaulle. Less occupied than Kafka by the explicit thematics of guilt and persecution, Beckett was nonetheless acutely sensitive to the processes of dehumanisation by which fellow human beings are suddenly stripped of their everyday anonymities and denigrated to the status of scapegoat-pariahs. As the purge of Nazi collaborators defined the civil life of the Republic after 1945, Beckett took the measure of ideologies that mimicked the logic of Nazi racism. They manifest in his work in the stubborn tenacity of 'instrumental reason' as a means of relating to others: Pozzo's relation to Lucky, Hamm's to Clov, Bom's to Pim, Willie's to Winnie and so on. That these patterns can be carbon dated to the Anglo-Irish origins of Beckett's literary imagination only adds to the depth of their image of twentieth-century political life. The British 'bestialisation' of the Irish is echoed in the Nazi treatment of Jews and in the Purge's attitude to collaborators – and anticipates the animalistic projection of Algerian revolutionaries.

That this post-war epoch of cynical rebuilding should be coeval with the enshrinement of a new set of universal, humanistic principles was an irony not lost on Beckett. If what best characterised the historical moment was a kind of 'transcendental homelessness' (to paraphrase Georg Lukács) – millions without homes, without families, without clear legal status – then the Universal Declaration of Human Rights, made by the United Nations General Assembly in Paris in 1948, provided that homelessness with a minimal assurance against murder, victimisation, torture, slavery, extrajudicial persecution and arbitrary arrest. The document is a globally significant one for the most disadvantaged; but without any real teeth, these assurances, unenforceable outside of the will of member nation states, seemed more like empty promises than guarantees. The very assurance in Article 15 that 'everyone has the right to a nationality' conjured up the inevitable exceptions: Europe's scattered Jews (now offered Israel), the collaborators and migrants. Furthermore, the Declaration rested on a view of the human being as scarcely more than a huddled animal, a conduit of suffering; as if war had stripped away centuries of material gains (through nationalist liberations, trade unionism, suffragism and socialism) in the definition of 'Man' as more than the sum of 'his' biological parts. The post-war era presented a denuded, 'pale, bare, fork'd animal' image of the human being, onto which liberal opinion and statecraft heaped its rhetoric of minimal rights and what we have come to call its 'biopolitical' management of social life.[4]

Beckett's masterpiece, *How It Is*, takes this late modern image of 'Man' and pushes it to a *reductio ad absurdum*. The narrator, who crawls haltingly forward through an infinite no man's land of mud (which may just be faeces), equipped only with a sack of tin cans and an opener, is 'man' at his most elemental and crude. Beyond this, one feels, it would be perilous to go in the reduction of human being to sheer being. Georg Lukcács complained that such an 'image of the utmost human degradation' exposes us to a 'triumphant nihilism'.[5] At one point, the narrator mentions in passing the godfather of modern German biology, Haeckel, whose 'great shadow' (*H*, 34–5) lies over this wasteland and this text: a promoter of the theory of Darwinian evolution, Haeckel also developed the 'recapitulation theory', according to which human ontogeny (the growth of the individual) recapitulates *in nuce* human phylogeny, the evolutionary development of the species out of non-humanity. Such a view of humanity, perched precariously over an inhuman abyss, found reaffirmation in the aftermath of Auschwitz; and it is the ontological underbelly of 'human rights' themselves.[6] Reduced to its mortal 'species being' as a creeping animal, 'man (I clung on on to the species we're talking of the species the human', *H*, 39) evacuates its dignity. Mercilessly, Beckett exposes 'man' to the logic of 'his' twentieth-century self-image as what Giorgio Agamben calls (after Roman law) *homo sacer*: the human animal as reptilian 'bare life', unworthy of sacrifice, always open to being eradicated.[7] He also, however, counterposes a contradictory axiom: 'in any case we have our being in justice I have never heard anything to the contrary' (*H*, 108); the marvel of *How It Is* is its stark juxtaposition of these two irreconcilable images of 'Man'.

Even as Europe staggered out of the mire of one imperial catastrophe, other superpowers were already sinking their claws into the 'arse' of the broken continent. The 1945 Yalta Conference, from which France was perforce excluded, split up the map of Europe between the United States and the Soviet Union with steely disregard for national sensitivities. Germany was divided between East and West. Poland, Hungary, Romania, Czechoslovakia and Albania were converted into 'people's republics' under the dominion of Moscow; the rest of Europe was increasingly under the economic and military jurisdiction of Washington – France more dramatically than any other state. Without American aid, reconstruction would have been impossible, and the Americans demanded strict conditions for any loans: austerity measures in the domestic economy, the weeding out of communist (mostly ex-Resistance) elements in the government and the removal of all barriers to American exports in the French market.[8] A new form of resistance, this time to American economic imperialism, became a habit of left-leaning intellectuals, but in the main, the deprivations of war had electrified French consumers to the seemingly limitless possibilities of Yankee materialism. Symbolised by the flood of cheap automobiles onto the streets of Paris and of cheap movies onto its screens, the new order was one of restless mobility, paper-thin glamour and a supermarket of styles.[9]

Modernisation, then, came in the form of speed and consumption, all at once, as an American import. Perhaps the most distinctive national response to this overnight transformation of the national culture was that of filmmaker Jacques Tati, whose character Monsieur Hulot is frequently abandoned to the liquid and streamlined contours of a 'modularised' and hypermodern spatial environment, and survives with his dignity intact only thanks to a spontaneous clownishness that holds this modernisation at bay for a precious instant. Tati deranges the 'system of objects' constitutive of the *societé du consummation* as a tacit anti-imperial critique.[10] Beckett nowhere openly 'represents' the Americanisation of France, but there is an argument to be made that his hapless figures of physical and moral alienation, adrift in a world without stable contours or knowable places, are comparably apt as allegories of life in post-war France. Certainly the tradition of American slapstick informs Beckett's sense of 'modern life', which would rapidly be converted into a metaphysic of 'absurdism' by the world's press – but which can be better understood as an extension of the lessons of Buster Keaton into that 'estrangement from American-inspired technological wizardry' that typified Beckett's own Eurocentric recoil into increasingly bourgeois respectability after the war.[11] What the clownish figures of *Godot* and even *Endgame* owe to the American slapstick cinema can never be overestimated. If Beckett's characters don't obviously inhabit the new French-American world, they are certainly driven by restless forward propulsion, an instinct for movement that is the formal shadow in the texts of an entire way of life. If they don't go to the movies, they work hard at conjuring up evanescent images on the porous screens of their minds, and in one extraordinary career move, Beckett would, in 1963–4, write and oversee the production of his one and only *Film*, starring Buster Keaton himself – an authorial alter ego who, in their only meeting, would out-Beckett Beckett in the stony impenetrability of his silence (*K*, 522).

Just as Europe was now divided between spheres of imperial and ideological influence, so France itself bore the scars of an internal politico-ideological torsion between Soviet Russia and the United States;

between communism and capitalism. Jean-Luc Godard, one of the greatest artists to emerge from this period in French history, characterised an entire generation of youth as the 'children of Marx and Coca-Cola', and this internalisation of a geopolitical cold war bears closer examination as a condition of Beckett's working life – even as he migrated increasingly between France, Germany and the United Kingdom. Again, this condition is best sensed negatively. If for Godard, the lesson was an inner schizophrenia, an impossible antinomy of pro-American little-red-book-carrying Maoism, for Beckett, a Spartan logic of subtraction operated. To the extent that the choice was one between the First and Second Worlds, Beckett could be said to have retreated from it as a false one. He suffered no fools of either party gladly, as witness the lampoon of a speech-stump Marxist in his story 'The End' – 'Union ... brothers ... Marx ... Capital ... bread and butter ... love. It was all so much Greek to me' (*CSP*, 94) – and the mockery of 'the language of the Western boardroom' in *Catastrophe*.[12] No doubt Beckett understood capitalist *and* communist power as two bureaucratic faces of the same coin, dominating human beings and reducing them to functions and automatisms. This can help explain his writing of the late play *Catastrophe* in support of Václav Havel's struggles against the Czech authorities, and his generous support of Polish dissident Antoni Libera. It can also explain his adamant refusal to 'represent' the everyday lifeworld of late capitalism itself – every image of which is in some sense an advertisement for it. As Gibson puts it, 'Both he [Beckett] and his characters give the impression of being quite simply indifferent; indifferent to the imperatives of capitalism, indifferent to the politics that opposes it'.[13]

Ideological withdrawal from the First and Second Worlds as models for artistic 'engagement' (in Sartre's term) might conceivably have led Beckett to support the emergent bloc of 'Third World' states (the term was coined at the Bandung Conference of 1955) as demographically superior 'neither/nor' nations, having survived many decades of European colonialism, and now making a claim for an alternate set of civic values. The single greatest historical event of the twentieth century is that protracted series of wars and declarations of independence that rocked the imperial centres from 1947 (Indian independence) to the repulsion of U.S. military might in Vietnam in 1975. As an Anglo-Irishman with no sympathy whatever for British rule, Beckett may be supposed to have been inclined to endorse anticolonialism as a viable alternative ideological formation bespeaking the political will of the majority of humankind. Indeed, he took a principled stand on the issue of South African apartheid, refusing almost all requests for staging rights of his plays there, on the ground that they should never appear before a legally segregated audience (see *K*, 636–41). Yet, despite the fact that he frequently vacationed in Tunisia (and was there when his Nobel Prize was announced in 1969), there is a striking silence in his recorded views on the most convulsive political episode in the life of the Fourth and Fifth Republics: the Algerian War of independence, 1954–62. This gruelling, drawn-out anti-imperial conflict led by the Algerian National Liberation Front (FLN), effectively led to the dissolution of the Fourth Republic and to the return of de Gaulle, eventually forcing a vote for the Algerian people, who elected for independence, but not before some million Algerian lives, and twenty-five thousand French ones, were lost. In one notorious incident on the mainland, Maurice Papon, a former Vichy collaborationist, led a police assault on a peaceful (if illegal) demonstration by thirty thousand pro-FLN Algerians in Paris, killing some 200 unarmed individuals. This Paris massacre, so reminiscent of the fate of the Commune, and of unnumbered incidents in Ireland, seems not to have left a trace on the recorded thoughts of Samuel Beckett. It is a strange silence, though perhaps we hear the injustice dimly echoed in works whose very titles – 'The Lost Ones' and 'Stirrings Still' – conjure up bleak vicinities peopled by stricken phantoms: 'Disappear and reappear in another where never. Nothing to show not another where never. Nothing but the strokes. The cries. The same as ever' (*CSP*, 261).

Again, the question arises of the value of 'situating' such abstract prose, which deliberately 'holds at bay the density of specific, historical time', in determinate social conjunctures – with named agents, historical props and casualty lists.[14] It is as if, in Beckett, the very confidence of historical naming and remembering is felt as a sham, subject to an immanent decay. 'History is kept outside because it has dried up consciousness' power to conceive it, the power to remember', wrote Adorno.[15] Though everything in him, as a Parisian ex-Resistance fighter for whom 'we have our being in justice', would have reviled the Paris massacre of 1961, there is no question of the event simply registering as such on his work. Rather, it disappears as concrete material, only to reappear as a moral shadow cast over the whole tenor of his aesthetic – its reluctance, its minimalism, its brittle abstraction from what 'merely' is. How much more is this true of that largest of contemporary historical terrors, 'the bomb' as such – the nuclear weapons whose stockpiling in the United States and the Soviet Union throughout the Cold War (ultimately in the pragmatic stalemate of 'mutually assured destruction', or MAD) threatened the existence of all life on earth? Adorno's point holds here, as we approach the 'non-representational' traumatic kernel of what cannot adequately be thought. *Endgame* is routinely presented as the 'play about the bomb' in Beckett criticism, a temptation that leads even as cautious a critic as Andrew Gibson to state that the 'thought of prodigious cataclysm is undoubtedly what fuels the appalled hilarity of *Endgame*'.[16] Adorno was perhaps more sober in his assessment that '*Endgame* is neither a play about the atom bomb nor is it contentless; the determinate negation of its content becomes its formal principle and the negation of content altogether'.[17] Yet it still seems somewhat presumptive and prescriptive even to go this far: *Endgame* is more properly a play about the bomb *because we want it to be*. Our historical need for a work of art that would resonate with the full annihilating terror of that apocalypse leads us into academic parlour games that the work itself stubbornly refuses. The play's insistence that nature is extinct, that 'all is zero' and 'nothing stirs', is contradicted by the presence and movement of its four players (*CDW*, 106–7). Our headlong desire to fill in the blank that hovers over their heads (to say 'Bomb!') is something the play wants us to reflect upon, critically; our wish to name the disaster is incompatible with the nature of the catastrophe on show, which seems rather to have been withdrawn from the logic of cause and effect.

And perhaps this is the richest of Beckett's history lessons. What 'shows' in the realm of news and public opinion – the course of national daily events, and beyond that the iceberg-tip evidence of world happenings that makes the papers – is in some sense not the real substance of history after all. Consider here the tumultuous events of May 1968, in Paris and the world. On the heels of the Tet Offensive in Vietnam, the Prague Spring and the collapse of the Bretton Woods arrangement, French students and workers erupted in a political carnival of strikes, occupations and demonstrations – occupying the Sorbonne, occupying the Renault factory at Cléon, fighting Paris police and reinventing everyday life with slogans, spontaneous mass singing and colossal marches. Affiliated events detonated around the world, in the United States, Latin America and elsewhere, in what looked like a decisive turning point in the struggle against global capitalism. But what did this lead to? Another round of elections: the replacement of one government by another; business as usual. In fact, certain sociologists have gone further and speculated that what 'May '68' finally put paid to was Fordism: the hierarchical and centralised chain of command in the workplace. In its stead emerged, more or less as a direct upshot of the protests, the logic of neoliberal flexibility:

The new capitalism triumphantly appropriated [the] anti-hierarchical rhetoric of '68, presenting itself as a successful libertarian revolt against the oppressive social organizations of corporate capitalism and 'really existing' socialism. This new libertarian spirit is epitomized by dressed-down 'cool' capitalists such as Microsoft's Bill Gates and the founders of Ben & Jerry's ice cream.[18]

Lost were the great moments of egalitarian logic, such as the declaration: 'The General Assembly of May 13 has decided that the University of Paris is declared an autonomous popular university and is permanently open, day and night, to all workers'. What rose from the ashes was a new, purified capitalism of digitised international transfers, deregulation, financialisation and predatory lending, keeping the world in thrall to money as never before. The absence from Beckett's writing of any 'affirmation' of May can be read as flinty sobriety rather than resignation. History's deeper passages, like Beckett's texts of disciplined 'lessness' and 'nothing', show scant regard for the punctual defiance of an inexorable process. The gesture of raising a head at the end of *Catastrophe* is atypical and relatively romantic by Beckett's standards, whose sterner grasp of the status quo is best exemplified by the pleasure-in-imprisonment that is the abstract scanning game of *Quad*, which raises the material logic of colour television to an allegorical Plato's cave: TV as destiny, a virtual entrapment between four corners, that can stand for a global generation's 'lostness' to spectacle.

At which point, it only remains to say that, due precisely to his disregard for historical particulars, and the remorseless acuity of his vision of a society held in thrall by power and abstraction, Beckett's oeuvre remains perhaps the most trenchantly 'timely' for a world – like ours – drained of existential depth and bereft of knowable coordinates. Parisian philosopher Alain Badiou, who perceives Beckett as responsible for some of the greatest truth of the twentieth century, has suggested that our world is no longer a world: 'capitalist nihilism has reached the stage of the non-existence of any world. Yes, today there is no world as such, only some singular and disjointed situations'.[19] It is in this horizon, of disjointed situations devoid of any meaningful coordination, that Beckett's abstract gestures 'worstward ho' come into full significance. *Endgame* turns out to have been a vision not of nuclear holocaust, but of our own late capitalist immanence, with no outside, no point of purchase to jimmy a crack open in the seamless 'grey' and no reliable memory with which to coordinate a reaction. Having held history at bay from his texts for forty-odd years after the destruction of Europe, Beckett has ended up as our historical era's greatest realist; because on them, in harrowing long exposure, the essential features of our 'civilisation' have cast their loveless shadows. 'All is zero'. *Commencez*!

NOTES

1 Andrew Gibson, *Beckett and Badiou: The Pathos of Intermittency* (Oxford: Oxford University Press, 2006), 73.
2 See Pascale Casanova, *Samuel Beckett: Anatomy of a Literary Revolution*, trans. Gregory Elliott (London: Verso, 2006), 75–103.
3 T. W. Adorno, *Prisms*, trans. Samuel and Shierry Weber (Cambridge: MIT Press, 1983), 34.
4 See Michel Foucault, *The Birth of Biopolitics: Lectures at the Collège de France 1978–1979*, trans. Graham Burchell, Michel Senellart (ed.) (Houndmills: Palgrave Macmillan, 2008).
5 Georg Lukàcs, *The Meaning of Contemporary Realism* (London: Merlin Press, 1979) 31, 66.
6 See Alain Badiou, *Ethics: An Essay on the Understanding of Evil*, trans. Peter Hallward (New York: Verso, 2002), 12.
7 Giorgio Agamben, *Homo Sacer: Sovereign Power and Bare Life*, trans. Daniel Heller-Roazen (Stanford: Stanford University Press, 1998).
8 See Robert Gildea, *France Since 1945* (Oxford: Oxford University Press, 2002), 8–12.
9 Kristin Ross, *Fast Cars, Clean Bodies: Decolonization and the Reordering of French Culture* (Cambridge: MIT Press, 1995), 15–70.
10 Jean Baudrillard, *The System of Objects*, trans. James Benedict (London: Verso, 2005).
11 Ibid., 46.
12 Andrew Gibson, *Samuel Beckett* (London: Reaktion, 2010), 142.
13 Gibson, *Samuel Beckett*, 156.
14 Gibson, *Beckett and Badiou*, 73.
15 T. W. Adorno, *Notes to Literature, Volume One*, trans. Shierry Weber Nicholsen (New York: Columbia University Press, 1991), 247.
16 Gibson, *Samuel Beckett*, 136.
17 T. W. Adorno, *Aesthetic Theory*, trans Robert Hullot-Kentor (London: Continuum, 2004), 325.
18 Slavoj Zizek paraphrasing Luc Boltanski and Eve Chiapello in 'The Ambiguous Legacy of '68', at http://www.inthesetimes.com/article/3751/.
19 Alain Badiou, *Polemics*, trans. Steve Corcoran (London: Verso, 2006), 34.

PART III
Milieus and Movements

CHAPTER 12

Modernism: Dublin / Paris / London
Paul Sheehan

Artistic movements are notoriously difficult to periodise, but there are at least two key dates ascribable to literary Modernism with which few critics would disagree. The first is 1922, generally seen as the movement's peak moment, its *annus mirabilis*; the second, September 1939, marks the outbreak of the Second World War and the consequent tapering off – if not outright cessation – of Modernism as an eventful historical phenomenon. Samuel Beckett, therefore, spends his formative years as a writer witnessing the twilight years of the movement that will determine his literary career. Yet from remarks made to Thomas McGreevy, the poet and critic with whom he had an intimate, unguarded correspondence, Beckett gives the impression that, far from being an acolyte of English literary Modernism, at least in its London-based version, he doesn't much like it. He snipes at T. S. Eliot in 1931 for his recent religious conversion; mentions reading Wyndham Lewis's *The Apes of God* and some of Ezra Pound's *Cantos* without any further comment; and twice dismisses D. H. Lawrence, first for his famously 'incendiary' prose (a 'tedious kindling of damp'), then for his moralism ('Coglioni Lorenziani' [Lawrentian balls]) (*L1*, 25, 66, 217–18, 250). Later in the 1930s, Beckett's attitude becomes more antagonistic. He describes Eliot's study of Dante as 'insufferably condescending, restrained & professorial', and admits to reading *Blasting and Bombardiering*, Lewis's autobiographical account of the war years and their aftermath, '4 pages at a time with considerable disgust' (*L1*, 531; *K*, 295).

It is true that Beckett is more reverent in his role as critic. Eliot and Pound, for example, are treated as iconoclastic radicals: Beckett hails *The Waste Land* as an archetype of the 'new' poetry (for its 'rupture of the lines of communication') and describes Pound's collection of critical works as 'a galvanic belt of essays, education by provocation, spartan maieutics') (*D*, 70, 79). But the disdain Beckett expresses to McGreevy about London's modernist establishment is clearly mutual. In 1932, he sends his first novel-length work, *Dream of Fair to Middling Women*, and a book of poems to Leonard and Virginia Woolf's Hogarth Press, and only receives a formal rejection slip in reply. The *Dream* manuscript is later reviewed by Edward Garnett, the English writer and champion of Joseph Conrad and D. H. Lawrence, for Jonathan Cape. Although conceding that Beckett 'probably is a clever fellow', he recoils from the work's formal oddities and stylistic idiosyncrasies. 'I wouldn't touch this with a barge pole', is his considered verdict (*LI*, 120).

Despite these well-documented antagonisms and setbacks, Beckett is still regarded as a paragon of Irish (or Franco-Irish) Modernism. The association persists through other forms of involvement, which subsequently underpin Beckett's modernist credentials. During the two years he spends in Paris, 1928–30, he becomes – thanks to the intercession of McGreevy – a close compatriot of James Joyce and a devoted member of his artistic circle. In addition, in 1931 (also thanks to McGreevy's contacts), Beckett publishes the most sustained non-fictional work of his career: a critical study of the French modernist par excellence, Marcel Proust. These two affiliations suggest that if Beckett had little time for the so-called modern movement, as it was then known, he was nonetheless enamoured of modernist writing in its other, non-English guises. His ambivalence is also telling in a more historical sense, as a symptom of how the literary-modernist narrative played itself out in the first half of the twentieth century.

From the early 1900s on, London is the breeding ground for a long parade of modernist talents. In 1908, for example, Ford Madox Hueffer (later Ford) founds *The English Review*, a literary magazine that gives many modernist writers their publishing debuts. At the same time, Italian futurist F. T. Marinetti delivers a series of high-profile lectures that earn him a great deal of public attention and notoriety. More discreetly, the Bloomsbury group takes shape under the guidance of Virginia Woolf and her sister Vanessa Bell, establishing a cultural enclave for a range of different writers (E. M. Forster, Roger Fry, Lytton Strachey) and a point of contact for such 'unaffiliated' figures as Katherine Mansfield and D. H. Lawrence. And then there is Ezra Pound. He leaves provincial America for the British capital in 1908, and spends the next twelve years there organising lectures, editing journals and publicising new writing, all the while honing his skills as a poet. His prodigious entrepreneurial energies are brought to bear on a panoply of modernist figures – some of whom are recruited into aesthetic programmes – that includes T. E. Hulme, H. D., W. B. Yeats, Wyndham Lewis, James Joyce and T. S. Eliot. When Pound takes his leave, in January 1921, literary London loses some of its dynamism. By the mid 1920s, Paris can lay greater claim to being the modernist capital, thanks in large part to the high-profile activities of the surrealist group, which publicly launches its manifesto in 1924.

Although Beckett spends more of the 1930s in Dublin and London than in Paris, the latter is undoubtedly his 'spiritual' home before it becomes his actual home in 1937. Beckett is also much more receptive to the exponents of Parisian Surrealism than he is to London's modernist elites. In 1932 he translates twenty-one poems and essays for a surrealist number of the Paris-based little magazine *This Quarter*, guest edited by André Breton.[1] The following year he meets Breton and poet Paul Eluard; 'Breton impressed him and Eluard inspires affection', reports Denis Devlin, the Irish poet.[2] Beckett's greater openness to French Modernism is made plain when, a short time after expressing his 'disgust' to McGreevy over Lewis's memoir, he tells him: 'I have read Sartre's *Nausée* & find it extraordinarily good' (quoted in *K*, 626).

After Joyce, Proust and (less notably) Surrealism, Beckett's most profound contemporary modernist encounters are not literary but painterly. For six months in 1936–7 he travels around Germany, visiting its galleries and museums, immersing himself in old masters, modern pioneers (Paul Cézanne, Wassily Kandinsky, Edvard Munch) and numerous works by German expressionist artists: Emil Nolde, Erich Heckel, Ernst Kirchner, Karl Schimdt-Rottluff, Paula Modersohn-Becker, Lionel Feininger, Otto Dix. Their compulsive fascination with the depredations of metropolitan life, in which basic human activities are treated as commodity forms (particularly sex, i.e., prostitution) and cruelty, mutilation and death ubiquitous, leaves a lasting impression on the thirty-year-old Beckett. The residuum of the German expressionist outlook is as discernible in *Murphy*, and its characterisation of the prostitute Celia, just as surely as it is in the television dramas of the 1960s and '70s and the late, spectral plays, *That Time* and *Footfalls*.

The collocation of Beckett and Modernism, from a historical perspective, can be telescoped into the years 1927–39; or from when Beckett first encountered the work of James Joyce, to the outbreak of war that drew a decisive line under the movement. The after effects of this period on Beckett's writing suggest a complex, multiform relationship to Modernism, which I propose to examine from three different angles: first, by considering him as a late modernist who both develops, and distances himself from, first-wave Modernism; then as a theatrical modernist, giving birth to the kind of drama that Beckett's (English-language) predecessors could not quite realise; and finally as a nomadic modernist, providing new ways to rethink questions of exile, translation and otherness in the post-war world.

LATE MODERNISM: AN ART OF INSUPERABLE INDIGENCE

To add the prefix 'post-' to an object or epoch, writes Marjorie Perloff, is to imply 'belatedness, diminution, and entropy'.³ The same could be said of the term 'late' – that it denotes an aftermath of sorts, an uncertain state of waning yet surviving, caught between continuation and expiration. 'Late Modernism' is therefore an unsettled, ambivalent redrafting of Modernism that challenges as well as advances, and Samuel Beckett is its exemplar. Lateness defines his career in two ways, historical and biographical. In the first place, Modernism has already 'happened' by the time he devotes himself unstintingly to writing in the post-war years, and to forging his unique aesthetic – the monological novels and novellas, and the ruthlessly pared-down drama. And second, this major work is not begun until Beckett is nearly forty, and then takes a further seven years to make its way into the publishing and theatrical worlds.

And yet, to identify Beckett as a 'late' modernist is something of a revisionist gesture, given that he is, strictly speaking, a modernist from the start. His first separately published work, *Whoroscope* (1930), is a failed attempt at a modernist poem, using all the Eliotic devices – allusion, obliquity, abrupt shifts of rhythm and register – to convey the sense of a private poetic language or code that only the initiated can decipher. *Dream of Fair to Middling Women* is similarly disorienting, and much more ambitious: a novel-length exploration of the mind and sexual misfortunes of Belacqua Shuah, whose name alludes to Dante's Belacqua, a minor character in the *Purgatorio*, and to the biblical Shuah, mother of Onan in the Book of Genesis. (The title, too, is a play on an early Tennyson poem, 'A Dream of Fair Women' [1833]). This dense referential tapestry is studiously modernist, even if Beckett was reluctant to admit as much. Instead he would insist, somewhat implausibly, that he had rejected the methods of Eliot and Pound, with their incessant quotations, allusions and reworkings of tradition. As he remarked to Brian Coffey, a fellow Irish writer, they were no more than 'jewel thieves' with their 'wholesale borrowing from others' (quoted in *B*, 100).

The work that Beckett produces in the rest of the 1930s – *More Pricks than Kicks* (1934), *Echo's Bones and Other Precipitates* (1935) and *Murphy* (1938) – adheres more or less faithfully to the Hiberno-modernist aesthetic patented by Joyce: comical, erudite, scabrous, rich in wordplay, dense with pastiche and linguistically exacting. Beckett's elaboration of this template yields a modernist style that is showy, ornate and acutely self-conscious, implicitly disclosing a kind of intellectual superiority. The literary tradition is treated as an endless resource to be played with, annexed and remade in his own mordant, impertinent image. In the post-war years Beckett retains some of these proto-Joycean elements, such as the comedy and the fastidiousness with language, but either modifies or repudiates the rest.

Late Modernism, then, at least as practiced by Beckett, is also to some extent a 'negative' Modernism, a negation of the aesthetic of virtuosity that defined his predecessors. In formal terms, this means cutting ties with the encyclopaedic, minutiae-laden Modernism that Joyce and Proust perfected in their most celebrated works. 'The more Joyce knew the more he could', remarks Beckett. 'I'm working with impotence, ignorance'.[4] One of his key innovations is the tentative, vacillating monological voice, emptying itself out at every turn, inexorably trying to neutralise its actuality through a frenzy of proposition and counter-proposition. Beckett's refiguring of his modernist heritage thus amounts to an aesthetics of subtraction, a gradual shedding of many of the literary conventions – psychological acuity, geo-historical context, narrative logic – that his predecessors contested yet retained.

There is, however, one modernist habit that Beckett takes up, albeit in his own unique way: the penchant for auto-poetics, that came to be realised in the form of the manifesto. As is now widely recognised, these literary 'tracts' were artworks disguised as declarations of principle, self-advertisements turned into aesthetic objects.[5] Following in the footsteps of F. T. Marinetti and his vehement, hyperbolic 'Futurist Manifesto' in 1909, came literary manifestoes for imagism (Pound and Flint), vorticism (Lewis and Pound), feminism (Mina Loy), dada (Tristan Tzara) and surrealism (Breton). Beckett's attitude to this kind of high-minded publicity stunt is, typically, ambivalent. On one hand, he (reluctantly) put his name to 'Poetry Is Vertical' (1932), a critical agenda contrived by Eugene Jolas for the Paris-based journal *transition*. On the other, although he never went in for self-exhibition the way, say, Lewis or Breton did, Beckett nonetheless produced several declarative texts that are manifestoes in all but name.

The *Proust* essay is one of the earliest, with its reflections on time, habit and memory, and their intermediation by suffering and boredom. Beckett also suggests that love and art are consubstantial with one another. In the course of channelling Proust, he refers to 'that desert of loneliness and recrimination that men call love'; then, several pages later, seems to revert to his own voice: 'The artistic tendency is not expansive, but a retraction. And art is the apotheosis of solitude'. The piece climaxes with an attack on realist and naturalist writers for 'worshipping the offal of experience ... content to transcribe the surface' (*P*, 54, 64, 78–9). Shortly after completing the essay, Beckett composed a kind of 'addendum' – a literary parody of a French modernist movement, *le concentrisme* ('*un prisme sur l'escalier*'), which he presented to Dublin's Modern Languages Society in November 1930 (*D*, 41).

Beckett, it would appear, had need of an interlocutor for his nascent poetics – and he found one in Axel Kaun, a publisher's assistant whom he met in Potsdam, during his German travels. Beckett's much-quoted letter to Kaun, sent from Dublin in July 1937, amplifies his thoughts on artistic retraction, solitude and surface. '[I]s literature alone to be left behind', he asks, compared with music and painting? Still using the interrogative mode, Beckett suggests a way forward: 'Is there any reason why that terrifyingly arbitrary materiality of the word surface should not be dissolved ... so that for pages on end we cannot perceive it as other than a dizzying path of sounds connecting unfathomable abysses of silence?' (*L1*, 518, 518–19). Beckett's subsequent career is the sustained response to this entreaty; though there is one more pause for reflection along the way.

In December 1949, *Transition Forty-Nine* published the *Three Dialogues*, a succinct codification of Beckett's post-war aesthetic. It consists of a (modified) transcription of conversations Beckett ('B') had with author and editor Georges Duthuit ('D'). Not just a vehicle for reflecting on contemporary art and criticism, these 'dialogues' are a rhetorical and performative tour de force – appropriately, given B's pessimism about communication, expression and certain other humanistic beliefs. The 'heroic' side of Modernism, with its dream of cultural reform, is entirely disowned; instead, B asks to be forgiven for relapsing into 'my dream of an art unresentful of its insuperable indigence'. In its most fully developed form, then, Beckett's late Modernism signifies a turn away from achievement, from communicative fealty and from what he calls 'the expressive vocation'. His replacement for these outmoded ideals, and for artistic proficiency in general, is 'fidelity to failure' (*P*, 112, 124, 125).

THEATRICAL MODERNISM:
THE PRINCIPLE OF DISINTEGRATION

Dublin's Abbey Theatre is often seen as the theatrical home of the Irish Literary Revival. Founded in 1903 by W. B. Yeats and Lady Augusta Gregory, it gave Beckett regular exposure to Irish drama, both historical and contemporary. So even though he was indifferent to the nationalistic character of the Revival, Beckett was a regular attendee at the Abbey from the mid 1920s to the early 1930s. Often this was a disheartening experience, as when he reports to McGreevy on plays he has seen by Austin Clarke ('truly pernicious'), Lady Gregory ('Vulgarly conceived & vulgarly written'), Richard Brinsley Sheridan ('positively lamentable') and Teresa Deevy ('the usual rubbish') (*L1*, 49, 49, 62, 122). Significantly, the Irish drama that does engage him is more modernist oriented – works by Sean O'Casey (*Juno and the Paycock* [staged in 1924], *The Plough and the Stars* [in 1926]), by W. B. Yeats (*The Resurrection, King of the Great Clock Tower* [both 1934], *Purgatory* [1938]) and by J. M. Synge (*The Well of the Saints, The Tinker's Wedding, The Playboy of the Western World* [1920s]).[6] These plays anticipate the down-at-heel Beckettian derelict, with their casts of lowborn, bedraggled plebeians; though Beckett's over-educated loners are, in other respects, worlds away from Synge's peasant-folk.

But despite the attention he gives to Irish drama, during the 1930s Beckett shows little interest in writing for the stage himself, focusing instead on fiction and poetry. An abortive attempt at a play about Samuel Johnson, 'Human Wishes' (circa 1940), is the only evidence of serious playwriting, before he begins *Eleutheria* in January 1947 (followed by *En attendant Godot* late in 1948). In fact, throughout this period Beckett seems more captivated by the cinema, particularly the silent cinema of Chaplin, Keaton and Harold Lloyd. Further, in the mid 1930s he steeps himself in writings by film theorist Rudolf Arnheim and filmmaker-theorists Vsevelod Pudovkin and Sergei Eisenstein. Unlike his theatre-going activities, this culminates in a vocational objective: in 1936, Beckett writes a letter to Eisenstein, requesting admission to the Moscow State School of Cinematography. Whilst admitting that he has no practical film experience, Beckett makes it clear that it is 'in the scenario and editing end of the subject that I am most interested' (*L1*, 317). But Eisenstein does not reply, and so the matter is dropped.

Beckett's preference for film over theatre, in this period, has a modernist aspect to it that goes beyond the technological modernity of the medium. It is to do with the fact that the theatre at this point has undergone a somewhat uneven development as a modernist form. Continental drama acquires some of the self-reflexive properties of the novel and the poem, thanks to Luigi Pirandello and Bertolt Brecht, who also bring to the stage troubling metaphysical and political conundrums. Antonin Artaud, too, hastens the modernist development of European theatre, though as a theorist and provocateur rather than a playwright. In the English-speaking world, by contrast, the theatre is much less revolutionary – especially when it comes to the dramatic works of the leading modernists. The verse dramas of Eliot and Yeats scarcely advanced the form, nor did Joyce's one attempt at playwriting, the quasi-Ibsenite *Exiles*, written in 1915, which not even Beckett could bring himself to admire. In America, Eugene O'Neill boldly incorporated myth, vernacular and post-Nietzschean despair into his plays, but without letting go entirely of either melodramatic excess or the humanistic longing for redemption.

Indeed, in the first half of the twentieth century there are perhaps two English-language attempts to make the drama as modernist as other literary forms. Although neither truly qualifies as a 'play', modernist or otherwise, each revitalises the German expressionist dramatic tradition. Wyndham Lewis's *Enemy of the Stars* appeared in the first issue of *Blast* (1914), and is often seen as the most original contribution to that anthology of execrations and affronts. Anticipating Beckett in its cruelty and clownish extravagance, two 'characters', Arghol and Hanp, battle it out in 'in a theatre of printed words'[7] that unfolds not via dramatic development but through spatial elisions, sudden transformations and textual breaches. The second instance, just as anti-mimetic, comes from Joyce. Following Melville's lead in *Moby Dick* ('Midnight, Forecastle'), Joyce presents the 'Circe' chapter of *Ulysses* as a playscript. An expressionist, phantasmagoric nightmare of sexual abasement, it adamantly matches its formal violations with transgressive subject matter (sadomasochism, fetishism, transvestism). Unlike Lewis's pitiless anti-drama, 'Circe' has been staged, albeit with mixed results.[8] Both pieces, however, are para-theatrical curios rather than fully realised works of modernist drama.

The theatre might be seen, therefore, as a 'solution' of sorts to Beckett's late modernist predicament. If his attitude to the novel is one of sedition, of gradually rendering it unusable as a narrative form (culminating in *The Unnamable* and *How It Is*), he sees the drama as a kind of opportunity – a way of evading the pressures of belatedness that haunt the post-war, modernist-inspired novelist and poet. As early as 1934, Beckett hints at how this might be achieved. It is occasioned by a review of Sean O'Casey's *Windfalls*, an *omnium gatherum* of verse, stories and (short) drama. Nestled amidst Beckett's typically fustian verbiage is a paragraph devoted to O'Casey's treatment of the 'one-act knockabout' – a vivid prefiguration of his own theatrical aesthetic. Beckett writes that O'Casey 'discerns the principle of disintegration in even the most complacent solidities, and activates it to their explosion. This is the energy of his theatre' (*D*, 82). The awareness that disintegration – as well as decomposition and (self-) dereliction – could be exploited to produce not dramatic torpor but theatrical 'energy' is the key that will unlock a host of new possibilities on the post-war stage.

NOMADIC MODERNISM: MOVEMENT WITHOUT ARRIVAL

Beckett's modernist years are marked by transnational mobility – across Dublin, Paris, London and several German cities. These movements give his incipient late-modernist outlook a clearly defined nomadic bearing, underscored by various kinds of politics of place that exacerbate his suspicion of governmental authority. Like Joyce and Yeats before him, Beckett experienced Dublin as anti-modernist and censorious. A 1934 essay addressing new legislation that prohibits 'unwholesome literature' shows Beckett's distaste for censorship in characteristically abstruse, sardonic and acerbic terms ('Sterilization of the mind and apotheosis of the litter suit well together') (*D*, 87). By contrast, the two years he spends in Paris at the end of the 1920s reveal a more cosmopolitan and polyglot world. The city offers living proof that cultural identity is not incompatible with artistic and intellectual reflection, nor is it something determined in advance by the dogmatic ordinances of church and state.

For Beckett, Parisian cosmopolitanism has both personal and professional coordinates, which occasionally overlap. So, on one hand, he befriends several members of Joyce's inner circle – Paul and Lucie Léon, Eugene and Maria Jolas – and becomes reacquainted with Alfred Péron, whom he had met at Trinity College, Dublin two years earlier, and Péron's future wife, Maya ('Mania') Lézine. On the other, the Jolases publish some of Beckett's earliest poetry, fiction and criticism in *transition*, a leading avant-garde literary magazine in the interwar years that they co-founded in 1927. Beckett also meets in Paris the American writer, publisher and activist Nancy Cunard, who commissions from him some translations for her major work, *Negro, an Anthology*. Published in 1934, the book celebrates and historicises black culture; Beckett's nineteen translations from the French include accounts of colonial history and imperialism in Madagascar, Haiti and the Congo.

But if *transition* and *Negro* heighten Beckett's sense of cultural diversity, his travels in Germany during 1936–7 reveal the repressed underside of European cosmopolitanism. As he soon discovers, many of the modernist pictures he wants to view have either been hidden or removed, due to Nazi abhorrence of *Entartung* (degeneracy). Official party policy since 1934, it reaches a head in 1937 when large numbers of paintings are confiscated and the notorious 'Degenerate Art' exhibition opens in Munich.

(In Berlin, trawling the city's art galleries, Beckett deems the trip a failure because '[a]ll the modern pictures are in the cellars') (*L1*, 397). Beckett's decision to join the French Resistance in September 1941, at the behest of Alfred Péron, is therefore in part a delayed reaction to the bigotry and injustice witnessed five years earlier.

London, however, impresses on Beckett what could be termed a politics of the self. In 1933, suffering acute anxiety symptoms and borderline paralysis, aggravated by his father's death in June, Beckett decides to undertake a course of psychoanalysis at the Tavistock Clinic in London. His willingness to commit himself to such a prolonged and demanding regimen – three sessions a week for nearly two years – suggests that his modernist-attuned mind has already been opened to the rigors of the analytical process. For Modernism and psychoanalysis are both deep-seated responses to modernity, both are quickened by crisis and both offer ways of traversing estrangement and otherness. Beckett's first-hand experience of this convergence thus leads him to a different kind of nomadic awareness: the self as rootless, vacillating and destitute, and 'homelessness' as not just a problem of dwelling, but also a condition of subjectivity.

Beckett takes the plight of the outcast as his starting point, peopling his work with what he will call a 'babble of homeless mes and untenanted hims' (*CSP*, 150). These characters inhabit a state of permanent 'in-betweenness', which reveals itself in Beckett's post-war writing through errancy, doubt, liminality, vagrancy and transience. As Gilles Deleuze and Félix Guattari define it: '[T]he in-between has taken on all the consistency and enjoys both an autonomy and a direction of its own. The life of the nomad is the intermezzo. Even the elements of his dwelling are conceived in terms of the trajectory that is forever mobilizing them'.[9] Itinerant and ambulant, exemplars of modernist alterity, Beckett's outsiders resist the single, fixed perspective and static identity. But their 'journeying' is never end oriented; whether confined to a room or aimlessly wandering, they are habituated to movement without arrival. Nor are their manifestations of difference reducible to racial, sexual, national, political or any other kind of attribute. Under the shadow of enduring exile and terminal dispossession, Beckett's nomadic Modernism presents otherness in its most elemental, which is to say, corporeal form. This constitutes perhaps the most enduring part of his late modernist legacy, and an apposite reminder of the equivocal influence exerted by his forebears.

NOTES

1 For a list of works, see Raymond Federman and John Fletcher, *Samuel Beckett: His Works and His Critics: An Essay in Bibliography* (Berkeley: University of California Press, 1970), 92–3.
2 In a letter to McGreevy (23 September 1933); quoted in *L1*, 169.
3 Marjorie Perloff, *21st-Century Modernism: The 'New' Poetics* (Malden: Blackwell, 2002), 2.
4 Israel Shenker, 1956 interview with Beckett. Reprinted in Lawrence Graver and Raymond Federman (eds.), *Samuel Beckett: The Critical Heritage* (London: Routledge, 1997), 162.
5 See Janet Lyon, *Manifestoes: Provocations of the Modern* (Ithaca: Cornell University Press, 1999), 5.
6 James Knowlson notes that Beckett saw 'most of the Synge revivals ... in the 1920s'. See Knowlson and John Pilling, *Frescoes of the Skull: The Later Prose and Drama of Samuel Beckett* (London: John Calder, 1979), 259.
7 David Graver, 'Vorticist Performance and Aesthetic Turbulence in *Enemy of the Stars*', *PMLA* (107.3: May 1992), 484.
8 *Ulysses in Nighttown*, adapted by Marjorie Barkentin, enjoyed commercial success but only limited critical support when it played off Broadway in 1958 and on Broadway in 1974.
9 Gilles Deleuze and Felix Guattari, *A Thousand Plateaus: Capitalism and Schizophrenia*, trans. Brian Massumi (Minneapolis: University of Minnesota Press, 1987), 380.

CHAPTER 13

The Joyce Circle

Sam Slote

The Joyce circle is anything but straightforward. If anything, it is more like the involute curlicue spiral Constantin Brancusi designed as a symbol of Joyce – when shown this design Joyce's father remarked that, 'The boy seems to have changed a good deal'.[1] Indeed, Joyce had changed since he left Ireland: unlike his experiences in Dublin two decades earlier, in the Paris of the 1920s Joyce enjoyed the luxury of defining his connections on his own terms. By the time he met Beckett, Joyce was comfortably ensconced in the literary *milieux* of Paris, which he twisted and tweaked to suit his own needs. As he told Arthur Power, he found Paris 'a very convenient city'.[2] Paris was certainly convenient in affording various factotums to promote his work and perform menial duties for himself and his family. Nora once said to Joyce that, 'If God Almighty came down to earth, you'd have a job for him'.[3] This quip anticipates Hélène Cixous's doctoral dissertation on Joyce, which argues that through his art Joyce supplements God with himself:

Joyce is attempting to set up a vision of his own, ex-centric as far as the Creation is concerned, a world which can escape from the Absolute which rules the world God has created. Everything which usually constitutes or contributes to the traps and net in which God holds the world and the mind captive, subjected to his Presence and Omnipotence, is endangered by Joyce's art.[4]

In his art, Joyce's circle trumps God's. Not just in his work, but in his Parisian life and days Joyce installed himself as an eccentric centre of varying schools and shoals of admirers, lackeys and sycophants. This was a heterogeneous and catholic crew, ranging from the willfully avant-garde coterie around Eugene Jolas's *transition* to Louis Gillet of the staid journal *La Revue des deux mondes*.[5]

Beckett's entrée into the Joycean web came through Thomas McGreevy, whose position he had inherited at the École Normale Supérieure in 1928. McGreevy had himself been pressed into service for the Joycean league earlier that year; hailing from the west of Ireland he was well received by the Galway-born Nora (*K*, 97). Beckett soon found himself enlisted in all manner of tasks for Joyce. The first two letters in the first volume of Beckett's correspondence are to Joyce and indicate at least some of the services he was providing. The first, written from Kassel and dated 23 March 1929, is about a revision to Beckett's essay on *Work in Progress* for *transition* 16–17 and also mentions that he was hunting for a book for Joyce. The second, dated 26 April, is an explication of some finer points of Greek conjugation (*L1*, 22–4).

Beckett's tasks for Joyce ranged from taking notes to accompanying him on walks through Paris and minding him when he got drunk (which was often enough) (*K*, 101–2). Beckett was hardly unique or alone in these tasks and he certainly was not Joyce's closest or most intimate *aide-de-camp* (the honour of that drudgery belongs to Joyce's Russian-born secretary, Paul Léon). Beckett was very much in awe of Joyce and took to adopting his gestures and sartorial habits (*K*, 101). However, Beckett was not uncritical towards the ways in which Joyce held his circle in thrall. In early 1930 he wrote to McGreevy that, 'I suppose the Gilberts and Carduccis would feel honoured if Joyce signed a piece of his used toilet paper (*L1*, 21)'.[6]

In 1954, when Ellmann was interviewing Beckett for his biography of Joyce, Beckett relayed the since much-circulated story about how he took dictation for *Work in Progress/Finnegans Wake*. During one bout of dictation, Joyce responded to a knock on the door with a phrase – 'Come in!' – that Beckett then duly transcribed and, ultimately, Joyce let this inadvertence remain within the text.[7] Beckett repeated the same story, more or less verbatim, to James Knowlson in 1989.[8] However, this phrase – even allowing for Wakean distortion – has not been located in any of the manuscripts that Beckett worked on or could have worked on. Furthermore, Beckett was only one of several amanuenses Joyce employed and most of the scribal work was performed by Léon. It is possible that Beckett had simply appropriated an event that had occurred to a different amanuensis and had simplified the compositional transaction in the interests of telling a good story. Therefore, the story could be true, but if so the scribe was (likely) not Beckett and the phrase was (probably) not 'Come in'.

At least one of Beckett's Joycean chores was more significant than this canard. In the late 1930s Joyce assigned Beckett to read and take notes from works by Fritz Mauthner and Hans Zimmer for possible incorporation into the *Wake*. Beckett's notes form a nexus between Joyce's work and Beckett's own. On one hand, some of these notes found their way into *Work in Progress/Finnegans Wake* and are thus 'the only material proof of

Beckett's contribution to the writing process of *Finnegans Wake*.[9] But, on the other hand, Mauthner's articulation of the fragility of human knowledge exerted an influence on Beckett's subsequent works, such as *Watt*. With Mauthner and Zimmer, Joyce's circle intersects with Beckett's.

The most significant tributary of Joycean circles for the young Beckett was Eugene Jolas, co-founder and editor of the journal *transition*. *Transition* was instrumental in aligning Joyce with the avant-garde quarters of the Parisian literary scene. Jolas, born in America of French and German parents, felt that 'English writing was undergoing a renewal in Paris and that a magazine was needed to further the cause of the literary resurgence'.[10] The idea for *transition* was that it should serve as a transatlantic link for the avant-garde. In 1949, Jolas coined the woolly term 'pan-romanticism' to name the variety of writings published by *transition*. '*Transition* contained elements of gothic, romantic, baroque, mystic, expressionist, Dada, surrealist, and, finally, verticalist modes of thinking. In the last phase, it tried to blend these traditions into a cosmic, four-dimensional consciousness'.[11] *Transition* was not so much a journal of *the* avant-garde, but rather a document of the various avant-garde*s* circulating and mingling (and not always without friction) in Paris in the 1920s and 1930s. While *transition* has often been mistaken for a journal solely dedicated to Joyce (and, indeed, Jolas and other *transition* regulars performed yeoman service in promoting and defending Joyce), there are some key differences. Jolas sought to harness the literary experimentations in *transition* into a full-fledged revolution, something he formalised into a manifesto, 'The Revolution of the Word', in 1929 – which appeared in the same issue as Beckett's first two published pieces.[12] He saw Joyce as a 'great example' for his revolution, but, perhaps unsurprisingly, Joyce declined to sign the manifesto.[13] As Régis Salado has pointed out, an incendiary production like 'The Revolution of the Word' is not entirely compatible with Joyce's posture of 'silence, exile and cunning'.[14] Thus, while the *transition* circle and the Joyce circle overlapped, they did not mesh and coincide completely.

Into this heady atmosphere Beckett submitted his first publications. Soon after their initial meeting, Joyce enlisted Beckett to write an article elucidating the importance of Dante, Bruno and Vico on *Work in Progress* for *transition*. *Transition* had been publishing various articles defending and illustrating various aspects of *Work in Progress* to a bewildered readership. These were largely directed by Joyce and in 1929 were published by Sylvia Beach's Shakespeare and Company as *Our Exagmination Round His Factification for Incamination of Work in Progress*. Beckett's background in Italian literature was the obvious reason why he was selected for the

Dante, Bruno and Vico essay. (McGreevy was another contributor and he wrote on the 'Catholic element' in *Work in Progress*.) As with most of the other contributions to the volume, Joyce's supervision was not passive.[15] Beckett was already well familiar with Dante but had to do some research on Bruno and Vico. He claims that Joyce was pleased with the final result but chided him for not doing enough with Bruno (*K*, 100). And so, with this article, Beckett made his first appearance in print as one of the disciples of Joyce's *Work in Progress*.

The general disposition of the *Exagmination* is an *apologia*; that is, the articles set out to explain that Joyce's *Work in Progress* does, despite its apparent obscurity, make sense. Beckett's argument is somewhat atypical of such defensiveness. He starts off by insisting that 'Literary criticism is not book-keeping' (*D*, 4). He then proceeds to argue how Joyce's 'position is in no way a philosophical one' (*D*, 7). Kevin Dettmar writes that in this essay, 'The Joyce that Beckett evokes ... sounds rather similar to the later Beckett: an artist who invokes systems only to smash them'.[16]

Beckett's short story 'Assumption' was published in the same issue of *transition* as his essay on *Work in Progress*. While thematically and stylistically unrelated to Joyce, it contains at least one line consonant with his counter-systematising analysis of *Work in Progress*: 'To avoid the expansion of the commonplace is not enough; the highest art reduces significance in order to obtain that inexplicable bombshell perfection' (*CSP*, 4). Even after Beckett left Paris in 1930, he continued his association with Jolas and *transition*. Subsequent issues of *transition* published his story 'Sedendo and Quiesciendo' (the only part of *Dream of Fair to Middling Women* published in his lifetime), various poems ('For Future Reference', 'Malacoda', 'Enueg II', 'Dortmunder' and 'Ooftish') and a review of Dennis Devlin's *Intercessions*. In a letter to Charles Prentice of Chatto and Windus, Beckett admitted that 'Sedendo' 'stinks of Joyce in spite of most earnest endeavours to endow it with my own odours' (*L1*, 81). Beckett and McGreevy were signatories to another of Jolas's manifestos, 'Poetry is Vertical', which appeared in *transition* 21. Not all of Beckett's submissions to *transition* were accepted: an essay on censorship in Ireland was declined as well as other works (*K*, 190).[17] After the war, *transition* was taken over by Georges Duthuit and Jolas remained as an editorial advisor. Beckett – along with Jean-Paul Sartre and Georges Bataille (who were hardly the best of friends) – served on the editorial committee of the new (and now properly capitalised) *Transition* (*K*, 369). The new *Transition* was more explicitly French than the internationalism of its predecessor and Beckett's contributions were more significant.[18]

Jolas's *transition* was hardly the only venue in which Beckett published his early works. As an aspiring writer, he pursued many different outlets, not all connected to Joyce. Beckett's other major contribution within the Joyce circle was not without controversy: the translation of 'Anna Livia Plurabelle' into French. Beckett should have known that the task of translating Joyce entailed acrimony. He was present at the celebration of the publication of the French translation of *Ulysses*, held at the Hôtel Léopold at Les-Vaux-de-Cernay on 27 June 1929. The three translators – Auguste Morel, Stuart Gilbert and Valery Larbaud – were notable by their absence: they grew to hate each other so much while working on the translation that they declined to attend the festivities and felicitations.[19] Beckett himself does not appear in the commemorative group photograph of the event – as he told James Knowlson, he was drunk 'under the table' (*K*, 103).[20]

In 1930 Beckett and his friend and former student Alfred Péron were approached by Philippe Soupault to translate a portion of 'Anna Livia Plurabelle' for the journal *Bifur*, founded the previous year by the dadaist Georges Ribemont-Dessaignes. Ribemont-Dessaignes convinced Joyce to be listed on the title page as one of the journal's 'conseillers étrangers'.[21] In August, Beckett submitted the translation to Soupault, although he admitted that, 'The more I think of it, the more I find it all very poor stuff' (*LI*, 39). According to Soupault's account of the matter, Beckett and Péron's translation was deemed unsuccessful and useful only as a 'premier essai' for a more meticulous and sensitive translation that was undertaken by an unwieldy phalanx that included himself, Paul Léon, Jolas, Ivan Goll and Adrienne Monnier, all working under Joyce's supervision.[22] This supposedly revised translation was eventually published not in *Bifur* but in the *Nouvelle Revue Française* in May 1931. Beckett and Péron's version does exist and was in preparation for publication in the December 1930 issue of *Bifur* before being withdrawn. Beckett and Péron heavily revised the translation as it was being prepared and the final version of their translation is actually, as Megan Quigley has demonstrated, 'nearly identical to the published "Anna Livia Plurabelle"' in *NRF*.[23] Evidently Soupault, with Joyce's endorsement, commandeered Beckett and Péron's work and understated their efforts. Daniel Ferrer and Jacques Aubert argue that the translocation of the translation was motivated by Joyce's 'public-relations strategy' to have his works appear in more respectable venues, such as *NRF*, as opposed to the merely avant-garde *Bifur*.[24] Knowlson writes that, in an interview with Beckett in September 1989, 'Almost sixty years later, he still felt slighted by the way in which his version had been underestimated and discarded' (*K*, 728 n43).[25]

When the translation was launched at Monnier's bookshop, La Maison des Amis des Livres, much to Beckett's annoyance Soupault introduced the translation with his own account of its genesis. During Monnier's reading from the translation, McAlmon grew somewhat uneasy and testy due to what he later described as the evening's 'dumbly worshipful' ambience. To signal his bemused contempt for the veneration, he lifted his hands in a gesture of mock prayer, an act which prompted Édouard Dujardin to rush across the room and slap him since he misconstrued the gesture as an insult to his wife.[26]

Translations and misunderstandings were not the only impediment between Joyce and Beckett in 1930. Nora resented Beckett for having hurt Lucia's feelings when he told her that he harboured no romantic feelings towards her and this resulted in a temporary exile from the Joyce family (*K*, 105; see also 156). When Beckett returned to Paris in the late 1930s, he resumed contact with Joyce. Joyce proved tremendously helpful and supportive after Beckett's stabbing by the pimp Prudent (*K*, 281–3). By now Beckett was becoming a more established writer: *Murphy* had been published and Joyce was impressed; he told his son Giorgio that 'I think he has talent' and he knew parts of the novel by heart.[27] Joyce even wrote a limerick about Murphy, 'There's a maevusmarked maggot called Murphy',[28] a bagatelle of a complement to Beckett's poem 'Home Olga', with its acrostic 'JAMES JOYCE' (*CP*, 8).

In late 1937 Joyce enlisted Beckett to write an article on *Work in Progress/ Finnegans Wake* for the *NRF* on the occasion of its publication. Initially Beckett agreed and he called it 'my parting gift to criticism' (*L1*, 565). However, he ultimately demurred. But, along with Giorgio, he did help correct the page proofs for the still-in-progress *Work in Progress*, for which he was paid 250 francs; '[Joyce] then supplemented it with an old overcoat and 5 ties!' (*L1*, 574). On 5 January 1938 he wrote McGreevy about Joyce, 'I don't feel the danger of the association any more. He is just a very lovable human being' (*L1*, 581). Beckett expressed an analogous sentiment to Martin Esslin in response to the vexing question of how Joyce had influenced him: 'his seriousness and dedication to his art influenced me'.[29]

The question of Joyce's influence on Beckett is, of course, not a simple one. Beyond stylistic affinities and shared linguistic and conceptual concerns, their rapport is often depicted in terms of consonant dispositions. In one of the more evocative passages in his biography of Joyce, Ellmann writes:

Beckett was addicted to silences, and so was Joyce; they engaged in conversations which consisted often of silences directed towards each other, both suffused with sadness, Beckett mostly for the world, Joyce mostly for himself. Joyce sat in his habitual posture, legs crossed, toe of the upper leg under the instep of the lower; Beckett, also tall and slender, fell into the same gesture.[30]

Ellmann's source for this is a 1953 interview with Beckett. In a 1989 interview with James Knowlson, Beckett paints a simpler picture of their silent interaction: 'There wasn't a lot of conversation between us. I was a young man, very devoted to him, and he liked me. And he used to call on me if he needed something. For instance, someone to walk with him before dinner'.[31] They had nothing to say simply because they had nothing to say and not because there was some groovy metaphysical bond that united them, as Ellmann's account implies.

Beckett's brief play *Ohio Impromptu* concerns the possibility of something being said when there is nothing, or little, to say. Written for a conference at Ohio State University on the occasion of his seventy-fifth birthday, it is difficult to not see this play as being, at least in part, Beckett reflecting on his relationship with Joyce, or perhaps, somewhat indirectly, it is Beckett's meditation on Ellmann's account of his relationship with Joyce. Two men, a listener and a reader, are seated at right angles at a white table and are described as being 'As alike in appearance as possible' (*CDW*, 445). Eugene Jolas remarked that Beckett 'resembled Joyce sometimes to such an extent that we were astonished'.[32] Of course, identity can be deceiving, as Moran remarked, 'As soon as two things are nearly identical I am lost' (*Mo*, 163).

In the play, the reader reads from a book a self-described 'sad tale' that begins with the line 'Little is left to tell' (*CDW*, 445) and ends with 'Nothing is left to tell' (*CDW*, 448), thereby suggesting that what little there is left to tell has somehow been told during the interval. The story concerns a man whose companion has gone, perhaps died. The remnant, solitary individual decides to move to a different location so as to no longer be reminded of the departed and thereby, perhaps, find some solace. This new home overlooks the Isle of Swans, which is where he goes to walk while wearing his black coat and Latin Quarter hat. These details explicitly recall Joyce: the hat is Stephen's Parisian accoutrement[33] and the Isle of Swans, or the Allée des Cygnes, was where Beckett and Joyce would not infrequently walk together (*K*, 665).[34] Now, this relocation fails to palliate the sorrows of the solitary individual, who dreams that his companion speaks to him 'unspoken words, Stay where we were so long alone together, my shade will comfort you' (*CDW*, 446). And so his translocation across Paris contravenes this imagined possibility of succour. After an interval, the man receives a visitor who reads to him from a book to comfort him, in a scenario that explicitly echoes the setup of the play with the listener and the reader. The story ends with the final visit and the tome's tale told one last time amidst 'Profounds of mind. Buried in who knows what profounds of mind. Of mindlessness. Whither no light can reach. No sound. So sat on as though turned to stone' (*CDW*, 448). A silent communion is the only rapport possible between these individuals, but it is unclear if this communion is a palliative or a supplement to the absence of such a palliative. Indeed, the mediation of the book between these two figures is precisely what might implicate Ellmann's biography into the play: the communion is enabled by a trace of what had been, a trace to which the narrative tends without ever reaching.

This suggests one way of revisiting the ancient chestnut apropos Beckett's relation to Joyce, which Beckett (supposedly) made to Israel Shenker: '[Joyce is] tending towards omniscience and omnipotence as an artist. I'm working with impotence, ignorance'.[35] Perhaps the key phrase here is 'tending towards': according to Beckett, Joyce doesn't so much achieve omniscience as *tends towards* it, just as Beckett doesn't so much achieve impotence – which, after all, cannot be achieved since such an achievement would be self-defeating. In this way, the figure for both writers would be the asymptote: the ever-closer approach that always falls short of attaining its goal. (And there would be some irony in having both these asymptotic writers commemorated by bridges in Dublin.) We see this in *Ulysses* – in one of Joyce's most Beckettian phrases – with Bloom's meditations of the minute scales of microbes and atoms, 'dividends and divisors ever diminishing without actual division till, if the progress were carried far enough, nought nowhere was never reached'.[36] The nought, the apotheosis of this Zeno's paradox, is asymptotic: something which is tended towards without ever being reached. This is also reminiscent of the enumeration of the picture of the broken circle in Erskine's room in *Watt*, a circle and its centre never meeting ever and ever again, and thus, not unlike Beckett, the gap in the Joyce circle, the impotence within the tendency towards omniscience.

NOTES

1 Richard Ellmann, *James Joyce*, rev. ed. (New York: Oxford University Press, 1982), 614.
2 Arthur Power, *Conversations with James Joyce* (Dublin: Lilliput, 1999), 60.
3 Ellmann, *James Joyce*, 699.
4 Hélène Cixous, *The Exile of James Joyce*, tr. Sally A. J. Purcell (New York: David Lewis, 1972), 701.

5 Initially Gillet dismissed *Ulysses*, but, after some courting by Joyce and Sylvia Beach, Gillet became quite laudatory in his praise for *Work in Progress/ Finnegans Wake*; see Louis Gillet, *Stèle pour James Joyce* (Paris: Sagittaire, 1946), 11–20 and Francine Lenne, 'James Joyce et Louis Gillet', *Cahier de l'Herne: James Joyce*, Jacques Aubert and Fritz Senn (eds.) (Paris: l'Herne, 1986), 151–75.
6 Gilbert's diary from this period reveals a more cynical attitude towards Joyce than Beckett allows for (Stuart Gilbert, *Reflections on James Joyce*, Thomas F. Staley and Randolph Lewis (eds.) (Austin: University of Texas Press, 1993).
7 Ellmann, *James Joyce*, 649.
8 James and Elizabeth Knowlson, *Beckett Remembering/Remembering Beckett* (New York: Arcade, 2006), 45.
9 Dirk Van Hulle, 'Beckett – Mauthner – Zimmer – Joyce', *Joyce Studies Annual* (10: 1999), 143–83, 149.
10 Dougald McMillan, *Transition 1927–38, The History of a Literary Era* (London: Calder, 1975), 16; see also Eugene Jolas, *Man from Babel*, Andreas Kramer and Rainer Rumold (eds.) (New Haven: Yale University Press, 1998), 87–93.
11 Eugene Jolas, 'Pan Romanticism in the Atomic Age', *Transition Workshop*, Eugene Jolas (ed.) (New York: Vanguard Press, 1949), 393–5, 393.
12 Eugene Jolas, 'Proclamation' [The Revolution of the Word], *transition*, (16–17: 1929), 1.
13 Eugene Jolas, *Man from Babel*, 108.
14 Régis Salado, '*Ulysses* de Joyce, laboratoire de la modernité. Étude de réception comparée dans les domaines français et anglo-saxon (1914–1931)', (unpublished doctoral thesis, Université de Paris X, 1994).
15 Ellmann, *James Joyce*, 613.
16 Kevin J. H. Dettmar, 'The Joyce that Beckett Built', *James Joyce Quarterly* (35.4–36.1L Summer–Fall 1998), 605–19, 607. See also Jean-Michel Rabaté, 'Dangerous Identifications, or Beckett's Italian Hoagie', *Joyce's Disciples Disciplined*, Tim Conley (ed.) (Dublin: UCD Press, 2010), 1–14.
17 See also *LI*, 112. The piece on censorship is 'Censorship in the Saorstat', *D*, 84–8.
18 See John Pilling and Seán Lawlor, 'Beckett in *Transition*', *Publishing Samuel Beckett*, Mark Nixon (ed.) (London: British Library, 2011), 83–95.
19 See John L. Brown, '*Ulysses* into French', *Library Chronicle* (20–21: 1982), 29–60.
20 See also Joyce's letter to Valery Larbaud, 30 July 1929 in *Selected Letters*, Richard Ellmann (ed.) (London: Faber and Faber, 1975), 344).
21 Daniel Ferrer and Jacques Aubert, 'Anna Livia's French Bifurcations', *Transcultural Joyce*, Karen R. Lawrence (ed.) (Cambridge: Cambridge University Press, 1998), 179.
22 Philippe Soupault, 'À propos de la traduction d'Anna Livia Plurabelle', *La Nouvelle Revue Française* (212: 1 May 1931), 633.
23 Megan M. Quigley, '"Justice for the 'Illstarred Punster": Samuel Beckett and Alfred Péron's Revisions of "Anna Lyvia Pluratself"', *James Joyce Quarterly* (41.3: Spring 2004), 473.

24 Ferrer and Aubert, 'Anna Livia's French Bifurcations', 180. Ferrer and Aubert did not consult all the extant drafts of Beckett and Péron's version and thus did not see the one effectively identical to the *NRF* version. This leads them to repeat, albeit in a qualified manner, Soupault's claim that Beckett and Péron's version was æsthetically insufficient; see also Megan M. Quigley, "Justice for the 'Illstarred Punster'", 473.
25 See also Beckett's letter to McGreevy, 29 May 1931 (*L1*, 78).
26 Robert McAlmon and Kay Boyle, *Being Geniuses Together* (London: Hogarth Press, 1984), 279–80; see also *K*, 128–9 and Ellmann, *James Joyce*, 637.
27 Ellmann, *James Joyce*, 701.
28 James Joyce, *Poems and Shorter Writings*, Richard Ellmann, A. Walton Litz and John Whittier-Ferguson (eds.) (London: Faber and Faber, 1991), 151.
29 James and Elizabeth Knowlson, *Beckett Remembering/Remembering Beckett*, 47.
30 Ellmann, *James Joyce*, 648.
31 James and Elizabeth Knowlson, *Beckett Remembering/Remembering Beckett*, 45.
32 Jolas, 'Proclamation', 174.
33 James Joyce, *Ulysses*, Hans Walter Gabler (ed.) (London: The Bodley Head, 1993), 3.174.
34 See also James and Elizabeth Knowlson, *Beckett Remembering/Remembering Beckett*, 44.
35 Israel Shenker, 'Moody Man of Letters', *The New York Times*, (6 May 1956), sec. 2: 1 and 3, 3. The authenticity of this 'virtual' interview has been much debated, although, as S. E. Gontarski has noted, 'the observations seem so accurate, so Beckettian, that it is difficult to believe that Shenker's information has no merit' (S. E. Gontarski, 'Samuel Beckett, James Joyce's "Illstarred Punster"', *The Seventh of Joyce*, Bernard Benstock (ed.) (Bloomington: Indiana University Press, 1982), 29–36, 31).
36 Joyce, *Ulysses*, 17.1067–9.

CHAPTER 14

Post–World War Two Paris

Shane Weller

Although he had first lived in Paris in 1928–30, when he held the post of *lecteur* in English at the École Normale Supérieure, and had made the city his permanent home in late 1937, the pre-war Samuel Beckett was associated for the most part with the city's expatriate Anglophone community, and in particular with those belonging to the Joyce circle and Eugene Jolas's English-language literary magazine, *transition*. In striking contrast, the post-war Beckett not only sought to establish himself as a French-language writer,[1] but also extended his acquaintance considerably among those at the heart of the cultural life of the French capital, involving himself as a writer, reader, translator and theatre spectator in the remarkable cultural renaissance that occurred during the economically harsh years following the German occupation.[2]

The Beckett who returned to Paris on 25 December 1945, following a period working at the Irish Red Cross Hospital in Saint-Lô and a number of fleeting trips to the capital in 1944–5, had not yet made the decision to write in French. While he had written poems in French before the war, what would prove to be a career-determining moment came only in March 1946, when, in the course of writing a short story in English, he drew a line across the page and continued in French. Its eventual title ('The End') notwithstanding, this first story in French proved anything but an end; indeed, it marked the beginning of an astonishing outburst of creative activity, later described by Beckett as a 'frenzy of writing'.[3] The word 'frenzy' is no overstatement, for between 1946 and 1951 he wrote three further short stories ('The Expelled', 'First Love' and 'The Calmative'), four novels (*Mercier and Camier*, *Molloy*, *Malone Dies* and *The Unnamable*), two plays (*Eleutheria* and *Waiting for Godot*), a series of thirteen short prose texts (*Texts for Nothing*), two art-critical essays on the Dutch painters Bram and Geer van Velde ('La Peinture des van Velde ou le monde et le pantalon' and 'Peintres de l'empêchement') and, with Henri Matisse's son-in-law, Georges Duthuit, the *Three Dialogues* on the painters André

Masson, Pierre Tal-Coat and Bram van Velde. In addition, he produced numerous (largely uncredited) translations for *Transition* magazine (the relaunched version of the pre-war *transition*, edited by Duthuit and with a focus on the visual arts).[4]

Despite this astonishing output, Beckett nonetheless found time to attend art exhibitions and theatrical productions and to familiarise himself with the most important artistic movements in post-war Paris. His engagement with this wider cultural world was, however, of a very particular nature. On one hand, he championed work that was yet to be accepted as important (above all, that of the painter Bram van Velde) and sought to remain unaligned with any particular literary movement or tradition. On the other hand, his growing reputation as a French-language writer resulted in his being located both by publishers of his work and by commentators on it within a decidedly French post-war literary-philosophical context. An attempt to place Beckett contextually can draw considerable support from the works he wrote in the years 1946–50, all of which engage with themes also central to the work of other writers and artists of the period: the nature and possibility of human freedom, the meaningfulness or otherwise of human existence, the predicament of human beings in a post–world-war, post-Holocaust world. In short, Beckett's relation to his cultural context in post-war Paris was, as we shall see, essentially ambiguous.

The liberation of Paris in August 1944 was followed by a period of political *épuration* (purging), with immediate consequences for the literary world, not least the suicide on 15 March 1945 of the novelist Pierre Drieu La Rochelle, who during the German occupation had taken on the editorship of France's most influential pre-war literary journal, *La Nouvelle Revue Française*. On account of its collaborationist stance, the *NRF* was closed down after the Liberation and did not reappear until 1953, when it was relaunched under the title *La Nouvelle Nouvelle Revue Française*.[5] The closure of the *NRF* left a significant gap in the literary-critical marketplace, a gap filled as early as October 1945 with the first issue of *Les Temps Modernes*. Established by Jean-Paul Sartre and Simone de Beauvoir, and published by France's most important literary publisher, Gallimard, this new review soon became the principal forum for the dominant literary and philosophical movement in Paris in the immediate post-war years: existentialism. In addition to Sartre and de Beauvoir, the two other most important figures in the French existentialist movement at this time were Albert Camus and Jean Genet, although the relationship of both these writers to the movement was complicated in various ways: Camus and

Sartre had rather different conceptions of the nature of human freedom and its political dimension, as would become clear on the publication of Camus' *The Rebel* in 1951; and Genet was championed by Sartre rather than actively seeking to join the existentialist cause.

French existentialism had emerged in the pre-war years, with Sartre's first novel, *Nausea*, published by Gallimard in 1938, followed by the short story collection *The Wall* (1939). Sartre's reputation was consolidated during the Occupation with the publication of his philosophical magnum opus, *Being and Nothingness* (1943), and the play *No Exit* (1944). Camus' breakthrough came in 1942, with the publication of both *The Outsider* and *The Myth of Sisyphus*. The years immediately following the war saw the publication of Sartre's widely read *Existentialism and Humanism* (1946) and his *Roads to Freedom* trilogy (1945–9), Camus' *The Plague* (1947), and de Beauvoir's *The Blood of Others* (1945), *All Men Are Mortal* (1946) and the landmark feminist volume *The Second Sex* (1949). As for Genet, his first novel, *Our Lady of the Flowers*, was published in 1944, followed by a second novel, *Miracle of the Rose* (1946), the play *The Maids* (1947) and the autobiographical *The Thief's Journal* (1949).

While there may have been significant philosophical and literary disagreements among the existentialists, most notably between Sartre and Camus, those associated with the movement shared a sense that the principal questions to be addressed both in literature and in philosophy concerned the nature of human freedom and the meaningfulness (or otherwise) of human existence. It is, of course, scarcely surprising that such questions should have become paramount at such an historical moment. As Sartre made clear in *Existentialism and Humanism*, his own founding principle was that existence precedes essence, and thus that human nature is not some ahistorical given, but is shaped by the individual in his or her specific historical context. For Camus, on the other hand, the overriding philosophical question was, as he put it at the beginning of *The Myth of Sisyphus* (1942), 'whether life is or is not worth living'.[6] Camus, who was associated not with Sartre and de Beauvoir's *Les Temps Modernes*, but rather with the journal *Combat*, also set the tone for things to come in the French theatrical world by placing the concept of the 'absurd' at the heart of his thinking.

Beckett took an interest in the work of the principal French existentialists, and thought highly of some of them. When he read Sartre's *Nausea* in May 1938, he adjudged it 'extraordinarily good'.[7] As for Camus' *The Outsider*, he thought it 'important', and, in a letter of 27 May 1946 to his former literary agent George Reavey, encouraged the latter to read it (*L2*, 32). Writing to de Beauvoir in 1946, he informed her that he had read her works, although he did not identify which ones and did not pass critical judgement on them. The extent of Beckett's connections with the Parisian existentialists is made clear in a letter of 21 October 1945 to his cousin Morris Sinclair, who was considering writing a study of the German philosophical influences on Sartre. Beckett wrote: 'I should be glad to help you and could introduce you to Sartre & his world' (*L2*, 22; 23, n1).[8]

Beckett's connections with the principal existentialists went beyond the appreciative reading of their works, however, for the first of his post-war French prose texts was published (in part) in *Les Temps Modernes* in July 1946.[9] Under the title 'Suite', the first part of what would eventually become 'The End' appeared alongside texts by Sartre, Genet, Francis Ponge and Henri Pichette.[10] An indication of Beckett's status at the time is the editors' decision to place his text last in the 1 July 1946 issue. That said, Beckett's appearing in *Les Temps Modernes* necessarily situated him for his first French readers within an explicitly existentialist context.[11] Furthermore, Sartre and de Beauvoir thought highly enough of Beckett's work to publish further texts by him in later issues of *Les Temps Modernes*; these included twelve poems written in French before the war and a pre-book-publication extract from *Malone Dies*.[12]

That Beckett was seen at the time as a writer with existentialist preoccupations is evident from reviews of his first French works in the early 1950s. For instance, in his review of *Molloy* in *Les Temps Modernes* in July 1951, Jean Pouillon declared that 'Here indeed we have a novel of the "absurd", to use a word which has become convenient, which is presented like an ordinary novel. [...] absurdity is not mysterious at all, it is, as Sartre wrote about *L'Étranger*, "nothing less than the relationship of man to the world"'.[13] There can be little doubt that the existentialist climate in France at the time was a major factor in the largely positive reception of Beckett's work. While he may have resisted the labels 'existentialist' and 'absurdist', Beckett's appreciation of works by Sartre and Camus before his own switch to French, his publication in *Les Temps Modernes* and the thematic concerns of the works he wrote between 1946 and 1950 all suggest strong affinities.

If Beckett was seen by some as continuing a line in French literature initiated by Sartre and Camus, by the early 1950s he was also being appreciated by, and taking an interest in, the work of two writers outside the existentialist fold, both of whom would have a profound impact on later twentieth-century French literary-philosophical culture: Georges Bataille and Maurice Blanchot. The latter's vision of Beckett, as expressed in an essay on *Molloy, Malone Dies* and *The Unnamable* first published in the *NNRF* in October 1953 and later collected in *The Book to Come* (1959), would ultimately be far more influential on the French reception of Beckett than that of the existentialists. Blanchot's first novel, *Thomas the Obscure*, was published in 1941, and was followed by two more full-length novels, *Aminadab* (1942) and *The Most High* (1948), and the short novel *Death Sentence* (1948), alongside the essay collections *Faux Pas* (1943), *The Work of Fire* (1949) and *Lautréamont and Sade* (1949). While *Thomas the Obscure* reads rather like an extended version of Mallarmé's *Igitur* (1869), *Aminadab* bears striking similarities to Kafka (as Sartre observed in his review of the novel shortly after its publication), and *The Most High* bears more than a passing resemblance to Camus' *The Plague*. As for Bataille, his major literary works, *Story of the Eye* (1928) and *Madame Edwarda* (1941), had been published pseudonymously, but, like Blanchot, in the post-war era he was published not only by Gallimard but also by Les Éditions de Minuit, Beckett's publisher. Like Blanchot, too, Bataille wrote admiringly of Beckett in the early 1950s, publishing a long essay on *Molloy* in the 15 May 1951 issue of *Critique*, the post-war journal he had founded.

Although it remains difficult to determine whether Beckett was familiar with Blanchot's novels of the period, his correspondence with Georges Duthuit reveals that in January 1951, at Duthuit's instigation, he read Blanchot's long essay 'Sade's Reason', from *Lautréamont and Sade*, together with Klossowski's *Sade My Neighbour* (1947) and the preface to Blanchot's first collection of critical essays, *Faux Pas* (1943), in which Blanchot makes a statement on the nature of the writer's predicament that is strikingly similar to the one made of the artist in the third of Beckett's *Three Dialogues* (1949) (see *L2*, 219). Blanchot expresses this predicament as follows: 'The writer finds himself in the increasingly ludicrous condition of having nothing to write, of having no means with which to write it, and of being constrained by the utter necessity of always writing it'.[14] Beckett's well-known articulation of the artist's predicament in 'Tal Coat', the first of the *Three Dialogues* (1949), reads: 'The expression that there is nothing to express, nothing with which to express, nothing from which to express, no power to express, no desire to express, together with the obligation to express' (*P*, 103). It is hardly surprising, then, that on 3 January 1951, having completed a translation of Blanchot's essay on Sade, Beckett should have written to Duthuit: 'What emerges from it [...] is a truly gigantic Sade, jealous of Satan and of his eternal torments, and confronting nature more than human-kind' (*L2*, 219). A few days later, Beckett communicated to Duthuit his view that, of all the French commentators on Sade whom he had recently read (Blanchot, Maurice Heine, Klossowski and Gilbert Lely), Blanchot was 'by far the most intelligent' (*L2*, 225). In contrast, he dismissed Klossowski's *Sade My Neighbour* as 'incomparably woolly rubbish' (*L2*, 225). Beckett's appreciation of Blanchot at this time is also evidenced by a remark made in a letter of 25 May 1951 from Beckett's partner, Suzanne Dumesnil, to his publisher, Jérôme Lindon, at Les Éditions de Minuit, regarding the awarding of the Prix des Critiques: 'To have been defended by a man like Blanchot will have been the main thing for Beckett, whatever the outcome' (*L2*, 254).

In the case of both the major existentialists and Blanchot, then, there is evidence to confirm not only Beckett's familiarity with their work, but also his appreciation of it. This is not to say, however, that his own post-war fiction was directly or consciously influenced by readings of Sartre, Camus, Bataille and Blanchot. Any such straightforward contextualising of Beckett's oeuvre would miss precisely the complexity of his relation to the literary world in which he found himself in post-war Paris. It is, rather, a matter of conjunctions that never quite settle into comfortably stable structures of determinable influence. A similar point can be made of Beckett's relation to those writers who came to prominence in the early to mid-1950s under the banner of the *nouveau roman*, especially Michel Butor, Alain Robbe-Grillet and Claude Simon, all of whom were, like Beckett, published by Les Éditions de Minuit. Robbe-Grillet's novel *A Regicide* was published in 1949, followed in 1953 by *The Erasers*, which won the Prix Fénéon in 1954. In February 1953, Robbe-Grillet published an essay on *Godot* in Bataille's journal, *Critique*, and, in a letter of 17 February 1953 to his publisher, Beckett described the essay as 'excellent, by far the best I have read'. He went on to enquire when *The Erasers* would be published (*L2*, 366).[15] While there are notable similarities in the ways that Beckett and Robbe-Grillet challenge the conventions of prose fiction and play on the detective fiction genre, these similarities do not resolve themselves easily into structures of determinable influence. That said, these similarities no doubt accounted for those authors published by Minuit being seen both by readers and by commentators in the 1950s as forming a group of sorts, sharing certain aesthetic principles (above all, that the traditional form of the novel, to which both Sartre and Camus remained committed, was no longer adequate). Furthermore, as was the case with the existentialists, so with the *nouveaux romanciers*, the very fact that Beckett's post-war French works could be placed in relation to them no doubt helped to ensure his remarkable success in post-war France.

Beckett's considerable interest in the visual arts, which led to his spending six months in Germany before the war (1936–7), continued into the post-war era, and took the form of regular visits to exhibitions, personal contact with artists, numerous translations (and revisions of others' translations) of writings on art for Duthuit's *Transition*, as well as the writing of art criticism. In January 1947, for instance, Beckett visited the Van Gogh exhibition at the Musée de l'Orangerie, as well as the Bonnard exhibition. Over two years later, in a letter of 9 June 1949 to Duthuit, he placed Van Gogh alongside Cézanne as a painter whose work he considered 'Apoplectic, bursting at the arteries', and thus quite unlike the kind of painting that Beckett was at that time championing, namely painting that was 'poor, undisguisedly useless, incapable of any image whatever' (*L2*, 166). Among those who also visited the 1947 Van Gogh exhibition was Antonin Artaud, recently released from the asylum at Rodez and living in Ivry, just outside Paris. Unlike Beckett, Artaud's assessment of Van Gogh, as expressed in *Van Gogh, the Man Suicided by Society* (published in late 1947), was entirely positive. In addition to his short book on Van Gogh, the other major public intervention by Artaud at this time was the reading from his own recent writings that he gave on 13 January 1947 at the Théâtre du Vieux Colombier. Just over a year later, on 4 March 1948, Artaud was found dead in his room at Ivry, on the walls of which were pinned many of his own drawings, including a number of remarkable self-portraits. Beckett's awareness of Artaud at this time is evidenced in a letter of 18 March 1948 to Thomas MacGreevy, which contains the laconic one-sentence paragraph: 'Artaud died the other day in Lucia's home at Ivry' (*L2*, 75).[16]

The immediate post-war years in Paris were a period during which Beckett devoted considerable energy to supporting the work of two painters who in the late 1940s were as little known in France as he was: brothers Geer and Bram van Velde, on whom he wrote two important essays. The first of these essays, 'La Peinture des van Velde or le monde et le pantalon', was commissioned by the magazine *Cahiers d'Art*, in anticipation of the Geer van Velde exhibition at the Galerie Maeght and the Bram van Velde exhibition at the Galerie Mai, both of which opened in March 1946.[17] The second essay, 'Peintres de l'empêchement', was published in *Derrière le Miroir* in June 1948. In these two essays, Beckett sought not only to take his distance from traditional forms of art criticism, but also to question the validity of any attempt to write about painting. At the same time, he proposed radical views on the van Velde brothers' art, and saw in Bram van Velde an artist who, in his opinion, was the first to break with the age-old conception of painting as having an object: according to Beckett, Bram van Velde painted that which made painting impossible.

As his extensive reflections on art, and above all on Bram van Velde, in his letters to Georges Duthuit in 1949 reveal, the paradoxicality of such a claim was not lost on Beckett. Although in his letters to Duthuit he expresses reservations about Bram van Velde's art that are not found in the *Three Dialogues*, Beckett nonetheless acknowledges that, for him, Bram van Velde's is a 'painting without precedent, in which as in no other I find what I am seeking, precisely because of this fidelity to the prison-house, this refusal of any probationary freedom'.[18]

Through his friendship with Duthuit, Beckett came into contact with some of the key figures in the post-war Parisian art world, including André Breton, to whom Duthuit introduced him in April 1948.[19] Duthuit took over editorial control of Eugene Jolas's *transition* magazine in 1947, changing its title by capitalising it, and redirecting its focus from the literary to the visual arts. While Jolas was retained as an editorial adviser, the editorial board now included Sartre, Bataille, the critic Max-Pol Fouchet, the philosopher Jean Wahl and the poet René Char; the young poet André du Bouchet was Duthuit's secretary for a time, and acquaintances included the artists Alberto Giacometti, Nicolas de Staël, André Masson, Pierre Tal-Coat, Jean-Paul Riopelle, Sam Francis and Norman Blum.[20]

When Beckett was first approached (by Maria Jolas) in the summer of 1947 to act as a translator for Duthuit's *Transition*, he declined the invitation, feeling that such work would interfere with what was proving to be an unprecedentedly fertile phase in his writing life.[21] However, his extremely precarious financial situation soon led him to reconsider this decision, and in the later 1940s he became Duthuit's principal translator, although insisting on not receiving credit for the translations (and the revisions of others' translations) that he undertook for the magazine. Translations by Beckett that appeared in *Transition* between 1948 and 1950 include those of texts by some of the major figures in post-war Paris, including René Char, Paul Éluard, Henri Michaux, Henri Pichette, Francis Ponge and Jacques Prévert.[22] Beckett's translation of Guillaume Apollinaire's poem 'Zone' was also first published in *Transition*.[23] In addition to alleviating his dire financial situation in the immediate post-war years, these translation duties ensured that Beckett remained in touch with developments in French literature, on which he expressed some strong views. For instance, he dismissed an essay by Ponge on Georges Braque as 'revolting',[24] and of a piece by du Bouchet, most probably on André Masson, Pierre Tal-Coat and Joan Miró, he wrote to Duthuit: 'My fondness for André warns me off any comment'.[25]

Beckett's relationship with Duthuit quickly developed into a close intellectual friendship, and from 1948 to 1952 Duthuit became his principal confidant on matters artistic. Beckett's letters to Duthuit, many of them written during the period when he was writing *L'Innommable*, contain extended reflections on aesthetics in general and on the art of painting in particular. These exchanges with Duthuit led in 1949 to the idea of the *Three Dialogues*, in which 'B.' and 'D.' exchange views on the work of André Masson, Pierre Tal-Coat and the (at that time) still largely unknown Bram van Velde. First published in the December 1949 issue of *Transition*, the *Dialogues* reveal Beckett to have had views on painting that were no less extreme than (if very different from) those expressed by Artaud two years earlier in *Van Gogh, the Man Suicided by Society*. And like the pre-war Artaud, the post-war Beckett would also intervene decisively in the world of French theatre.

If Paris saw a number of major art exhibitions in the immediate post-war years, it also witnessed some important new theatrical productions and, more significantly, the emergence of a number of new theatre directors who would go on to become major figures in the French theatrical world. Productions of works by writers at the heart of the existentialist movement included Sartre's *Dirty Hands* and Camus' *State of Siege* in 1948, and the latter's *The Just Assassins* in 1949. The existentialist theatre remained, however, for the most part decidedly traditional in its attachment to the idea of the well-made play. In contrast, a number of small theatres opened after the war in which far less traditional works were first performed. The key producers of these new, more theatrically challenging works included Roger Blin, Jean-Marie Serreau and Jean Vilar.

Among the most innovative playwrights of the period was Jean Genet. His play *The Maids* was first staged at the Athénée in 1947, in a production directed by Louis Jouvet, and *Death Watch*, co-directed by Genet, was staged at the Mathurins in 1949. As David Bradby observes, while both Sartre and Camus failed to find a new theatrical form, *The Maids* contained 'many of the features of the New Theatre of the 1950s', in which Beckett would be the leading figure.[26] Arguably the most important influence on the new theatre, Antonin Artaud, was not directly involved in it, although, as mentioned previously, on 13 January 1947 he appeared at the Théâtre du Vieux Colombier. In an extraordinary performance, Artaud recounted the story of his inner life and sought to read the texts 'The Return of Artaud the Momo', 'Indian Culture' and 'Centre Mère et Patron Minet'.[27]

A pre-war figure associated with Artaud whose work achieved a new audience in the immediate post-war years was Roger Vitrac. In 1926,

Vitrac had worked with Artaud towards a new kind of theatre (at that time called the 'Alfred Jarry Theatre', after the author of the *Ubu* plays), which was, as Martin Esslin puts it, to be 'a theatre of the fantastic and grotesque, of dream and obsession'.[28] From November 1946 to January 1947, a revival of Vitrac's *Victor, or, Power to the Children* ran at the Théâtre de la Gaîté-Montparnasse; Beckett saw this production shortly before he wrote his own first completed play, *Eleutheria* (written in January–February 1947), in which the main character is also named Victor. Another figure associated with Artaud was Roger Blin, who would produce *Waiting for Godot* in 1953 at Jean-Marie Serreau's tiny Théâtre du Babylone. Like Serreau, Blin had trained with the actor-director Charles Dullin, who, with his conception of 'total theatre', exerted considerable influence on Artaud in the 1920s; and, as Beckett was aware, Blin himself had been a friend of Artaud's. Thus, while Artaud's conception of a 'Theatre of Cruelty' might not have impacted directly on Beckett as a writer, it nonetheless passed by way of Blin into the original production of *Godot*, Lucky's speech in particular no doubt reminding some in the audience of the Artaud who had appeared at the Théâtre du Vieux Colombier six years earlier.

Just as he visited art exhibitions and concerts in the late 1940s, so, despite his dire financial predicament, Beckett took in some of the key theatrical productions, both classical and avant-garde.[29] In June 1948, for instance, he saw a production of Racine's *Andromache* at the Comédie-Française, and – crucially, as it would turn out, for his own future as a writer for the stage – he attended two performances of Roger Blin's production of August Strindberg's *The Ghost Sonata*, which ran at the Théâtre de la Gaîté-Montparnasse from 23 October 1949 to 13 February 1950. It has often been said that it was on account of seeing this production that Beckett subsequently offered *Godot* to Blin; less often noted is Beckett's decidedly negative view of Blin's production of the Strindberg play. As he wrote of Blin in a letter addressed to Duthuit on 27 February 1950: 'Nice fellow, very Montparnasse. I know him well by sight, great friend of Artaud [...]. Not very good either as actor or as director, if I am to judge by the *Sonata* that we saw, along with 17 other people, but great love of theatre' (*L2*, 182).

The first works of what would come to be labelled the 'Theatre of the Absurd' reached the stage in 1950; that is, after Beckett had completed *Godot* (written between October 1948 and January 1949). Three important new productions were staged in that year alone: Arthur Adamov's *The Great and the Small Manoeuvre*, in a production directed by Jean-Marie Serreau, at the Noctambules; his *The Invasion*, in a production directed by

Jean Vilar, at the Studio des Champs-Élysées; and Eugene Ionesco's *The Bald Prima Donna*, in a production directed by Nicolas Bataille, at the Noctambules. While Beckett had completed *Godot* prior to these productions, they nonetheless established an environment in which producers were more likely to consider staging Beckett. As early as 1948, Jean Vilar was prepared to contemplate a production of *Eleutheria*, although this came to nothing. Only two years later, however, it was clear that a new kind of theatre was emerging, within which Beckett would soon find his place. For a sign of just how much Beckett's status within Parisian literary circles had changed since his return to Paris after the war, one need look no further than his list of those to whom complimentary copies of the published text of *Godot* were to be sent in October 1952, before the play's production: this list included Arthur Adamov, Gaston Bachelard, Georges Bataille, Maurice Blanchot, Eugene Ionesco, Tristan Tzara and Jean Wahl.

According to Pascale Casanova, the post-war Beckett should be seen as a figure who sought 'to participate in the Parisian "factory" of modernity', the Paris to which he committed himself being 'the international capital of artists who refused to submit to a national vision. For Beckett, to live in the French capital and defend the art produced there was not in itself a choice in favour of France, which would repeat the nationalist assumption, but a demand for international (or anti-national) autonomy'.[30] It is precisely for this reason that it would be a mistake to see Beckett's switch to French in March 1946 as an attempt to locate himself squarely within a French literary tradition. Similarly, any analysis of his relation to his post-war Parisian context would fail to grasp the complexity of that relation were it not to emphasise his ambiguous relation to it. As we have seen, his post-war work undoubtedly bears traces of that context, but the identification of these traces in terms of influence or affinity would inevitably efface the contingent side to the relation between Beckett's post-war texts and their context, and would also underestimate what is among the most significant characteristics of Beckett's art, namely its resistance not only to nationalism, as Casanova argues, but also to various literary-philosophical '-isms', not least existentialism and absurdism. For Beckett, as he put it in his 'Homage to Jack B. Yeats' (1954), 'The artist who stakes his being is from nowhere' (*D*, 149).[31] Things are, however, not quite so simple. Not only did Beckett read, view and appreciate the works of writers and artists in post-war Paris, but, as we have seen, his oeuvre also shares with theirs a number of major preoccupations. Furthermore, the reception of his post-war works in the early 1950s was so positive not least because those works seemed particularly relevant in the context out of which they came and from which their author sought so assiduously to remove them. It is only by reflecting upon the ambiguous nature of Beckett's relation to his cultural context that one can begin to assess what it is that makes him seem, even today, a writer we cannot afford to ignore.

NOTES

1 As James Knowlson observes, the Beckett of 1946 was 'almost totally unknown as a French writer' (*K*, 359).
2 An indication of just how harsh the immediate post-war years in Paris were for Beckett is to be found in a letter he wrote to Thomas MacGreevy from his apartment at 6 rue des Favorites on 24 November 1947: 'No heating in this house for the 6th year in succession. Things are very bad, with a badness that won't lead anywhere I fear' (*L2*, 65).
3 Samuel Beckett, undated interview with Lawrence E. Harvey; quoted in *K*, 358.
4 Duthuit's post-war *Transition* described itself as 'the only English-language review entirely devoted to contemporary French writing'.
5 A (heavily censored) pre-book-publication extract from Beckett's *The Unnamable* was published under the title 'Mahood' in the 1 February 1953 issue of the *NNRF*, alongside texts by Valéry Larbaud, Jean Grenier, Roger Caillois and Saint-John Perse.
6 Albert Camus, *The Myth of Sisyphus*, trans. Justin O'Brien (Harmondsworth: Penguin, 1975), 11.
7 Letter to Thomas McGreevy, 26 May 1938, in *L1*, 626.
8 As James Knowlson observes, Beckett made Sartre's acquaintance before the war, through their mutual friend Alfred Péron (*K*, 359).
9 On the complications that arose regarding this publication, see Dirk Van Hulle, 'Publishing "The End": Beckett and *Les Temps modernes*', in Mark Nixon (ed.), *Publishing Samuel Beckett* (London: British Library, 2011), 73–82.
10 The texts alongside which Beckett's appeared included the final part of Sartre's 'Materialism and Revolution', an extract from Genet's *The Thief's Journal*, Francis Ponge's 'Ad Litem', and Pichette's 'Apoem I'.
11 It should be noted, however, that the story was placed for Beckett by his then literary agent, Jacoba van Velde, while he had assumed that it was to be published in another journal, *Fontaine*. Thus one cannot conclude that Beckett actively sought to rub textual shoulders with those at the heart of the existentialist movement; on the peritextual implications of this, see Van Hulle, 'Publishing "The End"', 76–7.
12 'Poèmes 38–39', *Les Temps Modernes* (November 1946); 'Quel malheur ...', *Les Temps Modernes* (September 1951).
13 Jean Pouillon, review of *Molloy*, trans. Françoise Longhurst, in Lawrence Graver and Raymond Federman (eds.), *Samuel Beckett: The Critical Heritage* (London: Routledge and Kegan Paul, 1979), 65.

14 Maurice Blanchot, *Faux Pas*, trans. Charlotte Mandell (Stanford: Stanford University Press, 2001), 3.
15 Robbe-Grillet's novel *The Erasers* was published by Minuit on 27 February 1953.
16 The Lucia to whom Beckett refers in this letter is Lucia Joyce, James Joyce's daughter.
17 The essay was published in *Cahiers d'Art* 20–1 (1945–6).
18 Letter to Georges Duthuit, 2 March 1949, in *L2*, 130.
19 As Rémi Labrusse observes, 'Although Beckett had probably introduced the van Velde brothers to Duthuit, he was himself most indebted to his friend for his new social life in the Parisian art world': Rémi Labrusse, 'Samuel Beckett and Georges Duthuit', in Fionnuala Croke (ed.), *Samuel Beckett: A Passion for Paintings* (Dublin: National Gallery of Ireland, 2006), p. 89.
20 Beckett had met Alberto Giacometti in the 1930s, but also spent time with him in the post-war years; see, for instance, Beckett's letter to Duthuit on 10 September 1951, in *L2*, 294.
21 See Beckett's letter to Maria Jolas, 2 August 1947, in *L2*, 58.
22 See John Pilling and Seán Lawlor, 'Beckett in Transition', in Mark Nixon (ed.), *Publishing Samuel Beckett* (London: British Library, 2011), 88.
23 In *Transition Fifty*, no. 6. This issue of *Transition* also contained extracts (in Beckett's own English translation) from *Molloy* and *Malone Dies*, neither of which had yet been published in the original French.
24 Letter to Georges Duthuit, 1 March 1949, in *L2*, 122. The essay in question was 'Braque, or Modern Art as Event and Pleasure'.
25 Letter to Georges Duthuit, April or May 1949, in *L2*, 148.
26 David Bradby, *Modern French Drama 1940–1980* (Cambridge: Cambridge University Press, 1984), 54.
27 See Évelyne Grossman, *Antonin Artaud. Un insurgé du corps* (Paris: Gallimard, 2006), 92–3.
28 Martin Esslin, *Artaud* (London: John Calder, 1976), 27.
29 In a letter of 4 January 1948 to Thomas MacGreevy, Beckett complained that he had not been able to afford to go to concerts or exhibitions since his return from Menton in September 1947; see *L2*, 73.
30 Pascale Casanova, *Samuel Beckett: Anatomy of a Literary Revolution*, trans. Gregory Elliott (London: Verso, 2006), 83.
31 The 'Homage' was first published, in French, in *Les Lettres Nouvelles* (April 1954).

CHAPTER 15

Staging Plays

Anthony Uhlmann

The concept of dramatic production which emerges through the works of Samuel Beckett and his practice as a director of his own plays seems openly antagonistic to those which have dominated twentieth-century assumptions. The ideas of the Russian director and theorist Stanislavski, and others such as Grotowski, have so colonised our understanding of theatre and acting practice that they have come to assume the status of laws of nature. Yet Beckett challenges both the role of the actor and the role of the director. In their place, he developed a different model of theatre practice, one which attempted to achieve a unified effect, with the actors, director and all other components subordinated to an expression inherent within and structured by the play text itself.

A convenient way of attempting to avoid anxieties around questions of 'intention' and authorial control which might be asked here is to admit, with James Knowlson, that an author's interpretation of his own work is not sacrosanct, and others are free to interpret Beckett's plays how they see fit, and this is apparent in performance history as the work of Kalb, Bradby and others shows.[1]

While Samuel Beckett's apparent desire for control over the performances of his plays during his lifetime, and the subsequent ongoing insistence of the Beckett Estate that his stage directions be closely adhered to, is well known, it is useful to detail the control Beckett extended over productions of his work while he was alive. In her biography of Beckett, Bair states that 'whenever possible, he tries to maintain absolute control over all productions; when not possible, he ignores them' (*B*, 675). Both Kenneth Tynan – when he changed the script of *Breath* – and JoAnne Akalaitis – when she tampered with the stage directions to *Endgame* – were threatened with legal action (*B*, 640–1).[2] In his letter to Akalaitis, who had changed the setting of *Endgame* to an abandoned New York subway car for her 1984 production, he stated that 'Any production which ignores my stage directions is completely unacceptable to me'.[3] Indeed, the stage directions to his plays, especially those written after *Happy Days* in 1961, might be seen to further emphasise Beckett's desire for control. Some of these plays include diagrams explaining movements of the characters and giving detailed instructions on the level and pitch of voice desirable. It is almost as if the plays have been 'blocked' within the text. As Enoch Brater notes: 'Stage directions multiply as Beckett begins to challenge the theater's traditional function as a collaborative and interpretive art'.[4] Brater concludes that 'What is at stake ... is ... control, how to translate Beckett's private image into the public forum that is theater'.[5] To quote from Deirdre Bair:

> For Beckett, the perfect stage vehicle is one in which there are no actors or directors, only the play itself. When asked how such theatre could be made viable, Beckett replied that the author had the duty to search for the perfect actor, that is, one who would comply fully with his instructions, having the ability to annihilate himself totally.
>
> 'Not for me these Grotowskis and Methods', Beckett storms. 'The best possible play is one in which there are no actors, only the text. I'm trying to find a way to write one'. (*B*, 544)

Continuing this theme elsewhere, Beckett stated, 'I hate this modern school of directing.... To these directors the text is just a pretext for their own ingenuity'.[6]

Traditionally the author has occupied a privileged position in relation to his or her own work (a position famously critiqued by Foucault and others). He or she is the centre, at once inside and outside the structure, and the function of this centre is to at once enable and limit the play of meaning. However, this author function has never been so wholly accepted in the theatre. The genre of theatre poses unique challenges to the authority of the author, as this authority is, to a large extent, usurped by the director and the actors who, in contextualising the writing for a specific performance, come between the written work and the audience. It is clear that, in working in the theatre, Beckett strove to challenge this established power structure, by, as it were, writing a unified expression into the texts themselves.

As Knowlson has noted, Beckett's notebooks 'reveal a careful choreography of word and gesture, sound and silence, movement and stillness ... all the different elements that are involved in staging a play ... are ... intricately integrated with the play's thematics'.[7] Speaking to Rosette Lamont in Paris in 1983, when asked how he began to write drama, Beckett replied: 'When I was working on *Watt* I felt the need to create for a smaller space, one in which I had some control of where people stood or moved, above all of a certain light. I wrote *Waiting for Godot*'.[8]

The concept of dramatic production which emerges through Samuel Beckett's practice as a director of his own plays seems openly antagonistic to those realist traditions developed by Stanislavski and others which have dominated twentieth-century assumptions.

Yet an alternative tradition might be found in the theories of English stage designer and theorist, Edward Gordon Craig. Writing in 1911, and strongly influenced by Heinrich Von Kleist's 1810 story (or essay in story form) 'On the Marionette Theatre', Craig suggested that acting was not an art because 'Art arrives only by design ... to make any work of art it is clear we may only work in those materials with which we can calculate. Man is not one of these materials'.[9] He argued that when ruled by emotion (as is the case with the 'realist' approach) actors lose control over their bodies and their voices, and, accordingly, what they produce is no more than a series of, perhaps interesting, accidents. As an alternative to 'realism' he envisaged the 'uber-marionette':

> The uber-marionette will not compete with life – rather it will go beyond it. Its ideal will not be the flesh and blood but rather the body in trance – it will aim to clothe itself with a death-like beauty while exhaling a living spirit.[10]

The difference between Craig's and Stanislavski's approaches can be summarised through an illuminating anecdote from Christopher Innes' book on Craig:

> By 1907 Stanislavski was ... in search of a deeper kind of realism that would reflect 'the life of the human spirit'. But his experiments with symbolist drama ... had been unsuccessful. The acting techniques he had developed for internalizing emotion and translating unexpressed thoughts into physical action were useless for plays that had abstract figures and no subtext.... Maeterlinck had complained [to Stanislavski] that the mystical level of his Bluebird fantasy was totally missing [from Stanislavski's production]. So, prompted by Isadora Duncan ... and impressed by the first copy of [Craig's book] *The Mask*, Stanislavski invited Craig to direct *Hamlet* for the Art Theater.[11]

Although the two men worked closely on the project, and Stanislavski had a great deal to do with the rehearsal of the actors, it is interesting that Stanislavski felt the need to call upon Craig. He clearly realised the limitations of his own ideas in productions of a certain type of play. From this it might be further argued that Beckett considered his style of direction, in which he wanted to precisely control the movements and voice quality of his actors, as necessary to the adequate production of his drama.

Craig considered his own Kleistian idea of uber-marionette as 'an impossible state of perfection', and claimed that he was looking to the actors to perfect their own craft.[12] Yet Beckett, who had a strong interest in Kleist's 'On the Marionette Theatre', seemed to push these ideas even further and made every effort to attempt to realise this impossible state of perfection. His direction might have been an attempt to impose it. Needless to say, circumstances would intervene in each performance, and the 'perfection' would never quite be achieved[13] – still, the actors were rehearsed to perform particular gestures at precise moments, to place their hands in exact positions, to walk in a particular manner, to use the exact tone of voice for the repetition of certain phrases. Beckett demanded an extraordinary self-control from his actors.

Beckett professed admiration for Kleist's story 'On the Marionette Theatre' on more than one occasion and indicated that he was seeking to develop some of its insights into his own performance practice. James Knowlson tells us Beckett visited Kleist's grave in 1969, and knew lines from *The Prince of Homburg* by heart (*K*, 569). He also outlines how Beckett made use of and referred to 'On the Marionette Theatre' while rehearsing the production of *Happy Days* he directed at the Schiller-Theater in Berlin in 1971, in arguing that 'precision and economy would produce the maximum of grace' (*K*, 584). Then again, in 1975, while assisting at the production of his television play *Ghost Trio*, Beckett spoke with both the principal actor Ronald Pickup and with Knowlson about the importance of Kleist's marionette story to understanding what he was attempting to do in this piece. As Knowlson describes it, Beckett more or less recounted Kleist's story in total. Firstly, he outlined how the principles of grace and harmony related to the puppets detailed in the story might be applied to the processes he was attempting to develop. Then he recounted the third part of Kleist's story concerning the bear that, in lacking self-awareness, and so human self-consciousness, therefore possesses both a more precise grace and a more comprehensive intuition with regard to the movement of bodies than any self-conscious person might (*K*, 632–3).

Beckett's breaking with Stanislavskian procedures is partly to do with the problematisation of meaning. Method actors want to know why they do things; they crave 'motivation' and they need to make sense of the character's actions, even if that sense is that the character is irrational. This approach not only makes it difficult to control the pace of a performance (important to the musical structure of the works),[14] but might be seen as reductive, especially when it is applied to a system which seems to highlight the impossibility of such reduction. Because a unified expression (or a line of intention) is written into Beckett's play text, Beckett, when he directed his own plays, had no choice but to see his actors as puppets. The interpretations of their roles, have, in large part, like the director's, already been written.

Due to the demand for faithfulness to his vision it is perhaps not surprising that there were a number of actors and directors with whom Beckett habitually worked. Among his favourite actors were Patrick Magee, Jack MacGowran, Billie Whitelaw and Madelaine Renaud, and among his favourite directors were Donald McWhinnie, Alan Schneider and Walter Asmus. On the whole he inspired these select with loyalty which seemed to be built, speaking on a professional, rather than a personal level, on the belief that while Beckett set definite limits to the interpretation of his plays within which the actor or director might work, an acceptance of these limits was both challenging and liberating. This point has been made by Whitelaw and by MacGowran and Schneider.[15]

The notion that he was 'trusting' his directors with his plays is underlined by Beckett's American director, Alan Schneider:

[A]ll of his texts – and that word includes both dialogue and stage directions – have always been 'Sam's' to me, a marriage in absentia, in which I have loved, honoured and obeyed as though he were always with me.[16]

Schneider's situation differed from some of the other directors I have mentioned because he only ever worked directly with Beckett on the screenplay *Film*. Though he met with Beckett often and spoke with him at length about his productions, Beckett was never present at Schneider's rehearsals, and so Schneider deferred directly to the stage directions. It is interesting to contrast Schneider's views with the comments of Donald McWhinnie, who worked more directly with Beckett:

He's very free about stage business, about areas of dialogue, about whether Hamm is mad, for example. But about certain areas of the text, and about the importance of rhythm, he is rigid.... There's a kind of musical guide to the structure of his speech that is more important than the interpretation of his speech.... He wants to get it as exact as the human instrument can get it.[17]

As Brater has noted, what is involved here is clearly a concern with control, with the insistence on the setting down of certain limitations.

Knowlson and Chabert, among others, suggest that the changes Beckett made in directing his own plays should be taken into account.[18] That is, because of the way in which Beckett perceived his plays, with the role of the director severely limited because of the presence of a unified expression within the texts, his own direction, in which important changes are made, should be seen as a continuation of the writing process.

Production notebooks which Beckett prepared for the Schiller-Theater performances of *Krapp's Last Tape*, *Endgame*, *Waiting for Godot* and the Royal Court production of *Happy Days*, along with productions of his late shorter plays were published by Faber and Faber in the late 1980s and early 1990s, and although these are now largely out of print and rare, they are held in many libraries. The originals of these notebooks are held in 'The Samuel Beckett Collection' of Reading University, and their publication was a project overseen by James Knowlson.

An examination of the various changes Beckett introduced into the productions he directed reveals that they might be divided into three main types. First are changes made to come to terms with specific problems of staging a particular production of a play. As Knowlson notes, 'Beckett has always been willing to modify his text in the light of difficulties encountered or highlighted by the process of staging a play'.[19] For example, in the Berlin production of *Krapp's Last Tape* Rick Cluchey was unable to pronounce 'Connaught' and so the word 'Kerry' was substituted.[20] Neither Madeleine Renaud nor Billie Whitelaw fitted the description of Winnie outlined in Beckett's text, yet their talents as actors were seen to offset this deficiency and so that stage direction was ignored (*B*, 599). Because of Pierre Chabert's 'relative youth, Beckett dressed him in a frayed dressing-gown to hide his tall frame, a toque to hide his abundant hair, and black half-gloves that evoke premonitions of death'.[21] Also included in this category of changes are those which Beckett described as 'variations' rather than true changes, such as Hamm being given white glasses instead of dark.[22] These changes were prompted by necessity, and so couldn't be said to be attempts to modify the original unified expression.

A second class of change includes changes made to emphasise a thematic contrast. Beckett seems to have used contrast as an organising principle. In his productions of *Krapp* Beckett consistently emphasised the thematic contrasts between light and dark, motion and stillness, silence and noise.[23] To assist in this contrast he simplified the action at the beginning of the play, removing material that was not 'relevant' to the play of these contrasts.[24] In directing *Endgame* he added stage directions which designated Clov's place on stage as being halfway between Hamm and the door to the kitchen, and this emphasised the contrast between his desire to leave Hamm and his inability to leave Hamm.[25] In directing Billie Whitelaw in *Happy Days* Beckett sharpened the contrast between the first and second acts. Through the use of makeup and Whitelaw's tones of voice Winnie's vitality in act one seemed much diminished in act two.[26] In *Godot*, Beckett substituted a stone for the 'low mound' of the original, to emphasise the contrast between Vladimir, associated with the tree, lightness, the air, and Estragon, associated with the stone, heaviness of spirit, the earth.[27] Such changes as these might be considered the addition of 'emphasis'. As such they are an important means of establishing views as to how Beckett endeavoured to structure his plays. He also worked closely with the actors in establishing voice, and a contrast of voice, so that, for example, moments of vitality would stand out from the flat grey tones which provided the general background.[28] Such emphasis then, might be seen as, in part, an interpretation of the works, as it seems to achieve an underscoring of elements already present.

A third category of changes might also be said to be concerned with emphasis. The use of repetition, like the use of contrast, might be regarded as an organising principle in Beckett's work.[29] The production notebooks seem largely organised around motif or repetition.[30] Beckett often mentioned that he was attempting to achieve something akin to musical structure, and his use of repetition as a playwright, and the emphasis he put on this repetition as a director, are clear attempts to approximate a motif-oriented musical structure.[31] Ruby Cohn has outlined Beckett's five-point approach to the direction of his plays in Germany. The first point was concerned with the correction of the original German translation by Elmar Tophoven.[32] Many of the emendations Beckett made to Tophoven's translation consisted of changing variant phrases to exact repetitions.[33] This brought the German text more into line with the English and French versions where exact repetitions are used.[34] In rehearsing his actors Beckett would often insist that these repeated phrases be repeated in exactly the same tone of voice.[35] In directing *Footfalls* he wanted M to assume Amy's voice and V to assume May's 'equating May with Amy'.[36] He also added a number of gestures, and Pierre Chabert has stated that Beckett never added a gesture to the performance without having that gesture repeated.[37] He was also keen to have the actors draw attention to the gestures by making them in an elaborate, or non-realistic manner so that the audience might recognise the gesture when it was repeated and become aware of the repetition.[38]

It is also apparent that these ideas of repetition and contrast interconnect. I have mentioned that the 'changes' Beckett made to include more repetition, or highlight contrast are changes to do with 'emphasis'. More than this however, one formal device is linked to the other. A tone of voice might be used repetitively for the majority of the play so that, when there is variation, the contrast, and the meaning implicit in that contrast is made more apparent.[39] In the same way, the play of contrasts, such as the light/dark imagery apparent in *Krapp*, are so emphasised that we become aware of their repetition. While directing *Endgame* in Germany Beckett told his actors that 'There are no accidents in *Endgame*; everything is built on analogy and repetition'.[40] Having quoted this statement Ruby Cohn goes on to suggest that analogy and repetition supply symmetry to Beckett's production of *Endgame*.[41] Explicit in the symmetry she details is a notion of pairing, which can inevitably be linked with dichotomy. In repetition there is always contrast. Something can never be done 'the same' as before. The status of a phrase or action is immediately altered once we realise it is being repeated. As Estragon states (in a phrase that seems to allude to Heraclitus' stream where it is impossible to stand in the same water twice): 'It's never the same pus from one second to the next' (*CDW*, 56). Such repetition makes the audience aware of patterning, of a limiting structure. The characters inhabit a world in which habit establishes not only a sense of order, but also limitation, and such limitation, if necessary to their survival, is also necessarily oppressive. Beckett wanted his actors to imagine a fourth wall in *Endgame*, at the proscenium arch: he was not using this so much as the standard theatrical device, but because he wanted his actors to be aware of their confinement, the limitations of their world, which he further emphasised by removing all reference to Clov going outside to fetch sand.[42] These spatial limitations are underscored by the limitations apparent through habit and repetition. These oppressive limits eventually succeed, not only in *Endgame*, but in *Godot*, *Krapp*, *Happy Days*, *Play*, *Rockaby* and other of the plays, in throwing the characters back upon themselves. The repetition of action and word is like a gradual constriction; with each repetition, the noose is pulled tighter until something gives or fades. Winnie's position in *Happy Days* is emblematic of the constriction I refer to. Repetition then, at once establishes a sense of order and unease. Chaos is admitted to form.

I would suggest that many of the changes Beckett made to his productions of his plays were made in an effort to emphasise or highlight formal characteristics already apparent in the texts of the plays, and help to construct a unified field of meaning. His direction, then, might be described as a attempt to organise or stage an expression rather than offering an interpretation. His direction consisted of the direction of the potentials for understanding that at once enable and limit meaning.

NOTES

1 James Knowlson (ed.), *Happy Days: Samuel Beckett's Production Notebook* (London: Faber and Faber, 1985), 13. Jonathan Kalb, *Beckett in Performance*

(Cambridge: Cambridge University Press, 1989). David Bradby, *Waiting for Godot (Plays in Production)* (Cambridge: Cambridge University Press, 2001).
2 Enoch Brater, *Why Beckett* (London Thames and Hudson, 1989), 84, 107.
3 Ibid., 107.
4 Ibid.
5 Ibid.
6 Ibid.
7 Knowlson, *Happy Days*, 13.
8 Dougald McMillan and Martha Fehsenfeld, *Beckett in the Theatre: The Author as practical Playwright and Director. Volume 1: From* Waiting for Godot *to* Krapp's Last Tape (London: John Calder, 1988), 15.
9 Edward Gordon Craig, *On the Art of the Theatre* (New York: Theatre Arts Books, 1956), 55–6.
10 Ibid., 84–5.
11 Christopher Innes, *Edward Gordon Craig* (Cambridge: Cambridge University Press, 1983), 149–50.
12 Ibid., 124.
13 See James Knowlson, 'State of play: performance changes and Beckett scholarship', *Journal of Beckett Studies* (10: 1985), 111–12; Ruby Cohn, *Just Play: Beckett's Theater* (Princeton: Princeton University Press, 1980), 266, Brater, *Why Beckett*, 83; Ruby Cohn, 'Beckett's German *Godot*', *Journal of Beckett Studies* (1: Winter 1976), 48.
14 See Martin Esslin, 'Review: *Godot*, the Authorized Version (Schiller Theater Company at the Royal Court Theatre)', *Journal of Beckett Studies* (1: Winter 1976), 99.
15 Billie Whitelaw, 'Practical aspects of theatre, radio and television: Extracts from an unscripted interview with Billie Whitelaw by James Knowlson. A television recording made on 1 February 1977 for the University of London Audio-Visual Centre' *Journal of Beckett Studies* (3: Summer 1978), 89, Alan Schneider, '"Any Way You Like, Alan": Working with Beckett', *Theatre Quarterly* (V.19: 1975), 35–6.
16 Ibid., 28.
17 McMillan and Fehsenfeld, *Beckett in the Theatre*, 176.
18 Pierre Chabert, 'Samuel Beckett as Director', in James Knowlson (ed.), *Theatre Workbook 1, Samuel Beckett: Krapp's Last Tape. A Theatre Workbook edited by James Knowlson*, trans. M. A. Bonney and James Knowlson (London: Brutus Books Limited, 1980), 85–6; James Knowlson (ed.), *Happy Days: Samuel Beckett's Production Notebook* (London: Faber and Faber, 1985), 12.
19 James Knowlson, 'State of play', 108.
20 James Knowlson (ed.), *Theatre Workbook 1*, 26.
21 Ruby Cohn, *Just Play*, 248.
22 McMillan and Fehsenfeld, *Beckett in the Theatre*, 190–1, 178.
23 See James Knowlson (ed.), *Happy Days*, 16–17; James Knowlson, '*Krapp's Last Tape*: The Evolution of a Play, 1958–75', *Journal of Beckett Studies* (1: Winter 1976), 50–65.

24 James Knowlson, '*Krapp's Last Tape*: The Evolution of a Play', 52.
25 McMillan and Fehsenfeld, *Beckett in the Theatre*, 194–5.
26 See Knowlson, *Happy Days*, 16–17.
27 Cohn, *Just Play*, 262; Walter D. Asmus, 'Beckett directs Godot', *Theatre Quarterly* (V.19: 1975), 21.
28 Walter D. Asmus, 'Practical aspects of theatre, radio and television. Rehearsal notes for the German premiere of Beckett's 'That time' and 'Footfalls' at the Schiller-Theater Werkstatt, Berlin (directed by Beckett)', trans. Helen Watanabe, *Journal of Beckett Studies* (2: Summer 1977), 86; Billie Whitelaw, 'Practical aspects of theatre, radio and television: Extracts from an unscripted interview with Billie Whitelaw by James Knowlson. A television recording made on 1 February 1977 for the University of London Audio-Visual Centre' *Journal of Beckett Studies* (3: Summer 1978), 87; Pierre Chabert, 'Samuel Beckett as Director', in James Knowlson (ed.), *Theatre Workbook 1*, 89–90.
29 See Walter D. Asmus, 'Beckett directs Godot', 23; Pierre Chabert, 'Samuel Beckett as Director', 102.
30 See James Knowlson (ed.), *Happy Day*, and see Asmus, 'Beckett directs Godot', 25.
31 Cohn, *Just Play*, 231, 270; Pierre Chabert, 'Samuel Beckett as Director', 88; Whitelaw, 'Practical aspects of theatre, radio and television', 89.
32 Ruby Cohn, *Just Play*, 236.
33 Ruby Cohn, 'Beckett's German *Godot*', 42.
34 Ruby Cohn, 'Beckett's German *Godot*', 41; Ruby Cohn, *Just Play*, 236.
35 Ruby Cohn, *Just Play*, 242.
36 Ibid., 271.
37 Pierre Chabert, 'Samuel Beckett as Director', 102.
38 Ruby Cohn, *Just Play*, 231.
39 Walter D. Asmus, 'Practical aspects', 86; Billie Whitelaw, 'Practical aspects of theatre, radio and television',87; Pierre Chabert, 'Samuel Beckett as Director', 89–90.
40 Ruby Cohn, *Just Play*, 241.
41 Ibid.
42 McMillan and Fehsenfeld, *Beckett in the Theatre*, 191, 225, 193.

CHAPTER 16

Working on Radio

Ulrika Maude

Charles Juliet once questioned Samuel Beckett about the time he spent in Ussy-sur-Marne in the solitude of his modest country home. He wondered what Beckett did 'when nothing happens'. Beckett simply replied, '[t]here is always something to listen to'.[1] Over the years, he made frequent mention to Juliet of the increasing significance hearing held for him: 'The eyes are now much less important', he commented.[2] On one occasion, relatively late in his life, Beckett even confessed to enjoying 'the sound made by the cartloads of beets passing by on the road outside'.[3]

Beckett's work for the radio makes explicit his lifelong interest in sound and hearing, implicit in his second-person narratives and prose fragments and foregrounded in much of his drama. The six years Beckett spent writing for the radio between 1956 and 1962 form a central part of his career, not only because he wrote a total of six radio plays and also adapted Robert Pinget's play *La Manivelle* for BBC radio, but also because radiophonic motifs seem to permeate so much of his oeuvre. His work also features various sound technologies – loudspeakers, switchboards and magnetic audiotape, with which Beckett first became familiar through his work for the radio.[4] Beckett famously stated of his first radio play, *All That Fall* (1956), that 'whatever quality it may have [...] depends on the whole thing's *coming out of the dark*'.[5] If '*coming out of the dark*' is an opportune trope for Beckett's radio plays, it also serves to characterise a good number of his television, stage and prose works. Plays such as *Eh Joe* (1966), *Footfalls* (1975), *Ghost Trio* (1975) and *A Piece of Monologue* (1979) and prose texts such as *Heard in the Dark I* and *II* (1970s) and *Company* (1980) all centre on the figure of a voice from the dark that fixes either the protagonist or the spectator/reader of Beckett's work.

When in June 1956 the BBC invited Beckett to write a play for the experimental Third Programme, he rose to the challenge and wrote *All That Fall* in the space of three months. The play is set in the fictional town of Boghill and centres on Maddy Rooney's arduous walk to the railway station to meet her blind husband, Dan, and the couple's laborious trek back home. On the way to the station, Maddy meets a number of friends and acquaintances with whom she discusses ailing relatives and her own ill health. Once Maddy reaches the station, she discovers that Dan Rooney's train has been delayed. It transpires that a child has fallen on the track and lost his life. Dan Rooney's silence and his possible stake in the incident are left ambiguously unresolved. The play's title comes from Psalm 145: 'The Lord upholdeth all that fall and raiseth up all those that be bowed down'. When Maddy Rooney quotes the psalm at the end of the play, she and her husband '*join in wild laughter*', for almost everything in the village of Boghill seems to take a fall (*CDW*, 198).

The first mention Beckett made of *All That Fall* appears in a letter he wrote to Nancy Cunard in July 1956: 'Never thought about Radio play technique but in the dead of t'other night got a nice gruesome idea full of cartwheels and dragging feet and puffing and panting'.[6] As his letter implies, Beckett was fascinated by the opportunity radio provided to experiment with non-verbal sounds such as animal noises, music, footfalls, humming, murmurs and laughter – all of which figure prominently in the final version of the play. *All That Fall* also relies heavily on the various affective and embodied qualities of the human voice, which appear in the play as stage directions such as '*Sobbing*', '*Brokenly*', '*Exploding*', '*Coolly*', '*Aggrieved*' and '*Tearfully*' (*CDW*, 176–8). When, on 27 September 1956, Beckett sent the completed play script to Charles John Morris at the BBC, he included a brief covering letter in which he emphasised that the play 'calls for a rather special quality of bruitage [sound effects]'.[7] On 18 October 1956, in another letter, Beckett suggested that he should 'meet the bruiteur, before the production, and talk it over'.[8] Still, the sound effects continued to preoccupy Beckett, and on 18 December he wrote to the play's director, Donald McWhinnie, insisting on a 'realistic nucleus' for the various animal sounds that feature in the play. Beckett opposed McWhinnie's idea of man-made animal sounds and expressed his concern that 'If they are badly imitated the result will be atrocious'.[9] As it turned out, McWhinnie did use man-made sounds for the '*Sheep, bird, cow, cock*' in the final production of the play (*CDW*, 172). Although delighted by a number of McWhinnie's directorial decisions, Beckett stated in a letter of 14 January 1957: 'I didn't think the animals were right'.[10] Beckett's extraordinary emphasis on the sound qualities of the play is striking, for it goes against the essentially speech-based tradition of radio drama. Similarly, Beckett's decision to include so many affective descriptors, verbs and adverbs, in the stage directions of *All That Fall* is conspicuous in an author who, in his later directorial work, famously insisted on the monotony of his actors' voices and the lack of affective 'colour' in the dialogue of his stage plays. Beckett's decision to emphasise the embodied and emotive qualities of the human voice in his first radio play goes against the dominant Western philosophical tradition, which has tended to obscure all traces of the voice's origin in the body. The sounds of physical exertion and effort, in turn, are particularly effective in 'embodying' the play's characters in the absence of the visual presence of a body on stage.

All That Fall, like Beckett's other radio plays, can be said to be a play about radio itself, for the dialogue is peppered with self-referential comments that draw attention to the play's radiophonic status. As many critics have pointed out, Dan Rooney's blindness is opportune for the acoustic medium of radio. When Mr Slocum and Tommy exclude Maddy from their conversation, she retorts, 'Don't mind me. Don't take any notice of me. I do not exist. The fact is well known', drawing attention to her own status as a word being, and to the fact that on the radio, silence means non-existence (*CDW*, 179). When Maddy later encounters Miss Fitt – the name itself a pun that draws attention to the sound qualities of language – she is annoyed by the manner in which her friend seems to ignore her, and retorts: 'Am I then invisible, Miss Fitt?' in a comment that again underscores radio's exclusive reliance on sound. Through Maddy's self-referential comments and the play's several references to people who are 'not really there at all', the text interrogates the status of the acoustically constructed characters it evokes.

If *All That Fall* focuses on Beckett's interest in sound, *Embers*, Beckett's second radio play, completed and first broadcast in 1959, can be said to thematise hearing, for Henry, the play's protagonist, spends his time listening to various sounds. Henry cannot stop speaking to himself, his dead father and his wife, Ada. He also narrates an apparently unrelated story of two men, Bolton and Holloway. In addition to Henry's voice, the auditor hears a dialogue between Henry and his wife, Ada, together with two scenes that feature the couple's daughter, Addie, and her music and riding masters. Either in the background, whenever a pause is indicated, or foregrounded by means of an increase in volume, the auditors hear the sound of the sea Henry is trying to escape. In addition, there is a sound of hooves, a drip, Ada and Henry's laughter and Addie's wail. Absent from the play is the sound of the embers that give the play its title, their '[s]hifting, lapsing, furtive like, dreadful sound', which Henry later refers to as the 'sound of dying' (*CDW*, 255).

While Beckett's first radio play, *All That Fall*, succeeded in creating a relatively realistic setting that, paradoxically, is more evocative of a naturalistic landscape than any of Beckett's stage plays, *Embers*, by contrast, presents the auditor with something far more audacious and experimental. For in this second radio play, the various sound spaces permeate one another in a process of sonorous overlap.[11] Throughout the play, we hear the sound of the sea even when the sound space is not that of the shore. This makes it difficult for the auditor to situate the events with any certainty, significantly complicating the play's spatial configuration. Something similar occurs with the characters of the play. We hear Henry's footsteps on the shingle, but do not hear those of his wife, Ada, which may well indicate that she is dead. As Beckett himself remarked of the play, '*Cendres* repose sur un ambiguïté: le personage a-t-il une hallucination ou est-il en presence de la réalité? La realisation scenique détruirait l'ambiguïté' ['*Embers* relies on ambiguity: are the characters hallucinations or are they real? A scenic realisation would destroy the ambiguity'.].[12] In *Embers*, Beckett exploits the fact that although sounds have a physical origin, they themselves are transitory and ephemeral. Partly because of the evanescent nature of the acoustic, hearing is more prone to miscalculations than vision.[13] Furthermore, we can also have a vivid acoustic memory or imagination: 'Auditorily, Beethoven was able to imaginatively "hear" an entire symphony at will. Even after deafness his "inner hearing" did not fail him as the magnificent Ninth Symphony so well shows'.[14] In sonorous experience, 'sensation, perception, emotion, interpretation and imagination mingle in connection with stimuli made up of sounds and silences, in a density that cannot always find appropriate words to describe it'.[15] Technology adds a further dimension to the duplicitous nature of sound in Beckett's work, for as Steven Connor has suggested, working for the radio attuned Beckett 'to the effects of interference or sonorous murk'. Connor speculates that 'for Henry the sea seems to be the sound of indeterminacy itself, corroding and decaying the clarity of signals: hence his desire for definite sounds that stand clear of their background'.[16]

Beckett's subsequent radio plays, *Rough for Radio I* and *Rough for Radio II*, were written in French in the early 1960s and did not appear in English translation until 1976.[17] As the titles indicate, they are less polished than the first two radio plays, and function more like sketches that bring to mind the radiophonic equivalent of Beckett's prose fragments.[18] Ruby Cohn reports that Beckett considered both of these plays unfinished, but that he also 'found a dramatic quality in that very incompletion'.[19] He never allowed *Rough for Radio I* to be broadcast. *Rough for Radio II* was produced by the BBC in 1976.

Rough for Radio I and *II* are perhaps most explicitly plays about radio itself. As Daniel Albright has put it, *All That Fall* is a 'meditation on the medium of radio' that 'makes no explicit reference to radio technology', whereas five years later Beckett 'sketched in French [...] playlets in which technology is in the foreground'. In *Rough for Radio I*, we encounter 'a machine incapable of providing heat or light, but pretty good at providing not-loud-enough sounds of voice and music'.[20] The music, furthermore, is continuous, 'Without cease', a point that the female visitor of the studio-like setting of the play finds 'unthinkable!' (*CDW*, 267). For Albright, the play is about Beckett imagining radio as a place:

In 1961 a radio was already an old-fashioned sort of apparatus, superseded by television, and so Beckett imagined radio as a slightly quaint and threadbare venue, with garbage piling up by the door; manned by a snooty butler or crank poorly trained in extinct codes of service. To step inside radioworld is to enter a place without heat or light, a virtual land of sound.[21]

Steven Connor has drawn attention to the switching of the knobs in *Rough for Radio I*, actions that activate the music and the voice in the play. These actions are accompanied by mechanical clicks as the knobs are turned: 'In a sense, they control the whole play, which then becomes an apparatus for tuning into the agon of listening to radio'.[22] In addition to radio technology itself, the play contains the rare appearance of a telephone in the Beckettian canon, an apparatus that in its early days was also controlled by a manned switchboard. The telephone calls in *Rough for Radio I* are made to the local doctor. We hear the '*Faint ping – as sometimes happens – of telephone receiver raised from cradle. Faint sound of dialling*', as if Beckett's original focus in writing the play had been on different sound technologies and their reconfiguration of space (*CDW*, 269). Both radio and telephone, after all, shrink the space between speaker and listener, enabling us to experience the intimacy of voice at a great distance.

In *Rough for Radio II*, Beckett associates the radio apparatus with pain and irritation, 'a medium produced by torturers for victims'.[23] Beckett is again interested in different sound effects: the lash of the whip, the bang of the cylindrical ruler on the table, the sound of the Stenographer's pencil, the 'sighs and sniffles of Animator and the nonverbal cries of the victimised Fox'.[24] The knobs and switches of *Rough for Radio I* have here been replaced by 'the swish and thud of pizzle on flesh' (*CDW*, 278). As Connor has observed, 'This may remind us that the principal reference for the word "switch", up until the nineteenth century, was to a whip or lash, usually made of a flexible twig or branch'.[25] Fox and his discourse, like a radio apparatus, is switched on and off, activated and deactivated in turn. 'Every listener to *Rough for Radio II* is put in the position of the Animator, trying to decode a tortured text, a text produced by torture'.[26]

Beckett's two remaining radio plays, *Words and Music* and *Cascando*, completed in 1961 and 1962 respectively, focus on the relationship between language and music. Both plays are strikingly experimental in exploring the role of music as a character or 'autonomous member of the cast of a play', and hence they instigate a new turn in Beckett's writing for the radio. Beckett's close friend, painter Avigdor Arikha, told James Knowlson that 'listening to music was essential to [Beckett]', an activity painter and author habitually shared: 'We had a period during which we listened to quite a bit of dodecaphonic music – Schoenberg, Berg, Webern (before 1959). But he always returned to romantic music – from Haydn to Brahms' (*K*, 495–6).

Words and Music was written in English, with an original score by John Beckett, the author's cousin. The play's first director, Michael Bakewell, summarised its plot in the following way: 'Croak, an aged tyrant, has two servants – Words and Music. He shouts out at them themes – "love", "age", etc., which they attempt to portray and which sharpen his memories of a woman once loved whose memory he cannot escape'.[27] The play, in other words, deals with two different signifying systems, a verbal, conceptual one and a musical, non-conceptual one; both Words and Music attempt to represent a different emotion, state or object. In the course of the play, we also hear the thump of a club, Croak's groans and the same striking emphasis on the emotive and embodied quality of the voices of Croak and Words that we first encountered in *All That Fall*: the descriptors '*Anguished*', '*Faltering*', '*Imploring*', '*Cold*' and '*Shocked*' all appear in the stage directions (*CDW*, 289, 291, 294). Words – also known as Joe – describes a post-coital woman, but otherwise the play is 'almost devoid of referential content'.[28] It contains two striking lyric poems by Beckett, one about ageing, and its preoccupation with love, age and the ghostly face of a former lover bring to mind Yeatsian themes, also evoked in Beckett's television play ... *but the clouds* ... (1976). The name Croak, although never heard in the radio production, evokes a dying man. *Words and Music*, as Ruby Cohn has suggested, is also a 'composition about composition'.[29] In 1987, the play was set to music by composer Morton Feldman.

Cascando was originally written in French and commissioned by Radiodiffusion-Télévision Française (RTF). RTF first approached Rumanian-born composer Marcel Mihalovici for a musical score for the radio. Mihalovici, who had recently made an opera of *Krapp's Last Tape*, turned to Beckett with the suggestion of a collaborative project.[30] As the seven surviving manuscript drafts of *Cascando* attest, Beckett was ambitious about the project, although he referred to it as 'an unimportant work'.[31] He sent the final typescript to Jérôme Lindon on 29 January 1962, while Mihalovici's score was completed on 30 December 1962, almost a year after Beckett's text.[32] The instruments for Mihalovici's score are 'flute, clarinets, piano, celesta, harp, percussion (two musicians: cymbal, tam-tam, gong, wood block, tambourine, triangle, 3 Chinese blocks, xylophone, marimba), first and second violin, alto, and violincello'.[33]

Like *Words and Music*, *Cascando* is a play for three 'characters', Opener, Voice and Music, but the non-verbal sounds that feature in the other five radio plays are missing from this final one. The figure of Opener in *Cascando* has taken the place of the power switch and the bull's pizzle in *Rough for Radio I* and *II*, turning the flow of Voice and Music on and off by uttering the phrases, 'I open' and 'I switch off' (*CDW*, 297).[34] The fragmented narrative uttered by Voice – about a character called Woburn – brings to mind a later version of Henry in *Embers*, haunted, deranged and plagued by storytelling and the sea. It is easy, therefore, to see why Yoshiki Tajiri has read both *Cascando* and *Words and Music* as plays that stage memory operating 'independently of the subject's intention'. The plays, he argues, conceive of the mind as a recording device in which consciousness 'is imagined to be mechanical and replaceable by recorded voices and music – the inner realm is infiltrated by prosthesis'.[35] Tajiri has emphasised the surrealist legacy present in such a thematic, and Albright, too, has foregrounded Beckett's surrealist 'instinct' in the play.[36]

Sound, as Jonathan Rée has observed, possesses a 'peculiar strength that light cannot rival: it can penetrate solid walls, boom through the depths of the ocean, go round corners, shatter delicate glasses, or force its way through the earth'.[37] Yet sounds are also evanescent and ephemeral, there and, in an instant, gone. The six years in which Beckett wrote for the radio enabled him to focus more closely on the duplicitous nature of sound and hearing, which he exploits to the full in his radio work. In the first two radio plays, *All That Fall* and *Embers*, Beckett's interest is precisely on the phenomenology of sound and the perceptual particularities of hearing and listening. In *Rough for Radio I* and *II*, he turns his attention to sound technologies and the spatial reconfigurations they effect. In *Words and Music* and *Cascando*, finally, Beckett's focus is on music and its role as a non-conceptual signifying system. Throughout his writing for the radio,

Beckett is concerned with the distinctive nature of sonorous perception: the fragile, ghostly and discontinuous soundscapes it evokes.

NOTES

1 Charles Juliet, *Conversations with Samuel Beckett and Bram van Velde* trans. Janey Tucker (Leiden: Academic Press Leiden, 1995), 155.
2 Ibid., 147.
3 Ibid., 163.
4 Beckett adapted Robert Pinget's play *La Manivelle* to BBC radio as *The Old Tune*. The play, which in Beckett's adaptation acquired an Irish context and characters, was first broadcast on the BBC on 23 August 1960, directed by Barbara Bray with Jack MacGowran and Patrick Magee in the roles of Cream and Gorman, respectively. *The Old Tune* is reproduced in *CDW*, 335–49.
5 Beckett to Barney Rosset of Grove Press on 27 August 1957, used as the epigraph to Clas Zilliacus, *Beckett and Broadcasting: A Study of the Works of Samuel Beckett for and in Radio and Television*, Acta Academiae Aboensis, Ser. A, Humanoira 51:2 (Åbo, Finland: Åbo Akademi, 1976).
6 Beckett to Nancy Cunard, 4 July 1956, *L2*, 631.
7 Beckett to Charles John Morris, 27 September 1956, *L2*, 656.
8 Beckett to Charles John Morris, 18 October 1956, *L2*, 656.
9 Beckett to Donald McWhinnie, 18 December 1956, *L2*, 688.
10 Beckett to Donald McWhinnie, 14 January 1957, quoted in *K*, 433. For McWhinnie's view on the man-made animal sounds, to do with an unwillingness to create a 'visual picture', 'together with the importance of creating the correct rhythm for the work, impossible to achieve through the use of "real" animal sounds', see McWhinnie, *The Art of Radio* (London: Faber, 1959), 133–4.
11 See Ulrika Maude, *Beckett, Technology and the Body* (Cambridge: Cambridge University Press, 2009), 57.
12 Quoted in Rosemary Poutney, '*EMBERS*: An Interpretation', *Samuel Beckett Today/Aujourd'hui* (2: 1993), 270. My translation.
13 See Maude *Beckett, Technology and the Body*, 57.
14 Don Ihde, *Listening and Voice* (Athens: Ohio University Press, 1976), 121.
15 Edith Lecourt, 'The Musical Envelope', in *Psychic Envelopes* Didier Anzieu (ed.), trans. Daphne Briggs (London: Karnac Books, 1990), 212.
16 Steven Connor, 'I Switch Off: Beckett and the Ordeals of Radio', in Debra Rae Cohen, Michael Coyle and Jane Lewty (eds.) *Broadcasting Modernism* (Gainesville: University Press of Florida, 2009), 290.
17 *Rough for Radio II* was in fact written between *Words and Music* and *Cascando*.
18 *Rough for Radio I* first appeared in French in 1961 as *Esquisse radiophonique*. The play was first published in English as 'Sketch for Radio Play' in *Stereo Headphones* 7 (Spring 1976). *Rough for Radio II* was written in French in the early 1960s as *Pochade radiophonique*.

19 Ruby Cohn, *The Beckett Canon* (Ann Arbor: University of Michigan Press, 2005), 274.
20 Daniel Albright, *Beckett and Aesthetics* (Cambridge: Cambridge University Press, 2003), 111–12.
21 Ibid., 113.
22 Connor, 'I Switch Off: Beckett and the Ordeals of Radio', 285.
23 Albright, *Beckett and Aesthetics*, 114.
24 Cohn, *The Beckett Canon*, 274.
25 Connor, 'I Switch Off: Beckett and the Ordeals of Radio', 286.
26 Albright, *Beckett and Aesthetics*, 118.
27 Cited in Zilliacus, *Beckett and Broadcasting*, 100.
28 Cohn, *The Beckett Canon*, 270.
29 Ibid., 268.
30 Zilliacus, *Beckett and Broadcasting*, 118.
31 The manuscripts are held in the Theater Collection of Harvard College Library. Beckett to Herbert Myron, 21 September 1962, cited in Zilliacus, *Beckett and Broadcasting*, 118.
32 John Pilling, *A Samuel Beckett Chronology* (Basingstoke: Palgrave, 2006), 158; Zilliacus, *Beckett and Broadcasting*, 131.
33 Zilliacus, *Beckett and Broadcasting*, 132.
34 Albright, *Beckett and Aesthetics*, 120.
35 Yoshiki Tajiri, *Samuel Beckett and the Prosthetic Body: The Organs and Senses in Modernism* (Basingstoke: Palgrave, 2007), 165–6.
36 Albright, *Beckett and Aesthetics*, 120.
37 Jonathan Rée, *I See a Voice: A Philosophical History of Language, Deafness and the Senses* (London: Harper Collins, 1999), 38.

CHAPTER 17

Working on Film and Television
Graley Herren

As a fledgling writer, Samuel Beckett was himself a critic.[1] He later downplayed his criticism to Ruby Cohn as 'mere products of friendly obligations or economic necessity', dismissing the lot as 'disjecta' (D, 7). In the present context, however, it bears considering what 'residua' lingered on from his 'disjecta'. The critical frame of mind and interpretive strategies Beckett tested out during these formative years – rereading as occasion for reinvention – would develop into his signature methodology in the mature creative work. S. E. Gontarski identifies 'a central tenet of Samuel Beckett's creative spirit, a creative life marked by a series of reinventions, or better by a pattern of serial reinvention'.[2] Gontarski refers primarily to Beckett's reinventions of personal and professional personae. I wish to expand the notion of 'serial reinvention' to characterise the work itself, as Beckett extended his oeuvre diachronically by excavating the synchronic strata of past works on which it was built. Beckett establishes a signature working method in his film and television plays whereby he returns to the past, not as homage or oath of allegiance but rather as creative leaping-off point, as occasion for reinvention.

Nowhere is this methodology of serial reinvention displayed more graphically than in his corpus for film and television. Between 1963 and 1989, Beckett committed an enormous amount of creative energy to (re)conceiving and (re)producing work for the big and small screens. He composed original screenplays for one film – *Film* (1963) – and five television pieces – *Eh Joe* (1965), *Ghost Trio* (1975), *...but the clouds...* (1976), *Quad* (1981) and *Nacht und Träume* (1982). He was also heavily involved in mounting screen productions, serving either as director, co-director or consultant to the director on *Film* (1964); four productions of *Eh Joe* [*He Joe*] [two in German (1966, 1979) and two in English (1966, 1989)]; two productions each of *Ghost Trio* [*Geistertrio*] [in English (1977) and German (1977)] and *...but the clouds...* [*...nur noch Gewölk...*] [in English (1977) and German (1977)]; one production each of *Quad* [*Quadrat I + II*] [in German (1981)] and *Nacht und Träume* [in German (1983)]; a film adaptation of his stage play *Play* [*Comédie*] [in French (1966)]; and a television adaptation of his stage play *What Where* [*Was Wo*] [in German (1986)]. Important critical studies have placed Beckett's screen work firmly within the contexts of their media productions [primarily with the British Broadcasting Corporation (BBC) in England and Süddeutscher Rundfunk (SDR) in West Germany]. Clas Zilliacus initiated this effort with his seminal book *Beckett and Broadcasting* (1976), and Jonathan Bignell offers the most extensive evaluation of the institutional media contexts in which the screen work was originally conceived, produced and broadcast in his book *Beckett on Screen* (2009). Vital as the BBC context is to a full appreciation of the teleplays, however, Bignell concedes that these enigmatic experiments for the medium constitute aberrations to some degree: 'Beckett's television work and adaptations of his theatre plays became increasingly exceptional rather than typical, increasingly marginal rather than high-profile'.[3] He adds, 'The plays, and *Film* too, look strikingly anachronistic in relation to the contexts in which I place them'.[4]

Bignell's admirable study places Beckett's screen works within the important contexts of their institutional production at the BBC and their critical reception (or conspicuous lack thereof) in television studies. For my part, in what follows I concentrate on two other useful contexts which help account for the comparatively alien and anachronistic qualities of Beckett's film and television work. These pieces seem out of place because they are oriented steadfastly towards the past, engaged in dialectical reconsiderations – and reinventions – of a number of formative influences. Elsewhere I have elaborated at length upon important influences from and dialectical exchanges with literature (e.g. Dante, Shakespeare and Yeats), music (e.g. Beethoven and Schubert) and painting (e.g. the 'Agony in the Garden' tradition).[5] In this chapter, I limit my focus to philosophical and psychological contexts for understanding the film and television plays. There is nothing new in looking at Beckett through these lenses, which are two of the more familiar disciplinary approaches in Beckett studies. But these perspectives are rarely applied to Beckett on screen (with the exception of *Film*), despite the fact that these works contain some of the most philosophically and psychologically suggestive works in his entire dramatic canon.

PHILOSOPHICAL CONTEXTS

Beckett's earliest cinematic interest dates back to his youth. He was an early devotee of silent films, especially the comedies of Charlie Chaplin and Buster Keaton. His early enthusiasm deepened, so much so that by early 1936 he had embarked upon an intensive self-directed study of film theory, culminating in an unsuccessful appeal to study under pioneering Soviet filmmaker Sergei Eisenstein at the Moscow State School of Cinematography.[6] Beckett's first opportunity to work in cinema would have to wait almost three decades. In April 1963 he began composing his only piece written specifically for the big screen, the reflexively titled *Film*, solicited and produced by his American publisher, Barney Rosset, for his fledgling Evergreen Theatre film project. During the summer of 1964, he made his first (and last) trip to the United States to collaborate with director Alan Schneider during the shooting of this (almost) silent film, starring screen legend Buster Keaton. *Film* must be regarded as only a qualified success – Beckett himself called it an 'interesting failure'[7] – but it nevertheless demonstrates his commitment from the start to interrogating the philosophical nature of the medium.

BERKELEY: BEING AND PERCEPTION

Film examines the relationship of being and perception, taking its impetus from eighteenth-century Anglo-Irish philosopher George Berkeley, the Bishop of Cloyne. In *The Principles of Human Knowledge*, Bishop Berkeley divides all existence into two categories, sensible objects and spirits (or minds, or souls). For all objects, he asserts, '*esse est percipi*' ['to be is to be perceived']; for all spirits, '*esse est percipere*' ['to be is to perceive']. The published screenplay consists chiefly of Beckett's notes, diagrams, concerns and a summary of the action (there is no dialogue save for one whispered 'shh!'). There Beckett transcribes Berkeley's dictum, '*Esse est percipi*', as well as his own disclaimer below: 'No truth value attaches to above, regarded as of merely structural and dramatic convenience' (*CDW*, 323). The dramatic conflict of *Film* derives from a tantalising loophole Beckett finds in Berkeley's perception-based thesis: if one can avoid all perception, might one then effectively cease to be? Beckett summarises the plot in one sentence: 'Search of non-being in flight from extraneous perception breaking down in inescapability of self-perception' (*CDW*, 323).

GEULINCX: WITHDRAWAL INTO THE 'INNERMOST SANCTUM'

Though not acknowledged as overtly as Berkeley, another palpable philosophical influence in *Film*, and in the teleplays as well, is Arnold Geulincx.[8]

What chiefly endured for Beckett from Geulincx was his acceptance of ignorance as the basic human condition, his ethic of humility and his advocacy for ascetic withdrawal and rigorous self-examination. Consider for instance Geulincx's promotion of diligence as 'an intense and continuous *withdrawal of the mind* (no matter what its current business) from external things into itself, into its own *innermost sanctum*, in order to consult the sacred Oracle of Reason'.[9] This philosophical image most directly anticipates M's 'little sanctum' in *...but the clouds...*, where he retreats from the world in order to summon his private oracle of his imagination, W (*CDW*, 419–22). In a broader sense, an 'innermost sanctum', into which one escapes from the world for the purposes of intense, imaginative, compulsive contemplation, serves ubiquitously as the serial precondition of *Eh Joe*, *Ghost Trio*, *...but the clouds...* and *Nacht und Träume*.

BERGSON: MEMORY AND HABIT

Once ensconced in their respective little sanctums, M and his televisual brethren habitually dwell upon their memories. Memory is the primary preoccupation of Beckett's late work, and that theme is developed with acute intensity on screen. The media of film and television lend themselves intrinsically to this theme because both function like memory itself. Actions registered as images are recorded and are thus made readily accessible and infinitely repeatable, reanimating the past and absent as if live and present. Yet these purportedly true images are subject to all manner of editorial manipulation, selection, condensation and distortion, resulting in sights and sounds that are less archival records from the past than expedient fantasies for the present – remembering as reinvention. The conceptual antecedents for Beckett's treatment of film and television as 'memory machines' can be traced back to theories of memory and habit articulated by modern French philosopher Henri Bergson. In *Matter and Memory*, Bergson posits a theoretical 'pure perception' that would collapse all meaningful distinctions between subject and object: 'let us place ourselves face to face with immediate reality: at once we find that there is no impassable barrier, no essential difference, no real distinction even, between perception and the thing perceived'.[10] Practically speaking, however, one's confrontation with reality is always refracted through memory: 'In fact, there is no perception which is not full of memories. With the immediate and present data of our senses we mingle a thousand details out of our past experience. In most cases these memories supplant our actual perceptions, of which we then retain only a few hints, thus using them merely as "signs" that recall to us former images'.[11] Beckett's disdain for habit is well known. In *Proust* he acerbically observes, 'The laws of memory are subject to the more general laws of habit.... Habit is the ballast that chains the dog to his vomit. Breathing is habit. Life is habit' (*P*, 19). Vladimir declares more succinctly in *Waiting for Godot* that 'habit is the great deadener' (*CDW*, 84). This understanding of the relationship between memory and habit, conceptualised by Bergson and inflected with Proustian (and Geulingian) scorn, deeply informs the teleplays.[12] One can see its visible and verbal reiteration, for instance, in the 'Pre-action', 'Action' and 'Re-action' sections of *Ghost Trio*. A male Figure (F) waits in his 'familiar chamber' (*CDW*, 408) for 'her', presumably some lost loved one from his past. Accompanied by occasional narration from a weary Voice (V) and sporadic interjections from music by Beethoven, F retraces his habitual patterns through the room, a compulsive exercise in rote repetition. While there are certain subtle variations in the pattern over the course of the teleplay, and an understated power struggle between F and V for formal control of that pattern, F ends the play in the same room with the same obsessions, no closer to resolution or reunion than he was when he began (which by the look of him might well have been centuries ago). *Quad* dispenses with dialogue and any discernible character or conflict, opting instead for mechanistic repetitions expressed through the carefully choreographed movement of four players along the coordinates of a quadrangle (*CDW*, 451–3). Yet even in this sparest of teleplays, the debilitating effects of habit are manifestly evident. Beckett appended a 'sequel' in the studio, sans percussion accompaniment, colour and speed, a repetition meant to suggest that the pointless routine continues on, perhaps for another 'ten thousand years' (*K*, 674), asymptotically wearing down but seemingly never concluding.

Perhaps the best example of the distorted interplay between memory and habit appears in *...but the clouds....* M attempts nightly to conjure up the face and voice of W, a beloved woman he has lost from his past. But the teleplay sends very mixed signals about his success. M attests to his abject failure: W either appears only momentarily and then disappears, appears and briefly lingers, appears and lingers long enough to mouth out a few inaudible words or – 'by far the commonest, in the proportion say of nine hundred and ninety-nine to one, or nine hundred and ninety-eight to two' (*CDW*, 421) – fails to appear at all. Or so we are told. What we see is actually quite different. Within the brief span of twenty minutes, we see W appear on screen eight times, and always right on cue when summoned by M. Nevertheless, consider *how* she appears: faint, disembodied, blind and mute. He has learnt how to recollect her dependably from his memory, but through the mechanical transfer she is stripped of all the attributes that made her inspirational and worth summoning in the first place. In other words, she is reduced to a paltry simulacrum, and his efforts to apprehend her merely '*habit interpreted by memory* rather than memory itself'.[13]

PSYCHOLOGICAL CONTEXTS

Freud: Mourning and Melancholia

Beckett cited his father's death as the impetus for seeking psychotherapy in the 1930s, so one can reasonably infer that working through this grief was one feature of his sessions with his therapist, Wilfred Bion. Be that as it may, there is no disputing the growing concern in his fiction and drama with loss, absence, longing, regret and the ever contentious interplay between the not-properly-born and the not-quite-dead. His treatment of these themes displays familiarity with Freud's theories on mourning, first articulated in his seminal essay 'Mourning and Melancholia'. Freud distinguishes two general responses to the death of a loved one: normal mourning and melancholia. Initially the normal mourner and the melancholic subject exhibit similar symptoms, though melancholics additionally suffer from 'self-reproaches and self-revilings' and 'a delusional expectation of punishment'.[14] Through the psychological work of mourning, the normal mourner is eventually able to assimilate the loss, detach his libidinal connection with the lost love object and form new libidinal attachments; in layman's terms, he moves on and learns to love again. Not so for the melancholic. Owing to ambivalent feelings of both love and hate originally directed towards the lost object, the melancholic cannot reconcile himself to the loss. Instead, he effectively keeps the dead object alive – inside his ego. The internalisation process formulated in 'Mourning and Melancholia' was pivotal to Freud's formulation of the superego developed soon thereafter, and it would later prove instrumental to Melanie Klein's object-relations theories. Freudian melancholia also provides a crucial subtext to *Eh Joe*.

Beckett's first teleplay might just as well have been called 'Night of the Living Dead'. Joe sits silently in his lonely room, where he is assailed by a feminine voice-over, simply labeled Voice in the script. She berates him for his infidelities, mocks his religious beliefs and finally captivates him with an excruciating description of the suicide of 'the green one', a former lover who apparently killed herself after Joe jilted her. Voice identifies herself as another former lover, long since departed, who returns as the latest in a series of voices to haunt Joe:

> You know that penny farthing hell you call your mind.... That's where you think this is coming from, don't you.... That's where you heard your father.... Isn't that what you told me? ... Started in on you one June night and went on for years.... On and off.... Behind the eyes.... That's how you were able to throttle him in the end.... Mental thuggee you called it. [...] Then your mother when her hour came. [...] Others.... All the others.... Such love he got.... God knows why.... Pitying love.... None to touch it.... And look at him now.... Throttling the dead in his head. (*CDW*, 362–3)

Voice's taunt that Joe only thinks these dead voices are emanating from his mind hints that the real story is more complicated than that. What we actually witness in *Eh Joe* amounts to a case study in chronic melancholia. Joe's relationships have always been tainted by ambivalence, 'Pitying love' as Voice puts it. Beginning with the primal loss of his father and mother, and continuing through the loss of several subsequent attachments, melancholic Joe cannot accept the loss of these ambivalent loves and instead incorporates them into his own self. Having relocated these lost objects internally, to what Nicolas Abraham and Maria Torok, building upon Freud, call the subject's 'intrapsychic tomb', Joe is devoted paradoxically to murdering the undead he himself is responsible for keeping alive.[15] Voice's verbal lacerations represent an ingenious dramatic correlative to the 'self-reproaches and self-revilings' of melancholia. Joe takes his sadistic impulses towards objects (father, mother, lovers) and redirects them inward just as Freud describes, persecuting himself through ventriloquism while sadistically 'throttling the dead in his head'.

Rank: Birth Trauma and Regression Fantasies

If Beckett means to recapitulate primary anxieties first encountered in earliest childhood, then, one might well ask, why are his characters *so damned old*? Perhaps this indicates the lifelong inability of these particular characters to come to terms with psychological dilemmas encountered from the beginning of life. Like May in *Footfalls*, whom Beckett characterised as having never been properly born, these haunted characters remain perpetually doomed to revolving but never resolving their primary anxieties.[16] A still more severe diagnosis would be that primary anxiety is fundamentally insoluble: no one can ever truly resolve it because none of us was properly born. This is the central premise of Otto Rank's *The Trauma of Birth*, a highly influential book that Beckett studied in his 'Psychology Notes'. Rank posits that the first libidinal attachment stems from the physical attachment of the foetus to the mother in the womb. This original condition is perceived (if only in retrospect) as ideal, one of complete unity between subject and object in which all the needs of the foetus are perfectly satisfied. The forcible detachment from the mother during birth is thus perceived as a catastrophic eviction, the 'trauma of birth'. 'Birth was the death of him', as Beckett phrases it in *A Piece of Monologue* (*CDW*, 425). According to Rank, the lingering effects from this trauma, combined with regression fantasies of returning to the womb, dictate the terms for all the postnatal subject's deepest fears and desires: 'just as the anxiety at birth forms the basis of every anxiety or fear, so *every pleasure has as its final aim the re-establishment of the intrauterine primal pleasure*'.[17]

Beckett himself claims to have recovered intrauterine memories during his sessions with Bion, though his sensations contrast sharply with typical idealisations: '"I used to lie down on the couch and try to go back in my past. [...] I certainly came up with some extraordinary memories of being in the womb. Intrauterine memories. I remember feeling trapped, of being imprisoned and unable to escape, of crying to be let out but no one could hear, no one was listening. I remember being in pain but being unable to do anything about it' (*K*, 177). One wonders whether these so-called memories reveal more about his postnatal ambivalence towards May Beckett than about his actual prenatal sensations. His personal associations with the intrauterine condition certainly prefigure those of his young adulthood in Ireland – suffocation, imprisonment and helplessness – an inherited condition passed on to his brood of artistic creatures. Whereas Rank interprets the newborn's first cry (memorably featured in Beckett's *Breath*) as a howl of protest against the trauma of being born, for Beckett one's existence before birth is reckoned as no less traumatic. When Beckett appropriates images and ideas from Rank, as he frequently does in the teleplays, he does so in such a way that indulges regression fantasies only to expose how they ultimately exacerbate primal anxieties.

Beckett's works are commonly read in the context of after-life scenarios: hell, purgatory, urns, ghosts; my own emphasis on mourning is a variation on this same tendency. Less familiar, but no less valid, are the before-life connotations of several works, particularly among the late drama. If *Eh Joe* invites consideration in terms of the 'intrapsychic tomb', then *Film*, *Ghost Trio*, ...*but the clouds*... and *Nacht und Träume* equally suggest regression fantasies of the womb. The latter teleplay enacts a longing for maternal love and reunion with keen fervour. A Dreamer (A) is sequestered in a dark room. There he hums, then sings, a line from Schubert's lied 'Nacht und Träume' before falling asleep. In his dream, his dreamt self (B) is nurtured by a pair of helping hands: they wipe his brow with a cloth, give him sup from a cup and embrace him. In a repetition of the dream, the entire sequence is repeated, but even slower and in close-up, heightening the sense of longing (*CDW*, 465–6). While the teleplay is undoubtedly replete with religious and artistic connotations, there is no denying the primal urges for maternal affection: the dreamt self gazes upward at an 'invisible face' (*CDW*, 466), and this hovering presence provides him with sustenance, swaddles him and hugs him. The verse sung from Schubert, 'Holde Träume, kehret wieder! [Sweet dreams, come back again!]' further reinforces the regression fantasy of reuniting with the idealised primal love object.

Serial variations on the same dynamic are apparent in all of the film and television plays (with the exception of the always exceptional *Quad*). In *Film*, for instance, Beckett specifies that O retreats to 'his mother's room' (*CDW*, 332). The 'familiar chamber' of F in *Ghost Trio* (*CDW*, 408) is also highly suggestive of the womb, particularly as he keeps thinking he hears a woman's voice emanating from somewhere nearby outside his shelter. In this context it is also tantalising to read the long corridor connecting the 'familiar chamber' to the outside world as analogous to the birth canal, especially when it is navigated by a 'small boy' with 'hood glistening' (*CDW*, 413) like a newborn's caul. Both the setting and actions in *...but the clouds...*, previously considered from a Geulingian perspective, equally support an intrauterine interpretation. In fact, M's description of his 'begging of the mind' while enclosed in his sanctum strongly echoes Beckett's own memories from the womb: 'Then crouching there, in my little sanctum, in the dark, where none could see me, I began to beg, of her, to appear, to me' (*CDW*, 420). Finally, M's language in describing his exit from the sanctum is pregnant with the labour of (re)birth: 'until the time came, with break of day, to issue forth again, void my little sanctum' (*CDW*, 421–2).

As for the viability of maintaining these regression fantasies, or the consolation they ultimately provide, Joe's Voice can speak for them all: 'Cut a long story short doesn't work' (*CDW*, 366). O's flight from perception is thwarted, F's anticipated reunion never materialises and M's habitual conjuring tricks only yield ephemeral glimpses of the elusive woman he seeks. Even in the most indulgent of the fantasies, *Nacht und Träume*, where a maternal presence does seem to arrive and accommodate all the subject's basic needs, the dream fades away in the end, proving its illusory nature and leaving the Dreamer not reunited in the idealised womb but alone again in his dark and empty room. The pattern of regressive retreat in these works only serves to trigger primal anxieties rather than alleviate them. Rank speaks to this dynamic in his consideration of the common childish fear of a dark room. Likewise for Beckett's screen protagonists, the retreat into the room as fantasized re-enactment of regression into the womb proves futile, only throwing their suffering into sharper relief. Just as the screen works consistently depict the failure of memory, they also depict, in what amounts to much the same thing, the *failure of fantasy*. This failure is many-layered, stemming from the irrepressibility of the external world, the inescapability of self-perception and the irreversibility of the birth trauma. But for Beckett, contra Rank, the failure of the regression fantasies also stems from the unwelcome discovery that, far from 'an experience of extreme pleasure', the womb may have been a miniature torture chamber wherein the foetus was familiarised with proto-traumas in preparation for the traumatic life to come.

NOTES

1. Beckett's one full-length critical monograph was *Proust*, originally published by Chatto and Windus in 1937. He also published numerous occasional pieces of criticism on art and literature, gathered together as *Disjecta: Miscellaneous Writings and a Dramatic Fragment*, Ruby Cohn (ed.) (New York: Grove Press, 1984).
2. S. E. Gontarski. 'Introduction', in S. E. Gontarski (ed.) *A Companion to Samuel Beckett* (Chichester: Wiley-Blackwell, 2010), 4.
3. Jonathan Bignell, *Beckett on Screen: The Television Plays* (Manchester: Manchester University Press, 2009), 8.
4. Ibid., 10.
5. For my extended studies of each film and television plays, originals and adaptations, see Graley Herren, *Samuel Beckett's Plays on Film and Television* (New York: Palgrave Macmillan, 2007).
6. See Samuel Beckett to Sergei Eisenstein, March 2, 1936 (*L1*, 317–18). For a consideration of the influence of film theorists Eisenstein, Pudovkin and Arnheim on Beckett's *Film*, see Matthijs Engelberts, 'Film and Film: Beckett and Early Film Theory', in Linda Ben-Zvi and Angela Moorjani (eds.) *Beckett at 100: Revolving It All* (Oxford: Oxford University Press, 2008), 152–65.
7. Maurice Harmon (ed.), *No Author Better Served: The Correspondence of Samuel Beckett and Alan Schneider* (Cambridge: Harvard University Press, 1998), 166.
8. Arnold Geulincx, *Ethics. With Samuel Beckett's Notes*. Trans. M. Wilson; Han van Ruler, Anthony Uhlmann, and Martin Wilson (eds.) (Leiden: Brill, 2006 [1675]), 329.
9. Ibid., 320, my emphasis.
10. Henri Bergson, *Matter and Memory*, Trans. N. M. Paul and W. S. Palmer (New York: Macmillan, 1912 [1896]), 291.

11 Ibid., 24.
12 Geulincx addresses habit most directly in his section and annotations on 'Disposition', where he asserts that 'to do something *easily* [Beckett's emphasis in his notes] is not necessarily to do good, nor is *to be accustomed* to do something necessarily to do good.... And what further proof do we need that the nature of Virtue is not derived from disposition?' (319). In the same annotation, Geulincx remonstrates, 'Familiarity, or love of the commonplace, are passions by which the greater part of the vulgar are continually moved' (319).
13 Henri Bergson, *Matter and Memory*, 95.
14 Sigmund Freud, 'Inhibitions, Symptoms and Anxiety', in James Strachey (ed.) and trans *The Standard Edition of the Complete Psychological Works of Sigmund Freud*. Vol. 20. (London: Hogarth Press, 1975 [1926]), 244.
15 Nicolas Abraham and Maria Torok, 'Mourning *or* Melancholia: Introjection *versus* Incorporation', in N. T. Rand (ed.) and trans. *The Shell and the Kernel*. Vol. 1. (Chicago: University of Chicago Press, 1994 [1972]), 130.
16 During rehearsals for his 1976 Schiller-Theater Werkstatt production of *Tritte* [*Footfalls*] in Berlin, Beckett compared May to one of Carl Jung's patients. Directorial assistant Walter Asmus reports Beckett's exchange with actress Hildegard Schmahl: 'In the thirties, he says, C.G. Jung, the psychologist, once gave a lecture in London and told of a female patient who was being treated by him. Jung said he wasn't able to help this patient and for this, according to Beckett, he gave an astonishing explanation. This girl wasn't *living*. She existed but didn't actually live. According to Beckett, this story had impressed him very much at the time'. Knowlson identifies this lecture given on 2 October 1935, the third in a series delivered by Jung at the Tavistock Clinic in London, which Beckett attended with his therapist, Wilfred Bion (*K*, 170). In the discussion period after the lecture, Jung said of this patient, who died young, 'she had never been born entirely' (C. G. Jung, *Analytical Psychology: Its Theory and Practice (The Tavistock Lectures)* (New York: Pantheon, 1968), 107). Beckett alludes even more directly to Jung's memorable comment in *All That Fall* (*CDW*, 196).
17 Otto Rank, *The Trauma of Birth* (New York: Martino, 2010), 17.

PART IV

'The Humanities I had': Literature

CHAPTER 18

Irish Literature

Seán Kennedy

When Samuel Beckett's novel *Murphy* was published in 1938, it was the subject of a somewhat bemused review in *The Dublin Magazine*:

Murphy comes in the guise of a novel. But it is more a study in words and phrases, the characters being secondary affairs. [...] And as it is not a novel, neither is it, as the title would indicate, Irish. Murphy, the chief character, hardly exists at all as a human being, so it would be difficult to label him with any nationality.[1]

In 1951, however, a Cork-based literary journal, *Irish Writing*, was able to publish excerpts from the no-less-obscure novel *Watt* without misgiving.[2] Elsewhere, in 2004, scholars C. J. Ackerley and S. E. Gontarski described Beckett as a 'consummate European', whereas, in 1991, the organisers of the Beckett Festival in Dublin aimed to 'give back some of the fundamental Irishness' to his work.[3] All of which is to say that Beckett's relationship to Irish literature was obscure from the outset and that questions persist. Is Samuel Beckett an Irish writer? The question is not, perhaps, a particularly interesting one, and may also be unanswerable due to the many contexts in which it might conceivably be posed. What precisely is Irish literature? Are we including work in the Irish language? Are we referring to writing before or since Beckett, or both? Does it include *all* writing done in Ireland? Might, for example, *The Faerie Queene* qualify? As the controversy over the *Field Day Anthology of Irish Writing* (1991) demonstrated, the exact provenance of the phrase 'Irish writing' is notoriously difficult to recover, and so is the nature of Beckett's relationship to it (whatever it may be).[4]

When seeking to address the issue, the 1934 essay 'Recent Irish Poetry' might seem the obvious place to begin, in that it addresses our theme directly, but I want to start with a short story, 'Walking Out', written around 1931, and with Belacqua Shuah's encounter with a tramp in the

Dublin mountains. It is an encounter somewhat complicated for him by the fact that his dog has peed on the tramp's trousers:

'Good evening' he [Belacqua] piped in fear and trembling 'lovely evening.'

A smile proof against all adversity transformed the sad face of the man under the cart. He was most handsome with his thick, if unkempt, black hair and moustache.

'Game ball' he said.

After that further comment was impossible. The question of apology or compensation simply did not arise. The instinctive nobility of this splendid creature [...] disarmed all the pot-hooks and hangers of civility. Belacqua made an inarticulate flourish with his stick and passed down the road out of the life of this tinker, this real man at last. (*MPTK*, 104)

In an obvious parody, Beckett takes aim here at the entire discourse of the 'imaginary Irish peasant' that provided much of the stock-in-trade imagery for the early writings of the Irish literary revival.[5] He quietly contrasts this 'real man' with W. B. Yeats's fisherman, the man who was 'but a dream', and situates him beyond the stifling effects of bourgeois civilisation.[6] A variation on the trope of the noble savage, the Irish peasant harkened back to a time when, as Yeats saw it, there was an instinctive sympathy between the aristocratic class and their rural charges. As Adrian Frazier demonstrates, the ideology of the Abbey Theatre grew increasingly conservative on the issue of property, framing the more extreme demands of Irish nationalism as an ill-conceived challenge to a natural/aristocratic order based on benevolence, property and propriety.[7] This reading of history was motivated by the nationalist successes of the land war, which effectively dismantled the economic basis of landlordism and left the landlord classes (and those affiliated with them) facing an uncertain future. Confronting the prospect of expropriation and demise, Frazier argues, the revivalists 'turned to literature to forge in new circumstances identities that were no longer secured in material and social realities'.[8]

Typically, Beckett is situated over and against this initiative – as a member of the Protestant upper middle classes and as one of the revival's great critics – but in this passage Belacqua Shuah is rendered complicit with revivalist ideology. One of the main effects of Yeats's '[d]ream of the noble and the beggar-man' was to obscure the issue of class and of class inequality in a divided Ireland, and Belacqua's 'inarticulate flourish' ratifies that gesture here.[9] In what may be read as a condensed expression of the class-based disavowals and privileges of revivalist ideology generally, Belacqua is assured by the 'instinctive nobility' of the tramp and persuades himself that any issue of 'compensation simply did not arise'. The issue of compensation was of course central to nationalist agitation as well as the various initiatives aimed at settling the land question, but this homeless creature, apparently, needs nothing.[10] Beckett is having fun, of course, and much of the comedy of *More Pricks than Kicks* stems from Belacqua's rebellion against his privileged background, the 'grand old family's Huguenot guts', but in this brief exchange Beckett encodes an entire disposition towards the Irish peasant and implicates our 'dirty low-church Protestant', however obliquely, in the politics of Protestant ascendancy (*MPTK*, 73, 159).[11]

Beckett may have had grave reservations about the ideology of the revival, but he was also aware of a shared background – what Pierre Bourdieu would term an 'ontological complicity' – with many of its chief proponents, and so his dialogue with their signature achievements was intense.[12] The passage cited previously quietly signals the possibility that Beckett may even have been indebted to certain aspects of the revival, itself not inherently inimical to modernism, complicating any reading of him as merely disdainful of its achievements.[13] Certainly, he was a regular attendant at the Abbey throughout the 1920s and 1930s, and whilst he found much of the fare to be 'vulgarly conceived and vulgarly written' (*L1*, 49), especially, as with Lady Gregory's *Devorgilla*, when it doubled as thinly veiled political allegory, he knew the repertoire extremely well.[14] In this sense, Murphy's wish that his ashes be flushed down the toilet at the Abbey, 'if possible during the performance of a piece', was both a wry insult perpetrated from beyond the grave and an admission of familiarity, even intimacy (*M*, 168). Beckett is neither Belacqua nor Murphy, of course, but reading the evidence we must admit the significance of the revivalists as both goad and guide.

W. B. Yeats is a case in point. Beckett's early writings are full of wry references to Yeats's work, as in the parody of 'The Tower' in *Dream of Fair to Middling Women* (1932), but he was notoriously evasive on the subject of Yeats's importance to him.[15] Anyone who reads only 'Recent Irish Poetry' will come away with an unduly negative sense of it. In 1952 he told Aidan Higgins flatly that he had 'never read much Yeats', but even a cursory scan of the oeuvre makes this an extraordinary claim.[16] In 1957, he told Herbert Martyn Oliver White that he was 're-reading' Yeats's poems, whilst insisting to Mary Hutchinson a year later that Yeats's symbolism was 'something I wish to forget'.[17] He baulked at Mario Rossi's description of the spirit of Lady Gregory as 'coextensive with the spirit of Ireland' (*L1*, 370) and told Hans Naumann as late as 1954 that it was 'impossible' to speak of Ireland 'with moderation' because he 'loathe[d] that romanticism'

(*L2*, 465). However, in 1956, he suggested Yeats's *Plays for Dancers* or *The Hawk's Well* as viable alternatives to the work of Eugène Ionesco on a bill with his *Acte sans paroles* (*L2*, 685). To make some sense of this, we need to distinguish between the legacy of Yeats the revivalist, peddling the 'Irish Romantic Arnim-Brentano combination', and Yeats the mature poet and experimental playwright (*D*, 76). Yeats's verse plays in particular had a lasting impact on Beckett's conception of the theatre and contained, in his estimation, 'much great poetry' (*D*, 76). *At the Hawk's Well* (1917) was a personal favourite. Yet he also developed a deep regard for many of Yeats's poems, including 'The Tower', indicating the distance he had travelled from *Dream of Fair to middling Women*.[18]

Elsewhere in *Dream*, Beckett also provided a memorable spoof of the Abbey mode, in particular the work of J. M. Synge: '"The mist", she sneered, "an it rollin' home UP the glen and the mist agin an' it rollin' home DOWN the glen"' (*D*, 197). Of all the revivalists, however, it may have been Synge that Beckett admired most, precisely because his dialogue with the governing forms of revivalist writing was fraught.[19] Joe Valente has recently traced Synge's continuing dissent from what he terms the 'noble impracticality' of revivalist mythology, analysing the *Playboy of the Western World*, for example, as a 'satiric gloss' on Lady Gregory's recovery of the Cuchulain myth.[20] For Valente, Synge's plays constitute subtle critiques of revivalism that 'bear far more affinity to the postmodern theater of Beckett than to the Irish National Theatre in which they played', and he provides compelling evidence of Synge's rejection of the 'organic standard of authenticity' that underlay the ideology of revivalism more generally.[21] Beckett was not entirely taken in by Synge – he considered *The Aran Islands* (1907) 'sentimentalisation' – but the drama provided him with a sophisticated formal and ideological critique of the revival and its governing modes (*L1*, 207). This may be why, in 'Love and Lethe', a disconsolate Belacqua is said to have 'thought of Synge and recovered his spirits' (*MPTK*, 95).

All of which alerts us to one of the central aspects of Beckett's relationship to Irish writing: the aspect of form. As Emilie Morin suggests, both Yeats and Synge influenced Beckett because of their 'leaning towards avant-garde experiment'.[22] Beckett conceived of writing in formal as well as thematic terms, and the issue of form provides one way of focusing his relationship to Irish writing at this time. Theodor Adorno's contention that the 'unsolved antagonisms of reality return in artworks as immanent problems of form' applies with particular force to the period surrounding the birth of the Irish Free State,[23] and, as Sinéad Mooney has argued,

'Recent Irish Poetry' reveals Beckett to be 'profoundly involved' in contemporary debates on 'the question of appropriate literary forms for the new state'.[24] Yeats, Synge and Seán O'Casey all mattered both as critics of Irish nationalist politics and because of their experiments with form. This is why, to take a familiar example, Beckett praised O'Casey's capacity to 'discern the principle of disintegration in even the most complacent solidities' and activate it 'to their explosion', and why he refused to provide an appreciation for George Bernard Shaw's anniversary, famously preferring 'a sup of the Hawk's Well, or the Saints', or a whiff of Juno' (*D*, 82). He did not deny Shaw's status as a 'great playwright', but he did imply that the Shavian 'well-made play' – what he terms 'the whole unupsettable apple-cart' – was inferior to the more experimental work of the revivalists because it remained oblivious, at the level of form, to the crises underlying modernist artistic practice (*L1*, 623). What was most admirable about O'Casey's *Juno* was its 'dramatic dehiscence, mind and world come asunder in irreparable dissociation – "chassis"' (*D*, 82). To Beckett's mind, the 'complacent solidities' of a Victorian episteme had fallen apart and where art did not follow suit it ceased to be credible (*D*, 70–6).

In Ireland in the 1920s and 1930s, however, the dominant artistic form was social realism, a naturalist mode that garnered global attention by way of the Cork school of Sean O'Faolain, Frank O'Connor and Daniel Corkery. Beckett followed their work, and was not entirely averse to the realist impulse in Irish literature, preferring it, in fact, to the twilight impulse of the early revivalists.[25] In 'Recent Irish Poetry', for example, he praises F. R. Higgins's poetry for its 'good smell of dung', which he finds 'most refreshing after all the attar of far off, most secret inviolate rose' (a reference to Yeats's early poem, 'The Secret Rose') (*D*, 73). He also admitted to having enjoyed Daniel Corkery's *The Hidden Ireland* and *The Threshold of Quiet*.[26] The problem, however, was that social realism in Ireland quickly reified into a cultural dominant that foreclosed on many of the possibilities that modernist art had identified and exploited (*D*, 73).[27] In *Synge and Anglo-Irish Literature* (1931), for example, Corkery had no qualms about putting Irish writing in the service of Irish reality, a reality he saw as constituted by the triumvirate of religion, nationalism and the land, and no such service was to be expected from Beckett.[28] Hence his insistence that 'the artist who stakes his being is from nowhere, has no kith'. In Beckett's view, Irish art needed to 'withstand the stock assimilations to holy patrimony, national and other', where the term 'withstand' gives a sense of the potency of the forces he is describing and was, to a significant extent, having to withstand himself (*D*, 149). Beckett did not mean that art should not be cognizant of social reality, only that, as Adorno later formulated it, art's 'double character as both autonomous and *fait social*' should be 'incessantly reproduced on the level of its autonomy'.[29] In the 1920s and 1930s, to generalise somewhat, there was a sense that Irish writing should contribute to national culture, and even writers routinely critical of the state, such as O'Faolain and O'Connor, could still be recuperated – as social critique – for the state-building project.

A survey of the literary journals of the period makes this clear. In the 1920s and 1930s, even before his mature vision had taken hold, the form of much of Beckett's work ensured continuing problems with the leading purveyors of Irish literature. George Russell (AE) found him simply inassimilable to the aesthetic of *The Irish Statesman*, for example, a journal that refused political affiliation whilst it explicitly linked its vision for Irish art to its vision for an Irish state under Cumann na nGaedhael.[30] Beckett sent along a few pieces in the 1920s and, judging by Russell's response, was deemed to have little to offer in either realm (art or politics).[31] *The Dublin Magazine*, under the editorship of Seumas O'Sullivan, was perhaps a more promising prospect with its emphasis on 'absolute individual liberty', but it too conceived of Irish writing as having a pivotal role to play in 'fostering the creative side of the national individuality', and Beckett's work was rarely deemed amenable to that project either. Beckett read the magazine with considerable interest and wrote regularly to McGreevy of its contents, but his submissions were routinely rejected or censored by O'Sullivan, who wanted writing that would help Ireland 'gain the power of expressing her nobler values in the world'. It is not difficult to see how this agenda counselled against Beckett's inclusion. Later, when the poems of *Echo's Bones* (1935) were reviewed in *The Dublin Magazine*, they were described in somewhat puzzled terms as the product of a 'very private, personal idiom', at a time when, as we have seen, the search for an artistic self was often conceived as an aspect of the search for a national self.[32] There is an important sense in which, in the 1920s and 1930s, Beckett's work was formally illegible as Irish writing.[33]

Brian Coffey and Denis Devlin were also largely excluded from debates about Irish writing, for reasons similar to those that excluded Beckett, and much has been made of his treatment of them in 'Recent Irish Poetry' as 'the nucleus of a living poetic in Ireland' (*D*, 75). Beckett certainly felt more of an affinity with them than with any of the naturalists, and they all tended to be grouped together (alongside Thomas McGreevy) as modernists, but Beckett's letters reveal much ambivalence about the nature and extent of their poetic achievements (*L1*, 456). In 1933, he lamented meeting both of them with their 'pockets full of calm precious poems', and he was hugely disappointed with Devlin's *Intercessions* (1937) (*L1*, 166). Although he found it 'an agreeable change from all the Hymns Ancient and Modern' (*L1*, 264), he found most of the poems 'overimaged', indeed 'cut adrift from the imaged altogether' (*D*, 94), confiding to McGreevy that the metaphysical poems were 'awful' (*L1*, 549). Coffey's Thomism also bewildered him; he found it 'ambling and incoherent', and he often confessed that he could not follow what Coffey was saying: 'Perhaps the problem is common, the problems, but stated so differently that no headway is possible' (*L1*, 361). He later drew closer to Coffey, and told McGreevy that he preferred Coffey's poems to Devlin's, but one gets the sense that he had grave and lasting reservations about both.[34] He certainly respected their dedication to the craft and considered them friends. He also named them as 'the nucleus of a living poetic in Ireland'. However this public judgement must be tempered by the private correspondence. If their work provided the basis for a modernist poetics in Ireland, to Beckett's eyes it still seemed a rather slender achievement: a judgement similar, of course, to that levied against Beckett's own poems of the period.[35]

'Here form *is* content, content *is* form'. With this early act of homage in 'Dante...Bruno.Vico..Joyce', Beckett made clear his admiration for Joyce's formal experimentation in *Ulysses* and *Finnegans Wake*. Decrying the 'decadent' demand for a form 'strictly divorced from content', Beckett rejects the common conception of form as an 'arbitrary and independent phenomenon'. Instead, as with Joyce, it should respond to 'a strict inner determination': 'When the sense is sleep, the words go to sleep. When the sense is dancing, the words dance' (*D*, 27). Beckett's later comments about Shaw demonstrate the enduring significance of this early insight, and Joyce was an important influence on his quest to find a 'form to accommodate the mess'.[36] Even as Beckett demurred from other aspects of Joyce's project, he retained this emphasis on formal integrity. As he told Israel Shenker, he found Kafka troubling because 'the form is classic, it goes on like a steam-roller – almost serene',[37] and he stated elsewhere of Kafka that he felt 'wary of disasters that let themselves be recorded like a statement of accounts'.[38] It would be difficult to overstate the significance of Joyce's Irish writing to Beckett's development, and it was his understanding of form as itself a mode of artistic expression that struck Beckett particularly.

Flann O'Brien's work mattered, too, especially *At Swim-Two-Birds*, which combined exhilarating formal experimentation with a sustained parody of the revivalist impulse. Rolf Breuer suggests that Beckett 'was influenced only by the structure of the novel and was not interested in the plot or the Gaelic folklore elements', but this seems a little strong.[39] He would certainly have had occasion to enjoy both, though it was undoubtedly the structure of the book – with its profusion of competing narratives – that distinguished the book in Beckett's eyes. As Breuer suggests, many aspects of Beckett's post-war narrative style recall O'Brien's text directly, as when he interpolates commentary on the progress of the story: 'Conclusion of the foregoing' (*At Swim*) becoming 'End of recall' (*Molloy*).[40] He also points up significance of the 'Chinese box structure' for both writers, whereby tales erupt within tales qualifying the authority of teller and tale.[41] For Beckett, as we have seen, it is only when 'form itself becomes a preoccupation' that art can be said to be adequate to its task, and O'Brien's work offered a stunning example of the pre-eminence of Irish modernism in this regard.[42] That said, O'Brien's regular disparagements of Joyce meant that he and Beckett did not develop any significant intellectual relationship, and Joyce's was always the pre-eminent achievement in Beckett's eyes.

In 1954, however, he explained to Hans Naumann that the most important influence that Joyce had on him was 'moral': 'He gave me, without in the least wishing to do so, an insight into what the words "to be an artist" mean' (*L2*, 465). Beckett sensed early on that the Joycean project was, in some sense, 'virtually the opposite' of his own (*L2*, 465), famously observing that Joyce was 'tending toward omniscience and omnipotence' whereas he was 'working with impotence, ignorance'.[43] One important difference between the two, relevant in the present context, was that Joyce's revolution of the word was also keyed in to a vision for the Irish state, which became an important point of divergence for Beckett.[44] As Michael Rubenstein has suggested, Joyce may or may not have been nationalist but he was certainly 'statist', and *Ulysses* reconceptualises the Irish state in ways that go beyond what he terms, after Pierre Bourdieu, the 'collective structures of invention' offered by nationalism. For Rubenstein, *Ulysses* posits a 'utopian vision' of citizenship rooted in state structures (waterworks, sewers, gasworks) and predicated on an indebtedness to infrastructure that appears only in the form of the payments that enable it: taxes.[45] Writing at a time when large parts of Dublin were being destroyed in the 1916 Rising, Joyce was never merely indifferent to the fate of Ireland.[46] In 'Ithaca' particularly, the sphere of civic finance marks an alternative mode of imagined community by which citizenship is refigured in terms of a civic, as opposed to a national debt (or debt to the nation).[47] When Beckett demurred from the terms of Joyce's project he also evaded this 'weak utopian' aspect of the work.[48] To generalise again, what links Joyce, Yeats and the revivalists is that they are all recuperable for some variant of the Irish state-building project, but it is notoriously difficult to read Beckett in this way. Indeed, if we think infrastructurally, most of Beckett's works have a rather quizzical relationship to the trappings of modernity – they contain more caves and chamber pots, for example, than electric circuits or sewers – and one of the more stubborn urges of the Beckettian vagrant is to establish himself in a place of stasis beyond civic debt (think of 'The End' or 'The Expelled'). Where Joyce explodes the bourgeois fantasy of autonomy by exposing our indebtedness to infrastructure, Beckett's vagrants long for little other than autonomy, even if their quest to be free inevitably founders, fails or fizzles out.[49] It is not incidental that Beckett's mature works bear such an oblique relationship to Ireland, and we can take it that the impulse to uncouple art from national context derived to no small extent from the manner in which the two had been conflated in Irish literature. Beckett routinely told Thomas McGreevy in the 1940s to write more for himself and 'less for Ireland' (*L2*, 79).

'Work, work, writing for nothing and yourself'.[50] This was the advice Beckett gave to another Irish writer, Aidan Higgins, who was clearly in awe of his achievements and seeking to liberate himself from the available traditions of Irish writing. Beckett was an obvious (if reluctant) exemplar, given his ex-centric relationship to the whole business, and an enduring theme in Irish responses to Beckett has been gratitude for the extent to which he remained unconscriptable to the Irish scene. Aidan Higgins discerned in Beckett's work 'an impossible freedom', implicitly contrasting him with Yeats and praising him for his artistic courage.[51] 'He belonged to no establishment', John McGahern has remarked, which was why he 'meant most to us'.[52] In a culture apparently obsessed with issues of origin and identity, where the 'Irishness' (or otherwise) of one's writing seemed to be all that mattered, Beckett offered hope of an artistic practice not entirely conditioned by political imperatives, and this was one of the most enduring aspects of his legacy.[53] This is not to say that Beckett simply transcended issues of Irish provenance, or that Ireland didn't matter because Beckett 'had no interest in being an Irish writer'.[54] Rather, after the war, the impulse to withstand assimilation to Irish culture became a governing impulse of the work itself, one expressed in formal as well as thematic terms. If Beckett's work was mostly illegible (and hence ineligible) as Irish literature in the 1920s and 1930s, it would become even more difficult to locate it in an Irish tradition after the war. Yet we have long been aware of a stubborn Irish remainder that will not go away, and generations of writers after Beckett, including many Irish ones, have discerned in his refusal of overt social commentary an eerily powerful reservoir of political critique. '[E]ven in the most extreme refusal of society', Adorno has argued, 'art is essentially social and not understood when this essence is misunderstood'.[55] In this sense, if Beckett's writing might be said to be Irish by way of its preoccupation with form (hardly unique to Ireland), there is an odd sense in which it might even be Irish in its extreme refusal of Irish society.[56] Certainly, its relationship to Irish literature remains to be explicated rather than dismissed.

NOTES

1 Quoted in Seán Kennedy, 'Beckett Publishing in Ireland, 1929–1956', in Mark Nixon (ed.), *Publishing Samuel Beckett* (London: British Library Press, 2011), 65.
2 Ibid., 68.
3 C. J. Ackerley and S. E. Gontarski, 'Foreword', in C. J. Ackerley and S. E Gontarski (eds.), *The Grove Companion to Samuel Beckett* (New York: Grove Press, 2004), xv. Michael Colgan quoted in Matt Wolf, 'National Pride in the Waiting Game', *The Times*, 16 October 1991.
4 See Claire Bracken, 'Becoming-Mother-Machine: The Event of Field Day Vols IV & V', in Patricia Coughlan and Tina O'Toole (eds.), *Irish Literature: Feminist Perspectives* (Dublin: Carysfort Press, 2008), 223–44.
5 See Edward D. Hirsch, 'The Imaginary Irish Peasant', *PMLA* (5: 1991), 1116–33.
6 W. B. Yeats, 'The Fisherman', in *Collected Poems* (London: Macmillan, 1973), 167.
7 Adrian Frazier, 'The Ideology of the Abbey Theatre', in Shaun Richards (ed.), *The Cambridge Companion to Twentieth Century Irish Drama* (Cambridge: Cambridge University Press, 2004), 33–46.
8 Adrian Frazier, 'Irish Modernisms', in John Wilson Foster (ed.), *The Cambridge Companion to the Irish Novel* (Cambridge: Cambridge University Press, 2009), 181.
9 W. B. Yeats, *Collected Poems*, 369.
10 For a history of land initiatives in the period up to 1905, see Andrew Gailey, *Ireland and the Death of Kindness: the Experience of Constructive Unionism, 1890–1905* (Cork: Cork University Press, 1987).
11 See Seán Kennedy, '"Yellow": Beckett and the Performance of Ascendancy', in Ruth Connolly and Ann Coughlan (eds.), *New Voices in Irish Criticism 5* (Dublin: Four Courts Press, 2005), 177–86.
12 On the topic of habitus as ontological complicity, see Pierre Bourdieu, *Pascalian Meditations* (Cambridge: Polity Press, 2000), 163. For an overview of Beckett's interest in the writers of the revival, see Emilie Morin, *Samuel Beckett and the Problem of Irishness* (New York: Palgrave Macmillan, 2009), 21–54.
13 See Emer Nolan, 'Modernism and the Revival', in Joe Cleary and Claire Connolly (eds.), *The Cambridge Companion to Modern Irish Culture* (Cambridge: Cambridge University Press, 2005), 157–72.

14 For a sense of Beckett's intimate knowledge of the Abbey program, see John Pilling, *A Samuel Beckett Chronology* (London: Routledge, 2006). For Beckett's frustration with the Abbey's penchant for state allegory, see James McNaughton, 'The Politics of Aftermath: Beckett, Modernism and the Irish Free State', in Seán Kennedy (ed.), *Beckett and Ireland* (Cambridge: Cambridge University Press, 2010), 62.
15 'It is time I learnt, he thought. I will study in the Nassau Street School, I will frequent the Railway Street Academies' (*Dream*, 137).
16 To Higgins, 29 October 1952 (Harry Ransom Humanities Research Center, University of Austin, Texas. Hereafter HRHRC).
17 To Oliver, 15 April 1957 (TCDMS3777). To Hutchinson, 21 January 1958 (HRHRC).
18 Beckett was in the habit of reciting from the plays and poems as late as the 1980s, see Anne Atik, *How it Was* (London: Faber & Faber, 2001).
19 James Knowlson, 'Beckett and John Millington Synge', in James Knowlson and John Pilling (eds.), *Frescoes of the Skull: The Later Prose and Drama of Samuel Beckett* (New York: Grove Press, 1980), 260.
20 Joe Valente, *The Myth of Manliness in Irish National Culture, 1880–1922* (Urbana: University of Illinois Press, 2010), 128.
21 Ibid., 128, 129.
22 Morin, *Samuel Beckett and the Problem of Irishness*, 25.
23 Theodor Adorno, *Aesthetic Theory* (London: Continuum Books, 1997), 7.
24 Sinéad Mooney, 'Kicking against the Thermolaters: "Recent Irish Poetry"', in Seán Kennedy (ed.), *Samuel Beckett Today/Aujourd'hui*, Historicising Beckett (2005), 30–1.
25 Beckett kept tabs on O'Faolain and O'Connor, viewing them as 'inseparable', but when he read their work in *The Dublin Magazine* he 'flinched at every 4th page'. Beckett to McGreevy, 5 May 1935 (TCDMS100902/75).
26 In a letter to Richard Seaver, dated 15 May 1959 (HRHRC).
27 See Joe Cleary, 'This Thing of Darkness: Conjectures on Irish Naturalism', in *Outrageous Fortune* (Dublin: Field Day Publications, 2005), 111–79.
28 Daniel Corkery, *Synge and Anglo-Irish Literature* (Cork: Cork University Press, 1931).
29 Adorno, *Aesthetic Theory*, 6.
30 See Nicholas Allen, *George Russell and the New Ireland, 1905–30* (Dublin: Four Courts Press, 2003), 144–73.
31 Seán Kennedy, 'Beckett Publishing in Ireland, 1929–1956', in Mark Nixon (ed.), *Publishing Samuel Beckett* (London: The British Library, 2011), 61.
32 Ibid., 61–2.
33 For a long time, he also remained illegible in Irish studies. See Ronán McDonald, 'The Ghost at the Feast: Beckett and Irish Studies', in Seán Kennedy (ed.), *Beckett and Ireland* (Cambridge: Cambridge University Press, 2010), 16–30.
34 In a letter dated 9 January 1936, quoted in John Pilling, *A Samuel Beckett Chronology* (London: Routledge, 2006), 55.

35 Derek Mahon, 'A Noise like Wings: Beckett's Poetry', *Irish University Review* (14.1: 1984), 88–92.
36 Quoted in Tom Driver, 'Beckett by the Madeleine', in Lawrence Graver and Raymond Federman (eds.), *Samuel Beckett: The Critical Heritage* (London: Routledge and Kegan Paul, 1979), 219.
37 Quoted in Israel Shenker, 'An Interview with Beckett', in Lawrence Graver and Raymond Federman (eds.), *Samuel Beckett: The Critical Heritage* (London: Routledge and Kegan Paul, 1979), 148.
38 In a letter to Hans Naumann, dated 17 February 1954. See *L2*, 465.
39 Rolf Breuer, 'Flann O'Brien and Samuel Beckett', *The Irish University Review* (37.2: Autumn/Winter 2007), 343.
40 Ibid., 344.
41 Ibid., 344–5.
42 Driver, 'Beckett by the Madeleine', 219.
43 Shenker, 'An Interview with Beckett', 148.
44 On Beckett's resistance to 'the creation of a nation-state devoted to the construction of a capitalist form of modernity', see Gregory Dobbins, *Lazy Idle Schemers: Irish Modernism and the Cultural Politics of Idleness* (Dublin: Field Day Publications, 2010), 162.
45 Michael D. Rubenstein, '"The Waters of Civic Finance": Moneyed States in Joyce's *Ulysses*', *Novel* (Summer 2003), 295.
46 See Enda Duffy, 'Disappearing Dublin: *Ulysses*, postcoloniality and the politics of space', in Marjorie Howes and Derek Attridge (eds.), *Semicolonial Joyce* (Cambridge: Cambridge University Press, 2000), 37–57.
47 Michael D. Rubenstein, '"The Waters of Civic Finance": Moneyed States in Joyce's *Ulysses*', *Novel* (Summer 2003), 297.
48 On Joyce's weak utopian impulse, see ibid.
49 'They clothed me and gave me money. I knew what the money was for, it was to get me started. When it was gone I would have to get more, if I wanted to go on' (*CSP*, 78).
50 In a letter dated 22 April 1958 (HRHRC).
51 Aidan Higgins, 'Foundering in Reality: Godot, Hamlet, Papa and Three Bashes at Festschrift', *The Irish University Review* (14.1: 1984), 101 and 100. Quoted in Denis Sampson, 'A Conversation with John McGahern', *The Canadian Journal of Irish Studies* (17.1: 1991), 22.
52 Quoted in Denis Sampson, 'A Conversation with John McGahern', 22.
53 For more on this, see Seán Kennedy, 'Samuel Beckett's Reception in Ireland', in Mark Nixon and Matthew Feldman (eds.), *The International Reception of Samuel Beckett* (London: Continuum, 2009), 64–6.
54 David Weisberg, *Chronicles of Disorder: Samuel Beckett and the Cultural Politics of the Modern Novel* (Albany: SUNY Press, 2000), 176. Indeed, Gregory Dobbins reads *Murphy* precisely as 'a satire of the way in which intellectuals devoted to traditional forms of intellectual work lie to themselves in order to create the illusion that they have somehow transcended the material conditions they inhabit'; see Dobbins, *Lazy Idle Schemers*, 170.

55 Adorno, *Aesthetic Theory*, 442.
56 See what Ronán MacDonald terms Declan Kiberd's 'provocative' claim that Beckett is the first truly Irish playwright because of his freedom from 'factitious elements of Irishness'. *Inventing Ireland* (London: Jonathan Cape, 1995), 531; McDonald, 'The Ghost at the Feast', 22.

CHAPTER 19

English Literature

Mark Byron

Samuel Beckett's relationship with the literature of his mother tongue is understandably complex. His education at Trinity College, Dublin and his subsequent autodidactic course of study served to provide him with a broad range of literary genres and textual exemplars across the history of the English language. His study of English literature in the earlier phases of life was complemented by that of other modern European languages such as Italian and French, and later, German and Spanish. The long shadow of his fellow Dubliners, especially James Joyce, was cast across his first forays into literary composition, and he conducted his mature literary life largely displaced from any significant Anglophone community. Beckett's literary precocity and longevity meant that he drew deeply from the experiments of modernism and wrote through a number of cultural phases, perhaps most notably French existentialism, postmodernism and postcolonialism, with which he has been associated and against which he has been measured. Beckett's mediation of the English language and Anglophone literature is characterised by a general shift from his earlier works, in which direct intertextual reference and stylistic emulation tend to prevail, to the later, more subtle and critically reflective deployments of literary genres, tropes and stylistic echoes, operating in a truly polyglot and immanent compositional milieu. Beckett's use of source material is recursive across his career: whilst there are significant differences in method and tone between the earliest works composed in English and later works that mediate English and French (and occasionally German), even very late works draw on literary concepts and materials honed in Beckett's formative years at Trinity and in London.

Beckett's reading in, and mediation of, English literature centres largely upon the classics of British literature (including canonical Irish and Anglo-Irish writers), with North American literature filling a surprisingly small role in his literary sensibility. The few exceptions to this rule, such as Edgar Allan Poe and Herman Melville, play relatively modest roles in his literary worldview. Beckett did read some of his American literary contemporaries, or otherwise came into contact with them in the various literary circles of London and Paris: most notably T. S. Eliot and Ezra Pound. His comment regarding Gertrude Stein's 'logographs' in the famous letter to Axel Kaun of 9 July 1937 is one of very few substantive references to her work (*LI*, 515, 519). Beckett's readers have their favourite intertextual references – such as the 'wild surmise' of Keats's sonnet, 'On Looking into Chapman's Homer', or 'pandemonium', a word introduced into the English language in Milton's *Paradise Lost*, both appearing in *The Lost Ones*; the 'vile jelly' of *King Lear* appearing in *Ill Seen Ill Said*; and so on – or instances of otherwise notable literary curiosity, such as the fact that Beckett found *Tristram Shandy*, a novel seemingly tailored to his literary temperament, irritating 'in spite of its qualities'.[1] Beckett's literary preferences were shaped very directly by his education, and his practices span a spectrum from straightforward quotation to deep critical response and compositional emulation.

The recent availability of numerous notebooks dating from his Trinity College, Dublin days and afterwards in London, Germany and Paris, have substantially enlarged the understanding of Beckett's reading tendencies and preferences. His note-taking methods also shed light on the kinds of uses to which he was to put his sources. The promise of full transcriptions of Beckett's literary manuscripts also opens the way for increased familiarity with his composition methods, including how they may have changed across his career, permitting a deeper awareness of specific textual filiations.

BECKETT'S LITERARY EDUCATION

Not much is known of Beckett's earliest education in English literature: James Knowlson recounts one story from Beckett's school days at Portora Royal School, concerning a night-time recital of Conan Doyle's story 'The Speckled Band'. Beckett and a friend also memorised Keats's 'Ode to a Nightingale' on a walk outside of school grounds (*K*, 45, 42). Little further information, beyond a precocious desire to read, has yet come to light. However scholars such as Frederik Smith have been able to trace Beckett's instruction in English literature at Trinity College in the first two years of his degree, by a process of reconstructing extant syllabus material.[2] Beckett's first-year tutor in 1923 was A. A. Luce, editor of George Berkeley, who passed on to Knowlson the kinds of examination papers Beckett faced in the Junior Exhibition of that year: 'prospective students were held responsible for Shakespeare's *Merchant of Venice*, Milton's *Paradise Lost*, Book I, and chapters of Alexander H. Thompson's *History of English Literature*, including "The Age of Anne – Pope, Swift, and the Augustan Poets"; "The Great Novelists of the Eighteenth Century"; and "The Dawn of Romantic Poetry"'.[3] Prior to choosing his honours programme in French and Italian in 1925–6, Beckett engaged in an intensive study of English Literature from Chaucer (to whom he would return in the *Dream* notebook) up to and including the eighteenth century. His curriculum of 1925 saw a particular concentration in Augustan literature, especially Addison, Pope, Dryden and Swift.[4] This course of study was not comprehensive but proved to be formative. Beckett maintained a correspondence with the English Department at Trinity College throughout his life, attested by numerous letters in the Trinity College Library archive, including letters to Herbert White, professor of English Literature (1939–60) in the years 1955–63, and letters between Beckett and R. B. D. French, senior lecturer in English Literature, in 1959–60, 1963 and 1969–72.[5]

Beckett's education in English Literature divided between his formal schooling at Portora Royal and Trinity and his autodidactic course of study in Dublin, Paris and London in the early 1930s. He tells Thomas McGreevy in a letter of May 1930 of his return to Keats – 'I like him the best of them all, because he doesn't beat his fists on the table' (*L1*, 21). This affiliation to Keats remained with Beckett throughout his career, evident as late as 1977 in the unpublished story draft 'The Voice'. In that manuscript, Beckett produces an abbreviated history of English literature, beginning with reference to such Anglo-Saxon poems as *The Wanderer* and *Beowulf*. He makes serial reference to Keats's 'Ode to a Nightingale', producing a sequence of subtle word patternings in emulation of Keats's poetic diction that demands the most intimate knowledge of the poem: 'Beckett is quoting by heart, in both the emotional and mnemonic senses of the word'.[6]

Beckett's self-directed course of study in English Literature in the early 1930s is preserved in a manuscript suite presented by Edward Beckett and Caroline Beckett Murphy to Trinity College, Dublin in 1997, part of the so-called 'Notes Diverse Holo'. He took these notes from Emile Legouis and Louis Cazamian's textbook, *A History of English Literature*, maintaining its order of chapter titles and general organisation as might befit an historical study of literary development with an eye towards genre and mode.[7] The contents of Beckett's fifty-nine pages entail mostly headings by period and author, cross-referenced with Legouis and Cazamian's textbook and the occasional comment. The subject matter ranges from Anglo-Saxon through all the major historical periods to the Pre-Raphaelites, the

'Irish Twilighters' and 'Sir Henry Newbolt Collected Bilge'.[8] Emphasis falls upon certain authors, particularly Chaucer, Dunbar, Shakespeare, Milton and Dryden. This exhaustive method of note-taking entailed certain risks of redundancy and diminishing returns. John Pilling has noted in the context of the *Whoroscope* notebook that 'there is perhaps no comparable example of a modern author so prepared to undertake such labour-intensive enterprises, when in the nature of things he could not be certain that they would prove in any way fruitful'.[9] Formidable achievement, exhaustive permutation and potential futility conjoin early in Beckett's autodidactic methods, ready for transfer into a fully fledged aesthetics.

BECKETT'S CANONICAL INTERACTIONS

Whilst the fullest catalogue of Beckett's reference to and emulations of various writers in the history of English literature is not yet complete, recent annotative work on Beckett's texts and studies of recently available manuscripts have furthered scholarly understanding of the relation between literary composition and Beckett's documentary record. In addition to abundant literary identifications in the general scholarship, Beckett Studies is privileged by recent work on several of Beckett's notebooks – Mark Nixon's study of Beckett's German diaries, Matthew Feldman's study of Beckett's interwar notes, and John Pilling's work on the *Whoroscope* notebook and *Dream* notebook[10] – as well as assiduous annotative work on individual texts, such as Pilling's *Companion to Dream of Fair to Middling Women*, Chris Ackerley's *Demented Particulars* and *Obscure Locks, Simple Keys*, as well as Ackerley and S. E. Gontarski's *Companion to Samuel Beckett*.[11] The critical truism has long held sway to beware 'the neatness of identification' between source material candidates and Beckett's work. Equally, a converse fuzziness of identification entails its own limitations, illustrated in recent controversies concerning the uses of textual evidence and the strength of identification and association.[12] Any argument for direct literary influence requires a firm evidential grounding, keeping in mind that hermeneutic evidence – often associative, and indicative of mood, tone and style – might not be confined to strict empirical evidence in all cases. Renewed scholarly attention to the processes and assumptions of evidentiary use is of great utility in matters of literary influence and emulation.[13]

This sharpened conceptual framework within which to document literary influence and emulation potentially alters the valencies of particular instances of influence, as well as the perceived tone and import of literary reference in Beckett's work per se. Yet the rich scholarship of the last half century remains valuable in its own right, and provides essential groundwork for new understanding of literary influence. The sheer weight of Beckett criticism precludes an assiduous account of the range and kinds of Anglophone literary influence upon Beckett's writing, but merits an indication of its contours. It is broadly understood that Beckett's particular proclivities in reading and annotating English literature during his student days and into the 1930s are overtly reflected in his earlier literary efforts prior to the Second World War, but that these literary influences (and most other influences from philosophy, psychology, theology, and of course, other literatures) are used sparingly thereafter, and are often largely submerged in the later works.

Keeping in mind the changing rates of Beckett's reading of and reference to specific authors, genres and literary periods over his long career, significant elements of literary influence can be outlined summarily. Beckett read vigorously in Elizabethan and Jacobean tragedy in 1935–6. Pilling catalogues the many plays and authors covered in this autodidactic programme of reading and note taking, preserved in the *Whoroscope* notebook: Francis Beaumont and John Fletcher (both single author and collaborative works), Thomas Dekker, Christopher Marlowe, Thomas Middleton, John Ford, Philip Massinger, Ben Jonson and William Shakespeare, as well as the comedies of George Farquhar and the poetry of John Donne.[14] Beckett also read the prose works of Thomas Nashe, George Peele and Robert Greene – the latter providing the source for Beckett's Augustinian chiasmus: 'Neither despair (1 thief saved) nor presume (only 1 saved)'.[15] At this time he also began a schematic reading of eighteenth-century novelists, including Tobias Smollett, Henry Fielding and Samuel Johnson's *Rasselas*.

Beckett's earlier works are replete with Shakespearean references too abundant to enumerate, but many of which are opportune deployments of specific phrases or images. There are occasional sightings in the later works, such as the 'vile jelly' of *King Lear* in *Ill Seen Ill Said*. Beckett's most abiding concern with Shakespeare is that of 'unaccommodated man' in *Watt* and the Trilogy[16]: this notion, best exemplified in *Lear*, recurs explicitly in the figure of Hamm in *Endgame* (who also recalls an attenuated Hamlet as well as Richard III), but might be seen in several other plays where characters yearn for tragic affect, or otherwise devolve into tomfoolery (*Krapp's Last Tape*, *Acts Without Words I* and *II* and even *Breath*). Another significant engagement with Shakespeare, both rhetorically and thematically, occurs in Pozzo's 'born astride the grave' speech in Act II of *Waiting for Godot*, which clearly emulates a number of Macbeth's speeches late in that play, not least 'Tomorrow and tomorrow and tomorrow'.

An abiding interest in prose works of the seventeenth century is in evidence not only in Beckett's early note taking, but in plays and stories spanning his career. The lifelong fascination with Robert Burton's *Anatomy of Melancholy* (1621) begins in earnest in the more than 300 entries in the *Dream* notebook of 1930–1, mostly taken from Part II of Burton's work concerning love and religious melancholy.[17] Although most overt references to Burton occur in the early works, particularly *Murphy*, residual inklings arise in such late works as *Ill Seen Ill Said*. Burton complements such other influential figures as Democritus and Schopenhauer in shaping Beckett's singular, and often ironic, pessimism. Sir Thomas Browne also occupies Beckett's attention, the evidence for which only arises in the later prose, particularly *The Lost Ones*[18] – Browne's *Garden of Cyrus* (1658), subtitled 'the Quincuncall, Lozenge, or Net-Work Plantations of the Ancients, Artificially, Naturally, Mystically Considered', finds its latter-day echo in the chiasmic arrangement of the tunnels within the cylinder – and *Play*, in which the three characters, figuratively buried in their tawdry iterative history as they are physically interred in giant pots, recall Browne's *Hydrotaphia, Urn Burial* (1658), a study of newly discovered sepulchral urns in Norfolk.

The influence of Jonathan Swift upon Beckett's literary career is profound and well documented: his first sustained contact was at Trinity College (said to still possess the volumes of Swift containing Beckett's marginalia), and he reread much of Swift's work in 1933 – certainly *Gulliver's Travels*, and probably *Tale of a Tub* and *Journal to Stella* – as well as at later times in his life.[19] In early 1933 Beckett rode his Swift bicycle out to Portrane Lunatic Asylum in Dublin, near the ruined tower (on its mound or motte) where Dean Swift was said to keep his 'motte' (lover) Stella. This episode is memorialised in the poem 'Sanies I', composed during Easter of that year.[20] Frederik Smith notes that the common critical tendency to treat Beckett and Swift as spiritual confederates is helpful to an understanding of neither writer, but the direct influence of Swift's dim view of humanity is evident in Beckett's early works, particularly *Murphy*. Among other direct gestures to Swift, the final, disastrous boat trip and ensuing massacre of Lady Pedal by the asylum attendant Lemuel, at the end of *Malone Dies*, conflates a nod to *Tale of a Tub* with the title character of *Gulliver's Travels*.

The Augustan literary sensibility has come to be that most closely associated with Beckett in the Anglophone tradition, in part the consequence of recent scholarship and renewed access to Beckett's working notebooks. The occasional reviewer – Edwin Muir in 1934 and Kenneth Rexroth in 1956 – noted such affinities in Beckett's work, with the latter boldly proclaiming a view that now seems altogether contemporary: '[Beckett] has a mind of singular toughness and stability – a mind like an eighteenth-century Englishman, as sly as Gibbon, as compassionate as Johnson, as bold as Wilkes, as Olympian as Fielding. I don't mean that he is "as good as" a mixture of all these people. I mean he is their moral contemporary'.[21] When asked, Beckett expressed no dissatisfaction at being thought of in the company of Swift, Fielding and Sterne.[22] His reading in eighteenth-century prose in the 1930s is evident in the preponderant references to Fielding, Swift and Johnson in the earlier prose works up to and including *Murphy*, in letters to Thomas McGreevy in the 1930s and in the *Whoroscope* notebook (all of which also include consistent reference to Pope). Beckett read Jane Austen in February 1935: in letters to McGreevy he mentions how 'the divine Jane [...] has much to teach me' and speaks of his admiration for her style.[23] The submerged networks of literary reference in *Watt* – the novel drafted in the following decade and published belatedly in 1953 – are still to be adequately understood, especially if the six manuscript notebooks and their abundant reserves are included. There exists a complex system of reference to Joyce's *Ulysses*, especially the Oxen of the Sun and Cyclops episodes, but a strong identification with various narrative moments in Tobias Smollett's *Humphrey Clinker* is also evident: the correlated names such as Quin and Watt, and characters paired in dyads of mutual dependency, often due to physical liability, are among the more obvious examples. Beckett's commerce with the novels of Sterne was both durable and foundational to his practice as a novelist. He adapted stylistic and narratological elements from *Tristram Shandy* and *A Sentimental Journey through France and Italy*, recalibrating the novel as a field of self-aware and self-derogating *inventio*.[24]

Beckett's affinities with Samuel Johnson are well documented: his confession to Deirdre Bair that 'it's Johnson, always Johnson, who is with me' (*B*, 272) places the melancholic lexicographer at or near the summit of Beckett's literary affinities. Beckett owned a 1799 edition of the *Dictionary* of 1755, as well as *Rasselas* and other works, including Boswell's biography and Hester Thrale's *Anecdotes of the Late Samuel Johnson, LL.D.*[25] Beckett's attempt to write a play in the mid 1930s on the Johnson-Thrale household, *Human Wishes*, has been thoroughly documented.[26] Whatever influence this abortive treatment had on Beckett's later drama, it bears Johnson's shade at one remove. The sheer volume of this material – three notebooks and collected manuscript and typescript material – indicates a single-minded attempt to master the details of Johnson's life and the general tone of his work. Beckett's interest in Johnson's medical condition, especially his impotence (from the 1937 discovery of Johnson's medical journal), and later, in his melancholy and fear of aphasia and encroaching insanity, are 'sublimated' into *Watt* and the novels of the Trilogy.[27] Further evidence for Beckett's interest in Johnson's biography, and the way it had become naturalised in his thought, may be found in the way Beckett associates Boswell's maxim, '*vitam continet una dies*' ('a single day contains the whole of my life') with Georges Belmont in a letter dated 8 August 1951 (*L2*, 278). A week later, Beckett wrote to tell Mania Péron '[j]e relis Boswell dans la belle édition de Birkbeck Hill' (*L2*, 281), where he also refers to the recent publication of several Boswell manuscripts found in Malahide Castle in 1930 and 1936.

Beckett's negotiations with his nineteenth-century literary forebears are remarkable for their sparsity. He read Dickens, referring to 'the old childish absorbtion [*sic*] with which I read Treasure Island and Oliver Twist' in a letter to Thomas McGreevy in September 1931, and evident in his description of ineffectual human agents as 'Pickwicks' (*L2*, 92, 179). Beckett also read George Eliot, giving *The Mill on the Floss* backhanded praise for its 'seedy' humour (*L2*, 240). Beckett read *Moby Dick* in the summer of 1932 (*K*, 161) in a sequence of reading that also included Thackeray's *Vanity Fair*, Aldous Huxley's *Point Counter Point* (of which Beckett was scurrilously if summarily withering in his assessments) and Fielding's *Joseph Andrews* and *Tom Jones*. There is no record of his having read Hawthorne, Whitman, Dickinson or most other significant American writers of the nineteenth century. One can only speculate on what might have transpired at such intellectual and literary encounters.

BECKETT AND HIS CONTEMPORARIES

The young Beckett engaged intensively with the literary life of his city. His circle included a number of prominent and rising poets and writers, including several of whom were subjects of his published critical appraisal: Denis Devlin, Thomas McGreevy, Brian Coffey, Austin Clarke and others. Drama occupied a pivotal place in his literary development: whilst a student at Trinity, he and Geoffrey Thompson would frequent the Abbey Theatre, attending premières of Sean O'Casey's *Juno and the Paycock* and *The Plough and the Stars*, as well as W. B. Yeats's Sophoclean adaptations, *Oedipus the King* and *Oedipus at Colonus*. He also saw productions of canonical playwrights, such as R. B. Sheridan, revivals of J. M. Synge's plays – a significant influence upon his own dramatic development – as well as many plays by contemporary playwrights, such as Lennox Robertson and Brinsley Macnamara (*K*, 56–7). Beckett, like Joyce, dismissed the Celtic Revival – 'cut-and-dried sanctity and loveliness' (*D*, 71) – and gave no sign of any knowledge of prominent contemporaries such as Elizabeth Bowen.

His engagements with currents in modernist American literature were equally sparse: there is brief mention of T. S. Eliot in 'Recent Irish Poetry'[28] and frequent, passing mention in letters to McGreevy. Beckett reviewed Ezra Pound's *Make It New*, 'Ex Cathezra', but wrote little else concerning modernist American poets (or British poets for that matter). In a letter to Patricia Hutchins of 18 December 1953, Beckett recounts his one regrettable meeting with Pound in 1929: 'The only time I remember having met Pound was one evening at dinner with the Joyces in the Trianons, Place de Rennes. He was having great trouble with a fond d'artichaud and was very aggressive and disdainful' (*L2*, 437). Beckett made scant reference to contemporary American playwrights, except to comment on their commercial success – or otherwise – such as the observation that Eugene O'Neill's *Desire Under the Elms* was 'flopping' in Paris in a letter to Pamela Mitchell of 25 November 1953 (*L2*, 421). The glaring absence of opinion of or commerce with contemporary Anglophone poets, novelists and playwrights, especially later in his career, is consistent with Beckett's earlier turn from English to predominantly French literary sustenance after the Second World War. He drew on his earliest and most intimate absorption of English literature at Trinity College in the 1920s and by virtue of his own energies in London in the 1930s, rarely migrating into the nineteenth century, and almost never across the Atlantic. Beckett's shift to French as his preferred language of composition in the late 1930s is reflected in his reading predilections at the time: having internalised an English literary sensibility at university and by his own devices – a sensibility particularly shaped by Renaissance drama and eighteenth-century fiction – Beckett immersed himself in the literary heritage of his adopted home on his way to becoming, in his own way, an authentically French writer.

NOTES

1 Beckett to Thomas McGreevy, 5 August 1938, quoted in *K*, 295. Knowlson indicates that Beckett later wrote to William York Tyndall (on 15 January 1963), expressing high praise for the novel (*K*, 762, n168).
2 Frederik N. Smith, *Beckett's Eighteenth Century* (Houndmills: Palgrave, 2002), 11–16.

3 Ibid., 12.
4 Ibid., 14.
5 See Jane Maxwell, 'Catalogue of the Samuel Beckett Manuscripts at Trinity College Library, Dublin', in Matthijs Engelberts, Everett Frost and Jane Maxwell (eds.) *Notes Diverse Holo, Samuel Beckett Today/Aujourd'hui* (Amsterdam: Rodopi, 2006), 183–99.
6 P. J. Murphy, 'On First Looking into Beckett's *The Voice*', in John Pilling and Mary Bryden (eds.) *The Ideal Core of the Onion: Reading Beckett Archives* (Reading: Beckett International Foundation, 1992), 75.
7 Emile Legouis and Louis Cazamian, *A History of English Literature*, trans. Helen Douglas Irvine, 2 vols. (London: J. M. Dent & Sons, 1926–7). See 'TCD MS 10970: English literature' in *Notes Diverse Holo*, 105–11.
8 Maxwell, 'Catalogue of the Samuel Beckett Manuscripts at Trinity College Library, Dublin', 110.
9 John Pilling, '"For Interpolation": Beckett and English Literature', in *Notes Diverse Holo*, 206.
10 Mark Nixon, *Samuel Beckett's German Diaries 1936–1937* (London: Continuum, 2011); Matthew Feldman, *Beckett's Books: A Cultural History of Samuel Beckett's 'Interwar Notes'* (London and New York: Continuum, 2006); John Pilling, 'From a (W)horoscope to *Murphy*', *The Ideal Core of the* Onion, 1–20, and *Beckett's Dream Notebook* (Reading: Beckett International Foundation, 1999).
11 John Pilling, *A Companion to* Dream of Fair to Middling Women (Tallahassee: Journal of Beckett Studies Books, 2004); Chris Ackerley, *Demented Particulars: The Annotated* Murphy (Tallahassee: Journal of Beckett Studies Books, 1998) and *Obscure Locks, Simple Keys: The Annotated* Watt (Tallahassee: Journal of Beckett Studies Books, 2005); Chris Ackerley and S. E. Gontarski, *The Grove Companion to Samuel Beckett* (New York: Grove, 2004).
12 See P. J. Murphy, *Beckett's Dedalus: Dialogical Engagements with Joyce in Beckett's Fiction* (Toronto: University of Toronto Press, 2009).
13 See especially Feldman, *Beckett's Books*.
14 John Pilling, '"For Interpolation": Beckett and English Literature', in *Notes Diverse Holo*, 207–32.
15 Quoted in Pilling, 'For Interpolation', 218.
16 Ackerley and Gontarski, *The Grove Companion to Samuel Beckett*, 523.
17 Ibid., 75.
18 See P. J. Murphy, 'The Nature of Allegory in "The Lost Ones," or the Quincunx Realistically Considered', *Journal of Beckett Studies* (7: 1982), 71–88; and David Porush, 'Beckett's Deconstruction of the Machine in *The Lost Ones*', *L'Esprit Créateur* (26.4: 1986), 87–98.
19 Smith, *Beckett's Eighteenth Century*, 18 and 28.
20 Ibid., 29; see also *L1*, 150.
21 Kenneth Rexroth, 'The Point is Irrelevance', *Nation* (14 April 1956), 325; quoted in Frederik N. Smith, *Beckett's Eighteenth Century*, 3.
22 William York Tindall, *Samuel Beckett* (New York: Columbia University Press, 1964), 37.
23 Letters of 14 and 20 February 1935, in *L2*, 249–56.

24 Smith, *Beckett's Eighteenth Century*, 48–9; see generally Chapter 3, 'Beckett and the Eighteenth-Century Novel', 47–67.
25 Ackerley and Gontarski, *The Grove Companion to Samuel Beckett*, 283–4.
26 Smith, *Beckett's Eighteenth Century*, especially 110–31; Lionel Kelly, 'Beckett's Human Wishes', in *The Ideal Core of the Onion*, 21–44; and Stephen John Dilks, 'Samuel Beckett's Samuel Johnson', *Modern Language Review* (98.2: 2003), 285–98.
27 Dilks, 'Samuel Beckett's Samuel Johnson', 284.
28 Both reviews are reprinted in *D*, 70–6 and 77–9.

CHAPTER 20

French Literature

Angela Moorjani

For influential French writer, critic and publisher Maurice Nadeau, the Irish Samuel Beckett was the greatest living French writer of the post-war period.[1] This chapter explores how this Irishman morphed into a major French writer. His impassioned interest in and then practice of French writing had their beginnings in the honours programme in modern literature (French and Italian) at Trinity College, Dublin in the 1920s, after which two years in Paris as a *lecteur d'anglais* immersed him in the modernist and surrealist ferment of the French capital, the intellectual excitement of the École Normale Supérieure and the avant-garde literary circles – both Anglophone and Francophone – orbiting around James Joyce. Taking it all in, he began to write: an essay on Joyce, a short story, poems – including his *Whoroscope* on René Descartes and time – and a study of Marcel Proust, most of which were published or about to be by the time he returned to Dublin in fall 1930 to take up a lectureship at Trinity in French literature. On resigning after little over a year to return to Paris to devote himself to his first novel, he interlaced it with often witty or mordant asides about the French writers he had recently studied or taught. At the same time, he was soon to apprentice himself to the ones he admired most among them, intent as he was on freeing himself from the overwhelming influence of Joyce evident in his early writing. Composing poetry in French soon after moving permanently to Paris in 1937 at age thirty-one, Beckett was to make his own avant-garde contributions to French literature in his post-war fiction and drama. Begun during his undergraduate years and lasting a lifetime, his passionate and learned engagement with French writing mingled with other literatures – Irish, English, Italian, German, Classical Greek and Latin, Russian, Spanish, among others – reverberating throughout his oeuvre. In turn, Beckett's influence on the entire spectrum of French literature and the arts in the second half of the twentieth century and beyond is incontrovertible, placing some writers in the same predicament as the young Beckett in relation to Joyce.

HONOURS IN FRENCH LITERATURE

Some of the French flavour of Beckett's writings can be traced back to the prescribed books listed in the *Dublin University Calendar* for 1923 to 1927, the years Beckett took the examinations for honours in modern literature, including the final moderatorship. Candidates choosing French as one of their two honours languages were required to study in detail the following works, here listed in chronological order, but grouped differently for the nine scheduled term examinations: *La chanson de Roland*; selections from Maurice Scève's *Délie* of neoplatonic and Petrarchan inspiration, Ronsard's poetry and Montaigne's *Essays*; five specific plays by Corneille, four by Racine, seven by Molière, La Fontaine's *Fables* and the first part of Honoré d'Urfé's pastoral *L'Astrée*; several plays by Marivaux, Florian's *Les arlequinades* and Émile Faguet's *Dix-huitième siècle*; selections of romantic poetry by Hugo, Vigny and Musset and four of the latter's plays, three assigned novels and five short stories by Balzac, poems by Leconte de Lisle and the minor symbolist Francis Vielé-Griffin and prose selections from Sainte-Beuve, Théophile Gautier's *Voyage en Italie*, several of Maupassant's *contes* and Ernest Renan's *Souvenirs de jeunesse*.[2]

Skimpy on the Middle Ages, with only *Gormont et Isembart* and *Aucassin et Nicolette* required, the moderatorship list in French for 1927, the year Beckett took and topped in the exam, simply states for the sixteenth through eighteenth centuries that candidates were expected to show 'first-hand acquaintance with the principal works of Ronsard, Corneille, Molière, Racine, and Marivaux'.[3] The list becomes more specific (and more eclectic) for the nineteenth and early twentieth centuries, including several novels each by Balzac, Stendhal and Gide, the 'Combray' section of Proust's *Du côté de chez Swann*, selected poems by Leconte de Lisle, Paul Verlaine, symbolist poets Francis Jammes and Henri de Régnier, the minor symbolist turned religious poet Louis Le Cardonnel and the poets in Robert de la Vaissière's anthology of twentieth-century poetry. The list includes several largely forgotten works: Le Cardonnel's poems, Marcel Schwob's novels, Régnier's tales and Henri Pourrat's World War I poem *Les montagnards*, while omitting some of the more notable authors of the canon.

Finally, among the requirements for honours and the moderatorship were, for French, a grounding in the history of French literature to be gleaned from Trinity College professor Thomas Rudmose-Brown's *Short History of French Literature* and parts of Gustave Lanson's *Histoire de la littérature française*, the latter a standard and popular manual.

Rudmose-Brown, known to have fostered Beckett's interest in French literature, was particularly concerned with literary *art* and the movements that cultivated it.[4] This emphasis and his partiality to particular figures in the canon – Scève, Ronsard, Racine, Marivaux and certain symbolist and modernist writers – may help to explain some, if not all, of the astonishing absences on the reading lists. This is not to imply that the young Beckett's exposure to French literature was limited to his study of the prescribed texts, extensive as this obviously was. Many more authors were discussed in the curriculum, and the student notes of Beckett's teaching and his letters and early writings attest to his esteem (or lack of it) for many of them. (More on this later.)

The lasting appeal several figures of the French Renaissance had for Beckett harks back to his undergraduate years. In his early fictions, he gave cameo appearances to Maurice Scève, Louise Labé, François Rabelais and Pierre de Ronsard – 'the finest of all lyric poets in French' in Rudmose-Brown's view[5] – and he would evoke them in conversation in later years along with Joachim du Bellay.[6] The Rabelaisian flavour of Beckett's *Murphy* was apparent to British author and critic Herbert Read, who found it to be 'in the true Rabelaisian vein ... the rare and right combination of learning and licence' (quoted in *K*, 217). Beckett had as a matter of fact been rereading and taking notes on Rabelais's *Pantagruel, Gargantua* and *Le tiers livre* while composing his novel.

On the other hand, following the lead of the reading lists and Rudmose-Brown's *Short History*, Beckett gave the rich literature of the French Middle Ages short shrift, with brief mentions of the *chansons de toile* and the thirteenth-century *chantefable Aucassin et Nicolette* in *Dream of Fair to Middling Women* (*Dream*, 84, 165, 199) and reverberations of Provençal troubadour forms in his *Echo's Bones*.

APPRENTICESHIP IN FRENCH LITERATURE

On graduating from Trinity College, Beckett worked on a research essay (whereabouts unknown) focusing on the founder of French unanimism, Jules Romains, and sometime unanimist Pierre Jean Jouve, whose early work Beckett particularly admired (*K*, 75–6). Taken up by avant-garde modernism on arriving in Paris in 1928 and befriending Joyce, Beckett switched his focus to a doctorate on Joyce and Proust at the École Normale, but such an investigation on a living writer being considered inappropriate, he failed to obtain the required permission (*K*, 101). Instead, he penned an essay on Joyce and having read the entire *A la recherche du temps perdu* through twice (*L1*, 35) – a feat in itself – and consulted critics, he wrote the study of Proust that Charles Prentice published as a Dolphin Book in 1931. Beckett commentators have tended to read his *Proust* in the way Beckett later read Gide's essays on Dostoevsky, suggesting to his students that the essayist reveals more about himself than about his subject.[7] As a consequence, Proustian parallels in Beckett's fiction and plays are a rich vein of investigation in Beckett studies. He obviously also dipped into Henri Bergson at the time, as in a letter to Charles Prentice of 14 October 1930, he proposed to expand the conclusion of his *Proust* to 'separate Proust's intuitivism from Bergson's' (*L1*, 52), and a year later, in his course at Trinity, he contrasted Bergson's and Proust's conceptions of time.[8]

Beckett's interest in modern French poetry awakened by Rudmose-Brown was given a further boost by the surrealist 'revolution' under way in the Paris of the twenties and thirties. He was to translate several surrealist writings, including texts by André Breton, Paul Eluard and René Crevel for *This Quarter*'s 1932 surrealist issue and more poems by Eluard for George Reavey's *Thorns of Thunder*,[9] leading critics to trace the influence of surrealism on Beckett's oeuvre.[10] Beckett's focus, however, was not limited to contemporary writers and thinkers during his two years at the École Normale. His study during this time of Descartes and his biographers had far-reaching effects on his writing, of which his 1930 *Whoroscope* poem was only the beginning. The allusions to the French rationalist philosopher pervading his oeuvre (despite unfounded views to the contrary) gave rise to still unresolved critical controversies on Beckett's stance on Cartesianism and its sequels.

The notes taken by students in Beckett's courses on French literature at Trinity from the fall term of 1930 through the fall term of 1931 attest to the in-depth preparation of his lectures and the modernist insights he brought to his material. The lecture notes are scarce on his Romantics to Modernism course about which he admitted in an 11 March 1931 letter to Thomas McGreevy that, reading only Rimbaud at the moment, he was pained by the need to spell matters out for his students (*L1*, 73). In comparing the romantics unfavourably to the later symbolists and dadaists in a subsequent course, Beckett disparaged the former's artificial and orderly fabrications in favour of the latter's artistic disorder, complexity and intuitive vision.[11] Accordingly, many of Beckett's references to the French romantics are tinged with irony, with Alfred de Musset a favourite early target (*Dream*, 70). On the other hand, he heaped praise on Sainte-Beuve's *Volupté* (*L1*, 145) and in later years brought up Gérard de Nerval and

Chateaubriand's *René* in conversation.[12] Beckett's early self-writing in French shares striking affinities with the romantic autofictions of these three authors, and as is well known, he was to draw on Alphonse de Lamartine's 'L'isolement' for the title of *Le dépeupleur*. Whatever he studied, taught or read appears to have stayed with him permanently.

Beckett taught Baudelaire, Rimbaud and Verlaine as precursors of symbolism, whereas Jules Laforgue was a symbolist, he explained, owing to his evocation of moods.[13] Beckett's lifelong regard for these four poets and for Stéphane Mallarmé and modernist Guillaume Apollinaire is apparent from his reciting their poetry by heart, echoing it in his own poems, whether in English or French and weaving their words into his plays and fictions until the very last.[14] Just one early and one late example: reverberations of Baudelairian *ennui*, Rimbaud's *Illuminations*, and Apollinaire's 'Zone' in Beckett's 1931 poem 'Enueg I'; and Mallarmé's *Igitur* and 'Le tombeau d'Edgar Poe' evoked in *Mal vu mal dit* of 1981. Beckett translated Rimbaud's 'Bateau ivre' in 1932, and his translation of Apollinaire's 'Zone' first appeared in 1950 in *Transition*.

For Beckett's Racine and the Modern Novel course, which he taught in the fall Michaelmas term of 1931, on the other hand, there are three different sets of student notes.[15] Focusing on Jean Racine's modernity was not as unusual as it would first appear when understood within the context of the modernist revival of classical models between the two world wars. Beckett identified Stendhal, Flaubert and Dostoevsky as the forerunners of the modern novel, defining their and Proust and Gide's modernity (and eventually Racine's) as deriving from their complexity, their acceptance of the inexplicable and the incoherent and their rejection of the causalities and motivations to which the young lecturer objected in Balzac's realist novels and Corneille's plays. Beckett may have derived this appreciation of modernism in part from the post-symbolist aesthetics of Remy de Gourmont, who in his *Pages choisies* (prescribed moderatorship reading in some years) asserts that '[art] develops and grows in the obscurity of the Self' and like the individual, it is 'anomalous, illogical, and incomprehensible'.[16]

In the young Beckett's critique of Balzac, he broke rank with his teachers at Trinity who placed five Balzac novels and as many of his short stories on the honours reading lists while omitting Flaubert, a lopsided choice informed most likely by the pronounced preference of Balzac over Flaubert and other French novelists in Irish literary circles at the time.[17] In condemning Balzac's 'snowball act', or the tendency to render reality comprehensible through a chain of circumstances, Beckett is siding with French avant-garde attacks on the realist novel.[18] Allusions to Balzac, nevertheless, were to crop up periodically in Beckett's texts, such as the fatal skin of *La peau de chagrin* in *Molloy* and Balzac's mystical *Louis Lambert* split into the Louis and Lambert peasant families in the French and English versions respectively of *Malone meurt*.

As one would expect from Beckett's preference of Stendhal and Flaubert over Balzac, his involvement with them is not limited to intertextual winks.[19] Remarking in his lectures on Stendhal's 'incoherent duality', his split into an eighteenth-century 'encyclopedist' and a mystic,[20] Beckett was no doubt aware of his affinity with the author of *Le rouge et le noir* in portraying the everyday travails of his 'dud' mystics, beginning with Belacqua (*Dream*, 186). A more extended engagement with Flaubert, on the other hand, is Beckett's first novel written in French *Mercier et Camier* (1946), which by its title and verbal mischief smacks of *Bouvard et Pécuchet* (*K*, 361). He spoke 'passionately' of Flaubert's work and example in later years.[21]

The influence of Gide on Beckett had barely been explored before Le Juez's recent presentation of Beckett's 1931 lectures. As I queried elsewhere, one can't help wondering what his stature would have been in Beckett studies had Beckett completed the monograph on Gide that he proposed to several publishers in the thirties.[22] The young lecturer held Gide's *Les faux-monnayeurs* [*The Counterfeiters*] of 1926 to be the 'greatest book since Proust'.[23] Later he was to adopt many of this novel's antirealist techniques, some announcing the experimental *nouveau roman* of the 1950s and 1960s: the use of *en abyme* structure; metafictional procedures such as the writer mirrored in the text; and maintaining complexity, uncertainty and incoherence by the shifting relation between writer, personages, narrative and reader.[24]

The other major focus of Beckett's 1931 lectures is, of course, Racine's drama. His remarkable lectures on the most renowned of seventeenth-century French dramatists, if indebted to Rudmose-Brown and the extensive literature in French on Racine, also reveal that, in teaching the classical dramatist through the lenses of the modern novel, Beckett was fashioning Racine as a predecessor for his own experimental drama and fiction. A number of Racinian devices in Beckett's plays have been examined at some length: the classical unities, the importance of pairs and allusions to a Jansenist hidden god[25] and, more recently, the resonances of the Racinian tragic universe and tragic form in Beckett's theatre[26] and an 'Orestean conception of desire'.[27] In my view, Beckett's fictional pseudo-couples, too, hark back to Racine's antagonistic dialogues between protagonists and confidants, which for the young Beckett are a dramatic device for staging a divided protagonist's interior monologue.[28] Beckett was to put the Racinian soliloquy *à deux* to gripping use in both his drama and fiction, as he did the 'Gidean' Racine's focus on the *clair-obscur* of unfathomable mind.[29] Beckett's rereading of Racine's plays in 1956 (*K*, 426) would lead to further refinements in his subsequent monological plays. Together with Racine and Descartes, critics are investigating other traces of the classical canon in Beckett, among them the works of Molière and Pascal.[30]

In addition to Proust, Gide, the 'modernist' Racine and Stendhal and Flaubert as the forerunners of the modern novel, Beckett 'created' for himself a number of additional French modernist precursors in the Borgesian sense.[31] While teaching at Trinity, Beckett discovered Jules Renard's *Journal*, considered one of the major works of *fin de siècle* France. He was to quote not only Renard's mordant aphorisms in his own texts, but to apprentice his writing to facets of Renard that he admired, among which are his unflinching depictions of bodily functions and physical decline and his dry and economical style, so different from his own at the time still modelled on Joyce's. Indeed, Renard's struggle against language, his 'being silent in writing', are considered forerunners of the 'literature of silence' of the 1940s, the time of Beckett's impoverishing switch from English to French.[32] The paths of the two writers converge in other ways, especially writing as self-writing or autofiction, its desubjectifying effects, its pact with silence, the abject and death and the irony and playfulness of textual manoeuvres. *Malone meurt*'s unconventional use of the diary form, its unblinkered depictions of peasant life and its playful writing in the face of bodily infirmity and death resonate with Renard's *Journal*.

Among other modernist writings with a palpable influence on Beckett are Paul Valéry's *La soirée avec Monsieur Teste* of 1896 and the novels of the 1930s Beckett read fresh off the press: André Malraux's *La condition humaine* (1933), cited in *Murphy*, Louis-Ferdinand Céline's 'superbly overwritten' *Mort à crédit* of 1936 (quoted in *K*, 231) and Sartre's 'extraordinarily good' *La nausée* of 1938 (*L1*, 626). About Céline's immensely popular and influential first novel *Voyage au bout de la nuit* of 1932, we know that Beckett read it some time in the thirties (*B*, 275). His interest in Céline's artistry was to last into the 1980s.[33]

These novels along with Albert Camus's *L'étranger* of 1942, which Beckett recommended to friends[34] and whose author he preferred to Sartre,[35] contributed experimental techniques and philosophical and social concerns to Beckett and other French writers' post-war oeuvre. The lines that connect *La nausée* with *Watt*, for instance, have been often noted, and the impact of Sartrean existentialism, Camus's notion of the absurd and Céline's introduction of the rhythms, sounds, diction and syntax of Parisian street French into literary writing, for instance, would be difficult to overstate. Understandably, critics in the 1960s sought to understand Beckett's oeuvre in terms of existentialism and absurdism: what it means to be in the world, the experience of contingency and nothingness, the sense of the absurd and anguish in the face of death, the obligations of authenticity and freedom. This approach has its merits, no doubt, as there are undeniable affinities, but it also has its limits, particularly in view of Sartre and Camus's post-war conversion to humanism, which the post-war Beckett contests even more than before the war. As for Céline, Ruby Cohn early on rightly remarked that 'Céline has shaped [Beckett's] French idiom'.[36] In turn, Beckett perceived a similarity between his *Mort à crédit*, with its at the time decried obscenities, and Rabelaisian technique (*K*, 231). Beckett's French writing of the 1940s would further intensify this modernist revival of Rabelaisian mockery and licentiousness in a popular register.

Celebrated by the surrealists, the even more licentious and libertine Marquis de Sade was increasingly the focus of attention from the late 1920s onward. Long interested in Sade, Beckett in 1938 first considered and then decided against translating Sade's *Les 120 jours de Sodome*, 'one of the capital works of the 18th century' (*L1*, 604, 605, n 4). He alludes to the *120 jours* in his Belacqua fictions and spiked *Murphy* with oblique intertextual allusions to Sade's novel.[37] In the early fifties, at the time Beckett was doing translations for Georges Duthuit's *Transition*, he worked on a piece on Sade (whereabouts unknown) translating several Sadean texts and using a passage from Maurice Blanchot's *Lautréamont et Sade* (1949), which he declared by far the most intelligent of the essays on the marquis. In contrast, he particularly disliked Pierre Klossowski's *Sade mon prochain* of 1947 (*L2*, 210, 216, 221, 223). The presence of Sade has been detected as late as *Mal vu mal dit*.[38]

Beckett's engagement with the eighteenth century extends to several other figures, of which only a few examples can be cited here. He adopted in his own fiction the narrator's witty intrusions in Denis Diderot's *Jacques le fataliste et son maître* (*K*, 165), and alludes to Diderot's novel in the master–valet relationship of *Eleutheria*'s M. Krap and Jacques. In *Dream*, he cites 'the coagulum of continuous bees' from Diderot's *Le rêve de d'Alembert* (*Dream*, 167–8), with Diderot's materialist and vitalist transformation of Spinoza's monism influencing Moran's view of his bees in Beckett's *Molloy*.[39] Further, Beckett's taste for Sébastien Chamfort's witty and disillusioned maxims led him to write doggerel versions in English in the 1970s of several of these. During the same decade, he entered two lines into his 'Sottisier' Notebook from Voltaire's equally disillusioned 'Poème sur le désastre de Lisbonne' (1756), an attack on optimism Voltaire later intensified in *Candide*, which Beckett quoted in his 1929 satire 'Che Sciagura'.[40] Only lack of space limits further instances of Beckett's lifelong passion for French literature and his creation of precursors from the Renaissance through the modernists that inform his powerful writing in French.

BECKETT'S FRENCH WRITING (BRIEF GLIMPSE)

When in 1946 Beckett returned to Paris after the war and began writing fiction and then drama in French, the movements of the post-war literary landscape that most closely affected his writing included the literature of (impossible) testimony about the horrors of the war and the Shoah; the literature of social and political commitment running the gamut from Catholic intellectuals, humanist existentialists and militant Marxists; and the already mentioned avant-garde literature of silence associated with Maurice Blanchot and Georges Bataille. How is one to explain that despite the fame of Sartre and Camus and the affinities among Beckett, Blanchot and Bataille – the shared belief in an obligation to write in the face of nothingness;[41] a radical critique of language and the attraction of silence; an ahumanistic unknowingness; the abject as material for artistic expression (Beckett and Bataille), and the notion of a timeless and ghostly space of writing conceived as a dying without end (Blanchot and Beckett), a ghostliness intensified in the post-war Beckett – Maurice Nadeau nevertheless looked upon Beckett as the greater French writer? Could it be that his texts are more 'writerly' owing to their dense poetic weave, formal complexity and an Irish-French writer's hybridity of style(s), high and low, humorously melancholic, Rabelaisian (or Sadean) and Mallarméan, and the interweaving of diverse cultural memories and a sense of dispossession with a Barthesian rapture of the unknowable before letting it all unravel, one minute it's there, the next minute gone?

The publication of *Molloy* in 1951 made Beckett a celebrated new voice in French literature, as most of the twenty-five writer-practitioners of *critique savante* who reviewed it situated Beckett on the outer limits of pre-war and post-war experimental writing going beyond Céline, Sartre, Camus or Jean Genet in his portrayal of the disaster of being human through the collapse of language and body. Some recognised in this radical impoverishment and exhaustion a witnessing to the horrors of the war.[42] At the same time, *Molloy*'s formal innovations are credited as preparing the way for the publication of the *nouveaux romanciers*, but that is the topic of a different chapter in this collection. Similarly, the run of *En attendant Godot* in 1953 led to the recognition of Beckett as one of the major innovators of a *nouveau théâtre*, rewriting the classical drama of Racine, the symbolist and static theatre of Maurice Maeterlinck and Antonin Artaud's post-surrealist theatre of cruelty, but that too is a subject surveyed in a separate chapter, as are his subsequent experiments with various media and his stunning legacy in literature and the arts. About this Irish-French writer's extraordinary renewal of the French literary archive much remains to be explored.

NOTES

1 Maurice Nadeau, *Grâces leur soient rendues* (Paris: Albin Michel, 1990), 366.
2 Anon., *Dublin University Calendar* (Dublin: University Press Hodges, Figgis, 1925), 108–9, 113–14.
3 Anon., *Dublin University Calendar*, 1926, 136.
4 T. B. Rudmose-Brown, *A Short History of French Literature: From the Beginnings to 1900* (Dublin: Educational Company of Ireland, [1923]), vii.
5 Ibid., 26.
6 Anne Atik, *How It Was: A Memoir of Samuel Beckett* (London: Faber and Faber, 2001), 49, 87.
7 Brigitte Le Juez, *Beckett before Beckett*, trans. Ros Schwartz (London: Souvenir Press, 2009), 35.
8 Rachel Dobbins Burrows, 'Notes of the Lectures of Samuel Beckett on Gide and Racine', Michaelmas 1931 (Trinity College Library Dublin, TCD MIC 60, 1931), 9.
9 Thomas Hunkeler, 'Beckett face au surréalisme', *Samuel Beckett Today/ Aujourd'hui* (17, 2006), 40–2.
10 e.g. Daniel Albright, *Beckett and Aesthetics* (Cambridge: Cambridge University Press, 2003).
11 Burrows, 'Notes of the Lectures of Samuel Beckett on Gide and Racine', 3–9.
12 Atik, *How It Was: A Memoir of Samuel Beckett*, 87.
13 Aileen Conan, 'Beckett Notes', 1931 (Trinity College Library Dublin, TCD MS 11354/1), 3.
14 Atik, *How It Was: A Memoir of Samuel Beckett*, 49, 78, 88, 119, 122, 127.
15 The three sets of manuscript student notes are Rachel Dobbins Burrows' at Trinity College Dublin (TCD MIC 60), and Leslie Daiken's and Grace McKinley West's at the University of Reading (UoR Daiken 1/2 and UoR JEK A 4/2/4). Burrows' manuscript notebook is extensively quoted and summarised in Le Juez (2009), so that in quoting from her book it is Burrows' notebook that is cited directly or indirectly. A transcription of the McKinley notes is found in James Knowlson and Elizabeth Knowlson, *Beckett*

Remembering/Remembering Beckett (New York: Arcade Publishing, 2006), 307–13.
16 Remy de Gourmont, *Pages choisies* (Paris: Mercure de France, 1922), 199, my translation.
17 Le Juez, *Beckett before Beckett*, 23–4.
18 Burrows 'Notes of the Lectures of Samuel Beckett on Gide and Racine', 40, 48.
19 For the latter, see C. J. Ackerley and S. E. Gontarski, *The Grove Companion to Samuel Beckett: A Reader's Guide to His Works, Life, and Thought* (New York: Grove Press, 2004), 199, 541.
20 Le Juez, *Beckett before Beckett*, 29.
21 Atik, *How It Was: A Memoir of Samuel Beckett*, 49.
22 Angela Moorjani, 'André Gide among the Parisian Ghosts in the "Anglo-Irish" *Murphy*', *Samuel Beckett Today/Aujourd'hui* (21, 2009), 209.
23 Le Juez, *Beckett before Beckett*, 43.
24 This discussion of Beckett's apprenticeship to Gide and the one to follow on Racine and Renard draw on my three recent essays on Beckett's Parisian ghosts: Moorjani, 'André Gide among the Parisian Ghosts in the "Anglo-Irish" *Murphy*', 209–22; 'Beckett's Racinian Fictions: "Racine and the Modern Novel" Revisited', *Samuel Beckett Today/Aujourd'hui* (24, 2012), 41–55; 'Beckett's Parisian Ghosts (continued): The Case of the Missing Jules Renard', *Limit/e Beckett* (1, 2010) Web.
25 Vivian Mercier, *Beckett/Beckett* (New York: Oxford University Press, 1977), 76–7, 82.
26 Danièle de Ruyter, 'Fascination de la tragédie racinienne: résonances dans *Oh les beaux jours*', *Samuel Beckett Today/Aujourd'hui* (24, 2012), 57–71.
27 Shane Weller, 'The Anethics of Desire: Beckett, Racine, Sade', in Russell Smith (ed.), *Beckett and Ethics* (London: Continuum, 2008), 102–8.
28 See Leslie Daiken, 'Manuscript Notes on Beckett's TCD Racine Lectures', in 'French Literature' Notebook (Beckett International Foundation, University of Reading, Daiken 1/2, 1931) 16 and Moorjani, 'Beckett's Racinian Fictions: "Racine and the Modern Novel" Revisited', 47.
29 Le Juez, *Beckett before Beckett*, 37–9.
30 See the special issue of *Samuel Beckett Today/Aujourd'hui* (24, 2012) on 'Early Modern Beckett'.
31 Jorge Luis Borges, 'Kafka and His Precursors', trans. James E. Irby, *Labyrinths* (New York: New Directions, 2007), 201.
32 Jean-Paul Sartre, 'L'homme ligoté: notes sur le *Journal* de Jules Renard', *Situations, I* (Paris: Gallimard, 1947), 271–2.
33 Charles Krance, 'Remembrance of the Last Twenty Years', in Knowlson and Knowlson, *Beckett Remembering/Remembering Beckett*, 264–5. An additional (recovered) influence has recently surfaced. In 1950, Beckett thought of changing the name of Godot after suddenly recalling, much to his dismay, Marcel Jouhandeau's 1926 novel *Monsieur Godeau intime* (*L2*, 210). The novel is still in print.

34 John Pilling, *A Samuel Beckett Chronology* (Houndmills, UK: Palgrave Macmillan, 2006), 125, 200.
35 Knowlson and Knowlson, *Beckett Remembering/Remembering Beckett*, 252.
36 Ruby Cohn, *Samuel Beckett: The Comic Gamut* (New Brunswick: Rutgers University Press, 1962), 100.
37 Richard Begam, 'Beckett's Kinetic Aesthetics', *Journal of Beckett Studies* (16.1 and 2, 2007), 50–8.
38 Ibid., 59, n 8.
39 Angela Moorjani, 'The Dancing Bees in Samuel Beckett's *Molloy*: The Rapture of Unknowing', in Mary Bryden (ed.), *Beckett and Animals* (Cambridge: Cambridge University Press, 2012).
40 Samuel Beckett, 'Sottisier' Notebook (Beckett International Foundation, University of Reading, MS 2901, 1976–1982), 3. For other relatively infrequent citations of both Voltaire and Rousseau, see Ackerley and Gontarski, *The Grove Companion to Samuel Beckett*, 618, 491 and Yoshiyuki Inoue, '"Little People" in *Le dépeupleur*: Beckett and the Eighteenth Century', *Samuel Beckett Today/Aujourd'hui* (19, 2008), 226–8.
41 Critics have commented on the similarity between Blanchot's statement in his *Faux pas* of 1943 that 'the writer finds himself in the increasingly ludicrous condition of having nothing to write, of having no means with which to write, and of being constrained by utter necessity of always writing it. [...] Nothingness is his material' (Maurice Blanchot, *Faux pas*, trans. Charlotte Mandell [Stanford: Stanford University Press, 2001]), 3 and Beckett's later, 'The expression that there is nothing to express, nothing with which to express, nothing from which to express, no power to express, no desire to express, together with the obligation to express' (*D*, 139). We now know that Beckett was aware of Blanchot's *Faux pa*s (*L2*, 210).
42 See Angela Moorjani, 'Beckett's *Molloy* in the French Context', *Samuel Beckett Today/Aujourd'hui* (25, 2013).

CHAPTER 21

Italian Literature
Daniela Caselli

In a letter to Thomas McGreevy on 31 January 1938, Beckett writes:

> I understand your anxiety to clarify his [Jack B. Yeats's] pre and post 1916 painting politically and socially, and especially in what concerns the last pictures I think you have provided a clue that will be of great help to a lot of people, to the kind of people who in the phrase of Bergson can't be happy till they have 'solidified the flowing', i.e. to most people. [...] You will always, as an historian, give more credit to circumstances than I, with my less than suilline interest and belief in the *fable convenue*, ever shall be able to do. However you say it yourself on p. 34. (*L1*, 599)

Samuel Beckett, to tell what is by now a *fable convenue*, learned Italian as an undergraduate student of modern languages at Trinity College Dublin (1923–7). He learned it well, as demonstrated not only by the first class degree he received, but also by the notebooks found by Edward Beckett and Caroline Beckett Murphy after Beckett's death and now held at Trinity College Dublin. Seven of such 'schoolboy notebooks' (catalogued and partially transcribed in 2006 by Everett Frost and Matthijs Engelberts with Jane Maxwell)[1] deal with Italian literature: MS 10962 is devoted to Machiavelli and Ariosto and mostly derives from J. A. Symonds' textbook on Italian literature;[2] MS 10963 summarises the largest part of Dante's *Inferno* and a rich selection of canti from *Purgatorio*; MS 10963a is devoted to sections of *Inferno*, the 'ponete mente almen com'io son bella' canzone from *Convivio* (which will reappear in Beckett's essay on Proust) and other excerpts from the same work, a passage from *Inferno* V and line 95 from *Purgatorio* XI; MS 10964 engages with the *Paradiso*, abruptly ending with the disconsolate (but for the Dante scholar also heartening) jotting after Canto XXVIII: '[Don't understand a word of this]'. The subject is 'stuck', like Belacqua in 'Dante and the Lobster', and his ironic exit parallels that of B. in *Three Dialogues* (*L1*, 208). The notes match those 'beslubbering' the text of the *Comedy* in the Enrico Bianchi edition for Salani, which is called 'ignoble' in *Dream of Fair to Middling Women*, occasionally also referring to the Scartazzini-Vandelli 1922 text (*Dream*, 51).[3] MS 10965 is devoted to Carducci and hosts a two-page-long essay comparing the virtues (or otherwise) of Giosué Carducci's poetry and Gabriele D'Annunzio's short prose (MS 10965a): Carducci, that 'intolerable old bitch', as the 1932 *This Quarter* version of 'Dante and the Lobster' puts it, is here a 'sun worshipper' ('adoratore del sole') whose freshness is deemed inspiring ('ispira la sua freschezza!').[4] D'Annunzio's sensationalist short prose is judged, on the other hand, to be 'ributtante' ('revolting') and his realism 'immondo' ('filthy'). The overblown rhetoric praising Carducci in an Italian which partially echoes Symonds' patriotic sentiments and aesthetic judgements cannot be fully trusted as an indication of Beckett's own opinions, however. In the notebook hosting the essay we encounter an unsourced quotation from Carducci claiming: 'Sono tentato di far due altre poesie su Assisi e San Francesco' ('I am tempted to make two other poems about Assisi and Saint Francis').[5] Beckett, puncturing the inflated rhetoric of his essay, now comments:

No-one but a verse manufacturer could express himself like that. Imagine Leopardi being 'tempted' to write poetry! Or Shelley writing for Italy: 'I'd rather like to write a poem about the Lombard plain but I can't think of a rhyme for "Euganean"'. Carducci, with all his enormous & complicated meters, was not a poet. His work is stamped with a desperate subconscious effort.[6]

Only a few years later, in a July 1930 letter to McGreevy, Beckett fashions his own identity, defending his choice to read Schopenhauer and rejecting Carducci and Barrès in favour of Leopardi and Proust:

I am reading Schopenhauer. Everyone laughs at that. Beaufret & Alfy etc. But I am not reading philosophy, nor caring whether he is right or wrong or a good or worthless metaphysician. An intellectual justification of unhappiness – the greatest that has ever been attempted – is worth the examination of one who is interested in Leopardi & Proust rather than Carducci & Barrès. (*L1*, 33)

Beckett's view of D'Annunzio, on the other hand, remains virtually unaltered, even though in 1930 his language ruthlessly and confidently mimics, rather than squeamishly distancing itself from, the D'Annunzian diction:

I was reading D'Annunzio on Giorgione again and I think it's all balls and mean nasty balls. I was thinking of Keats and Giorg[i]one's two young men – the Concert and the Tempest – for a discussion of Proust's floral obsession. D'A. seems to think that they are *merely* pausing between fucks. Horrible. He has a dirty juicy squelchy mind, bleeding and bursting, like his celebrated pomegranades. (*L1*, 41)

The textual evidence on Ariosto and Machiavelli also indicates their ongoing relevance in the early Beckett. MS 10966 expands on the acumen of Niccolò Machiavelli's political thought and the creative genius of his literary antithesis, Ludovico Ariosto; in early March 1936, Beckett still describes Ariosto as 'the greatest literary artist (as distinct from poet) of them all perhaps' (*LI*, 319); a few weeks earlier, on 6 February, he had quoted Machiavelli to McGreevy:

Have just read the *Mandragola* & started *Clizia*. He apologises as *uom saggio e grave*, for writing so frivolously, in what de Sanctis calls 'cattivi versi ma strazianti'. I quote them because I think they will please you:

> Scusatelo con questo, che s'ingegna
> Con questi van pensieri
> Fare il suo tristo tempo più soave:
> Perchè altrove non ave
> Dove voltare il viso:
> Chè gli è stato interciso
> Monstrar con altre imprese altra virtue,
> Non sendo premio alle fatiche sue.

I want to get hold of Folengo & Berni and the Cardinal of Bibbiena (*La Calandra*) and the theatre of *Bruno* & much else besides. [...] Translate Fracastoro's *Sifilide* e poi mori. (*LI*, 313–14)

Referring to Francesco de Sanctis' *Storia della letteratura italiana*,[7] Beckett confidently puns with local proverbs ('vedi Napoli e poi muori' / '[first you] see Naples and then [you can] die'), refers to salacious writers of the Italian renaissance and quotes from the play's witty prologue, which defends writing as alleviating one's melancholia in the sad absence of other ways of proving one's abilities. Machiavelli's *Storie fiorentine* is mentioned a couple of months later:

He [Maurice Sinclair] has dug out some more Italian books for me, including the *Storie fiorentine*, which pleases me greatly; and I found some for myself at Webb's, left in by some little Jez called Boyle or Doyle, lepping fresh from Florence, including the accounts of Dante by the Villani, Boccaccio, Aretino & Manetti brought together in one volume. I have been reading wildly all over the place, Goethe's *Iphigenia* & then Racine's to remove the taste, Chesterfield, Boccaccio, Fischart, Ariosto & Pope! (*LI*, 324, see also 361)

In full *More Pricks Than Kicks* mode, thanks to the 'little' Jesuit Boyle, or Doyle, 'lepping fresh from Florence', Giuseppe Lando Passerini's *Vite di Dante* (published by Sansoni in Florence in 1917) can please Beckett as greatly as Machiavelli's eight books on the history of Florence.

As this 'swift survey of the question' indicates, the presence of Italian literature in general and Dante in particular goes well beyond Beckett's college years. If we look at further archival evidence, the 1930s *Whoroscope* and

Dream notebooks are peppered with fragments from Dante; intriguingly, the first fifteen sections of UoR MS 3000 (the *Whoroscope* notebook) point in the direction of what will eventually become *Murphy*, drawing a parallel between the protagonists' journey and that of Dante and Virgil along the Purgatorial cornices only to instruct: 'But keep the whole Dantesque analogy out of sight', thus conjuring up Dante's presence while claiming to erase it.[8] UoR MS 5000 (the *Dream* notebook) reproduces the famous lines from *Purgatorio* IV (98–9, 11, 118–19, 127–35) in which Belacqua, a slothful soul crouched in a foetal position under a rock, addresses Dante, who is climbing mount Purgatory, and gently mocks his ascent. Belacqua's textual life will be long and eventful in the Beckett oeuvre, ranging from 'Dante and the Lobster' to *Company*; in this manuscript we find the important sections on Belacqua by two early commentators of the *Comedy*, Benvenuto da Imola and the Anonimo Fiorentino (items 311, 313, 314), as they appear in Paget Toynbee's *Dictionary of Proper Names and Notable Matters in the Works of Dante* (1898), which will be elaborated upon in *Dream of Fair to Middling Women*, *Murphy*, *How It Is* and *Company*.[9] The characterisation of Belacqua as a Florentine lute maker contemporary to Dante is not encountered in the *Comedy*, in fact, but in these commentaries, which adopt the genre of the novella to 'insert frivolous spirals' on the brief apparition of the crouched, slothful shade in Dante's Antepurgatory. The frequent critical confusion between the *Comedy* and its commentaries mirrors the way in which *Dream* conflates them: Dante's Belacqua merges into Benvenuto's and the Anonimo's and together they shape the unstable protagonist of *Dream* who is, naturally, declared to be not quite there: 'there is no real Belacqua [...] there is no authority for supposing that this third Belacqua is the real Belacqua' (*Dream*, 121–2).

Belacqua here also produces 'Mr Beckett' as the 'author', which is embroiled in the narrative teleology he wants to question. At the end of *Dream*'s chapter 'UND' 'a voice comes to one [in the dark]'; just as Dante in *Purgatorio* IV first hears a voice and only later can identify Belacqua as the speaker crouched in the shadow of a big stone, so the reader does not at first know where 'L'andar su che porta?' comes from. In *Purgatorio* IV, Belacqua replies to Dante's question about the reasons for his lazy posture by saying: 'O frate andare in sù che porta? / ché non mi lascerebbe ire a' martìri / l'angel di Dio che siede in su la porta' ('O brother, what's the use of going up? For God's angel who sits at the gate would not let me pass to the torments'). In *Dream* we read: 'L'andar su che porta? ... Oh but the bay, Mr Beckett, didn't you know, about your brow' (*Dream*, 141). 'Mr Beckett', anticipating B. in *Three Dialogues* and Sam in *Watt*, becomes part of the fictional world of the novel while also remaining the author of the literary text we are reading: Mr Beckett is now mocked as being 'laureate', sporting 'his bay about his brow' like Dante does in his famous portrait. 'L'andar su' always brings something, even when 'we do not quite know where we are'; narrative progression cannot simply be negated (*Dream*, 9).

We can push this insight further and argue that Dante is central, just like in the *Whoroscope Notebook*, to the interplay between absence and presence in the Beckett oeuvre. For instance, in a letter Beckett wrote to McGreevy on 4 January 1948, he claims: 'I haven't read Dante in years', a statement apparently confirmed by another letter written two months later:

Yes I received your *Dante* article and reading it was reminded of our old talks 20 years ago in Paris. Not because the article owed anything to me, but because it was you. I felt you constrained, as in all your work for The Record, and found myself wishing again you were writing more for yourself and less for Ireland. I know you are doing what you want to do, in a sense. But it must leave you often with a starved feeling. (*L2*, 75)

And yet, only a few months later, in a letter to Georges Duthuit, we read: 'Connaissez-vous le cri commun aux purgatoriaux? *Io fui*' (*L2*, 90), mirroring the purgatorial and infernal associations of the Italian simple past tense linked to both French and English versions of *Rough for Radio II/Pochade radiophonique* and *Text for Nothing 6/Texte pour rien 6*:

Je fus, je fus, disent ceux du Purgatoire, ceux des Enfers aussi, admirable pluriel, merveilleuse assurance. Plongé dans la glace, jusqu'aux narines, les paupières collées de larmes gelées, revivre ses campagnes, quelle tranquillité, et se savoir au bout de ses surprises, non, j'ai dû mal entendre.

I was, I was, they say in Purgatory, in Hell too, admirable singulars, admirable assurance. Plunged in ice up to the nostrils, the eyelids caked with frozen tears, to fight all your battles o'er again, what tranquillity, and know there are no more emotions in store, no, I can't have heard aright.[10]

In a letter of 1949, again to Duthuit, we find a description of the same icy ninth circle, followed by a quotation in Italian of *Inferno* XXXII, 13–15, and a confident aside on the 'very dubious interpretation [...] but one to which I am attached', that Count Ugolino has 'eaten his young' (*L2*, 111–12).[11]

In *How It Is*, a much later text often recognised as 'Dantean', and which I have argued to be a performance, not without humour, of the *Inferno*,[12] the unstable narrative position occupies for a while the 'Belacqua posture' occurring in many other Beckett texts[13]:

knees drawn up back bent in a hoop I clasp the sack to my belly I see me now on my side I clutch it the sack we're talking of the sack with one hand behind my back I slip it under my head without letting it go I never let it go. (*H*, 10)[14]

And again:

asleep I see me asleep on my side or on my face it's one or the other on my side it's preferable which side the right it's preferable the sack under my head or clasped to my belly clasped to my belly the knees drawn up the back bent in a hoop the tiny head near the knees curled round the sack Belacqua fallen over on his side tired of waiting forgotten of the hearts where grace abides asleep. (*H*, 24)[15]

This modification of the 'Belacqua episode' is also reproduced in a letter Beckett writes to Kay Boyle on 29 August 1960:

Belacqua for me is no more than a kind of fetish. In the work I have finished he appears 'basculé sur le côté las d'attendre oublié des cœurs où vit la grâce endormi' (cor che in grazia vive), and I hope that's the end of him.[16]

This is not the end of Belacqua, however: he is also referred to in part two of *How It Is/Comment c'est*, and 'the old lutist' is still able to wrench a 'wan smile' from Dante in *Company/ Compagnie* (*NO*, 44).[17] Belacqua, whose dubious origins were debated at length in *Dream* and its notebook, critiques the possibility of origins and originality while bringing us back to the external authority of Dante's *Comedy*. The slothful soul of *Purgatorio* IV contributes to the larger question in Beckett of where meaning comes from and if, indeed, it comes from anywhere.

These 'Belacqua episodes' are a few of the many examples that could be used to demonstrate that Dante is the most long-lasting and productive Italian presence in the Beckett oeuvre. My previous analysis of the English and French prose has brought to light the extended wanderings of Dante's texts in Beckett, and Séan Lawlor's work on the poetry has confirmed these findings.[18] As part of a wider discussion of the Italian context, aside from passing references to authors such as Castiglione and Poliziano in 'Dante... Bruno.Vico..Joyce', or Mario Praz's *La carne, la morte e il diavolo* in the *Dream* notebook, or the juicy attacks against Papini's views on Dante now collected in *Disjecta*, one should also remember the importance of early nineteenth-century poet Giacomo Leopardi.[19] Since there are no surviving notebooks for the years 1928–30, the textual occurrence of Leopardi in the early works (together with, among others, Schopenhauer)[20] has no archival correlative, but his presence can be traced in 'Dante...Bruno. Vico..Joyce', in which 'Sopra il monumento di Dante che si preparava in Firenze' is employed as shorthand to describe Dante's origins; in *Proust*, possibly the work that takes Leopardi most seriously, using half a line from

'A Se Stesso' as an epigraph and mobilising Leopardi's poetics of desire against Schopenhauer; in *Dream of Fair to Middling Women*, in which we find Belacqua wallowing in the 'gloomy' poet in the dim light of 'Le Ricordanze'; and in *Molloy*, where the occurrence of 'non che la speme / il desiderio è spento', again from 'A se stesso', allows us to measure the distance separating this novel from the more earnest *Proust*:

> It was she [Lousse] dug the hole because I couldn't, though I was the gentleman, because of my leg. [...] I had so to speak only one leg at my disposal, I was virtually one-legged, and I would have been happier, livelier, amputated at the groin. And if they had removed a few testicles into the bargain I wouldn't have objected. For from such testicles as mine, dangling at mid-thigh at the end of a meagre cord, there was nothing more to be squeezed, not a drop. So that *non che la speme il desiderio*, and I longed to see them gone, from the old stand where they bore false witness, for and against, in the lifelong charge against me. (*Mo*, 33)

The passage squeezes every last drop out of Leopardi's 'A Se Stesso', a poetic distillation of the incurious seekers' 'deux besoins': lacking and amputated, the line mirrors the narrator's reality and desires. Molloy's 'leg' is not just his 'bad leg' but what makes him a gentleman (his 'manhood'); the desired amputation is, suggestively, to take place 'at the groin' – his 'few' testicles ('nothing to write home about') should also go. It is hard to resist the temptation to utter 'speme', Joyceanly, aloud: it sounds remarkably like 'sperm', adding an aural dimension to the equivocation.[21] After all, in a letter to David Hayman of 22 July 1955 Beckett recounts as an amusing anecdote 'once quoting to Joyce Leopardi's *E fango è il mondo*, to which his instantaneous and sole reaction consisted in seizing on the association *Il mondo – immonde*.' (*L2*, 537) The existential 'lifelong charge against me', the mark of 'someone interested in' Leopardi, Proust and Schopenhauer, is incorporated, both seriously and obscenely, through a paradoxically mutilated Leopardi.

To give credit to circumstances, then, Beckett's undergraduate studies at TCD, his work on Dante under the guidance of his private tutor, Bianca Esposito, and his 'reading wildly all over the place' provide a biographical and historical context for his remarkable knowledge of Italian literature in general and of Dante Alighieri in particular, whose presence extends from the Dublin years to the alleged 'last farewell to the old lutist' in *Company*, and beyond. But, if we remain Bergsonianly and Beckettianly unhappy with 'solidifying the flowing', we have to realise that manuscripts and correspondence, aside from their non-exhaustive nature, cannot simply be taken as material evidence but need to be interpreted. In line with the high modernist claim we found in Beckett's 1938 letter to McGreevy, unlike what happens for 'most people', the presence of intertextual references to Italian literature refuses to act as 'context' if we take context, Beckettianly, as having a tendency to act as a freezing agent, turning movement into tableau. As I have argued more extensively elsewhere, finding a Dante intertext might be highly satisfying for the critic turned detective, but it never produces a 'eureka effect', because it does not restore full meaning to an obscure or lacking text. On the contrary, the presence of Italian literature in Beckett is yet another way in which the relationship between what belongs to the text and what comes from outside is complexly scrutinised.

The apparent stability that context seems able to provide also presents us with a wider political problem, betrayed by the history of the possible uses one can make of it: in our case, the mastery of Italian (and French and German) languages and literatures has been seen either as part of that 'turning away from the local' that characterises a European Beckett (a Beckett who freed himself from the stifling provinciality of Ireland)[22] or recuperated as the sign of the genuine Irish exile, whose lack of affiliation and 'inorganic' landscape paradoxically signal national belonging.[23] Italian literature in general and Dante in particular were, for modernists as differently placed on the political spectrum as Pound, Eliot and Joyce, a move towards a transnational aesthetic project. In Beckett (who disliked Eliot's professorial first essay on Dante), Dante, and Italian literature as a whole, do not stand for a specific principle, either of affiliation or negation. This is why it is a moot point to debate how much Italian literature Beckett actually knew or how well he represents Dante in the twentieth century. Italian literature in Beckett illustrates how the paradoxical consistency of the Beckett oeuvre derives from its being made of odds and ends, disjecta, residua, fizzles, foirades and remains of abandoned work[s], which resist against being reconstituted into the wholeness which 'context' promises us.

Italian literature in Beckett thus presents us with a recurrent problem: we cannot dismiss the Italian (or Irish, or English, and the list could of course go on) elements in the oeuvre, but we have to resist stabilising them into a reassuring idea of 'context'. Indeed, we are led to question context's seductively explicative role: context might be of great help to many people, but the Beckett oeuvre both invites and disappoints contextual readings; it does not want to stop the flow. With the benefit of hindsight, we can now see that criticism might well have been guilty of celebrating Beckett's genius by abstracting it from any kind of historical framework (performing, in turn, a now familiar historical move), but the Beckett oeuvre stubbornly refuses to produce itself as a figure emerging from a well-defined background: history is questioned in Beckett, as the 1938 letter indicates, rather than 'given credit to'.

The role of Dante and Italian literature in Beckett can be summed up in the words of *Ill Seen Ill Said/Mal vu mal dit*, in which the eye 'will return to the scene of its betrayal. On centennial leave from where tears freeze' / 'reviendra sur les lieux de ses trahisons. En conge séculaire de là où gèlent les larmes' (*NO*, 63).[24] The frozen tears of the intertwined treacherous brothers immersed in the ice of Cocytus in *Inferno* XXXII (encountered also in an early 'Dante' Notebook, in *Text 6* and *dread nay*) lead us back to the impossible choice between saying and betraying ('ill saying') and self and other (the I looking at itself).[25]

The last farewell to Dante is a 'return to the scene of its betrayals' because the Beckett oeuvre does not just tell us, as Beckett does to George Reevey in 1938: 'All going well, though I don't know exactly where' (*L1*, 592), but also performs the inability to fully belong, to fully be there, to have the matter fully explicated and 'wrapped up in a notion' for us. Context – in our case the Italian context – cannot tell us where things were going to go for Beckett or dilute that uncomfortable and yet essential sense that one does not really know where one is when reading Beckett. Finding Dante, or Leopardi, or even an entertainingly despised D'Annunzio or Papini in Beckett does not freeze our readings into a critical Cocytus, but keeps us toiling up the cornices of mount Purgatory. A reading of Italian odds and ends is an opportunity to ask how they participate in the ongoing question of what belongs and what does not in the Beckett oeuvre, of how the outside becomes incorporated and the belonging estranged. A 1949 letter to Duthuit discussing Bram van Velde's art places this dilemma precisely in Dantean terms:

> His painting is, if you will, the impossibility of reconnecting. There is, if you like, refusal and refusal to accept refusal. That is perhaps what makes this painting possible. For my part, it is the *gran rifiuto* that interests me, not the heroic wrigglings to which we owe this splendid thing.[26]

The exegetically undecidable 'great refusal', of which the nameless shade in the Antechamber of Inferno is guilty, indicates an 'interest' in 'what lies beyond the outside-inside where he does his striving, not the scale of the striving itself'. The artist, after all, has to resist two great temptations, 'celle du réel et celle du mensonge'.[27]

NOTES

1 Matthijs Engelberts, Everett Frost and Jane Maxwell (eds), *Samuel Beckett Today/Aujourd'hui* 'Notes Diverse Holo' (Amsterdam: Rodopi, 2006).
2 For Everett Frost the manuscript, dating from late summer/autumn 1926, was 'compiled as part of private lessons or "grinds" in the language school run by Bianca Esposito in preparation for the Moderatorship examinations in Modern Literature given in the Michaelmas term (October 1926) in Trinity College Dublin'. J. A. Symonds, *Italian Literature*. Variously identified as vol. V or vol. IV part II of *The Renaissance in Italy* (1875–86), depending on whether it is enumerated as a five-volume or seven-volume set. Engelberts, Frost and Maxwell, *Samuel Beckett Today/Aujourd'hui* 'Notes Diverse Holo', 30, 37.
3 The typescript of *Dream of Fair to Middling Women* held at the UoR reads 'the Fiorentia edition in the ignoble Salviani'. See Daniela Caselli, '"The Florentia edition in the ignoble Salani collection": A Textual Comparison', *Journal of Beckett Studies*, (9.2, 2001), 1–20 and Matthijs Engelberts, Everett Frost and Jane Maxwell (eds), 'The Promise of Dante in the Beckett Manuscripts', *Samuel Beckett Today/Aujourd'hui* 'Notes Diverse Holo', (16, 2006), 237–57.
4 Samuel Beckett, 'Dante and the Lobster', *This Quarter* (December 1932), 222–36, 230.
5 Samuel Beckett, TCD MS10965, fol. 30.
6 See Daniela Caselli, 'Thinking of "A Rhyme for Euganean": Beckett in Italy', in Mark Nixon and Matthew Feldman (eds), *The International Reception of Samuel Beckett* (London: Continuum, 2009), 209–33.
7 Francesco De Sanctis, *Storia della letteratura italiana* [1870–1] (Turin: Einaudi-Gallimard, 1996). For a discussion of De Sanctis's mediating authority in *Proust*, see Terence McQueeny, *Samuel Beckett As Critic of Proust and Joyce* (Chapel Hill: University of North Carolina, 1977, unpublished doctoral thesis).
8 Daniela Caselli, *Beckett's Dantes: Intertextuality in the Fiction and Criticism* (Manchester: Manchester University Press, 2005) and Engelberts, Everett Frost and Maxwell (eds), 'The Promise of Dante in the Beckett Manuscripts', 237–57.
9 John Pilling, *Beckett's* Dream *Notebook* (Reading: Beckett International Foundation, 1999), 43–5; Daniela Caselli, '"Looking It Up in My Big Dante": A Note on "Sedendo and Quiescendo"', *Journal of Beckett Studies* (6.2, Spring 1997), 85–93. In MS 5000 we also find lines from *Paradiso* XXXI, 83–4, XXX, 22–4 and 31–3, XXIX, 12 (items 1081, 1082, 1083), *Inferno* XXX, 128 (item 1096) and *Paradiso* III 10–18 (item 1097), quotations that can be traced back again to the two sources for the Trinity College Dublin Dante notebooks, the 'ignoble' Salani edition and the Scartazzini-Vandelli 1922 edition.
10 Samuel Beckett, *Nouvelles et textes pour rien* (Paris: Les Éditions de Minuit, 1958), 172; *CSP*, 124.
11 This interpretation was prevalent among nineteenth-century commentators.

12 The text mentions Belacqua, the Paolo and Francesca episode from *Inferno* V, *Inferno* III and XXXIV. Many critics describe it as 'Dantean'; among others, see Ruby Cohn, *Back to Beckett* (Princeton: Princeton University Press, 1973), 232; William Hutchings, '"Shat into Grace" Or, A Tale of a Turd: Why It Is How It Is in Samuel Beckett's *How It Is*', *Papers on Language and Literature. A Journal for Scholars and Critics of Language and Literature*, (21.1, Winter 1985), 64–87, 79; John Fletcher, *Samuel Beckett's Art* (London, Chatto & Windus 1971) 118; Michael Robinson, 'From Purgatory to Inferno: Beckett and Dante Revisited', *Journal of Beckett Studies*, (5, Autumn 1979), 79; Jean-Pierre Ferrini, *Dante et Beckett* (Paris: Hermann, 2003). For a fuller discussion of these positions, see Daniela Caselli, *Beckett's Dantes*.
13 See, for example, *Dream*, 66; *MPTK*, 38–9, 47; *M*, 51; *T*, 11; *CDW*, 65; *CSP*, 177, 179; *NO*, 44–5.
14 And Samuel Beckett, *Comment c'est* (Paris: Les Éditions de Minuit, 1961), 14.
15 And Beckett, *Comment c'est*, 37.
16 Samuel Beckett to Kay Boyle, 29 August 1960, HRHRC, University of Texas, Austin.
17 And Samuel Beckett *Compagnie* (Paris: Les Éditions de Minuit, 1985), 84.
18 Séan Lawlor, '"Alba" and "Dortmunder": Signposting Paradise and the Balls-Aching World', *Samuel Beckett Today/Aujourd'hui*, (18:2007), 227–40; and 'The "Dream" Poems: Poems in Personae', *A Companion to Samuel Beckett* ed. S. E. Gontarski (Oxford: Wiley-Blackwell, 2010), 228–43. In the first decade or so of Beckett's career, Dante is often mentioned in the correspondence; see *LI*, II, 187–9.
19 Daniela Caselli, 'Beckett's Intertextual Modalities of Appropriation: the Case of Leopardi', *Journal of Beckett Studies* (6:1, Autumn 1996), 1–24; republished in revised form as 'Beckett and Leopardi', *The Beckett Critical Reader* ed. S. E. Gontarski (Edinburgh: Edinburgh University Press, 2013).
20 Lawrence Harvey, *Samuel Beckett: Poet and Critic* (Princeton: Princeton University Press, 1970), 34; John Pilling, *Beckett Before Godot* (Cambridge: Cambridge University Press, 1997), 11; Everett Frost, 'Preface', in Engelberts, Everett Frost and Maxwell (eds), 'The Promise of Dante in the Beckett Manuscripts', 21–2.
21 Anecdotal evidence has Beckett fond of repeating this verse in old age. André Bernold, *L'amitié de Beckett 1979–1989* (Paris: Hermann Editeurs de Sciences et des Arts, 1992).
22 Samuel Beckett to Morris Sinclair, 5 May 1934: 'No sooner do I take up my pen to compose something in English than I get the feeling of being "de-personified", if one may use such a marvellous expression' [...] If only Dublin were unfamiliar, then it would be pleasant to settle somewhere nearby' (*LI*, 205).
23 Samuel Beckett to Thomas McGreevy, 14 August 1937: 'God knows it doesn't take much sensitiveness to feel that in Ireland, a nature almost as inhumanly inorganic as a stage set' (*LI*, 540).

24 Samuel Beckett, *Mal vu mal dit* (Paris: Les Éditions de Minuit, 1981), 32.
25 TCD MS 10963, fo. 79. Samuel Beckett, 'dread nay', *CP*, 33.
26 Samuel Beckett to Georges Duthuit, 9 March 1949, *L2*, 136. Dante also negotiates aesthetic ideas in the correspondence with Duthuit, see letter of 26 May 1949, *L2*, 154.
27 *D*, 150. In the past the 'gran rifiuto' was mostly interpreted as the cowardly abdication of Pope Celestino V, a reading now disputed.

PART V

'The Humanities I had': Arts

CHAPTER 22

Contemporary Visual Art

Nico Israel

Imagine what might have happened if Beckett's 1933 application letter for a job as an assistant at London's National Gallery of Art, written 'in a moment of gush' (*L1*, 166), had been taken seriously – if the brilliant but ill-at-ease Irishman had been interviewed and offered a position and if he had begun his curatorial career with a comprehensive exhibition on, say, Romantic landscape painter Caspar David Friedrich, whom the young Beckett greatly admired, or, more boldly, a retrospective of the work of the painters of Germany's Die Brücke group. One might go further along this flight of fancy and conjure Beckett's long tenure at the august museum, during which time he becomes one of the first in a then deeply conservative English museum scene to exhibit some of the major movements in mid to late-twentieth-century visual art – Abstract Expressionism, Arte Povera, Minimalism, Earthworks, Performance Art. Almost immediately upon embarking on this flight, however, one recognises how heavily each of these movements was influenced by the ideas of, or associated with, the novelist and playwright Samuel Beckett.

So perhaps the proper fate for this capricious little scenario is that it be shoved back, Krapp-like, into a drawer of files containing others generated by Beckett's fitful 1930s missives in search of an alternative to 'writing books that no one will read' (*L1*, 362): inquiring about a job as a London advertising copywriter; offering to serve as an apprentice to filmmaker Sergei Eisenstein in Moscow; and applying to teach Italian in Cape Town or French in colonial Bulawayo, Southern Rhodesia – each of which letters is legendary among Beckett scholars. Yet while his desire to, say, become a commercial airplane pilot may have been fleeting – this was alluded to, as were most of these alternative careers, in correspondence with his Irish confidant Thomas McGreevy – Beckett's interest and involvement in the history of visual art and in contemporary art and indeed, his influence on subsequent generations of visual artists, have been profound and lasting.[1]

In this chapter, I explore Beckett's engagement with visual art – especially contemporary art – over the course of his career: his interest in the art of the '20s and '30s; his art criticism of the mid '40s to the mid '50s; motifs of visual art in his novels and plays; and his collaborations with painters and sculptors – ending the essay by speculating about his impact on visual artists he did not know. In doing so, I try to think about both Beckett and the visual art of the twentieth century in relation to what philosopher Jacques Rancière calls 'the distribution of the sensible' – 'the system of ... forms determining what lends itself to sense experience[:] a delimitation of spaces and times, of the visible and the invisible'.[2] In their distinct but related delimitation of spaces and times, visibility and invisibility, both Beckett and the visual art of his era are shaped by this 'system' and contribute to it, revising it and offering new horizons of possibility for understanding what is meant by the ontological, the ethical and the political.

That said, neither rubric, 'Beckett' or 'Contemporary Visual Art', is a stable formation. While some persistent preoccupations can be found over the course of Beckett's long writing career, the 'early' Beckett of *Whoroscope* or *More Pricks than Kicks* (to say nothing of *Proust* or 'Dante...Bruno. Vico..Joyce') is hardly identical to the 'late' Beckett of *Ohio Impromptu* or *Worstward Ho*. Likewise, while 'Contemporary' by definition is fugitive, the very idea of 'Visual Art' itself transformed: the struggle with the commodifiable art object that to a great extent shaped early to mid twentieth-century art was, by the decade in which Beckett died, largely abandoned, with artists never quite defeating or relinquishing that object (hence the return in the 1980s of earlier modernist movements with 'neo-' and 'post-' prefixes attached, and the extraordinary rise, well after the emergence of Conceptual Art, of the monetary value of works in the international art market). 'Beckett' and 'Contemporary Visual Art' are moving targets, not always moving in the same direction, and the familiar if oxymoronic mainstay of Beckett criticism, 'increasing minimalism', simply won't suffice when considering, seriously, the metamorphosis of visual art from the 1920s through the 1980s – despite the increasing 'theatricality' of art after Minimalism.[3]

The Paris to which Beckett moved as a twenty-three-year-old in 1929 had long been established as the capital of the visual art world. It not only possessed one of the finest art collections in the world in the Louvre, which, according to Beckett's biographer James Knowlson, Beckett often visited, but had been home to generations of would-be innovators and provocateurs from the Impressionists' and Post-Impressionists' registering of the artist's ocular data to Cubists' planar experiments to Dadaists' stridently anti-bourgeois and anti-art detonations to Surrealists' attempt to unleash the unconscious onto canvas and paper and more broadly into the political sphere. Beckett certainly was aware of and kept abreast of the then current directions in contemporary art; there would have been no way to have translated André Breton or Paul Eluard, as Beckett did, without knowing the work of Max Ernst, Salvador Dalí and Man Ray. Beckett's familiarity with (but by no means allegiance to) Surrealism and other France-based international vanguardist projects continued through the 1930s. However, he spent much of the early part of that decade in Dublin and London, where the visual art scenes were still comparatively stodgy, and it was not until his six-month 1936–7 trip to Germany, as the recent publication of parts of his diaries from this period reveal, that his passionate interest in visual art reached its zenith. In Germany Beckett saw works by the Dutch old masters and the German Romantics, of whom he had been fond since his Dublin student days, and he visited the great collections of Egyptian, Islamic and Indian art in Berlin. Especially, he actively sought out the work of such Expressionists as Karl Schmidt-Rottluff, Ernst Ludwig Kirchner, Karl Ballmer and Emil Nolde, even though their work was already subject to Nazi censorship and ridicule. (In the Moritzburg in Halle in January 1937, Beckett saw the 'Schreckenskammer des Entarteten' [Chambers of Horrors of Degenerate Art], precursor to the notorious Entartete Kunst [Degenerate Art] exhibition in Munich later that year.) The sojourn to Germany appears to have crystallised Beckett's commitment to the most experimental of visual art, including works that seemed, rather than elaborately expressive and deliberately ugly, relatively 'simple', like those of Paul Klee and Wassily Kandinsky. Perhaps through their comparative restraint, Beckett began to see a way out of the 'maximal' dimension of the writers whose influence was still most pressing on him, and on whose work he had written, namely Joyce and Proust.

Upon his return to Paris in the later 1930s, Beckett got involved in a more visual arts-oriented milieu. He was to become personally acquainted with Kandinsky, Francis Picabia and Alberto Giacometti, as well as with an officially 'retired' Marcel Duchamp, with whom he is said to have played chess.[4] After the Nazi occupation of Paris, Picabia's daughter Jeanine would help draw Beckett into the underground resistance group Gloria SMH, whose exposure entailed Beckett and his companion (later wife) Suzanne's fleeing to the south of France, where they would stay from

1942–5. The deeply isolated and lonely years Beckett and Suzanne spent waiting out the war in Rousillond'Apt were, according to Knowlson, only somewhat ameliorated by their friendship with other refugees from Paris, including Polish-born French painter Henri Hayden and his wife, Josette (*K*, 298). Hayden was a moderately well-known artist whose work had gone through a number of phases mirroring the history of avant-garde art (Post-Impressionism, Cubism etc.) and had collaborated with Erik Satie. In Roussillon, most days Hayden painted close to where Beckett worked on the novel *Watt*, and the two men frequently shared lunch and discussed art and literature.

The bulk of Beckett's writing about visual art emerged in the decade after the end of the war, between 1945 and 1954 – the period in which he started to write literature in French and in which the novel trilogy of the later 1940s (*Murphy*, *Malone Meurt* and *L'innomable*) and the play *En Attendant Godot* began to attract wider notice. Beckett later disavowed this post-war art writing, suggesting that it was produced out of financial need and/or fidelity to friendships; nonetheless, as is the case with the also-later-disavowed essays on Proust and Joyce, his art writing is exceedingly instructive.

Beckett's best-known critical writing on visual art appears in the 'Three Dialogues' published in the journal *transition* in 1949. The heavily stylised 'dialogues', which are actually an edited version of a correspondence written over several months, took place between Beckett and his friend Georges Duthuit, a highly regarded French art historian. The author of a well-received book on Coptic Byzantine art, Duthuit, was married to the daughter of Henri Matisse and was an editor of *transition*. The exchange between Beckett and Duthuit concerns their disagreement over now-little-discussed painters Pierre Tal-Coat and André Masson (whose work Duthuit admired and Beckett did not) and Bram van Velde (Beckett's friend, whose work Beckett then admired and Duthuit did not particularly). More important, in his evaluation of these painters' work, Beckett begins to articulate an aesthetic, or, better, an anaesthetic theory – the necessary stutter here issuing an important rejoinder to, or at least hesitancy over, hasty generalisation.

In one of the 'dialogues', for example, Beckett (who, it will be recalled, was formerly enthralled by expressionism) famously argues for the necessity of an artist to confront 'that there is nothing to express, nothing with which to express, nothing from which to express, no power to express, no desire to express, together with the obligation to express' (*D*, 138).

Discussing the 'plane of the feasible' with Duthuit he describes 'an art turning from it in disgust, weary of its puny exploits, weary of pretending to be able, of being able, of doing a little better the same old thing, of going a little further along a dreary road' (*D*, 138). Later, he writes of his 'dream of an art unresentful of its insuperable indigence and too proud for the farce of giving and receiving' (*D*, 141). In a short essay on van Velde from the same year, also drawn from the correspondence with Duthuit (and later published in the 1960 book *Bram van Velde*), Beckett claims that 'to be an artist is to fail, as no other dare fail', this 'fidelity to failure' being both impossible and necessary, indeed obligatory (*D*, 145). Clearly such carefully written epigrammatic comments, emblematic of much of Beckett's 'art criticism', pertain not only to the work of van Velde, who Beckett dubiously claims was 'the first to desist from aestheticised automatism' but, as many readers of Beckett have recognised, even more so to Beckett's own oeuvre, especially around the time of the first novel trilogy and *Texts for Nothing*. Whether the epigrams ought to be taken as an all-encompassing 'statement of purpose' (or of purposive purposelessness) is another matter. As Oppenheim correctly asserts, Beckett's 'preoccupation with failure has all too often been made to stand for a philosophy of art', a philosophy that Beckett, 'in renouncing writing on art', which he did in the mid 1950s, 'made the sincerest effort to avert'.[5] For Oppenheim, Beckett offers 'a non-conceptual approach to art wherein the need for its definition is undone not only by the very inadequacy of expression [he] continually addresses ... but by the futility of attempting to give form to what already is meant to exist as such'.[6]

Thus what is immediately noticeable in rereading Beckett's most active period of art criticism, in which he wrote also on Bram van Velde's brother Geer and on Hayden and Jack Yeats (many of which essays were later collected in *Disjecta*), is their almost complete lack of description of the works putatively under consideration. There is virtually no analysis of size, scale, shape, line or colour, and likewise no comparison to precursor or contemporaneous works or movements. The closest Beckett will come to these staples of art history and art criticism is in the van Velde dialogue, where he offers, amid other epigrammatic reflections, this wry offhand question (without a question mark): 'for what is this coloured plane, that was not there before' (*D*, 145). To this he immediately offers a deadpan response: 'I don't know what it is, having never seen anything like it before. It seems to have nothing to do with art, in any case, if my memories of art are correct' (*D*, 145). Amid this scene of bewilderingly dual 'thrownnesses' – the thrownness both of the work of art in relation to Beckett, and Beckett's own, given the specific task of having to say something about that art – the evasion of description (save for calling it a 'coloured plane') negates 'art' as typically understood but nevertheless affirms art's being in the world and its effects, despite art's tendency (like criticism's) towards inadequacy or downright botchedness. It is surely no accident that Beckett deployed the Jewish joke of the fastidious but incompetent tailor (whose unsatisfying punch line is 'But, sir, look at the world and look at your trousers') first in his writing on the van Veldes and then, some ten years later, with very slight emendation (a change of personal pronouns from 'your' to 'my'), in Nagg's soliloquy in *Endgame*. Art, like the faulty trousers, can be 'looked at' – and indeed, according to his artist friend Avigdor Arikha, Beckett would look at artworks with extreme concentration for an hour at a time (*K*, 186) – but that does not make them any more legible or comprehensible than the 'world' itself.

In fact, one might consider the strikingly stationary, and often silent, images from so many of Beckett's plays akin to painterly tableaux – the kind that can and must be looked at for a long time: Hamm, at the beginning and end of *Endgame*, with his bloody handkerchief covering his face like a figure from Pieter Bruegel the Elder's *Lepers*; *Happy Days*' Winnie, up to her bosom, then neck, in a mound of earth, looking like part of a Gustave Doré illustration of a later canto from Dante's *Inferno*, against a Dalí-like 'laughably earnest bad imitation' of a sky; *Not I*'s brightly lit mouth, appearing out of the void, as though a Meret Oppenheim *vagina dentata*, or the same play's unnamed 'Auditor' in hood and djellaba, again as though from Doré's *Inferno*; the television play *Nacht and Träume*'s dejected dreamer, who resembles Dürer's angel of Melancholy, though devoid of all of his tools for understanding the world.[7]

Yet if one is to do justice to the plays' (and the art criticism's) complexity, one must hold this idea of picture or image in tension with the dubiety with which Beckett generally treats the faculty of vision, a dubiety that infuses Beckett's description of van Velde's coloured plane having 'nothing to do with art'. To wind back to *Endgame* for a moment, note the opening stage descriptions:

Bare interior.
  Grey Light.
  Left and right back, high up, two small windows, curtains drawn.
  Front right, a door. Hanging near door, its face to wall, a picture.
  Front left, touching each other, covered with an old sheet, two ashbins.
  Center, in an armchair on castors, covered with an old sheet, Hamm. (*CDW*, 92)

These 'directions' describing the claustrophobic vacancy of Hamm and Clov's world are highly pictorial in themselves; it is as though they have been painted with quick brushstrokes. Yet to complicate matters, at their very heart they depict a recto-verso picture, whose image, like the images outside the window, remains obscure and perplexing, withheld both from their viewers acting within the play and those witnessing the actors acting. Is this image too painful for Hamm or Clov (or anyone else) to look at, too reminiscent of a former world (or horizon of possibility), or is it rather that 'art', like 'nature' (to which, according to Kant, art bore an intimate relation) has 'forsaken' the world? This notion of a pictoriality that refuses or at least challenges its purpose, referentiality, comprehensibility and aestheticised effect can also be recognised as operating in much of Beckett's fiction as well, where the overall greyness and reduction of external stimuli nevertheless serve to highlight, El Greco-like, particular bodies in particular situations: the head trapped in a jar in *The Unnamable*; the pinned and wriggling victim (then perpetrator, then victim) of 'can opening' in *How it Is*; the confined, practically imprisoned figures of the late narrative trilogy.

In any case, by the time Beckett's works began to reach a broader audience in the later 1950s, the trajectory 'from' Visual Art 'to' Beckett's literature and theatre was becoming, if not exactly reversed, at least more equilibrial. In a legendary example of Beckett's work impacting a visual artist, Jackson Pollock reportedly saw *Waiting for Godot* three times during its 1956 run on Broadway and, during Lucky's speech, once wept so loudly and profusely he had to flee the theatre.[8] Beckett's eventual fame led to collaborations not only with such friends as Arikha and Hayden but with internationally celebrated artists. In 1963 Giacometti knew *Godot* well enough to design the set for a Beckett-directed production of the play with a single sculpted barren tree. In the later 1960s, Ernst illustrated a trilingual edition of *From an Abandoned Work*, creating several lithographs, including the astonishing *Tête – Pour Beckett*. The following decade saw Jasper Johns take a stab or series of stabs at *Foirades*, a text Beckett translated into English (as *Fizzles*) for the occasion; Johns' thirty-three etchings and aquatints ('plus color lithograph endpapers') were hailed by several art critics for opening a new direction in Johns' work. One collaboration from the 1980s must be singled out for its aptness: the book created by minimalist Robert Ryman responding to Beckett's *Nohow On* trilogy (*Company, Ill Seen Ill Said, Worstward Ho*). Ryman had dedicated himself since the early 1960s to creating monochromatic white and off-white paintings on a variety of media, including canvas, wood and paper but also linen, burlap, steel, fibreglass, aluminum and vinyl. He doesn't so much 'illustrate' Beckett's late trilogy (avoiding, *pace* Johns, excerpting words from the novels) as provide a sort of blank context – usually multiply white paintings, which stand juxtaposed, faceless face to face, with the text of Beckett. Given that Beckett signed the 550 volumes Ryman produced in 1989, the year of Beckett's death, there is a gently epitaphic quality to the effort.

To be sure, the entire generation of Minimalists, including sculptors like Carl Andre, Dan Flavin and Robert Morris, shared with the later Beckett a commitment to a certain 'less is more' objectivity and phenomenality, and, such as Beckett, they had read, and owed much to the work of, Merleau-Ponty, especially the latter's conception of a post- or non-Cartesian embodied type of viewing. But Beckett's impact on later twentieth-century art did not expire with Minimalism. In fact, although Lois Oppenheim makes a strong case for Beckett's linguistic painterliness (drawing on Merleau-Ponty to substantiate her claim), and although there are real affinities between Beckett's writings and theatre and Italian Arte Povera (which went further than minimalist painting in attacking the bourgeois conventions of painting, extending to ripping the canvas itself), it is in later twentieth-century Performance and Earthworks, which in part fled painting and sculpture for their associations with singular artistry, that Beckett's work has left its most durable impression.

In 1968, post-minimalist/proto-performance artist Bruce Nauman created a sixty-minute black-and-white video, *Slow Angle Walk (Beckett Walk)*, in which Nauman walks back and forth in his studio with exaggeratedly stiff legs and his arms clasped behind his back in front of a fixed camera turned on its side, the camera recording both the walking movements, and, equally often, merely the room punctuated by the sound of footsteps. The obsessive pattern of Nauman's movements – he kicks one leg up at a right angle, pivots a quarter turn, falls forward hard, sticks out the rear leg again at a right angle behind and begins the sequence again – indicates the existence of a set of rules whose rationale is never spelled out. In the *Walk*, Nauman condenses motifs from many Beckett texts: *Act Without Words*' repeated gestures, *Molloy*'s shifted stones, *The Unnamable*'s narrator's (imagined) circuitous ambulations, and Buster Keaton's post-slapstick movements in *Film*.[9]

A couple of years later, Robert Smithson and a hired construction crew created the earthwork *Spiral Jetty* on the north end of the Great Salt Lake in Utah. In the hallucinatory film in which Smithson documented the making of the jetty, Smithson reads a long passage from early in *The Unnamable* as a voice-over for a scene shot in The Hall of Late Dinosaurs at New York's American Museum of Natural History. In the essay he wrote that followed in 1972 – the earthwork, film and essay were together called *The Spiral Jetty* – Smithson makes clear how much of the film and even the earthwork itself were drawn from Mahood's projected spirallings inward and outward in the first trilogy's last text. In *The Spiral Jetty*, Beckett's 'All has proceeded, all this time' (*T*, 289) resonates not just with an individual life or human history, but is extended to geological time, the history of stones, extinction.[10]

Nauman's and Smithson's works, produced in the Vietnam War period and long recognised as bringing about a decisive change in the direction of then contemporary art, were, of course, created while Beckett was still actively writing; in fact Beckett would survive Smithson (who died in a plane crash) by sixteen years. In the decades since Beckett's death, his works' impact on artists has been less direct, though still readily perceptible. For the 100th anniversary of Beckett's birth, the Museum of Contemporary Art in Chicago and the Centre Pompidou in Paris launched major exhibitions in which artists contributed art directly or indirectly inspired by Beckett. Two 'installation' works bear special mention. In Chicago, Cuban artist Tania Bruguera presented *Endgame Study #7* (2006), one of a number of works she created over several years on Beckett's play. For *Study #7*, she placed a speaker and a microphone on a microphone stand on each of the balconies situated above the large gallery exhibition space on two of its sides, facing each other but separated by some thirty metres. The microphones were wired in such a way that viewers who chose to speak into one of them could do so, but their voices were projected only into the opposite balcony's speaker and heard by someone who could not fully be seen. Likewise, the speaker adjacent to the microphone registered the sounds of the auditor. This created a sense of mediated (and potentially false) intimacy while also evoking the tradition of grand public political speeches delivered from balconies. The gallery space was itself left empty, save for a single quotation from the play printed in large type on the floor: 'I'll give you just enough to keep you from dying'. In Paris, British artist of Palestinian origin Mona Hatoum exhibited her *Corps Étranger*. In a large darkened room a looped video displayed apparently abstract, sometimes erotic and often disgusting images; the images, the viewer discovers upon reading the wall text, were produced through a medical endoscopic tour of the inside of Hatoum's body: throat, oesophagus and further down the digestive tract.

With its multiple Mouth-like apertures and apparent terminuses, this tour proceeded as if 'from impenetrable self to impenetrable unself / by way of neither'. These recent projects by internationally recognised mid-career artists go beyond mere homage to Beckett; they decisively challenge 1990s installation art's supposed 'relational aesthetics'[11] by raising the stakes of what Martin Harries has called 'destructive spectatorship'[12] – precisely the kind of spectatorship Beckett's theatre engendered.

NOTES

1 Some of the many critics who have written perceptively about Beckett and the visual arts include James Acheson, Alan Ackerman, Daniel Albright, Leo Bersani, Herbert Blau, Pascale Casanova, Ruby Cohn, Renee Riese Hubert, Dougald McMillan, Breon Mitchell, Marjorie Perloff, Peggy Phelan, Jessica Prinz, Carol Schloss and Nigel Spivey. Lois Oppenheim's *The Painted Word* is, to date, the most comprehensive study in this field.
2 Jacques Rancière, *The Politics of Aesthetics: The Distribution of the Sensible*, trans. Gabriel Rockhill (London, Continuum 2004), 13.
3 My focus on 'contemporary' art is in no way intended to suggest that pre-twentieth-century art (especially of the Renaissance and by the old masters) did not shape Beckett's writing, or that he did not refer to these works, consciously or unconsciously, in his literature or theatre. (It could fairly be said that Beckett was drawn to 'extreme' work of all historical moments.) Rather, because that influence has been widely recognised, it seems more productive to pursue a relatively neglected dimension in Beckett criticism. In regards to my square quoting of 'theatrical': this was the adjective through which critic Michael Fried famously dismissed early Minimalist sculpture.
4 Although Beckett had earlier included Kandinsky on his short list of the greatest living artists, he seems in a 1949 essay on Bram van Velde to ridicule what he calls the 'every man his own wife experiments of the spiritual Kandinsky'. 'Every man his own wife', it will be remembered, was *Ulysses*' Buck Mulligan's comical title for a play, discussed in the 'Scylla and Charybdis' episode. The play, subtitled *A Honeymoon in the Hand*, inverted the interdiction of fornication in Corinthians 7:1. Thematic connections between Beckett and Giacometti are explored in Matti Megged's *Dialogue in the Void: Beckett and Giacometti*.
5 Lois Oppenheim, *The Painted Word: Samuel Beckett's Dialogue with Art* (Michigan: Michigan University Press, 2000), 93.
6 Ibid., 93.
7 Knowlson sees both *Nacht and Träume* and *Ohio Impromptu* as indebted to Rembrandt. For Knowlson's description of how Beckett distills, abstracts or modernises pre-modernist painterly images see *K*, 609–10.
8 Ruth Kligman, *Love Affair: A Memoir of Jackson Pollock* (Michigan: Michigan University Press, 1999), 69. I write 'reportedly' because Kligman, once Pollock's lover, has been accused of frequent exaggeration and self-aggrandizement.

9 *Samuel Beckett/Bruce Nauman*, a major exhibition at Vienna's Kunsthalle in 2000, explored connections between the two artists. It is not clear whether Beckett knew of Nauman's work, but that the two artists were at times mining the same vein is clear. Consider Beckett's 1975 play *Footfalls*, in which May obsessively paces back and forth, the pacing diagrammed in the text of the play. Other late 1960s performance artists whose works show a clear debt to Beckett are Paul McCarthy and Vito Acconci, both of whom amplify scenes of degradation and abjection via repeated gestures and movements, especially quasi-erotic ones.
10 See Nico Israel, 'At the End of the Jetty', *Journal of Beckett Studies* (20.1: 2011), 1–31.
11 See Nicolas Bourriaud, *Relational Aesthetics* (Paris: Les Presses du Réel, 2002).
12 See Martin Harries, *Forgetting Lot's Wife: On Destructive Spectatorship* (New York: Fordham University Press, 2007).

CHAPTER 23

Music

Catherine Laws

Samuel Beckett's love of music is well documented. He enjoyed playing the piano, married a professional pianist and counted a number of musicians amongst his friends. He regularly attended concerts and clearly relished discussing the relative merits of performances. His letters, as well his notes on philosophy and other reading, attest to the extent of his listening to and thinking about music, as well as to the strong opinions and preferences that resulted: 'Beethoven's Quartets are a waste of time'; Furtwängler is 'murderous', his trio producing 'a frenzy of impotence' (*L1*, 68, 182, 470). Moreover, his tastes were broad; while Beckett's great love was for music of the late Classical and early Romantic periods, throughout his life he listened widely.

In particular, Beckett's friendship with composer Marcel Mihalovici and Mihalovici's wife, pianist Monique Haas, resulted in his acquaintance with a wide range of music from the early mid twentieth century: especially Debussy, Ravel, Hindemith, Stravinsky and Bartók (*K*, 496). Beckett also showed interest in the music of Schönberg, Berg and Webern (*L2*, 146), and listened to their music with Avigdor Arikha (*K*, 496). Similarly, Everett Frost remembers discussing 1950s *musique concrète* with Beckett during their work on a production of *All That Fall*.[1]

The question, then, is how any of this fed into Beckett's writing. What follows here is an attempt to give an overview of this complex topic, but also to use specific instances to demonstrate the depths at which Beckett's thinking about music – about philosophical, formal and expressive considerations and about the activity of listening – penetrates his writing.

Many of those involved with Beckett's work have commented on its musicality. Interviews with actors and directors more often than not include some reference to the musical character of the texts. George Devine sums up the prevailing attitude: 'One has to think of the text as something like a musical score wherein the "notes", the sights and sounds, the pauses, have their own interrelated rhythms, and out of their composition comes the dramatic impact'.[2] The working relationship between Beckett and actress Billie Whitelaw provides an example of this approach, and Whitelaw described herself as the musical instrument upon which Beckett would 'play the notes.'[3] No doubt much of this derives from the terms in which Beckett attempted to convey his dramatic vision; Ruby Cohn (amongst others) commented on Beckett's tendency to use musical terminology in rehearsal,[4] while Whitelaw noted Beckett's preference for directing by 'conducting' the lines.[5]

Arguably these analogies operate on a surface level, suggesting a relationship to musical practices or their influence without necessarily telling us much about the specifically musical qualities that might result. Nevertheless, certain comments reach deeper, implying that this 'musicality' is closely bound up with Beckett's use of language and particularly his attitude towards meaning. For example, a number of performers relate the musical effect to Beckett's determination that his characters and their words or actions cannot be explained and that performers should avoid imposing an interpretation in the traditional sense. Rehearsing *Footfalls* with Rose Hill, Beckett announced: 'We are not doing this play realistically or psychologically, we are doing it musically',[6] while David Warrilow is uninterested in the 'whys' of performance: 'I know that if an actor gets up onstage and starts to play the meaning of the thing it dies, it just dies'.[7]

From this perspective, Beckett's use of musical terminology suggests an approach to performance that treats characters, words and stage directions as given; their relative articulation in sound and space – intonation and rhythm, repetition and variation – rather than meaning, becomes the focus of rehearsal, as in music. At this level, the general perception of Beckett's texts as musical relates closely to the question of meaning in his work and his preference for exploring *how*, rather than *why*, something should be said or done.

Despite this, even by the early 1990s it was still difficult to find anything more than brief passing comments on the topic of Beckett and music. General references to the musicality of Beckett's language were abundant in Beckett studies, with critics often copying Beckett's use of musical terminology or employing loose analogies with musical forms or practices. However, there was very little consideration of quite what this meant or why it should be of interest. The 1998 publication of *Samuel Beckett and Music*, edited by Mary Bryden, changed things, providing the first book-length study, and in the twenty-first century a growing body of work has sought to get to grips with the topic.

However, this is a complex task. Music is not a singular entity in Beckett, but is manifested in different ways: thematised as an 'idea' or a formal or expressive model; as actual music in the plays, whether prerecorded or sung by characters; as references to music and musicians; and through the musicalising of language effected by attention to qualities of sound and rhythm and increasing use of forms of structural variation and motivic development. These manifestations are rarely independent of one another, and it is often hard to establish where Beckett's language demonstrates the influence of music and where the relationship instead lies in his use of certain tropes and structures held in common at a deep formal or broadly analogous level by music and language.

MUSIC AS CATALYST

Beckett's 1931 study of Proust was his most extended piece of literary criticism. It shows Beckett to be using *A la recherche du temps perdu* to think through the possibilities for literature. Music has a role to play in this, and while there are dangers in reading *Proust* as a broader credo applicable throughout Beckett's oeuvre, in certain respects the ideas persist beyond this slim monograph.

Beckett was probably the first to suggest that 'Music is the catalytic element in the work of Proust' (*P*, 92), acknowledging the significance of the fictional composer, Vinteuil. Moreover, Beckett's reading of Schopenhauer, especially in mid 1930, fed into this work: he was the first to discuss the influence of Schopenhauer upon *A la recherche*. In some respects Proust adopts Schopenhauer's idealist vision of music as 'by no means like the other arts, namely a copy of the Ideas, but *a copy of the will itself*, the objectivity of which are the Ideas'.[8] However, Beckett inserts into Schopenhauer's metaphysical stance the idea that 'This essential quality of music is distorted by the listener, who, being an impure subject, insists on giving a figure to that which is ideal and invisible' (*P*, 92).

On the one hand, as Thomas Mansell says, the Beckett of *Proust* is clearly attracted to the possibility of music as transcendence.[9] Nevertheless, John Pilling's observations are equally true: ultimately, Beckett is 'either unable or unwilling to attribute to music such a benign and curative role' as Proust: for Beckett, as soon as the listener enters into the equation, all is lost.[10] This reflects his generally pessimistic critical stance but also the unresolved division in Beckett's thinking about music, in both *Proust* and the work that followed. At this point, there is no apparent means of reconciling the desire to project music as idealised, abstract and transcendent with the complexity of its material operation and its subjective appropriation by listeners.

Significantly, this disjunction persists into Beckett's fictional oeuvre. It is most explicitly apparent in his early fiction, particularly *Dream of Fair to Middling Women*, but a preoccupation with listening is more pervasive. The image of the listener recurs as an object of attention in Beckett's plays, poetry and prose. Sometimes, as in *Ghost Trio*, Beckett dramatises the act of listening to music. Elsewhere it is a voice that is listened to; that of a reader, as in *Ohio Impromptu*, or the protagonist's own recorded voice, as in *Krapp's Last Tape*. Often, though, the voice is ambiguous, emerging from the darkness without clear origin or identity; perhaps the listener's own voice – the unstoppable voice in one's head – or that of another: real, imaginary or remembered. Notably, it is the listener and the act of listening that Beckett foregrounds, as much as (sometimes above and beyond) what is heard. Beckett commented more than once that as he grew older the sense of hearing was becoming more important, and titles such as *Heard in the Dark*, *Stirrings Still* or *Sounds* emphasise the auditory.[11] Beckett asks what it is to listen, and this has a reflexive quality; we experience the dramatisation of our own act of listening: its performativity.

'THE MOST REGRETTABLE SIMULTANEITY OF NOTES': THE ILL-TEMPERED NOVEL

Beckett's thinking through of ideas about music is extended in his early novel *Dream of Fair to Middling Women*, completed in 1932. With an aspiring writer, Belacqua, as its protagonist, the novel works playfully with creative authority and the expression of literary aspirations. Music is influential here: Beckett draws into his text somewhat abstruse fragments of philosophies of tuning, melody and harmony, derived selectively from Pythagoras in particular, via French musicologist Louis Laloy's idiosyncratic study of Chinese music.[12] This strange web of imagery is used to contrast rational, coherent systems with complexity and chaos; the ideal unity of 'melodic' novelistic composition, 'a little book that would be purely melodic' (*Dream*, 10), in which characters would toe the line and do as the narrator wishes, with the raucous cacophony of misaligned harmonics that occurs when they interact, 'thickening the ruined melody' (*Dream*, 117). Music, in this way, offers two models for a writer: the narrator's depiction of music is of a linear, unified model of cause and effect, whereas Belacqua's preference is for music of discontinuity, fragmentation, unpredictability.

Significantly, Belacqua's literary ideals are apparently exemplified by the music of Beethoven: 'The experience of my reader shall be between the phrases, in the silence, communicated by the intervals, not the terms of the statement.... I think of Beethofen [*sic*], ... where into the body of the music he incorporates a punctuation of dehiscence, flottements, the coherence gone to pieces, the continuity bitched to hell' (*Dream*, 137–8). Belacqua refers to Beethoven's music positively, as an 'incoherent continuum', wherein artistic utterance articulates a hovering at the edge of a void of meaning. He even incorporates two snippets of musical notation from Beethoven's Seventh Symphony; a tiny phrase that acts, in the first movement, as a sudden held moment, interrupting the swirling momentum of the orchestral *tutti*. This idea of a 'Beethoven pause' comes to exemplify a state of 'in betweenness' beyond ordinary representation (or 'between the terms'); a state Belacqua associates with true experience and seeks to capture in his writing. Later, in 'Ding Dong' in *More Pricks Than Kicks* (which reworks some of *Dream*), Belacqua says he 'lived a Beethoven pause' (*MPTK*, 38).

Beethoven's more fragmentary treatment of often quite simple motives, relative to his predecessors and contemporaries, perhaps explains Beckett's somewhat idiosyncratic characterisation, and some of his reading on the composer portrayed the works in this way.[13] There is also, though, a sense of Beckett being drawn to ideas of the man himself; to Beethoven as the symbol of what a composer might be, or come to stand for. The traditional image of Beethoven-hero standing alone on the brink of an era, personifying the disintegration of musical Classicism and impending Romanticism, perhaps sheds additional light on Beckett's representation of the music as 'in between', beyond grasp.

However, the link from the Pythagorean tuning model to Beethoven comes from Schopenhauer. The emphasis on discontinuity and unpredictability echoes Schopenhauer's quite particular notion that 'a symphony by Beethoven presents us with the greatest confusion which yet has the most perfect order at its foundation'.[14] Moreover, Schopenhauer follows his paragraph on Beethoven by relating his metaphysical account to music's physical properties, reminding us of the basic ratios of Pythagorean tuning. And the subsequent steps of his argument are echoed in *Dream*, from ideas of melody and harmony through to the invocation of a Beethoven symphony as the supreme manifestation of the strivings of the will.

In this way, Beckett seems to be thinking *through* these strangely linked musical models – Pythagoras's, Laloy's and Schopenhauer's – as part of his exploration of what his writing might do. Moreover, these metaphors persist into Beckett's more mature work, as he continues to contrast chaos and flux with order and ratiocination. The narrator's desire for coherent 'melodic' form anticipates Neary's aspirations towards 'Apmonia' in *Murphy* (*M*, 3), and Beckett's more detailed study of Pythagoras later in the 1930s feeds directly into Neary's founding of a Pythagorean academy in Cork,[15] now brought into play with ideas from Occasionalism and Greek Atomism.[16] Beyond this, as Heath Lees has shown, metaphors of tuning persist into *Watt*, again used to contrast system with the chaos of experience.

Beethoven continues to serve as a useful reference point, initially in *More Pricks Than Kicks* and the much-quoted letter to Axel Kaun (1937):

> Is there any reason why that terrifyingly arbitrary materiality of the word surface should not be dissolved, as for example the sound surface of Beethoven's Seventh Symphony is devoured by huge black pauses, so that for pages on end we cannot perceive it as other than a dizzying path of sounds connecting unfathomable chasms of silence? (*LI*, 518–19)

There is a danger in attaching undue weight to this letter. Nevertheless, its contents are revealing with regard to Beckett's recourse to German Romanticism, including its re-emergence in a far more self-conscious, deconstructed form in late plays such as *Ghost Trio* and *Nacht und Träume*. Moreover, in a broader sense the preoccupation with the relative expressive and meaningful capacities of language and music resurfaces throughout Beckett's work, most explicitly in the radio plays *Words and Music*, *Esquisse Radiophonique* (*Rough for Radio I*) and *Cascando*, all written in 1961.

'KINDLY TUNE ACCORDINGLY': THE LISTENING SELF

Underlying Beckett's invocation of Beethoven in *Dream* is a questioning of artistic agency and authority, a preoccupation that continually resurfaces but re-emerges in specific relation to Beethoven over forty years later, in the television play *Ghost Trio* (first broadcast in 1977). Here, the unusual treatment of music and listening corresponds to the broader interrogation of the relationship between the body, imagination and subjectivity. As a result, music plays a more sophisticated, less idealised role.

A female voice, V, directs our viewing of a bare room, in which a silent, unnamed male figure, F, waits, apparently for a female visitor. Mostly, the camera position and F's (minimal) movements are prompted by V. However, at times the action 'disobeys' or pre-empts the voice, destabilising her authority. The self-conscious production of action undermines any verisimilitude and undercuts any pathos: we are left unsure as to whether this situation ever 'really' existed, and instead the articulation of the scene becomes as much the subject of the play as the tension of F's waiting and listening.

The music supports this ambiguity. Snippets of the *Largo* of Beethoven's *Piano Trio* Op.70 No.1 'The Ghost' are heard, associated with F's hunching over a cassette player. However, the music comes and goes in a subtly unrealistic manner, not always related to the proximity of the camera but more in relation to his assumption and resumption of the listening pose. Moreover, the extracts of the *Trio* do not stop and start in a naturalistic fashion: instead, Beckett makes very particular choices, fragmenting and re-ordering the original.[17] The music does not simply represent the awaited woman, in a straightforwardly sentimental fashion; instead, its uncertain origins support the focus on creative agency, implying that it is F's listening that is productive, summoning the musical phrases. In this the play gains a poignant, elegiac quality beyond simple nostalgia. The music of this play is not only ghost-like in character but haunts us (and Beckett) with insubstantial intimations of imaginative agency, drawing on and resituating the redemptive Romantic spirit of the music.

'SHIVERING THROUGH THE GRIM JOURNEY AGAIN': BECKETT AND SCHUBERT

If Beethoven is a significant point of reference for Beckett, Schubert is nevertheless the composer to whom he refers most frequently. Specific works are invoked in some of the early stories: in 'Walking Out' Belacqua and Lucy 'sit up to all hours' listening to *An die Musik* (*MPTK*, 113) (and Beckett copied this piece into his *Whoroscope* notebook),[18] while in 'Ding Dong' the reference to 'A great major symphony ... fulcrate on the middle C' (*MPTK*, 42) calls to mind Schubert's 9th. Throughout his life, Beckett held a particular love of Schubert's lieder, sometimes singing them to his own accompaniment.[19] He listened repeatedly to *Winterreise*, especially, and references to winter journeys are found in *Texts for Nothing* 2 and 12, and especially at the end of *What Where* (1983) commissioned for the Autumn Festival in Graz, where *Winterreise* was partly composed: 'It is Winter./ Without journey'.

A number of writers have considered the significance of Schubert to Beckett, observing a certain commonality of thematic concerns: lone figures journeying through barren landscapes, ambiguous encounters along the way, the persistent desire for the comfort of company in the face of ultimate isolation and the hovering presence of death.[20] However, in Beckett's radio play *All That Fall* (written in 1956) and in his television play *Nacht and*

Träume (1982) we hear Schubert's actual music, and here the writer's understanding – and use – of its specific characteristics is most apparent. As in *Ghost Trio*, Beckett seems interested in what we *do* with music; how active listening involves an imaginative engagement with the expressive content of (especially Romantic) music; an engagement that is productive, constituting a working through or imaginative enactment of selfhood in the world.

In *All That Fall* the precise qualities of the soundscape were of great concern to Beckett.[21] However, it is the framing of Maddy's journey with extracts from Schubert's 'Death and the Maiden' – the lied or quartet movement[22] – emanating from the 'ruinous old house' of a 'very old woman', that supports the themes of the play: birth, youth and fertility versus barrenness, sterility, physical decline and death. As in *Ghost Trio* the music operates not entirely realistically; it is apparently located in the house, yet continues to grow louder or softer even when Maddy stops moving. It is as if it is the degree of attention to the music that brings it into focus, rather than the acoustical fact of its relative proximity. Again, the music projects absence – dead children and the 'poor woman' – but also invokes the productive powers of the imagination, in this case via Maddy's conjuring of her own ambiguous other(s): the suffering woman and the looming figure of death. This creates a lyrical and affective counterpart to what cannot quite be said.

More broadly, as has recently been much discussed, Beckett's relationship to Romanticism is complex and contradictory. He is distrustful of heroic transcendence and dismissive of the sentimentalism of much Romantic writing,[23] and yet the references persist.[24] Beethoven, figured as the Romantic visionary, is useful to Beckett, but he finds an equally close affinity with the decidedly unheroic strain of German Romanticism, with melancholic figures isolated in an indifferent world; those in Schubert's lieder, or the paintings of Caspar David Friedrich. There is, then, a strong link between Beckett's sense of the gap between the self and the world and his attraction to particular strains of Romantic music. If Beethoven's music provides confirmation of the limits of rational thought and the irreconcilability of subject and object, Schubert's seems to reinforce the paradox that results: that, as Paul Lawley puts it, 'the comfort of company is itself the occasion for suffering'.[25]

'SUCH ARE OUR TRANSPORTS'

Clearly, the solace provided by music is never complete or simple for Beckett[26]: 'never a rapturous or transformatory force'.[27] And underlying

Beckett's use of music and ideas about music is a nagging preoccupation with what music can do, explored in relation to the ongoing struggle with the limits of language. In this respect Beckett considers, works through and ultimately goes beyond the conventional Idealist (and subsequently Modernist) positioning of music as the transcendent 'beyond' of language. One might well argue that Beckett's disintegrating language results in part from an impulse towards a state of music, stripping away the referential, representational complexities of language. Certainly, a play like *Words and Music* seems to imply that music can access the true essence of ideas, in contrast to the distorted, mediations of language: 'Music always wins', he said.[28] The subsequent increasing musicality of Beckett's language is a logical consequence of this, manifested through a combination of fragmentation, speeds of articulation which make ordinary comprehension difficult (*Not I* is a great example), structures of repetition and association that foreground the sounding qualities of language (as in *Play*, amongst other dramatic works) and, in some of the late works, the evolving of lines from the implications, both sonic and semantic, of an initial phase, word or monosyllable (as in *Worstward Ho*, generated motivically from the first phoneme, 'on', and its negation, 'no').

Nevertheless, the complexities of Beckett's uses of music acknowledge the inevitable failure of this drive towards abstraction. The residual traces of reference and grammatical function are always significant. Even in texts as fragmented as 'Ping', 'Lessness' or 'What is the Word', the rhythmic ebb and flow of the phrases and the textual impulsion are intimately bound up with the inability absolutely to divorce individual words from their conventional associations, grammatical, cultural and memorial. Moreover, Beckett's focus on our subjective engagement with music, through listening, reflects back to us the complexities of its action in the world; music may signify differently to language, but does so equally messily. Inevitably, then, music is not simply 'Music', an indivisible higher idea. Indeed, the very striving towards a hopelessly idealised notion of music is one facet of Beckett's broader aesthetics of failure: that of the subject's inability to disentangle from the chaotic experiencing of meaning.

BECKETT AND COMPOSERS

The context of Beckett's approach to music, as outlined earlier in this chapter, might explain two potentially contradictory things: that Beckett never truly collaborated with a composer on the production of a new work, and the continuing attractiveness of his work to composers.

Music

Studies of Beckett's work certainly contain references to Beckett 'collaborating' with composers. However, one might define these instances more as cooperation. In those instances when Beckett's plays require the composing of new music (as in *Acte sans paroles I*, *Words and Music* and *Cascando*), its role and scope is defined by the author. The music can be (and has been) realised with different stylistic features and various instrumentations; the specific characterisation of the music can, of course, vary. Moreover, the first versions were written with specific composers in mind: Beckett's cousin John for *Acte sans paroles I* and *Words and Music*, and Marcel Mihalovici for *Cascando*. However, none of these versions have become synonymous with the plays (and John Beckett withdrew his contributions), and ultimately the questions explored here are not dependent upon individual compositional choices. As such, each work continues to exist in the imaginary form of 'Beckett's play', above and beyond the contribution of any one composer.

Beckett was relatively generous in his granting of permission to composers seeking to produce musical settings of his work (*K*, 655). Nevertheless, the closest he came to collaboration was his interaction with Mihalovici during the composition of a chamber opera based on *Krapp's Last Tape*. Even here, the play was already fully formed when the composer started work, and accounts suggest that Mihalovici wrote the music with some consultation but relatively independently (*K*, 467).[29] The two subsequently worked together with German translator Elmar Tophoven to adapt the text–music relationships, and James Knowlson sketches this scenario as a possible source for *Words and Music*, suggesting that the play 'bears the imprint of these struggles to bring the two different elements together' (*K*, 496). If so, the relationship between art forms was something of a tussle for dominance. Moreover, it seems that, despite his loyalty to his friend, privately the operatic *Krapp* was not really to Beckett's taste (*K*, 468).

Ultimately, none of these processes, nor the substantial settings sanctioned by Beckett (those by Morton Feldman, for example) genuinely stand as true collaborations. However, this is not to suggest that Beckett was indifferent to contemporary musical developments in general or to the specifics of composers' engagement with his work. In particular, Everett Frost's debates with Beckett about possible composers for new productions of *Words and Music* and *Cascando* confirmed Beckett's interest in the work of a diverse range of contemporary composers.[30]

The international range and the diversity of compositional approaches to Beckett's work testifies to the extent of his musical legacy. There are now dozens of Beckett-related compositions, and some critical commentary in this area (most notably in Bryden's book). For some composers the attraction relates to Beckett's sensitivity to the sounding qualities and the rhythmic patterns of words and silences. Often, though, composers, like many actor and directors, connect their sense of Beckett's musicality more broadly and loosely to the question of meaning. Berio and Glass are good examples here, and American composer Roger Reynolds refers to 'a curious, piquantly unreliable balance between blunt immediacy and nagging ambiguity'.[31]

For other composers, the attraction has more to do with the ideas and images of Beckett's work, most particularly his concern with the impossibility of making sense of one's experience of being, along with the unfeasibility of abandoning that attempt.[32] However, I would argue that this is in itself intimately bound up with the approach to language and the experiencing of the resultant effect as peculiarly musical: Beckett's breakdown of language and his ever-increasing sensitivity to sound are consequences of his struggle to find a means of representing the fragmentation and chaos of being. In this respect we come full circle: back to the idea that Beckett's ongoing exploration of music is always, if in different ways, bound up with the question of meaning.

NOTES

1 E-mail to the author, 7 March 2007.
2 Alan Schneider, 'Working with Beckett', in S. E. Gontarski (ed.) *On Beckett: Essays and Criticism* (New York: Grove Press, 1986), 249.
3 James Knowlson, 'Extracts from an Unscripted Interview with Billie Whitelaw by James Knowlson', *Journal of Beckett Studies* (3: 1978), 89.
4 Ruby Cohn, *Back to Beckett* (Princeton: Princeton University Press, 1973), 153.
5 Linda Ben-Zvi (ed.), *Women in Beckett: Performance and Critical Perspectives*, (Urbana: University of Illinois Press, 1990), 6.
6 James Knowlson, 'Beckett as Director', in S. E. Wilmer (ed.) *Beckett in Dublin* (Dublin: The Lilliput Press, 1992), 13.
7 Jonathan Kalb, *Beckett in Performance*, (Cambridge: Cambridge University Press, 1989), 229.
8 Arthur Schopenhauer, *The World as Will and Representation*, 2 vols. trans. E. F. J. Payne, (New York: Diver, 1969), I, 257.
9 Mansell, Thomas. 'The Significants of Music in the Work of Proust'. Unpublished, 4.
10 John Pilling, '*Proust* and Schopenhauer: Music and Shadows', in Mary Bryden (ed.) *Samuel Beckett and Music* (Oxford: Clarendon, 1998), 177.
11 Charles Juliet, *Conversations with Samuel Beckett and Bram van Velde*, trans. Janey Tucker (The Hague: Academic Press Leiden, 1995), 147, 152.

12 See Séan Lawlor, 'Louis Laloy's *La Musique Chinoise*', *The Beckett Circle* (20.1: Spring 1998), 10–11; Séan Lawlor, '"Alba" and "Dortmunder": Signposting Paradise and the Balls-aching World', *Samuel Beckett Today/Aujourd'hui* ('*All Sturm and no Drang*': *Beckett and Romanticism*) (18: 2007), 227–40; John Pilling (ed.), *Beckett's* Dream *Notebook* (Reading: Beckett International Foundation, 1999); and John Pilling, *A Companion to* Dream of Fair to Middling Women, *Journal of Beckett Studies* (12.1–2: 2003).
13 John Pilling's work on Beckett's 'Dream Notebook' reveals Beckett's note taking from Romain Rolland's *Vie de Beethoven* (1903). Some of Beckett's Beethoven references suggest additional reading (especially Thayer), and his library included Leopold Schmidt's *Beethoven: Werke und Leben* (1924) and the collection of conversations, *Beethoven im Gespräch*.
14 Arthur Schopenhauer, *The World as Will and Representation*, 2 vols. trans. E. F. J. Payne (New York: Diver, 1969), II, 450.
15 Matthew Feldman, *Beckett's Books: A Cultural History of the Interwar Notes* (London: Continuum, 2006), 68.
16 C. J. Ackerley, *Demented Particulars: The Annotated* Murphy, *Journal of Beckett Studies* (7: 1998), 106–8, 115–16.
17 See Catherine Laws, 'Beethoven's Haunting of Beckett's *Ghost Trio*', in Linda Ben-Zvi (ed.) *Drawing on Beckett: Portraits, Performances, and Cultural Contexts* (Tel Aviv: Assaph, 2003), 197–214.
18 C. J. Ackerley, and S. E. Gontarski, *The Grove Companion to Samuel Beckett* (New York: Grove Press, 2004), 516.
19 Ibid., 515.
20 Michael Maier's work is especially insightful, both in this specific context and with respect to the broader relationship between Beckett and music: Franz Michael Maier, *Becketts Melodien: Die Musik und die Idee des Zusammenhangs bei Schopenhauer, Proust und Beckett* (Würzburg: Königshausen & Neruman), 2006.
21 See Clas Zilliacus, *Beckett and Broadcasting*, (Åbo, Finland: Åbo Akademi, 1976), 69.
22 Beckett specifies Schubert's' 'Death and the Maiden', but there is some uncertainty as to which work he was referring: the lied to a text by Matthias Claudius, composed by Schubert in 1817 (D.531), or the *String Quartet in D Minor* (D.810) from 1824, which uses the theme from the lied as the basis for the second movement variations. Critics do not agree on this. The original BBC production by Donald McWhinnie uses extracts from the string quartet. In researching his American production for Voices International, Everett Frost found no comments on the choice of music in the BBC Written Archive. Frost used the lied.
23 Mark Nixon, 'Beckett and Romanticism in the 1930s', *Samuel Beckett Today/Aujourd'hui* ('*All Sturm and no Drang*': *Beckett and Romanticism*) (18: 2007), 64.
24 Dirk Van Hulle and Mark Nixon, 'Introduction', *Samuel Beckett Today/Aujourd'hui* ('*All Sturm and no Drang*': *Beckett and Romanticism*) (18: 2007), 9.

25 Paul Lawley, '"The Grim Journey": Beckett Listens to Schubert', *Samuel Beckett Today/Aujourd'hui (Samuel Beckett: Endlessness in the Year 2000)* (11: 2001), 258.
26 In a letter of 1 August 1956, Beckett wrote to his American publisher, Barney Rosset, 'The electrophone dispenses its balm. This week we get the *Dicterliebe* and *Winterreise*. Such are our transports' (*L2*, 644).
27 Mary Bryden, 'Beckett and the Sound of Silence', in Mary Bryden (ed.) *Samuel Beckett and Music* (Oxford: Clarendon, 1998), 42.
28 Katherine Worth, 'Words for Music Perhaps', in Mary Bryden (ed.) *Samuel Beckett and Music* (Oxford: Clarendon, 1998), 16.
29 Ruby Cohn, *A Beckett Canon*, (Ann Arbor: University of Michigan Press, 2005), 248.
30 E-mail to the author, 7 March 2007. Frost remembers Beckett referring to Pierre Schaeffer, Edgard Varèse, Olivier Messiaen, Arvo Pärt and Krzysztof Penderecki, amongst others. Frost finishes: 'I have no idea of his actual likes and dislikes amid all that.... But he was certainly not hostile to – then – contemporary, post Cageian, efforts in "new music"'.
31 Don Gillespie (ed.), *Roger Reynolds: Profile of a Composer* (New York: Peters, 1982), 9.
32 Morton Feldman and Richard Barrett are two contrasting examples.

CHAPTER 24

Cinema

Matthijs Engelberts

1936: TO MOSCOW!

In 1936, Beckett is certainly *writing* (he is finishing what will become his first published novel, *Murphy*), but professionally, he is surely not a *writer* yet – even if he has published a number of poems, several short stories and a book on Marcel Proust. So in July, at thirty years old, he appears to be on the lookout for at least the semblance of a career, and hopes that he is not 'too stupid about machines to qualify as a commercial pilot' (*L1*, 362) – a professional project he apparently did not pursue any further. Earlier that year, however, he cherished another professional perspective, one less unrelated to his artistic endeavours. His correspondence from the very beginning of 1936 shows that he has taken an interest in film; and in early March he has already decided that he wants to go to Moscow 'for a year at least' (*L1*, 317), in order to take courses at the State Institute of Cinematography. 'Mastering modern machines' is perhaps the (modernist) goal that Beckett's quest leads to as he plans to be a pilot or a filmmaker, but he nevertheless appears to prefer artistic technology to the motorised vehicles – and the weapons – that fascinated the futurists. And so, on 2 March 1936, a former 'lecteur d'anglais at École Normale, Paris' (assistant teacher of English), as Beckett presents himself, writes a letter to Sergei Eisenstein, the theorist and filmmaker whose *Battleship Potemkin* brought him to world fame at the end of the 1920s, asking him to admit to the Soviet film school one 'Samuel Beckett', author of a few essays and books – Beckett quotes the titles of most of his publications in his short letter after mentioning his year in Paris as a student teacher.

The Moscow film school, founded in 1919, was no longer the only option in 1936, given that the Academy of Motion Pictures Arts and Sciences, just two years after its own foundation, created a film school in 1929 at the University of Southern California (today's USC School of Cinematic Arts). But even if Beckett knew of this option, he already held a university degree and had actually resigned from his post at Trinity College Dublin (not without applying, however, for a university position in Cape Town in 1937 – 'How I dread getting that job' (*L1*, 548), as he confides to a friend). Furthermore, he was interested in the theoretical and experimental developments taking place primarily in (eastern) Europe, more so probably than in the majority of the films coming out of the studio system that led to the foundation of the Academy in California by Louis Mayer of Metro-Goldwyn-Mayer (MGM). Indeed, by January 1936, Beckett had read 'a lot of works on cinema' (*L1*, 305), as he says. He quotes texts by Vsevolod Pudovkin, Rudolf Arnheim and Sergei Eisenstein: all English translations of recent books and articles written in Russian and German by European filmmakers and theorists thrilled by the still quite new medium of film, energetically defending it as an art medium and eager to influence its development in order to exploit its artistic possibilities and heighten its status.

However, notwithstanding his interest in this experimental, modernist strand in cinema and theory, what Beckett seems to want to learn most is not primarily film theory or experimental techniques, but more basically 'how to handle a camera, the higher trucs of the editing bench, & so on' (*L1*, 311), as he writes in February. In January, he had wondered how to get 'into a decent studio, or even a bad one, simply to pick up the trade', and went on asking: 'Se munir d'un scénario?' ('Arm oneself with a script?') (*L1*, 307). Apparently, Beckett thinks he most needs basic practical training: he is eager to know the 'actual tricks of photography' (*L1*, 307), and not primarily the up-to-date theory with which he recently familiarised himself through his reading. In fact, he might as well have followed Hitchcock's example as set in the early 1920s and started at the bottom in a film studio – Hitchcock set off as a title card designer. But Beckett was more involved in his writing than Hitchcock (who, indeed, started off by writing stories as well), and was more involved in international art theory, all of which directed his attention to Moscow. He was, as well, in a position to perhaps live without a salary for quite some time. As a result, he never even mentions the idea of accepting a job in a studio in London or elsewhere. Not being 'too stupid about machines' is in itself apparently not attractive enough as a goal for Beckett, who wants to learn a practical and yet art-related job *only* under the guidance of reputed artistic film-makers.

So it is 'To Moscow!' – for at least a while. As the characters in Chekhov's *Three Sisters*, although perhaps less persistently, Beckett repeats his desire after having written his letter to Eisenstein: at the end of March he specifically recalls his plans and the recent letter, stating boldly: 'I have had no reply. Will probably go soon whether or no' (*L1*, 324). What is striking in the application that Beckett sends addressed to 'Monsieur' (a standard French salutation in a letter otherwise written in English that also ends with a polite formula in French) is that the applicant (Beckett) seems to waver about what he wants to do in cinema: write or direct. Without mentioning his language and literary studies at Trinity College Dublin, he does clearly stress the fact that he has a literary orientation. Beckett mentions his collaboration with Joyce, his publications on Joyce and Proust, his volume of short stories and, finally, *Echo's Bones*, his collection of poems. He then writes:

I have no experience of studio work and it is naturally in the scenario and editing end of the subject that I am most interested. It is because I realise that the script is function of its means of realisation that I am anxious to make contact with your mastery of these, and beg you to consider me a serious cinéaste worthy of admission to your school. I could stay a year at least. (*L1*, 317)

It is without a doubt only 'natural' for a beginning writer to first underline his literary competence before foregrounding his wish to become a 'serious cinéaste', but since Beckett emphasises the script in the main paragraph of his application, he seems on one hand to suggest that he, as a writer who wishes to learn how to *write film screenplays*, would need to know 'how to handle a camera' (as he wrote to his friend), whereas, on the other hand, he also seems to value being considered a 'serious cinéaste' who would be *shooting films*. It is, obviously, possible to write *and* direct films, but Beckett's highlighting of the screenplay seems to indicate that he hesitates deciding whether he wants to be a writer – of film scripts, in this case – or a filmmaker. It is, anyway, quite markedly a man of letters and languages who writes to 'monsieur' Eisenstein requesting admittance to the Moscow film school. Beckett's letter exemplifies his knowledge of languages; he mentions his publications and emphasises his literary involvement. His self-fashioning is that of a literary author who wishes to master the 'means of realisation' of cinema.

Jay Leyda has noted that Eisenstein probably never received Beckett's letter, but the end of Beckett's short love story with the Moscow film school is less dependent on 'fate' (which, in this case, would mean illness and political trouble for Eisenstein) than the story of the unanswered letter would seem to suggest.[1] When Beckett is on his trip to Germany, only a year after his extensive readings in contemporary film theory, he relates in just three sentences in an otherwise long letter written from

Berlin that a friend 'prepared a place for me at the Court of Eisenstein in Moscow'. Having heard of Beckett's interest in the Moscow film school, a friend indeed asked the brother of French writer André Malraux to contact Eisenstein. However, nine months after having written to Moscow himself, Beckett is by all appearances not interested any more in what he now views as being a sort of film courtier. 'I did not answer', he writes in a factual and what may seem rather blunt way about the letter in which he learned he would now be accepted at the State Institute of Cinematography, 'Moscow is another journey' (*L1*, 423). And so Beckett continues his trip through Germany, a trip primarily devoted to museums and galleries, turning away – at least professionally – from the modern machine that captures movement. Old and new visual art (yet mostly still images and in fact mainly painting) thus supersede Beckett's sudden surge of interest in the moving image, to which he was nevertheless to return after becoming a professional writer.

1963: TO NEW YORK...

Professionally, cinema thus seems only for a short while to have intrigued Beckett, who nevertheless seriously considered a stay of a year 'at least' at what is now known as the oldest film school in the world. And yet, Samuel Beckett was indeed to be a film-maker – for a while, if by being a film-maker we understand working in cinema in a professional setting. More than twenty-five years after his letter to Eisenstein, in 1963, Beckett had become a professional author in every respect for more than ten years, after Minuit decided to publish the French trilogy and after the publication and successful staging in 1953 of *En attendant Godot* in Paris. In early 1963, his American publisher, Barney Rosset, concocted a project in New York intended to allow the publishing house and three of its authors to broaden their scope: Harold Pinter, Eugène Ionesco and Samuel Beckett were commissioned to write film scripts for production by an offshoot of Rosset's company, Grove Press. Beckett's quite quick reply to this 'tempting offer' (*K*, 451) made by Rosset at the end of February is ready to be read in May, only about six weeks after he first started devising the scenario for a short movie of some thirty minutes. From a very early stage of the composition, Beckett's film was to be called, simply, *Film*; and even if in every art medium that Beckett worked in he highlights the conditions of that medium to some extent, *Film* is probably the work most markedly structured around the medial conditions of a particular art, cinema, with special and constant reference to the history of film. *Film* is not only a short silent movie shot in black and white when sound and colour had become the current and by far the most mainstream format in cinema for three decades; the short moreover stars a lead actor known primarily from the era of silent film, Buster Keaton, who of course brings up memories of a specific cinematic genre. And finally Beckett casts the camera in a striking role that highlights its function as a looking device, as a revealing eye.

If one compares *Film* to Beckett's readings of cinema theory in the thirties, it becomes quite clear that the way he is dissecting the medium as he understands it and the way that he is toying with its history are to a large extent inspired by the early cinema theory he had delved into twenty-five years earlier, when he thought for a while that the Moscow film school would be the answer to his professional riddle. This is not so much because he follows a specific theory or comments on a set of ideas that can be traced to the work of a single theorist or film-maker, but because *Film* brings to the fore the general debate raging at the early stage of film theory.[2] In these first decades, the proponents of cinema sang the praises of the possibilities of the moving image; film theorists did certainly not all agree on *how* it should be used, but it was definitely clear for them *that* the film camera opened up intriguing new perspectives for art and society (and their enthusiasm was certainly to some extent an answer to the critics of the photographic and moving image, who disdained a low art of mechanical reproduction and facile effects). The new mechanical eye that caught motion was the fascinating object of desire for the early theorists. In *Film*, Beckett does not recreate the fervour that seized those who defended cinema in the early decades, but he does indeed very markedly highlight what was at the core of the enthusiasm of the early theorists: eye and motion. In *Film*, a figure wearing a long overcoat and a flat hat with a handkerchief that covers part of his face seems to hurry to an old apartment, trying to avoid seeing other people, and eventually locking himself up in a room. Here, he tries to suppress 'all extraneous perception', as the published scenario of *Film* has it: even the parrot's and the goldfish's eye, filmed in remarkable close-ups, frighten him so much that he hides the animals (*CDW*, 323). He then looks at photographs of himself during his life, tears them up and dozes off, exhausted by his fears and of having fled being looked at. The camera then finally turns around him (his face not having been shown yet), and he suddenly wakes up, terrified by what he sees, or rather by what is looking at him: the camera in front of him *is he*, his *self* looking at *himself*.

What *Film* shows, then, is an apparently threatening look that follows one who tries to flee it; and in the end, the looking eye appears to be the one who flees himself. The old man is also the looker who forces himself to see himself and to be aware of himself. 'All extraneous perception suppressed, animal, human, divine, self-perception maintains in being'. The first sentence of the scenario clearly states what is at stake in the short movie; the film itself shows how remarkably the 'eye' of the camera is thematised as 'the look of the self', as consciousness, and how motion is linked to 'the look', since the character played by Buster Keaton tries throughout the film to escape from the self who pursues him. What *Film* also shows, therefore, is that this focus on looking and motion for Beckett no longer inspires a hymn-like praise, as it used to do for many film-makers and film theorists in the beginning of cinema. The character in *Film* is the 'man with the movie camera', so to speak, as in the title of Dziga Vertov's monumental song of praises to the documenting and enchanting powers of the camera. But here man is not set free by the camera and its possibilities; he is instead confronted with a consciousness of his existence that makes him suffer. It may even seem that *Film*, while acknowledging the (symbolic) power of the eye and while thematising motion, ends on the suppression of sight and motion itself: the man is unable to bear the weight of 'the look', the 'gaze' which has arrested his last movement in the rocking chair to which he has retreated.

Film clearly invites philosophical interpretations linked to its thematising of 'the look' and consciousness, not only because its epigraph comes from Berkeley (*esse est percipi*, being is being seen), as almost every essay on *Film* underlines, but also because the contemporary context in which *Film* was written has produced (sloganised) thought in the form of Sartre's 'l'enfer, c'est les autres' (hell is the others), a motto that is moreover conspicuously linked to the look in Sartre's play *Huis clos* (*No Exit*).[3] Beckett would seem to be showing in *Film* that first, 'hell is oneself'. Piercing through the looking glass confronts one with oneself. However, as far as Beckett's interest in film is concerned – both the self and cinema are confronted with themselves – it should be underlined that *Film* does not only foreground sight and motion (the 'camera eye' pursuing a fleeing victim), but also other issues intensely debated in the twenties and thirties in cinema: sound, colour and the close-up. In that period, most theorists indeed commented on the changes produced by the introduction of sound and colour. Arnheim was perhaps the most radical opponent to sound in the movie picture, but others like Eisenstein also feared that sound – the word – would turn film, which for them was the art of the moving image first, into screened theatre, recorded theatrical productions that would not stress enough the, in their eyes, visual nature of film, and thus harm its specific artistic quality. Colour was also thought by some theorists to be a comparable danger in that it would create a naturalistic kind of filming that would put the art of film at risk.[4] What was on the contrary an essential technique in film, for some of the early theorists, if not the most distinctive feature of cinema, was the close-up; it is for instance telling that the early British film review, which Beckett read in the thirties, is called *Close Up*. Seen against this background, *Film* noticeably enters into a dialogue with these early conceptions of cinema. It is almost as if Beckett materialises the old idea – *his* old idea, too, if we consider his echoing of it in his 1936 correspondence (*LI*, 311–12) and his later statements in the 1960s – that cinema should also have pursued the road of black-and-white, silent film and continued to explore what were thought to be its distinctive features.[5]

However, it should be noted that the anachronistic qualities of *Film* do not only refer to early cinema, but that their use in 1963 also contributes to creating the 'unreal' quality that Beckett had in mind for his short film, as he writes in the scenario (*CDW*, 323). Beckett is not simply continuing a debate from the 1930s; he is using the old ideas – which he certainly does not reject, as we have seen – in order to make the world of his short film appear awkward: comic but also slightly out of place. The distance between the perceiver and the perceived that is the crux of the structure of the movie is thus repeated in the distance that the film creates between the 'usual' reality that the moviegoer expects in a cinema and the 'unreal' world that she or he watches in *Film*. To the uneasy split self corresponds an uneasily split reality.

Film was not a success in the cinema, and for several reasons, among which was the lack of cinematic experience of the director, Alan Schneider, Beckett's American theatre director, who did, however, have at his disposal a professional and experienced shooting team. Beckett, as a novice screenwriter, was of course also inexperienced, although clearly interested to be less so, since he was present during the entire shooting in New York. Beckett and Buster Keaton did not get on very well and had a different approach of film-making. Moreover, in cinema, shorts are not easily accepted and distributed by the majority of the existing structures, especially experimental shorts and, in some periods, especially films considered as 'literary'.[6] This experience, however, did not prevent Beckett from taking advantage of another offer he received only a year after having started work on the *Film* script. In 1964, young film-maker Marin Karmitz asked Beckett via his French publisher Jerôme Lindon if he could make a film version of *Comédie* (*Play*), which had premiered in Paris. Beckett, who was on principle very clearly opposed to 'adaptation' in the usual sense, but who often nevertheless accepted proposals coming from people he knew or did not want to disappoint, agreed and worked intensely with the twenty-six-year-old, still largely unknown Karmitz, on what would be not so much an adaptation as a cinematographic equivalent of the stage play.[7] The short is an intricate and elaborately crafted film version of the 1964 French theatre production. Both sound and image were processed after being recorded, and the meticulous editing adds to the visual experience – an experience quite different from the theatrical one in staged productions based on the published text. Still, the audience at the Venice film festival where the short premiered in 1966 booed the film, and the critic of the Rome newspaper *Il Messagero* wrote that it had managed to change 'pure theatre into pure non-cinema'.[8] This witty judgement may seem less enlightening when one realises that Beckett's theatre has been called 'anti-theatre' and that at the time, this designation was used as a positive aesthetic judgement for art that transcends the boundaries of accepted practices. Beckett had been working *with* as much as *against* the medium he used in the different arts that he explored. But in film, this strategy was now rejected for the second time by professionals from the field of cinema. Beckett's anti-novels and anti-theatre were acclaimed, but his anti-cinema did not bring him the success that an experienced film-maker like Alain Resnais had shared with contemporary French novelists: Marguerite Duras, for instance, who had written the script for their *Hiroshima mon amour* (1959), and Alain Robbe-Grillet who had written *L'Année dernière à Marienbad* (1961).

1965–1985: TELEVISION

And yet, Beckett was not to abandon his – albeit intermittent – desire to have access to the field of screen arts. Since the 1950s, television had developed into an ever more present mass medium, and in the beginning of the 1960s, Beckett had already imagined what kind of productions he thought would work on the small screen (*not* his theatre plays, in his view) (*K*, 435–6). Even before both *Film* and *Comédie* were screened in public, Beckett started writing his first television play, *Eh Joe*, in 1965, at the age of almost sixty. He was to conceive of four more short plays for television and to assume full directorial responsibility as well as to adapt his play *What Where* for television in 1985, all while he continued to write prose fiction and drama during the next twenty years or so.[9] Clearly, modern cameras continued to exert their influence over Beckett at times.

BEYOND FILM

That continuing attraction raises the question of whether Beckett was also influenced by film in his novels and short stories, before or after his excursions in screen arts. This general topic has not received any sustained attention in criticism, as far as I know, but an answer would have to take into account three considerations that appear hard to sidestep.

First, it seems clear that Beckett does not so conspicuously exploit 'cinematic' techniques as other writers have done, whether they worked in the early period of film or later on. There is very clearly a 'camera eye' in *Film*, but there are for instance no chapters called such in Beckett's novels, as there are in Dos Passos's *USA* trilogy, nor any (structural) references to cinema in Beckett's work. French novelists of Beckett's era, both from the immediate post-war years such as Camus and indeed Sartre, as well as the opposing and later *nouveau roman* (*new novel*) authors of the 1950s and '60s, with writers (and film-makers) such as Robbe-Grillet, were known for their use of narrative and descriptive styles thought to stem from and to refer to the film camera. Beckett does not seem to partake in this often explicit projection of cinema onto literature. At the same time it should be underlined that his work after World War II could roughly be said to have an 'aural' quality until the sixties, and in some cases a much more 'visual' quality later. *Ill Seen Ill Said* for instance thematises the gaze much more than the voice or the word, notwithstanding its title. Finally, however, it is also worth noting that the visual qualities of (part of) Beckett's writing cannot simply be traced back to his interest in the screened moving image and its technologies only. It would be very odd to disregard Beckett's well-documented, long-term interest in and involvement with painting; and it would seem just as implausible to ignore Beckett's theatre, which increasingly exploits visual effects and which from the end of the fifties already includes two scenarios for 'silent theatre', the *Acts without words*. Beckett starts acting as the (billed) director of his plays in the mid sixties, when he also becomes involved in film-making; 'visuality' in his work is surely not exclusively traceable to his interest in screen arts.

Finally, it is also very clear that Beckett was drawn to the screen, if somewhat intermittently: 1936, 1963, 1985 for his last television production; taking into account the 'intermittences of the heart' (Proust), Beckett was intrigued by the possibilities of screen media until the end of his life.

NOTES

1 Jay Leyda (ed.), *A Premature Celebration of Eisenstein's Centenary* (Calcutta: Seagull, 1988), 59.
2 In 1936, Beckett has written to Eisenstein, but in the same month he also writes that what 'I would like to learn under a person like Pudovkin is how to handle a camera' (*LI*, 311). This points to a general interest in what is taught at the Institute of Cinematography, just as Beckett's reading testifies to a general interest in modern film theory, and not to an interest in a specific theory of one of the teachers in Moscow.
3 Gontarski is probably the first to underline this possible reference to French intellectual discourse of the war and immediate post-war years; S. E. Gontarski, *The Intent of Undoing in Samuel Beckett's Dramatic Texts* (Bloomington: Indiana University Press, 1985), 103.
4 For further details about the way Beckett uses early film theory in his only film scenario for the big screen, see '*Film et Film*: Beckett et les premières théories cinématographiques', Sjef Houppermans (ed.), *Samuel Beckett Today/ Aujourd'hui, Présence de Beckett* (17 : 2006), 331–50 and '*Film and Film*: Beckett and Early Film Theory', Linda Ben-Zvi and Angela Moorjani (eds.), *Beckett at 100: Revolving It All* (New York: Oxford University Press, 2008), 152–76.
5 Caroline Bourgeois (ed.), *Comédie/Marin Karmitz/Samuel Beckett* (Paris: Editions du Regard, 2001), 19–22.
6 For the literature–film competition in the case of Beckett's *Film*, see Matthijs Engelberts, 'From *Film* to literature: theoretical debates and the critical erasure of Beckett's cinema', in Daniela Caselli (ed.), *Beckett and Nothing: Trying to Understand Beckett*, (Manchester: Manchester University Press, 2010), 160–75.
7 This French short made in collaboration with Karmitz, who was to become one of the best known and biggest (independent) film producers and owners of cinemas in France, was forgotten for more than thirty years after its initial riotous premiere at the Venice film festival in 1966, to such an extent in fact, that it was not mentioned in Knowlson's 1996 biography. It is, however, lovingly documented in Caroline Bourgeois (ed.), *Comédie/Marin Karmitz/Samuel Beckett* (Paris: Editions du Regard, 2001), and discussed in Graley Herren, *Samuel Beckett's Plays on Film and Television* (New York: Palgrave MacMillan, 2007), 175–81.
8 Bourgeois, *Comédie/Marin Karmitz/Samuel Beckett*, 27.
9 For a discussion of Beckett and adaptation, with special reference to *What Where*, see Matthijs Engelberts, *Défis du récit scénique: Formes et enjeux du mode narratif dans le théâtre de Beckett et de Duras* (Genève: Droz, 2001), 235–46.

CHAPTER 25

Popular Culture

Jane Goodall

During the run of the 2009 British production of *Waiting for Godot*, starring Ian McKellan and Patrick Stewart, widespread media interest in the celebrity cast led to new levels of public interest in the play. McKellan enjoyed a cult following for his portrayals of Gandalf in *Lord of the Rings* and Magneto in *X-Men*, and Stewart carried the aura of *Star Trek*. Tickets for *Godot* quickly sold to the fan base for these mass-market sagas, and in interviews about the production, McKellan and Stewart spoke of a mission 'to take all this to the people'. Not everyone rejoiced in the cultural boundary crossing. Elisabeth Mahoney, writing in *The Guardian* (13 March 2009) found their comments 'repellently smug'. 'That kerfuffle you can hear', she said, 'is Beckett turning in his grave'.[1]

Beckett's relationship with traditions of popular culture was fraught with apparent contrariness. His evident love of clown routines, vaudeville patter, punch lines and slapstick did not extend to tolerance of high spirits or impromptu rapport with the audience in performances of his plays. He was, as Fehsenfeld and Overbeck comment in their introduction to the first volume of his letters, 'amazed and often dismayed by the popularity of his own work' (*L1*, lxxxi). *Waiting for Godot* represents a turning point in Beckett's association with popular culture in the public mind. While resonances of vaudeville are evident in his earlier work, in *Godot* they present themselves with a new insistence. And as performed elements, expressed through the bodies and voices of actors, they took on a life that Beckett, with all his near pathological animus against vitality, could not entirely contain, even when he assumed directorial control.

Had it not been for this inevitable surfacing of popular elements in productions of *Godot*, it is arguable that Beckett's works might never have gained a viable following. Distressed as he was by persistent rejection of his early narrative works, the determination to get them published was not accompanied by any apparent concern about the extent of their appeal to a readership. A rejection of *Dream of Fair to Middling Women* by Grayson and Grayson in 1932 was accompanied by advice he caricatured as to 'be a good boy in future and compose what I was well-fitted to compose – a best-seller' (*L1*, 135). Five years later, he reported that 'responses of small as well as large audiences are becoming more and more mysterious to me and, what is worse, less significant' (*L1*, 517). The success of *Godot* bred antipathetic reactions in him that were at times virulent. Walter Asmus recalls sitting next to him in rehearsal, when there was a sudden outburst: "'Walter I *hate* this play". Just like that. I was scared. He looked at me so wildly'.[2]

There were escalated stress levels in Beckett's reaction to many things. As his plays came to be widely performed, his stringent views on what would – but mainly what would not – be true to the script became legendary, and the confinement of the actor's expressive capacity reached extremes with his direction of Billy Whitelaw in *Not I* in 1973. *Godot* continued to attract performers whose background was primarily in comedy and variety performance, but it provided them with no licence to exploit the qualities that had made them popular in their own domains. The increasing austerity of his subsequent dramatic works gained Beckett a different kind of audience, drawn from literary and academic circles and from amongst theatre practitioners who found the aesthetic experiments compelling.

If *Godot* was a turning point in Beckett's public reception because of its evident popular affiliations, from Beckett's own point of view it may represent something like a u-turn, a culmination of his attraction towards the classic elements of vaudeville – clowning, slapstick, misfired choreography, monologue, cross-talk, crude jokes, cheap punch lines and ditties – followed by an increasingly persistent return to the more abstruse tendencies of his early prose works. During the 1960s and '70s, theatrical interpreters went one way and the author went the other. Writing with hindsight about the original Paris production he directed in 1953, Roger Blin acknowledged that his initial idea of setting the play in a circus tent would have been a fundamental error. 'Ninety per cent of the *Godots* put on in the world fall into this trap'.[3] David Bradby observes that the tendency has been far less common since the 1970s, but the McKellan–Stewart approach to promoting the play indicates that a circus tent is not prerequisite to a kind of popularisation that might make the author turn in his grave.[4]

Yet it is not to be denied that there are strong leanings towards popular culture forms throughout Beckett's work, and if its audience and readership are to be sustained, these are the elements we may need to emphasise by way of introduction. Many of us who teach Beckett have resorted to a focus on the vaudeville elements to provide students with a way in. Few students would respond well to an approach that involved plunging straightaway into a maelstrom of Proust, Descartes and Spinoza.

I once took a studio class in which we extracted some pages from *Watt*: the episode in Part Three where the members of a college grants committee attempt to exchange glances but proceed to demonstrate that 'when five men look at one another, though in theory only twenty looks are necessary, every man looking four times, yet in practice this number is seldom sufficient, on account of the multitude of looks that go astray' (*W*, 150). And so it begins:

Mr.Fitzwein looks at Mr.Magershon, on his right. But Mr.Magershon is not looking at Mr.Fitzwein, on his left, but at Mr.O'Meldon, on his right. But Mr.O'Meldon is not looking at Mr. Magershon, on his left, but, craning forward, at Mr.MacStern, on his left but three at the far end of the table. (*W*, 150)

This process continues over the next couple of pages, elaborated with details of Mr.MacStern's right ear, Mr.de Baker's hairless sinciput, the boils on the back of Mr.Magershon's neck, and the 'disgusting' right side of Mr.O'Meldon's face. Midway through the adventure, a note of exasperation is struck:

Thus of the five times four or twenty looks taken, no two have met, and all this craning forward and backward and looking to the right and to the left has led to nothing, and for all the progress made by the committee in this matter of looking at itself, its eyes might just as well have been closed, or turned towards heaven. Nor is this all. (*W*, 152)

There follows a further two pages of intensified effort on the part of the quintet, punctuated by silent but pungent farts and increasingly tangled intentions before the narrator offers a summation:

And all this comes of lack of method, which is all the less excusable in a committee as committees, whether large or small, are more often under the necessity of looking at themselves than any other body of men, with the possible exception of commissions. (*W*, 153)

It takes an experienced and patient reader to appreciate the comedy of this on the page, drawn out as it is over some sixteen hundred words in compacted syntax. But realised as a stage mime, with the five figures going through each of the motions described, accompanied by a narrative commentary from an actor with an ear for the sharper tonal accents and a capacity to build acceleration through the intricacies of the denser passages, the extract can be converted into an effective comic sketch. From a teaching point of view, the benefits of this approach are double edged. Some students may be won over to seek a closer acquaintance with Beckett's work, but others who do not might be left with no sense of the philosophical dimensions of what they have encountered. The technical parody of serial reasoning and satirical allusions to Descartes' *Discourse on Method* may seem to them rather beside the point. Why not just go with the vaudeville?

There is evidence that Beckett himself found ready pleasure in variety theatre, comedy films and genre literature, pleasure of a kind missing from his more sophisticated cultural engagements. In a letter to Tom McGreevy in 1931, he writes of 'the old childish absorption with which I read *Treasure Island* and *Oliver Twist*' (*L1*, 90). Popular cultural tastes displayed in his youth were typical of what passed through the filters of a highly selective social environment: Gilbert and Sullivan operas, silent comedy films, Sherlock Holmes stories, Sexton Blake comics and the annual pantomime at the Gaiety Theatre.

These tastes were not left behind in adulthood. Mira Avrech, an Israeli journalist Beckett became friendly with in Berlin in the late nineteen sixties, wrote of how she ceased to feel intimidated by his cultural standing when she saw the Agatha Christie and Perry Mason paperbacks stacked in his room.[5] In James Knowlson's account, the thriller stash also included Edgar Wallace, a favourite of Beckett's father, and one of the key writers for *Union Jack*, the weekly comic to which Beckett was addicted in his primary school years (*K*, 31, 533). Allusions to silent movies are scattered through his early fiction and testify to a continuing fascination with the figures of Laurel and Hardy, Charlie Chaplin, the Marx Brothers and Buster Keaton.

Beckett's letters provide frequent comments on his theatregoing. He followed the rather earnest literary repertoire at the Abbey Theatre and the Gate Theatre in Dublin, but more often than not was left fulminating about what he had just sat through. Rougher and more popular forms of theatre, by contrast, seem to have afforded him ready amusement. Bill Cunningham, a friend from Beckett's Dublin years, remembers him being so caught up in a whodunnit by C. S. Forester (of Hornblower fame) at the Gate Theatre in the early 1920s that he stood up in his seat and interjected.[6] Thirty years later, Beckett's responses to a music hall performance in Islington featuring a nude chorus girl on a bicycle and a Mr Dooley monologue on the topic of castor oil, were similarly immediate, judging by the account of Irish novelist Aiden Higgins. Higgins characterises Beckett as a culturally divided personality. 'Sam lives in two worlds, he lives in the rough, tough world very much and he lives in the abstract world, too, and there he was bored. Sometimes he gets bored with the abstract world and he wants to join the rough stuff'.[7]

From the remarks Beckett makes in his letters, something more intense than boredom comes into play in many of his reactions to more elevated works of theatre, music and literature. In October 1930, he saw a poetic comedy by Austin Clarke – 'truly pernicious' – and *Dervorgilla*, 'a gutter snippet' by 'that old poisse' Lady Gregory (*L1*, 49). A triple bill of plays by Corneille and Bergson at Trinity College in February the following year might have gone worse, he says, though 'the inevitable vulgarisation leaves one exhausted and disgusted' (*L1*, 68).

Beethoven's Pastoral symphony left the impression that the composer poured into it 'everything that was vulgar, facile and childish in him' (*L1*, 197). And the Seventh Symphony under Furtwängler's baton came across as 'rather like a fried egg, or, if you prefer, like a foot put in it' (*L1*, 182). Reading matter was a constant source of irritation; Dostoevsky's *The Possessed* is riddled with 'clichés and journalese', not all of which can be attributed to the 'foul translation'; Darwin's *On the Origin of Species* is 'badly written catlap' (*L1*, 79, 111).

It seems Beckett has a constant tussle with over-developed critical faculties that prompt him to make hawkish attacks on what passes for great literature and artistry in the world at large. A division between the rough and the cerebral in his nature may be partly to account for this, and it is easy to read that division as one in which natural inclination gravitates towards the rough and the popular, while education, upbringing and the European intellectual milieu in which he spent his adulthood drew him in another. But by his own account, the tensions were more loaded than that. In a letter to Thomas McGreevy in March 1935, he writes of how during his time at Trinity College, his critical reactions reached 'a crescendo of disparagement':

The misery and the solitude and apathy and the sneers were the elements of an index of superiority and guaranteed the feeling of arrogant 'otherness'.... It was not until that way of living, or rather negation of living, developed such terrifying physical symptoms that it could no longer be pursued, that I became aware of anything morbid in myself. (*L1*, 258–9)

These physical symptoms, reported on in previous letters, included a succession of abscesses, piles, phlegm on the lungs, heart palpitations and sweaty panic attacks. 'Rough Beckett' did not just inhabit a world of vulgar pleasures; he sank into a morass of gross physicality, beset by complaints that rendered the body obscene and abject. When the critical censures of the 'superior man' are typically laced with terms of disgust – 'foul', 'facile', 'vulgar' – and gutter imagery, it seems clear that some form of psychical division is at work. Beckett's analyst, Wilfred Bion, was trying to help him address this, but the writings Beckett produced before and during the period of treatment (1933–5) themselves constitute a set of skirmishes with the dichotomies of mental and physical being. The figures in his early prose works are often gutter dwellers, prone to dwelling at length on matters of excretion, masturbation, infection and ambient detritus, yet the scenarios in which they are caught up have overt metaphysical resonances.

While Beckett's leanings towards popular culture may serve to provide some comic relief in this rather forbidding mix, they are also deeply intertwined with the more esoteric components of his works. There is no simple pattern of high culture and low culture influences pulling against each other. The dynamic is one of torsion rather than oppositional tension, and involves some perverse twists: the slapstick is not necessarily comedic, while the philosophy often leans towards farce. Detective figures appear in duos, like clowns – or vice versa. It is hard to tell Holmes and Watson from Laurel and Hardy when they are stranded in some scene deserted by the train of events on which they depend for any continuing momentum in the world.

Why burden oneself with an umbrella, said Mercier, and not put it up as required?
    Quite, said Camier.
    Put it up now, in the name of God, said Mercier.
    But Camier could not put it up.
    Give it here, said Mercier.
    But Mercier could not put it up either.
    This was the moment chosen by the rain, acting on behalf of the universal malignity, to come down in buckets. (*M&C*, 19)

Mercier and Camier, the double act from Beckett's first French novel, make desultory progress through a succession of incidents that afford moments of farce, smatterings of rhythmic cross-talk, a few crude jokes and a random killing, but the succession fails to lock into a sequence of the kind that allows either hilarity or suspense to build up. It is as if Beckett has identified the path of the tension wires in the popular form and pulled them out, to leave the central characters stranded without the capacity to engage in any articulated line of action. Of course there are compensatory injections of philosophical parody and existential confrontation. What makes the popular form popular has been clinically removed, but another dynamic takes its place, something quite unfamiliar in the realms of aesthetic form.

In the late 1940s, in the few years before he embarked on the writing of *Godot*, Beckett produced a range of prose works in which he seems drawn to exploring what is funny about existentialism and what isn't funny about vaudeville. 'First Love', one of the *Quatre nouvelles*, originally written in French in 1946, presents the tragic-comedy of incarnation as a blend of slapstick, depravity and obsessive-compulsive disorder. It begins with the narrator visiting his father's grave. In the English translation, Beckett added a touch of pub humour – 'Personally I have no bone to pick with graveyards' – before embarking on an extensive rumination on the morbidity of living bodies (*CSP*, 25). As the story line meanders off into the wider world of the living, the narrator continues to offer a running commentary on all his physical functions – or rather dysfunctions – from the lavatorial through to the sexual and alimentary, and the strange anatomical processes involved in speech. He finds himself a room where he has an argument with the landlady about the chamber pot.

> She came back with a kind of saucepan, not a true saucepan for it had no handle, it was oval in shape with two lugs and lid. My stewpan, she said. I don't need the lid, I said. You don't need the lid? She said. (*CSP*, 41)

So far, so funny. But there is much more of it, in a continuous stream of words over several pages unbroken by paragraphing or any other structuring device, so that the experience of reading it rather resembles that of listening to some rambling anecdote in a bar. Except that, when the voice breaks off from recounting the particulars of what happened next, it locates itself somewhere quite outside the world of everyday socialised consciousness, in a mental universe where Dante and Geulinx are the reference points:

> It took me a long time, my lifetime so to speak, to realise that the colour of an eye half seen, or the source of some distant sound, are closer to Giudecca in the hell of unknowing than the existence of God, or the origins of protoplasm, or the existence of self, and even less worthy than these to occupy the wise. (*CSP*, 43)

The narrator's lifetime is one without borders, strung between a birth that is not complete and a death that may or may not have already taken place. No stable cognitive order can be maintained in it. As Anthony Uhlmann comments, at stake is an attempt to create a literary form 'that does justice to the idea of an absence of order, and absence of system'.[8]

Form is of the essence here, and one of the enduring obsessions is how to impose it on the human body. Bodies in Beckett are never functionally integrated. 'The Expelled', the sequel to 'First Love', begins with the protagonist being thrown out into the street with his hat sailing after him: a scene that might easily belong in a Chaplin movie. It takes some pages of mental processing before he is on his feet, exhibiting a silly walk that would outdo that of Chaplin at his craziest:

Stiffness of the lower limbs, as if nature had denied me knees, extraordinary splaying of the feet to right and left of the line of march. The trunk, on the contrary, as if by the effect of a compensatory mechanism, was as flabby as an old ragbag, tossing wildly to the unpredictable jolts of the pelvis. (*CSP*, 50)

Biological humanity is in permanent need of splints or casts to discipline it into some kind of alignment, but when transferred to the stage, this requirement has the effect of quelling any physical comedy. We have characters encased in urns and dustbins; half buried in a mound; strapped to an apparatus that prevents anything but the mouth from moving. The stage in itself becomes a field of constraint, a euclidian space in which every pace is measured according to an exact geometry, and every word – and breath – subject to split-second timing.

These are disciplines well understood by comic performers, particularly those specialising in clowning, mime and vaudeville cross-talk. In performance, their skills are exploited to produce escalating hilarity, but considered purely as discipline, they are no laughing matter. The Swiss clown Grock, acknowledged as a 'major influence' on *More Pricks than Kicks*, was trained in boyhood as a tumbler and as a virtuoso on the violin who could play some two dozen other instruments with casual aplomb (*L1*, 208). Grock was the son of a watchmaker and his hallmark tricks were consummate feats of timing. One of these was to shuffle on stage in his outsized, misshapen shoes and baggy pants, carrying a miniature violin, and make some business of attempting to stand on a small bentwood chair. Eventually – and precariously – he would succeed, but the moment he began to play, the seat of the chair fell through. Apparently undeterred, he would continue the music from inside the broken frame, smiling inanely at the accelerating rhythms, then in one bound and without missing a beat, he leapt to perch on the back of the chair, feet resting on the frame of the seat, legs crossed. Still smiling.[9]

From the point of view of technique, such a performance is pure clinical control. There is no room for the slightest variation of balance, rhythm or sequence. Every breath must be timed. In the Beckett world, this is an irresistible paradox. Grock, whose signature walk evokes the condition of Duck's disease that so fascinated Beckett, needed no urn or mound to contain the disorderly body. He made his own straitjacket.

It is these clinical elements of technique – precision timing and spatial exactness – that transfer to Beckett's theatre works. Lucien Raimbourg, a former music hall player who played Vladimir in Blin's original production of *Godot*, brought to it 'the rigour and awareness of a man who has worked before a public infinitely more demanding than a theatre audience'. In *Godot*, the rigour and alertness must be divided off from the more vibrant aspects of the music hall tradition.[10] There is no place for the warmth and spontaneity of audience engagement; the feedback loop as spectators are caught in ever more helpless laughter and the performer adds to the stage business to wind up the hysteria. Bert Lahr, one of the great artists of the feedback loop, may have disconcerted his popular following when he played Estragon in Alan Schneider's 1956 production of *Godot*, but the technical demands of the work were second nature to him, and it gave expression to those melancholic qualities that so often underlie the comedian's art. As his son, critic John Lahr, observed, he 'had an understanding of the pathos and meaning of the play that went beyond critical generalities. Lahr lived with silences: his understanding of language was commensurate with Beckett's precise, philosophical use of it'.[11]

The backlash effects of public exposure on comic performers are well known; some of the most celebrated have exhibited personalities of legendary difficulty in personal life. With an unflagging commitment to paradox, Beckett's work taps into the reclusive, depressive and obsessive qualities in them that are the inverse of what makes them popular yet are integral to their capacity as entertainers. He is the austere taskmaster, they the trained conscripts, endlessly stripped of any extraneous talents or energies they may be trying to smuggle in. In one instance, though, the dynamic was reversed. Roger Blin's account of the first meeting between Beckett and Buster Keaton prior to the shooting of *Film* reveals Beckett in the role of suitor, trying to make some social connection, while Keaton mimes an imaginary four-handed poker game that has been going on for decades with opposing players who are now deceased. He breaks off only to issue peremptory calculations on the playing time of the script. On the way home, says Schneider, 'I worried considerably about Keaton'.[12] Of course, he need not have done so. During the shooting, Keaton proceeded, both on and off screen, to deliver one of the defining renditions of Beckett's dramatic vision.

NOTES

1 Elisabeth Mahoney, 'For Godot's Sake', *The Guardian*, 13 March 2009. http://www.guardian.co.uk/culture/tvandradioblog/2009/mar/13/godot-mckellen-stewart-today-programme.
2 Interview with Walter Asmus, in James and Elizabeth Knowlson (eds.) *Beckett Remembering/Remembering Beckett*, (London: Bloomsbury, 2006), 192.
3 Roger Blin, *Souvenirs et propos*, 85, quoted in David Bradby, *Beckett, Waiting for Godot: Plays in Production* (Cambridge: Cambridge University Press, 2001), 58.
4 David Bradby, *Beckett, Waiting for Godot: Plays in Production*, l (Cambridge: Cambridge University Press, 2001), 227.
5 Mira Avrech, 'A Friend Recalls Affectionately a Shy Nobel Prize Playwright Named Samuel Beckett', *People* (15:14, 13 April 1981), 76. Also at http://www.people.com/people/archive/article/0,,20079029,00.html. Knowlson's account of the relationship in *Damned to Fame* gives the name as Mira Averech, but Avrech is the name under which the article is published.
6 Bill Cunningham, in James and Elizabeth Knowlson (eds.) *Beckett Remembering/Remembering Beckett* (London: Bloomsbury, 2006), 28.
7 Aiden Higgins, in James and Elizabeth Knowlson (eds.) *Beckett Remembering/Remembering Beckett* (London: Bloomsbury, 2006), 140.
8 Anthony Uhlmann, *Samuel Beckett and the Philosophical Image* (Cambridge: Cambridge University Press 2006), 61.
9 Video clips of Grock in performance are online at *Grock and the Berio Sequenza V*, http://www.osborne-conant.org/Grock.htm.
10 Jacques Lemarchand, notice published in *Figaro Litteraire*, 17 January 1953, reprinted in Lawrence Graver and Raymond Federman (eds.), *Samuel Beckett: the Critical Heritage* (London: Routledge 1997), 99.
11 John Lahr, quoted in Bradby, *Beckett, Waiting for Godot: Plays in Production*, l, 91.
12 Alan Schneider, 'On Directing Film', in *Film by Samuel Beckett* (London: Faber and Faber, 1972), 67–8.

PART VI

'The Humanities I had':
Systems of Knowledge and Belief

CHAPTER 26

Philosophy

Matthew Feldman

The conjunction 'Beckett and philosophy' is now some six decades old. Following the unexpected success of *Molloy* and particularly *Waiting for Godot* in the early 1950s, French *philosophes* were first off the mark in taking a 'broadly philosophical approach' to Beckett's work.[1] Maurice Nadeau in *Combat* and Georges Bataille in *Critique* set the tone in 1951 – the latter calling *Molloy* a 'sordid wonder' – with Jean-Paul Sartre, Gabriel Marcel and Claude Mauriac weighing in on *En Attendant Godot*, and Maurice Blanchot praising *L'Innomable*.[2] The trend quickly became transnational with influential readings like Georg Lukács's *The Meaning of Contemporary Realism* in 1957 and, in the next year, Theodor Adorno's 'Trying to Understand Endgame'. Variously seeing in Beckett's works evidence of existentialism, absurdism or nihilism – all of which, incidentally, Beckett explicitly rejected vis-à-vis his works – early philosophical readings may now appear somewhat dated; but then again, they are closely bound up with Beckett's pivotal, post-war recognition as a major twentieth-century European writer.

At the end of the 1950s, less celebrated but perhaps more significant than the conjoining of Beckett and philosophy by European philosophers, was the 1959 American special issue of *Perspective*, edited by Ruby Cohn. Often credited as the start of Beckett studies in English, here too, philosophical readings were the order of the day, encapsulated by Hugh Kenner's celebrated essay in that collection, 'The Cartesian Centaur'.[3] As this suggests, René Descartes took centre stage in this view – and many subsequently – on interpretations of Beckett's employment of philosophy. Yet if this proved to be an overstatement, with Beckett's philosophical interests recently shown to be much wider than Cartesianism, it has been a remarkably durable one. At one point, the *de rigueur* philosophical interpretation

I am grateful to the Bergen Research Foundation and the University of Bergen, Norway for a Senior Research Fellowship with the 'Modernism and Christianity' project that has facilitated the writing of this chapter.

of Beckett's work, the role of Cartesianism in Beckett's work has almost certainly been overstated.[4] Without doubt 'Whoroscope', Beckett's first published poem in 1930, based upon the life of René Descartes, demonstrated some knowledge of Cartesian philosophy. However, this was inductively applied to a reading of Beckett's work as a whole, creating the misleading impression that, as both online sources and the *Encyclopaedia Britannica* have it, Descartes was 'Beckett's favourite philosopher'.[5] If this critical tradition has been recently eclipsed in favour of a more empirical approach, however, other early accounts were remarkably prescient in delimiting Beckett's eclectic interest in philosophical ideas:

> His world is a syzygy, and for every laugh there is a tear, or every affirmation a negation. His art is a Democritean art, energized precisely by the dialectical interplay of opposites – body and mind, the self and other, speech and silence, life and death, hope and despair, being and non-being, yes and no.[6]

And no doubt, Beckett's interests in philosophy were diverse. To but scratch the surface: his first essay from 1929, in praise of Joyce's then unfinished *Finnegans Wake*, contained Giordano Bruno and Giambattista Vico in the title; in 1930, an award-winning ninety-eight lines of verse parodied the life of René Descartes; and in the next year, Beckett's only academic monograph, *Proust*, was so steeped in the philosophy of Arthur Schopenhauer as to distort the eponymous author's *À la recherche du temps perdu* ostensibly under examination.[7] Other philosophers name checked across Beckett's subsequent work, to name only some of explicitly cited in his writings, include Thales of Miletus in the 1932 poem 'Serena I' (later included in Beckett's 1935 poetry collection, *Echo's Bones*); idiosyncratically 'windowless' Leibnizian monads feature in the novel *Murphy* from 1935–6; a long-unpublished dramatic fragment from 1940, *Human Wishes*, is based around the life of Samuel Johnson; Immanuel Kant's 'fruitful bathos of experience' is provided in German in the Addenda to *Watt* from 1945; Arnold Geulincx appears in the short story 'The End' and the first novel of the 'Beckett Trilogy', *Molloy*, over the next two years; Aristotle, 'who knew everything', makes an appearance in *Texts for Nothing* from 1951; the occasionalist philosopher Nicolas Malebranche is cited in 'The Image' and *How It Is* in the later 1950s; while Fritz Mauthner 'may be it' in *Rough for Radio II*, first published in 1975.[8]

Moreover, this eclecticism may be because, as he informed his first biographer, Deidre Bair, 'he did not study philosophy' as a student at Trinity College, Dublin (*B*, 694). Despite sounding suspiciously like Beckett's notorious disavowals of philosophical knowledge in his rare interviews – 'I am not a philosopher'; and still more memorably, 'I never read philosophers / Why not? / I never understand anything they write'[9] – Beckett was on the level with Bair, and set out to educate himself about Western philosophy over the next decade.

Critics know this because of the 'archival turn' signalled by the 1996 authorised biography *Damned to Fame: The Life of Samuel Beckett*. Assessing the importance of Beckett's 'siege in the room' in the six years following 1945 – which undoubtedly laid the groundwork for his later international fame – James Knowlson concludes: 'the notion of "THE Revelation" also obscures several earlier and less sudden or dramatic revelations. [...] The ground had been well prepared' (*K*, 353). Although Beckett was to famously embrace 'impotence and ignorance' in his post-war writings, this was built atop a substantial amount of self-directed learning between roughly 1929 and 1938. That is to say, seeking ignorance implies prior knowledge. Put another way, Beckett's was a very philosophical ignorance, as Anne Atik's recent memoir attests: 'He feared erudition swamping the authenticity of a work, and constantly warned against that danger for other artists, having had to escape from it himself'. If Beckett's 'mature' literature after 1945 may be seen as a revolt against the assumed omniscience and assumed benevolence of Western knowledge (like the defiant use of the phrase 'I don't know' fully 140 times in 'The Trilogy'),[10] then this is partly due to his gathering of ammunition over the previous generation. That this knowledge was kept concealed through veiled allusions in his post-war work should not obscure that, in the end, Beckett was armed with a formidable grasp of Western knowledge.

Amongst this store of knowledge – ranging from European languages (Latin, French, Italian and, from the mid 1930s, German) and literature to psychology, painting and history – Beckett's engagement with Western philosophy stands out for several reasons. First, as has become clear in the long wake of Knowlson's biography, Beckett took reading notes and transcriptions from a wide variety of European philosophers across the late 1920s and 1930s. As this suggests, second, this was an extensive and sustained encounter, one detectable across Beckett's writings – here subtly, there overtly. Third and finally, this immersion in Western philosophy was an important feature in Beckett's interwar development (to a degree that will be long debated in Beckett studies), and is correspondingly a key reason for so many readers' view that this is a philosophical novelist, dramatist and poet *par excellance*. With these points in mind, a brief biographical accounting of Beckett's interwar engagement with several key philosophers is in order.

Of course, philosophy was inscribed into the very title of Beckett's first extant publication, praising James Joyce's ongoing *Work in Progress* (ultimately *Finnegans Wake*) in his 1929 essay 'Dante...Bruno.Vico..Joyce'. Giordano Bruno receives scant consideration, and instead Vico's idiosyncratic philosophy of history clearly excited Beckett's interest, with the author of *The New Science* described as an '*innovator*'. Yet in keeping with a pattern later repeated in many of his borrowings from Western philosophy, Beckett deployed Benedetto Croce's secondary source on Vico rather more extensively than the then untranslated *Scienza Nuova*. Simply put, Croce's Vico appears more significant for Beckett's literary purposes than Vico himself.[11] This was also the case with Beckett's pastiche on the life of Descartes the next year: fellow TCD alumnus J. P. Mahaffy's synoptic *Descartes* forms the most important source for 'Whoroscope' – rather than either Adrien Baillet's expansive, two-volume 1691 biography or Descartes' actual writings.[12]

It was at this time, in preparation for his commission to write a short monograph on Marcel Proust, that Beckett met a lifelong love: Arthur Schopenhauer. The latter's pessimism coloured the 1931 *Proust* and beyond; Beckett confided to his friend Thomas McGreevy six years later: 'I always knew he was one of the ones that mattered most to me [...] a philosopher that can be read like a poet, with an entire indifference to the apriori forms of verification. Although it is a fact that judged by them his generalisation shows fewer cracks than most generalisations'.[13] Also relevantly, as the influence of James Joyce upon Beckett waned in the early 1930s, so too did the former's effect on what the latter called, in August 1931, 'the old demon of notesnatching' – that textual raiding of words and phrases taken to its logical conclusion in *Finnegans Wake* and so unmistakeable in the abortive *Dream of Fair to Middling Women*. Taking a somewhat charitable view of 'philosophy', Robert Burton's *Anatomy of Melancholy*; Thomas à Kempis's *The Imitation of Christ*; Jules de Gaultier's (again synoptic) *De Kant à Nietzsche*; and St Augustine's *Confessions* were all plundered for use in Beckett's first novel; for example, fully 132 consecutive items derive from Beckett's notebook towards *Dream*, with John Pilling finding fully thirty-eight of these allusions making their way into the revamped collection of stories published in 1934, *More Pricks Than Kicks*.[14]

This wider approach towards the acquisition of knowledge changed markedly with the *pièce de résistance* of 'Beckett and philosophy': 267 pages, mostly recto and verso, comprising the 'Philosophy notes'. Likely compiled during 1932–3, these notes are a mélange of typed and handwritten entries ranging from Thales of Miletus (often seen as the first Western philosopher) to its self-described undertaker, Friedrich Nietzsche – all headed by a striking colour map of ancient Greece, with the names and locations of philosophers placed meticulously in boxes.[15] As this suggests, especial focus is given to what the short text *All Strange Away* later phrased as 'ancient Greek philosophers ejaculated with place of origin when possible suggesting pursuit of knowledge at some period'. In fact, Beckett's focus on early Greek philosophy extended to some 200 notebook sides, summarised from at least four introductory sources. Amongst Beckett's expansive notes – for example, entries on Democritus of Abdera run to ten sides, while those on Aristotle comprise nineteen – the 'Philosophy Notes' reproduce many of the earliest debates, dialectics and developments from ancient Greece. In turn, these were heavily employed across Beckett's work, from Neary's Pythagorean utterances in *Murphy* right through to the Sophists' paradoxes opening *Endgame* twenty years later ('which kernel of grain by being added makes the heap?') and much more besides.[16] Although Beckett's engagement with early Greek philosophy has yet to fully marinate amongst scholars in Beckett studies, it is clear that this will be a fruitful area of research for many years to come.

More specifically, of these philosophical summaries far and away the most important to Beckett was Wilhelm Windelband's revised 1901 *A History of Western Philosophy*. Beckett took more notes from this source than any other we know about – more than Dante's *Inferno*, the Bible; everything. In fact, some three-quarters of the one hundred twenty thousand words comprising the 'Philosophy Notes' are taken from Windelband's summary; even more significant, the period of Western philosophy between Roman antiquity and 'The Philosophy of the Nineteenth Century' is solely mediated by *A History of Philosophy*. Thus, Beckett's 'Philosophy Notes' is something of a double act: a mosaic of ancient Greek and Roman thinking, deriving from several secondary texts (including Windelband); and Beckett's summary of *A History of Philosophy*'s summary of the doctrines and systems ostensibly shaping Western philosophy thereafter. Moreover, from this second half, detailed notes on medieval nominalism (part of which went by the deliciously Beckettian name 'terminism' thanks to William of Occam) and the doctrine of Immanuel Kant certainly had closer attention given to them in Beckett's excerpts and summaries. As with Schopenhauer, Beckett returned to both of these subjects later in the 1930s, as recorded by his wide-ranging commonplace notebook, the 'Whoroscope' Notebook, kept during these years.

It also seems that *A History of Philosophy* introduced Beckett to the ideas of a number of philosophers he then followed up in the original over the next three years. Interestingly, Beckett seems to have focused particularly upon writings by a assorted array of post-Cartesians: G. W. Leibniz, Baruch Spinoza, Bishop George Berkeley and Arnold Geulincx. While accepting the theology of none, many of the doctrines advanced by these philosophers were read, noted and used in Beckett's subsequent writings. Erik Tonning has usefully traced Leibniz's monadism, first encountered in late 1933, to a number of Beckett's post-war dramatic works, while Spinoza was briefly held out as a possible 'solution & a salvation' upon reading his *Ethica* in September 1936, later rendered as the 'counsel of an Israelite on the subject of conation' in *Malone Dies*.[17] For his part, Berkeley's *Three Dialogues between Hylas and Philonaus*, read around the same time, plays an intertextual role in Beckett's own *Three Dialogues*, while the Bishop's celebrated motto, 'esse est percipi', prefaces the script of the 1964 arthouse (and Beckett's only) film, *Film*. While research continues to probe into what, and where in his writings, Beckett's specific philosophical debts to these thinkers resides – not least due to the wealth of new archival material made available in the wake of Knowlson's biography – it is increasingly clear that post-Cartesian philosophy (rather than that by Descartes himself) was deeply engaged and deployed by Beckett. Just how seriously, and indeed how *philosophically* – rather than *artistically*, which is another key question – these and other doctrines were incorporated in Beckett's work, however, remains subject to fundamental debate in Beckett studies.[18]

Arnold Geulincx is different entirely. The discovery of some fifteen thousand words of typed transcriptions from Geulincx's oeuvre, mostly taken from his *Ethics*, has only reinforced a sense of the Occasionalist philosopher's fundamental importance to Beckett. His 'beautiful Belgo-Latin' of human negation – expressed by the maxim 'wherein you have no power, therein neither should you will' ('*Ubi nihil vales ibi nihil veils*') – was championed in *Murphy* and reformulated in numerous post-war works; perhaps persisting, as Anthony Uhlmann suggests, as philosophical images of ineffable Geulingian movement in Beckett's work (cradles, rocking chairs, grandfather clocks and so on).[19] Furthermore, as a flurry of letters from early 1936 attests, it was not only the ineffability of movement and the absolute incommensurability of mind and body that Beckett found of interest in this esoteric, little-known seventeenth-century philosopher. Geulincx's pragmatic solution also seemed to appeal: a philosophical acceptance of human ignorance; one leading to the supreme virtue of humility. In the event, however, it was knowledge of Geulincx's iconoclastic mix of rationalism and mysticism that helped get the stalled

Murphy finished in 1936, and he remained someone to whom Beckett owed an explicit, often acknowledged philosophical debt thereafter.

Appearing to conclude Beckett's engagement with Western philosophy during this period was a jump into the twentieth century. In spring 1938, roughly halfway between the completion of *Murphy* and the start of *Watt*, Beckett transcribed some five thousand words from Fritz Mauthner's enormous *Beiträge zu einer Kritik der Sprache* [*Contributions to a Critique of Language*]. Mauthner's was a linguistic scepticism far more radical than that of his selected precursors – the nominalists, Vico, Kant and Schopenhauer, all of whom Beckett had encountered by this point – essentially holding that all language is a (bad) metaphorical translation from consciousness. Consequently, Mauthner argued that language was a good vehicle for poetry, but a bad one for knowledge acquisition, as Beckett aptly summarised in a letter to Linda Ben-Zvi four decades later: 'For me it came down to: Thought words/Words inane/Thought inane/ Such was my levity'.[20] Later in 1938, Beckett then read his acquaintance Jean-Paul Sartre's novel *Nausea* – which he found 'extraordinarily good' – before moving onto the 1936 *Imagination*, Sartre's self-published MA thesis on the dynamism of thought, which concludes: 'an image is *a certain type of consciousness*. An image is an act, not some thing. An image is a consciousness of something. [...] A pheomoenological description of the structure known as "an image" would have to be the next step'.[21] With hindsight, this may be seen as a programme Beckett was to take up in his subsequent works, as with the start of his 1965 short story 'Imagination Dead Imagine':

No trace anywhere of life, you say, pah, no difficulty there, imagination not dead yet, good, imagination dead imagine. Islands, waters, azure, verdure, one glimpse and vanished, endlessly, omit. Till all white in the whiteness the rotunda. (*CSP*, 182)

Given his notoriously opaque post-war literature, there is little agreement as to what Samuel Beckett got out of the varied philosophers in the 1930s, let alone his wider debt to 'Western philosophy' from that point on. However, Beckett's readings – and correspondingly, writings (especially his periodic non-fiction, collected in *Disjecta*) – from philosophy during the interwar years nonetheless reveal notable themes that echo across Beckett's fiction and drama. This ranges from subject–object relations (self–other, consciousness–world and so on) to doctrines whereby knowledge is folded upon itself, such as the 'doctra ignorantia' of mediaeval nominalism; the 'ineffability' of outer movement in Occasionalist thinking; and the sceptical philosophy of language found in Mauthner and others.

Favourite phrases were reused as 'tags' and one-liners in Beckett's writings, both as (rare) recommendations for the study of his work, as well as 'little phrases that seem so innocuous', but which 'rise up out of the pit and know no rest until they drag you down into its dark'; in the case of *Malone Dies*, referring to Democritus' maxim: '*Nothing is more real than nothing*'.[22] More generally, and while by no means decontested in Beckett studies, it seems that Beckett's philosophical didacticism during the 1930s helped provide the tools with which he was to subsequently and so memorably assault rational, systematic thought: think of *Watt's* 'mixed choir', for example, which Watt hears singing the weeks in a non-leap year (52.285714; leap years contain 52.1428571 weeks) (*W*, 26).

Thus, ultimately, when it comes to philosophy in Beckett's works, one hand giveth and the other taketh away. Protestations of ignorance by his narrators, no less than by Beckett himself, are enveloped within a philosophical 'docta ignorantia', linguistic scepticism and metaphysical agnosticism that are, at bottom, deeply learned. Returning full circle to *Molloy*, Beckett's breakout novel, here too declarations of not knowing are interspersed with philosophical conundrums (like the constrained freedoms of mind and will):

[O]nce again I am I will not say alone, no, that's not like me, but, how shall I say, I don't know, restored to myself, no, I never left myself, free, yes, I don't know what that means but it's the word I mean to use, free to do what, to do nothing, to know, but what, the laws of the mind perhaps, of my mind, that for example water rises in proportion as it drowns you and that you would do better, at least no worse, to obliterate texts than to blacken margins, to fill in the holes of words till all is blank and flat and the whole ghastly business looks like what it is, senseless, speechless, issueless misery. (*Mo*, 9–10)

Later, speaking broadly of wisdom – that 'eudeomistic slop' prized by Aristotle as the summit of virtue and happiness – the epononymous Molloy laments: 'my ideas on this subject were always horribly confused, for my knowledge of men was scant and the meaning of being beyond me' (*Mo*, 55, 38).

Yet if Molloy's confusion is evocative of many 'Beckettian' voices and places ranging across an oeuvre itself lasting six decades, this has little impinged upon the long-standing philosophical analyses of critics, approaching Beckett under such titles as 'Samuel Beckett: The Search for Self'; *Samuel Beckett and the Meaning of Being*; 'What is Man? The Search for Reality'; and most recently, 'Conclusion: The Beckett Absolute Universal'.[23] And with similarly fruitful results, philosophers and literary critics have long been energetic in suggesting that Beckett's post-1945

Philosophy

fiction could be said to exemplify – in the case of Wolfgang Iser's influential 'reader response' theory – or, in the case of post-structuralism, anticipate, a particular philosophical doctrine.[24] These and similar enquiries into the unique *mise en scène* of the 'Beckett Country' are set to long continue, with critics continuing to trace out philosophical influences, *zeitgeists* and legacies to – and not least, interpretations of – Beckett's writings. For the philosophy both in and behind Beckett's work calls out for critical attention, which may in turn remind readers that this most philosophical of authors was neither *sui generis* nor writing in an intellectual vacuum; for as Molloy has it: 'homo mensura can't do without staffage'.[25]

NOTES

1. Shane Weller, 'Beckett among the *Philosophes*: the Critical Reception of Samuel Beckett in France', in Mark Nixon and Matthew Feldman (eds.) *The International Reception of Samuel Beckett* (London: Continuum, 2009), 24.
2. See, respectively, Nadeau and Bataille, reprinted in Lawrence Graver and Raymond Federman (eds.) *Samuel Beckett: The Critical Heritage* (London: Routledge, 1999), 55–69; Jean-Paul Sartre, 'People's Theatre and Bourgeois Theater', in Michael Contat and Michel Rybalka (eds.), *Sartre on Theater*, trans. F. Jellinek (Quartet Books, London: 1976), 51; Marcel, Mauriac and Blanchot, reprinted in Lance St. John Butler (ed.) *Critical Essays on Samuel Beckett* (Aldershot: Scholas Press, 1994), 19, 24, 86–92.
3. Hugh Kenner, 'The Cartesian Centaur', in Ruby Cohn (ed.) *Perspective* (Autumn 1959), 132–41.
4. See, for example, Edouard Morot-Sir, 'Samuel Beckett and Cartesian Emblems', in Edouard Morot-Sir (ed.) *Samuel Beckett and the Art of Rhetoric* (Chapel Hill: University of North Carolina, 1976), 25–104; Michael Mooney, '*Molloy*, Part 1: Beckett's *Discourse on Method*', in *Journal of Beckett Studies* (3: 1978) 40–55; and Roger Scruton, 'Beckett and the Cartesian Soul', in *The Aesthetic Understanding: Essays in the Philosophy of Art and Culture* (Manchester: Carcanet Press, 1983), 222–41.
5. For an argument that Cartesian influence upon Beckett is largely circumstantial and better recast in terms of a wider engagement with Western philosophy, see my 'René Descartes and Samuel Beckett', in *Beckett's Books: A Cultural History of Samuel Beckett's "Interwar Notes"* (London: Continuum, 2008), 41–57.
6. David Hesla, *The Shape of Chaos: An Interpretation of the Art of Samuel Beckett* (Minneapolis: University of Minnesota Press, 1971), 10–11.
7. See, respectively, 'Dante...Bruno.Vico..Joyce' in *D*; 'Whoroscope', in *CSP* and *Proust*, reprinted in *P*.
8. Philosophical references correspond to the following: Thales in *CP*, 21; Leibniz in *M*, 69–72; the *Human Wishes* fragment is reproduced in *D*; Kant's 'das fruchtbare Bathos der Erfahrung' comprises entry 31 of the fifty-five addenda items at the end of *W*, 222; Geulincx appears in 'The End', in *CSP*, 91, and in *T*, 51;

Aristotle appears in 'Text for Nothing VIII' in *CSP*, 134; Malebranche 'less the rosy hue the humanities' is cited in 'The Image', in *CSP*, 167, and retained in *H*, 30; and Mauthner is mentioned in *Rough for Radio II*, in *CDW*, 276.

9 See the 1961 interviews with Tom Driver and Gabriel d'Aubaërde, reprinted in Lawrence Graver and Raymond Federman (eds.) *Samuel Beckett: The Critical Heritage* (London: Routledge, 1999), 238–47.

10 Rubin Rabinovitz, *Innovation in Samuel Beckett's Fiction* (Chicago: University of Illinois Press, 1992), 33.

11 Samuel Beckett, 'Dante...Bruno.Vico..Joyce' in *D*, 20. For a fuller discussion of Beckett's use of Croce's *1911 La Filosofia di Giambattista Vico*, see my '"I am not a philosopher". Beckett and Philosophy: A Methodological and Thematic Introduction', in the *Sofia Philosophical Review* (4.2: 2010), 27–31.

12 See Francis Doherty, 'Mahaffy's Whoroscope', *Journal of Beckett Studies* (2.1: 1992), 21–37, which shows that 'the amount of material which can unequivocally be said to be from Baillet is small, compared to that which can be shown to be taken from Mahaffy' (28).

13 Samuel Beckett to Thomas McGreevy on 21 September 1937, cited in *L1*, 550. The most exhaustive account of Beckett's relationship with Schopenhauer to date is found in Ulrich Pothast's *The Metaphysical Vision: Arthur Schopenhauer's Philosophy of Art and Life and Samuel Beckett's own way to make use of it* (New York: Peter Lang, 2008).

14 For Beckett's 'Joycean' notes on St. Augustine, see John Pilling (ed.) *Beckett's Dream Notebook* (Reading: Beckett International Foundation, 1999), 11–30, quoted xiii; and for Augustinian allusions in Beckett's collection of short stories, see John Pilling, *Samuel Beckett's More Pricks Than Kicks: In a Strait of Two Wills* (London: Continuum, 2011), ch. 5. As was his wont, a few years later Beckett returned to Augustine, taking two dozen sides of notes from Joseph McCabe's *St. Augustine and His Age*, followed by Porphyry's 'on the Life of Plotinus and the Arrangement of his Work'; see *Samuel Beckett Today/Aujourd'hui* 16, 91–3.

15 These notes have been catalogued as the 'History of Western Philosophy' in *Samuel Beckett Today/Aujourd'hui* 16, 67–90; the map of Greek antiquarian philosophers is also reproduced there (76). For a broad introduction, see my 'Beckett's Poss and the Dog's Dinner: An Empirical Survey of the 1930s "Psychology" and "Philosophy Notes"', in *Beckett the European*, Dirk van Hulle (ed.) *Journal of Beckett Studies* (13.2: 2004), 69–93.

16 The quotation is one of several Sophist paradoxes recoded by Beckett's 'Philosophy Notes' in TCD 109/67/42, cited in my *Beckett's Books: A Cultural History of Samuel Beckett's "Interwar Notes"* (London: Continuum, 2008), 34.

17 Erik Tonning, *Samuel Beckett's Abstract Drama: Works for Stage and Screen, 1962–1985* (Bern: Peter Lang, 2008), ch. 6. Beckett's letter to Thomas McGreevy of 19 September 1936 is cited in my 'Beckett and Philosophy, 1928–1938' in *Samuel Beckett Today/Aujourd'hui* 22 (2010), 172; *T*, 218.

18 See, for example, chapters on Beckett's relationship with Henri Bergson, Arthur Schopenhauer, Immanuel Kant, George Berkeley, Gottfried Wilhelm

Leibniz, Arnold Geulincx, Samuel Johnson, linguistic scepticism, early Greek philosophy and nominalism, in Matthew Feldman and Karim Mamdani (eds.) *Beckett/Philosophy* in *Sofia Philosophical Review* (5.11: 2011).

19 Cited in the 'Introduction to Samuel Beckett's Notes to the *Ethics*' in Han van Ruler, Anthony Uhlmann and Martin Wilson (eds.) *Arnold Geulincx: Ethics, with Samuel Beckett's Notes*, trans. Martin Wilson (Leiden, Brill, 2006); see also Anthony Uhlmann, *Samuel Beckett and the Philosophical Image* (Cambridge: Cambridge University Press, 2009), ch. 5.

20 Samuel Beckett to Linda Ben-Zvi of summer 1978, cited in the latter's 'Fritz Mauthner for Company', in *Journal of Beckett Studies*, (9: 1984), 65–88, quoted 66.

21 Samuel Beckett to Thomas McGreevy, cited in my 'Beckett, Sartre and Phenomenology' in *Limit(e) Beckett* 0, available online at www.limitebeckett.paris-sorbonne.fr/home.html (last accessed 9 June 2011); and Jean-Paul Sartre, *Imagination: A Psychological Critique*, trans. Forrest Williams (Ann Arbor: University of Michigan Press, 1962), 146.

22 Beckett's suggestion to Sighle Kennedy of 14 June 1967 exemplifies this tendency – 'If I were in the unenviable position of having to study my work my points of departure would be the "Naught is more real ..." and the "Ubi nihil vales ..." both already in *Murphy* and neither very rational' – widely quoted and reprinted in *D*, 113; *T*, 193.

23 See, respectively, Martin Esslin, *The Theatre of the Absurd*, ch. 1 (London: Penguin Books, 1968); 'Introduction' to Paul Davies, *The Ideal Real: Beckett's Fiction and Imagination* (London: Associated University Presses, 1994); Lance St. John Butler, *Samuel Beckett and the Meaning of Being: A Study in the Ontological Parable* (London: MacMillan, 1984); and Eric P. Levy, *Trapped in Thought: A Study of the Beckettian Mentality* (New York: Syracuse University Press, 2007).

24 See, for example, Wolfgang Iser, *The Implied Reader: Patterns of Communication in Prose from Bunyan to Beckett* (London: The Johns Hopkins University Press, 1987), 164–79, and 257–73; and Anthony Uhlmann, *Beckett and Poststructuralism* (Cambridge: Cambridge University Press, 1999).

25 *T*, 63. The reference to 'homo mensura' is taken from the early Greek philosopher Protagoras' motto, 'Man is the measure of all things, of things that are that they are, and of things that are not that they are not', corresponding to Samuel Beckett's 'Philosophy Notes' in TCD 10967/45, cited in my *Beckett's Books: A Cultural History of Samuel Beckett's "Interwar Notes"* (London: Continuum, 2008), 36.

CHAPTER 27

Psychology

Laura Salisbury

'[W]e are, needless to say, in a skull', suggests the voice in *The Calmative* (*CSP*, 70). '[N]eedless to say', presumably, because the narrator is acknowledging a literalisation of what many have long suspected, that Beckett's texts can be understood as explorations of a human mind reduced to its most fundamental, and here most material, conditions – a mind reduced to a kind of bare life. Much of Beckett's work seems precisely interested in getting into the head and poking about, so to speak, perhaps with the hope of penetrating or even finally escaping from the difficulties encased within it. The homicidal Lemuel in *Malone Dies*, for example, subjects his cranium to a hailstorm of hitting not only because it 'is a bony part, and sensitive, and difficult to miss', but because, unlike the leg, it is also 'the seat of all the shit and misery' (*MD*, 97). *The Unnamable*'s explorations of 'the shit and misery' indeed turn decisively to the penetrated interiority of a skullscape, with images of disintegrated subjects 'surrounded on all sides by massive bone' resounding within that text (*U*, 65), but also ringing across the oeuvre and through to those white spaces of *Imagination Dead Imagine* and *All Strange Away* that are as cranial as they are architectural. As a number of interpreters have suggested, the very set of *Endgame*, with its two windows, two apertures, traces the shape of eye sockets that invoke a *memento mori*; but the implied skullscape also transforms the exhausted 'wriggles' of the work on stage into the compulsive back and forth of a mind. And if Beckett is indeed imagining what it might be to peer into the head and stage the workings of a psyche, it becomes vital to understand, with as much precision as possible, the complex intellectual and biographical contexts through which Beckett might have formed his particular sense of that mind's unvisible shape.

Looked at in one way, Beckett's invocation of the skull is a kind of literalism, but this explicitness hardly makes things simple, as the odd mimeticism at work in representing cranial interiority is paradoxically matched by ossified walls imagined and written at the limits of abstraction.

Beckett's long-standing and clear interest in examining the topography of the mind, often using dysfunction to render revealingly explicit the unexpected contours of its workings, indeed steadfastly refuses any turn to the psychological interiority that realist forms seem able to illuminate so clearly. In 1949, during the writing of *The Unnamable*, Beckett suggested to the art critic Georges Duthuit that an art, in this case a painting, that disconnects itself from the putative facile ease of representing the external world is not helped by a retreat to the inside, to a sense of an artist's or character's psychology. Beckett affirms, instead, that he is seeking a disconnected art – one in which 'the break with the outside world entails the break with the inside world', and where 'there are no replacement relations for naïve relations' (*L2*, 140).

Of course, Beckett goes on to acknowledge that links do remain – will remain – and he suggests he is doing nothing more than 'trying to point to the possibility of an expression lying outside the system of relations hitherto held to be indispensable' (*L2*, 140–1). But this articulated position is significant, for it suggests that Beckett's turn to scenarios that tempt interpretations linked to psychology, alongside his oddly disconnected, and then peculiarly reconnected, use of the technical materials of psychology and psychoanalysis, must be considered alongside the complexity of his non-relational aesthetic. Pondering the limits of his questionable learning, Beckett's Molloy indeed admits, 'Yes, I once took an interest in astronomy. I don't deny it. Then it was geology that killed a few years for me. The next pain in the balls was anthropology and the other disciplines, such as psychiatry, that are connected with it, disconnected, then connected again, according to the latest discoveries' (*Mo*, 37). Molloy, like his creator, it turns out, may be well versed in 'psychiatry', but it is precisely the connection, and indeed the disconnection, of such technical reading to other materials in the novel and to an inner world of intentions, actions and compulsions, that the text paradoxically both projects and screens from view.

The critical understanding of the fact that Beckett's work is explicitly concerned with the materials of psychology and psychoanalysis has undergone a series of paradigm shifts since his texts first received critical attention in the 1950s. There was an initial, broadly existentialist humanist, sense that Beckett was concerned with portraying the human mind thrown back on itself, stripped of those normative social habits that might mask its uninhabitable strangeness. This loosely psychological, though nevertheless insightful, conviction that the mind and its troubled relationship to a body was Beckett's primary material, was consolidated and extended in the next few decades as critics of various theoretical stripes undertook detailed and revealing readings of both the content and form of Beckett's work in relation to specifically psychoanalytic ideas. Anxious to understand the movements, enactments and articulations of the texts rather than simply to psychoanalyse author or characters, many scholars produced rich analyses of the performance of modes and drives within the work – modes, it turned out, that could usefully be understood through the ideas of psychoanalysis, even if they could not be reduced to them.

In 1976, for example, Julia Kristeva developed a Lacanian, feminist understanding of *First Love* and *Not I* not by diagnosing Beckett or his characters, but by using psychoanalysis to explore the evocation of a split speaking subject picking through the crumbling linguistic edifice of the paternal symbolic order.[1] The sense that certain psychoanalytic modes could usefully be aligned with the readings of Beckett's deconstruction of the subject that dominated in the 1980s and early 1990s was supplemented later in the decade, however, by work concerned explicitly with interpreting the appearance of the technical materials of psychology and psychoanalysis within Beckett's texts. J. D. O'Hara's 1997 *Samuel Beckett's Hidden Drives* illuminatingly worked to trace the shape of the intellectual 'scaffolding' that seemingly underpinned the work, analysing Beckett's 'use of Freudian psychology, moving from the many specific details in his texts to their actual or probable sources in Freud's writing'.[2] In the same year, Phil Baker also insisted that his own study was 'less a psychoanalytic "reading" of Beckett's work than an attempt to read the psychoanalytic and quasi-psychoanalytic material which is already present in certain texts'.[3] Baker was, however, usefully reluctant to imagine a straightforward correspondence between Beckett's works and the psychoanalytic materials they so clearly cite. It does not take much critical acumen to notice that the name of the odd figure of Obidil who appears in *Molloy* is formed from an anagram of libido, that Molloy has a seemingly Freudian notion of a 'fatal pleasure principle', or that the 'Davus complex' – that 'morbid dread of sphynges' – that appears in the Addenda of *Watt* is a citation of psychoanalytic material; but what is not at all clear, as Baker suggests, is precisely what the textual appearance of such terms might mean.

Baker helpfully insists that Beckett's uncertain incorporation of psychoanalytic materials into his texts is 'a form of unstably ironised citation; a mythic borrowing compounded by considerations of polarity and structure along the lines of Beckett's declared interest in "the shape of ideas" rather than their content'.[4] He thus implies that this material must be read according to Beckett's always complex, always ambivalent ingestion

Psychology 315

and expulsion of external textual authorities. This is not to say, however, that scholarship is not enriched by knowing, and understanding with precision, the details of Beckett's exposure to psychological and psychoanalytic materials. Jean-Michel Rabaté's work on the early Beckett's obvious knowledge of Gestalt psychology, of which he makes such parodic use in *Murphy*, serves as a useful example. In the mid 1980s, Rabaté noted Beckett's incorporation of specific names and concepts drawn from experimental and Gestalt psychology, and, by contextualising the references to the Külpe school of Kurt Koffka, Wolfgang Köhler, Henry Jackson Watt and Narziss Ach, he produced a highly illuminating account of *Murphy* that explored Beckett's ironic use of the idea that meaningful pattern and order might be immanent within the world.[5] As he has recently admitted, though, Rabaté found an all-too-tempting mirror of the novel's title in the name of a psychologist called Gardner Murphy, from whose book, Rabaté surmised, Beckett drew his material. Much later, James Knowlson, in his biography *Damned to Fame* (1996), revealed a cache of notes that Beckett took between 1934 and 1935 that proved Beckett had indeed read a work concerned with Gestalt psychology and psychoanalytic texts, but it was not Murphy's book; it was Robert Woodworth's *Contemporary Schools of Psychology* (1931) from which Beckett read, and then transcribed, the Gestaltist belief that '[n]ature runs to *organised* wholes' with the 'figure stand[ing] out naturally from the ground in relation to the fundamental distinction between them'.[6] Rabaté's reading of Beckett's parodic use of the idea of a putatively 'natural' relationship between figure and ground remains revealing, demonstrating as it does the shape of Beckett's artistic reworking of 'straight' technical materials; but it is clear that his argument can be both underpinned and extended by knowing the sources Beckett was using and transforming to produce his work.

In the 2000s, C. J. Ackerley and Matthew Feldman meticulously demonstrated that the archive could indeed support, in revealing detail, textual analyses informed by the psychological and psychoanalytic texts we now know Beckett read in the 1930s.[7] Feldman's path-breaking account of Beckett's interwar notes on philosophy and psychology (held in the archive at Trinity College Dublin) quoted many of Beckett's typed transcriptions of texts, usefully contextualising and glossing his sources. Suggestively, Feldman noted that Beckett seemed more interested in the general tenets of particular psychoanalytic theories than clinical cases,[8] and certainly his transcriptions of Bloomsbury psychoanalyst Karin Stephen's *Psychoanalysis and Medicine: A Study of the Wish to Fall Ill* (1933) that detail Freud's erotic phases, the Oedipus complex, neurotic processes, castration anxieties and Freud's second topography of the id, ego and superego, all imply an attempt to get to grips with psychoanalysis as an intellectual framework. Woodworth's *Contemporary Schools of Psychology* also offered Beckett a technical overview of a field in its account of the late nineteenth-century emergence of experimental psychology, behaviourism (including the work of Watson, Thorndike and Pavlov), neurological theories of the localisation of functions in the brain, the Gestalt psychology Rabaté finds most clearly translated into *Murphy* and accounts of the psychoanalytic theories of Alfred Adler and Jung. Beckett's knowledge of Freudian theory was, in turn, extended and deepened by his reading of Ernest Jones (mischievously represented as 'Erogenous Jones') and his *Papers on Psychoanalysis* (1923). There, Beckett encountered Freud's notion of the pleasure principle and the reality principle; the mechanisms of repression and the inevitable return of repressed material; detailed accounts of narcissism, melancholia and anal eroticism; Freud's understanding of dream work, instincts, drives and various perversions; a Freudian topography of the psyche; Freudian and Jungian theories of symbol formation; theoretical work on impotence and psychical anaesthesia; and detailed material on sublimation. Significantly, though, Beckett's subsequent notes on Jones's *Treatment of Neuroses* (1920) and its material on conversion hysteria and the psychogenic causes of physical ailments contain levels of detail and sardonic personal ejaculations that perhaps suggest some sort of identification with the symptoms presented. Without reducing the work to pathography, it nevertheless seems plausible that Beckett's underscoring of and seeming identification with the drive within neurotic compulsion (*Zwang*) that produces both paralysis and an overwhelming 'feeling of mustness' might offer a suggestive way of prizing open that famous, though cryptic, 'obligation to express' that compulsively haunts the work, alongside the oscillation between impossibility and demand that so many of the texts seem to enact.[9]

Whilhelm Stekel's *Psychoanalysis and Suggestion Therapy* (1923) was quickly condensed by Beckett into the noting of a few terms (including '[a]cithisia, i.e., inability to sit down', which reappears in the figure of Cooper in *Murphy*). Even though Beckett was to complain of Alfred Adler's 'onetrack mind [*sic*]' (*L1*, 246), *The Neurotic Constitution* (1921) was attended to in far greater detail, with the sense that the neurotic's will is both narcissistically engorged as a will to power and paralysed in symptoms seeming to hold Beckett's attention. But perhaps it is Beckett's final notes on Otto Rank's *The Trauma of Birth* (1929) that most clearly offer a theoretical frame through which many of his later aesthetic concerns might usefully be understood. Rank suggests that all neurosis is an expression of the trauma of birth as the baby is expelled from intrauterine calm, from the realm of pure pleasure, into the world. For Rank, as for Freud, the pleasure principle and the death drive are chiastically folded into one another, with pleasure's aim to return the organism to the state of quiescence that precedes birth becoming compellingly elided with an unconscious fantasy of the experience of death. Beckett's engagement with the notion of a 'wombtomb' certainly preceded his reading of Rank, appearing as it does in *Dream of Fair to Middling Women*; but, as Angela Moorjani puts it, our understanding of the ways in which 'the Beckettian text (after *Murphy*) repeatedly tries and fails to effect a birthing into death in a rapturous celebration of the always deferred return to nothing' is enriched by knowing the details of one of the theoretical models Beckett might have been exploring in relation to those demands that seem to emerge as drives within his texts.[10]

There remains, though, the vexed question of the relationship between theoretical ideas, the citation of psychoanalytic concepts or their performance in texts and Beckett's biographical experience. For it is clear that Beckett's contact with psychology and psychoanalysis was lived beyond any sealed space of theoretical reading. Feldman convincingly argues that Beckett's note taking functioned as a form of self-diagnosis, or at least an attempt at self-analysis,[11] for at the point of their writing the young Beckett was desperate to understand the symptoms – heart palpitations, panic, paralysis, boils and cysts and various intestinal complaints – that plagued him. Both at the time and since, these symptoms have been read by friends, critics, biographers and even by Beckett himself as part of what would now be labelled an 'anxiety disorder'. Beckett's letters reveal a close but difficult relationship with his mother, but it was the death of his beloved father that seemed to provoke a crisis. Beckett told Knowlson:

After my father's death I had trouble psychologically. The bad years were between when I had to crawl home [from Paris to Dublin] in 1932 and after my father's death in 1933 [...] I was walking down Dawson Street. And I felt I couldn't go on. It was a strange experience I can't really describe. I found I couldn't go on moving [...] So I went into the nearest pub and got a drink just to stay still. And I felt I needed help. [...] [Geoffrey Thompson] recommended psychoanalysis for me. (*K*, 172–3)

Believing psychoanalysis to be illegal in Ireland at the time, Beckett persuaded his mother to subsidise psychotherapy in London. It is unclear whether Thompson recommended Wilfred Ruprecht Bion specifically to Beckett, for the two had undertaken training together at the Institute of

Medical Psychology in 1932; but it is clear that Bion had not yet undergone formal psychoanalytic training. Beckett, however, was obviously attached to the idea of having an 'analyst' and to a sense that psychoanalysis was the work he was doing with Bion, as he consistently referred to Bion in those terms. Although this was not yet the Bion who would undertake a training analysis with Melanie Klein and prove such an extraordinary, though eccentric, force in the development of theories of object relations in British psychoanalysis, he nevertheless saw Beckett on the couch for three sessions a week between 1934 and 1935. Analyst or not, their work with dreams, memories and fantasies that Beckett details in letters and later to Knowlson demonstrates that Bion offered Beckett a profoundly psychoanalytically oriented psychotherapy. Beckett was initially hopeful, speaking of 'analysis' as the 'only thing that interests me for the moment, and that is how it should be' (*L1*, 183). And this hope, which most likely coincided with the inception of his psychology notes, suggests that Beckett's reading, note taking and, presumably, his pondering on neurotic symptoms are hard to interpret as simply disinterested intellectual pursuits.

In later years Beckett was to admit that the therapy with Bion did help him:

I think it helped me perhaps to control the panic. I certainly came up with some extraordinary memories of being in the womb [...] I used to go back to my digs and write notes on what had happened, on what I'd come up with. I've never found them since. Maybe they still exist somewhere. I think it all helped me to understand a bit better what I was doing and what I was feeling. (*K*, 177)

Alongside Bion's clinical notes, this material has not been found; still, even without a material archive of Beckett's experience of therapy, there are seemingly clear links to be drawn between Beckett's symptoms and experiences and the explorations of his psychology notes. And yet, though there is a temptation to follow Beckett in his attempts at self-diagnosis, or at least to piece together his understanding of his symptoms, such impulses must be tempered with the fact that Beckett rejected the therapy rather than work it through to a finish. Beckett's own refusal of what Bion would later come to understand as the analyst's capacity to make links between material for the patient, is something that might usefully alert critics to the fact that relations, connections and links seem always to be occasions of complexity and ambivalence in Beckett's work.[12]

Critical readings of Beckett's relationship with Bion and the links to be made between their mature work range from impulsive yet suggestive,[13] to reserved, careful and clearly evidenced assessments both of what might have survived of Beckett's interest in psychoanalysis and how Bion and Beckett might each have used the work between them following the termination of the therapy.[14] For it remains clear that psychoanalytic ideas – the tropes, frames and expressions of drive – were something to which Beckett persistently returned, in the work, if not in the world. An example that has received a good deal of critical attention is Beckett's retention of a fragment of the lecture by Jung at the Institute of Medical Psychology (Tavistock Clinic) that he attended with Bion in 1935. Although at the time he worried in a letter to his friend Thomas McGreevy about Jung's mysticism and gently professed him to be 'less than dirt under Freud's nails' (*L1*, 82), a dislocated fragment of the lecture, of which he suggestively gives no account in the letter, resounds in the work as far as the 1960s. In conversation with Charles Juliet in 1968, Beckett indeed connects, with extraordinary candour, one of Jung's clinical examples discussed that night with a sense of his own dilemma:

I have always felt as if, inside me, someone had been murdered. Murdered before my birth. I had to find this murdered being. Try to give him life … Once I attended a lecture by Jung – he spoke of one of his patients, a young girl [...] And then, as if speaking to himself, and surprised by the discovery he had made, he added: 'In fact, she had never been born'. I have always had the feeling that I too had never been born.[15]

The key phrase, 'never been properly born', echoes in the oeuvre, repeating as a still-born fragment in the Addenda to *Watt*, reappearing (with slight difference) in *All That Fall* and seeming to structure *Footfalls* almost entirely. Beckett specifically told Charlotte Joeres, who played Mother, and Hildegard Schmahl, who played May in *Footfalls*, of the link to Jung's lecture (*K*, 616, 618); but, as ever with Beckett's citation of psychoanalytic materials, the strange repetition in the work of ideas, phrases and experiences that part of Beckett gave up on decades earlier, seems to rearrange, to retranscribe, that seemingly aborted, failed experience, somehow demanding that a link be made with psychoanalysis, even as the shape of that link is occluded. The uncanny return to and reworking of psychoanalytic material, a retranscription that might even be read through the Freudian trope of *Nachträglichkeit* – a present working through that retroactively constructs the meaning of past memories – indeed suggests that psychoanalysis remained an experience and a discourse limned with significance for Beckett. When in 1935 Beckett predicted, accurately as it turned out, that the analysis would not continue much after Christmas, he admitted: 'I don't expect the troubles I hoped first and foremost to get rid of via analysis will be gone then any more than they are now. Tant pis. I must use me to them' (*LI*, 283). Without reducing his aesthetic work to biography or to an acting out of psychopathology, it is precisely the complexity of the way in which Beckett might have 'used himself' to his symptoms by using them in the work, sometimes repeating them as content but more significantly enacting their contradictory and implicated drives at the level of artistic form, that criticism might still usefully submit to its own remembering, repeating and working through.

Beckett himself never gave up on representing in his work the odd discontinuities, alarming slippages and surprising vicissitudes of the relationship between mind and body, nor did he ever give up aesthetically on the task of imagining what it would mean to peer into the head. That Beckett remained compelled by the workings of the mind, and indeed the oddly magical translation of brain matter into all that is immaterial in the human, until the end is tellingly staged in his conversations with Lawrence Shainberg in 1981. Shainberg sent Beckett a copy of his book about neurosurgery and, to his astonishment, received a response almost straight away from the older author. In their meetings that followed, Beckett asked enthusiastic yet specific questions:

Whenever I saw him, he questioned me about neurosurgery, asking, for example, exactly how close I had stood to the brain while observing surgery, or how much pain a craniotomy entailed, or, one day during lunch at rehearsals: 'How is the skull removed?' and 'Where do they put the skull bone while they're working inside?'[16]

The sense that this is more than the curiosity of the amateur is suggested by the fact that Beckett went on to link the work of the brain surgeon with his own writing practice: 'I have long believed that here in the end is the writer's best chance, gazing into the synaptic chasm'.[17] His imagined attention to the fundamental units out of which all human experience is composed seems to affirm that the relationship between the mind, material brain and body remained Beckett's fundamental object of concern.

The turn to the synapse, to neurology rather than psychology or psychoanalysis, perhaps suggests that even Beckett was influenced by the cognitive revolution of the second half of the twentieth century and the new dominance of neuroscience. But maybe this is too much of a leap, for it is clear, as far back as *Murphy*, that Beckett was interested in those odd imbrications of minds and bodies, ideas and matter, at work in modes of psychological and neurological dysfunction. Beckett seemingly never wavered from the belief that disorder suddenly renders in gritty, resistant relief the fundamental strangeness of even putatively 'normal' functioning; indeed he articulated to Shainberg the artistic value of a subjectivity that is somehow damaged – denuded of the powers that allow the world to slip by in a space of cognitive ease:

> It's a paradox, but with old age, the more the possibilities diminish, the better chance you have. With diminished concentration, loss of memory, obscured intelligence – what you, for example, might call 'brain damage' – the more chance there is for saying something closest to what one really is. Even though everything seems inexpressible, there remains the need to express. A child needs to make a sand castle even though it makes no sense. In old age, with a few grains of sand, one has the greatest possibility.[18]

And this context of 'brain damage' – neurological and psychological dysfunction – has recently provided scholars with another lens through which to consider Beckett's account of mind and bodies written to and beyond their normative limits. Finding in Beckett's work enough space for a chiselling out of underexplored crannies of human experience, in the last few years critics have examined the use of textual strategies that mime the extraordinary shapes of schizophrenic language, aphasia, Parkinson's disease, Tourette's syndrome and Cotard's syndrome, amongst others, to render explicit Beckett's usefully particularised questioning of the locus of the human subject and the limits of its capacities.[19]

As the quotation demonstrates, however, 'diminished concentration, loss of memory, obscured intelligence', though perhaps suggestive of new set of explorations for Beckett studies, maintains a highly ambivalent relationship to the idea of an intellectual, even a disciplinary, context into which the materials of psychology, neurology and psychoanalysis might easily fit. For 'brain damage' indeed accords with the well-documented sense that Beckett became increasingly suspicious of, though nevertheless remained clearly compelled by, knowledge and intellectual frames as his work matured. In a letter to Duthuit in 1949, Beckett was already suggesting that 'to want the brain to function is the height of crassness [...] The brain has better things to do, stopping and listening to itself, for example' (*L2*, 149). Forcing the brain to stop functioning with its transparent ease and reflexively to take itself as an object, demanding that the swerves that underpin the processes of thought and feeling should extrude into consciousness, using the neurologically damaged body to give revealing, expressive shape to drives and demands that would otherwise remain invisible, Beckett's textual experimentation indeed uses the context of psychological, psychoanalytic and perhaps even neurological ideas to enable a thinking that would allow something new to be seen about the relationships between psyche and soma. But the thinking and feeling about thinking and feeling that Beckett's writing produces, though clearly emergent from an intellectual context, also resists that context in ways that paradoxically both frustrate and offer a possibility. Beckett's steadfast refusal of straightforward relations and neat identifications indeed demands that his works' retranscription of the materials of psychology and psychoanalysis be understood as operating beyond the frames, and indeed beyond the psychological security, of any simple staging of technical knowledge.

NOTES

1 Julia Kristeva, 'The Father, Love, and Banishment', *Desire in Language: A Semiotic Approach to Literature and Art*, trans. Thomas Gora, Alice Jardine and Leon S. Roudiez (Oxford: Basil Blackwell, 1980), 148–58.
2 J. D. O'Hara, *Samuel Beckett's Hidden Drives: Structural Uses of Depth Psychology* (Gainesville: University of Florida Press, 1997), 10.
3 Phil Baker, *Beckett and the Mythology of Psychoanalysis* (London: Macmillan, 1997), xii.
4 Ibid., xiv.
5 Jean-Michel Rabaté, 'Quelques figures de la première (et dernière) anthropomorphie de Beckett', in Jean-Michel Rabaté (ed.) *Beckett avant Beckett: essays sur le jeune Beckett 1930–1945* (Paris: Presses de l'Ecole Normale Supérieure, 1984), 135–51.
6 Trinity College Dublin MS 10971/7/12. Quoted in Laura Salisbury, '"Something or Nothing": Beckett and the Matter of Language', in Daniela Caselli (ed.) *Beckett and Nothing: Trying to Understand Beckett* (Manchester: Manchester University Press, 2010), 222.
7 C. J. Ackerley, *Demented Particulars: The Annotated 'Murphy'* (Tallahassee: Journal of Beckett Studies Books, 2004); Matthew Feldman, *Beckett's Books: A Cultural History of Beckett's Interwar Notes* (London: Continuum: 2006).
8 Feldman, *Beckett's Books*, 96.
9 See Laura Salisbury, *Samuel Beckett: Laughing Matters, Comic Timing* (Edinburgh: Edinburgh University Press, 2012), 86–91; Shane Weller, 'Staging Psychoanalysis: *Endgame* and the Freudian Theory of the Anal-Sadistic Phase', in Erik Tonning, Matthew Feldman, Matthijs Engelberts and Dirk Van Hulle (eds.) *Samuel Beckett: Debts and Legacies*, Samuel Beckett Today/Aujourd'hui (22: 2010), 135–47.
10 Angela Moorjani, 'Beckett and Psychoanalysis', in Lois Oppenheim (ed.) *Palgrave Advances in Beckett Studies* (Houndsmills: Palgrave Macmillan, 2004), 174.
11 Feldman, *Beckett's Books*, 96.
12 For a reading of Beckett's split from Bion through Bion's understanding of the patient's 'attacks on linking' see Steven Connor, 'Beckett and Bion', *Journal of Beckett Studies* (17: 2008), 9–34.

13 See, for example, Didier Anzieu, 'Beckett and Bion', *International Review of Psycho-Analysis* (16: 1989), 163–9.
14 See, for example, Lois Oppenheim, 'A Preoccupation With Object-Representation: The Beckett-Bion Case Revisited', *International Journal of Psycho-Analysis* (82: 2001), 766–84.
15 Charles Juliet, *Conversations with Samuel Beckett and Bram van Velde*, trans. Tracy Cooke et al. (Champaign: Dalkey Archive Press, 2009), 13.
16 Lawrence Shainberg, 'Exorcising Beckett', *Paris Review* (104: 1987), 102.
17 Ibid.
18 Ibid., 103.
19 See, for example, the work gathered under the theme of 'Beckett, Language and the Mind' in Elizabeth Barry's special issue of the *Journal and Beckett Studies* (17: 2008).

CHAPTER 28

The Bible

Chris Ackerley

Samuel Beckett told Tom Driver in 1961 that he had no religious feeling: 'Once I had a religious emotion. It was at my first communion. No more'. Its efficacy at times of crisis, he said, was that of an old school tie.[1] Likewise, Belacqua's first communion has come and gone, leaving in his breast 'a void place and a spacious nothing' (*Dream*, 185). Wylie's 'ecstasy of compassion' leaves him feeling 'purer than at any time since his second communion' (*M*, 35); compare Joyce's *Portrait of the Artist*, Napoleon to his generals: 'Gentlemen, the happiest day of my life was the day on which I made my first communion'.[2] Beckett's scepticism, or deep agnosticism, did not preclude an intense interest in religion. His close readings of the Bible (the King James, with forays into the Vulgate, *La Sainte Bible* and obscure secondary sources) reflect a lasting fascination with the paradoxes of faith. Moran's body, its soul appeased when dispatched by Father Ambrose's portable pyx, feels 'ravenous' (*Mo*, 101), like Elijah in the wilderness, fed by ravens (1 Kings 17:4–6).[3] The 'Beckett country' is such a wilderness, riddled with theological quags, and the Bible a dubious *vade mecum*, a Protestant guide to wider European traditions (both catholic and Catholic) that if not distinctly living were yet not 'wholly dying', as Beckett remarked of Jeremy Taylor.[4]

Raised (like Belacqua) 'a dirty low-down Low Church Protestant highbrow', Beckett's 'cogging in the Synod' (*MPTK*, 163, 151) indelibly marked his early writings. Like Krapp, he may have 'fallen off the pew' when still 'in short trousers' (*CDW*, 222–3), but fragments of indoctrination recur, in the Protestant rituals of Arsene's 'short statement' in *Watt*, for instance, or in memories of bedtime prayers in *Dream* (*Dream*, 8–9) and 'Serena II', recalled in *Company* (*NO*, 21). Mrs Rooney, in *All That Fall* (*CDW*, 184), confuses 'Nearer My God to Thee', played as the *Titanic* went down, with 'Rock of Ages'. *How It Is* (*H*, 10) recalls a child kneeling on a veranda, hands clasped in prayer, and the mother's eyes, burning with severe love, when he looks to the sky whence no help cometh (Psalm 121:1). A photo of this survives into *Film*, where O tears it up in a vain attempt to escape apperception.⁵ These are poignant touches, but the Bible affords a more enduring testimony to Beckett's fascination with the faith that he might ridicule and resent, but could not ignore.⁶

Beckett's biblical allusion follows the trajectory of his wider aesthetic. Early writings reflect an impulse that is broadly literary, philosophical and ironic, where religious echoes abound, but are often obscure or ostentatious. The middle period, from *Watt* to *How It Is*, constitutes a substantial body of religious literature, in which biblical allusions question and qualify a Christianity that is, Beckett's comments to the contrary notwithstanding, more than a familiar mythology.⁷ Then, like literary echoes and other rhetorical effects, biblical references diminish in the later writings, as religious sentiments fade to residua (ill said, ill heard); yet, like a faint *miserere*, biblical images, often deriving from music and the visual arts, shape a subtle iconography. This triangulation is not triage, as 'middle' works like *All That Fall* (1957) are 'early' in all but date and 'later' works imitate earlier with a subtle typology (as the New Testament the Old); but it permits pragmatic distinctions between biblical touches that are broadly baroque, thematic or iconic, matching a changing aesthetic.

Like the mercies of Youdi, Beckett's biblical allusions are so abundant that, in this short benediction, their proper documentation is impossible.⁸ I propose to discuss the typical and the arcane, to identify patterns of signification arising as biblical verses create narratives or become motifs. Hence, a small set (thirteen seems auspicious) of 'Beckett's Bible Stories' if you wish, parables if you prefer, with no didactic purpose other than to attest their tragi-comedic qualities. There are many such ('Billions', as Estragon would say), but the few numbered here must bear witness for those unheard.

I. RAHAB

Beckett's early poetry invokes Rahab, an harlot saved when Jericho was destroyed (Joshua 2:1–25, 6:22–5) because she had hidden the Israelite spies among the flax stalks on her rooftop. She was told to bind a line of scarlet thread in her window that she and her family might be spared, and so it came to pass. In *Whoroscope*, 'Rahab of the snows' becomes 'Christina the ripper', the Swedish queen who 'murdered' Descartes by making him rise early on winter morns (*CP*, 4). 'From the Only Poet to a Shining Whore' shows Dante addressing Rahab, whom he places in heaven (*Paradiso* 9.112ff), to the jealous fury of blissful Beatrice at seeing such a woman saved.⁹ The comedy is exquisite, but Harvey misses the joke, calling Rahab 'a figure of the saving power of faith'.¹⁰ Beckett soon tired of what he described to Tom McGreevy (17 July 1930) as 'the Rahab tomfoolery' (*L1*, 25), but in 1931 she returned, in *Dream*, bedroom visit from nice Asia lady, the 'geisha Rahab', as Yang Kuei-Fei, Chinese concubine of the T'ang Emperor, Hsüan Tsung, hanged by his eunuch on a pear tree when her adopted son and lover rebelled (*Dream*, 53).¹¹

2. 'OHOLIBA CHARM OF MY EYES'

'Hell Crane to Starling', despite its Dantean title (*Inferno* V.40–51, Paolo and Francesca, the birds emblems of their infidelity), rehearses tales of Old Testament whoredom and adultery, traduced into Oirish.¹² The speaker woos 'Oholiba charm of my eyes', a name to conjure the whoredoms of Aholah and Aholibah (Ezekiel 23:1–4), with promises of an ass (Ezekiel 23:20), stout and pommes *impurées* (mashed murphies, all puns intended). He sings Hippolytus, who refused to pollute his father's bed when enticed by Phaedra; and Reuben, son of Jacob, who lay with his father's concubine, Bilhah (Genesis 35:22), and boasted of it ('Bilah always blabs'). The setting is a cave above Tsaor, or Zoar (Genesis 19–30), where Lot lay with his daughters, as drunk as Noah, the one man worth saving from the destruction of Sodom and Gomorrah (one might speculate about the unworthy). Combining scriptural irreverence with a witty parody of the Twilighters ('a bloody fine ass / lepping'), the poem offers the first of many vistas of Bally, as seen from the Dublin hills, a city of the plain ('Saorstat' was irresistible). Boisterous and irreverent, but not, as Harvey opines, a 'lecherous leer',¹³ the poem generated another, 'To My Daughter', where identical imagery assumes a different intonation as Beckett reflects bitterly on his recent affair with Mary Manning, now a distant Aholiba content with her comely donkey: Mary had returned to her husband in Boston and borne the daughter who might have been, but was not, Beckett's child.¹⁴

3. TRUE SAYINGS

Belacqua's frequent sentiment, when rehearsing received ideas, is 'that was a true saying', echoing the Anglican Communion Service and Timothy 1:15: 'This is a true saying, and worthy of all men to be received, That Christ Jesus came into the world to save sinners'. In 'Dante and the Lobster' (*MPTK*, 5), 'Yellow' (*MPTK*, 155) and *Dream* (40), it is a dubious consolation. Like Molloy, Belacqua is no enemy to the commonplace, but he is outdone by the parson of 'Draff', verily a master of the art. Assuring Smerry that in 'no time' she will meet Bel in 'Paradize' (Luke 23:43), he covenants her with 'Therefore be glad' (Psalms 32:11), and rides off 'like a weaver's shuttle', oblivious to Job 7:6: 'My days are swifter than a weaver's shuttle' or to his bicycle as a 'Swift' (*MPTK*, 170–1). On the day of 'committal' (Burial of the Dead), delayed by 'casting out devils' (Mark 3:22), he arrives 'in the nick of time' (oblivious to 'Old Nick') and 'in a muck sweat' (oblivious to Bella Cohen), piety subverted by the profane (*MPTK*, 175). By the mercy of God he is slow to wrath (James 1:19), responding mildly to Hairy's 'O Anthrax ... where is thy pustule' (1 Corinthians 15:55: 'O death, where is thy sting?'): 'She has been through the fire' (2 Kings 21:6). Evicted from the car (*MPTK*, 178), and unable to 'cock up the other cheek' (Matthew 5:39), he assures Hairy and Smerry that there shall be no more death or sorrow or crying (Revelation 21:4); the word unheard is 'pain'. Abandoned, he stands in the road, almost hoping they might be forgiven (Luke 23:34: 'Father, forgive them; for they know not what they do'). Of such is the Kingdom of Heaven.

4. MURPHY ON THE JOBPATH

If misery be virtue, then Job is Beckett's burden, as he draws less consolation from it than any other book. Its extravagant language was his first temptation; he succumbed fatally in 'Text', section 3, where Job ceases not his lamentations.[15] An unworthy token (Job 21:29) 'of Godcraft', he lacks the behemoth's strength, the 'hippopot's cedar tale / and belly muscles'[16]; or the 'flashneezing' of Leviathan,[17] the 'non-suppliant airtight alligator'.[18] Another temptation was arcane detail: Job's wife is unnamed in the Bible, but the Smeraldina has 'a Rasima look in her shrunken eyes' (*Dream*, 5); William Cooper's *Flagellation and the Flagellants* tells how Job's wife, Rasima, urges him to curse God and die.[19] Murphy's is a nominalist crisis structured by the very name of the Lord's afflicted: he seeks a body-tight mind, but a deplorable susceptibility to Celia and ginger biscuits binds him to the Big World. Celia cannot be his muse (*serenade, nocturne, alba*) and a working girl (Murphy finds this irrational); so he must find a JOB to support them both: an intrusion of the macrocosm into the freedom of the microcosm. Comforting himself with maieutic saws, such as 'How can he be clean that is born?' (Job 15:14), Murphy succumbs; and, setting out on the 'job-path', becomes (to the false comforters of the Blake League) an object of derision, a man of sorrows and acquainted with grief (*M*, 47).

5. ARSENE'S SHORT STATEMENT

William James offered Whitman's *Song of Myself* to illustrate the 'sporadic' mystical experience[20]; Arsene's 'short statement' in *Watt* (39–64) is akin, an epiphanic sunlit moment in and out of time, when 'Something slipped' (*W*, 35). It is not an illusion, though Arsene is buggered if he can understand how it could have been anything else (*W*, 37). The crisis is anticipated, orchestrated and mediated by biblical echoes. The dark ways 'in his head, in his side, in his hands and feet' intimate the wounds of Christ; there is a stirring 'beyond coming and going' (Psalms 121:8); the 'moment' suggests 1 Corinthians 15:52: 'In a moment, in the twinkling of an eye ... we shall be changed' (*W*, 32). Arsene 'witnesses and is witnessed' (*W*, 34); he tries to tell an uncomprehending Watt something of that ineffable, unattended moment. His phrasing is biblical[21]; Mr Knott (61) neither comes nor goes, but abides (Psalms 61:7); life as a shadow (Psalms 144:4); the vanity of human wishes (Ecclesiastes 1:2). A little wind (Acts 2:2) comes and goes; Arsene is afflicted from the crown of his head to the soles of his feet (Job 2:7); his regrets, from the Anglican Confession, concern what he has not said and what he has done ill (63). This, Beckett's first great monologue, is the harbinger of the Unnamable and Lucky, in whom the scapegoat's agonies find further expression.

6. ANTHROPOMORPHIC INSOLENCE

Mr Knott's various incarnations in the manuscripts leave traces in the final text. That 'on Sunday he did not rise at all' (*W*, 72) is less Genesis 2:2, God resting after the creation, than the setting of a sun god. He enters the garden at the end of Part II, coming and going amidst the hardy laurels, allowing Watt to catch a glimpse, 'as it were in a glass', as in an eastern window at morning, and a western window at evening. Watt once saw his master (*W*, 125) 'face to face' (1 Corinthians 13:12: 'For now we see through a glass, darkly; but then face to face'); but more typically at a distance and fugitively, or sideways on, or 'even from behind': compare Exodus 33:23, where the Lord puts Moses into a rocky clift, saying, 'thou shalt see my back parts: but my face shall not be seen'. Anthropomorphic identification persists into 'nightly displacements' of 'almost one minute' whereby Mr Knott in his circular bed annually rotates almost completely ('almost' reflecting the incommensurability between 360 degrees and 365 days) (*W*, 179).[22] Although Beckett's fascination with biblical arcana endured, some oddities did not find overt expression. In the *Sottisier Notebook*, of the late 1970s, he recorded (almost with disbelief) from *La Sainte Bible* Jehovah's reproof (Deuteronomy 10:16) of the uppity Children of Israel: 'Circoncisez donc le prépuce de votre coeur'. In the King James this becomes: 'Circumcise therefore the foreskin of your heart, and be no more stiffnecked'.[23] Like the back parts of the Lord, with which it should not be associated, this loses little in translation, but may be seen as indicative of Beckett's later iconography, the Image partially freed from the chains of language.

7. BIBLICAL TITLES

An epigraph is a frame, a window on its world. Beckett, like a good monad, uses few, Leopardi's 'E fango è il mondo' ('The world is mud'), to *Proust* (1931), an exception, though the 1965 Calder reprint deleted that.[24] Titles are epigraphs, but of Beckett's early works only *More Pricks than Kicks* (1934) is biblical, Saul's 'road to Damascus' experience (Acts 9:5, 26:14). The next was *First Love*, Revelation 2:4: 'Nevertheless I am somewhat against thee, because thou hast left thy first love'; an allusion not present in the French, in *Premier amour*, for *La Sainte Bible* reads 'première charité'. Other titles intimate religious themes: 'The Expelled' (2 Samuel 14:14, but also Eden); 'The End' (Lamentations 4:18, 'our end is near'); *The Unnamable* (the apophatic sense of God as beyond utterance); and *Godot*, that miscegenation of an English deity and a French diminutive. *All That Fall* is the first drama with an explicit biblical title (one that works in French): Psalms 145:14, 'The Lord upholdeth all that fall and raiseth up all those that be bowed down'. This elicits wild laughter, but the fall of sparrows (Matthew 10:31) and of 'a little child' (Luke 18:16) sustain a minor chord of pity, the only ethical value that Beckett (following Schopenhauer) allowed in a fallen world. Other works follow: 'Come and Go': Psalms 121:8, 'The Lord shall preserve thy going out and thy coming in'; 'Enough': 1 Kings 19:4, 'It is enough now, O Lord, take away my life'; *Company*: Psalms 55:14, 'We took sweet counsel together, and walked unto the house of God in company'; and 'All Strange Away': Genesis 35:2, 'Put away the strange gods that are among you'. 'Not I' (1972) dramatises a motif that Beckett had made his own, 'I in the accusative' in *Texts for Nothing* on trial as both subject and object (*not I, not me*). It echoes 1 Corinthians 15:10, the authority by which Paul speaks: 'yet not I, but the grace of God which was with me'. A major theme, both aesthetic and religious, of Beckett's middle period is the Voice and the authority contingent on its location (within or without). Further consideration is warranted.

8. I, OF WHOM I KNOW NOTHING

The title of *L'Innommable/The Unnamable* intimates the true saying that God is beyond the nameable; that His mystery is ineffable and His name is death; that He is the ultimate aporia. *The Unnamable* is more deeply saturated in biblical allusion than any other Beckett text, both in specific echoes of chapter and verse and in general references to words like 'wilderness' and 'witness'; more so in English than in the French original. As Beckett rewrote it he cultivated, either as conscious rhetoric or because in his native language biblical cadences came more naturally, a mode of expression bearing constant witness to the Bible as an implied authority. The opening paragraph invites exegesis of the 'not I'; the narrative voice tries to 'speak of things of which I cannot speak', as John 14:10: 'the words that I speak unto you I speak not of myself; but the Father that dwelleth in me, he doeth the works'. He is 'obliged to speak', as in Job 7:11: 'Therefore I will not refrain my mouth; I will speak in the anguish of my spirit; I will complain in the bitterness of my soul'. These injunctions align his predicament with a biblical tradition that is a composite of Job and Jeremiah, John and Paul, where the need to 'utter' in the anguish of the spirit combines with the sense of 'being spoken' by a voice whose authority lies beyond the self, whatever that self might be. The Unnamable's problem is to define and locate the voice, which is either *within*, and thus potentially schizophrenic, or *without*, and so embodying (if that is the metaphor) a transcendent authority. These allusions are equally explicit in the French original, which suggests that Beckett tried to define from the outset a sense of the Unnamable's voice in terms of the mysterious authority by which it speaks. However, in the manuscript the opening questions, 'Où maintenant? Quand maintenant? Qui maintenant?', are absent.[25] Likewise, 'Moi, dont je ne sais rien', the 'I, of whom I know nothing', a key text for the entire novel, is not in the manuscript, which suggests that only in retrospect did Beckett insert it, as the 'thesis statement' of a paragraph of some nine thousand words. Beckett may have found his theme only in the act of writing, but once it was found (as defined by biblical authority) he proceeded quickly and without substantial revision.

9. ONE OF THE THIEVES WAS SAVED

Although *En attendant Godot* was written as an interlude between *Malone meurt* and *L'Innommable*, it ignores the trilogy's great theme, the Voice. Beckett, as so often when writing for new media, reverted to familiar themes, such as the two thieves, the repentant one (Dysmas) saved, the other (Gestas) damned. Beckett recorded in the Whoroscope Notebook: 'Never despair (1 thief saved) / nor presume (only 1 saved)', the shape of that idea less Augustine than Robert Greene.[26] Neary remembers 'also one thief was saved' (*M*, 132); Malone considers this 'a generous percentage' (*MD*, 83). Christ tells the repentant thief, 'Verily I say unto thee, To day shalt thou be with me in paradise' (Luke 23:43); Vladimir worries that only one evangelist speaks of his being saved, though all four were there, or 'thereabouts' (*CDW*, 14).[27] He is wrong to say that 'two don't mention any thieves at all', for Matthew 27:28ff tells of two thieves crucified, and how they mocked Christ; Mark 15:27–8 mentions them, saying that the scripture is fulfilled, Christ numbered among the transgressors; while John says they crucified Christ, 'and two other with him' (19:18). Even so, a *reductio* of rationality takes 'an even chance' to 12.5 per cent, and this without calculating 'thereabouts'. Beckett discussed with Tom Driver 'the dramatic qualities of this theology', saying that if there were only darkness all would be clear, but because there is light it becomes inexplicable.[28] Hence his favoured stage iconography as director, with patterns of light and dark reflected in the shadows cast by images of Pozzo between the two tramps, and settings reflecting his fascination with paintings of the Crucifixion and Descent from the Cross; but which downplayed comic absurdity such as Estragon's foot 'swelling visibly' to suggest the 'mound' as Golgotha: 'Ah, yes, the two thieves' (*CDW*, 14). Production history thus reflects the wider aesthetic transition from the baroque to the thematic.

10. EVERYTHING HAS AN END...

Save, in 'Avant *Fin de partie*', progenitor of *Endgame*, the sausage, which has two.[29] Every ending implies a new beginning: Hamm's opening gambit, 'Finished, it's nearly finished', echoing Christ's last words from the cross (John 19:30), begins each new theatrical enactment of a world running down but which is poised against the biblical covenant of the life to come (Clov's was always that). The story of Noah (Genesis 6–10) is a crucial element. Ham, second son of Noah, is cursed by his father (Genesis 9:25); and Hamm, son of Nagg (Luke 3:25, the genealogy of Christ), returns that curse. Ham's biblical destiny is to build the Ark (Genesis 6:14), and hence Hamm imagines making a raft, to be carried away to other (he hesitates) mammals; Clov's 'God forbid' extinguishes that faint flicker (*CDW*, 109). Extinction of the flea, the dog, the rat (half) and the small boy ensures that humanity will not start all over again, as after Noah's flood. Beckett in

Murphy had used Proverbs 30:15 and the horse leech's daughter to inscribe a closed system in which the 'quantum of wantum' cannot vary (*M*, 38); the universe of *Endgame* has moved from that principle of equilibrium towards a post-nuclear winter, running down to an unimaginable zero as the irreversible laws of thermodynamics insist: 'Something is taking its course' (*CDW*, 98,107). Clov comments: 'I love order. It's my dream. A world where all would be silent' (*CDW*, 120). What can resist this vision? What is there to keep us here? Hamm gives the only conceivable answer: 'the dialogue' (*CDW*, 121).

II. TEASERS

A recent visitor to New Zealand who lost her crucifix wrote to a local newspaper of her attempt to replace it. The sweet young thing behind the counter thought, yes, they had some crosses, and returned with a selection: 'Look,' she said, 'some of them even have a little man on them'. In the light of this, consider the following:

(i) Genesis 38:1–10: Why should Belacqua Shuah in 'What a Misfortune' wish to marry 'at the Church of Saint Tamar' (*MPTK*, 115)?
(ii) Acts 9:5: *More Pricks than Kicks* was not Beckett's chosen title, but *Draff* was deemed too obscure. The biblical echo disappears in the posthumous translation to *Bande et sarabande* (1994), of which Beckett approved since 'Bande' (Fr. *bander*, to have an erection) retained musicality (prick-song, sarabande) without loss of obscenity (compare *La dernière Bande*). 'Draff' is from Thomas à Kempis, *The Imitation of Christ* (III.xv), of the Prodigal Son and fallen Angels.[30] Which now of these three, thinkest thou, is the best title?
(iii) 2 Corinthians 9:15: 'Thanks be to God for his unspeakable gift'. Watt's world gradually becomes 'unspeakable' (*Watt*, 71). Write a dissertation on this paradox.
(iv) Proverbs 13:12: 'Hope deferred maketh the heart sick; but when the desire cometh, it is a tree of life'. Not in *En attendant Godot*, but crucial (no pun intended) to the English text (*CDW*, 11). Do French readers have an even chance?
(v) Job 3:3: 'Let the day perish wherein I was born, and the night in which it is said, There is a man child conceived'. Compare 'Serena I', and, noting Mr Tyler's flat tyre, consider if his curse against the wet Saturday afternoon of his conception implies a perished condom (*CDW*, 175).

The Bible

(vi) Job 7:21: 'For now shall I sleep in the dust'. Moran's grey hen sits in the dust from morn to night, 'Like Job, haha' (*Mo*, 105). The Unnamable's next 'vice-exister' will be a billy in a bowl, his arse in the dust (*U*, 26). Explain this echo.

(vii) Proverbs 26:11: 'As a dog returneth to its vomit, so a fool returneth to his folly'. In *That Time*, an old man returns to Dublin, seeking Foley's Folly, where he had hidden as a child. Krapp sees the various fools that once he was, but not the fool that he is. Use the biblical echo (*P*, 19) to critique such folly.

(viii) 1 Kings 18:44: 'There ariseth a little cloud'. Malone, raising his eyes as the Psalmist advises, sees no hope (*MD*, 15); Vladimir sees nothing wonderful (*CDW*, 78). What is the covenant of the little cloud?

(ix) Luke 12:20: 'Thou fool, this night thy soul shall be required of thee'. Consider 'the passion of Our Joe', and whether the capitalised 'Our' (which Beckett wanted, but did not get in 'Eh Joe') is warranted.

(x) Ecclesiastes 1:2: 'All is vanity'. Hamm comments: 'Perhaps it is a little vein' (*CDW*, 101). How is this pun handled in the French and German translations?

(xi) Psalms 103:15–16, and Isaiah 40:16: 'flower of the field', echoed in *Watt* (116), *Endgame* (*CDW*, 112), *How It Is* (*H*, 67),'Enough' (*CSP*, 188), and 'From an Abandoned Work' (*CSP*, 155). Which biblical verse is Beckett's preferred source?

(xii) Matthew 16:18: 'Thou art Peter, and upon this rock I will build my church'. Name *four* Beckett characters who in some sense 'peter out in the stones'.

(xiii) Isaiah 7:16: 'For before the child shall know to refuse the evil, and choose the good, the land that thou abhorest shall be forsaken of both her kings'. Beckett noted on the manuscript of 'For to end yet again' a reference to 'Isa.vii.16'.[31] Without this prompt, is the biblical reference detectable? With it, is anything clarified?

12. ICONOGRAPHY

Biblical echoes become fewer and fainter in Beckett's later works, as memory replaces allusion and religious sentiments fade to dust. Yet, even in the last attenuated texts, they leave a trace. *Ill Seen Ill Said* (1981) depicts an old woman in an empty lot; images arise with difficulty, their meaning obscure; the narrative eye witnesses her life even as it (both eye and life) is reduced to silence. This enigmatic text is secular in its obvious intent, yet full of details demanding exegesis: the field as 'the inexistent centre of a formless place', both the Potter's Field (Matthew 27:8) and God as a sphere whose centre is everywhere and circumference nowhere; words like 'stray' intimating *lost sheep*, not quite shorn of their biblical intent; phrases such as 'as they list' (John 3:8), 'going out or coming in' (Psalm 121:8), 'darkly' (1 Corinthians 13:12), 'eye of flesh' (Job 10:4); stones like whited sepulchres (Matthew 23:27); suggestions of Golgotha; the earth faintly quaking, as at the crucifixion (Matthew 27:51); and a silver buttonhook, 'pisciform' and hung like a crucifix (*NO*, 57), not unlike the silver knife-rest of *Molloy* and *Malone Dies* which intimates a Christ between two thieves. Listed thus, their religious import is overwhelming; in the text, their presence is more subtle and less insistent. But even in Beckett's later, ostensibly barren and desolate works, biblical authority remains a point of reference, not a salvation from despair but nonetheless *there*.

13. FOR DUST THOU ART

Beckett's most insistent biblical sentiment draws on Genesis 3:19: 'for dust thou art, and unto dust shalt thou return', to which he returns (a fool to his folly) throughout his entire oeuvre. One compelling evocation is Fizzle 8, 'For to end yet again', the eschatology of a world turned to dust, in which, surrealistically, two white dwarfs appear (like dying stars), disturbing the obscurity before leaving a world of stillness and silence, as the dust settles again. Yet, for one brief moment, it was disturbed, a trace was made, as brief witness to what once was. Beckett's last work, 'What is the Word?', reflects similar desolation, the struggle to express, to leave a trace. According to John 1:1, in the beginning was the Word; according to Beckett (*M*, 43), in the beginning was the pun, as better accommodating the chaos; in the end, as the dust falls back into place, the mystery remains.

NOTES

1 Tom Driver, 'Beckett by the Madeleine', in C. J. Ackerley and S. E. Gontarski, *The Grove Companion to Samuel Beckett: A Reader's Guide to His Works, Life, and Thought* (New York: Grove Press, 2004), 479.
2 James Joyce, *A Portrait of the Artist as a Young Man* (Harmondsworth: Penguin, 1964), 47.
3 All references to the Bible, unless otherwise specified, are to the King James Authorised Version. See Milton, *Paradise Regained* (II.269), horny-beaked ravens: 'Though ravenous, taught t'abstain from what they brought'. The etymology is fanciful.

The Bible

4 Ackerley and Gontarski, *The Grove Companion to Samuel Beckett*, 479.
5 The photograph, taken by a neighbour, appears in *B*, opposite 114.
6 Ackerley and Gontarski, *The Grove Companion to Samuel Beckett*, 52.
7 Colin Duckworth, *Angels of Darkness* (London: George Allen, 1972), 18.
8 My 'Samuel Beckett and the Bible' (1999) lists, text by text, and by chapter and verse, Beckett's biblical allusions; I have drawn on these tablets extensively, though the listings are incomplete and little is made of their thematic implications. See C. J. Ackerley, 'Samuel Beckett and the Bible', *Journal of Beckett Studies* (9.1: 1999), 53–125.
9 'From the Only Poet to a Shining Whore', first published by the Hours Press (1930), then in Lawrence Harvey, *Samuel Beckett, Poet and Critic* (Princeton: Princeton University Press, 1970), 306–7.
10 Ibid., 305.
11 H. A. Giles, *The Civilization of China* (London: Williams and Norgate, 1911), 85–7.
12 Harvey, *Samuel Beckett, Poet and Critic*, 303–4.
13 Ibid., 273.
14 'To My Daughter' is in the Leventhal papers (1.i) at the Harry Ransom Humanities Center, University of Texas at Austin. I discuss the poem in C. J. Ackerley, 'Lassata Sed: Samuel Beckett's Portraits of his Fair to middling Women', *Samuel Beckett Today/Aujourd'hui: Pastiches, Parodies & Other Imitations/Pastiches, parodies & autres imitations* (12: 2002), 68–9.
15 Harvey, *Samuel Beckett, Poet and Critic*, 288–96.
16 Job 40:16–17: '[H]is force is in the navel of his belly. He moveth his tale like a cedar....'
17 Job 41:17: 'By his neezings [sneezings] a light doth shine....'
18 Job 41:125–26: 'His scales are his pride, shut up together as with a close seal. / One is so near to another, that no air can come between them'.
19 Ackerley and Gontarski, *The Grove Companion to Samuel Beckett*, 477.
20 William James, *The Varieties of Religious Experience* (New York: New American Library, 1958), 304.
21 For a detailed commentary, see C. J. Ackerley, *Obscure Locks, Simple Keys: The Annotated* Watt (Edinburgh: University of Edinburgh Press, 2010), 57–86.
22 The confusion of 'minute' and 'degree' was not corrected until the French translation of *Watt* (1969; though the Minuit edition says '1968'). Matters cited here are discussed in Ackerley, *Obscure Locks*.
23 Ackerley and Gontarski, *The Grove Companion to Samuel Beckett*, 51.
24 'Les Deux besoins' (1938), 'La Peinture des van Velde' (1946) and *Three Dialogues* (1949) are other exceptions, but like *Proust* these are essays; the stricture holds for other genres.
25 I discuss these matters in Ackerley, 'Unnamable's First Voice', *Journal of Beckett Studies* (2: 1993), 53–8.
26 Ackerley and Gontarski, *The Grove Companion to Samuel Beckett*, 593.
27 Compare 'There's an even chance. Or nearly' (*CDW*, 19).
28 Ackerley and Gontarski, *The Grove Companion to Samuel Beckett*, 393–4.

29 Ibid., 34.
30 Similar titles include 'Human Wishes', combining Samuel Johnson with Ecclesiastes; and 'Fancy Dying', echoing Jeremy Taylor's *Holy Dying*. See Ackerley and Gontarski, *The Grove Companion to Samuel Beckett*, 149, 266, 557.
31 Mary Bryden, *Samuel Beckett and Religion* (Basingstoke: Macmillan, 1998), 105–6; the BIF (University of Reading) archival reference is UoR MS 1552, 2.

CHAPTER 29

The Occult

Minako Okamuro

I

Occultism in Beckett's work is nearly invisible, its presence neither overt nor obvious, and this explains its neglect in Beckett studies. The invisibility, however, does not imply an indifference towards the occult. Occultism is fundamentally not disclosed, as the very word 'occult' derives from the classical Latin 'occultus', which means 'secret, hidden from the understanding, hidden, concealed'.[1] Imagery and symbolism, therefore, have played the most significant role in transmitting occult thought, and in particular, alchemical or Hermetic philosophy. In this chapter, I will focus on exposing the rich lode of hidden alchemical allusions in Beckett's works and exploring the occult dimension of the world to which they afford access.

Alchemy is popularly regarded as a pseudoscience devoted to the transmuting of base metals into gold or silver. Yet this conception encompasses only one aspect of the alchemical tradition. More generally, alchemy concerns the transformation of materials from cruder, less refined states into more perfect, purified forms in a circular movement that alchemists reproduced in their vessels. The microcosm of the alchemist's vessel that contains such materials corresponds to the macrocosm of God's creation. The alchemist is the creator in the microcosm, pursuing the transmutational process of the Great Work (the Magnum Opus), which has a spiritual as well as a material dimension. Prominent nineteenth-century occult revivalist Éliphas Lévi (the pseudonym of Alphonse-Louis Constant), whose influence extended to Surrealism in the twentieth century, defines the Great Work as 'the creation of man by himself, that is to say, the full and entire conquest of his faculties and his future, especially the perfect emancipation of his will'.[2]

Between World War I and World War II in Paris, the Surrealists pursued a fascination with esoteric traditions such as alchemy, Gnosticism and Tantra, premodern thought systems that served as a source of artistic inspiration. In his second Surrealist manifesto, published in 1930, André Breton wrote, 'I would appreciate your noting the remarkable analogy, insofar as their goals are concerned, between the surrealist efforts and those of the alchemists'.[3]

In 1928, Beckett moved to Paris, taking up the post of lecturer in the École Normale Supérieure, where he was introduced to James Joyce, whose 'Work in Progress' was being published serially in the journal *transition*. Beckett soon started to write for the journal, in which many of the writings and manifestoes of the Surrealists appeared. Although Beckett maintained a distance from the Surrealists because of their coolness towards Joyce's 'revolution of the word', he participated in the ferment of experiment and innovation that surrounded Surrealism (*K*, 107). The young Beckett would naturally have encountered the contemporary interest in occult sciences such as alchemy and astrology in the milieu.

It is noteworthy that Beckett seems to have drawn upon the central idea of alchemy in his first published work, the essay 'Dante...Bruno. Vico..Joyce' included in *Our Exagmination Round his Factification for Incamination of Work in Progress* (1929); a collection of articles to support Joyce's 'Work in Progress', later entitled *Finnegans Wake*. In 'Dante... Bruno.Vico..Joyce', Beckett refers to the Hermetic thought of Giordano Bruno, a Renaissance philosopher, mathematician and astronomer:

> The maxima and minima of particular contraries are one and indifferent. Minimal heat equals minimal cold. Consequently transmutations are circular. The principle (minimum) of one contrary takes its movement from the principle (maximum) of another. Therefore not only do the minima coincide with the minima, the maxima with the maxima, but the minima with the maxima in the succession of transmutations. Maximal speed is a state of rest. The maximum of corruption and minimum of generation are identical: in principle, corruption is generation. (*D*, 21)

Although Beckett makes no explicit reference to alchemy in this passage, alchemical implications may be discerned in his discussion of 'transmutations' as 'circular', in that the process of distillation and sublimation takes a circular form in alchemy. Moreover, Beckett refers to the idea represented in the passage as 'Giordano Bruno's treatment of identified contraries' (*D*, 20). 'Identified contraries', or the union of opposites, is the key concept of alchemy.

Beckett learned from Bruno to see two things as contrary to each other not in a split state but in as 'one and indifferent'. As an astronomer, Bruno not only accepted Copernican heliocentricity but more radically proposed the infinity of the universe. For Bruno, the infinitely extended universe was nonetheless One. Specifically, he embraced the Hermetic idea of the unity of the All in the One, which originated from the 'miracles of the One Thing' inscribed on an emerald tablet in Phoenician characters and attributed to Hermes Trismegistus, or the Egyptian Thoth. The document reads:

> That which is Below corresponds to that which is Above,
> and that which is Above corresponds to that which is Below,
> to accomplish the miracles of the One Thing.
> And just as all things have come from this One Thing,
> through the meditation of One Mind,
> so do all created things originate from this One Thing
> through Transformation.[4]

For Beckett, the ideas of the identification of contraries and the 'miracles of the One Thing' were the key to transcending Cartesian dualism. He therefore embedded them in works ranging from his early poems and prose writings to his later teleplays.

II

Beckett's early works allude to alchemy rather explicitly. Beckett's poem 'For Future Reference', written in 1929 and published in *transition* 19–20 (1930), begins as follows:

> My cherished chemist friend
> lured me aloofly
> down from the cornice[5]
> into the basement
> and there:
> drew bottles of acid and alkali out of his breast
> to a colourscale accompaniment
> (mad dumbells spare me!)
> fiddling deft and expert
> with the doubled jointed nutcrackers of hen's ovaries.[6]

The poem may seem enigmatic. By placing the mysterious 'nutcrackers of hen's ovaries' in an alchemical context, however, it becomes apparent that the 'chemist' handling them represents an 'alchemist', a meaning that the word 'chemist' conveyed from the sixteenth century to the eighteenth century. Hens and eggs are among the most important symbols in alchemy, as the hermetically sealed vessel used in the process of alchemy is called the 'philosopher's egg'. The vessel is placed in the athanor, the furnace of the philosopher, and maintained at a constant temperature, much as an egg is warmed in the nest by a hen sitting on it.[7] The reconciliation of opposites that occurs in the philosopher's egg is the essence of alchemy.

The poem presents the chemist as an ambivalent figure. The narrator calls him 'my cherished friend', but is smitten, smashed and crushed by him. Then, the scene abruptly shifts from the basement to a rocky swimming spot where the narrator seems to be learning and practicing the high dive. Notably, the narrator associates diving with 'Bruno's identification of contraries':

> over the stream and the tall green bank
> in a strong shallow arch
> and his face all twisted calm and patient
> and the board ledge doing its best to illustrate
> Bruno's identification of contraries
> into the water or on to the stones?[8]

The high dive in a rocky spot is an ambivalent act, at once attractive but dangerous; the possibility of death makes the dive thrilling. Yet it is not only in relation to this ambivalence that the diving board does 'its best to illustrate Bruno's identification of contraries'. The act of diving from the high board into the water below represents the conjunction of higher and lower realms, which echoes the miracles of the One Thing.[9] Fifty years after he wrote 'For Future Reference', Beckett again referred to diving in *Company* (1980): 'You stand at the tip of the high board. High above the sea. In it your father's upturned face. Upturned to you. You look down to the loved trusted face. He calls to you to jump. He calls, Be a brave boy' (*NO*, 12). This passage reflects Beckett's love for and fear of his father, which transfer to the ambivalent feelings of the narrator of the poem for the 'chemist friend'. Hence, for Beckett, the act of diving symbolises a longing for an alchemical reconciliation of contradictory feelings.

The 'miracles of the One Thing' is further developed into a poem in *Dream of Fair to Middling Women* (written in 1932, published in 1992).[10] In the novel, the phrase 'one with the birdless cloudless colourless skies' which appeared in 'Assumption' is developed in the following poem created by Belacqua:

> At last I find in my confused soul,
> Dark with the dark flame of the cypresses,
> The certitude that I cannot be whole,
> Consummate, finally achieved, unless

> I be consumed and fused in the white heat
> Of her sad finite essence, so that none
> Shall sever us who are at last complete
> Eternally, irrevocably one,
>
> One with the birdless, cloudless, colourless skies,
> One with the bright purity of the fire
> Of which we are and for which we must die
> A rapturous strange death and be entire,
>
> Like syzygetic stars, supremely bright,
> Conjoined in the One and in the Infinite! (*Dream*, 70)

In this poem, the narrator (Belacqua), who holds darkness in his 'confused soul', becomes 'one with the bright purity of the fire' through his fusion in the 'white heat' of his beloved's (Smeraldina-Rima's) 'essence' and 'a rapturous strange death'. This process corresponds to the three stages of transmutation in alchemy; *nigredo*, *albedo* and *rubedo*, which occur in the athanor, the furnace in which the Great Work is carried out, heated by the secret fire. In the initial stage, called *nigredo*, or the blackening, the body of the impure metal is killed. This death is followed by a long process of decay, which lasts until all is putrefied and dissolved into a 'dark' liquid. The next stage, *albedo*, or the whitening, occurs after the blackened matter is washed to whiteness by the mercurial waters of fire. The final stage, *rubedo*, or the reddening of the white matter of the Stone, represents its union with the spirit. In this union, the supreme chemical wedding of the male sulphur and the female mercury in the heat of the fire, the body is resurrected into eternal life.[11] Similarly, Belacqua is conjoined with Smeraldina-Rima 'in the One and in the Infinite' that seems to bear the connotations of 'miracles of the One Thing'.[12] The narrator of the novel describes their reunion as 'the vilest and basest excesses of sublimation of a certain kind', and their 'mystical adhesion' in ecstasy and agony is called 'a sentimental coagulum'; the terms 'sublimation' and 'coagulum' are often used in alchemical contexts (*Dream*, 69–70).

Belacqua thinks that Smeraldina-Rima has the magical power to work a 'miracle' on him, although it is a miracle that is 'on tap in the nearest red-lamp'. With his use of words such as 'miracle' and 'magic' in comical and sexual contexts, Beckett seems to be making fun of Belacqua, who desires physical union with Smeraldina-Rima.

In the novel a hen appears to which Belacqua compares Smeraldina-Rima (*Dream*, 35). In view of this, the following comment by Belacqua merits consideration: 'There is a long poem waiting to be written about hens and eggs. There is a great subject there, waiting to be written' (*Dream*, 192). By the time he wrote *Dream of Fair to Middling Women*, Beckett had already written a long poem employing the 'hens and eggs' motif: *Whoroscope* written and published in 1930. In the poem, the 'hens and eggs' motif no longer plays a secondary role.

Whoroscope mockingly portrays Descartes as he is waiting for an egg to develop. Beckett's own notes explain that 'Descartes [...] liked his omelette made of eggs hatched from eight to ten days; shorter or longer under the hen and the result, he says, is disgusting' (*CP*, 5). Beyond this biographical explanation, however, an additional meaning of the egg can be discerned. Descartes' care for the hatching of the egg – the philosopher's egg in the literal meaning – resembles that of an alchemist attending the transmutation that occurs in the philosopher's egg. In Beckett's ironic treatment, Descartes, who developed a dualistic system of mind and matter, becomes an alchemist who is to reconcile the separated. A sense emerges of Beckett's vision of the great philosopher as persiflage.

The philosopher's egg is often represented as spherical. In *Murphy*, Beckett further developed the motif of the egg in the large hollow sphere of Murphy's mind, which is itself made up of 'above and beneath' (*M*, 70), and is also 'hermetically closed to the universe without' (*M*, 69). The phrase 'hermetically closed' is not simply an idiom here, because in alchemy the philosopher's egg is usually closed with a Hermetic seal. The egg-sphere image eventually becomes the big talking ball in *The Unnamable*, which calls itself an 'egg'.

As I have shown, early Beckett works such as 'For Future Reference', *Dream of Fair to Middling Women* and *Whoroscope*, written at the peak of the wave of Modernist occultism around 1930, are informed by such central alchemical notions as the chemical wedding, the conjunction of opposites, the miracles of the One thing and the philosopher's egg. From his beginnings as a writer, Beckett registered the suffering accruing to the dualities of existence as a differentiated self, the experiences of love and fear, light and dark, consciousness and the unconscious, body and mind, physical and platonic love and life and death. To transcend dualism, which reason could not surmount, the young Beckett turned to the alchemical reconciliation of contraries. Beckett's feelings towards alchemy were ambivalent in his youth, entailing interest and suspicion, hope and despair, sympathy and antipathy. Nonetheless, 'Bruno's identification of contraries' would emerge as a fundamental principle of Beckett's world throughout his life.

III

In Beckett's later works, the idea of the identification of contraries developed into the concept of the 'wombtomb'. *Texts for Nothing* (*Textes pour rien*, 1955) offers a clear framing of the notion: 'Yes, I'd have a mother, I'd have a tomb, I wouldn't have come out of here, one doesn't come out of here, here are my tomb and mother, it's all here this evening, I'm dead and getting born, without having ended, helpless to begin, that's my life' (*CSP*, 137–8). Vladimir articulates a similar viewpoint in *Waiting for Godot* (*En attendant Godot*, 1952): 'Astride of a grave and a difficult birth. Down in the hole, lingeringly, the grave-digger puts on the forceps' (*CDW*, 84). The protagonist of *A Piece of Monologue* (1981) succinctly conjoins birth and death in asserting, 'Birth was the death of him' (*CDW*, 425). In *Worstward Ho* (1983), the narrator says, 'The whole narrow void. No blurs. All clear. Dim clear. Black hole agape on all. Inletting all. Outletting all' (*NO*, 114). This description is closely analogous to the wombtomb as an ambivalent hole that gives birth and engulfs life.

The identification of contraries may also inform the development of wheel imagery in Beckett's works. In *Texts for Nothing*, the narrator conceives of his memory as a turning wheel: 'What thronging memories, that's to make me think I'm dead, I've said it a million times. But the same return, like the spokes of a turning wheel, always the same, and all alike, like spokes (*CSP*, 128). This echoes the memory wheel in Joyce's *Finnegans Wake* (1939): 'Now by memory inspired, turn wheel again to the whole of the wall'.[13] Interesting, Joyce regarded *Finnegans Wake* itself as 'an engine with one wheel', oddly, a wheel that is square. In a letter to Harriet Shaw Weaver dated 16 April 1927, he wrote: 'I am making an engine with only one wheel. No spokes of course. The wheel is a perfect square. You see what I am driving at, don't you? I am awfully solemn about it, mind you, so you must not think it is a silly story about the mouse and the grapes. No, it's a wheel, I tell the world. *And* it's all *square*'[14] (emphasis in the original). Here Joyce apparently alludes to the idea of the quadrature, or squaring, of the circle. In alchemy, the transformation of the square into a circle symbolises the transformation of the four elements into the alchemical quintessence or fifth element.

Beckett's *Quad* (1981), a mime for television written in 1980,[15] represents that symbolism most remarkably. In the teleplay, four players repeat geometrical movements on a square divided by two diagonals into four triangles. The players emerge one by one in sequence to pace counter-clockwise along the sides and diagonals, avoiding the centre. When all of the players are avoiding it at the same time, they seem to form a circle around something invisible at the centre. The pattern the players trace suggests a 'mandala', a form that usually consists of a combination of squares and circles, and sometimes triangles.[16] In particular, *Quad* bears a close resemblance to one of the 'mandala dreams' that Jung analyses from an alchemical viewpoint in *Psychology and Alchemy*.[17]

The narrative of the sixteenth mandala dream of Jung's patient reads, 'Many people are present. They are all walking to the left around a square. The dreamer is not in the centre but to one side'.[18] In this dream, people walk counter-clockwise around a square. Jung assumes that the square arises from a circle that appeared in the patient's previous dream, and interprets the dream from an alchemical point of view by applying the idea of the quadrature, or squaring, of the circle. The synthesis of four into one is one of the main preoccupations of alchemy.[19] The squaring of the circle is the way from chaos to unity, the method by which the four elements represented by the sides of the square can reach a higher unity in circular form. *A Dictionary of Alchemical Imagery* reads:

During this circulation, the elements earth, air, fire and water are separated by distillation and converted into each other to form the perfect unity, the fifth element. This conversion takes place by unifying the qualities that each element has in common: earth which is cold and dry may be united with water through the common quality of coldness since water is cold and moist (or fluid), water may be united with air through heat, since fire is hot and dry. In another alchemical metaphor, this process is described as the transformation of the square (four elements) into the circle (the united fifth element).

This process of transformation, of successively converting the elements into each other, is often compared to the turning of a great wheel.[20]

Through the gyratory movement of four players on a square of *Quad* indeed constitutes an iconographic image of a turning wheel, or more precisely, a turning square wheel.[21]

In his explanation of the dream, Jung states that 'The left, the sinister side, is the unconscious side. Therefore a leftward movement is equivalent to a movement in the direction of the unconscious, whereas a movement to the right is "correct" and aims at consciousness',[22] and so, 'Presumably the leftward circumambulation of the square indicates that the squaring of the circle is a stage on the way to the unconscious, a point of transition leading to a goal lying as yet unformulated beyond it. It is one of those paths to the centre of the non-ego which were also trodden by the medieval investigators when producing the lapis'.[23]

In *Quad*, the players may be pointing in the direction of the unconscious, like the walkers in the dream, to unite the opposites: consciousness and the unconscious, and body and mind. Surmounting Cartesian dualism was Beckett's lifelong desire; why, then, do the players avoid the centre? Jung interprets the mandala symbols in a series of the patient's dreams as archetypal images that depict a centralising process, the production of a new centre of personality. He calls this process 'individuation' and this centre the 'self', emphasising that the individual is not only the centre but also the whole circumference, embracing both consciousness and the unconscious. As the centre of this totality, the self is different from the ego, which is only the centre of consciousness. Since the square expresses in particular the complete symmetry of consciousness and the unconscious, its centre represents the unity of the self. This centre is, however, unrecognisable. Jung writes, 'Often one has the impression that the personal psyche is running round this central point like a shy animal, at once fascinated, always in flight, and yet steadily drawing nearer'; yet he adds, 'I trust I have given no cause for the misunderstanding that I know anything about the nature of the "centre" – for it is simply unknowable and can only be expressed symbolically through its own phenomenology, as is the case, incidentally, with every object of experience'.[24] This ambivalence is reflected in the centre represented in *Quad*, at which the players repeatedly aim, only to veer away as they near it.[25]

Hugh Kenner once called a man riding a bicycle in Beckett's works 'the Cartesian Centaur', saying, 'This being rises clear of the muddle in which Descartes leaves the mind-body relationship. The intelligence guides, the mobile wonder obeys, and there is no mysterious interpenetration of function'.[26] Yet many of Beckett's figures have lost their bicycles, as Kenner says, 'If it is never a shiny new substantial bicycle, always a bicycle lost, a bicycle remembered'.[27] Most significant to my argument is Kenner's observation that 'on its two wheels it [a bicycle] performs its essential function',[28] and therefore, it is wheels that enable the existence of the Cartesian Centaur whose body and mind are in harmony in Beckett's world. The Beckett figures who lost their wheels instead describe spirals or circles; Mahood on crutches in *Malone Dies* (*Malone meurt*, 1951) executes a converging spiral, Molloy progresses in spirals in *Molloy* (1951), the surrogate of *The Unnamable* (*L'Innommable*, 1953) describes a spiral on the surface of a sphere and in *Endgame* (*Fin de Partie*, 1957), Clov pushes Hamm's chair with casters around the room, as Hamm says, 'Right round the world!' and 'We'd need a proper wheel-chair. With big wheels. Bicycle-wheels!' (*CDW*, 104).

This longing for wheels in the alchemical context might be understood to represent an unconscious but tireless, since it is never fulfilled, desire for an alchemical transmutation to surmount Cartesian dualism and integrate the split self.

NOTES

1 *Oxford English Dictionary*, Third Edition, March 2004; Online version September 2011.
2 Éliphas Lévi, *Transcendental Magic: Its Doctrine and Ritual*, trans. A. E. Waite (York Beach, ME: Samuel Weiser, 1999), 113.
3 André Breton, *Manifestoes of Surrealism*, trans. Richard Seaver and Helen R. Lane (Ann Arbor: University of Michigan Press, 1972), 175.
4 Dennis William Hauck, *The Emerald Tablet: Alchemy for Personal Transformation* (New York: Penguin, 1999), 51–2.
5 A 'cornice' often appears in alchemical illustrations, sometimes as a feature of Solomon's Temple, said to have been built with the aid of the philosopher's stone.
6 Samuel Beckett, 'For Future Reference', *transition* 19–20 (1930), 342–3. The revised version of the poem is included in *The Collected Poems of Samuel Beckett: A Critical Edition*, Seán Lawlor and John Pilling (eds.) (London: Faber, 2012), 233–4.
7 See Stanislas Klossowski de Rola, *Alchemy: The Secret Art* (London: Thames and Hudson, 1973), 11.
8 Beckett, 'For Future Reference', 343.
9 About Beckett's traumatic dreams of diving lessons, see Lawrence Harvey, *Samuel Beckett: Poet and Critic* (Princeton: Princeton University Press, 1970). About Beckett's antipathy for W. R. Tetley, a science and swimming teacher at Portra Royal School, see *C*.
10 This poem first appeared in 'Sedendo et Quiescendo' (*transition* 21, 1932), which was later included in *Dream of Fair to Middling Women*.
11 This explanation of the three stages is based on the writings of Abraham and Klossowski de Rola.
12 Knowlson points out that the description of Smeraldina-Rima, 'She is, she exists in one and the same way', is based on St Augustine's *Confessions* (*K*, 109).
13 James Joyce, *Finnegans Wake* (London: Faber, 1975), 69.
14 James Joyce, *Letters of James Joyce*, vol. 1, Stuart Gilbert (ed.) (New York: The Viking Press, 1966), 251.
15 On 27 January 1980, Beckett told Ruby Cohn that he had invented a crazy, textless piece for TV. See John Pilling, *A Samuel Beckett Chronology* (London: Palgrave Macmillan, 2006). 210.
16 The term 'mandala' denotes a ritual diagram used in Buddhism and Hinduism, particularly in Tibetan Buddhism and Tantric yoga, as a 'yantra', or aid to contemplation. According to Jung, however, mandalas are found not only in

Eastern traditions, but in cultures around the world, and are among the oldest religious symbols of humanity.
17 Susan D. Brienza observes the mandala-like characteristics of *Quad*. She does not relate the mandala to Jung in this discussion, but refers to Jungian psychology in a subsequent discussion of *Quad*. Although Brienza offers a valuable approach, her argument extends only to the analogy of the pattern traced in *Quad* to mandala drawings in general. About *Quad* and Jung's mandala, see Minako Okamuro, '*Quad* and the Jungian Mandala', *Samuel Beckett Today/Aujourd'hui* 6 (1997), 125–34.
18 C. G. Jung, *Psychology and Alchemy*, trans. R. F. C. Hull (Princeton: Princeton University Press, 1968), 124.
19 See C. G. Jung, *Mysterium Coniunctionis: An Inquiry into the Separation and Synthesis of Psychic Opposites in Alchemy*, trans. R. F. C. Hull (Princeton: Princeton University Press, 1970), 3, 9.
20 Lyndy Abraham, *A Dictionary of Alchemical Imagery* (Cambridge: Cambridge University Press, 1998), 137–8.
21 Regarding the influence of Joyce and W. B. Yeats, see Minako Okamuro, 'Turning a Square Wheel: Yeats, Joyce and Beckett's Quad', in Hiroko Mikami, Minako Okamuro and Naoko Yagi (eds.) *Ireland on Stage: Beckett and After* (Dublin: Carysfort Press, 2007), 87–106.
22 Jung, *Psychology and Alchemy*, 127.
23 Ibid., 127–8.
24 Ibid., 218.
25 This image of 'the turning of a great wheel' also brings to mind the rhythm of the ritual dance in Yeats's 'Rosa Alchemica', which is described as 'the wheel of Eternity'. Furthermore, the 'Great Wheel' is the central idea in Yeats's work of occult philosophy, *A Vision*, in which he presents a figure captioned 'The Great Wheel' that consists of triangles, squares and circles; in effect, the Great Wheel is portrayed as a mandala.
26 Hugh Kenner, *Samuel Beckett: A Critical Study* (London: John Calder, 1961), 121.
27 Ibid., 117.
28 Ibid., 128.

CHAPTER 30

Science and Mathematics

Hugh Culik

The work of Beckett studies often takes scholars through texts littered with fragments of expert knowledge. We stumble across the names of obscure psychologies (the Wurzburg School in *Murphy*), Pythagorean concerns with irrational numbers, an allusion to the seventeenth-century proto-calculus of Craige (*Molloy*), stellar evolution (*How It Is*), a formula for extracting cube roots (*Watt*), performances of specific aphasias (*Godot*), allusions to phrenology (*Mercier and Camier*) and the neurological symptoms of diseases (*Murphy*, *Watt*, *Footfalls* and elsewhere). Recognising the traces of larger scientific systems has been part of Beckett studies since the work of Sighle Kennedy. Her 1971 *Murphy's Bed* initiated studies of not only Beckett's specific astronomical and astrological references, but also the participation of his work in a larger cultural anxiety about the limits of language and the failure of language as a tool for representation. This dual focus has gained momentum for some forty years; a recent manuscript that identifies specialised medical allusions runs forty-nine single-spaced pages, and lists of mathematical allusions can grow to even greater lengths. Recent work on Beckett's interests in these fields and on his knowledge of arcane psychologies and of aphasiology are even more sustained mappings of his familiarity with the history and developmental turning points in the sciences and mathematics.

Whatever the variety of these scholarly investigations, almost all connect the scientific materials to concerns with the limits of representation and the nature of negation. Drawing upon notions of undoing (Gontarski), erasure and mutual exclusion (Iser), the scholarship often addresses the paradoxical ability of language to express the excruciating failure of words. Beckett's tactic is to invoke, erode and then negate the representational aspirations of systematic knowledge, a negation that paradoxically embodies its representational incapacity in words. Allusions to the sciences and mathematics embed the text in the world of socially held knowledge, but they only serve as an opportunity for failure, a failure that itself becomes the next subject of the text. The tactic resembles a recursive formula in mathematics. Such formulae draw a number from a particular 'domain' of numbers, apply the formula to generate a 'range' of answers and then use the output as the next input. The outputs become the inputs, and the procedure begins to form an infinitely large circle of self-reference. Definitions become circular procedures explained in terms of themselves. Similarly, Beckett's texts draw upon the domain of systematic sciences, apply techniques that problematise their consistency and completeness and then subject the result to the same tactic. This recursive process often begins with allusions drawn from the domain of historical moments when the sciences and mathematics recognised that their aspiration to systematic completeness and consistency was failing. Thus, Beckett's works both comment upon and participate in a cultural anxiety about the limits of representation.

In Beckett's works, the traces of systematised knowledge entrap the reader by seeming to promise a path back to a nameable referent, a referent available through some specific mathematical or scientific system. The readers' expectations are raised and then denied, often by invoking pairs of sciences with claims to the same phenomena: philosophy and neurology; neurology and phrenology; mathematics and logic; Wurzburgian psychology and psychoanalysis; astrology and astronomy. The systems compete for the same phenomena, and their contrasts suggest the incompleteness and inconsistency of each other. For example, the Cartesian allusions in *Murphy* focus on the integration of mind and body through the regulatory function of the soul, housed – at least according to Descartes – in the brain's pineal gland. Allusions to dualistic philosophy abound, and the novel seems Cartesian. This neatness of identifications totters when Murphy proves to have all the symptoms of a pineal gland tumour. Thus, the systematic philosophical claims and the medical syndrome compete for the same phenomena and seem to be incommensurable; the two systems – neurology and occasionalist philosophy – are as distinct as mind and body, but without any conceptual integration. Neither can claim completeness because the other engages the phenomenon in different terms. The readers' archaeological work of discovering fragments of expertise, identifying sources and reconstructing origins discovers a gap not only between the two systems but also between the phenomena and language itself. More important is that the contrast and interplay of these two systems of meanings creates a third position occupied by the reader, a position which recapitulates the reading itself as within the contexts of the novel. Occasionally, this aspect of Beckett's tactics suggests a sort of solipsistic logos, but his use of the sciences and mathematics (especially the work of Kurt Gödel) goes beyond solipsism to demonstrate the presence of an extra-linguistic Real.

The text becomes – in part – the readers' work to realise Beckett's traces, a process that problematises the very processes it invokes. The reader plays various interpretive games as signalled by the allusions, finds them negated and returns to the starting point. There, the process of failed representation itself becomes an item in the expanding field of the text's contexts. This changes the readers' relationship to the representational impulse because the systematic disciplines that have been tracked and compared prove independent of each other. They recall the two clocks of Geulincx's neo-occasionalist metaphor that display the same time, toll the same hour, but have no connection; their coincidental parallels are contained within the observer. Throughout Beckett's work, parallel systems negate each other's claims to consistency and completeness. They neither connect to each other nor do they fully map the Real. They are, at most, iterations of the representational impulse, that is, of the drive towards successful language. As each fails, the reader finds that their simultaneous disconnection and reiterative drive paradoxically point towards the unnamable. In a different context (the concept of the zero in mathematics), Brian Rotman notes that the zero emerges in the thirteenth century through 'isomorphic' appearances in mathematics, painting and commerce. The zero becomes 'a sign about signs, a *meta-sign*, whose meaning is to indicate, via a syntax which arrives with it, the absence of certain other signs'.[1] Similarly, in *Murphy*, the readers' changed relationship to the two systems (neurology and philosophy) becomes a larger, complex system that returns to the representational impulse with a new term that will suffer its own failure. As a structural element, it appears in the parallel acts of *Waiting for Godot*, the 'Molloy' and 'Malone' sections of *Molloy*, and elsewhere. The double structure – and indeed the doubling of characters – both serves and reflects the notion of revealing limitations through contrast, and the result is that the text becomes a 'meta-sign' for functions of a non-linguistic Real.

The torturous relationship of failure and function is often literalised. In *More Pricks Than Kicks*, Belacqua's horror at the wedding gift of two clocks recognises both the general problem of the unbridgeable gap between systems and the similar gap between self and other that his impending marriage will not bridge. The two do not become one; rather, like Murphy and Celia, their love for each other is 'a striking case of love requited' (*M*, 12). Images and allusions simultaneously differentiate and integrate as they drive forward by provoking yet another reading that becomes enfolded in the text. As *Watt*'s narrator notes of the sequences that abound in Mr Knott's house, 'Here then was another series' (*W*, 123). Each new explanation is a potential rupture in the aspiration for a closed system of meaning that is both consistent and complete. In *Watt*, the picture in Erskine's room is 'A circle, obviously described by a compass, and broken at its lowest point.... In the eastern background appeared a point, or dot.... How the effect of perspective was obtained, Watt did not know' (*W*, 109). After speculation about the picture's origins, ownership and the artist's intentions, he begins to weep 'at the thought that it was ... a circle and a centre not its centre in search of a centre and its circle respectively, in boundless space, in endless time' (*W*, 110). Issues of perspective, series and relationship erupt as he considers the series of lovers, caretakers and dogs at Mr Knott's house. The house contains both Mr Knott, that is, naught; and the naught/Knott has the binding function of a knot that holds together the discrete items in the various series. Again, the novel is naming the nothing as Democritus had: 'Nothing is more real than nothing', a phrase that appears in both *Murphy* and *Imagination Dead Imagine*. The scientific and mathematical allusions are heuristics; they function to make visible this absence, an absence figured through a place that is Knott/naught/not/knot. Not only are any system's representational claims frustrated, but the reader's continuous displacement problematises the process without denying the existence of a referent. Rotman's history finds that the zero problematises the hope that a 'field of entities' exists prior to 'the meta-sign which both initiates the signifying system and participates within it as a constituent sign'.[2] Beckett's series of counter-poised sciences – like the contexts that produced the zero – find 'the simple picture of an independent reality of objects providing a pre-existing field of referents for signs conceived after them ... cannot be sustained'.[3] Each iteration can precipitate some new complex of signs, but they will not be conclusive. The strategy emphasises the functioning of the text, and in this it proves closely allied to sciences whose development required a similar understanding. Among such sciences are neurology and aphasiology.

Chapter 6 in *Murphy* offers a model of the 'Murphy mind'. Partly parodic, partly serious and intensely recursive, it resonates with the representational anxieties that characterise Beckett's texts. The images prefigure other novels, especially the figures of the drama. The model begins recursively: 'Murphy's mind pictured itself as a large hollow sphere, hermetically closed to the universe without' (*M*, 69). As with the image in *Watt*, the image is a simple closed figure, but this time without an opening. What is outside is understood to only be an exteriorisation of the internal.

It is explicitly an escape from 'the idealist tar' (*M*, 69). A set of binaries and fusions follow that seems to suggest that within the mind is a gradient running from the mental to the memory of physical experience. It concludes 'that his mind was a closed system, subject to no principle of change but its own, self sufficient and impermeable to the vicissitudes of the body' (*M*, 70). This solipsistic system is critiqued when the narrator notes that the interior world needs the world exterior to this supposed plenum: 'A man is in bed, wanting to sleep. A rat is behind the wall at his head, wanting to move. The man hears the rat fidget and cannot sleep, the rat hears the man fidget and dares not move' (*M*, 71). The possibility of motion in a plenum perplexed Descartes, and the Murphy Mind preserves that concern; of course, Murphy also has the motion of his rocking chair where he comes alive. The distinctions multiply, and the section calls Murphy 'a point in the ceaseless unconditioned generation and passing away of line'. To this is added 'Matrix of surds' (*M*, 72). Beckett invokes the mathematical notion of the 'surd', the term for irrational numbers. Irrational numbers literalise many other concerns with the limits of naming, and they connect the Cartesian allusions to other mathematical allusions that eventually extend the works beyond solipsistic paralysis by a literary codification resembling the work of contemporary logicians.

These other mathematical allusions serve as emblems of the representational gaps in systematic languages. Frequently, they reference the Pythagoreans and their struggle with irrational numbers. The Pythagoreans are especially appropriate because they viewed the world as 'number'. It not only could be represented through numbers, but it was number. The vulnerability of their system was its ignorance of numbers that were 'irrational', that is, which could not be represented as ratios of integers. The Pythagoreans required that any point on a line could be named as the ratio of two whole numbers; hence, the term 'rational numbers'. The rationals could be used to describe geometric figures, and such demonstrations were genuinely religious performances of nature's reality. On the other hand, points on the number line that could not be named as ratios of integers were a decided threat, and of course, there is an infinite supply of just such numbers: $\sqrt{2}$, π and a host of others. The vaunted Pythagorean Theorem ($a^2 + b^2 = c^2$ where a and b are the sides of a right triangle and c is the hypotenuse) produces such numbers and undermines the cult's aspiration towards pure representation. These are 'irrational numbers', and are as genuinely numbers as any other. To the Pythagoreans, they represented a gap in the naming system upon which they would build a complete and consistent system. The irrationals were a sort of mathematical aphasia for which they had no cure. Beckett refers to irrational numbers in *Murphy*, *Proust*, 'Dante...Bruno.Vico..Joyce' and elsewhere. They are present by implication in his pervasive references to the methods – series, approximations and the tricks of number theory – that seek to circumvent the 'irrational' relationship between the sides and hypotenuse of a right triangle. In the irrational numbers, Pythagorean aspirations for a representational system, and the collapse of that project, is a parallel to the failure of language to represent the world. In other mathematical and scientific allusions, Beckett turns to contemporary work that had managed to reconceptualise the gap, the zero, the failure, not as silent, but as demonstrably unnamable and thus Real.

Beckett's use of scientific and mathematical knowledge has at least three aspects: 1) it opens the texts into a world of referential, material reality; 2) the allusions have a structure of opposition and cancellation that limits the representational lure; 3) the subjects to which he alludes are themselves consciously struggling with the limits of representation. Beckett's allusions embody the incommensurability of words and things, the gap between self and other, and they force the readers to participate in processes that make their own responses a part of the works' context. There are other dimensions to these allusions; some, such as the literalisations of Parkinson's Disease in *Murphy* and in *Footfalls*, have autobiographical roots in Beckett's mother's protracted illness, but even these are as systematically problematised as those that seemingly are less authorial. In all cases, the sciences and mathematics of Beckett's texts instantiate two great realms: the systems of meaning and the buzzing, blooming confusion of the world. They establish his major terms, and then it is in his use of neurology and mathematical logic that the work evades solipsism. These terms become like the single side of the Möbius strip that we can hold between our fingers; its paradoxical singularity indicates that, like a circle, it has only one edge, but unlike the circular definitions of recursion, its 'sides' constantly communicate. It is the figure traced in the pacing of May in *Footfalls*, a topology further expressed in allusions to neurology and the work of Kurt Gödel.

Beckett's technique – to treat systemic disciplines as heuristic methods whose function is to approximate the real – is naturally drawn to the neurosciences because as Robert Young notes, the work of that field became modern when it understood the brain in terms of the function of particular brain regions. To emerge as a new form of discourse about the mind/body, neurology had to forsake the abstract categories of philosophy – especially Cartesian dualism – and openly embrace the notion of function. David de Giustino finds that this shift began with phrenologists such as Gall, a figure who appears in *Watt* as a piano tuner who cannot restore the instrument, and in *Mercier et Camier* accompanied by the symptoms of syphilis and fragments of phrenology's history. Beginning with the phrenologists and culminating in modern neurology was a transformative approach to studying the mind: the brain is what it does, and what it does informs what it is. Beckett's use of the sciences is similarly functional, and it references the scientific fields concerned with the same issue.

Neurological allusions enable Beckett to literalise the functional nature of language, especially when they perform the linguistic distortions – the aphasias – that accompany some brain injuries. Using neurology to perform a functional strategy in the work is another iteration of the representational aspiration. But it is as model of representation, a gesture towards the unnamable compulsion towards language, that neurology, and especially the aphasias, make various appearances.[4] The neurological destruction of memory manifested in Korsakow's syndrome, the Weirnicke's aphasia of Lucky and the defective memory of Didi and Gogo seem to share a failed attempt to recall a permanent and stable world. The (dys) function of language in the text reveals the limits of representation just as the dysfunction of speech of a patient reveals the nature of an injury. Beckett's interest in gestalt psychology – particularly in the short-lived Wurzburg School[5] – recognises that the roots of gestalt psychology in the neurological work of Kurt Goldstein offered a notion of 'global function', a concept that distinguishes between the larger integrating capacity of the organism (the self) and discrete injuries and losses of function. The conflict between the localisation of function and a holistic approach is a central problematic of neurology.[6] The 1934 publication of Goldstein's *The Organism* not only conceptualised that paradox in fruitful ways, but also its publication is nearly contemporaneous with the publication of Kurt Gödel's Incompleteness and Inconsistency theorems in 1931. There, a similar concern emerges with discontinuities between discrete systems and their larger relationship.

Kurt Gödel's work responded to a problem that had vexed mathematicians for about sixty years: how to build a wholly consistent and complete arithmetic system, and indeed to find out if it were possible. Frege, Russell and Hilbert were among those deeply involved in the question. While the question was highly technical, it also carried whispers of an anxiety about representation. A major, ongoing project was to demonstrate that mathematics might be a purely syntactic system without reference to the material world. In 1931, Gödel's first theorem demonstrated that axiomatic systems necessarily produce true statements that can be neither proven nor disproven; his second theorem demonstrated that such systems would necessarily contain contradictions, that is, be inconsistent. While his work addresses a purely mathematical problem, it should also be read metaphorically and as an analogue of Beckett's concern with the limitations of explanation and symbolic systems. Gödel's work abruptly ended the quest for a formal language that did not have to reach outside of itself. In a fashion roughly analogous to the plenum mind of *Murphy*'s Chapter 6, the vision of a closed system proved impossible. In the neurological work of Kurt Goldstein, the art of Beckett and the mathematics of Gödel, a common concern with comparative systems, failure and representation proves central, and Beckett references their work.

Rebecca Goldstein carefully argues that Gödel's theorems succeeded, in part, because he considered the aprioricity of mathematics the central issue. His demonstration of incompleteness and inconsistency does not signal chaos; rather, it proves arithmetic truths exist that lie outside of any formalised arithmetic system; Rebecca Goldstein notes, 'the criteria for semantic truth could be separated from the criteria for provability'; this was an argument for mathematical Platonism. Like Beckett's unnamable, it has an extra-linguistic existence. The cultural framework and the meta-mathematical significance of Gödel's work did not argue for the absence of any extrinsic order to the world.[7] Rather, Gödel's theorem exposed defects in a mathematical project to convert mathematics into a self-referential system whose orderliness would be its internal consistency and completeness. By demonstrating that arithmetic systems were not closed systems, mathematics itself could be opened to meta-mathematical claims. His theorems participate in a specialised discourse, but it shares in a more widespread anxiety about representation and the nature of language. Goldstein notes:

> The structure of Gödel's proof, the use it makes of ancient paradox [the liar's paradox], speaks at some level, if only metaphorically, to the paradoxes in the tale that the twentieth century told itself about some of its greatest intellectual achievements – including, of course, Gödel's incompleteness theorems. Perhaps someday a historian of ideas will explain the subjectivist turn taken by so many of the last century's most influential thinkers, including not only philosophers but hard-core scientists, such as Heisenberg and Bohr.[8]

The work of major scientists, mathematicians and Beckett can be triangulated with three symbolic systems: as isolated, internally ordered syntactic systems; as accompaniments of experience in the material world, or as representations of the real. Beckett was drawn to the key meta-mathematician whose work describes the limits of mathematical representation through an elegant demonstration that arithmetic systems – axiomatic systems – were inevitably inconsistent and incomplete and then used those failures as a proof of existence.

Beckett recognises the emergence of representational problems and indicates his familiarity with Gödel's work in a letter to Axel Kaun: 'for the time being we must be satisfied with little. At first it can only be a matter of somehow finding a method by which we can represent this mocking attitude towards the word, through words. In this dissonance between the means and their use it will perhaps become possible to feel a whisper of that final music or that silence that underlies ALL' (*D*, 172). Beckett proves politely sceptical of Joyce's 'Apotheosis of the word' by suggesting that the solution lay in acting like 'that mad (?) mathematician who used a different principle of measurement at each step of his calculation'. The reference seems to be to Gödel's deployment of a system that creates specialised numbers for the symbols and the functions within them. Nagel and Newman explain how this second order system enabled him to move back and forth between the rules of arithmetic statements and the codes that represented them. The process uses 'a different principle of measurement at each step of [the] calculation', as Beckett notes in his letter. His interest in this contemporary work resembles other interests in the obscure 'Algebraic theology' of John Craige, Pythagoras, number theory (in *Watt*) and other mathematical matters. Each involves failure: Craige was interested in predicting the Apocalypse on the basis of the loss of belief in the gospels; Pythagoras feared the gaps in the number line represented by the irrational numbers and Gödel identified the incompleteness and inconsistency of axiomatic, arithmetic systems. All share an interest in the failure and negation, but they respond to the threat with complex tactics. Beckett recognises and uses their struggles as part of his own concerns with the nothing.

Beckett's 'work' instantiates a large network of activity – cultural, generic, linguistic, scientific, mathematical – that models the representational aspiration. The iterations of sciences and mathematical problems historicise the meaning making process and problematise the representational aspiration not only of these fields, but of language itself. The paired discourses of Beckett's work suggest an inflection point, a point where the negations produced by the contraries of competing systems such as astronomy and astrology, phrenology and neurology and neurology and philosophy make their turn towards a muted optimism. The gaps between word and world become an opportunity to perform a negation via methods that reveal an order beyond the discovery of failure. In the sciences and in mathematics, the result of discovering and exploiting such inflections led to disciplinary innovation. Beckett both participates in and comments upon this key feature of his historical moment through the work of his texts.

NOTES

1 Brian Rotman, *Signifying Nothing: The Semiotics of the Zero* (Stanford: Stanford University Press, 1987), 1.
2 Ibid., 27.
3 Ibid.
4 Laura Salisbury, '"What Is the Word": Beckett's Aphasic Modernism', *Journal of Beckett Studies* (17:2008), 78.
5 Jean-Michel Rabaté (ed.) *Beckett avant Beckett: essais sur le jeune Beckett 1930–1945* (Paris: Presses de l'Ecole normale superieure, 1984), 135–51.
6 Oliver Sacks, 'Preface', in Kurt Goldstein (ed.) *The Organism* (New York: Urzone, 1995), 7–14.
7 Rebecca Goldstein, *Incompleteness: the Proof and Paradox of Kurt Gödel* (New York: Norton, 2005), 51; Andrew Gibson, *Beckett and Badiou: The Pathos of Intermittency* (New York: Oxford University Press, 2007), 174.
8 Rebecca Goldstein, *Incompleteness*, 51.

PART VII

Language and Form

CHAPTER 31

Language and Representation
Daniel Katz

The question of language and representation is especially complex in relation to Samuel Beckett for three noteworthy reasons. The first complicating factor is Beckett's activity as a bilingual author. His drafting of texts in both French and English and his subsequent auto-translation of them means that for Beckett any idea of 'language' as system or metaphysical abstraction has to be measured against the varying particularities of the different languages – French and English – of his texts. 'Language' as a generality or universal structure is in this way relativised by the specifically different problems and procedures one discovers when comparing any Beckett text in its French and English versions. For all Beckett's interest in language as such, virtually no passage in Beckett allows us to consider language in the absolute, simply because such a passage will be a contingently French or English rendering of something that can exist, and does exist, in a parallel version. If Beckett's texts in manifold ways point to the resistance of language to meaning and reference, and vice versa, they also show that this resistance itself can be transferred from one particular language to another, that any statement about language as a whole must be made from within a particular language and that this positioning has its own retinue of effects and implications. As against an ideal placelessness of disinterested theoretical inquiry, Beckett's texts mark themselves as French, English and, very often, Irish. This emphasis on languages, in the plural, in addition to language, lends Beckett's project a cultural and historical specificity which its philosophical complexity can too easily lead a reader to ignore. Beckett never lets us forget that any speculation about language happens not in 'language' but in a specific language, at a specific time.[1]

In addition to linguistic diversity, Beckett's generic diversity, as a major author of both prose and drama, is a supplementary complicating factor. In fiction, of course, language is the only means of representation, the only element in which the work exists at all; whatever a novel might present as 'visual' or 'material' nonetheless only comes to be represented by way of the language which conveys it. As Beckett relentlessly emphasised, in a novel or story there is quite simply no extra-linguistic element. Therefore, by questioning the status of its own words, discourse or narration, a fictional text can cancel or erase the entirety of its construct; if not reduce itself to nothing, then leave a trail of its own unsayings: 'affirmations and negations invalidated as uttered, or sooner or later', as *The Unnamable* puts it in presenting a programme to which the novel largely adheres (*U*, 1). Likewise, the second half of *Molloy*, though structurally quite different, achieves a similar effect when Moran's final words erase the premise of the narrative which has taken him to the point where those words can be uttered. Beckett's fiction is obsessional in its interest in invalidating the framing of its own utterance and inscription, and in addition to middle-period works like the trilogy and *Texts for Nothing*, very late pieces like *Company* and *Worstward Ho* also propose analogous self-cancelling manoeuvres.

But in the theatre (or television), obviously, language holds an entirely different status, being only one signifying element within a framework which exceeds and contains it, and which can in fact dispense with it entirely, as Beckett's silent works point out. Within a theatrical setting, language no longer dominates the entire ontology of the work in question, and to transpose the kinds of paradoxes Beckett's narrators offer in the prose to a character present on the stage would fundamentally alter their import, which partially explains why Beckett's stage characters tend to speak so differently from his prose 'voices'. Language on the stage can be subordinated to the visual, spatial and material, and in stage directions emphasising repeated and inverted patterns of movement and gesture, Beckett's theatre often physically stages the kinds of relationships the prose builds up through patterns of clause, sentence and paragraph. On Beckett's stage, people can be seen to move the way syntax so often does in the prose. Where these two parallel aspects of Beckett's architectonics meet, however, is in the fact that in the theatre language is subject not only to competing claims of space and matter, but also, quite radically in Beckett's case, to the impositions of time. It is not the noiseless printed page but the theatre which is the space of silence in Beckett, and not only because by presenting something materially 'there' in front of the spectator, the stage can dispense with language as a mediating means of representation. More than this, it is because the theatrical performance and not the silently read book allows for the enforced application of *time* to the linguistic unit, breaking it, shaping it and interrupting it in a manner that a blank space on a page can hardly approximate. Among his other achievements as a playwright, Beckett is the great technician of the pause, the materialised linguistic rupture. Any linguistic unit is structurally temporal in that phonemes and morphemes need to be deployed in sequence, and that word order determines meaning, but this logical temporality is attacked by pressures on the aural temporality of the spoken word on Beckett's stage, by both the pause and its dialectical obverse, speed. Indeed, in this respect the massively hurried and nearly incomprehensible speech in *Not I* can be seen as a variation of the temporality of the pause; in fact, the two modes are related as early as *Waiting for Godot*, in the concatenation of Didi and Gogo's elongated, interrupted dialogues and Lucky's logorrheic flow.

In many respects, then, when it comes to language and representation, Beckett's fiction and his theatre each attack and ironise the other's premise. The theatre counters the self-enclosed narrative worlds of the fiction by positioning them within a physical space which cannot be annulled by utterance, which implicitly invalidates the auto-invalidations of the prose. Conversely, the fiction re-encloses the theatre within the space of an imagining or 'fabling' source, staging and enclosing its own staging of the artistic scene. In a larger pattern of affirmation and negation, in Beckett fiction and theatre each call to the other as a necessary negation of each genre's premises, as Beckett posits them.

But the third and most important complicating factor is that few writers at any time and in any medium have ever questioned as insistently, explicitly and profoundly as Beckett the questions of language and representation in their work. These problems, or to use Beckett's own related term, that of expression, are at the heart of his entire project.[2] In recognition of this, there is a long-standing critical tradition of seeing this project as in some manner an assault on a language which would inevitably 'lie', in favour of a truer form of representation, such as, say, mathematics, or short of that, quite simply silence. As Molloy puts it when discussing his own discourse, 'I am merely complying with the convention that demands you either lie or hold your peace' (*Mo*, 89). In such a reading, Beckett emerges as the anti-Joyce, rejecting the latter's 'apotheosis of the word' for a more sceptical and indeed ethical position, inclined to the sorts of 'truth' that language might inevitably obscure (*L1*, 519). The support for and terms of such an argument are found in Beckett's famous 'German letter' of 1937 to Axel Kaun, a letter whose notoriety is due not only to the powerful position Beckett there articulates, but also to its having been published in *Disjecta* in 1984, at a time when much less of the correspondence and archival materials of all kinds were available. Beckett writes: 'It is indeed getting more and more difficult, even pointless, for me to write in formal English. And more and more my language appears to me like a veil which one has to tear apart in order to get to those things (or the nothingness) lying behind it.... To drill one hole after another into it until that which lurks behind, be it something or nothing, starts seeping through – I cannot imagine a higher goal for today's writer' (*L1*, 518). From such a statement, it is tempting to conclude that Beckett's main goal is a familiar, sceptical one: to rend the lying veil of language to reveal the ineffable truths lying behind it. However, such a position is in some ways problematic, and not only because Beckett himself later dismissed the letter as 'German bilge' (*D*, 170). First of all, let us note that when this letter (written in German) first dismisses language as 'pointless', it refers to a specific language: 'formal English'. While the claims about language made here doubtless have a general extension, it is hardly beside the point that Beckett singles out his use of English as unsatisfactory while experimenting with composing in a foreign language, just a few years before making the shift to French. Among other things, then, this letter, which also explicitly concerns itself with translation, is about the possibility of productive interference between various languages, not only 'language' in general. But even more to the point is the position with which this letter flirts, short of entirely endorsing, in its evocation of 'nothingness': not so much that language falls short of real and substantive presences, feelings and impressions which it can only distort, mediate and hide, but rather that it exceeds the nothingness, the negativity, which lies behind representation. In other words, Beckett's problem is not that language would be a supplement, a secondary sign, falling short of the real, but that language, too real, obscures the irreality which it cannot abide. And this leads to the central issue for Beckett: Is this irreality subject to any representation of any kind, and can it even be made to fit within an ontological regime in which the problem of representation can be posed?

Beckett explores this question in *Watt*, in the famous scene of the Galls, father and son, piano tuners by trade. On the face of it, the convoluted episode, defined as a highly suspect account, could be seen as another example of language inevitably 'lying' about or distorting experience: 'foisting a meaning there where no meaning appeared' (*W*, 64). But Beckett takes great pains to emphasise in this extraordinary passage that, strictly speaking, there is no meaning that exists in any form prior to its representation, or narrativisation, within the novel. It is not that the telling of the story fails to live up to the events experienced, but that the construction of the narrative itself takes the place of a kind of 'something' which can't quite be called an 'experience' at all. The novel instead asserts 'that nothing had happened, with all the clarity and solidity of something' (*W*, 63) while specifying that 'the only way one can speak of nothing is to speak of it as though it were something' (*W*, 64). The incident of the Galls, then, in its totality, is simply one of Watt's various attempts to elaborate the 'nothing' by way of a representation which is inherently figural, as emphasised by the 'as though' of the preceding phrase. And the novel insists that the success of these attempts tends to be provisional, leading Watt to concoct entire series of narratives aimed at handling the same material, which in turn presents a thorny question: 'one is sometimes tempted to wonder, with reference to two or even three incidents related by Watt as separate and distinct, if they are not in reality the same incident, variously interpreted' (*W*, 65). The 'events' Watt recounts, then, are essentially unconnected with the 'nothing' that prompted them; concerning what 'really happened' at the Knott residence we know nothing, but only how Watt at various points used language and narrative to 'exorcise' the events that otherwise would have tormented him, as that is the effect of the events that 'continued to mean nothing ... right up to the end' (*W*, 64): 'For there we have to do with events that resisted all Watt's efforts to saddle them with meaning, and a formula, so that he could neither think of them, or speak of them, but only suffer them, when they recurred' (*W*, 65). This passage is remarkable for a number of reasons. First of all, it asserts that the purpose of linguistic representation is less to convey meaning or information than quite simply to alleviate suffering, by the very construction and solidification of meaning – any meaning – in and of itself. Thus, another of Watt's accounts is presented this way: 'Not that for a moment Watt supposed that he had penetrated the forces at play, in this particular instance, or even perceived the forms that they upheaved, or obtained the least useful information concerning himself, or Mr Knott, for he did not. But he turned, little by little, a disturbance into words, he had made a pillow of old words, for a head' (*W*, 99). Language and representation, then, have a function beyond that of conveying information or solidifying knowledge, but act in and of themselves as a palliative, or to use another Beckettian term, a calmative, possessed of powers which seem to border on the somatic. This performative or even auto-performative valency of language, present throughout Beckett, arises from what *Company* calls 'fabling', and not from any serious relationship to a prior content which language must come to represent. And indeed, this leads to a second crucial implication of how these passages from *Watt* represent what is anterior to language and representation in the first place: not as a primal experience, or an ineffable feeling or impression, but rather as something which is not only 'unspeakable' (or unnamable, perhaps) but also quite literally 'unthinkable', as such or in itself. In this way, Beckett marks a clear difference with certain sorts of phenomenological or existentialist thinking prominent at the time *Watt* was written, as he refuses to posit anything, with the very important exception of suffering, as pre-representational at all. That is to say, for Beckett 'experience' is almost always already *within* the regime of language and representation, and not a prior essence which gives rise to them. And this in turn implies that if language must be viewed as suspect, it is not because it is in some way insubstantial with regard to what it represents, as in the classic realist critique, but quite the contrary; it is not insubstantial enough.

This is the position most powerfully articulated in the *Three Dialogues* with Georges Duthuit of 1949, where B calls for 'The expression that there is nothing to express, nothing which to express, nothing from which to express, no power to express, no desire to express, together with the obligation to express' (*D*, 139). Certainly, the question of representation should not be too hastily equated with that of expression, but Beckett's stance is compelling here and characteristic of problems he works through incessantly in the prose, especially the trilogy. Clearly, here as in *Watt* there is no coherent and entire interiority which it would be the task of language to exteriorise successfully. On the contrary, it would seem to be the very inadequacy of language which gives it its chance and value, which allows it to do justice to the 'nothing' at the heart of both what is expressed and what does the expressing. Such a position is entirely in line with the imperative to 'fail better' from the late *Worstward Ho*, showing how closely Beckett cleaves to this thinking through to the very end. Here, the 'missaid' words strive after a 'better worse', in the desperate attempt to 'fail better', to which the greatest threat is nothing other than the propensity of language to be successful: 'The words too whosesoever. What room for worse! How almost true they sometimes almost ring! How wanting in inanity! Say the night is young alas and take heart' (*NO*, 99). In this nearly final text, Beckett acknowledges the extent to which its concerns have been a constant for him: 'All of old. Nothing else ever. Ever tried. Ever failed. No matter. Try again. Fail again. Fail better' (*NO*, 89). This last invocation again very clearly echoes the *Three Dialogues*, where B declares that 'to be an artist is to fail, as no other dare fail ... failure is his world and the shrink from it desertion, art and craft, good housekeeping, living' (*D*, 145). What remains to be seen is how *Worstward Ho* sketches the modality of this failure in terms of language, expression and representation. It does so by moving from a language that would be 'missaid', false-sounding and inane, to the evocation of one which would forego expression as representation entirely. First of all in this process, words as something 'said' or 'missaid' are replaced by a vision of language as a kind of somatic production, a bodily fluid: 'Not to know what it is the words it says say. Says? Secretes' (*NO*, 104). This idea is carried forward as the text increasingly refers to language as 'ooze', an ooze that by oozing of its own disappearance would give itself the lie: 'No ooze for when ooze gone' (*NO*, 112). And indeed, if to be an artist is to fail, it is because no language can succeed in marking its own erasure. As in *Three Dialogues*, the simple absence of expression is not enough; there must be the impossibility to express along with the 'obligation to express'. Thus *Worstward Ho* at once suggests 'Blanks for when words gone' and affirms 'Nothing save what they [words] say', leaving us within a very old Beckettian problem: the text's 'blanks' can only be spelled by the very words those blanks are meant to replace (*NO*, 104). And this in turn means that even if we had those blanks, they would enter into the field of language and representation by the very fact of replacing the absent words, rather than remaining in a simple opposition to them. Part of the problem with 'silence' for Beckett, is that in this manner it also 'speaks'.

In parallel to this paradox, however, as we have seen, there is a manner in which *Watt*'s 'pillow made of words' and the secreted 'ooze' of *Worstward Ho* evoke a relationship to language which is not representational at all, but somatic and indeed, almost biochemical. If the traditional concept of 'expression' places in parallel the literal exhalation of air from the lungs in the form of words with a metaphorical exteriorisation of a psychic interiority, Beckett's serious joke is to replace this metaphor with one stressing the exteriorisation of the body's physical interiority; verbal expression is placed on a par with tears, sweat and the body's other excretions, precipitates, disjecta. In this conception, language seems not to represent its expressive subject as a double, or a sign, but rather, as it leaks or oozes out, to support it like a pillow or perhaps in some way house it. The 'ooze' of *Worstward Ho* and the snail-like progress of the text as a whole are reminiscent of Francis Ponge's 'Notes pour un coquillage', where Ponge calls on artists to abandon monumental representations of the human and its form in favour of the creation of dwelling spaces or shells on the human scale; dwellings, moreover, that can be made of words. In language not unlike Beckett's, Ponge praises those writers whose 'monument is made of the true secretion common to the human mollusc, of the thing most in proportion and suited to its body, yet the most different imaginable from its form: I mean speech'.[3] And this is a sort of speech which creates shells that outlast the creatures that secreted them, as Ponge goes on to note, and can be used by others that take up residence there.

Ultimately, then, language not only represents but also constructs and creates, 'oozes' in a manner independent to the reference which it nevertheless implies. Expression as ooze means language, failing as subjective mirror or voice (which is all to the good, even all to the better), exists expressively as trace, as *Texts for Nothing* suggests: 'there is nothing but a voice murmuring a trace. A trace, it wants to leave a trace' (*CSP*, 152). In this way, the tracing language for Beckett is as much indexical as symbolic; a mark and not a representation of its source. Yet the traces work in another sense too, leaving tracks and establishing patterns and networks in a manner which tends to join the verbal and the spatial as procedures of mapping and charting, delineating spaces such as the cylinder of *The Lost Ones*, or effecting the ghostly demarcations of *Stirrings Still* or *Footfalls*. Such modes of mapping are made palpable in the late stage plays, *Quad I* and *Quad II*, wordless pieces which approach dance. These works, which are empty of speech and mark only space and time through the geometric patterns of the figures' movements and the careful synchronization of their footsteps, can seem wholly autotelic and self-referential, 'representing' only the enclosed framework of their own motions and performance. There is not the slightest possibility of psychologising the 'players' into representational characters, nor is there any indication of how the entire spectacle could be a 'fable' or tale, devised by one of Beckett's anti-expressivist sources. Again, typically of Beckett, rather than have narrative progression, even implicit, the movements of the players traversing the square and cutting across it diagonally stress repetition and circularity. Yet the circuitry of the modular movements is governed by one literally central 'problem' that Beckett's diagrams and notes isolate: this is the space Beckett designates as 'E', the central point in the square of the stage where the diagonal lines traversed by the players cross, and where the players themselves, given their synchronization, would collide.[4] Beckett's laconic suggested solution to this problem is as follows: 'E supposed a danger zone. Hence deviation', a deviation embodied in the recorded Stuttgart production, to which Beckett's script alludes, as a vertiginous, last-minute swerve on the part of the players (*CDW*, 453). The bodies of *Quad*, then, run through the paces of a manic trajectory punctuated by a spatially central moment of *avoidance* of their doubles and counterparts, who come careening towards them. The tensions and pleasures of the piece derive from that moment of missed encounter with the serial, specular double, charging head-on, and then only dodged through a swoon-like manoeuvre which fails both to break the rhythm of the trajectory and to impede the reoccurrence of the non-encounter. Albeit multiplied and let loose in frenetic motion and noise, the players of *Quad* re-enact and present again in allegorical form the dynamics of the Beckettian pseudo-couples, so familiar from the earlier drama and prose. Footsteps become the wordless speech of allegorical representation.

NOTES

1 For further discussion of this see the next chapter. Also see Chapter 26 for a discussion of Fritz Mauthner, a philosopher of language in whom Beckett took a strong interest.
2 So much is this the case, that to give a bibliography of critical examinations of these issues in Beckett would largely amount to listing every significant study of his work.
3 Francis Ponge, *Le parti pris des choses, suivi de Proêmes* (Paris: Editions Gallimard, 1948), 77; my translation. Ponge's French reads, 'parce que leur monument est fait de la véritable sécrétion commune du mollusque homme, de la chose la plus propotionnée et conditionnée à son corps, et cependant la plus différente de sa forme que l'on puisse concevoir: je veux dire la PAROLE'.
4 'Problem' is Beckett's own term. See *CDW*, 453.

CHAPTER 32

Self-Translation

Corinne Scheiner

Beckett and Vladimir Nabokov are two of only a few exceptional authors to engage in literary bi-discursivity, that is, continual creation in two languages throughout their careers. Several aspects of Beckett's practice distinguish it from the practices of others that fall under the broader category of literary bilingualism or multilingualism. First, unlike many modernists who preceded him – for example, Joyce, Eliot and Pound – who employed polyglot quotation as a stylistic device in their works and thus produced what might be called a bilingual or multilingual text, Beckett wrote separate texts in more than one language, yielding an extraordinarily bilingual corpus.[1] Second, he wrote bilingually throughout his career, never abandoning his native tongue, as did most authors who wrote in more than one language, for example Joseph Conrad and Arthur Koestler.[2] Beckett's moves between English and French as the language employed for the primary version of a given text are not unidirectional (from one to another) but bidirectional (back and forth). Thus, these moves do not signal a renunciation of the native language, but rather initiate an integral reworking of his literary idiosyncrasies into a bilingual mode of production. Third, Beckett has earned a marked degree of recognition in both of his literary traditions; far from being viewed as foreign, his texts (both the original and self-translated versions) have become part of the English-language and the French-language literary canons. Indeed, it is precisely this mastery of two cultures and an awareness of two different sets of readers that allow Beckett to move back and forth between French and English as his two languages of composition. Last, the works of Beckett are fairly evenly distributed between English and French and thus yield a bilingual corpus, one further complicated when one takes into account the translations of the texts. Beckett actually created four different sets of texts: those written in English, those written in French, the French translations and the English translations. The relations of these texts to one another as interconnected elements of the bilingual oeuvre and, in particular, the act of self-translation, the most vivid physical manifestation of the bilingual corpus, are central to Beckett's poetics.

Beckett's bi-discursive practice was possible due to his fluency in French, which he studied at a small kindergarten school near Foxrock and then at Portora Royal School in Enniskillen. His honours subjects at Trinity College in Dublin were French and Italian. While French would become the language in which he composed nearly half of his works, as well as the language into and from which he translated his own texts, his first translation to appear in print in the journal *This Quarter* in 1930 was from Italian to English, a translation of Eugenio Montale's poem 'Delta'. It was thus often as a translator that Beckett found his way into print in the early years, and he continued to translate the works of others throughout his career, translating from French, German, Italian and Spanish into English and, in one notable case, from English into French, translating 'Anna Livia Plurabelle' (a section from Joyce's *Finnegans Wake*, at that point titled *Work in Progress*) with Alfred Péron (1931). His published translations into English include poems by French surrealists Breton, Eluard and Crevel, which appeared in *This Quarter* (1932); a variety of texts for Nancy Cunard's *Negro* (1934); numerous poems and articles that appeared in George Duthuit's review, *transition* (1948–9); essays and poems commissioned by UNESCO for an homage to Goethe (1949) and for an *Anthology of Mexican Poetry* (1951); a radio play by Robert Pinget, *La Manivelle* (*The Old Tune*) (1960); and selected poems by Alain Bosquet (1963). As Knowlson notes, 'Beckett did far more translations than anyone has ever realized, for many of them appeared, at his own request, unsigned' (*K*, 369). These published translations of others' works fall into two main categories: those done to earn money to support himself, primarily those undertaken early in Beckett's career or immediately following the war, and those done at the request of friends, such as those of Bosquet's poems. In addition to translating literary and scholarly works, Beckett engaged in the translation of information reports as part of his role in the Resistance movement during World War II.

In his 1931 essay on Proust, Beckett quotes, translates and, via parentheses, expands on a remark made by the narrator in Proust's *Le temps retrouvé*, 'Le devoir et la tâche d'un écrivain sont ceux d'un traducteur': 'The duty and the task of a writer (not an artist, a writer) are those of a translator' (*P*, 84). It is thus perhaps not surprising that Beckett's activity as a translator was not limited to translating the works of others, but that self-translation was a central part of his bi-discursive practice. Beckett began translating his own works as early as 1936, when he translated his poem 'Cascando' from English to German. He then translated his short story 'Love and Lethe' from English into French in 1938, possibly with help from Péron. Neither translation was published. From 1938 to 1940, Beckett collaborated with Péron on the translation of *Murphy* from English to French. Following World War II and an incredibly productive period in which he wrote *Mercier et Camier*, the trilogy (*Molloy*, *Malone meurt* and *L'Innommable*) and *En attendant Godot*, among others, Beckett continued to collaborate on the translations of his texts, working on the translation of *En attendant Godot* into German with Elmar Tophoven, and on the translation of *Molloy* into English with Patrick Bowles. Although Beckett collaborated on the translations of some of his later works (most notably with Pinget on the French translations of *All That Fall* and *Embers*, with Tophoven on the German translation of *Fin de Partie* and with Ludovic and Agnès Janvier on the French translation of *Watt*), in 1953 he made the decision to translate both *En attendant Godot* and *Malone meurt* into English on his own. In the case of *En attendant Godot*, his French editor, Jérôme Lindon, had received many requests 'for permission to translate or "adapt" [the play] into English.... Worried by the very sound of the word "adaptation" and anxious about the quality of any resulting translation, Beckett decided to set about translating the play himself' (*K*, 398). In contrast, in the case of *Malone meurt*, Beckett 'tried to work at a revision of Patrick Bowles' translation of *Molloy*; then, finding it easier to translate himself than to revise someone else's work, he started to translate *Malone meurt*' (*K*, 402).

Apart from these cases in which Beckett translated collaboratively, usually with close friends, and from a few texts translated by others (including Tophoven's German translations of *Footfalls* and *That Time*, which Beckett reviewed, and Edith Fournier's French translation of *Worstword Ho*, which she did after his death), Beckett translated his own works from and into English and French[3] throughout the rest of his career and often oversaw or checked the translations of his texts into German and Italian. The time lag between initial composition and self-translation varies: the longest is that of *Mercier et Camier*, which Beckett wrote in 1946 and translated into English nearly forty years later; in contrast, Beckett began to translate *Company* (1980) into French almost immediately upon completion of the English manuscript. In fact, the manuscripts of *Company* and *Compagnie* share a single notebook. Connor contends that the shorter the length of time between composition and translation, the closer the correspondence between the two versions of a given text, whereas the longer the length of time, the greater the 'changes in [Beckett's] outlook, stylistic priorities and attitude towards the originals' and thus an 'increase in disparity between original and translation'.[4] However, regardless of the time lag between composition and translation, one aspect of Beckett's practice of self-translation is consistent: like all translators, he introduces changes into the translated texts, for translation is, in and of itself both literally and figuratively, a form of rewriting; however, unlike other translators, Beckett as self-translator need not justify any of these changes no matter how big or small and no matter their nature, for his status as the author of the text provides him with the authority to make them.[5] The changes may concern the rendering of individual words and phrases, the deletion, addition or elucidation of small or large sections of the text and/or systemic decisions regarding style or cultural specificity. These changes are significant in that they reveal the choices Beckett makes in translating his own texts and allow for a (re)construction of the poetics of self-translation that guide him.

In her ground-breaking article, 'Samuel Beckett Self-Translator', the first to address Beckett's practice of self-translation and to systematically examine the textual changes necessarily introduced in the process of translation, Cohn remarks that when translating the works of others, as for example in the case of his translations of the poems that appeared in *transition 1948*, Beckett is 'able to translate without modifying'.[6] In doing so, she draws attention to the prevailing view (both then and now) that a 'good' translation is one that is literal or word for word, hence faithful to the original. Lest Beckett's translations of his own texts be deemed therefore 'poor' in comparison, she is quick to remark that, despite the changes that Beckett interpolates into his translations of *Murphy*, *En attendant Godot*, *Fin de partie* and the novels of the trilogy, 'It is ... important to insist for each work that the translation is in the main faithful, and even brilliant'.[7] The faithfulness of Beckett's self-translations upon which Cohn insists does not appear to be Beckett's concern. Indeed, it is clear from accounts of his collaborations that Beckett does not seek to produce literal, word-for-word renderings of his texts. Rather, he clearly understands the process of self-translation to be one of rewriting. In describing the process of translating *Molloy* with Beckett, Bowles states that 'it was not a translation as that term is usually understood. It was not a mere matter of swapping counters, of substituting one word for another ... Time and again, Beckett said that what we were trying to do was to write the book again in another language – that is to say, write a new book'.[8] Agnès Janvier expands on Beckett's specific goal in translating his texts, commenting that when translating *Watt* with Beckett and her husband, 'Il [Beckett] est parfois arrivé à des résultats très éloignés du texte anglais, mais qui fonctionnent en fait de la même manière, et c'était de ces déplacements apparents que naissait la fidélité vraie' ['He sometimes arrived at results far removed from the English text, but that in fact function in the same way, and it was from these apparent displacements that true fidelity arose'.].[9] The type of faithfulness or equivalence that Beckett appears to seek in translating his works is therefore what Nida terms functional equivalence, that is, Beckett's goal is to make 'the translation approach more closely what one thinks or experiences from the original', not to achieve the formal equivalence that Cohn implicitly identifies as the aim of translation.[10]

As Federman notes, the type of analysis undertaken by Cohn has been the norm: 'Usually one studies the Beckett twin-texts to observe if the meaning has changed as the text passes from one language to the other, or to note omissions, deletions, or additions, to delight in the way Beckett translates his own puns or renders a typical Beckettian play-on-words'.[11] Hokenson and Munson assert that most studies have arrived at the same conclusions as Cohn and 'agree on certain consistent patterns of translative practice', to wit: 'the French is more reduced and the English more amplified, the English has added colour and detail of objects and situations, where the French is more colourless and spare, the English narrator is more differentiated as a distinct presence where the French narrator seems a neutral cipher'.[12] What is important then is that 'the *types* of divergence between French and English clearly operate in both directions (whether translating from French to English or English to French)', and thus may be seen as a divergence between the different languages themselves.[13]

McQueeny rightly argues that this approach is too limited: '[textual] changes, additions, deletions, variations in tone and meaning, however, cannot all be accounted for by the ineluctable tendencies of the language in question. Beckett's bilingualism allows him to play upon the different *génies* of the two languages, but he also seems to approach each work with a distinct strategy of translation that goes beyond matters accessible to comparative stylistics'.[14] While Hill asserts that 'it is far from self-evident that Beckett's practice as a self-translator can be reduced to a single uniform strategy', in comparing the original and self-translated versions of Beckett's texts, it is in fact possible to identify at least one general principle that guides him and therefore may serve as a basis for articulating his poetics of self-translation: cultural transposition.[15] Regardless of the text's primary language of composition or of the time lag between the two versions, Beckett seeks not only to rewrite a given text in a new language, but also to inscribe the text into a new cultural field of reference

Self-Translation

so that it may resonate for the new reader. In his call for a definitive study of Beckett's poetics of self-translation, it is precisely these 'resonances and equivalences', that is, 'how certain linguistic elements are transformed in the process of translation, but also how certain cultural, philosophical, and literary allusions, and even quotations, are not simply translated but transposed into a French or an English context to produce a totally different set of cultural, philosophical, or literary connotations', that Federman sees as essential to Beckett's activity as a self-translator.[16] Beckett's handling of these 'resonances and equivalences' oftentimes may be attributed to his awareness of the two linguistically and culturally distinct readerships, English-speaking Irish and French. These references draw on a wide range of elements belonging to what may be termed shared cultural knowledge.

Some references appeal to the reader's familiarity with geographical locations or with certain cultural institutions and structures, such as units of measurement, currency and time or particular customs and practices. For example, Cohn notes that in translating *En attendant Godot* into English (*Waiting for Godot*), Beckett substitutes 'Connemara for Normandie, Puncher for Poinçon, Feckham Peckham Fulham Clapham for Seine Seine et Oise Seine-et-Marne Marne-et-Oise in Lucky's tirade'.[17] In replacing the French topographical references, be they to real or to imaginary locales, with Irish or English-language ones, Beckett '[appeals] to the changed nationality of the audience'.[18] In the English version of *Molloy*, Beckett renders 'un petit Trianon' as 'a charming home', removing the reference to a French landmark that is unlikely to evoke any associations for the English-speaking Irish reader and replacing it with a more generic and, hence, accessible descriptor; in the same text, he translates 'Isigny' as 'Blackpool', replacing the French seaside town with a British one. As Simpson illustrates, Beckett does not employ these strategies solely in his translations of his prose texts but in his dramatic works as well. For example, in the French translation of *Happy Days* (*Oh les beaux jours*) 'Borough Green' becomes 'Fougax-et-Barrineuf' and in the French translation of *Play* (*Comédie*) 'Ash and Snodland' become 'Sept-Sorts et Signet'. One of the most interesting examples of Beckett's handling of topographical references in translation may be found in the second sentence of the opening paragraph of *Murphy*. The English version reads: 'Murphy sat out of it, as though he were free, in a mew in West Brompton'. In the French version, Beckett renders this as 'Murphy, comme s'il était libre, s'en tenait à l'écart, assis, dans l'impasse de l'Enfant Jésus, West Brompton, Londres'. Fitch discusses this passage and remarks that:

[W]e have here a copy-book model of the standard alternative procedures for the translation between languages ... which explains the at first inexplicable expansion of the single English proper names into three distinct elements, including the latter. One can either retain proper names in their original form – 'West Brompton' – or have recourse to the target-language transcription of them ('Londres' for the implicit 'London') needed for the information of the French reader. Given that neither of these names would render the Catholic connotations that the London district of West Brompton, with its well-known oratory, has for the English-speaker, the latter are made explicit by the name 'l'impasse de l'Enfant-Jésus', with the added advantage for Beckett of slyly suggesting that Catholicism is a dead end. If this procedure aims at reproducing as far as possible for the French reader the connotations of the name 'West Brompton' for the English reader, it does so, it should be noted, far more explicitly, while adding to the original the snide attack on Catholicism through the pun on the term 'impasse'.[19]

While Fitch sees the translation of this sentence as somehow falling outside the scope of translation proper, it serves as a perfect example of the myriad of ways in which Beckett engages in cultural transposition and rewrites his text.

In addition to topographical references, nearly all of Beckett's texts are replete with allusions that draw from a general store of cultural knowledge and he once again engages in cultural transposition when translating these items. For example, in the French *Murphy*, he translates 'shillings' as 'francs', 'one o'clock' as '13 heures' and he converts traditional British measurements into metric ones; similarly, in the English translation of *Malone meurt* (*Malone Dies*), he translates 'kilos' as 'stone'. In addition to converting units of measurement and time, Beckett replaces references to the French reader's larger cultural frame of reference with ones to English-speaking Irish culture in the English versions of both *Molloy* and *L'Innommable* (*The Unnamable*). For example, in both translations he renders 'jours de fête' as 'bank holidays'; similarly, in *The Unnamable*, he replaces the reference to the French school system, 'en sixième', with one from the British, 'in the lower third'. Beckett's practice of cultural transposition is especially evident in his translation of references to items, in particular brand names, specific to a given culture. In general, he replaces items likely to be unfamiliar or lacking in associative chains of meaning for the new reader with items that appeal to the new reader's own cultural frame of reference. For example, in both *Malone Dies* and *The Unnamable* the French 'Guignol' becomes the very British 'Punch and Judy', in the French version of *Play* (*Comédie*), 'Lipton's tea' becomes 'l'Eléphant' and in the English *Fin de partie* (*Endgame*), 'biscuit classique' becomes 'Spratt's medium'.

Beckett approaches the translation of the literary allusions in his texts in a similar manner. In the main, he replaces the existing allusions with new ones that draw on the new reader's cultural store of knowledge; for example, the reference in *En attendant Godot* to Voltaire is replaced in *Waiting for Godot* by one to Bishop Berkeley. However, one example in particular gets to the heart of the principle of cultural transposition underlying Beckett's poetics of translation: his rendering of *Le Dépeupleur* as *The Lost Ones*. The title is a neologism but one that, as Fitch points out, 'recalls ... a literary allusion to Lamartine's famous line "Un seul être vous manque, et tout est dépeuplé"'.[20] Fitch then reminds the reader of Pilling's opinion regarding the English version's change of title: 'One reason for the disparity between the French and English titles is doubtless the fact that Beckett could not rely on his English readers catching the allusion to the line of Lamartine's ... which is embedded in the coinage'.[21] Indeed, Pilling's remark serves as a fitting summary of the principle of cultural transposition that governs Beckett's decisions in translation: in certain instances, Beckett wants his readers, both English-speaking Irish and French, to catch the allusions, be they topographical, cultural or literary. As these examples show, Beckett accomplishes this cultural transposition in several different ways, frequently employing more than one of these strategies within the same translation: (1) he replaces unfamiliar references with ones familiar to the new reader; (2) he retains the references present in the first version but, recognising that these references are likely unfamiliar to the new reader, he offers more information; and (3) he interpolates additional references drawn from the new reader's culture.

Beckett's practice of cultural transposition follows from an overarching poetics of self-translation that views translation as rewriting, a creative act, and hence a central part of his bilingual production. Thus, it is perhaps not surprising that this rewriting extends to the 'original' text when Beckett self-translates some of his late works. For example, both *Company* and its French translation (*Compagnie*) were published in the same year, 1980, but due to revisions of the English text that Beckett made while engaged in the translation, the French text appeared first. The cover of the first English edition therefore intriguingly informs the reader that *Company*, although 'written in English, has already been translated by the author and revised in the light of the French text'.[22] Similarly, an examination of the manuscript notebooks of *Mal vu mal dit* and *Ill Seen Ill Said* (both of which were also published in the same year, 1981) clearly reveals that Beckett began translating into English even as he composed the French text. The types of rewriting that constitute Beckett's practice of self-translation raise the issue of the (ontological) status of a self-translated text. A self-translation appears somehow different than a traditional translation: it is perhaps more 'original', a result of the author having translated it, and yet not quite an 'original', for it is, after all, a translation of another text. Thus, a self-translation seems to fall somewhere between an 'original' and a translation, sharing aspects of each, yet not fully identical with either. Equally problematic is the relationship that holds between the two versions of each of the texts and, as a result, some scholars, particularly those who work in only one language, opt not to address or only to make passing reference to the existence of two versions, treating them as interchangeable. Others, like Fitch, view Beckett's bilingual production in terms of 'one work, two texts' and thus collapse the duality of the bilingual work into a single, unified whole. The two versions of a given work have a complementary relationship and it is only 'in the coming together of the two' that we may begin to have 'an adequate representation of "what the author had in mind"'.[23] Still others, like Connor, claim that 'translation and original can be seen as organically continuous with one another'.[24] Given Beckett's view of self-translation, and by extension, translation, as rewriting, it is clear that each self-translated text must be viewed as a work in its own right as well as in relation to the original from which Beckett translates it.

In their article, 'Seeing in Depth: The Practise of Bilingual Writing', Sarkonak and Hodgson employ the notion of 'the stereographic effect' or 'seeing in depth' as a metaphor for the practice of bilingual writing.[25] Shattuck develops this idea in his study on Proust: 'Depth, or what is called in optics penetration effect, cannot be found in a single *instantané* [snapshot]. The visible world reaches us through a double take based on the stereographic principle. Two slightly different versions of the same "object" from our two eyes are combined subjectively with the effect of relief ... Physiologically and psychologically and metaphysically, *to see* means to see with or against or beside something'.[26] While Sarkonak and Hodgson apply Shattuck's understanding of depth to individual bilingual texts, this concept perfectly fits with the literary bi-discursivity of an author like Beckett. For him, this 'double take' occurs as a result of having two languages and two cultures at his disposal. In terms of his literary production, his continual creation in both languages coupled with his self-translations give rise to two versions of the same 'object'. In the bringing together of the two versions, of reading one *against* or *beside* the other, Beckett's bilingual poetics are imbued with greater depth and understanding.[27] This is nowhere more evident than in the act of self-translation, in which Beckett revisits, rewrites and produces multiple versions of his texts.

NOTES

1. Beckett did imitate/parody Joyce's stylistic device of polyglot quotation in his first novel, *Dream of Fair to Middling Women*, and in his first collection of short stories, *More Pricks than Kicks*.
2. Many scholars have claimed that Beckett did abandon his native tongue, yet this claim is not borne out when one examines Beckett's corpus as a whole.
3. According to Knowlson, after having translated his texts into French, Beckett often 'sent a copy of his typescript to Mania Péron [Alfred Péron's widow] for her views, accepting some minor revisions of the French' (*K*, 508).
4. Steven Connor, *Samuel Beckett: Repetition, Theory and Text* (Oxford: Basil Blackwell, 1988), 89.
5. Michael Molnar terms this authority 'noetic licence', 'the right denied the ordinary translator of altering the original': 'Noetic Licence in Brodsky's Self-Translation', *Russian, Croatian and Serbian, Czech and Slovak, Polish Literature* (37.2–3: 1995), 333.
6. Ruby Cohn, 'Samuel Beckett Self-Translator', *PMLA* (76: December 1961), 616.
7. Ibid., 620.
8. 'Patrick Bowles on Beckett in the Early 1950s', in James Knowlson and Elizabeth Knowlson (eds.) *Beckett Remembering/Remembering Beckett: A Centenary Celebration* (New York: Arcade Publishing, 2006), 109.
9. Ludovic Janvier and Agnès Vaquin-Janvier, 'Traduire avec Beckett: *Watt*', *Revue d'esthétique*: 'Samuel Beckett' (1986), 59.
10. Elmar Tophoven, 'Translating Beckett', in Dougald McMillan and Martha Fehsenfeld (eds.) *Beckett in the Theatre: The Author as Practical Playwright and Director*, vol. I (London: John Calder; New York: River Run Press, 1988), 324.
11. Raymond Federman, 'The Writer as Self-Translator', in Allen Warren Friedman, Charles Rossman and Dina Sherzer (eds.) *Beckett Translating/ Translating Beckett* (University Park: The Pennsylvania State University Press, 1987), 9. Many scholars have examined individual texts and the changes they undergo in translation. Fewer have followed Cohn's initial attempt to examine multiple texts. Those that have include Henry Cockerham, 'Samuel Beckett, Bilingual Playwright', in Katherine Worth (ed.) *Samuel Beckett the Shapechanger* (London: Routledge and Kegan Paul, 1975), 141–59; Ekundayo Simpson, *Samuel Beckett, traducteur de lui-même: aspects de bilinguisme littéraire* (Québec: Centre international de recherche sur le bilinguisme, 1978); Raymond Federman; Brian Fitch, *Beckett and Babel: An Investigation into the Status of the Bilingual Work* (Toronto: University of Toronto Press, 1988); Steven Connor; Lori Chamberlain, '"The Same Old Stories": Beckett's Poetics of Translation', *Beckett Translating/Translating Beckett*, ed. Allen Warren Friedman, Charles Rossman, and Dina Sherzer (University Park: The Pennsylvania State University Press, 1987); Michaël Oustinoff, *Bilinguisme d'écriture et auto-traduction: Julien Green, Samuel Beckett, Vladimir Nabokov* (Paris: L'Harmattan, 2001); and Bruno Clément, *L'Oeuvre sans qualities: Rhétorique de Samuel Beckett* (Paris: Seuil, 1994).

12 Jan Walsh Hokenson and Marcella Munson, *The Bilingual Text: History and Theory of Literary Self-Translation* (Manchester: St. Jerome Publishing, 2007) 192, 193.
13 Ibid., 193.
14 Terence McQueeny, 'Beckett, Chamfort, and the Wastes and Wilds of Self-Translation', *Literary Review* (30.3: Spring 1987), 413.
15 Leslie Hill, *Beckett's Fiction: In Different Words* (Cambridge: Cambridge University Press, 1990), 46.
16 Federman, 'The Writer as Self-Translator', 13.
17 Cohn, 'Samuel Beckett Self-Translator', 616.
18 Ibid. However, Beckett does not transpose the text entirely, for as Cohn points out, 'in both versions the two tramps have associations with France' (616).
19 Fitch, *Beckett and Babel*, 42.
20 Fitch, *Beckett and Babel*, 111, n17.
21 James Knowlson and John Pilling, *Frescoes of the Skull: The Later Prose and Drama of Samuel Beckett* (London: John Calder, 1979), 157.
22 Samuel Beckett, *Company* (London: John Calder, 1980), described in Joseph Long, 'The Reading of *Company*: Beckett and the Bi–Textual Work', *Forum for Modern Language Studies* (32. 4: October 1996), 315. It is precisely this revision and this back and forth between the two texts that prompt Charles Krance to speak of 'transtextual confluence' with respect to Beckett's bilingual oeuvre and his practice of self-translation: 'Traces of Textual Confluence and Bilingual Genesis: *A Piece of Monologue* and *Solo* for Openers', *Samuel Beckett Today/Aujourd'hui: An Annual Bilingual Review/Revue annuelle bilingue* (2: 1993), 134.
23 Fitch, *Beckett and Babel*, 101.
24 Connor, *Samuel Beckett: Repetition, Theory and Text*, 88.
25 Ralph Sarkonak and Richard Hodgson, 'Seeing in Depth: The Practise of Bilingual Writing', *Visible Language* (27.1/2: Winter/Spring 1993), 9.
26 Roger Shattuck, *Proust's Binoculars: A Study of Memory, Time and Recognition in "À la recherche du temps perdu"* (New York: Vintage, 1963), 42–4, quoted in Sarkonak and Hodgson, 'Seeing in Depth: The Practise of Bilingual Writing', 9.
27 Charles Krance's series of bilingual variorum editions provide the reader with exactly this opportunity. Dirk Van Hulle and Mark Nixon's Beckett Digital Manuscript Project (http://www.beckettarchive.org/) continues the work of Krance's variorum editions.

CHAPTER 33

Theatre Forms

Enoch Brater

It may seem counterintuitive that Beckett's work, justly and famously celebrated in the international theatre community for its miniature, even minimalist scale, should reveal itself to be a richly textured demonstration of an entire series of weighty dramatic forms. In this regard the plays can be considered the work of a 'synthesiser' as much as an 'analyser', though the playwright behind the mask, distinguishing himself from James Joyce in this matter, liked to emphasise the latter at the expense of the former.[1] As early as *Waiting for Godot*, the orchestration of a variety of inherited conventions are already in play, and more often than not their practical implications for performance can be observed in something like sharp relief. So much so that the first generation of Beckett critics, most notably Ruby Cohn, was quick to seize upon them as a way to understand what was happening – and the how and the way it was happening – on the redrawn parameters of his stage (*The Comic Gamut* was the first of Cohn's landmark studies that sited the dynamics of the *mise en scène* in familiar tropes drawn from the long history of dramatic representation in Western theatre).[2] And as Beckett's fascination with restructuring the techniques of rendering stage time on stage space developed and matured over the next three decades of his playwriting career, his preoccupation with controlling the shape of his dramatic form became ever more deliberate, precise – and unpredictable.

As with the accomplishment of any artist of this magnitude, it is probably a good idea to separate the individual works into their successive periods of composition in order to view the achievement as a whole more clearly. The four major plays beginning with *Godot* and ending with *Happy Days* are of course the logical place to begin such a retrospective. In these frequently produced pieces Beckett displays a heady combination of well-known stage techniques, though in each case the synthesis is entirely original. *Godot* is essentially a four-hander, plus the sudden appearance of a walk-on fifth character, the Boy-actor, who appears to signal the closure of both of the play's two parts. The set is equally economical, perhaps even more so: a rock, a tree and the stark simplicity of an unspecified country road. The site seems to suggest that we could be anywhere. Modifications here will be nothing if not minute, but nonetheless crucial – the moon suddenly rises, artificial yet real (a nice lighting effect), and a few leaves inexplicably materialise to decorate and destabilise a tree as the curtain opens on the second act. Props, by contrast, are generous in their vigorous distribution: a radish (black – Gogo likes only the red ones), bowler hats, a picnic basket, chicken bones, a half-hunter, one memorable carrot and an uncorked bottle that elicits an incongruous toast, Pozzo's 'Happy days!' (*CDW*, 26). Keeping stock of so many props can be a nightmare for any assistant stage manager (no wonder Sam Shepard is often regarded as one of Beckett's heirs). Much is made out of almost nothing – and that *almost*, in terms of the possibility of theatre, is pretty much the whole point.

Along the way *Godot*'s strategy relies on the steady exploitation of any number of traditional devices to pinpoint and achieve its most impressive theatrical effects. Dancing, for instance, perhaps western theatre's most seminal form, will be rendered in this case as a dithyramb of an entirely different sort, this one variously called 'the hard stool' and 'the net'. As in Shakespeare, for one, classical allusions abound: we hear of caryatids and the figure of Atlas, even though the paternity of this mythological being is misattributed to Jupiter in the play's first French and English editions.[3] Motives and cues for passion, however, will be placed temporarily on hold, though 'traces blurs signs' remain (*CSP*, 193), signifiers that may very well signify nothing; it is these that the audience is likely to find most tantalising as the drama, such as it is, unfolds. Less makes more surprisingly possible. References (inferred? debunked? both?) steadily accumulate, but with no fixed point on offer – Yeats, Verlaine, *The Gospel According to St. Matthew*, Shelley, all the way back to fifth-century B.C.E. Heraclitus, the weeping philosopher.[4] Meanings may not proliferate, but irony certainly does.

Theatre has always done this. In the modern repertory, Chekhov references *Hamlet*; Pirandello references himself. And it is hard to imagine the ending of a Shakespeare comedy without a dance, Bottom's 'Bergomask' for example (very unlike Lucky's), to wrap up the romantic tensions that finally settle down in the joyful celebration near the conclusion of a work like *A Midsummer Night's Dream*. Theatre likes to reference all that comes before it; it especially likes to reference itself.

The dialogue in *Waiting for Godot*, in shape and form, seems particularly drawn to both a remembrance and recalibration of things past.

Stichomythic lines are all the rage, those quick, short, pointed give-and-take one-liners designed for rapid and in this case an actor's typically comic delivery. 'That wasn't such a bad little canter', a character congratulates his partner and himself, followed by a well-timed silence, isolating and extending a single moment's most arresting effects. *Godot*, it could be argued, plays its silences extremely well; these are rarely nothings, but rather the gateway to pregnant *nothings in particular*. Stage silences like this make the void sound full. Beckett similarly ponders the aesthetics of other elements in *Godot*'s expansive theatre vocabulary. Big-ticket items like monologues and soliloquies will be deployed tactfully and richly, unlocking previously undiscovered formal potentials. Lucky's thinking speech, a parody both hilarious and frightening, deflates itself almost as soon as the extravaganza gets going. This is all supposed to be high-minded, something more substantial and certainly more dignified than a fitful dance; at least that's the way logic and stage logistics are assumed to have functioned in the past. Soliloquies, on the other hand, seem to have been protected from such unglamorous intrusions. Vladimir's at the end of the play is strictly by the book. Beckett seems to know at this early point in the repertory when it's best to leave well enough alone (he will revisit their possibilities in the haunting speeches he composes for his grand soliloquisers in the late, great dramas of the 1970s and '80s).

Asides, which derive from Attic comedy, have always been something of a metatheatrical trick, a wink and a nod and an entre nous to the audience to remind its members that they are in fact watching – and hearing – a play. Asides can also remove two characters from the rest of the crowd: think of Macbeth pulling Banquo literally 'aside' to comment on what the weird sisters have just told them (it's a complicated scene for the actor – a word to Banquo, a word to the company as a whole, another word to himself). Compared to his use of asides in *Endgame* – 'An aside, ape! Did you never hear an aside before' (*CDW*, 130) – Beckett employs them with considerable discretion in *Godot*, though he will deploy them to light(e)ning effect, and in both senses of the word. Gogo complains more than once to the audience (but also, speaking aloud, to himself): 'Hurts! He wants to know if it hurts!' Complicating the moment and the dramatic convention, is Didi meant to hear this too? (We could of course ask the same question of Claudius concerning Hamlet's 'A little more than kin, and less than kind.').[5] And when a blind Pozzo falls to the ground in the second act and cries out for help, asides are very much to the point as Gogo and Didi ponder the hermeneutics of a possible act of charity their fallen man is never meant to hear. Earlier in the play they were also out of earshot when they wondered if his name was Bozzo or perhaps even Gozzo, a family whose mother 'had the clap'.

Other metatheatrical devices in *Godot* are keyed to physical movement and dramatic action. Vladimir runs offstage to take an elaborately announced pee, in production sometimes rushing out the door at the rear of the auditorium to do so ('End of the corridor, on the left') as the hectic absurdity of classic farce more than once intrudes. *Commedia dell'arte* techniques are likewise in the air (no pun intended): someone farts and fouls the air as four major characters are laid out unceremoniously on the ground, a dubious position for line delivery few other playwrights might risk. Vaudeville, too, as style and schtick, makes any number of other arrangements possible, including the mimed exchange of bowler hats, head lice never to be forgotten. The figure of the Clown is transformed several times in the play, as it will be again in *Krapp's Last Tape*; so too for the Fool, though just who should be assigned this hat in *Waiting for Godot* is a matter of interpretation. Is the Boy a misplaced Epilogue, or merely a soon-to-be-abused Messenger, like his brother? 'I don't know, Sir'. And just who provides the choral element to whom will be a matter of constant renegotiation. Why limit yourself, the play seems to be saying, to the unforgiving devices and monotone language of picayune realism? Who before Ibsen would have asked for a real door anyway? Come on, *Godot* implores us, get a (stage) life.

That same stage life is in some ways even more noteworthy in *Endgame*, whose very title suggests a serious reduction in forces, though not necessarily in terms of the viability and volatility Beckett builds into his dramatic forms. Set indoors – locked is probably the more appropriate verb – the limits of this world and the roles the characters pursue within its bounds are now more clearly the limits of the proscenium ('Me – ([Hamm] *yawns* – to play'). And 'dialogue' is what keeps four players there. Hamm is the 'heavy', like Pozzo before him, but in this go the self-dramatising Hamlet-*manqué* is worried about show-biz complications like the late development of 'an underplot' and the 'warming up' for what is supposed to be the big moment of his 'last soliloquy'. This ham actor is nothing if not competitive. Clov's virtuoso performance of his grand monologue only a few moments before has obviously thrown him for a loop.

Beckett's control over the formal elements of his composition in *Endgame*, including the celebrated mime with which Clov opens the play, are so well integrated within the narrative drive of the piece that it is easy to lose sight of their derivation, provenance and constant manipulation. Stage images speak volumes, and Beckett's in this case exercise a powerful pull on our dramatic imagination. Representations of isolation have appeared on stage before (in Sophocles, Strindberg and Büchner for example), though rarely have they been rendered quite so claustrophobic (Sartre's *No Exit* and Pinter's menacing rooms would be the contemporary analogues). In *Waiting for Godot* '[their] man' doesn't come; in *Endgame* Clov can't or won't and doesn't go, this despite a busy preparation for leave taking, soon revealed as neither more nor less than stage and stagy business. It may be, as Clov says, 'easy going', but not so from this patriarchal 'shelter', even when the actor dresses for the part. *Endgame* conspires with other theatrical tropes as well, not the least of which is the seated figure on stage.[6] Shakespeare's 'throned' monarchs cast an envious shadow on much that happens – or doesn't – in this work. Hamm even knows how to speak the language of such fictive royals, substituting a 'nightman' for Richard's missing 'horse' and appropriating Prospero's 'Our revels now are ended' for a line of his own (he goes so far as to borrow Prospero's staff for a prop, too, one he relishes and enlivens). *Endgame* even makes its move to take *King Lear* one step further, turning epic tragedy on its head by transforming it into a reconfigured chess match: this king also lacks a queen, has lost his knights (see the line from *King Richard III* referred to earlier), just as a reimagined Kent, still uncomfortable playing the part of a pawn, nurtures his master but in this take whines, winces and bitterly complains.[7] Blindness on this board is as terrifying as Gloucester's, and 'shelter' on the heath, where Shakespeare's desperate characters seek refuge from a storm, is no more promising than this one: 'Can there be misery – ([Hamm] *yawns*) – loftier than mine? No doubt. Formerly. But now?' Beckett's Hamm is speaking in strictly theatrical terms.

So much dramatic history is built into *Endgame* that the wonder is it never succumbs to the weight that in the hands of another writer might have threatened to bring it down. That also holds true for *Krapp's Last Tape*, where the shape of what might have been a sentimental little scene is saved by the use of a mechanical recording device. The play so much wants to be a monologue (Beckett originally conceived it as such for the great Irish actor Patrick Magee),[8] even though its form and structure resists any standard definition of the term. As in *Endgame*, *Krapp's Last Tape* begins with an extended mime, the figure of a seedy old man dressed like a clown shuffling about, eating a banana and discarding its skin (slipping, too), fiddling with keys, banging into things and opening drawers, finally moving into the darkness backstage to uncork an unseen bottle. The guy's a drunk, and he will become progressively more so under the influence as his story develops. This mime's big event is the location of 'box … thrreee.… spool … five.… Spool! … Spooool!' the particular tape that contains the private history Krapp has been searching for (*CDW*, 216). He wants to hear the past recaptured, in this instance on the electronic recording tape he can hold in his hand. Technology upstages Proust. But no sooner does he load the machine than the monologic structure abruptly falls apart. What we are about to hear is a duet, the voice of the past commenting on the present, just as the present makes its statement on the past. They do so as much through tone and inflection (Krapp-at-39) as by movement and gesture (Krapp-at-69). This is a PowerPoint presentation in the guise of a dialogue staring the form of monologue down.

There will be no dancing here – what has there been in Krapp's life to dance about? – though in its place there will be some attempt at singing. On the dusty tape torn from the past the obsessively self-recorded self will wonder if he ever sang; he will do so on this night, however, when he performs a lively but drunken rendition of a famous Protestant hymn ('Ah these wasps!' Maddy Rooney lashes out in *All That Fall*) (*CDW*, 177). Theatre has a lot of resources, and Beckett uses them to much advantage to make Krapp come alive, if only as a dynamic stage presence. He, too, was once capable of quoting Shakespeare, recycling *Othello*'s 'chrysolite' to capture the sheer intensity in the glance and gaze of a lover's wan eyes (the image still haunts him, thirty years on). 'What remains of all that misery? A girl in a shabby green coat, on a railway-station platform?' The atmosphere of memory is minimalist, but no less elegant for being so. 'We drifted in among the flags and stuck', the soundscape rolls on, gaining emotional force, body and texture as it does so. 'The way they went down, sighing, before the stem! [*Pause.*] I lay down across her with my face in her breasts and my hand on her. We lay there without moving. But under us all moved, and moved us, gently, up and down, and from side to side'. With each playback the romantic passage of the girl in the punt reinscribes and reinvigorates itself, insinuating its validity as a storyline halfway between reality and fiction. Krapp tried so hard to be a writer after all. Now his recordings only prompt memories, not emotions; even the memories of emotions are difficult to recall. So what we have in *Krapp's Last Tape* is not one monologue, but two; past and present recitals reflect and refract one another in vibrant but previously unimagined counterpoint. Both monologues, moreover, march to their own beats, framing and illuminating the other to establish, then sustain, a persuasive dialogue of their own. And as they do so they highlight not memory, but rather the memory of memories, less substantial but more agonisingly acute. In this deceptively simple work Beckett seizes upon the resources of the one-character play, transforms the shape of dramatic monologue and makes it uniquely his own.

Happy Days will be equally thrilling from a strictly formalist point of view. Even Beckett's innovations trigger innovations, and this time he pursues the porous border separating monologue from soliloquy. As the drama and her day begin, Winnie awakens to the sound of an alarm clock, prays to the so-said Almighty and then gracefully attends to her toilette. Things are running down, but also out. Buried up to her waist and the next day up to her neck in a mound of unforgiving earth, she wants to believe she is talking for the remainder of the day to Willie, who remains all but hidden from the audience's view until the close of the play, when he appears in formal attire dressed, so to speak, to kill. 'Just to know that in theory you can hear me even though in fact you don't is all I need', Winnie rambles but also explains. 'Just to feel you there within earshot and conceivably on the qui vive is all I ask ... not to be just babbling away on trust as it were not knowing and something gnawing at me. *(Pause for breath.)* Doubt' (*CDW*, 148). Elsewhere Winnie tries to sound more self-assured and moderately if temporarily more secure, characterising the dynamics of her less than enviable situation as 'paradise enow'. Monologue such as this presupposes an onstage listener, but Willie proves at best a most reluctant one. There is much else he has had to ignore, not the least of which is his wife's fling with 'His Grace and Most Reverend Father in God Dr Carolus Hunter', 'dead in a tub'. 'Charlie Hunter!' Winnie muses, closing her eyes and remembering the happy times she sat on his knees 'in the back garden at Borough Green, under the horse-beech'. Later she reminisces about her 'first ball' under the rafters with a 'Mr Johnson, or Johnston, or perhaps I should say *Johnstone*. Very bushy moustache, very tawny. *(Reverently.)* Almost ginger!'

Uneasy about her speechifying as she so often is, Winnie may be yet another one of Beckett's delusional monologuists. From time to time in a low-level panic she even questions whether or not her listener is actually there at all, prompting him to react and elicit one of his cryptic one-liners, 'Castrated male swine' and 'Opening for smart youth' among the best of them. A dialogue of sorts momentarily intrudes to get her through this day: 'Have you gone off me again? *(Pause.)* I do not ask if you are alive to all that is going on, I merely ask if you have not gone off on me again. *(Pause.)* Your eyes appear to be closed, but that has no particular significance we know. *(Pause.)* Raise a finger, dear, will you please, if you are not quite senseless. *(Pause.)* Do that for me, Willie please, just the little finger, if you are still conscious. *(Pause. Joyful.)* Oh, all five, you are a darling today'. After such a limited but nonetheless encouraging exchange, she can proceed with an 'easy mind', perhaps even with her signature but always enforced cheerfulness. In the second act, when she can no longer turn her torso to check up on her man, she will crave such assurance even more: 'I used to think ... *(pause)* ... I say I used to think that I would learn to talk alone. *(Pause.)* By that I mean to myself.... *(Smile.)* But no. *(Smile broader.)* No no. *(Smile off).* Ergo you are there'. Willie likely nods off again, before her unacknowledged solo resumes. But this is a formal consideration she does not wish to pursue; for if that is indeed the case, she is talking alone, soliloquising, once more into the void.

Stage speech structured like this is by no means unprecedented. In the first act of *Othello* Iago passes in and out of a soliloquy-like state in his encounter with Roderigo, the 'gulled gentleman' who can barely follow what this 'super subtle' Venetian is saying. He is therefore licensed to think aloud within the confines of a single speech, in-between his imprecations to 'put money in thy purse'. Roderigo rushes off to sell all his land. 'Thus do I ever make my fool my purse', Iago soliloquizes in a moment of self-revelation that also serves as an emblem of his self-aggrandisement and cruelty. Unlike Shakespeare's villain, however, always in full command of his rhetorical strategy (he will spend the rest of the play retooling and refining the devices of language in order to reduce the Moor to a Roderigo-like state), Winnie is barely conscious of her variable dialogic state. Beckett cautioned his actress not to make her 'too capable' a woman, citations from *Cymbeline* and *Romeo and Juliet* notwithstanding.[9]

Just as Beckett's *Happy Days* defies any simple categorisation of monologue and soliloquy, so too does it alter any preconception about how movement constitutes meaning on a given performance space. In this piece the actor's body is deliberately and literally restrained, and that is indeed to put it mildly. Act two makes things even worse, for in this diminution the female player is merely a talking head, set against a 'trompe-l'oeil backcloth to represent unbroken plain and sky'. She fared much better in act one, where even in the same 'blazing light' she could at least play around with the contents of a handbag. And it is indeed amazing to see what she does with it. Not since *The Importance of Being Earnest* has a handbag played such a crucial part in advancing a play's dramatic action. Winnie never wavers; even when she despairs that gravity isn't what it used to be, or when her body sinks further into the growing mound, she still finds in the movement of her eyes and even more so in the deployment of words a complex repertory of highly communicative gestures. Beckett has made demands on the actor's physical restraint before, most notably in *Endgame*, where only one character can walk, albeit in a stride both painfully stiff and staggering. 'But you can move', Hamm reminds Clov from his retrofitted wheelchair: 'Then move!' he suddenly shouts. Nell and Nagg, the 'accursed progenitor[s]' who long ago crashed on their tandem and lost their shanks, have meanwhile been warehoused in onstage trashbins. Minimalist that he is, this playwright has always been intrigued by how little physical action has to occur on stage for a full dramatic display to develop and unfold. Here, too, Beckett considers the untapped potential of certain other dramatic forms, in this case those abstracted from Racine. In *Phèdre* and *Bérénice* the characters speak their lines mostly standing stock still, letting the alexandrines do all the work. Winnie got it right: 'What a curse, mobility'.

Happy Days brings to conclusion the first great period of Beckett's revolutionary work for the stage; and it is nothing if not remarkable how quickly he took to writing for such a demanding performing arts medium. In four major plays Beckett tests the limits of what a serious dramatist might still be able to do within an existing framework of inherited dramatic forms. And for a moment the palette seems to have been exhausted as to what he might be able to do with them next. Having transformed and refined – redefined really – the rules and regulations of a stubborn genre, Beckett becomes more of an analyser than a synthesiser as he embarks on a new creative path that displays both the inclination and the wherewithal to break them down further, if not completely. In the transitional works that follow *Happy Days* the playwright's formalist credentials are therefore at full stretch, perhaps too much so. Short in their playing time and to some extent largely experimental in nature, these complex works have been appropriately characterised as 'dramaticules', a term that implies their dimension and scale but not the scope of the theatrical ambition they contain (*CDW*, 351).

Come and Go is a case in point. In this work the image is poised to be arresting in its ultimate visual display. Three women sit '*Very erect, facing front, hands clasped in laps*' as 'soft' lighting illuminates the drama of their present isolation centre stage (CDW, 354). There is no background and therefore no context; even their ages are 'undeterminable'. And as we study the image, we wonder just what these female figures are doing there. This is a far cry from the richly detailed tableau informing the emotional resonance of the outdoor scene that brings down the curtain on Chekhov's *Three Sisters*, or the naturalistic effects later subverted by Edward Albee in *Three Tall Women*. In Beckett the image as rendered is far more fragile, and the tight space is uncertain. Full-length coats, buttoned high ('dull violet', 'dull red', 'dull yellow') as well as 'drab' hats and 'Light shoes with rubber soles' might be on other platforms a dead giveaway, but in this case they aren't. The tension in *Come and Go* is instead sharply focused on rhythmic pacing. Varied patterns of movement, repeated turn and turnabout by three women on a circumscribed set, destabilise the image before it reconstitutes itself to return to its original form, the same but somehow subtly different. Only then do we realise that their paths have converged only to complete the 'rings' they have just traversed around Beckett's stage. This is enough, more than enough really, as they conclude by holding hands 'in the old way'. Three pairs of hands clasp and rest on three laps as Flo intones the ambiguous curtain line: 'I can feel the rings'.

How does Beckett do this?

First and foremost, in *Come and Go* he suppresses dialogue and allows a narrative of sorts to emerge from physical movement itself. Shifting the equation between movement and meaning, as well as their priorities in fostering a unique dramatic representation, Beckett tests the viability of a form that seems to exist halfway between a skit and a sketch. Much is at stake, for this piece wants us to reimagine the province of mime with the intrusion of the briefest of words hell-bent on disguising minor interior variations: 'Does she not realize?'/'God grant not'; 'Has she not been told?'/'God forbid'; and finally 'Does she not know?'/'Please God not'. There is, then, just enough dialogue to keep the hybrid going, as though its peculiar momentum was derived from some animated puppet show, this time with no strings attached. The tableau proves remarkably vivant, but at the same time shadowed by a series of prompts whose effects prove to be not only oddly askew, but ominous. Allusions, for example, evoke a visual iconography at once highly theatrical and threatening, the most obtainable being the 'weird sisters' from *Macbeth*. Here the 'three', updated, are fated to meet again (Verdi's opera calls them *Le Sorelle Vagabonde*). This time, however, *nomen est omen*, the name is the signifier. Ru, Vi and Flo take their names from the suicidal Ophelia's mad speech in *Hamlet*. This does not sound promising. Retracing each other's steps and spinning a net of words, the same term that describes Lucky's dance in *Waiting for Godot*, such fatefully gendered protagonists defy any prohibition to hear no evil, speak no evil, see no evil. In the course of this highly condensed drama, they may in fact be called upon to perform all three. Theirs is no idle gossip.

This also holds true for *Play*, where the integrity of an unanticipated visual image is similarly empowered to signal any number of strange theatrical tactics. 'Adulterers take warning, never admit' (*CDW*, 310): three actors who might otherwise have been protagonists in a French farce, one man and two women, now find themselves potted in urns, '*Faces so lost to age and aspect as to seem almost part of urns*'. Just as Nabokov said of Emma Bovary, the bourgeoisie never seems to tire of exploring 'a most conventional way to rise above the conventional'.[10] But there is certainly nothing conventional about their situation on this stage, which is simultaneously sinister and droll. The piece requires intense coordination and concentration on the part of its actors; none of the players in this drama can miss a beat.

Where exactly are we now? Some previously unchartered territory in Dante's hell might be a good guess. Equally devoted to the primacy of movement, and movement before meaning, *Play* assigns that role exclusively to the spotlight, which becomes a principal personality in its own right. This may be 'just play', in all its irony, ambiguity and wit, but there will be no ambivalence concerning the spotlight's control over the play's canned speakers, always at the mercy of omniscient illumination. When the spotlight tires of their lame renditions detailing the antics of an adulterous affair, involving as it does the inevitable subterfuge of perfume, suspect bodily scents, uncontrollable jealousy and the final insult of all, the hiring of a private detective who is eventually paid off, it promptly shuts the speakers down and moves on to the next instalment in an all-too-familiar soap opera, now magically defamiliarised. Without the movement of the spotlight, then, there is in fact no real 'play', 'just' or otherwise, for these talking heads yearn to be heard as much as seen. In a pinch, even mumbling will do, as when they speak all together, rendering them unintelligible. And for these players, planted on stage as they are, this is a punishment worse than silence.

In *Play*, as in *Come and Go*, Beckett renews his licence to pursue the flexibility of dramatic form, now understood as something inherently, perhaps even supremely, spatial and mathematical. In the final stage of his playwriting career, he will raise the bar even higher, composing a series of works that make us rethink everything we thought we knew about certain limits and possibilities for theatrical representation. By way of illustration, let us begin with the question of stage time. This has always been understood in its problematic relation to time as it passes before us in the real world. Aristotle in his *Poetics* valorised this as one of the three dramatic unities, so much so that he admired Sophocles above all others, as in his plays there was the closest approximation between time as it passed on stage and time as it was experienced in the world outside the play. Western theatre has of course travelled a long road since Aristotle, and no more so than in its strategies for violating the unity of time. Shakespeare was one of its principal violators, but no more so than fourth-wall realists like Ibsen and Chekhov, the inventors of theatrical modernism. All three playwrights have in common the condensation of real time to meet the contingencies of their various performance spaces. Every cup-and-saucer does this, too: *My dear, let me draw the curtains. We have been sitting here talking all afternoon.* The entire scene, however, lasts hardly a quarter of an hour.

Something else is at work, and profoundly so, in Beckett's late style for the theatre, where the concentration of emotional richness is at a premium. Here, too, though time never stands still, he expands the moment rather than contracts it, extending its temporality to make the instant seem much larger and grander than it actually is. Reversing our normal expectations for the movement of time on stage, and suggesting a new template for unities and disunities of time, works like *Not I* and *Rockaby* and *Footfalls* always seem in performance much longer than they actually are, and not because of their *longueurs*. The dramatic moment redoubles its affective force to become something less fleeting, more lasting, more substantial and far more weighty. What results is haunting. *Not I*, in fact, may be the longest eighteen minutes in theatre history. *Rockaby*, clocking in at fourteen minutes, fifty seconds, is not much shorter.[11] Duration on stage may have never played itself out quite like this before.

Such a recalibration of stage time on stage space will achieve its most impressive effect in the use and orchestration of soliloquy. Beckett's characters in his late plays are not so much thinking aloud as they are attempting to communicate 'Thoughts, no, not thoughts. Profounds of mind' (CDW, 448). This is a subtle difference, but one that will have enormous repercussions as each of these short dramas runs its course. Stage space is reassembled to track and trace the space of human consciousness, offering us a new opportunity to consider what a soliloquy is and what it might become as delivered in performance. Many metaphors have been used to describe what Beckett has in mind here: 'spots of time', 'a pulsation in the artery', Joyce's 'epiphany', even a vulgarisation like 'it suddenly flashed on me'. But not before Beckett has a playwright attempted to capture this fleeting moment and contain it in the shape of a new dramatic form. The effect can be unsettling, but also startling. His ghost-like soliloquisers, alone, wounded and isolated as they are on a very empty space, therefore have an awful lot to act, to do and to perform as they expand the dramatic moment to encompass the entirety of a play itself.

Asked in 1981 by an eager audience member if he could describe the difference between Beckett's 'full-length' plays and the short works he was now composing for the stage, American director Alan Schneider responded as follows: 'All of Mr. Beckett's plays are full length. Some of them are shorter than others, but they're are full length. None of them is half-length'.[12] Schneider's remark in some ways goes to the heart of the matter concerning the dynamics of duration as we might be able to observe them at work in the modern theatre. Beckett's last plays, including the well-named *That Time*, offer us precisely sustained images challenging any preconceptions we might still have concerning the relationship between time and space as they figure in the mechanics necessary to their stage representation. Genre and media considerations are paramount; it is hard to imagine, for example, what Beckett's late plays would look like without his immersion in television technology, where the spare, exact and Spartan pictographs designed for screen transmission in masterful works like *Ghost Trio* and ... *but the clouds* ... reach for and finally achieve a different but equally compelling impact on the live stage. Beckett's dramatic forms are always in dialogue with themselves regarding the aesthetics of their constant negotiation. Formalism, yes, without which 'the mess' outside the theatre can never 'accommodate' itself to the contingencies of mood and atmosphere and gesture within the compelling framework of a performing arts medium. In his plays, as elsewhere in the vast resources to be found in his writing, Beckett's 'forms' are therefore 'many', and many indeed, 'in which the unchanging seeks release from its formlessness'.[13]

NOTES

1 Martin Esslin quoted Beckett on this point during his presentation at the symposium on *Rockaby*, State University of New York at Buffalo, 8 April 1981.
2 Ruby Cohn, *Samuel Beckett: The Comic Gamut* (New Brunswick: Rutgers University Press, 1962).
3 See C. J. Ackerley and S. E. Gontarski, (eds.), *The Grove Companion to Samuel Beckett* (New York: Grove Press, 2004), 28.
4 For a catalogue of such references in *Waiting for Godot*, see Enoch Brater, *The Essential Samuel Beckett* (London: Thames & Hudson, 2003), 75.
5 All references in my text to Shakespeare's plays are taken from *The Riverside Shakespeare*, second edition (Boston: Houghton Mifflin, 1997).
6 See Enoch Brater, *Ten Ways of Thinking About Samuel Beckett: The Falsetto of Reason* (London: Methuen Drama, 2011), 69–85.
7 On the relationship between *King Lear* and *Endgame*, see Jan Kott, *Shakespeare Our Contemporary*, trans. B. Taborski (New York: Norton, 1974), 127–68.
8 See Enoch Brater, *The Essential Samuel Beckett* (London: Thames & Hudson, 2003), 91.
9 See ibid., 102.

10 See Julian Barnes, *Flaubert's Parrot* (New York: Vintage, 1990), 91.
11 For the running times of *Not I* and *Rockaby*, see Enoch Brater, *Beyond Minimalism: Beckett's Late Style in the Theater* (New York: Oxford University Press, 1987), 23, 167.
12 Alan Schneider, speaking at the symposium on *Rockaby*, 8 April 1981.
13 See Tom Driver, 'Beckett by the Madeleine', *Columbia University Forum* (4: Summer 1961).

PART VIII

Reception and Remains

CHAPTER 34

Initial Reception

James Gourley

The literary career of Samuel Barclay Beckett was, by any standard, a wild success. Beckett was awarded the Nobel Prize for Literature in 1969, was the recipient of numerous international literary prizes and was a writer whose every new work aroused huge interest in literary (and non-literary) circles. Beckett's texts have become a byword for importance in theatre and prose. Despite this unbridled success, Samuel Beckett's career is generally judged as the struggle of a writer unsuited to the commercial realities of publication, whose tortured writing, and the difficult brilliance that emerged regularly, nonetheless obscures an inherent failure on the part of both the author and his critics.

In this chapter, I examine the critical successes and failures of Beckett's writing career, using the Second World War as a marker for a transformation in the critical approach to Beckett's work. This chapter cannot provide complete coverage of the critical reception of Beckett's work, as the international reach of Beckett's oeuvre makes a complete documentation in the space provided impossible. Considering this, I point the reader to the recent publication of a volume that deals with the subject of this chapter in great detail, the thoroughly researched collection of essays edited by Mark Nixon and Matthew Feldman, *The International Reception of Samuel Beckett*.[1] The volume does more justice both to specific detail and theoretical considerations than is possible in this chapter. Readers should also examine the chronology at the beginning of this volume that sets out in skeletal form aspects of the publishing history of Beckett's works.

In *The International Reception of Samuel Beckett* Nixon and Feldman ask a crucial question:

[W]hat is to be 'received'? Is it artistic success or failure, expression or inexpression, speech or silence?[2]

To this we may add two further questions; how are we to define reception? And, where does reception begin and end? This chapter will focus on a generally (although not exclusively) European reception of Beckett's work and focus primarily on the 1940s and '50s as the crucial period to examine in Beckett reception. There are, of course, entire subjects that must be ignored because of space constraints on this chapter. The works cited provide further examination of issues I am unable to address here.

PRE-WAR

The critical response to Samuel Beckett's pre-war writing is characterised by a widespread, although not universal, ambivalence. The young Irishman, moving restlessly between Ireland and the Continent, and between fiction and criticism, did not achieve the success he so earnestly desired. Beckett's first foray into publication occurred in 1929, after his initial solidifying experiences in Paris and the beginnings of his friendship with James Joyce. The young Beckett was asked to contribute an essay to a volume on Joyce's *Work in Progress* to emerge, in 1939, as *Finnegans Wake*. Beckett's contribution to the volume was the essay 'Dante...Bruno.Vico.. Joyce'. The essay not only assumed the title that Joyce had proposed to Beckett, but also distilled the essence of Beckett's discussions with Joyce and Joyce's explanations of the *Wake*.[3] Little critical response to Beckett's essay occurred, notwithstanding the burgeoning notoriety of Joyce's final work. Despite the significance attributed to this essay in both Joyce studies and Beckett studies since its republication in *Disjecta* in 1983, the effect of this work was minimal at the time. Post-war Beckett criticism lionised Beckett's claim that in *Finnegans Wake*: 'form *is* content, content *is* form' or 'direct expression', both of which the common reader may be 'too decadent to receive', and argued that a similar impetus exists in Beckett's work (*D*, 27, 26). Despite being an important source for modern Beckett criticism, the response to Beckett's essay was at the time close to complete critical silence.

A more creative exercise was Beckett's 1931 monograph on Proust, which utilised Beckett's critical faculties to reconsider the main focuses of *A la recherché du temps perdu*. Beckett concluded that time was the primary concept of Proust's work, what he called the 'double-headed monster of damnation and salvation' (*P*, 1). The work received a number of brief reviews, the most notable written by Imagist F. S. Flint. The review epitomises faint praise, with Flint concluding: 'If we could understand this essay, we might be able to praise it'.[4] Beckett's inability to produce work that received critical approval is, of course, linked with his lack of comfort in the academic world – a world he was more than happy to leave behind, and did so shortly after *Proust* was published. The publishers of *Proust* reflected the liminal status of their author by only being willing to publish a trade edition, eschewing the possibility of a signed, limited edition, which would have only been profitable for an author with a higher critical profile (*K*, 113–14).

It is instructive that Beckett's first published piece of creative work, the poem 'Whoroscope', received much warmer analysis than its critical counterparts. 'Whoroscope' was produced in 1929, supposedly as a last-minute entry into Nancy Cunard and the Hours Press' poetry competition, for a poetic composition on the subject of time. Considering Beckett's temporal focus in *Proust* it is no wonder he was successful, with the poem so taking Cunard and the other judges (including Richard Aldington) that it was immediately awarded first place, and the £10 prize (See *K*, 110–13). Even this minor success was not enough to wrestle the young Beckett out of his 'initial marginality', reflected not only in the minimal critical attention focused on him – but also in the difficult position Beckett was in – in limbo between the academic and creative worlds.[5]

After fleeing Dublin, and finally rejecting an academic career for literary pursuits, Beckett faced a difficult time in the period leading up to the outbreak of the Second World War. The early success of *Whoroscope* was put into perspective by the struggles Beckett had to find publishers for his work. After labouring intensely on *Dream of Fair to Middling Women*, Beckett saw the manuscript repeatedly turned down, perhaps because of the likely threat that the novel would fall foul of the censors (*K*, 159–61, 165). The novel was finally published, after Beckett's death, in 1992. *More Pricks than Kicks* was published in London in 1934, although its readership was proscribed by its quick censorship in Ireland.[6] After even more painful struggle including, reputedly, rejection from forty-two publishers, *Murphy* was published in 1938.[7] *More Pricks than Kicks* received a few minor reviews, with the *Times Literary Supplement* identifying a 'fresh talent ..., though it is a talent not quite sure of itself'.[8] *Murphy* garnered more critical attention, including a review by Dylan Thomas, who saw it as 'difficult, serious, and wrong' with the 'serious' being the redeeming of the three determinations.[9] The *TLS* still identified talent in its review of *Murphy*, this time paired with knowledge, although a writer that required 'a theme of more depth and substance'.[10]

Beckett's often marginalised other publication of this period is his collection of poetry, *Echo's Bones, and Other Precipitates*. This collection caused Beckett considerable heartache, not only because of the lack of critical interest (indeed the young man had given up on publishing the collection for economic gain) but because of the personal subject matter of the poems, including a rumination on his father's death in 'Malacoda' (see *K*, 222). By this point Beckett was beginning to perceive the negative reaction to his works as reflective not simply of a disinterest on the part of the critical sphere, but also as reflective of some lack inherent to the works themselves. Thus James Knowlson reports on Beckett's later dismissal of *Echo's Bones*, the author calling it the 'work of a very young man who had nothing to say and the itch to make' (quoted in *K*, 223). It is perhaps with the benefit of hindsight that we can interpret this critical disregard that Beckett experienced pre-war as another precipitate towards the fractured form of his works that emerged after World War Two.

The commercial and critical difficulties that the young Beckett was encountering on his way to literary success, combined with his personal conflicts with mother and country, would have made his lack of success doubly galling. These problems, however, were ultimately supplanted by the Second World War, during which Beckett remained in France, participating in the Resistance; he then spent the final years of the war in Roussillon, outside Paris. Having written *Watt* in this period of waiting for the war to end, it was only after the war concluded that Beckett was to experience what Knowlson called his 'frenzy of writing' which was to change forever the critical reaction to the young author's work.

POST-WAR

Beckett's first attempts at publishing post-war replicated his experiences from before the war, with publishers in the United States and the United Kingdom rejecting *Watt*. The novel was to be published in 1953, after up to twenty rejections on both sides of the Atlantic.[11] Things began to change for Beckett, however, when Tristan Tzara read *Molloy* in manuscript form, and 'admired it greatly'; although his influence was not sufficient to see the novel published (*K*, 377). The spectre of rejection was alleviated when Beckett's work was discovered by Jérôme Lindon, of Les Éditions des Minuits, who admired both Beckett's prose and plays, and agreed to publish them. The publication of the first two parts of the 'Trilogy', *Molloy* and *Malone meurt*, began the avalanche of positive critical response that Beckett craved. French critics responded positively to the complexity of these two works, and although there were contractual issues, and publishers to be found in the United States and the United Kingdom, things began to turn for the young Irishman.

Initial Reception

As critical notice of Beckett's work increased so did the length of reviews, and most significant, the importance of the reviewers assigned to Beckett's work. Perhaps the most significant review of *Molloy* was written by Maurice Nadeau, who had a reputation for identifying talented writers earlier than other critics. Indeed, Nadeau was a committed supporter of Beckett's work, assisting in early radio productions of his plays, and recommending Beckett's work for literary prizes.[12] Nadeau wrote, in his review of *Molloy*, of the influence he anticipated for Beckett, describing him as an:

> Ironic genius, subtle charmer, humorist besides which the most famous black humorists pale, champion of the Nothing exalted to the height of the Whole, and conversely, giant conqueror of an elusive reality, he took us along with him into this forest. We too will only come out of it on our elbows and our knees. It will take years.[13]

Nadeau exalts both author and work, and his review is indicative of the reception of *Molloy* and more generally Beckett's post–World War Two output. Indeed, it is the 'reality' of Beckett's works that enraptured his reviewers, with Georges Bataille, the famous author and essayist, commenting on *Molloy*:

> There is in this reality, the essence or residue of being, something so *universal*, these complete *vagabonds* we occasionally encounter but immediately *lose* have something so essentially indistinct about them, that we cannot imagine anything more anonymous. So much so that this name *vagabond* I have just written down misrepresents them.[14]

Aside from the positivity of Bataille's review, it is his observations on Beckett's use of language that are most important. Indeed, this issue is addressed not through examination of the language Beckett uses, but through the language that Bataille is called to use, examining the resonances and accretions of 'vagabond', which make the term simultaneously appropriate and inappropriate.

Despite the success of Beckett's novels published after the Second World War, it is only with the huge success of his plays that the no longer young Irishman gained the fame and critical attention that his works have maintained to this day.[15] The successful premiere of *En attendant Godot* at the Théâtre de Babylone changed everything. Despite the confusion that met the initial performances, reviews were generally positive, and the play moved quickly into production in Europe and the United States. The burgeoning popularity of the play signified the apotheosis of a significant shift in modernist theatre practice. *Godot* eventually took Paris by storm, followed by Germany, whilst the first British production was a disaster, a critical response that Beckett was, by this time, thoroughly inured to.[16] Cecil Wilson and Milton Shulman were two rays of hope for the production, both producing positive reviews (*K*, 415). The tide turned, however, with Kenneth Tynan and Harold Hobson's reviews, both equivocal in their praise (*K*, 415). The theatregoing public began to embrace the production, and Beckett's critical reputation prospered not just on the continent but in the United Kingdom as well. The critical perception of Beckett's work, and the profits that his play was producing meant that the play's reputation could withstand a few further setbacks, especially the infamous marketing of *Waiting for Godot* (the 'laugh hit of two continents') in Miami, which was redeemed by the play's success on Broadway (*K*, 420, 422). From this point on, Beckett's theatrical success meant that he was financially secure, and the critical reaction to his work solidified his reputation as a serious, if difficult, modern writer.

The critical response to Beckett's work was generally positive throughout the late 1950s and '60s. *All that Fall* was one of the two BBC nominations for the Prix Italia, whilst *Embers* won the RAI prize, the 1959 Prix Italia (*K*, 433, 446). Both *Endgame* and *Krapp's Last Tape* were critical successes throughout Europe as they emerged, and Beckett, along with Jorge Luis Borges, was awarded the Prix International des Critiques, or, Prix Formentor, in 1961 (*K*, 458, 485). Beckett was now at the height of his fame, and the critical response was indicative of this. The Prix International des Critiques came with a $10,000 prize, which Beckett, now financially comfortable, used to support his friends and artistic acquaintances. Perhaps the only sour note in these years was the mixed reviews the Paris premiere of *Happy Days* received, although the negative reviews were perhaps evidence of a rejection of the manipulation of the theatrical form that Beckett experimented with in this work; the play was, nevertheless, received warmly elsewhere.

The positive critical reception of Beckett's post–World War Two work culminated in 1969 when the Swedish Academy decided to award him the Nobel Prize for Literature. Beckett's citation read: 'for his writing which – in new forms for the novel and drama – in the destitution of modern man acquires its elevation'. The recognition and publicity that the award produced was no doubt uncomfortable, especially in the short term. His wife, Suzanne, viewed it as a 'catastrophe', just as Jérôme Lindon advised the pair 'to go into hiding' (*K*, 570). Nevertheless, the Prize was an important recognition which guaranteed sales for Beckett's works and allowed publishers to profit on an author they had earlier taken a risk with. Indeed,

Knowlson suggests that Beckett decided to accept the award (albeit in absentia) partly in recognition of Maurice Nadeau 'and others' who had nominated Beckett for the prize regularly from twelve years prior to his success (*K*, 573).

Beckett's critical reception and literary success culminated in an emerging view of his work, beginning in the late 1950s, which seeks to understand the Beckettian oeuvre as somehow reflective of *all*. Northrop Frye, in a review of the first collected publication as 'Trilogy' of *Molloy, Malone Dies* and *The Unnamable*, makes the observation that in Beckett's work character is not individual, but rather 'the ego is stripped of all individuality and is seen merely as representative of all of its kind'.[17] Indeed Frye will later observe, when examining the consciousness of *The Unnamable*, that the 'voice' may be 'our own subconscious if we acquire the trick of listening to it'.[18] Finally, the persistence of the voice allows Frye to conclude that the silence, which he sees in *The Unnamable*, is the 'role of serious writing'.[19] Despite the pessimism of this statement, a critic such as Frye epitomises the importance with which Beckett's work is viewed and simultaneously illustrates the paradigmatic shift that his creative work engendered, not only in Europe but throughout the world.

NOTES

1 Mark Nixon and Matthew Feldman (eds.), *The International Reception of Samuel Beckett* (New York: Continuum, 2011); see also P. J. Murphy et al., *Critique of Beckett Criticism: A Guide to Research in English, French, and German* (Columbia: Camden House, 1994).
2 Ibid., 3.
3 See Letter to Joyce, *L1*, 7.
4 F. S. Flint, quoted in L. Graver and R. Federman, *Samuel Beckett: The Critical Heritage* (London: Routledge, 1997), 41.
5 Nixon and Feldman, *The International Reception of Samuel Beckett*, 2.
6 See Seán Kennedy, 'Samuel Beckett's Reception in Ireland', in Nixon and Feldman, *The International Reception of Samuel Beckett*, 57.
7 See Linda Ben-Zvi, *Samuel Beckett*, (Boston: Twayne Publishers, 1986), 14; cf. *K*, 248.
8 No author attributed, quoted in Graver and Federman, *Samuel Beckett: The Critical Heritage*, 44.
9 Dylan Thomas, quoted in ibid., 47.
10 No author attributed, quoted in ibid., 46.
11 See *K*, 396.
12 See *K*, 386, 392.
13 Maurice Nadeau, quoted in Graver and Federman, *Samuel Beckett: The Critical Heritage*, 54.

14 Georges Bataille, quoted in Graver and Federman, *Samuel Beckett: The Critical Heritage*, 55, italics original.
15 Indeed, as Nixon and Feldman observe, it is still *Godot* that drives the general critical impression of Beckett's work throughout the world. See Mark Nixon and Matthew Feldman, 'Introduction: "Getting Known" – Samuel Beckett's International Reception', in Nixon and Feldman, *The International Reception of Samuel Beckett*, 5.
16 See *K*, 386, 392, 414–15.
17 Northrop Frye, quoted in Graver and Federman, *Samuel Beckett: The Critical Heritage*, 209.
18 Ibid., 213.
19 Ibid., 214.

CHAPTER 35

Influence

Michael D'Arcy

Samuel Beckett's writing suggests a persistent suspicion of the notion of literary influence, even as the problem of influence would continue to haunt his work and its reception. His 1929 essay 'Dante ... Bruno. Vico ... Joyce' is devoted to establishing James Joyce's indebtedness to the three precursors mentioned in the title, but it is striking that Beckett avoids the term 'influence'. He prefers instead to speak of 'reverberations', 'reapplications', similarities and parallels (*D*, 20, 30). Moreover, despite the confidence with which Beckett declares the presence of Italian philosophers Giambattista Vico and Giordano Bruno in Joyce's *Work in Progress* (which would become *Finnegans Wake*), the essay maintains an awareness of the problematic nature of its central task. Beckett's first sentence announces, 'The danger is in the neatness of identifications' (*D*, 19), signalling the difficulty inherent in the project on which he is embarking. The essay's opening paragraph indicates, however, that the enterprise will go on nonetheless. After referring to the illegitimate identification of 'philosophical abstraction and the empirical illustration', an identification he sees in the work of Vico, Beckett continues, 'And now here I am with my handful of abstractions, among which notably: a mountain, the coincidence of contraries, the inevitability of cyclical evolution, a system of Poetics, and the prospect of self-extension in the world of Mr. Joyce's "*Work in Progress*"'. These 'abstractions', derived from the work of the authors under discussion, are apparently unavoidable for Beckett in his approach to the 'particulars' of *Work in Progress*, even as the identification of abstraction and particular 'empirical illustration' is seen as 'unjustifiable'. We are already confronted here with a typically Beckettian double bind, as the critical problem of reading relationships of literary indebtedness is framed in terms of the dilemma of a necessary, but illegitimate, identification of 'abstraction' and 'empirical illustration'.

The struggle with the spectre of literary influence would continue to inform Beckett's writing in various ways. In 1931, on the subject of his unpublished short story 'Sedendo et Quiescendo', he admitted to Charles Prentice, his editor at Chatto & Windus, 'of course it stinks of Joyce in spite of most earnest endeavours to endow it with my own odours'.[1] As his biographer James Knowlson puts it, Beckett came to 'the certainty that he had to dissociate himself at an early stage from Joyce's influence' (*K*, 353). Later in his life Beckett recognised the importance for him of Joyce's 'heroic achievement',[2] though he characteristically deflected more specific suggestions of influence on his work – in 1967, for example, he wrote to critic Sighle Kennedy, 'I simply do not feel the presence in my writings as a whole of the Joyce & Proust situations you evoke' (*D*, 113). This negative response to scenarios of specific literary indebtedness appears in other forms in Beckett's writings. On reading the work of French writer Charles Juliet in 1968, Beckett's advice was 'Distance yourself both from yourself and from me'.[3] In 1955, he wrote to critic David Hayman, commenting on the latter's doctoral thesis on Joyce, 'I think perhaps you derive Joyce's use of the technique of suggestion too directly and exclusively from the symbolists and Mallarmé. The device after all is as old as writing itself' (*L2*, 537). These comments may be read as expanding on Beckett's earlier hesitation to make 'identifications' in tracing Joyce's relationships to previous authors. Beckett's letter suggests this connection to 'Dante...Bruno. Vico..Joyce', in his framing of Hayman's work as involving the 'identification in FW [*Finnegans Wake*] of Mallarmean elements'. As in Beckett's Joyce essay, such identification has its perils, even as it appears unavoidable (at least for the literary critic), a point he makes to Hayman somewhat diplomatically: 'sometimes you seem rather to strain the point and solicit your texts, but I think you could hardly have done otherwise. For you had not only to resist the special pleading to which all thesis is an invitation, but at the same time texts into which almost anything can be read'.

Beckett's letter to Hayman, like 'Dante...Bruno.Vico..Joyce', indicates that the problem of influence is tied to the larger issue of literary interpretation. The Joyce essay conceives of its interpretations as coterminous with the tracing of relations of literary indebtedness, and suggests that while this may be a necessary task, it is to be performed with a certain reluctance. In this regard the essay looks forward to Beckett's later work preoccupied with the problem of interpretation and its ineliminability. Beckett the literary critic who appears in 'Dante ... Bruno.Vico ... Joyce' anticipates, for example, the figure of Watt, who is compelled to interpretation, even as he evinces no enthusiasm for what the novel's narrator describes as 'this pursuit of meaning in this indifference to meaning' (*W*, 62). *Watt* proposes one important line of response to this situation.

This work is Beckett's first novelistic elaboration of the narrator or protagonist as a listener-interpreter, a scenario that would find its fullest development in *The Unnamable*, where the narrator is cast as a transcriber of a series of misunderstood or almost-understood sounds or voices. At this point we are returned to the question of literary influence, given that the voices heard by Beckett's protagonists or narrators frequently involve allusions to other texts.[4] Beckett's vision of the subject as a listener-interpreter emerges as centrally concerned with the dynamics of textual transmission and reception, or the writer's subjection to cultural context and literary precursors. More specifically, it has been argued that *The Unnamable*'s difficulties with voices reveal Beckett's 'desire to break free from the linguistic community of writers who have preceded him', and in particular that at issue here is Beckett's fraught relationship to his great modernist precursors, Joyce being the most imposing of these figures.[5] Leaving aside the question of how specifically one should locate the source of *The Unnamable*'s voices, the least one could say is that Beckett's voices tie the subject firmly to the world of textual dissemination, and this scenario becomes one way for him to think about literary inheritance and influence. To conceive of these relationships in such terms is to frame them as ambiguous, intermittent and, at least in part, indecipherable.

In this way Beckett's work is already mapping – without providing any apparent solutions – central coordinates of a dilemma that is animating contemporary scholarship addressed to the problem of his legacies, influence or persistence. Beckett's voices point us at once to specific literary connections – his relationships to Joyce, Marcel Proust, St Augustine and others – even as they exceed these connections, or remain entangled with nagging problems of intertextual undecidability. Relations of literary influence, involved as they are with Beckett's voices, are only partially readable, or undecidedly readable. If Beckett's work suggests this point, this is clearly a problem that extends into the travails of contemporary scholars faced with the issue of Beckett's influence. The problem raised here, in a nutshell, is how to talk about something at once pervasive and elusive. John Brenkman writes that Beckett's influence extends 'to minimalists and Menippeans, postcolonial fabulators and trailer-park realists'.[6] In his account, Peter Boxall includes Irish sitcoms, contemporary dance and visual art, not to mention literature from across the globe.[7] A very short list of writers whose work has been linked to that of Beckett would include novelists Paul Auster, John Banville, Thomas Bernhard, J. M. Coetzee, Don DeLillo, B. S. Johnson and Kenzaburo Oe; poets Thomas Kinsella, Derek Mahon and Paul Muldoon; and playwrights Edward Albee, Brian Friel,

Athol Fugard, Václav Havel, Sarah Kane, Suzan Lori Parks, Harold Pinter and Tom Stoppard. Beckett's influence starts to resemble the voices that swell the pages of *The Unnamable*, and to address it is to talk about something that resists being tracked down and domesticated in the abstractions of literary criticism.

Faced with this critical gauntlet, the following discussion takes as its focus Beckett's relationship to the form of the novel and a series of engagements with this form that follow in his wake. In the spirit of his approach to the question of influence, the methodological position informing this account is a compromised one. If the relationships suggested here are not always authorised by 'empirically defensible connections with Beckett's art', the underlying proposition is that Beckett's fiction opens up or enables specific pathways in the history of the novel and that these are at least partially readable in the authors considered.[8] More specifically, the strain of novelistic experiment sketched here, in which Beckett plays an indispensible role, elaborates an acute awareness of the novel as a frail and fallible form. In the aftermath of Beckett, the novelists under consideration – B. S. Johnson, V. S. Naipaul, J. M. Coetzee and Thomas Bernhard – develop ways of scrutinizing, negating and perpetuating operations often ascribed to the novel: the invention of plot, the elaboration of an exemplary meaning of individual experience, the creation of individuated characters and the representation of their interaction with concrete (social) environments.

Writing in 1962 in *The Spectator*, British novelist B. S. Johnson locates Beckett in a tradition that includes Rabelais, Cervantes and Sterne, arguing of Beckett, 'admiration or loathing of him is an indication of whether the reader is really interested in the novel as a form, or merely in being told a story'.[9] Johnson's 1964 novel *Albert Angelo*, with its epigraph from Beckett's *The Unnamable*, suggests important links to the Irish author's engagement with the novel form. The conclusion of Johnson's novel subjects the conventions of the genre to withering scrutiny, beginning with the sudden interjection, which interrupts a passage of relatively conventional psycho-narration, 'OH, FUCK ALL THIS LYING!' The ensuing section of the novel, titled 'Disintegration', indicates that 'all this lying' includes the creation of characters, 'telling stories' and the writer's imposition on complexity of 'his own pattern, an arbitrary pattern, which must falsify, cannot do anything other than falsify'.[10] *Albert Angelo* thus offers a vehement interrogation of the components of the literary form we have just traversed, at the same time that this novel, its post-Joycean experimentation notwithstanding, remains attached to these conventions.

The ground for this scenario has been prepared by Beckett, a point implicitly recognised by Johnson's epigraph from *The Unnamable*. After denigrating a series of characters going back as far as Murphy, Beckett's passage cited by Johnson evokes a 'lucidity' that would transcend such fictional surrogates: 'there is nothing else, let us be lucid for once, nothing else but what happens to me, such as speaking, and such as seeking, and which cannot happen to me, which prowl around me, like bodies in torment' (*U*, 109).[11] The passage, in particular its evocation of a series of figures that 'prowl around' the narrator, leaves the transcendence of novelistic artifice, especially of novelistic character, very much in doubt. If Johnson develops on this situation, more generally *Albert Angelo* elaborates on Beckett's framing of the novel as a compromised but inescapable literary form. This novelistic programme is manifest already in Beckett's first published novel, *Murphy* (1938), which treats the conventions of novelistic realism and the *Bildungsroman* as a series of discredited obligations to be fulfilled in a perfunctory and mocking way. In the work of both authors, the novel goes on, but in a version of that form that continually signals its own infirmity and absence of legitimacy.

One way that Johnson frames this vision of the novel is by insisting on the inimical relationship between what *Albert Angelo* refers to as 'the fragmentariness of life' and the ordering of imposed forms, in particular those of the novel. The world is too big, too disjointed and complicated for the novel; any novelistic representation of it thus appears as inadequate and misrepresenting or – to use Johnson's terms – as 'lies, lies, lies'. And, in a point especially reminiscent of Beckett, this complexity that the novel fails to encompass is framed in terms of the banal details of bodily functions.[12] The novel thus becomes a privileged venue to register a disjunction between meaningful forms and the fragmentariness of life, and this position centrally informs the self-denigration we see in *Albert Angelo*. The novel appears to be faced with a choice between unenviable alternatives – to continue to impose its falsifying 'pattern', or to embrace fragmentariness and incoherence to the point of its own dissolution.

This is a dilemma framed by Beckett in his early novel (unpublished in his lifetime) *Dream of Fair to Middling Women*. The protagonist, Belacqua Shua, announces the problem and proposes, perhaps overconfidently, a solution: 'The reality of the individual ... is an incoherent reality and must be expressed incoherently'.[13] If this programme of incoherent expression avoids the 'falsity' that the novel ascribes to the nineteenth-century novels of Balzac and 'the divine Jane', it remains questionable whether it is possible to write a novel on this model.[14] *Watt* (1953), Beckett's last novel written directly in English before his turn to French in the 1940s, sharpens the horns of the dilemma involved here, notably in the account of Watt's encounter with a family of piano tuners, the Galls. This incident is subsumed within a random and unmasterable flux of phenomena, 'and became a mere example of light commenting bodies, and stillness motion, and silence sound' (*W*, 60). At the same time, the very designation of the event as an encounter with a family of piano tuners already performs a novelistic domestication of these intricacies. The novelistic creation of character, encounter and incident (however desultory this creation) appears as quite possibly an arbitrary imposition of form: 'were there neither Galls nor piano then, but only an unintelligible succession of changes, from which Watt finally extracted the Galls and the piano, in self-defence?' (*W*, 65).

Watt thus evokes Watt's inability to represent a fragmentary reality with which he is confronted, suggesting by implication that the forms of the novel are inimical to such representation. What Watt (or *Watt*) fails to adequately represent is also figured here in terms of the experience of the human body. Beckett's fiction, or certainly the work produced in the 1940s and 1950s, registers this somatic experience but also indicates that the form of the novel is unequal to the task of representing it. In *The Unnamable*, for example, the narrator's inevitable recourse to novelistic conventions, 'the resorts of fable' and the creation of characters, apparently serves to distract attention from his 'pains', given that the pains of his characters 'are nothing, compared to mine, a mere tittle of mine' (*U*, 14). Beckett's narrator discusses his 'pains' and physical situation, but this description remains a novelistic distraction from (rather than an adequate representation of) physical suffering. The account of the narrator's bodily situation is condemned as 'mean words', invented, the narrator suggests, 'to escape from me' (*U*, 16).

Elements of these novelistic experiments are developed in a different register in the fiction of Trinidadian-British novelist V. S. Naipaul. His 1967 novel *The Mimic Men* returns us to the scenario of artistic failure in the portrayal of its protagonist, Ralph Singh, as a failed memoirist. Referring to the opening narration we have just read, the novel's narrator – who is also apparently its protagonist – states, 'These are not the political memoirs I saw myself composedly writing in the evening of my days. A more than autobiographical work, the exposition of the malaise of our times pointed and illuminated by personal experience'.[15] While framed in terms of an autobiographical project, this literary ambition points to a central function that has been ascribed to the novel form – to fashion an exemplary meaning for individual experience. In a gesture similar to what we have observed in Beckett and Johnson, Naipaul thus registers the inherited formal and thematic imperatives of the novel, even as his work raises the question of its own negative relationship to these imperatives. One reason why *The Mimic Men* is ambiguous in its address to this problem is the complication raised by the scenario of the protagonist as failed writer – it is unclear to what extent we should identify the novel we are reading with the book that Singh talks about writing. This interpretive ripple, familiar to readers of Proust, is also at issue in Beckett's fiction. For example, if we take Watt as a figure for the novelist, as my discussion would suggest we do, a complication raised here is the uncertain relationship between the novel we are reading (*Watt*) and the interpretive and representational problems of its protagonist (Watt).

Naipaul's novel also discusses (its own) literary failure through its portrayal of the writer's inability to do justice to a history of 'disorder', which is framed in terms of the dislocations of imperialism and colonialism. Complicating this account is a narrative thread focussed on an experience of involuntary memory. In a moment reminiscent of Proust's famous scenes of involuntary memory, the narrator describes how his writing emerges from a memory, of a scene several decades earlier, 'forcing itself to the surface'. But this apparently epiphanic memory is also framed as an unwilled eruption of disorder. Writing appears here in an inimical relationship to such memory: the narrator speaks of this activity as 'abolishing' the disturbance of his interruptive memory.[16] Writing emerges as a frail imposition of form, and Naipaul's narrator comes to conceive of his literary labours in terms of the cultivation of calm or 'anaesthetizing order'.[17] Beckett's work manifests a similar attitude to involuntary memory, conceiving of it as involving an unpleasant intrusion of suffering or painful affect, and also suggests that a corollary to this view of memory is a conception of writing as anesthetising: his story 'The Calmative' states at the outset, for example, 'I'll try and tell myself another story, to try and calm myself' (*CSP*, 61). For both novelists, this conception of involuntary memory as painful or disturbing becomes one way to frame the disorder and fragmentation that the novel at once registers and resists.

South African-Australian novelist J. M. Coetzee has acknowledged Beckett's importance for him, commenting in an interview, 'Beckett has meant a great deal to me in my own writing – that must be obvious. He is a clear influence on my prose'.[18] To attempt to frame this connection more specifically, we can return to the question of the novel's relationship to the body. Coetzee's *Waiting for the Barbarians* (1980) is centrally concerned with the impotence, irrelevance or guilt of culture vis-à-vis suffering and atrocity. The protagonist and narrator, referred to only as the Magistrate, retreats into a solipsistic appreciation of 'the classics' as the colonial administration he works for carries out a string of atrocities under his watch. The novel is not set in any recognisable geographical or temporal location, but its exploration of state-perpetrated torture suggests an indirect reference to the South African context of the 1970s, where the Security Police routinely carried out acts of torture. The Magistrate makes several attempts to transcend the confines of his solipsism and political quietude, but at the conclusion of the novel he apparently remains ensconced in isolation, 'toying' with his hobbies. These include the attempt to write a history of his outpost, a project that deteriorates into what he describes as the 'devious', 'equivocal' and 'reprehensible' 'locutions of a civil servant with literary ambitions'.[19]

As in the novels discussed earlier, Coetzee's portrait of artistic failure is arguably a commentary on the novel form and its awareness of its own limitations. *Waiting for the Barbarians*, unlike the Magistrate's lyrical evocations of the outpost in the examples of his writing given in the novel, does not ostensibly ignore the issue of state-perpetrated atrocity. Coetzee's writings indicate, however, that the dilemma faced by the novel, when confronted with the problem of the representation of torture and suffering, is not to be overcome by detailed descriptions of atrocity. He makes this point in a 1986 essay titled 'Into the Dark Chamber: The Writer and the South African State', which argues that the writer faced with a history of state-perpetrated torture faces unenviable alternatives – to ignore the 'obscenities' of the state, or to attempt to represent this obscenity, which involves 'following the state ... making its vile mysteries the occasion for fantasy'. The writer's 'challenge' in this situation, Coetzee continues, is 'how to imagine torture and death on one's own terms'.[20] If *Waiting for the Barbarians* represents one such attempt to imagine torture 'on one's own terms', this attempt involves the recognition – suggested in the portrayal of the Magistrate and his literary equivocation – of the novel's inadequacy before the history it confronts. Coetzee's fiction, like that of Beckett, thinks about its representational limits through the evocation of the novel's relationship to the suffering, infirm or fractured body: if the novel cannot properly represent this somatic dimension, in the hands of these authors it is preoccupied with registering this inadequacy. To frame this situation in other terms, intrinsic to these novelistic scenarios is an aspiration towards that which the novel form fails to comprehend. It is in terms of such an aspiration that we can understand, for example, *The Unnamable*'s reference to 'the last words, the true last' (*U*, 133), *Albert Angelo*'s stated ambition 'to tell the truth about me about my experience', and the Magistrate's evocation of a time in which he will abandon his 'literary ambitions and begin to tell the truth'.[21] If *Waiting for the Barbarians* ends on an ostensibly pessimistic note, the novel's recognition of its own limitations, especially vis-à-vis the suffering body, carries with it a normative and ethical dimension.

While his work has often been compared to that of Beckett, Austrian writer Thomas Bernhard's only recorded comment on the Irish author presents a teasing ambiguity: 'as far as I am concerned, Beckett has been dead for ten years, he merely sends brief messages from the hereafter'.[22] This equivocal remark only gains in complexity when we consider that it was made in a 1982 interview, seven years before the deaths of both authors in 1989. Whether one reads this comment as a somewhat snide evaluation of Beckett's later work, an indication of Bernhard's own diminishing engagement with the Irish writer or as a more complicated evocation of a strange temporal logic associated with Beckett's work and its reception, the remark points us to a central preoccupation of Bernhard's 1983 novel *The Loser* – the agonistic nature of relationships between artists. Bernhard's novel takes the form of a jagged first person narration that describes the relationships between three musicians – Glenn Gould, the narrator and a figure simply identified as 'Wertheimer'. The latter two characters have in common the fate of being 'destroyed' by Gould, in the initial sense that their musical careers are effectively over from the moment they hear him playing Bach's Goldberg Variations. In a scenario that recalls the novels discussed earlier, artistic failure becomes coterminous with literary production, as both the narrator and Wertheimer become writers following the frustration of their musical ambitions. Their literary projects – Wertheimer's is titled *The Loser*; the narrator's is described as a 'bungled essay' titled 'About Glen Gould' – are inseparable from their authors' conviction of the failure of their writing, and both projects are continually threatened by or subject to deletion and destruction by their authors. While Wertheimer apparently destroys his work, the final eradication of the work of the narrator is constantly postponed, even as this work is subject to perpetual destruction and recommencement.

This scenario of literary infirmity is developed performatively in Bernhard's cultivation of a stylistic awkwardness that overlaps with a sardonic subversion of novelistic conventions. For example, the narrator's constant recourse, in relating the speech of Wertheimer, to the formulation 'he said, I thought' calls attention to conventions of narrative point of view and character construction and undermines these conventions in the very awkwardness of its handling of them. Beckett's *Watt* performs a similar operation in its narrator's explication of the relationship between what he knows and 'what Watt knew', and the convoluted logic by which these two realms can be identical (*W*, 105–6). More generally, Bernhard's novel recalls Beckett's operations of literary creation that are coterminous with their undoing, operations manifest, for example, at the conclusion of *Molloy*: 'I went back into the house and wrote, It is midnight. The rain is beating on the windows. It was not midnight. It was not raining' (*Mo*, 184).

The narrator of *The Loser* declares that both he and Wertheimer were destroyed by Gould, but the novel indicates that there are different kinds of destruction: the only character left standing is the narrator, Wertheimer having committed suicide and Gould having been killed 'by the impasse he had *played* himself into for almost forty years'.[23] For Bernhard's narrator, and for the other novels discussed in this chapter, the posture of artistic failure, infirmity and self-negation is inseparable from a paradoxical self-perpetuation. But *The Loser* is also a story of artistic agon, and this returns us in conclusion to the problem of literary influence. If Bernhard apparently needed to figuratively kill off Beckett years before his death, a similar relationship is suggested in the fact that the narrator of *The Loser* is writing about a dead artist. The complexity of this relationship is indicated by Bernhard's conclusion, which leaves us with the narrator about to listen to a recording of Gould playing the Goldberg Variations. The passage underlines that Gould is dead, as the scenario of listening to a recording of his music contrasts with the encounters with his live playing described earlier in the novel. But this conclusion also evokes a submission to the work of the artistic antagonist and his uncanny afterlife, as Gould's music stretches into the future beyond the limits of the novel, appearing like the work of Beckett as a message 'from the hereafter'.

NOTES

1 See *LI*, 81. 'Sedendo et Quiescendo' was eventually published in the journal *transition* in 1932.
2 Samuel Beckett, quoted in James Knowlson and Elizabeth Knowlson (eds.), *Beckett Remembering/Remembering Beckett* (London: Bloomsbury, 2006), 47.
3 Charles Juliet, *Conversations with Samuel Beckett and Bram Van Velde*, trans. Janey Tucker (Leiden: Academic Press, 1995), 153.
4 See, for example the references in *Molloy* to 'distant music' (*Mo*, 18) and 'the famous flies' (*Mo*, 25). The former passage arguably alludes to the 'distant

music' of Joyce's 'The Dead'; Beckett's reference to the 'famous flies' alludes to an episode from Marcel Proust's *In Search of Lost Time*. Other passages that suggest the connection between literary inheritance and Beckett's voices include Watt's encounter with the voices of the 'mixed choir' as he lies in a ditch. See *W*, 26. This passage alludes to an incident from 'The Legend of Knockgrafton', a story attributed to folklorist T. Crofton Croker and collected by W. B. Yeats. See Sighle Kennedy, 'Spirals of Need: Irish Prototypes in Samuel Beckett's Fiction', in Kathleen McGrory and John Unterecker (eds.) *Yeats, Joyce, and Beckett: New Light on Three Irish Writers* (Lewisburg: Bucknell University Press, 1976), 159.

5 Michael Valdez Moses, 'The Sadly Rejoycing Slave: Beckett, Joyce, and Destructive Parody', *MFS* (31.4: 1985), 671–2.
6 John Brenkman, 'Innovation: Notes on Nihilism and the Aesthetics of the Novel', in Franco Moretti (ed.) *The Novel Volume 2: Forms and Themes* (Princeton: Princeton University Press, 2006), 829.
7 Peter Boxall, *Since Beckett: Contemporary Writing in the Wake of Modernism* (London: Continuum, 2009), 10–13.
8 In the first chapter of *Beckett's Literary Legacies*, Matthew Feldman writes, 'the essays here, ultimately, all commence from empirically defensible connections to Beckett's art, which precedes the subsequent interpretations about Beckett's influence'. Matthew Feldman, 'After "The End" of Samuel Beckett: Influences, Legacies, and "Legacees"', in Matthew Feldman and Mark Nixon (eds.), *Beckett's Literary Legacies* (Newcastle: Cambridge Scholars Press, 2007), 8.
9 See James Knowlson and Elizabeth Knowlson (eds.), *Beckett Remembering/ Remembering Beckett* (London: Bloomsbury, 2006), 284.
10 B. S. Johnson, *Albert Angelo* (New York: New Directions, 1964), 163–71.
11 Quoted in B. S. Johnson, *Albert Angelo* (New York: New Directions, 1964), 5. For the original passage from *The Unnamable*, see *U*, 109.
12 Johnson, *Albert Angelo*, 169–70.
13 *Dream*, 101. This novel was written in 1932 and published for the first time in 1992.
14 *Dream*, 119. Referring to Jane Austen, Beckett wrote to McGreevy in 1935, 'Now I am reading the divine Jane. I think she has much to teach me'. See *L1*, 250.
15 V. S. Naipaul, *The Mimic Men* (New York: Vintage, 2001), 10.
16 Ibid., 97, 292.
17 Ibid., 39, 291.
18 J. M. Coetzee, *Doubling the Point: Essays and Interviews*, David Attwell (ed.), (Cambridge: Harvard University Press, 1992), 25.
19 J. M. Coetzee, *Waiting for the Barbarians* (London: Vintage, 2004), 169.
20 Coetzee, *Doubling*, 364.
21 B. S. Johnson, *Albert Angelo*, 167; Coetzee, *Barbarians*, 169.
22 Quoted in Michael Jopling, '"Es gibt ja nur Gescheitertes": Bernhard as Company for Beckett', *Journal of European Studies*, (27: 1997), 49. In a recently published 'farewell letter' to Beckett, German theatre director Walter

Asmus indicates that Beckett read and apparently appreciated Bernhard's work. Walter D. Asmus, 'Farewell Beckett: A Letter of Farewell to Walter Beckett', *Journal of Beckett Studies* (19.1: 2010), 105.
23 Thomas Bernhard, *The Loser*, trans. Jack Dawson (Chicago: University of Chicago Press, 1991), 5.

CHAPTER 36

Notebooks and Other Manuscripts

Dirk Van Hulle

In the second half of the twentieth century, an implicit hierarchy insinuated itself into literary studies, suggesting that 'theory' was the truly intellectual part of literary studies, whereas philological scholarship was regarded as mere preparatory spadework. In David Hayman's introduction to a collection of essays on 'Genetic Studies in Joyce', this implicit hierarchy shone through: 'Those who limit themselves to the philological tasks may perhaps see themselves as doing necessary spadework for which we others may be grateful, but we should not confuse this sort of activity with criticism. Unless the implications of such findings are used to disclose something about the text and its procedures, theirs is an endstopped activity'.[1] Although Hayman acknowledged that philological spadework, including 'source hunting', is 'a first step toward genetic criticism at its best', he did create a dividing line between 'scholars' and 'critics', 'they' versus 'we'.[2]

Joyce studies were very early in responding to French genetic criticism; the response in Beckett studies was more gradual. The 1980s did see the publication of pioneering studies on the writing process of Beckett's plays, combining 'spadework' with 'criticism', such as S. E. Gontarski's *The Intent of Undoing* and Rosemary Pountney's *Theatre of Shadows*, but these studies did not explicitly use genetic criticism as a theoretical framework. In contrast to Joyce studies, Beckett studies' delayed reply to French *critique génétique* had the advantage that the encounter was less burdened by the legacy of late twentieth-century academic politics, dichotomies and hierarchies.

These hierarchies continue to make themselves felt, but a twenty-first-century approach to genetic criticism within Beckett studies may choose to build bridges instead of overemphasising the dichotomy between scholarship and criticism. As Pierre-Marc de Biasi indicated in his seminal essay 'Toward a Science of Literature: Manuscript Analysis and the Genesis of the Work', genetic criticism consists of two components.

(1) The main aim of the 'genetic' part is to decipher, to render visible and readable what is observed on the page. (2) The 'critical' component involves the reconstruction of the genesis from a chosen perspective.[3] Both these aspects crucially complement each other, and both have at least one element in common: they start from material traces of the writing process, such as marginalia, notes, manuscripts, typescripts, galleys and proofs.

In Beckett's case, many of the surviving documents are publicly accessible, to a large extent thanks to donations by the author himself, notably to Trinity College, Dublin and to the University of Reading. On 2 July 1969, W. O'Sullivan, Keeper of Manuscripts at Trinity College, Dublin, sent a typed letter to Samuel Beckett to thank him most heartily for his great kindness to the Manuscript Room: 'Very different indeed from the "scraps" you promised R. B. D. [Robert B. D. French] were the items you sent us. As far as I can judge they seem to give a pretty wide sampling of your writing over the years, 1954 to 1963'.[4] Six days later, Beckett replied that he was glad to hear the odds and ends – as he called them this time – gave the keeper of manuscripts pleasure, and he promised him that if any other manuscripts turned up he would give them to him with the same heart and a half. With the same heart and a half, however, he also generously gave manuscripts to James Knowlson when he organised his Beckett exhibition in Reading in 1972. At regular intervals, Beckett gave him more 'items', as he tended to refer to them. He seldom wrote the word 'manuscripts' in full, but either abbreviated it as MSS or simply referred to the manuscripts as 'stuff'.[5]

In the meantime, however, several manuscripts had already been bought and sold again by antiquarians or collectors such as Jake Schwartz.[6] As a result, Beckett's manuscripts are now dispersed over several holding libraries on both sides of the Atlantic. In 1979, Richard L. Admussen undertook a meritorious attempt to catalogue *The Samuel Beckett Manuscripts* on a global scale. The catalogue is not exhaustive, but it describes the documents relating to Beckett's works as a whole, rather than the holdings of one particular archive.

One of the practical difficulties of genetic research is that the documents pertaining to one particular work are often divided over several archives. Beckett's publicly available manuscripts are held at various holding libraries (in the following list – a preliminary part of the Centre for Manuscript Genetics' ongoing work on a more exhaustive online catalogue of Beckett's manuscripts – the abbreviations are mainly based on Admussen 1979 and Cohn 2001):

BC: The John J. Burns Library at Boston College (Chestnut Hill, MA) has numerous manuscripts and typescripts, located among the papers of Calvin Israel, Barney Rosset, Robert Pinget and Alan Schneider.

BnF: The Bibliothèque nationale de France (Paris) notably keeps the copybook with the complete first draft of *En attendant Godot* (also correspondences such as Beckett's letters to Jacoba van Velde).

CU: The Columbia University Rare Book & Manuscript Library recently acquired the Barney Rosset papers.

HRC: The Harry Ransom Humanities Research Center (Austin, Texas) holds the second largest Beckett collection (mainly among the Samuel Beckett papers, but also in the Carlton Lake Collection), described by Carlton Lake in *No Symbols Where None Intended: Samuel Beckett at the Humanities Research Center*.[7]

HU: The Houghton Library at Harvard University holds interesting Beckett material, such as manuscripts and typescripts of *Cascando*, several versions of an English translation of *Fragment de théâtre*, a one-page typescript fragment of *Waiting for Godot* and an early manuscript of *Embers*.

ICU: The University of Chicago Library, Illinois, holds typed copies of 'Yoke of Liberty' ('Moly'), 'Enueg I', 'Dortmunder' ('Cassel Revisited') and 'Echo's Bones' among the Morton Dauwen Zabel papers.

IMEC: The Institut mémoires de l'édition contemporaine (IMEC, Caen) holds the papers of publishing houses such as Les Éditions de Minuit and John Calder.

InU: The Lilly Library at Indiana University, Bloomington, has papers of Breon Mitchell, Richard Seaver and Calder & Boyars and a large collection of Beckett material, including an incomplete manuscript and galleys of *Molloy*; marked proofs of the trilogy; manuscripts, galleys and proofs of *How It Is*, *Come and Go*, *Imagination Dead Imagine*, *Lessness*, *The Lost Ones*, *Mercier and Camier*.

MBU: The Howard Gotlieb Archival Research Center at Boston University (Boston, MA) holds carbon typescripts with autograph corrections of the Grove Press typescript of *How It Is*.

McM: McMaster University, Hamilton, Ontario, Canada, holds the Merlin files and also some manuscript material, including typescripts of 'Dortmunder' and 'Whoroscope'.

MoSW: Washington University, St. Louis, Missouri, acquired its first Beckett typescript (*All That Fall*) in 1965 through book dealer Henry Wenning, and gradually built an important collection with numerous manuscripts and typescripts, especially of Beckett's shorter works (such as *Bing*, *Cascando*, *Imagination Dead Imagine*, *Eh Joe*, *Le Dépeupleur*) and of translations, catalogued by Sharon Bangert.[8]

NhD: Dartmouth College, Hanover, New Hampshire, holds the Lawrence Harvey archive, including material relating to *Dream of Fair to Middling Women*, *Mercier et Camier*, *Eleutheria* and several shorter pieces.

NSyU: Syracuse University, New York, holds not only miscellaneous Beckett material, but also the Grove Press records.

NYP: The Berg Collection of the New York Public Library inludes a corrected copy of *Echo's Bones and Other Precipitates*, two notebooks and two typescripts of *The Lost Ones*.

OSU: The Ohio State University Rare Books and Manuscripts Library has a large collection, comprising the so-called Tara MacGowran notebook; an annotated English edition of *Watt*; notebooks, typescripts and page proofs of the French *Watt*; manuscripts and typescripts of *Fin de partie* and of Beckett's translation, *Endgame*; a notebook and typescripts of *Happy Days*; notebooks, typescripts, galleys and page proofs of *How It Is*.

SB: The Donald C. Davidson Library at the University of California, Santa Barbara, California, holds typescripts of *Eleuthéria*, *Mercier et Camier* and *Premier amour*.

TCD: Trinity College, Dublin, keeps many of Beckett's reading notes on philosophy and psychology (discussed by Matthew Feldman in *Beckett's Books*), including his notes to Geulincx and several notebooks with drafts, such as the Kilcool fragments, manuscripts of (preparatory stages of) *Fin de partie*, *Rough for Radio* II, *Imagination Dead Imagine*, catalogued by Everett Frost and Jane Maxwell.[9]

UoR: The *Beckett International Foundation* at the University of Reading (UoR), which grew out of the exhibition organised by James Knowlson in 1971, holds the largest collection of Beckett manuscripts in the world, catalogued in *Beckett at Reading*.[10]

YU: Yale University Library, New Haven, Connecticut, has notes, manuscripts, typescripts, galleys and page proofs of *Sans* (*Lessness*).

Ruby Cohn mentions several of these holding libraries in *A Beckett Canon*. They are briefly discussed in the footnotes, which reflects the perceived difference between the published versions of the works, discussed in the main body of the text, and their manuscripts; or between the canon and what S. E. Gontarski has called 'the grey canon'. But the fact that the manuscripts are discussed at all in *A Beckett Canon* shows that the canon is gradually 'greying', more recently also thanks to the edition of the letters and initiatives such as the Beckett Digital Manuscript Project (BDMP, www.beckettarchive.org), which aims to reunite the dispersed manuscripts, in the form of digital facsimiles and transcriptions.[11]

To the list of libraries, at least one other library should be added: Beckett's own library in his apartment at the Boulevard Saint Jacques in Paris, for the earliest inception of Beckett's own texts often took place in the margins of other authors' texts.

MARGINS: READING NOTES

Beckett sometimes wrote in the margins of the books he read, initially to work on his vocabulary by looking up translations, but sometimes also to comment on the content. Even if the annotation is limited to a mere pencil line in the margin, it can signal a thought that was later transformed into an idea for a passage in one of Beckett's own works. Thus, for instance the underlined sentence 'Blue-eyed cats are invariably deaf' from Darwin's *On the Origin of Species* was incorporated literally in 'What a Misfortune'. Beckett did however highlight the 'foreign' origin of the line by making the 'colossal Capper' quote Darwin's line 'for no other reason than that the phrase had been running in his mind and now here was a chance to discharge it on a wit' (*MPTK*, 125). In *Dream of Fair to middling Women*, he similarly drew attention to textual *Fremdkörper*. For instance, when he employed Proust's metaphor of the zone of evaporation (marked in his copy of *À la Recherche du temps perdu*), the passage is followed by the metafictional comment 'We stole that one. Guess where' (*Dream*, 191–2).

This kind of 'theft' was a technique Beckett had learned from Joyce. Beckett applied it, not only to passages he marked in his books, but also to so-called non-marginalia (passages that derive from a page *not* marked in a book otherwise annotated by Beckett). Thus, in Beckett's otherwise marked copy of Darwin's *On the Origin of Species*, Beckett did *not* mark the sentence 'Even Ireland has a few animals, now generally regarded as varieties, but which have been ranked as species by some zoologists' in the second chapter of Darwin's *On the Origin of Species*, but he did incorporate it literally in his story 'Draff' (*MPTK*, 171).

NOTEBOOKS

a. Intertextual Notes

Apart from the marks (pencil lines and dog ears) in his copy of Darwin's *Origin of Species*, Beckett also took notes from it in his so-called Whoroscope Notebook.[12] There is a clear development in the way Beckett made notes, especially noticeable when one compares the Dream Notebook (early 1930s) to the Whoroscope Notebook (mid to late 1930s), both preserved in Reading. In Daniel Ferrer's distinction between 'marginalists' (writing in the margins of books) and 'extractors' (writing in separate notebooks; Ferrer 2004), the second category could be subdivided into 'notesnatchers' and 'excerptors'. Beckett fits in with all of these categories, but then again, one should perhaps specify *which* Beckett one is referring to. The young Beckett is generally more of a Joycean 'notesnatcher', whereas the slightly older Beckett (in his late twenties, early thirties) is more of an 'excerptor':

Samuel Beckett, 1. marginalist
       2. extractor: a. 'notesnatcher'
            b. excerptor

Beckett, the notesnatcher, for instance, took notes from Pierre Garnier's *Onanisme seul et à deux sous toutes ses forms et leurs conséquences* in his Dream Notebook.[13] On the verso pages, Beckett has taken notes from Jean-Baptiste Bouvier's *Dissertatio in Sextum Decalogi Praeceptum et Supplementum ad Tractatum de Matrimonio*, a copy of which still survives in his personal library.[14] According to Bouvier, one of the first threats to chastity was 'luxuria' (lust), or the inordinate appetite of venereal pleasure. Beckett jotted down the definition in Latin, without any reference to the source text (*De luxuria in genere* [...] Rectè definitur, Appetitus inordinatus delectationis venereae'),[15] in the manner of 'that odious and still today insufficiently malestimated notesnatcher', as Joyce described 'Shem, the Penman' in *Finnegans Wake*.[16]

Beckett, the excerptor, started taking his distance from this approach and sometimes excerpted, translated or paraphrased a longer passage, such as Bouvier's episcopal advice with regard to a question on masturbation:

Quaeritur 1.° ad quid teneatur homo qui evigilans advertit se pollutionem experiri. R. Debet mentem ad Deum elevare, eum invocare, signo crucis se munire, nihil ad expellendum semen positive facere, delectation voluptatis renuntiare.[17]

Beckett translated the passage as follows:

Quaeritur I° What shall he do who is aware that he is about to experience pollution?
 R. He shall elevate his mind to God, invoke him, signo crucis se munire [arm himself with the sign of the cross], abstain from all voluntary exoneration, renounce the delectation of voluptuousness.[18]

This procedure became more conspicuous in the second half of the 1930s, for instance in his *Faust* notes[19] or in his Whoroscope Notebook, which notably contains extensive excerpts from Fritz Mauthner's *Beiträge zu einer Kritik der Sprache*, one of the books he explored for Joyce in 1938 and which 'greatly impressed' him, as he told Hans Naumann on 17 February 1954 (*L2*, 462, 465).

b. Conceptual Notes

The first few pages of notes in the Whoroscope Notebook are of yet another nature. They could be categorised as 'conceptual notes'. In the first fifteen sections of the Whoroscope Notebook, discussed by Daniela Caselli in 'The Promise of Dante in the Beckett Manuscripts', Beckett conceived of a Dantesque 'Journey through the "careers" like D. & V. along the Purgatorial cornices, except that V. goes back, H goes out'.[20] Apart from H (modelled after Virgil), a certain X was also mentioned. But while Beckett was making these conceptual notes, he wrote a note to himself, comparable with what, in genetic Proust studies, is called a 'note de rédaction': 'But keep whole Dantesque analogy out of sight'. The sixteenth section ('Exordium I: X, naked, bound with silk scarves to a chair ...') can be read as prefiguring *Murphy*, and in De Biasi's typology it might even qualify as an 'initial workplan' or 'scenario'.[21] But making a distinction between section 16 and the preceding ones would imply a teleological perspective: only retroactively, after having read the published version of *Murphy*, is it possible to denote section 16 as a 'scenario' that conceptually underpins the opening pages of the novel and to 'discard' the others as ideas that did not directly make it into the published text, but at the time Beckett was taking these notes, they all played a role in the conceptualisation of a future work.

To some extent even the distinction between an intertextual note and a conceptual note is an artificial imposition. For instance, the note 'Kritik des reinen Quatsches' may be merely a playful, pseudo-Joycean jotting referring to Kant's *Critique of Pure Reason*.[22] But in combination with the twist to Kant's definition of art, further in the notebook ('Zweckmässigkeit ohne Zweck' / (Kant) / Quatsch: 'Zweck ohne Zweckmässigkeit' / (?)'), the 'Kritik des reinen Quatsches' may be considered a conceptual note, indicating that, at some point in Beckett's career, 'Quatsch' may have been a shorthand term for a vague project, which later turned out to be a dead end.[23]

DRAFTS: CREATION, DECREATION

Conceptual notes are relatively scarce in Beckett's manuscripts, which is indicative of his writing method. Louis Hay and Almuth Grésillon have suggested two general categories of writing: 'écriture à programme' and 'écriture à processus'.[24] Beckett writing practice is clearly less 'programmatic' than Emile Zola's or Thomas Mann's, and comes much closer to a Proustian 'écriture à processus'. Although Beckett disapproved of the 'theory of *Correspondances*, that trusty standby of all the Romantics from Hoffmann to Proust' in the review 'Schwabenstreich' (published in the *Spectator* of 23 March 1934; *D*, 62), he defended Proust one month later in his review (also in the *Spectator*) of Albert Feuillerat's *Comment Proust a composé son roman*. Beckett deprecated Feuillerat's attempt to stress the uniformity and cohesion, the 'stock-in-trade exactly of the naturalism that Proust abominated' (*D*, 64). Instead, he drew attention to the 'uncontrollable agency of unconscious memory', the 'full complexity' of the book's 'clues and blind alleys' and the way Proust communicated his material 'in dribs and drabs' (*D*, 65). To some extent, Beckett may have been riding a hobbyhorse by emphasising the notion of complexity and downplaying the fact that Proust first wrote the opening and closing parts of the *Recherche* and 'filled' the entre-deux later on. But the recent edition of Proust's *Cahiers* does show that Proust worked with 'textual units', which he could shuffle around at any time during the process of writing.

Beckett's preference for the 'dribs and drabs' method is reflected in a tendency to work with short scenes. For instance, in one of his late copybooks, the so-called Super Conquérant Notebook, Beckett tried out a scene between two people, starting from the suggestion of reading a Shakespeare sonnet to each other.[25] The scene never developed into a published text or play, but it illustrates Beckett's practice of writing in 'scenes'. This tendency also applies to his prose. For instance, the 'scene' of an old man sitting with his head in his hands at a table in *Stirrings Still* already appears (in a rough form) in the Sottisier Notebook.[26] Similarly, the first so-called Kilcool fragment in the 'Héraklès' exercise book, opens with a 'woman's face alone in constant light. Nothing but fixed lit face and speech',[27] prefiguring the lit mouth of *Not I*.[28] The Kilcool fragments are not the 'first draft' of *Not I*; they contain several elements that could just as justifiably prefigure *That Time* or *Footfalls*. But that does not diminish the power of the initial image. In Beckett's case, such a 'scene' of inception is often visual. In *Worstward Ho*, this method of working with scenes becomes thematic. First, three scenes are suggested (presented as shades); then gradually they are 'denarrated', as Brian Richardson calls this procedure.[29] This method of denarration has a genetic equivalent, which comes close to what S. E. Gontarski has dubbed 'the intent of undoing'. This procedure is more complex than what Beckett presented as 'taking away', contrasting his method to Joyce's constant 'adding' (*K*, 352). In order to be able to 'denarrate', he needed to narrate first. Sometimes a narrated piece is 'taken away' in a later phase, such as the sixteen-page description of

Ballyba's faeces-based economy in the notebook with the first manuscript of *Molloy* (HRC) or the eight-page slapstick conversation on the question whether 'it' is worthwhile (*est-ce que c'est la peine*) in the manuscript of *En attendant Godot* (BnP). Very often, however, the words are not literally 'taken away', but 'taken back', so that the genesis is driven by the tension between narration and denarration, the statement and its deletion, creation and decreation.

MARGINS REVISITED: REREADING NOTES

The 'intent of undoing' also implies that a deletion can, in its turn, be undone again. Thus, for instance, the sentence 'Leave him or not alone again unwaiting' was first crossed out in a *Stirrings Still* typescript, and subsequently reinstated by means of the word 'stet' in the left margin.[30] As his own first reader, Beckett was also a marginalist, writing in the margins of his own texts. And this practice did not stop at the 'pass for press' moment. Beckett also applied it in his capacities of translator and director. The prompt copy of *En attendant Godot* preserved at TCD or the annotated Grove Press and Faber editions of *Krapp's Last Tape* contain all kinds of marginal notes, additions and revisions. So do the notebooks with translations, such as the six *Mercier and Camier* notebooks, and the so-called theatrical notebooks, edited under the general editorship of James Knowlson.[31] For instance, as the last page of Beckett's theatrical notebook of the Schiller Theater production of *Waiting for Godot* shows, Beckett even wanted to 'undo' a few leaves of the tree: 'TREE / Was not right (3 branches). / Two branches only, *two* leaves / 3rd couple'.[32]

Beckett's works came into being in an area of tension between composition and decomposition, through many layers of revision. From most of these layers we still have textual traces, in the form of holograph manuscripts or otherwise. Even a dog-eared page can be part of the 'fossil record'. Thus, for instance, Beckett earmarked a page in Darwin's *On the Origin of Species* in the chapter on the 'Imperfections of the Geological Record'. The large number of Beckett's notebooks and other manuscripts differs considerably from the scarcity of traces in Darwin's fossil record, but even the seemingly abundant manuscript record is only an imperfect record of the creative and decreative processes behind the textual genesis of Beckett's world, to which at least one of the sentences on the dog-eared page in his copy of the *On the Origin of Species* is equally applicable: 'We should not forget that only a small portion of the world is known with accuracy'.[33]

NOTES

1 David Hayman, 'Genetic Criticism and Joyce: An Introduction', in David Hayman and Sam Slote (eds.) *Probes: Genetic Studies in Joyce* (Amsterdam: Rodopi, 1995), 8.
2 Ibid., 8.
3 Pierre-Marc de Biasi, 'Toward a Science of Literature: Manuscript Analysis and the Genesis of the Work', in Jed Deppman, Daniel Ferrer and Michael Groden (eds.) *Genetic Criticism: Texts and Avant-textes* (Philadelphia: University of Pennsylvania Press, 2004), 42.
4 TCD 4664a/1.
5 UoR JEK 3 March 1973, 1 March 1976, 14 June 1977.
6 Dirk Van Hulle and Mark Nixon '"Holo and unholo": The Beckett Digital Manuscript Project', in *Samuel Beckett Today/Aujourd'hui* (18: 2007).
7 Carlton Lake, *No Symbols Where None Intended: Samuel Beckett at the Humanities Research Center* (Austin: The University of Texas at Austin, 1984).
8 Sharon Bangert, *The Samuel Beckett Collection at Washington University Libraries: A Guide* (St. Louis: Washington University Libraries, 1986).
9 Everett Frost and Jane Maxwell, 'Catalogue of "Notes Divers Holo[graph]"', *Samuel Beckett Today/Aujourd'hui* (16: 2006), 19–181. Anthony Uhlmann has edited Beckett's notes to Geulincx, which are published in Arnold Geulincx, *Ethics. With Samuel Beckett's Notes*, Han van Ruler, Anthony Uhlmann and Martin Wilson (eds.), trans. Martin Wilson (Leiden: Brill, 2006 [1675]).
10 Mary Bryden, Julian Garforth and Peter Mills, *Beckett at Reading: Catalogue of the Beckett Manuscript Collection at the University of Reading* (Reading: Whiteknights Press and the Beckett International Foundation, 1998).
11 S. E. Gontarski, 'Greying the Canon: Beckett in Performance', in S. E. Gontarski and Anthony Uhlmann (eds.) *Beckett after Beckett* (Gainesville: University Press of Florida, 2006), 141–57.
12 UoR MS 3000.
13 John Pilling (ed.) *Beckett's 'Dream' Notebook* (Reading: Beckett International Foundation, 1999), 59, notes 422ff.
14 For a full account of the books and marginalia in Beckett's personal library, see Dirk Van Hulle and Mark Nixon, *Samuel Beckett's Library* (Cambridge: Cambridge University Press, 2012).
15 Jean-Baptiste Bouvier, *Dissertatio in Sextum Decalogi Praeceptum et Supplementum ad Tractatum de Matrimonio* (Paris: Facultatis Theologiae Bibliopolas, 1852), 9.
16 Joyce, James. *Finnegans Wake* (London: Faber and Faber, 1939), 125.
17 Bouvier, *Dissertatio in Sextum*, 65.
18 Dream Notebook, note 447.
19 UoR MS 5004–5005.
20 Whoroscope Notebook, quoted in Daniela Caselli, 'The Promise of Dante in the Beckett Manuscripts', *Samuel Beckett Today/Aujourd'hui* (16: 2006), 237–57.

21 Pierre-Marc de Biasi, 'What is a Literary Draft? Toward a Functional Typology of Genetic Documentation', in Yale French Studies 89, 'Drafts' (1996), 34–5.
22 Whoroscope Notebook, 22r.
23 Ibid., 60r.
24 Louis Hay, 'Die dritte Dimension der Literatur: Notizen zu einer 'critique génétique', *POETICA* (16.3–4: 1984), 307–23.
25 UoR MS 2934, 1v–2r.
26 UoR Ms 2901.
27 TCD MS 4664.
28 10r; quoted in S. E. Gontarski, *The Intent of Undoing in Samuel Beckett's Dramatic Texts* (Bloomington: Indiana University Press, 1985), 135.
29 Brian Richardson, *Unnatural Voices: Extreme Narration in Modern and Contemporary Fiction* (Columbus: Ohio State University Press, 2006), 87.
30 UoR MS 2935/3/5. *Stirrings Still/Soubresauts and Comment dire/what is the word*: an electronic genetic edition (Series 'The Beckett Digital Manuscript Project', module 1). Dirk Van Hulle and Vincent Neyt (eds.) (Brussels: University Press Antwerp (ASP/UPA), 2011), http://www.beckettarchive.org.
31 UoR MS 1396/4/17–22.
32 James Knowlson (ed.) *The Theatrical Notebooks of Samuel Beckett*, vol. 1; Dougald McMillan and James Knowlson (eds.) *Waiting for Godot* (New York: Grove Press, 1994), 393.
33 Charles Darwin, *On the Origin of Species by Means of Natural Selection or the Preservation of Favoured Races in the Struggle for Life* (London: Grant Richards, 1902), 275.

CHAPTER 37

Letters

Lois More Overbeck

Samuel Beckett wrote letters, over sixteen thousand of them in the sixty years of his writing life from 1929 to 1989. These comprise a unique corpus, itself a literary effort, by one of the central writers of the twentieth century. Beckett's letters travel the narrative arc of his own work, from the insecurities of a fledgling writer to a man who feels, frequently, that he has written himself out. The letters also reflect the cultural and social changes of the times, in Ireland, France, England and Germany – indeed internationally – as Beckett's work is widely published, translated and performed. By contrast to Beckett's frequent refusal to be interviewed about his work, the letters offer Beckett's own words about his work as it is written, published and produced.

BEGINNINGS

In the letters, we can overhear Beckett musing aloud, especially to close friends who share his creative life: Thomas McGreevy in the early years, Georges Duthuit in the post-war period, Alan Schneider from 1955 to 1984 in matters of theatre, and Barbara Bray – beginning in the late 1950s when she worked in BBC radio drama, and more intensely from the 1960s when she moved to Paris. What Beckett describes to McGreevy as the 'frail sense of beginning life behind the eyes' suggests the gradual dawning of the imaginative faculty, enough to go on with.[1]

Beckett often speaks of this impulse as hearing voices. To Barney Rosset, Beckett describes the beginnings of 'an attempt to go from where the Textes left me off' as hearing 'siren voices'.[2] In the soundtrack of Beckett's writing, the uttered voice is often accompanied by or articulates an inner voice. Beckett translated the opening of *Comment C'est* for Patrick Magee as 'From an Unabandoned Work' and described the work as 'the uttered voice, fragments of an inner voice ill heard'; to Alan Schneider, of *Eh Joe*, Beckett wrote of the 'dead voice inside his head'.[3] From *Krapp's Last Tape* and *Eh Joe* to *Rockaby* and *That Time*, the staged image reflects the tension between a listener and a disembodied voice. When his writing is going well, Beckett often speaks of it in an auditory sense. As he resumes work on 'Pim', he writes to Barbara Bray that he has him 'murmuring at last'.[4] Beckett uses the same term when he sends Ethna MacCarthy the radio play *Embers*, in the hope that 'there are bits that will murmur to you'.[5]

At other times the beginnings form as a visual image. Beckett mentions his idea for a one-act play to Belgian writer Henri Lefebvre: 'with three white faces (mouths) and lights. But my ideas ... '.[6] Several days later he writes to Robert Pinget: 'Very difficult, but I think I can get there. I'd like to talk to you about it'.[7] Though still unnamed as *Play*, Beckett's idea of 'faces and voices of two women and one man, provoked to speech (or silenced) by spots' has been worked out when he writes to Alan Schneider in August 1962.[8] At times the stage image is provoked by images from painting: that of *En attendant Godot* was inspired by *Two men looking at the Moon* by Caspar David Friedrich in the Galerie Neue Meister of the Zwinger Museum in Dresden; the stage image of *That Time* was suggested by Caravaggio's *The Decollation of Saint John the Baptist*, which Beckett saw in Valleta Cathedral, Malta, in 1971.

GERMINATION, AND THE EFFORT TO GO ON

Beckett's letter to Barbara Bray on 11 March 1959 says of writing what will eventuate as *Comment C'est*: 'I'm struggling along with the new moan.... Sometimes I think I'm getting on, then realise how far I am from it still'.[9] And on the next day, he writes similarly to Avigdor Arikha, 'The rhythm and the syntax of weakness and penury, not easy to catch. All the same, I am getting there a little better – 6th version of the beginning'.[10] Getting there, getting on. The life behind the eyes does not take form without trial and exploration, doubt and error.

'I finished first draft of first part of book and am beginning the battering before going on to second and third', Beckett writes to Barbara Bray on 15 April 1959.[11] Frequently the letters offer a minute chronology of the effort. When Beckett writes to Ethna MacCarthy on 22 April 1959, he says: 'I have to flog myself on now at the new work'.[12] On 26 May 1959, Beckett observes to Bray: 'I battle on here, average of half a page daily, in a year or so I might have a rough draft. The thing makes itself as it goes, but that's not the point alas'.[13] The verbs betray the exertion and the resistance: *battering*, *flog*, *battle*. Sometimes the 'struggle' is so discouraging that he just leaves it, writing to Thomas McGreevy the 'average of half a page – and very provisional – a day gets me down sometimes'.[14] The perspective from within is riddled with doubt: 'The result is very far from what I want but not quite bad enough to throw away'.[15] Beckett describes his accomplishment as 'bits and scraps & aborted fragments'.[16] A great deal is thrown away, or set aside in a drawer, never to be brought out again, or, sometimes much later, it may become a starting point for another work. Beckett writes to Barbara Bray in 1959: 'I don't know what period I'm in but I don't see how I can ever emerge'.[17] Similarly, the words from the opening of 'Text 9' of *Texts for Nothing* are carried on to the closing of that text, almost as a refrain: 'If I said, there's a way out there, there's a way out somewhere, the rest would come, the other words, sooner or later, and the power to get there, and the way to get there, and pass out, and see the beauties of the skies, and see the stars again' (*CSP*, 140).

Beckett takes soundings of his writing in process when he writes to trusted intimates. Letters to Barbara Bray, who as a scriptwriter and producer with the BBC operates within the world of radio drama, reveal a developing intimacy with Beckett's writing process. Bray has read several drafts of *Embers*, and it is to her that the final script is sent to be directed by Donald McWhinnie for broadcast on the *Third Programme*. Bray is uniquely placed at the production end of this radio script. When she challenges Beckett's choices, he explains his thinking about the title:

I decided on *Embers* because … it receives light in the course of the piece and … because embers are a better ebb than the sea's, because followed by no flow. The real title is the first line of the little poem, *Again the Last Ebb*, which I would accept, and *Embers* says that more or less in one word.

Beckett refers to his poem as 'Dieppe'. The letter to Bray continues: 'Bolton's room and the dying fire' are real, 'the sea and shore' unreal. Beckett is willing to settle, but not to compromise: '*Ebb* or *Again the Last Ebb* is acceptable' but '*The Last Ebb* alone would not do'.[18]

THE TESTING GROUND – PRODUCTION

Beckett folds his instinctive decisions about *Play* over and over as he writes to Barbara Bray and others. He and Alan Schneider had gone to Ulm in late May 1963 to see a rehearsal of the work directed by Deryk Mendel. Siegfried Unseld, Beckett's publisher at Suhrkamp Verlag, attended the June premiere and issued a report to Beckett about the production; in it he questioned the too real faces and debated the wisdom of Beckett's directive to repeat the whole play, together with a threatened third repeat of the *da capo* ending. Beckett had already come to his own conclusion about the faces in the urns. Following his return from Ulm, he revised the stage direction to read: 'Faces so lost to age and aspect as to seem almost part of urns. But masks forbidden'.[19] To Unseld who was concerned about the repetition and the *da capo* ending, Beckett wrote, 'What is needed is nothing less than a mad outburst of light and scraps of speech'; on the same day, writing to Barbara Bray, he defends this choice: 'I still feel that taken at right speed it is valid', yet to Alan Schneider, about three weeks later, Beckett comments: 'I am not at all sure of it myself and won't be till I work on a production'.[20]

Beckett's attitude about the centrality of production, indeed including his own involvement in production, is an outgrowth of his experience with *En attendant Godot*, which he felt was 'insufficiently "visualized" during writing'.[21] As it happened, the protracted preliminaries (the lengthy process of procuring a subvention for the first play, the beginning of rehearsals, the delay of production when a new theatre had to be found for the premiere) meant that the book was published before the play had been fully rehearsed and performed (*L2*, 234–5, 278, 323–4). Following the production at the Théâtre de Babylone, a second edition of *En attendant Godot* was prepared incorporating changes made during the production process.[22] Although he often spoke of writing the voices he heard in his head, for Beckett, the rhythms of speech spoken on stage and the physicality that articulated the stage space created a dynamic that lifted the script to life. Beckett wished to know whether this was successful before he could think of a play as finished.

Beckett's letters reveal the gradual shifts that take place between his original conception and the realisation of his work. A letter to George Devine indicates that Beckett had first imagined the voice of Krapp as emanating from the tape recorder, but then, closer to production, he determined that the recording must be played from the wings. When Beckett calls for a 'little island of light in the midst of darkness', he is creating a stage image. At the same time, since the play was written as a companion piece for *Endgame*, he is also accommodating the actual stage conditions – aware that the darkness will allow *Krapp's Last Tape* to be played on the same set.[23] Another impetus for writing this play was the voice of Patrick Magee, hence 'Magee monologue'. Beckett was entranced by the actor's voice, and he also had trust in Magee. To Devine he writes that he has not given detailed directions for 'Krapp's face as he listens, though this is a good half of the battle. Anyhow I didn't see it clearly. Expressiveness in blankness sums it up'.[24]

Letters also show Beckett writing himself into problems, for which he then must pursue a solution. The evolution of *Happy Days* offers such an instance: he writes to Bray on 4 October 1960: 'as I drove in the Paris rain [I think I solved] ... the problem of how to get her to speak without speaking to herself or to the public or to the merely imaginary interlocutor'.[25] Two weeks later, he describes the solution is 'to have a real interlocutor at the outset ... and then get rid of him for the rest of the play'; however, this idea begat another problem: '"he" is proving more difficult to dismiss than desirable ... I hope tomorrow (4th page) he'll be gone for keeps, except occasionally his voice – and unsolicited ejaculations'.[26]

From Godot to Willie to the late plays, absent presence becomes a dramaturgical feature. In *Eh Joe*, *That Time* and *Rockaby*, recordings present interior monologues that counterpoint the much reduced staged action. The tension between text and stage image is always critical. In 1976, Klaus Herm, who had acted the role of Krapp in Berlin, proposed a radio production. Beckett dismissed the possibility: 'In my opinion, *Damals* [*That Time*] as a radio play is out of the question, because of the loss of the picture, i.e. half of the whole thing! The listening face is an inextricable part. Otherwise it would no longer be a play, but only an aimless voice without any suspense'.[27] The listening presence, both on stage and in the audience, comes close to a Beckettian dramatic principle.

'NEARLY FINISHED'

Incubated behind the eyes, pursued through experiment: When do the results square up? When is a work finished? When, and on what terms, does Beckett let it go? The letters prove that the process is often riddled by doubt. On 10 April 1951, Beckett writes to his French publisher Jérôme Lindon of *L'Innommable*: 'I am trying to get it finished. But I am not getting it finished. Perhaps it will all have been for nothing'.[28] Of an early draft of what later becomes *Fin de partie*, Beckett confides to Pamela Mitchell (26 February 1955): 'The play is nearly finished, i.e. first draft.... Then all the fiddling and fussing. However I don't disown it – yet'.[29] About two weeks later, in response to her inquiry (13 March 1955), he writes again: 'Yes, I finished the play, but it's no good and I have to begin all over again'.[30] When, nearly a year later (22 February 1956), the word 'finished' appears in conjunction with *Fin de partie*, Beckett reports to Barney Rosset that it is 'to my great dissatisfaction, especially with Act 1. Am letting it cool off'.[31] Months later, in October 1956, writing of *Fin de partie* to Stefani Hunzinger at Fischer Verlag, Beckett indicates: 'I cannot settle the final text until after a certain number of rehearsals'.[32] Hesitant, even after he has put down the pen, Beckett writes of *Krapp's Last Tape* to Barney Rosset: 'I have finished the Magee monologue and sit looking at it with a fishy eye'.[33]

The long struggle with *Comment C'est* was an attempt to go on in French, on and beyond the prose of *L'Innomable*. When Beckett writes of completing a final revision of *Comment C'est* to Barney Rosset, he says, 'don't think I can do much more with it. I have no idea what it is worth'.[34] Two months later, Beckett writes to Aidan Higgins that he had finished 'or rather stopped a work in French after 18 months tedious struggle on and off, due out in December'.[35] And to Christian Ludvigsen, his Danish translator, he comments: 'It cannot be described as a novel nor as anything else, not even I fear as prose'.[36]

More and more, finishing and letting go becomes a collaborative issue. Beckett is encouraged by his publishers and supported by trusted directors – Alan Schneider and Donald McWhinnie in the case of *Happy Days*. To A. J. Leventhal, Beckett writes that Schneider had come over from London and is 'reading it for me as I write'; to Barbara Bray, Beckett reports that he has shown Alan Schneider a 'completed version of play.... I don't know how I finished it – working like mad in the morning'.[37] Schneider had some helpful technical suggestions which encouraged Beckett to write to Judith Schmidt, who worked with Barney Rosset at Grove Press, that although he would 'let it lie now for a few weeks, then have another wrestle with it', he thought he might be able to send it to Grove Press in April.[38] April came and went. Only in mid May did Beckett write to A. J. Leventhal that the play was 'practically finished – or as near as I can get to it'.[39] Almost apologetically he tells his former agent and Dutch translator Jacoba van Velde that he was not sure if *Happy Days* was 'any good; I had to do it, that's all. I could have done it better, but I wasn't able to'.[40] On 2 June 1961, Beckett announces the completion of *Happy Days*, but warns that 'the text won't be final until I've done some work in the theatre. Nevertheless I think it is already quite neat'.[41] Stefani Hunzinger proposed that *Happy Days* be produced by the Schiller Theater for the Berlin Festival; Beckett agreed, 'on the presumption that the project survives a close reading of the text – which is not certain'.[42]

With *Play*, the hesitations and reassessments follow a similar pattern. Having finished the first version of the play for 'three characters (mouths)', Beckett tells Barney Rosset that he is 'not satisfied with it and can't let it away just yet'. Of two minds, he hesitates further, and adds, 'But I don't think there's much more I can do to it.... I have no title yet'.[43] Finally in

October 1962, he is willing to tell Jacoba van Velde: 'I have finished a new play. Very short. A quarter of an hour. 10 months' work (intermittent, I grant you!) for fifteen minutes of boredom. It is called *Play*!'[44]

THE LAST WORD

When his writing of a work is finished, it is hard for Beckett to place himself again within the stream that is creation. To Arland Ussher, Beckett wrote: 'my unique relation [with my work] – and it a tenuous one – is the making relation. I am with it a little in the dark and fumbling of making, as long as that lasts, then no more'.[45] This detachment can be seen again and again in the effort it costs Beckett to take on the task of preparing to direct his plays. This process forces him to re-engage with the 'making' all over again, as if an outsider. He wrote to Mary Hutchinson in 1971 regarding his preparation for his production of *Glückliche Tage*, at the Schiller Theater Werkstatt in Berlin: 'Still prowling round that stranger's play looking for a chink'.[46]

Time ripens all perspectives. As Beckett completed the novel *Molloy*, he wrote to George Reavey that it had 'its place in the series, as will perhaps appear in time'; 'the series' was, at that time, the novels *Murphy*, *Mercier et Camier* (then still unpublished), and *Molloy*.[47] Later the definition of 'series' shifts as *Molloy*, *Malone meurt* and *L'Innommable* form a trio, though not a 'Trilogy'. In 1959, Beckett later writes to Barbara Bray that John Calder planned to publish the three novels together: 'I was told the 3 in 1 was imminent, Please God he doesn't call it a trilogy'.[48]

Beckett is none too kind to his work in retrospect, and perhaps readers should not take him at his word. When offers came to republish his early works – most often poems or short prose pieces – Beckett invariably asked that the date of original publication be given. At times, Beckett's later opinion of an early work exceeds even his usual tendency to self-deprecation. Of *Mercier et Camier*, Beckett writes in 1954 to Jérôme Lindon regretting that he is seriously considering it for publication by Editions de Minuit: 'It can always take its place, if you really want it, in a volume to be entitled *Posthumous Droppings*'. He adds that *Watt* in a French translation 'makes me go purple right down to the bones'.[49] Attempts to republish *More Pricks Than Kicks* suffered from a similar approach-avoidance. After much hesitation, agreements were concluded with Grove Press and John Calder. Then in October 1964, Beckett 'broke down half way through galleys', calling it a 'ghastly mistake on my part to imagine, not having looked at it for a quarter of a century, that this old shit was revivable'.[50] Production was halted then; only in 1970 did Beckett give way to the demands of his publishers and his readers and permit the reprint.

FINISHEDNESS

What about Beckett's own sense of himself as a writer? This too is subject to change. On 18 March 1948, Beckett wrote to Thomas McGreevy: 'I see a little clearly at last what my writing is about and feel I have perhaps 10 years courage and energy to get the job done. The feeling of getting oneself in perspective is a strange one, after so many years of expression in blindness. Perhaps it is an illusion'.[51] Perhaps. The years following *L'Innommable* proved bleak. Beckett wrote to Barney Rosset from his brother Frank's bedside in Dublin: 'I think my writing days are over. *L'Innommable* finished me or expressed my finishedness'.[52]

Later that year, Karl-Franz Lembke, a prisoner at Lüttringhausen who had translated *En attendant Godot* into German and who had organised productions of the play within the prison walls, wrote to Beckett. Beckett replied: 'My last work is from 50. Since then, nothing. That tells you how long I have been without words. I have never regretted it so much as now, when I need them for you'.[53]

Attempting one, and then another, of the short pieces that became *Textes pour rien* provided a window for Beckett, and the courage, once again, to begin again, on the way to what could not be known. From this effort came the next; this resulted in the landmark prose work *Comment C'est*. Still, the caution, the fear, never entirely lifts. In one of many such remarks, Beckett recounts to Alan Schneider: 'Tried to get going on something new, but in vain. Frankly don't see much hope of going on'.[54]

IN COLLABORATION

Beckett's letters also show half a lifetime's collaboration with editors and publishers. Although long in coming, when the relationships were established, Beckett could call Editions de Minuit, Grove Press, Suhrkamp Verlag, John Calder, and Faber and Faber 'my publishers' – for nearly fifty years. His professional relationships with editors and members of staff became personal. Although from time to time he could be impatient with each of them in turn, and did refuse some of their demands, Beckett also looked for guidance to Jérôme Lindon, Barney Rosset, Peter Suhrkamp and Siegfried Unseld, John Calder and Charles Monteith.

Some translation of his work was undertaken with others, such as that of *Molloy* with Patrick Bowles, some of the *Nouvelles* with Richard Seaver, and with Ludovic and Agnès Janvier in the case of *Watt* (with an earlier attempt at the same by Daniel Mauroc which was abandoned when Beckett thought it was not worth publishing in French) (*L2*, 416). The Janviers translated 'From an Abandoned Work'; *Krapp's Last Tape* was undertaken by Pierre Leyris; Robert Pinget translated *All That Fall* as *Tous ceux qui tombent*, and Beckett translated his radio play *La Manivelle* as *The Old Tune*. Beckett responded to the inquiries of Erich Franzen as he translated *Molloy* into German. With Elmar Tophoven and later Erika Tophoven, who became his German translators, Beckett worked closely for years – finding it advantageous that his translators lived in Paris. The letters also chronicle translations of Beckett's work into languages which he did not know, including those by Jacoba van Velde (Dutch), Christian Ludvigsen (Danish), C. G. Bjurström (Swedish), and Antoni Libera (Polish). These letters are informed by the difficulties of translation, well understood by Beckett from his own experience of translating the work of others, and most especially his own. From this deep sympathy, the letters to translators revisit the work with sometimes startlingly direct comment.

To his trusted directors, Alan Schneider and Donald McWhinnie, Beckett openly expresses his doubts about a work, and as he works as director for many of his later productions, as well as throughout the Süddeutscher Rundfunk productions of his television plays, the writing is laid bare and ways are found by author and the production team to realise the texts. Letters to theatre artists, to academics and even to some collectors of his writing also open new facets on Beckett's writing life. In mutual regard, Beckett supports other writers and artists in their striving and in their successes. His letters show him intervening on behalf of young writers with his own publishers, giving advice when pressed, encouraging when he can.

The letters reflect a long writing life, one led in public ways as well as in much-craved solitude. Beckett's letters show him engaged with others, and, in the richest sense, the letters engage us in his writing.

NOTES

1 Samuel Beckett to Thomas McGreevy, 6 February 1937, *L1*, 447. [NB, McGreevy had changed his name to MacGreevy and this is reflected in the second volume of the letters. To avoid confusion in this collection of essays we have chosen to standardise all references to Beckett's friend as 'McGreevy'. Samuel Beckett will hereafter be referred to as 'SB']

2 SB to Barney Rosset, 5 May 1959, Syracuse University, Special Collections Research Center, Grove Press Records.
3 SB to Patrick Magee, 26 February 1960, TCD, MS 11313/3. SB to Alan Schneider, 7 April 1966, Samuel Beckett and Alan Schneider, *No Author Better Served: The Correspondence of Samuel Beckett and Alan Schneider* (Cambridge: Harvard University Press, 1998), 201.
4 SB to Barbara Bray, 29 July 1959, TCD, MS 10948/1/40.
5 SB to Ethna MacCarthy, 22 April 1959, TxU, Leventhal Collection.
6 'Avec trois visages blancs (bouches) et des lumières. Mais mes idées ... ' SB to Henri Lefebvre, 12 May 1962, Du Bouchet Collection. All translations from French in this chapter are by George Craig.
7 'Très difficile mais je pense y arriver. J'aimerais à t'en parler'. SB to Robert Pinget, 15 May 1962, Boston College, John J. Burns Rare Book and Manuscript Library, Robert Pinget/Samuel Beckett Collection.
8 SB to Alan Schneider, 4 August 1962, Beckett and Schneider, *No Author Better Served*, 126.
9 SB to Barbara Bray, 11 March 1959, TCD, MS 10948/1/22.
10 'Le rythme et la syntaxe de la faiblesse et de la pénurie, pas commode à attraper. J'y arrive quand même peut-être un peu – 6me version du début'. SB to Avigdor Arikha, 12 March 1959, Indiana University, Lilly Library, Arikha Collection.
11 SB to Barbara Bray, 15 April 1959, TCD, MS 10948/1/27.
12 Ethna MacCarthy, 22 April 1959, TxU, Leventhal Collection.
13 SB to Barbara Bray, 26 May 1959, TCD, MS 10948/1/24.
14 SB to Thomas McGreevy, 19 August 1959, TCD MS 10402/222.
15 SB to Barbara Bray, 15 April 1959, TCD, MS 10948/1/27.
16 SB to Aidan Higgins, 17 May 1965, TxU, Higgins.
17 SB to Barbara Bray, 29 July 1959, TCD, MS 10948/1/40.
18 SB to Barbara Bray, 11 March 1959, TCD, MS 10948/1/22.
19 *P*, 307. SB wrote to Siegfried Unseld on 1 July 1963: 'C'est seulement au retour d'Ulm que j'ai fait ce changement et rédigé la note sur l'éclairage. Je ne les ai pas encore communiqués à Tophoven, mais ne tarderai pas à le faire, trop tard hélas pour votre édition' ('It was only after coming back from Ulm that I made this change and wrote the note about the lighting ... too late for your edition') (Literaturarchiv-Marbach, Suhrkamp Verlag).
20 'Il faut que ce soit un véritable affolement de lumière et de bribes vocales'; SB to Siegfried Unseld, 1 July 1963, Literaturarchiv-Marbach, Suhrkamp Verlag. SB to Barbara Bray, 1 July 1963, TCD, MS 10948/1/235. SB to Alan Schneider, 20 July 1963, Beckett and Schneider, *No Author Better Served*, 138.
21 SB to Christian Ludvigsen, 8 December 1966; Ludvigsen Collection.
22 *En attendant Godot* was printed by Editions des Minuit on 17 October 1952; the first reprint was September 1953. *L2*, 353.
23 SB to George Devine, 5 March 1958 [*for* 5 April 1958], TxU, English Stage Company Collection.
24 Ibid.

25 SB to Barbara Bray, 4 October 1960, TCD, MS 10948/1/114.
26 SB to Barbara Bray, 16 October 1960, TCD, MS 10948/1/116.
27 'Als Hörspiel kommt *Damals*, meiner Meinung nach, gar nicht in Frage, wegen des Verlustes des Bildes, d.h. der Hälfte des Ganzen! Das horchende Gesicht gehört untrennbar dazu. Sonst gibt es kein Stück mehr da, nur eine ziellose Stimme ohne Spannung'. SB to Klaus Herm, 18 December 1976, Herm Collection.
28 'J'essaie de m'en sortir. Mais je ne m'en sors pas. Je ne sais pas si ça pourra faire un livre. Ce sera peut-être un temps pour rien'. SB to Jérôme Lindon, 10 April 1951 in *L2*, 234.
29 SB to Pamela Mitchell, 26 February 1955, University of Reading, BIF, MS 5060/52.
30 SB to Pamela Mitchell, 13 March 1955, *L2*,531.
31 SB to Barney Rosset, 22 February 1956, in *L2*, 602.
32 'Je ne puis en établir le texte définitif qu'après un certain nombre de répétitions'. SB to Stefani Hunzinger, 20 October 1956, *L2*, 667–8.
33 SB to Barney Rosset, 5 October 1960, Syracuse University, Special Collections Research Center, Grove Press Records.
34 SB to Barney Rosset, 6 August 1960, Syracuse University, Special Collections Research Center, Grove Press Records.
35 SB to Aidan Higgins, 5 October 1960, TxU, Higgins Collection.
36 SB to Christian Ludvigsen, 7 October 1960, Ludvigsen Collection.
37 SB to A. J. Leventhal, 9 February 1961, TxU, Leventhal Collection; SB to Barbara Bray, 12 February 1961, TCD, MS 10948/1/137.
38 SB to Judith Schmidt, 12 February 1961, Syracuse University, Special Collections Research Center, Grove Press Records.
39 SB to A. J. Leventhal, 18 May 1961, TxU, Leventhal Collection.
40 '[Je ne sais pas ce que] ça vaut, je devais le faire, c'est tout. J'aurais pu le faire mieux mais je n'ai pas pu'. SB to Jacoba van Velde, 20 May 1961, BNF, 197941/76.
41 'Mais le texte ne sera définitif que lorsque j'aurai pu travailler un peu dans un théâtre. Je le crois néanmoins déjà assez précis'. SB to Jacoba van Velde, 2 June 1961, BNF, 197941/77.
42 'A supposer que ce projet résiste à l'examen du texte, – ce qui n'est pas sûr'. SB to Stefani Hunzinger, 7 June 1961, Fischer Verlag Collection.
43 SB to Barney Rosset, 26 July 1962, Syracuse University, Special Collections Research Center, Grove Press Records.
44 'J'ai terminé une nouvelle pièce. Très courte. Un quart d'heure. 10 mois de travail (intermittent d'accord!) pour 15 minutes d'ennui. Elle s'appelle PLAY!' SB to Jacoba van Velde, 12 October 1962, BNF, 197941/91.
45 SB to Arland Ussher, 6 November 1962, in *L1*, xi.
46 SB to Mary Hutchinson, 9 July 1971, TxU, Mary Hutchinson Collection.
47 SB to George Reavey, 14 May 1947, in *L2*, 55.
48 SB to Barbara Bray, 26 May 1959, TCD, MS 10948/1/124.
49 'Il peut toujours avoir sa place, si vous y tenez, dans un volume à intituler Merdes Posthumes ... m'empourpre jusqu'aux os'. SB to Jérôme Lindon, in Beckett in *L2*, 446.

50 SB to Barney Rosset, 20 October 1964, Syracuse University, Special Collections Research Center, Grove Press Records.
51 SB to Thomas McGreevy, 18 March 1948, in *L2*, 75.
52 SB to Rosset, 21 August 1954, in *L2*, 497.
53 'Mon dernier ouvrage, de 50. Depuis rien. C'est vous dire qu'il y a longtemps que je suis sans mots. Je ne l'ai jamais regretté autant qu'aujourd'hui, où j'en ai besoin pour vous'. SB to Karl-Franz Lembke, on or after 14 October 1954, in *L2*, 505–6.
54 SB to Alan Schneider, 20 February 1962, Beckett and Schneider, *No Author Better Served*, 121.

Index

à Kempis, Thomas
   The Imitation of Christ, 304
Abélard, Peter, 55
Abraham, Lyndy
   A Dictionary of Alchemical Imagery, 344
Abraham, Nicolas, 198
absences, 7
Ach, Narziss, 315
Ackerley, Chris, 48, 205, 315
   Demented Particulars, 221
   Obscure Locks, Simple Keys, 221
Ackerley, Chris and S.E Gontarski
   Companion to Samuel Beckett, 221
Adam, Charles and Paul Tannery
   Euvres de Descartes, 48
Adamov, Arthur, 170
   The Great and the Small Manoeuvre, 169
   The Invasion, 169
Addison, Joseph, 220
Adler, Alfred, 316
   The Neurotic Constitution, 316
Admussen, Richard L, 418
   The Samuel Beckett Manuscripts, 418
Adorno, Theodor, 50, 127, 132, 133, 208, 210, 214
   'Trying to Understand Endgame', 301
Akalaitis, JoAnne, 173
Albee, Edward, 407
   Three Tall Women, 389
Albrecht, Günter, 103
Aldington, Richard, 399
Algerian War of Independence, 132
Alsace, 111
Ancient Order of Hibernians, 67
Andre, Carl, 262
Andrews, Lancelot, 59
Apollinaire, Guillaume, 81, 233
   'Zone', 59, 167, 233
Aragon, Louis, 116
Aretino, Pietro, 243
Arikha, Avigdor, 260, 261, 266, 429
Ariosto, Ludovico, 241, 242, 243

Aristotle, 302, 305
   Poetics, 391
Arnheim, Rudolf, 145, 280, 284
Aron, Robert
   Décadence de la nation française, 78
Artaud, Antonin, 145, 168–9, 238
   Van Gogh, the Man Suicided by Society, 166, 168
Asher, Claudia, 106
Asmus, Walter, 177, 290
Atik, Anne, 303
Aubert, Jacques, 154
Aucassin et Nicolette, 230, 231
Aujourd'hui, 111
Auschwitz, 115, 127
Austen, Jane, 93, 224
Auster, Paul, 407
Avrech, Mira, 292

Bach, Johann Sebastian, 413
Bachelard, Georges, 170
Badiou, Alain, 50, 134
Baillet, Adrien, 304
   La Vie de Monsieur Des-Cartes, 48
Bair, Deirdre. *See* biographies of Beckett
Baker, Phil, 7, 314–15
   Beckett and the Mythology of Psychoanalysis, 12
Balibar, Etienne, 78
Ballmer, Karl, 104, 257
Ballyba, 25, 26
Ballybalfour, 14
Ballyogan Road, 7
Balzac, Honoré de, 409
Banville, John, 407
Barrès, Maurice, 242
Barth, John
   'The Literature of Exhaustion', 44
Bartók, Béla, 266
Bataille, Georges, 153, 163, 164, 165, 167, 170, 237, 301, 401
   Madame Edwarda, 164
   Story of the Eye, 164

Bataille, Nicolas, 170
Baudelaire, Charles, 27, 233
Bauer, Walter
    Die Notwendige Reise, 101
Beach, Sylvia, 53
Beamish, Annie O'Meare de Vic, 118
Beaufret, Jean, 48–9, 242
Beaumont, Francis, 222
Beckett Country, The, 26
Beckett, Edward, 220, 241
Beckett, Frank, 92, 435
Beckett International Foundation archive, 99
Beckett, John, 275
Beckett, May. *See* Roe, Maria
Beckett Murphy, Caroline, 220, 241
Beckett, Samuel (biographies of)
    Bair, Deirdre, 9, 12, 13, 48, 95, 173, 174, 224, 302
    Cronin, Anthony, 11, 66, 88, 93, 95
    Samuel Beckett, The Last Modernist, 9
    Gordon, Lois, 9
    Knowlson, James, 8, 9, 12, 15, 59, 90, 93, 94, 95, 151, 154, 156, 173, 174, 176, 177, 178, 219, 256, 258, 275, 292, 303, 306, 317, 318, 346, 371, 400, 403, 406, 418, 420, 425
    Damned to Fame, 42, 44, 315
    O'Brien, Eoin, 9, 16, 19
Beckett, Samuel (diaries)
    German diaries, 101–4, 105–7
Beckett, Samuel (film director, co-director or consultant)
    of *...but the clouds...*, 192
    of *Comédie*, 193
    of *Eh Joe*, 192
    of *Flim*, 192
    of *Geistertrio*, 192
    of *Ghost Trio*, 192
    of *He Joe*, 192
    of *Nacht und Träume*, 193
    of *...nur noch Gewölk...*, 192
    of *Play*, 193
    of *Quad*, 192
    of *Quadrat I + II*, 192
    of *Was Wo*, 193
    of *What Where*, 193
Beckett, Samuel (letters), 23, 42, 45–6, 48, 49, 50, 51, 58, 60, 61–2, 76, 81, 82, 91, 92, 94, 126–7, 165
    to A.J. Leventhal, 102, 433
    to Aidan Higgins, 433
    to Alan Schneider, 431, 435
    to Arland Ussher, 434
    to Axel Kaun, 100, 101, 144, 219, 271, 363
    to Barbara Bray, 429, 430, 431, 432, 433, 434
    to Barney Rosset, 428, 432, 433, 435
    to Charles Prentice, 153, 232
    to David Hayman, 247
    to George Reavey, 89, 249, 434
    to Georges Belmont, 225
    to Georges Duthuit, 61, 164, 166, 167, 169, 245, 249
    to Hans Naumann, 422
    to Harriet Shaw Weaver, 343
    to Herbert White, 220
    to Jacoba van Velde, 419, 433, 434
    to James Joyce, 45–6, 151
    to JoAnne Akalaitis, 173
    to Judith Schmidt, 433
    Ludvigsen, Christian, 433
    to Mania Péron, 225
    to Mary Hutchinson, 434
    to Mary Manning Howe, 102, 104, 107–8
    to Morris Sinclair, 90, 92, 102, 163
    to Nualla Costello, 89, 94
    to Pamela Mitchell, 226, 432
    to Patricia Hutchins, 226
    to R.B.D. French, 220
    to Sergei Eisenstein, 145, 279, 282
    to Simone de Beauvoir, 162
    to Stephani Hunzinger, 432
    to Thomas McGreevy, 88, 90–1, 96, 101, 107, 139, 151, 155, 166, 210, 220, 224, 225, 226, 232, 241, 242, 243, 245, 247, 255, 292, 293, 304, 319, 428, 429, 435
    to Ussher, Arland, 99
Beckett, Samuel (obituary), 1
Beckett, Samuel (pseudonym)
    Andrew Belis, 93
Beckett, Samuel (stage direction)
    of *Endgame*, 178, 180
    of *Footfalls*, 179
    of *Happy Days*, 178, 180
    of *Krapp's Last Tape*, 178, 179, 180
    of *Play*, 180
    of *Rockaby*, 180
    of *Waiting for Godot*, 178, 180
Beckett, Samuel (translations)
    for Nancy Cunard *Negro*, 93, 147, 371
    for *This Quarter*, 141, 232
    of *Anna Livia Plurablle*, 371
    of *Anthology of Mexican Poetry*, 371
    of Apollinaire's "Zone", 233
    of Arthur Rimbaud's "Bateau ivre", 233
    of Eugenio Montale, 46
    of Eugenio Montale's 'Delta', 371
    for *Formes*, 46
    for George Reavey's *Thorns of Thunder*, 232
    of Georges Duthuit's *Transition*, 167, 236
    of Giovanni Comisso, 46
    of Guillaume Apollinaire's 'Zone', 167

of James Joyce's 'Anna Livia Plurabelle', 154–5
of Joyce into French, 46
of Maurice Blanchot's 'Sade's Reason', 164
of Paul Eluard, 371
of poems for Duthuit's *Transition*, 371
of Raffaello Franchi, 46
of Rainer Maria Rilke's *Poems*, 93
of René Crevel, 371
of Robert Pinget's *La Manivelle*, 371
self-translation, 46–7
of *All That Fall*, 372
of 'Cascando', 372
of *Comment C'est*, 428
of *Company*, 372, 377
of *Embers*, 372
of *En attendant Godot*, 372, 373, 375, 377
of *Endgame*, 376
of *Fin de Partie*, 372, 373
of *Happy Days*, 375
of *La Manivelle*, 436
of *L'Innommable*, 376
of 'Love and Lethe', 372
of *Mal vu mal dit (Ill Seen Ill Said)*, 377
of *Malone meurt*, 372, 376
of *Mercier et Camier*, 372
of *Molloy*, 372, 373, 375, 376, 436
of *Murphy*, 372, 373, 375, 376
of *Play*, 375, 376
of *Watt*, 372, 373, 436
of UNESCO homage to Goethe, 371
Beckett, Samuel (works by), 55–6, 327
  ... but the clouds ..., 192, 195, 199, 393
'A Case in a Thousand', 16, 94
'A Piece of Monologue', 38, 199
Acte sans paroles, 208
Acte sans paroles I, 275
Acts without Words, 287
Acts Without Words I, 222
Acts Without Words II, 222
All Strange Away, 305, 312
All That Fall, 13, 20, 74, 266, 272, 273, 319, 324, 325, 329, 386, 402, 419, 436
'Arènes de Lutèce', 56–7
'Ascension', 57
'Assumption', 81, 153
Bing, 419
Breath, 173, 199, 222
'The Calmative', 160, 312, 411
The Capital of the Ruins, 120, 121, 122–3
Cascando, 25, 271, 275, 419
Catastrophe, 131, 134
'Censorship in the Saorstat,' 24, 71, 80, 93
"Che Sciagura", 71, 237
Come and Go, 389–90, 391, 419

Comédie, 285–6
Comment C'est, 429, 433, 435
Company, 7, 8, 13, 20, 244, 261, 324, 329, 340, 362, 365
Company notebook, 372
'Dante and the Lobster', 241, 242, 326
'Dante ... Bruno.Vico ... Joyce', 44–5, 48, 152–3, 211, 246, 256, 304, 338, 353, 398, 405, 406
'Dieppe', 99, 430
'Ding Dong', 22, 272
'Dortmunder', 153, 419
'Draff', 22, 421
Dream notebook, 422
Dream of Fair to Middling Women, 2, 20, 21, 26, 27, 29, 46, 48, 54, 71–2, 83, 88, 89, 139–40, 142, 153, 207, 208, 231, 236, 241, 244, 247, 269–70, 271, 289, 304, 317, 324, 326, 340–2, 399, 409, 419, 421
and Alfred Péron, 43
Dream of Fair to Middling Women notebook, 220, 221, 223, 246, 421
Echo's Bones and Other Precipitates, 23, 24, 93, 142, 210, 231, 281, 302, 399–400, 419, 420
Eh Joe, 192, 195, 197–8, 199, 200, 286, 419, 428, 429, 432
Eleutheria, 8, 145, 160, 169, 170, 236, 419, 420
Embers, 402, 419, 420, 429, 430
En attendant Godot, 425, 429, 431, 435
'The End', 8, 131, 160, 163, 213, 302
Endgame, 74, 130, 132–3, 134, 173, 222, 260–1, 305, 312, 331–2, 333, 345, 383, 384–5, 388, 402, 420, 431
Endgame, Production Notebook, 178
"Enueg I", 21, 233, 419
'Enueg II', 21, 153
essay in *Bram van Velde*, 259
'The Expelled', 160, 213
Film, 2, 38, 57, 130, 177, 192, 193, 194, 199, 200, 262, 282–5, 286, 287, 306, 325
Fin de partie, 420, 432–3
'Fingal', 22, 24, 26
'First Love', 127, 160, 295, 314
'The Fly', 57–8
Foirades/Fizzle with Jasper Johns, 261–2
Footfalls, 141, 198, 267, 319, 348, 353, 368, 372, 392, 424
From an Abandoned Work, 261
'From the Only Poet to a Shining Whore', 325
'For Future Reference', 8, 16, 23, 153, 339–40, 342
Ghost Trio, 176, 192, 195, 196, 199, 200, 269, 271–2, 273, 393
'Gnome', 93
Graff. See More Pricks than Kicks

Beckett, Samuel (works by) (*cont.*)
  Happy Days, 56, 174, 176, 260, 381, 387–9, 402, 432, 433
  Happy Days notebook, 420
  Happy Days, Production Notebook, 178
  Heard in the Dark, 269
  'Hell Crane to Starling', 326
  'Homage to Jac B. Yeats', 170
  'Home Olga', 155
  How It Is, 129, 146, 244, 261, 302, 324, 325, 333, 348, 419
  How It Is notebook, 420
  Human Wishes, 145, 224, 302
  Ill Seen Ill Said, 219, 222, 223, 261, 287, 333
  'The Image', 302
  Imagination Dead Imagine, 312, 351, 419, 420
  Krapp's Last Tape, 38, 178, 222, 269, 275, 324, 384, 385–7, 402, 425, 428, 431, 432, 433, 436
  Krapp's Last Tape, Production Notebook, 178
  'La Peinture des van Velde ou le monde et le pantalon', 160, 166
  Le Dépeupleur, 233, 419
  'Le monde et le Pantalon', 24
  lecture on Marcel Proust, 34
  Lessness, 274, 419, 420
  L'Innommable, 168
  The Lost Ones, 132, 219, 223, 368, 419, 420
  'Love and Lethe', 22, 27, 208
  Mal vu mal dit, 233, 236
  'Malacoda', 153
  Malone Dies, 8, 15, 69, 70, 160, 163, 223, 234, 235, 258, 308, 312, 330, 334, 345, 372, 400, 403, 434
  Malone meurt. *See Malone Dies*
  Mercier and Camier notebooks, 425
  Mercier et Camier, 20, 74, 160, 234, 294–5, 348, 354, 372, 419, 420, 434
  Molloy, 7, 13, 25, 37, 68, 94, 156, 160, 163, 164, 212, 234, 236, 237, 238, 301, 302, 308, 309, 313, 314, 324, 334, 345, 348, 350, 362, 363, 372, 400–1, 403, 414, 419, 425, 434
  Moran, Jacques, 14
  More Pricks than Kicks, 24–5, 89, 93, 94, 97, 142, 207, 243, 256, 271, 296, 304, 324, 329, 350, 399, 434
  Murphy, 26, 27, 38, 59, 72, 73, 83, 87, 88, 95, 96, 141, 142, 155, 205, 207, 223, 224, 231, 235, 236, 244, 258, 271, 279, 302, 305, 307, 315, 316, 317, 320, 324, 332, 342, 348, 349–50, 351–2, 353, 399, 409, 423, 434
  influence of London on the novel, 95–6
  publication, 97
  Murphy (translation into French), 46
  Nacht und Träume, 192, 195, 199–200, 260, 271, 273
  Not I, 274, 314, 363, 392, 424
  Ohio Impromptu, 156–7, 256, 269
  The Old Tune, 20
  'Ooftish', 153
  'Peintres de l'Empêchement', 2, 3, 160, 166
  'Ping', 274
  Play, 223, 274, 390–1, 429, 430–1, 433
  'Prayer', 57, 58
  Premier amour, 420
  Proust, 50–1, 60, 89, 115, 140, 143–4, 196, 232, 256, 268, 302, 304, 329, 353, 398–9
  Quad, 134, 192, 196, 200, 343–4, 345
  Quad I, 368–9
  Quad II, 368–9
  'Recent Irish Poetry', 24, 36, 44, 93, 205, 207, 209, 210, 226
  review of Denis Devlin's *Intercessions*, 99, 153
  review of Thomas McGreevy's *Poems*, 93
  Rockaby, 392, 429, 432
  Rough for Radio I, 271
  Rough for Radio II, 302, 420
  Rue de Vaugirard, 56
  'Sanies I', 25, 223
  'Sanies II', 23
  'Sedendo et Quiescendo', 46, 153, 406
  'Serena I', 302
  'Serena II', 21, 24, 324
  'Serena III', 21
  'Sonnet', 46
  "Sottisier" Notebook, 237, 424
  Sounds, 269
  Stirrings Still, 132, 269, 368, 424, 425
  'Suite', 163
  'Super Conquérant' notebook, 424
  'Tal Coat', 164
  Textes pour rien, 435
  Texts for Nothing, 58–9, 160, 259, 272, 302, 329, 343, 362, 368, 430
  That Time, 141, 333, 372, 393, 424, 429, 432
  Three Dialogues, 160, 164, 167, 168, 241, 244, 258–9, 306, 366, 367
  trilogy, 82
  The Unnamable, 8, 9, 10, 16, 36, 127, 146, 160, 163, 258, 261, 263, 301, 312, 313, 328, 329, 330, 342, 345, 362, 403, 407, 408, 409, 410, 413, 432, 434, 435
  ur-Watt notebooks, 27
  'The Voice' (unpublished), 220
  Waiting for Godot, 1, 55, 61, 74, 82, 94, 110, 115, 117, 118–19, 121, 122, 123, 130, 145, 160, 165, 169, 170, 174, 196, 223, 238, 258, 261, 282, 289–90, 295, 297, 301, 329, 330, 332, 343, 348, 350, 363, 372, 381–4, 385, 390, 401–2, 419, 420, 425
  1953 Paris production, 290

Index

1956 American production, 297
2009 British production, 289
premiere at Théâtre de Babylone, 401
Waiting for Godot, Production Notebook, 178
'Walking Out', 21, 22, 205–7, 272
Watt, 7, 8, 13, 20, 25, 27, 37, 46, 60, 74, 94, 119, 157, 174, 205, 222, 224, 225, 235, 244, 258, 271, 291–2, 302, 307, 308, 324, 325, 328–9, 332, 333, 348, 351, 354, 356, 364–6, 400, 406, 409–10, 411, 414, 420, 434
causality, 34
'What A Misfortune', 22, 421
'What is the Word', 274
What Where, 272, 286
Whoroscope, 34, 48, 81, 106, 142, 229, 232, 256, 304, 342, 399, 419
Whoroscope notebook, 221, 222, 224, 272, 331, 421, 422, 423
Words and Music, 271, 274, 275
Worstward Ho, 256, 261, 274, 362, 368, 372, 424
'Yellow', 22, 326
Beckett, William Frank. *See* father
Beethoven, Ludwig van, 193, 266, 270, 271–2, 273, 293
Piano Trio Op.70 No.1, 272
Bell, Vanessa, 140
Belmont, Georges. *See* Pelorson, Georges
Benjamin, Walter, 57
Ben-Zvi, Linda, 93, 307
Beowulf, 220
Berg, Alban, 266
Bergson, Henri, 29–38, 196, 232, 241, 293
Creative Evolution, 33, 37
influence on Beckett, 36
Matter and Memory, 33, 35, 195–6
Time and Free Will, 33, 35
Berio, Luciano, 276
Berkeley, George, 29, 219, 284, 306, 377
Beckett on, 36
The Principles of Human Knowledge, 194
Three Dialogues between Hylas and Philonaus, 306
Berlin Philharmonic concert, 92
Bernhard, Thomas, 407
The Loser, 413–14
Beyle, Marie-Henri, 230, 233, 234, 235
Le rouge et le noir, 234
Bifur, 46, 154
Bignell, Jonathan
Beckett on Screen, 193
Bion, Wilfred, 61, 90, 91, 96, 197, 199, 294, 317–19
birth, 9–10
Bistué, Belén, 47
Bjurström, C.G, 436

Blair, Eric. *See* Orwell, George
Blake, Sexton, 292
Blanchot, Maurice, 80, 163, 164–5, 170, 237, 301
Aminadab, 164
The Book to Come, 163
Death Sentence, 164
Faux Pas, 164
Lautréamont and Sade, 164
Lautréamont et Sade, 236
The Most High, 164
'Sade's Reason', 164
Thomas the Obscure, 164
The Work of Fire, 164
Blast, 146
Blin, Roger, 168, 169, 290, 297
Bloomsbury group, 140
Blum, Léon, 80, 83
Blum, Norman, 167
Boccaccio, Giovanni, 243
Bohr, Niels, 355
Bookman, The, 93, 94
Bor, G.T, 16
Borges, Jorge Luis, 402
Bosquet, Alain, 371
Boswell, James, 225
Life of Samuel Johnson, 224
Bouglé, Célestin, 47
Boulevard Saint Jacques, 58
Bourdieu, Pierre, 207, 212
Bouvier, Jean-Baptiste, 422
Dissertatio in Sextum Decalogi Praeceptum et Supplementum ad Tractatum de Matrimonio, 422
Bovary, Emma, 391
Bowen, Elizabeth, 226
Bowles, Patrick, 46, 100, 372, 373, 436
Boxall, Peter, 407
Boyle, Kay, 246
Bradby, David, 168, 173, 290
Brancusi, Constantin, 150
Braque, Georges, 167
Brater, Enoch, 174, 177
Bray, Barbara, 26, 428
Brecht, Bertolt, 145
Brenkman, John, 407
Breton, André, 141, 143, 167, 232, 257, 371
Nadja, 59
Breuer, Rolf, 211, 212
British Museum, 88
Brontë, Emily, 82
brothers, 15
Brown, Terence, 80
Browne, Sir Thomas, 223
Garden of Cyrus, 223
Hydrotaphia, Urn Burial, 223

Bruegel, Pieter
  Lepers, 260
Bruguera, Tania
  Endgame Study #7, 263
Bruno, Giordano, 302, 304, 338–9, 340, 342
Bruton, Robert
  Anatomy of Melancholy, 304
Bryden, Mary, 276
  editor of *Samuel Beckett and Music*, 267
Buchner, Georg, 385
Burgess, Anthony, 82
Burton, Robert
  Anatomy of Melancholy, 223
Butler, Lance St John
  Samuel Beckett and the Meaning of Being, 308
Butor, Michel, 165

Cahiers d'Art, 166
Calder, John, 419, 434, 435
Camus, Albert, 161, 162, 163, 165, 168, 236, 237, 287
  Combat (association with), 162
  The Just Assassins, 168
  L'étranger, 235
  The Myth of Sisyphus, 162
  The Outsider, 162
  The Plague, 162, 164
  The Rebel, 162
  State of Siege, 168
Caravaggio, Michelangelo Merisida
  Decollation of Saint John the Baptist, 429
Carducci, Giosué, 242
Carrel, Alexis
  L'Homme, cet inconnnu, 79
Casanova, Pascale, 170
Caselli, Daniela
  'The Promise of Dante in the Beckett Manuscripts', 423
Castiglione, Baldassare, 246
Cazamian, Louis, 220
Céline, Louis-Ferdinand, 53, 235, 236, 237
  L'École de cadavres, 80
  Mort à crédit, 235, 236
  Voyage au Bout de la Nuit, 59, 235
Censorship
  'Index of Forbidden Books in Ireland', 89
Cervantes, Miguel, 408
Cézanne, Paul, 92, 141, 166
Chabert, Pierre, 177, 178, 179
Chamfort, Sébastien, 236
chansons de toile. See *chansons d'histoire*
Chaplin, Charlie, 145, 193, 292, 296
Char, René, 60, 167
Chatto and Windus, 88, 89, 96, 153
Chaucer, Geoffrey, 220, 221

Chautemps, Camille, 111
Chekhov, Anton, 382, 392
  Three Sisters, 280, 389
children, absence of, 8
Christie, Agatha, 292
Churchill, Winston, 111, 118
Cioran, Emile, 1
Cixous, Hélène, 50
  dissertation on Joyce, 150
Clarke, Austin, 145, 225, 293
Clemenceau, Georges, 112
Close Up, 285
Cluchey, Rick, 178
Coetzee, J.M, 407
  'Into the Dark Chamber, The Writer and the South African State', 412
  Waiting for the Barbarians, 411–13
Coffey, Brian, 142, 210, 211, 225
Cohn, Ruby, 179, 192, 236, 267, 301, 373, 374, 375, 418
  A Beckett Canon, 420
  The Comic Gamut, 381
  editor of *Disjecta, Miscellaneous Writings and a Dramatic Fragment*, 259, 307, 363, 398
Collins, Michael, 68, 116
Combat, 80, 162, 301
Comisso Giovanni. See Beckett, Samuel (translations)
Connolly, Cyril, 95
Connolly, James, 78
Connor, Steven, 372, 378
Conrad, Joseph, 140, 370
Constant, Alphonse-Louis, 337
Cooldrinagh, 11, 12
Cooper, William
  Flagellation and the Flagellants, 327
Corkery, Daniel, 209
  The Hidden Ireland, 209
  Synge and Anglo-Irish Literature, 209
  The Threshold of Quiet, 209
Corneille, Pierre, 230, 233, 293
Costello, Nuala, 22, 23, 89, 94
Costelloe Stephen, Karin, 31–2, 36, 37
  'An Answer to Mr. Bertrand Russell's Article on the Philosophy of Bergson', 31
County Fermanagh, 14
Craig, Edward Gordon, 175–6
  The Mask, 175
Craige, John, 356
Crevel, René, 232
Crichton-Miller, Hugh, 90
Criterion, The, 93
Critique, 164, 165, 301
Croce, Benedetto, 304

Index

Cronin, Anthony. *See* Beckett, Samuel (biographies of)
Cuchulain, 67, 73
Cunard, Nancy, 48, 399
  Authors Take Sides on the Spanish Civil War, 81
  Negro, 93
Cunningham, Bill, 292
Cunningham, Valentine, 89, 91

da Imola, Benvenuto, 244
D'Annunzio, Gabriele, 242, 249
Dalí, Salvador, 257, 260
Dante, Alighieri, 15, 45, 48, 139, 142, 193, 241, 243–9, 295, 325, 391
  Convivio, 241
  The Divine Comedy, 241
  Inferno, 241, 260, 305
  Paradiso, 241
  Purgatorio, 142, 241
Darwin, Charles
  On the Origin of Species, 293, 421, 425
Das Innere Reich, 100
de Balzac, Honoré, 230, 233, 234
  La peau de chagrin, 234
  Louis Lambert, 234
de Beauvoir, Simone, 42, 161, 163
  All Men Are Mortal, 162
  The Blood of Others, 162
  The Second Sex, 162
de Biasi, Pierre-Marc
  'Toward a Science of Literature, Manuscript Analysis and the Genesis of the Work', 417
de Chateaubriand, François-René
  René, 233
de Chavannes, Puvis, 23
  Sailing Sailing Swiftly, 23
de Florian, Jean Pierre Claris
  Les arlequinades, 230
de Gaulle, Charles, 111–12, 114, 115, 116, 117, 120, 128, 132
de Gaultier, Jules
  De Kant à Nietzsche, 304
de Giustino, David, 354
de Gourmont, Remy
  Pages choisies, 233
de La Fontaine, Jean
  Fables, 230
de la Vaissière, Robert, 230
de Lamartine, Alphonse
  "L'isolement", 233
de Marivaux, Pierre, 230, 231
de Maupassant, Guy
  contes, 230
de Montaigne, Michel, 230
de Mortillet, Gabriel, 56–7

de Musset, Alfred, 230, 232
de Nerval, Gérard, 232
de Pellepoix, Darquier, 115
de Régnier, Henri, 230
de Ronsard, Pierre, 230, 231
de Sade, Marquis, 236, , *See* Donatien Alphonse François
  120 jours de Sodome, 236
  Les 120 jours de Sodome, 236
de Sanctis, Francesco, 243
  Storia della letteratura italiana, 243
de Staël, Nicolas, 167
de Valera, Eamon, 67, 68, 70, 72–3, 76, 77, 78
de Vigny, Alfred, 230
Debussy, Claude, 266
Dedalus, Stephen, 126
Deevy, Teresa, 145
Dekker, Thomas, 222
Deleuze, Gilles, 34, 50, 148
  on *Film*, 2
DeLillo, Don, 407
Democritus, 223, 305, 308
Dernières Nouvelles de Paris, 111
Derrida, Jacques, 50
Derrière le Miroir, 166
Descartes, René, 35, 48, 49, 229, 232, 235, 291, 301–2, 304, 306, 342, 345, 349, 352
  Discourse on Method, 292
Deschevaux-Dumesnil, Suzanne, 54, 165, 257, 402
Dettmar, Kevin, 153
Devine, George, 266, 431
Devlin, Denis, 107, 141, 210, 211, 225
  'The Statue', 107
Dickens, Charles, 225
  Oliver Twist, 225, 292
Dickinson, Emily, 225
Diderot, Denis, 236
  Jacques le fataliste et son maître, 236
  Le rêve de d'Alembert, 236
Dix, Otto, 141
Doirot, Jacques, 79
Donne, John, 222
Donnellan, Anne, 29
Doré, Paul Gustave, 260
Dostoevsky, Fyodor, 232, 233
  The Possessed, 293
Doyle, Arthur Conan, 292, 294
  'The Speckled Band', 219
Driver, Tom, 324
Dryden, John, 220, 221
du Bellay, Joachim, 231
du Bouchet, André, 167
Dublin Magazine, 93, 205, 210
Dublin University Calendar, 230

Duchamp, Marcel, 257
Dujardin, Édouard, 155
Dukes, Gerry, 13
Dullin, Charles, 169
Dunbar, William, 221
Durandet, Christian, 117
Duras, Marguerite
  Hiroshima mon amour, 286
Durer, Albrecht, 35
d'Urfé, Honoré
  L'Astrée, 230
Durkheim, Emile, 47
Durrieu, Margaritha, 105
Duthuit, Georges, 161, 166, 167–8, 258, 259, 313, 321, 428
  'Three Dialogues with Georges Duthuit', 2, 144
  Transition, 153

Earlsfort House, 13
Easter Rising, 13–14, 67–8, 69, 73
École Normale Supérieure, 42–3, 53, 76, 82, 150, 160, 229, 231, 232, 279, 338
Eisenhower, Dwight, 119
Eisenstein, Sergei, 145, 194, 255, 280, 281–2, 284
  Battleship Potemkin, 279
Eliot, George
  The Mill on the Floss, 225
Eliot, T.S, 53, 59, 93, 94, 139, 140, 142, 146, 219, 226, 248, 370
  The Waste Land, 139
Ellmann, Richard
  biography of James Joyce, 155–6, 157
  Nayman of Noland, 1
Elsner sisters, 13
Eluard, Paul, 81, 141, 167, 232, 257
En Attendant Godot. See Beckett, Samuel (works by): *Waiting for Godot*
Engelberts, Matthijs, 241
English Review, The, 140
ENS. *See* École Normale Supérieure
Ernst, Haeckel, 261
Ernst, Max, 257
Esposito, Bianca, 247
Esslin, Martin, 155, 169
Étoile, 113

Faber and Faber, 435
Faber Companion to Samuel Beckett, 50
Faguet, Émile
  Dix-huitième siècle, 230
Faolain, Sean, 209
Farquhar, George, 222
father, 8, 10–11
  death, 87
  marriage, 11

Federman, Raymond, 94, 374, 375
Fehsenfeld, Martha, 289
Feininger, Lionel, 141
Feldman, Matthew, 315, 317, 397
  Beckett's Books, 420
Feldman, Morton, 275
Ferrer, Daniel, 154, 421
Feuillerat, Albert
  Comment Proust a composé son roman, 424
Fíanna Fáil, 76, 77
Field Day Anthology of Irish Writing, 205
Fielding, Henry, 222, 224
  Joseph Andrews, 225
  Tom Jones, 225
Fiorentino, Anonimo, 244
Fitch, Noel Riley, 375–6, 377, 378
Flaubert, Gustave, 233, 234, 235
  Bouvard et Pécuchet, 234
Flavin, Dan, 262
Fletcher, John, 94, 222
Flint, F.S, 143, 398
  trans of Bergson's *An Introduction to Metaphysics*, 31
Foot, M.R.D, 113, 116
Ford, John, 222
Forester, C.S, 292
Formes, 81
Forster, E.M, 140
Foucault, Michel, 174
Fouchet, Max-Pol, 167
Fournier, Edith, 372
Franchi, Raffaello. *See* Beckett, Samuel (translations)
Francis, Sam, 167
Frankfurter Zeitung, 102
Franzen, Erich, 436
Frazier, Adrian, 206
Frege, Gottlob, 354
French and Beckett, 45
French Resistance, 109, 110, 112, 148
French, Robert B.D, 418
Freud, Sigmund, 12, 314, 315, 316, 317, 319
  'Mourning and Melancholia', 197
Friedrich, Caspar David, 255, 273
  Two Men Looking at the Moon, 429
Friel, Brian, 407
Frost, Everett, 241, 266, 275, 420
Fry, Roger, 140
Frye, Northrop, 403
Fugard, Athol, 408
Furtwängler, Wilhelm, 91, 102, 266, 293

Gaelic League, 67
Gall, Franz Joseph, 354
Gallimard, 161, 162, 164

Garcin, Jean, 117
Garnett, Edward, 140
Garnier, Pierre
    Onanisme seul et à deux sous toutes ses forms et leurs conséquences, 422
Gates, Bill, 134
Gautier, Théophile
    Voyage en Italie, 230
Genet, Jean, 57, 161, 162, 163, 237
    Death Watch, 168
    The Maids, 162, 168
    Miracle of the Rose, 162
    Our Lady of the Flowers, 162
    The Thief's Journal, 162
George, Stefan, 99
Geulincx, Arnold, 49, 194–5, 196, 200, 295, 302, 306, 350, 420
Giacometti, Alberto, 167, 257, 261
Gibson, Andrew, 82, 131, 133
Gide, André, 230, 232, 233, 234, 235
    Les faux-monnayeurs, 234
Gilbert, Stuart, 154
Gilbert, W.S and Arthur Sullivan, 292
Gillet, Louis
    La Revue des deux mondes, 150
Giorgione, 242
Glass, Philip, 276
Glencullen road, 13
Gloria Resistance Network, 54, 113, 116, 257, 400
Godard, Jean-Luc, 131
Gödel, Kurt, 350, 353, 354–6
Goebbels, Josef, 100, 102, 103
Goering, Hermann, 102, 103
Goethe, Johann Wolfgang von, 100–1, 127
    Dichtung und Wahrheit, 101
    Faust, 101–2
    Iphigenia, 243
Goldstein, Kurt, 354
Goldstein, Rebecca, 355
Goll, Ivan, 154
Gontarski, S.E, 48, 192, 205, 221, 348, 420, 424
    The Intent of Undoing, 417
Gordon, Lois
    The World of Samuel Beckett. *See* biographies of Beckett
Gormont et Isembart, 230
Graham, Douglas, 15
Great Depression, 91
Greene, Graham, 82
Greene, Robert, 222
Grésillon, Almuth, 423
Griese, Friedrich, 104
Griffith, Arthur, 67, 68
Grimm, Hans
    Volk ohne Raum, 104

Grohmann, Will, 105
Grotowski, Jerzy, 173
Grove Press, 435
Gruen, John, 10
Grutman, Rainier, 46
Guattari, Félix, 148
Guerne, Armel, 113
Guggenheim, Peggy, 81

H.D, 140
Haas, Monique, 266
Haeckel, Ernst, 129
Harries, Martin, 264
Harvey, Lawrence, 58
    Samuel Beckett Poet and Critic, 48
Hatoum, Mona
    Corps Étranger, 263–4
Havel, Václav, 131, 408
Hawthorne, Nathaniel, 225
Hay, Louis, 423
Hayden, Henri, 258, 259, 261
Hayman, David, 406
    'Genetic Studies in Joyce', 417
Heaney, Seamus, 61
Heckel, Erich, 141
Heidegger, Martin, 100
Heinemann, Karl, 103
Heisenberg, Werner, 355
Henriot, Philippe, 119
Heraclitus, 382
Herm, Klaus, 432
Hess, Rudolf, 102
Heyse, Hans, 104
Higgins, Aidan, 207, 213, 292
Higgins, F.R, 209
Hilbert, David, 354
Hill, Leslie, 70
Hill, Rose, 267
Hindemith, Paul, 266
Hitchcock, Alfred, 280
Hitler, Adolf, 77, 91, 102, 103, 109, 111, 116
    Mein Kampf, 102
Hobson, Harold, 402
Hodgson, Richard. *See* Sarkonak, Ralph and Richard Hodgson
Hoffman, Ernst Theodor Amadeus, 424
Hogarth Press, 89, 140
Hokenson, Jan Walsh, 374
Hölderlin, Friedrich, 99–101, 107
    'Der Spaziergang', 99
    Hyperion, 100
Home Rule movement, 65
Hueffer, Ford Madox, 140
Hugo, Victor, 230

Hulme, T.E, 31, 32, 36, 140
'Anti-Romanticism and Original Sin', 31
'Bergson's Theory of Art', 31
'Modern Theories of Art', 38
'The Philosophy of Intensive Manifolds', 31
trans of Bergson's *An Introduction to Metaphysics*, 31
Hunzinger, Stefani, 433
Hutchinson, Mary, 207
Huxley, Aldous
Point Counter Point, 225

Ibsen, Henrik, 384, 392
Il Messagero, 286
Imola, Benvenuto da, 244
Innes, Christopher, 175
Ionesco, Eugene, 170, 208, 282
The Bald Prima Donna, 170
Irish Parliamentary Party, 67
Irish Republic Army, 68
Irish Statesman, The, 46, 210
Irish Writing, 205
Iser, Wolfgang, 309, 348
Israel, Calvin, 419

James I of England, 14
James, Henry, 82
James, Willliam, 328
Jammes, Francis, 230
Janvier, Agnès, 372, 373, 436
Janvier, Ludovic, 436
Jessop, Thomas Edmund, 29
Joeres, Charlotte, 319
Johns, Jasper, 261
Johnson, B.S, 407, 408–9
Albert Angelo, 408, 409, 413
Johnson, Samuel, 93, 145, 224–5, 302
Rasselas, 222, 224
Jolas, Eugene, 44, 53, 81, 82, 147, 153, 154, 156, 160, 167
Our Exagmination Round His Factification..., 44
'Poetry is Vertical', 81, 143, 153
'The Revolution of the Word', 152
transition, 44, 150, 152, 153
Jolas, Maria, 147, 167
Jonathan Cape, 89, 140
Jones, Ernest
Papers on Psychoanalysis, 316
Treatment of Neuroses, 316
Jonson, Ben, 222
Jouve, Pierre Jean, 47, 231
Jouvet, Louis, 168
Joyce, Giorgio, 155

Joyce, James, 26, 27, 42, 44, 47, 49, 51, 53–4, 59, 65, 81, 109, 126, 140, 141, 142, 143, 146, 147, 150–7, 160, 211, 212–13, 218, 226, 229, 231, 235, 248, 257, 258, 281, 304, 370, 381, 392, 398, 405, 406, 407, 417, 421, 422, 424
A Portrait of the Artist as a Young Man, 8, 19, 44, 324
'Anna Livia Plurabelle', 46
'Apotheosis of the word', 356
'Circe' chapter of *Ulysses* as playscript, 146
comparison with Beckett, 19
'The Dead', 21
Dubliners, 21, 44
Finnegans Wake, 19, 21, 22, 155, 211, 302, 304, 338, 343, 371, 398, 405, 406, 422
influence on Beckett, 44–5
Our Exagmination Round His Factification for Incamination of Work in Progress, 152, 153, 338
Ulysses, 19, 24, 34, 146, 157, 211, 212, 224
Ulysses (French translation), 154
Work in Progress, 44, 45, 46, 151, 152, 153, 155, 304, 338, 371, 398, 405
Joyce, Lucia, 22, 23, 54, 155
Joyce, Nora, 150, 151, 155
Juliet, Charles, 319, 406
Jung, Carl, 96, 316, 319, 344–5
Psychology and Alchemy, 344

Kafka, Franz, 128, 164, 211
Kalb, Jonathan, 173
Kandinsky, Wassily, 141, 257
Kane, Sarah, 408
Kant, Immanuel, 261, 302, 305, 307
Critique of Pure Reason, 423
Karmitz, Marin, 285–6
Kassel, 101
Kaun, Axel, 100, 101, 103, 106, 356
Keaton, Buster, 130, 145, 194, 262, 283, 284, 285, 292, 297
Keats, John, 220, 242
'Ode to a Nightingale', 219, 220
'On Looking into Chapman's Homer', 219
Keitel, General Wilhelm, 114
Kennedy, Sighle, 348, 406
Kenner, Hugh, 345
'The Cartesian Centaur', 301
kindergarten, 13
Kinsella, Thomas, 407
Kirchner, Ernst Ludwig, 141, 257
Klee, Paul, 257
Klein, Melanie, 197, 318
Kleist, Heinrich Von
'On the Marionette Theatre', 176
The Prince of Homburg, 176

Klossowski, Pierre, 164
  Sade mon prochain, 236
  Sade My Neighbor, 164, 165
Knowlson, James. *See* Beckett, Samuel
  (biographies of)
Koestler, Arthur, 370
Koffka, Kurt, 315
Köhler, Wolfgang, 315
Kristeva, Julia, 314

La chanson de Roland, 230
La France au Travail, 111
La Nouvelle Revue Française, 161, 163
La Rochelle, Pierre Drieu, 161
La Victoire, 110
Labé, Louise, 231
Lady Gregory, Isabella Augusta, 144, 145, 207, 208, 293
  Devorgilla, 207
Laforgue, Jules, 233
Lahr, Bert, 297
Lake, Carlton
  No Symbols Where None Intended
  Samuel Beckett at the Humanities Research Center, 419
Laloy, Louis, 269, 270
Lamont, Rosette, 174
Landry, Adolphe
  La Revolution demographique, 79
Lanson, Gustave, 47, 50–1
  Histoire de la littérature française, 230
Larbaud, Valery, 154
Laurel, Stan and Oliver Hardy, 292, 294
Laval, Pierre, 111, 115
Lawley, Paul, 273
Lawlor, Séan, 246
Lawrence, D.H, 139, 140
Le Cardonnel, Louis, 230
Le Juez, Brigitte, 234
Le Matin, 110
Leconte de Lisle, Charles Marie René, 230
Lees, Heath, 271
Lefebvre, Henri, 429
Left Review, 70, 94
Legouis, Emile and Louis Cazamian
  A History of English Literature, 220
Leibniz, Gottfried Wilhelm, 49, 306
Lely, Gilbert, 164
Lembke, Karl-Franz, 435
Léon, Lucie, 147
Léon, Paul, 113, 147, 151, 154
Leopardi, Giacomo, 242, 246, 247, 249, 329
  'A Se Stesso', 247
Leopardi, Joyce
  E fango è il mondo, 247

Les Éditions de Minuit, 164, 165, 435
Les Temps Modernes, 161, 163
  ed by Sartre and de Beauvoir, 162
Leventhal, A.J, 102
Lévi, Éliphas. *See* Constant, Alphonse-Louis
Lewis, Wyndham, 140, 141, 143, 146
  The Apes of God, 139
  Blasting and Bombardiering, 139
  Enemy of the Stars, 146
Leyris, Pierre, 436
Lézine, Maya, 147
Libera, Antoni, 131, 436
Linderberg, Daniel, 80
Lindon, Jérôme, 165, 285, 372, 400, 402, 432, 434, 435
Listener, The, 94
Lloyd, Harold, 145
L'OEuvre, 110
London Mercury, The, 93
Lorraine, 111
Loy, Mina, 143
Luce, Arthur Aston, 29–30, 219
  Bergson's Doctrine of Intuition, 30, 32, 33–4, 35–8
  Berkeley's Immaterialism, 29
  influence on Beckett, 33, 34–8
Luchaire, Jean, 119
Ludovic, Janvier, 372
Ludvigsen, Christian, 436
Lukács, Georg, 128, 129
  The Meaning of Contemporary Realism, 301

MacCarthy, Desmond, 88
MacCarthy, Ethna, 429
MacDonald, Ramsay, 91
MacGowran, Jack, 116, 177
Machiavelli, Niccolò, 241, 242, 243
  Storie fiorentine, 243
Macnamara, Brinsley, 226
Maeterlinck, Maurice, 238
Magee, Patrick, 177, 385, 428, 431
Mahaffy, John
  Descartes, 48, 304
Mahon, Derek, 407
Mahoney, Elisabeth, 289
Mahood, E.P, 17
Malebranche, Nicolas, 49, 302
Mallarmé, Stéphane, 233, 406
  Igitur, 164, 233
  "Le tombeau d'Edgar Poe", 233
Malraux, André, 282
  La condition humaine, 235
Manetti, Giannozzo, 243
Mann, Thomas, 423
Manning Howe, Mary, 102

Manning, Mary, 11, 20, 326
Manning, Susan, 20
Mansell, Thomas, 268
Mansfield, Katherine, 140
maquis, 116–17, 119–20
Marcel, Gabriel, 301
Marinetti, F.T, 140
   'Futurist Manifesto', 143
Marlowe, Christopher, 222
Marquis de Sade, 59, 60
Marrus, Michael, 79
Marx Brothers, 292
Marx, Karl, 131
Mason, Perry, 292
Massinger, Philip, 222
Masson, André, 161, 167, 168, 258
Matisse, Henri, 258
Mauriac, Claude, 301
Mauroc, Daniel, 436
Mauthner, Fritz, 151, 152, 307
   Beiträge zu einer Kritik der Sprache, 107, 422
   Contributions to a Critique of Language, 307
Maxwell, Jane, 241, 420
Mayer, Louis, 280
McAlmon, Robert, 155
McGahern, John, 213
McGreevy, Thomas, 11, 20, 24, 26, 27, 44, 46, 47, 48, 49, 50, 51, 53, 80, 81, 88, 90, 92, 93, 94, 109, 139, 140, 141, 145, 150, 153, 210, 213, 225, 326, 428
   Poems, 93
McKellan, Ian, 289, 290
McNeill, D.B, 17
McQueeny, Terence, 374
McSwinney, Terence, 69
McWhinnie, Donald, 177, 430, 433, 436
Melville, Herman, 218
   Moby Dick, 146, 225
Mendel, Deryk, 430
Merleau-Ponty, Maurice, 42, 262
Michaux, Henri, 167
Michel, Henri, 113
Middleton, Thomas, 222
Mihalovici, Marcel, 266, 275
Miller, Henry, 82
Milton, John, 221
   Paradise Lost, 219, 220
Minuit, 165
Miró, Joan, 167
Mitchell, Breon, 419
Modersohn-Becker, Paula, 141
Molière. *See* Poquelin, Jean-Baptiste
Monnier, Adrienne, 53, 154, 155
Montale, Eugenio. *See* Beckett, Samuel (translations)

Monteith, Charles, 435
Mooney, Sinéad, 208
Moorjani, Angela, 238, 317
Morel, Auguste, 154
Morin, Emilie, 81, 107, 208
Morris, Robert, 262
mother, 8, 9, 11–12, 87
Moulin, Jean, 116, 117
Muir, Edwin, 224
Muldoon, Paul, 407
Munch, Edvard, 141
Munson, Marcella, 374
Murphy, Eva, 11
Murphy, Gardner, 315

Nabokov, Vladimir, 370, 391
Nadeau, Maurice, 229, 237, 301, 401, 403
Naipaul, V.S
   The Mimic Men, 410–11
Nashe, Thomas, 222
National Gallery in London, 88
Nationalgalerie in Berlin, 104
Nauman, Bruce, 263
   Show Angle Walk (Beckett Walk), 262
Naumann, Hans, 207, 212
Nazi Germany, 99, 100, 101, 102, 105, 107
negation, 2–3, 12
New Statesman, 89, 94
Newbolt, Sir Henry, 221
Nietzsche, Friedrich, 305
Nixon, Mark, 221
Nixon, Mark and Matthew Feldman
   The International Reception of Samuel Beckett, 397
Nobel Prize for Literature, 230, 397, 402–3
Nolde, Emil, 141, 257
non-relation. *See* negation
Nord, Philip, 79, 82, 83
Normaliens (students of ENS), 43
Nouvelle Revue Française, 154

O'Brien, Eoin
   The Beckett Country, Samuel Beckett's Ireland. *See* biographies of Beckett
O'Brien, Flann
   At Swim-Two-Birds, 211–12
Observer, The, 94
O'Casey, Sean, 209
   Juno and the Paycock, 145, 209, 225
   The Plough and the Stars, 145, 225
   Windfalls, 146
occlusion, process of, 3
O'Connor, Frank, 209, 210
Oe, Kenzaburo, 407
O'Faolain, Sean, 210

O'Hara, J.D
    Samuel Beckett's Hidden Drives, 314
Oliver, Herbert Martyn, 207
O'Neill, Eugene, 146
    Desire Under the Elms, 226
Oppenheim, Lois, 259, 262
Oppenheim, Meret, 260
Orwell, George, 95
    Down and Out in Paris and London, 95
Ory, Pascal, 81
    La Belle Illusion, 79
O'Sullivan, Seumas, 210
O'Sullivan, W.O, 418
Overbeck, Lois More, 289

Papini, Giovanni, 246, 249
Papon, Maurice, 132
Paris-Soir, 111
Parks, Suzan Lori, 408
Parnell, Charles Stewart, 67
Parson, Ian, 97
Parti Populaire Français, 79
Pascal, Blaise, 235
Passerini, Giuseppe Lando
    Vite di Dante, 243
Passos, Dos, 287
Pavlov, Ivan, 316
Paxton, Robert, 80
Pearse, Patrick, 67, 68, 69
Peele, George, 222
Pelorson, Georges, 76, 80, 82–3
    Le Kid, 82
Perloff, Marjorie, 142
Péron, Alfred, 43, 46, 81, 113, 116, 147, 148, 154, 371, 372
Persse, Isabella Augusta. See Lady Gregory
Pétain, Marshal, 111
Pétain, Philippe, 78, 82, 111–12, 115
Petsch, Robert, 101
Pferdmenges, Hans
    Deutschlands Leben, 104
Picabia, Francis, 257
Picabia, Jeanine, 257
Pichette, Henri, 163, 167
Pickup, Ronald, 176
Pilling, John, 46, 221, 222, 268, 304, 377
    Companion to Dream of Fair to Middling Women, 221
Pinget, Robert, 372, 419, 429, 436
Pinter, Harold, 282, 385, 408
Pirandello, Luigi, 145, 382
Poe, Edgar Allan, 218
Poliziano, 246
Pollock, Jackson, 261
Pompidou, George, 43

Ponge, Francis, 163, 167, 368
Pope, Alexander, 220, 243
Popular Front, 83
Poquelin, Jean-Baptiste, 230, 235
Portora Royal School, 13, 14, 219, 220, 371
    academic achievements, 14, 15
    influence on themes, 17
    names in literary works, 16–17
    social status, 15
    sporting achievements, 14–15
    teachers, 16
Pouillon, Jean, 163
Pound, Ezra, 59, 139, 140, 142, 143, 219, 248, 370
    Cantos, 139
    Make It New, 226
Pountney, Rosemary
    Theatre of Shadows, 417
Pourrat, Henri
    Les montagnards, 230
Power, Arthur, 150
Praz, Mario
    La carne, la morte e il diavolo, 246
prenatal memories, 10
Prentice, Charles, 88, 96, 232, 406
Prévert, Jacques, 167
Prosper, 113
Proust, Marcel, 47, 53, 140, 141, 143, 196, 229, 231, 232, 233, 234, 235, 241, 242, 247, 257, 258, 281, 287, 291, 304, 371, 378, 386, 407, 421, 423, 424
    A la recherche du temps perdu, 50, 232, 268–9, 302, 398, 424
    Du côté de chez Swann, 230
    Cahiers, 424
    Le temps retrouvé, 51, 371
Prudent (pimp), 155
psychotherapy, 12–13, 87, 90–1, 199
Pudovkin, Vsevelod, 145
Putnam, Samuel, 44, 46

Queneau, Raymond, 82
Quigley, Megan, 154

Rabaté, Jean-Michel, 315, 316
Rabelais, François, 231, 408
    Gargantua, 231
    Le tiers livre, 231
    Pantagruel, 231
Rabinovitz, Rubin, 94
Racine, Jean, 230, 231, 233, 234, 235, 238, 243, 389
    Andromache, 169
Ragg, T.M, 97
Raimbourg, Lucien, 297
Rancière, Jacques, 256

Rank, Otto, 201
The Trauma of Birth, 198–9, 316–17
Ravel, Maurice, 266
Ray, Man, 257
Read, Herbert, 231
Reavey, George, 89, 162
religion, 17
Renan, Ernest
    Souvenirs de jeunesse, 230
Renard, Jules, 235
    Journal, 235
Renaud, Madelaine, 177, 178
Resnais, Alain, 286
Rexroth, Kenneth, 224
Reynaud, Paul, 111
Rhône Valley, 111
Ribemont-Dessaignes, Georges, 154
Richardson, Brian, 424
Rimbaud, Arthur, 81, 232, 233
    Illuminations, 233
Riopelle, Jean-Paul, 167
Robbe-Grillet, Alain, 165, 287
    A Regicide, 165
    The Erasers, 165
    L'Année dernière à Marienbad, 286
Robertson, David, 14
Robertson, J.G
    A History of German Literature, 99, 101
Robertson, Lennox, 226
Roe, Maria, 11, 199
Roe, Mollie, 13
Roe, Samuel Robinson, 11
Roe, Sheila, 10
Romains, Jules, 231
Rommel, Erwin, 115
Ronsard, Pierre de, 231
Roosevelt, Franklin. D, 111
Roscelin, Jean, 55
Rosset, Barney, 194, 282, 419, 433, 435
Rossi, Mario, 207
Rotman, Brian, 350
Roussillon, 59–60, 110, 116, 117–18, 120, 258
Routledge, 97
Rubenstein, Michael, 212
Rudmose-Brown, Thomas, 29, 32, 72, 76, 231, 232, 234
    Short History of French Literature, 230, 231
rue des Favorites, 54, 58
Russell, A.E, 96
Russell, George, 71, 210
Russell, Lord Bertrand, 30–2, 354
    A History of Western Philosophy, 31
    'The Philosophy of Bergson', 30, 31
Ryman, Robert, 261, 262

Sainte-Beuve, Charles Augustin, 50–1, 230
    Volupté, 232
Saint-Lô, 110, 120–1, 126–7, 160
Sarkonak, Ralph and Richard Hodgson
    'Seeing in Depth, The Practise of Bilingual Writing', 378
Sartre, Jean-Paul, 42, 131, 153, 161, 162, 163, 164, 165, 167, 168, 235, 236, 237, 284, 287, 301
    Being and Nothingness, 162
    Dirty Hands, 168
    Existentialism and Humanism, 162
    Imagination, 307
    La nausée, 235
    Nausea, 162, 307
    Nausée, 141
    No Exit, 162, 284, 385
    Roads to Freedom, 162
    The Wall, 162
Satie, Erik, 258
Sauerlandt, Max
    Kunst der letzten dreißig Jahre, 105
Scève, Maurice, 231
    Délie, 230
Schapire, Rosa, 104
Schimdt-Rottluff, Karl, 141
Schmahl, Hildegard, 319
Schmidt-Rottluff, Karl, 257
Schneider, Alan, 177, 194, 285, 297, 393, 419, 428, 429, 430, 433, 436
Schönberg, Arnold, 266
Schopenhauer, Arthur, 49, 50, 101, 223, 242, 246, 247, 268, 270, 302, 304, 305, 307, 329
Schubert, Franz, 193, 200, 273
    Lieder, 101
    'Nacht und Träume', 200
Schumann, Gerhard, 104
Schwartz, Jake, 418
Schwob, Marcel, 230
Seale, E.G, 15, 17
Seaver, Richard, 419, 436
Serreau, Jean-Marie, 168, 169
Shainberg, Lawrence, 320–1
Shakespeare, William, 193, 221, 222–3, 382, 392, 424
    A Midsummer's Nights Dream, 382
    Cymbeline, 388
    Hamlet, 382, 390
    King Lear, 219, 222, 385
    King Richard III, 385
    Macbeth, 223, 383, 390
    Merchant of Venice, 220
    Othello, 386, 388
    Romeo and Juliet, 388
Shattuck, Roger Whitney, 378
Shaw, George Bernard, 71, 209, 211

Shelley, Percy Bysshe, 242, 382
Shenker, Israel, 157, 211
Sheridan, Richard Brinsley, 145, 226
Shulman, Milton, 402
Simon, Alfred, 1
Simon, Claude, 165
Sinclair, Boss, 91
Sinclair, Maurice, 243
Sinclair, Morris, 90, 92, 102
Sinclair, Peggy, 54, 87, 101
Sinn Féin, 68, 69
Smith, Frederik, 219
Smith, Russell, 223
Smithson, Robert
  Spiral Jetty, 262–3
Smollett, Tobias, 222
  Humphrey Clinker, 224
Sophocles, 385
Soupault, Philippe, 154–5
Soutes, 81
Spectator, The, 89, 93, 94, 408
Spenser, Sir Edmund
  The Faerie Queene, 205
Spinoza, Baruch, 49, 236, 291, 306
St. Augustine, 407
  Confessions, 304
Stanislavski, Constantin, 173, 175, 176
Starkie, Walter, 32
Stein, Gertrude, 219
Stekel, Whilhelm
  Psychoanalysis and Suggestion Therapy, 316
Stendhal. *See* Beyle, Marie-Henri
Stephen, Karin
  Psychoanalysis and Medicine, A Study of the Wish to Fall Ill, 315
Stephens, James, 13
Sterne, Laurence, 224, 408
  A Sentimental Journey through France and Italy, 224
  Tristram Shandy, 219, 224
Stevenson, Robert Louis
  Treasure Island, 225, 292
Stewart, Patrick, 289, 290
Stieve, Friedrich, 106
Stoppard, Tom, 408
Strachey, Lytton, 140
Stravinsky, Igor, 266
Strindberg, August, 385
  The Ghost Sonata, 169
Suhrkamp, Peter, 435
SuhrkampVerlag, 435
Suttill, Francis, 113
Swift, Jonathan, 220, 223, 224
  Gulliver's Travels, 223
  Journal to Stella, 223

Tale of a Tub, 223
Symonds, J.A, 241, 242
Synge, John Millington, 65, 208, 209, 226
  The Aran Islands, 208
  The Playboy of the Western World, 145, 208
  The Tinker's Wedding, 145
  The Well of the Saints, 145

Tackaberry, Thomas. *See* Portora Royal School: teachers
Tal-Coat, Pierre, 161, 167, 168, 258
Tati, Jacques, 130
Tavistock Clinic, 87, 90, 148
Taylor, Jeremy, 324
Temps Nouveaux, 111
Tennyson, Lord Alfred
  'A Dream of Fair Women', 142
Tetley, W.N. *See* Portora Royal School: teachers
Thackeray, William Makepeace
  Vanity Fair, 225
Thales of Miletus, 302, 304
Theatre of the Absurd, 169
thematic presences, 8
This Quarter, 46, 242, 371
Thomas, Dylan, 399
Thompson, Alexander H
  History of English Literature, 220
Thompson, Geoffrey, 16, 87, 88, 89, 95, 225, 317
Thorndike, Edward, 316
Thrale, Hester, 93
  Anecdotes of the Late Samuel Johnson, LL.D., 224
Three Dialogues with Georges Duthuit. *See* Beckett, Samuel (works by): *Three Dialogues*
Times Literary Supplement, 94, 399
Tonning, Erik, 306
Tophoven, Elmar, 179, 275, 372, 436
Tophoven, Erika, 436
Torok, Maria, 198
Toynbee, Paget
  Dictionary of Proper Names and Notable Matters in the Works of Dante (1898), 244
transition, 46, 53, 54, 57, 81, 143, 147, 151, 152–3, 154, 160, 161, 167, 258, 338, 339, 373,
  See also Jolas, Eugene
Transition, 144, 153, 161, 166, 167, 168
Trinity College, Dublin, 13, 14, 29, 51, 71, 76, 110, 147, 218, 219, 220, 223, 225, 226, 229, 231, 232, 233, 235, 241, 247, 280, 281, 293, 302, 315, 371, 418, 420
Trismegistus, Hermes, 339
Troubles, the. *See* Easter Rising, 1916
Tynan, Kenneth, 173, 402
Tzara, Tristan, 143, 170, 400

Uhlmann, Anthony, 295, 306
Ulm. *See* École Normale Supérieure
United Irish League, 67
Universal Declaration of Human Rights, 128
Unseld, Siegfried, 430, 431, 435
Ussher, Arland, 10
Ussy, 58, 59, 60–2

Valente, Joe, 208
Valéry, Paul
  La soirée avec Monsieur Teste, 235
Van Gogh, Vincent, 166
Van Hulle, Dirk, 101
van Velde, Bram, 161, 166–7, 168, 249, 258, 259, 260
van Velde, Geer, 57, 166, 259, 260
van Velde, Jacoba, 436
Verlaine, Paul, 230, 233, 382
  Autumn Song, 119
Vertov, Dziga, 284
Vichy, 79, 82, 111, 112, 115, 119, 128
Vichy avant Vichy, 79, 82
Vico, Giambattista, 48, 302, 304, 307, 405
Vielé-Griffin, Francis, 230
Vilar, Jean, 168, 170
Vinteuil, 268
Virgil, 244
Vitrac, Roger, 168–9
  Victor, or, Power to the Children, 169
Völkischer Beobachter, 101
Volontés, 82
Voltaire, 237, 377
  Candide, 71, 237
  "Poème sur le désastre de Lisbonne", 237
von Hellingrath, Norbert, 99
Von Kleist, Heinrich
  'On the Marionette Theatre', 175
Vsevolod, Pudovkin, 280

Wahl, Jean, 167, 170
Wallace, Edgar, 292
Wanderer, The, 220
Warrilow, David, 267
Watson, John, 316
Watt, Henry Jackson, 315

Weber, Eugen, 79
Webern, Anton, 266
Weil, Simone, 42
Wessel, Horst, 106
West, Rebecca
  Stange Necessity, 94
Wettach, Charles Adrien (Grock), 296–7
Whitelaw, Billie, 177, 178, 267, 290
Whitman, Walt, 225
  Song of Myself, 328
Wilde, Oscar, 14
  The Importance of Being Earnest, 388
Wilkes, John, 224
Wilson, Cecil, 402
Windelband, Wilhelm
  A History of Philosophy, 48, 305
Wohlwill, Gretchen, 104
Woodworth, Robert
  Contemporary Schools of Psychology, 315, 316
Woolf, Virginia, 140
Woolfe, Leonard, 89, 140
Wylie, Laurence, 117

Yeats, Jack B, 23, 88, 97, 107, 259
  Amaranthers, The, 24
Yeats, John Butler, 241
Yeats, W.B, 26, 27, 65, 71, 140, 144, 146, 147, 193, 206, 207–8, 209, 213, 382
  At the Hawk's Well, 208
  Exiles, 146
  Four Plays for Dancers, 208
  King of the Great Clock Tower, 145
  Oedipus at Colonus, 225
  Oedipus the King, 225
  Purgatory, 145
  The Resurrection, 145
  'The Second Coming', 23
  'The Secret Rose', 209
  'The Tower', 207, 208
Young, Robert, 353

Zilliacus, Clas
  Beckett and Broadcasting, 193
Zimmer, Hans, 151, 152
Zola, Emile, 423